"Benson makes a persuasive case for Stegner as the equal of Hemingway and Faulkner—not as a 'regional' writer of passing interest, but as a master stylist and imagineer whose novels, short stories, historical fiction, and nonfiction should be part of every well-read person's experience."
—*Buffalo News*

"Warmly engaging . . . a pleasant and entrancing biography."
—*The Raleigh News & Observer*

"Well-researched, highly readable, and informative . . . No one interested in Stegner will fail to glean plenty of news about his life and times."   —*The Bloomsbury Review*

"In this engrossing, elegant, and meticulously researched biography, Wallace Stegner is finally given his due—as one of the most influential conservationists of his century, as a writer of amazing virtuosity and depth, and as a teacher who nurtured and developed many of the most luminous writers in recent American fiction."

—Marc Reisner, author of *Cadillac Desert*

"Wallace Stegner's life was a gift to us all. He believed in what we call character—decency, willingness to work, to create, to preserve, to take care. Through witnessing the example of his life we begin to understand our own responsibilities. This is a truly useful book."   —William Kittredge

"As this book makes wonderfully clear, Wallace Stegner's heroic life belongs to the whole continent, not only the West where he has been revered."   —Bill McKibben

PENGUIN BOOKS

WALLACE STEGNER

Born and raised in San Francisco, Jackson J. Benson graduated from Stanford (Honors Humanities) and received his M.A. from San Francisco State University and his Ph.D. from the University of Southern California. From 1966 to 1997 he served as professor of English and comparative literature at San Diego State University, where he taught twentieth-century American literature. Twice a fellow of the National Endowment of the Humanities, Benson has received several awards for teaching excellence. He has published nine books on modern American literature, among them the authorized biography, *The True Adventures of John Steinbeck, Writer* (1984), which won the PEN-West USA award for non-fiction. *Wallace Stegner: His Life and Work* (1996) won the David Woolley and Beatrice Cannon Evans Biography award presented by Utah State University.

WALLACE STEGNER

His Life and Work

JACKSON J. BENSON

PENGUIN BOOKS

PENGUIN BOOKS

Published by the Penguin Group
Penguin Putnam Inc., 375 Hudson Street,
New York, New York 10014, U.S.A.
Penguin Books Ltd, 27 Wrights Lane, London W8 5TZ, England
Penguin Books Australia Ltd, Ringwood, Victoria, Australia
Penguin Books Canada Ltd, 10 Alcorn Avenue,
Toronto, Ontario, Canada M4V 3B2
Penguin Books (N.Z.) Ltd, 182–190 Wairau Road,
Auckland 10, New Zealand

Penguin Books Ltd, Registered Offices:
Harmondsworth, Middlesex, England

First published in the United States of America by
Viking Penguin, a division of Penguin Books USA Inc. 1996
Published in Penguin Books 1997

1 3 5 7 9 10 8 6 4 2

Grateful acknowledgment is made for permission
to reprint excerpts from the following copyrighted works:
Selections from *The Poetry of Robert Frost*, edited by Edward Latham.
By permission of Henry Holt and Company, Inc.
Big Rock Candy Mountain by Wallace Stegner. Copyright 1938, 1940,
1942, 1943 by Wallace Stegner. Used by permission of Doubleday,
a division of Bantam Doubleday Dell Publishing Group, Inc.
Crossing to Safety by Wallace Stegner. Copyright © 1987 by Wallace Stegner.
Reprinted by permission of Random House, Inc.
Recapitulation by Wallace Stegner. Copyright © 1979 by Wallace Stegner.
Used by permission of Doubleday, a division of Bantam Doubleday Dell Publishing Group, Inc.
Stegner: Conversations on History and Literature by Wallace Stegner and Richard W. Etulain
(revised edition; Reno: University of Nevada Press, 1983, 1990, 1996).
By permission of University of Nevada Press.
All other writings by Wallace Stegner are reprinted by permission of Mary Stegner.

THE LIBRARY OF CONGRESS HAS CATALOGUED THE HARDCOVER AS FOLLOWS:
Benson, Jackson J.
Wallace Stegner: his life and work / Jackson J. Benson.
p. cm.
Includes index.
ISBN 0-670-86222-5 (hc.)
ISBN 0 14 02.4796 3 (pbk.)
1. Stegner, Wallace Earle, 1909–1993. 2. Authors, American—20th century—Biography.
3. Western stories—History and criticism. 4. West (U.S.)—Historiography.
5. West (U.S.) in literature. I. Title.
PS3537.T316Z6 1996
813'.52—dc20
[B] 96–12757

Printed in the United States of America
Set in Walbaum MT
Designed by Brian Mulligan

For Anne and John Loftis,
scholars both, without whose kindness
and invariable hospitality this book
could not have been written

PREFACE

I first met Wallace Stegner in 1986. I had called him to ask if I could discuss doing a book about him. He had written a very generous review of my Steinbeck biography for the *Los Angeles Times*, and I was looking for a new project. He had several things in common with Steinbeck: they were Westerners, they were known for their integrity, they had a strong sense of place and a concern for the environment, and they had both either been looked down upon or ignored by the Eastern intellectual press. Like Steinbeck, Stegner was a world-class author who had been largely overlooked by the academic critics. Although I had read only a couple of Stegner's novels—*The Big Rock Candy Mountain* and *Angle of Repose*—a few of his short stories, and his nonfiction *Beyond the Hundredth Meridian*, I admired his work.

More importantly, perhaps, I felt I shared many of his values, and although I had only sketchy information about his life, on the basis of what I did know I admired him for what he had been able to accomplish coming out of an impoverished background. I respected him as a man who had strong principles and who had lived his life by them, one of those rare people who had never faked it or made excuses. In a world full of blowhards and show-offs, he seemed to me to be the real thing— someone a person could really look up to and admire.

When I first met him, we sat out in the sun on the brick patio in front of his house in Los Altos Hills surrounded by a profusion of oak trees and shrubs and the flowering vines that blocked off the view of the house from the driveway. He was tall and robust-looking, with broad shoulders, a full head of wavy white hair, and erect posture. He was seventy-seven and looked to be in his early sixties.

I was a bit intimidated by the meeting, but Wally (it was not long after our first meeting that he insisted I call him Wally) put me at ease almost at once. There was nothing arrogant in his manner, only the self-assuredness that came from having been in the public eye for many years. He treated me with the casual courtesy and plain speech he would use with an equal. I explained what I would like to do: to write a short book to begin with, which would outline his life and review his writings, and follow that some years later with full-length biography, attempting to make the second book as definitive as possible.

He made it clear that while he was happy to have books written about him, he was not comfortable at all with the idea of biography as it is usually written nowadays. He referred to the biographies that he had written, about John Wesley Powell and Bernard DeVoto, and stated that he had avoided personal details and had concentrated only on these men's careers and hoped I would do the same. We compromised: I told him that I would concentrate on the career in the first book and avoid anything overly personal in the second. He smiled and said that the second book might well come out after his death (he was aware that my track record for speed was not impressive; the Steinbeck biography had taken me thirteen years of research and writing), in which case he would trust my judgment about what to say and what to leave out.

Although I eventually discovered that he had had a very eventful and, to a large extent, unusual life, I worried at the beginning that there might not be much high drama. Wally was so straight that despite a story filled with achievement and adventure, his life might seem comparatively dull to some—particularly those conditioned by a *National Enquirer* public mentality. Except, that is, for his sense of humor. Many of his letters are sprinkled with it, as was his conversation. He saw clearly the absurdities of life around him, and no one was more aware of the follies of the local and national political scenes. He loved to play with words; puns, rhymes, and verses flowed effortlessly from his mouth when a playful mood struck him. No one who had so much energy right up until his mid-eighties could ever be dull—his level of activity throughout his life was amazing. When I was with him, he was nearly always working on several things at the same time, planning trips, and arranging a complicated speaking schedule. He was a man who never had a clean plate and it didn't seem to bother him. With all his activity, he never seemed to resent the time it took to sit down with me and be interviewed, sometimes for hours.

I spent several weeks a year, off and on, with him for nearly seven years, first interviewing him and then going over his papers in his home office, and I found myself impressed not only with his energy, but with his sense of purpose. He stayed at his old upright typewriter no matter how many interruptions he might have to suffer through. Furthermore, I soon discovered that he was simply, by far, the brightest man I've ever known. Fast—he never missed the point; witty—he always saw the contradictions and the ironies; sharp—invariably he cut away the dross to get to the heart of the matter. But what complemented his intelligence and made it even more impressive was an incredible memory, a vast storehouse of general knowledge, and a sharp eye for detail.

After he agreed to cooperate with me, he considered it one of his duties to arrange for my comfort. When I came to work, he would have a table and chair all set up for me. If I worked through lunchtime, he would arrange to feed me if he was home and didn't have guests. His study had no central heat, and it was his habit to light a little fire in his sheet-metal stove every morning to get rid of the chill, and then go to work. If I got there early enough, I would go through this ritual with him. But in any case, he supplied a little portable electric heater for me (which he, himself, did not use) in the event I needed it. Actually, except in the summer, it was colder than hell in there, but it was a matter of my pride that I too would refuse the heater.

Nevertheless, it was a joy to be in his company even if much of the time, during the last years when I was reading his papers, we sat ten feet apart and ignored each other—further testimony to his powers of concentration. Often, however, especially in the early mornings while warming our hands at the fire he had made from the twigs he had garnered during the previous few months from his garden (waste not, want not), we talked about cabbages and kings. Current events during the late 1980s (cabbages) and the Reagan years (kings) were particularly depressing for him; more cheerful conversations had to do with authors and books and comparing notes about teaching experiences. I ended up also telling him a good deal about my own life and family—for instance, that my grandfather was a civil engineer in Idaho and Wyoming working on the survey only a decade or so after John Wesley Powell. That my father was a lawman in the woods of far Northern California after the turn of the century. I spent a lot of time defending California, a state whose excesses and eccentricities Wally never really did become accustomed to.

I was shocked when one day he said to me that if he had to choose between living in Vermont or living in California, he would choose Vermont, and when he died, he wanted his and Mary's ashes to be spread on a Vermont hillside. This from the man who was called the dean of Western writers. But the exploitation, the explosion of population, the greed, and the environmental degradation just got to be too much for him, I think. The despoiling of the environment depressed him terribly, and he took it as a sign of what the future might well have in store for all of us throughout the country. Vermont, where he had spent most of his summers for decades, gained his admiration for the tough endurance of its people and for its wildness, a second growth that most of the drought-ridden West had not had. Vermont was far closer in spirit, if not in topography, to the Saskatchewan that he grew up in than suburban California.

I had completed about a third of my manuscript before he died. Writing about a subject who is still alive has its advantages and disadvantages. If I ran into a question, I could always go to the source itself— and the source had an excellent memory. The disadvantage of writing about a living person, I found, was the sense that he is always looking over your shoulder as you write, approving or disapproving—and that can be very intimidating. His standards were very high, and I wasn't at all sure that in the end my manuscript would please him.

I suppose that I got to know more about Wally than just about anyone except his immediate family in that he probably talked more about his life to me than he had to anyone else. But although he was very candid and forthright, he did project a sense of reserve: friendly and kind, but never too close. I had lunch with him a few times, saw him in social situations a few times, and heard him speak to audiences twice. (Many years ago when I was at Stanford I also heard him speak on a couple of occasions. I don't remember what he said, but I do remember a man of striking appearance—tall and upright, penetrating blue eyes with metal-rimmed glasses, and most memorable of all, that same shock of nearly white hair. It seemed to me thirty-five years later that he had changed hardly at all.)

I never did travel with him, although I almost had that opportunity. He was going to go back to Saskatchewan for the dedication of the house that he grew up in as a historical site and one that in the future, as a tribute to him, would be used to house aspiring Canadian writers. I told him that somehow I was going to get up there myself sometime, to look around and get the feel of the territory. He suggested that I meet him in Canada, and he would give me a tour of Eastend and take me out to the old homestead. I was delighted, and my wife and I made plans to meet him and Mary that June, which turned out to be two months after he died as a result of injuries suffered in an auto accident. That trip would have been a capstone to all of it, my years of work and the evolution of what I considered a rare friendship. I have never gotten to Saskatchewan. I'm not sure now that I could bear to go.

In consultation with Wally's widow, Mary, I decided not to go forward with the plan for two books, but to combine the two and write the full-length book right away. This, then, is the account of a very remarkable man, possibly the most accomplished person of American letters in our time—award-winning novelist, award-winning short story writer, award-winning historian, outstanding teacher and founder of one of the finest writing programs in the country, and for decades a leading voice in the fight to save our environment. At the end of his biography of William Faulkner, emphasizing the author's unique contribution to American literature, Joseph Blotner tells us that we are not liable to see his like again. That sentiment might be applied just as well to Wallace Stegner, applied with some sadness for the loss of a great man, but sadness, too, for the loss of the ideals and values that created him.

ACKNOWLEDGMENTS

I am in debt to the many people who gave of their time to talk to me about Wallace Stegner. I have listed and thanked many of them individually as sources in my documentation at the end of the book. The person above all to whom I am grateful is Wallace Stegner, who cheerfully took many hours out of a very busy schedule so that I might interview him for this book and who opened his files to me, allowing me to roam through them at will. His total cooperation made this biography possible. I would also like to thank his wife, Mary, for her help and support, as well as his son, Page. I would like to extend special thanks to Sherry Gray, who allowed me, through Wally, to share and use Wally's letters to Sherry's parents.

Several libraries helped me in my work, and I am particularly indebted to Everett L. Cooley, collections specialist at the Marriot Library at the University of Utah, and Margaret J. Kimball, head of archives and special collections at the Green Library at Stanford University. My profound gratitude goes out to Wendy Smith, who assisted me for many years and whose perceptiveness, good taste, and careful attention to detail are reflected on every page of this book. I appreciate the support I received from the chairs of the Department of English and Comparative Literature at San Diego State University, Dan McLeod and

Carey Wall, and the help and backing of the dean of the College of Arts and Letters, Paul J. Strand. Also, I wish to thank the National Endowment for the Humanities for a grant that gave me the time to finish this manuscript, and to thank Tom Lyon, Jim Maguire, and Warren French, who were kind enough to recommend me. A special thanks to Michael Cohen, who helped me with Sierra Club history and Stegner's participation in the club, and to Steven Tanner, who helped me by providing much material on Stegner's relationship to Ken Kesey.

Finally, I would like to express my gratitude to all those who studied Stegner's life and accomplishments before me and whose publications provided a solid foundation for my own work. In particular, I am in debt to Forrest and Margaret Robinson's pioneering book, *Wallace Stegner*, which gave me the basis for my own chronology; to Richard Etulain, whose *Conversations with Wallace Stegner* provided much material for my own book; and to Nancy Colberg, whose scrupulously detailed *Bibliography* I found indispensable.

CONTENTS

LIST OF ILLUSTRATIONS

INTRODUCTION:
Against the Grain –
A Heritage of Integrity

Until his death in the spring of 1993, Wallace Stegner had been for several decades one of a half-dozen of America's most accomplished writers. He won nearly every major award given to a writer except the Nobel Prize. His books have, on occasion, sold several hundred thousand copies, and they continue to sell—nearly all of his books are in print. He has been the kind of novelist who has absolutely devoted fans, who has been the favorite author of thousands of readers, and who, at the same time, has been generally recognized by reviewers and those in the book trade as a "serious" writer who has made a significant contribution to American letters. During the last decade of his life, in any bookstore in the country where he went for a signing, there were long lines waiting for him; when he gave a talk or a reading, he could pack an auditorium with people anxious to see and hear him.

But ask the notorious "man in the street," or your next door neighbor, and if you don't live in certain areas where Stegner's name has been frequently in the newspapers—in the San Francisco Bay Area or Salt Lake City—the chances are fairly good that he or she may never have heard of him. Stegner was famous, but he never became a national media celebrity. While he surpassed many of his contemporaries in the breadth of his work and in depth of vision, he has never achieved the superstar status accorded to the likes of Norman Mailer, John Updike, or Eudora Welty. He has been, perhaps, the greatest of our noncelebrity authors— a status that has been a matter of regret to both him and his admirers. Although an unassuming, soft-spoken man, he was also ambitious. It was painful for him when his Pulitzer Prize— and National Book Award— winning books weren't even reviewed by *The New York Times Book Review*, and although he was a man of generous spirit, it may well have hurt him that some of his students, such as Ken Kesey and Larry McMurtry, became better known than he while, arguably, they accomplished less in the breadth and quality of their work.

There are several reasons why Stegner's achievements have out-stripped their public recognition. With an awareness of our visual-media-dominated culture, one reason that comes to mind is that none of Stegner's novels has ever been turned into a motion picture. Add to that a lack of national TV exposure for the author himself, the sort of expo-sure on talk shows that has made Mailer and Updike celebrities. Nor did he ever appear on the cover of *Time* or *Newsweek*, an occasion that alone seems to explain the promotion of the relatively obscure (except to readers of *The New Yorker*) John Cheever to national prominence.

But behind the lack of publicity—itself perhaps an effect rather than a cause—there are other, deeper reasons that Wallace Stegner is not rec-ognized and respected as much as many think he should be. One factor that concerned Stegner himself has been a tendency to consider him a provincial and therefore limited in scope and appeal, a Westerner who wrote a great deal (although not exclusively) about the West—history, biography, travel, and fiction. His personal story, having been raised on a homestead at the end of the pioneer era, is an archetypally Western story. Regionalism has been, of course, a large part of the history of American literature, but there have been those writers, such as Steinbeck or Faulkner, who have transcended the borders of their region in the power of their work and in the universality of their themes, and those, by contrast, who have been thought of only in terms of their place—its culture, customs, dialect, and scenery.

While admitting his devotion to the West and its environment, Stegner always aimed toward a larger venue. (Two of his novels take place in Vermont and *The Spectator Bird*, which won the National Book Award, is mostly set in Denmark.) And while he was not so confident of his own accomplishment that he would place himself on the same level as William Faulkner, he did on several occasions compare his situation as a writer to that of Faulkner. The Southerner had been relegated by critical consensus to a minor role in our literature as a regional writer, an eccentric marked by a prolix style and the grotesque subject matter common to the fiction of his locale. Then in 1946, almost single-handedly, the critic Malcolm Cowley rescued Faulkner through a reappraisal of his work and propelled him toward his current position as one of the premier writers of the twentieth century. During his last years, Wallace Stegner hoped for his Malcolm Cowley, who would take him out of the category of regional writer.

The label has been limiting and frustrating, as well as causing mixed emotions: yes, he wanted to explode the myth and tell stories of the "real" West(s), but no, he did not want to be shunted aside as *merely* a Western writer. It may seem odd that largely due to Faulkner's celebrity, Southern writers have gained legitimacy in the eyes of the Eastern literary establishment, whereas writers of the West, regardless of the quality of their work, are usually ignored.

It is no accident that on one occasion when Stegner's *Wolf Willow* was shunted in a brief notice to the back pages of *The New York Times Book Review*, the lengthy front-page review was not devoted to an original work, but a compilation of the letters of Oscar Wilde. More recently, *The New York Times Book Review* printed its review of *Crossing to Safety*, Stegner's last novel, on page fourteen. Would a book of this quality (Doris Grumbach's review praised it inordinately) by any other recipient of the Pulitzer Prize and National Book Award have been accorded such treatment? Can one imagine Mailer, even with a bad novel, thrust into the back pages?

If one looks at a writer like Ken Kesey, whose reputation has been largely built by one novel, *One Flew Over the Cuckoo's Nest*, one sees a novelist who made it not just because he wrote a wonderful book, but because that book also just happened to find a huge, sympathetic audience among the rebellious, anarchistic youth of the 1960s. So, too, with the less wonderful, but often very engaging books of Jack Kerouac,

William Burroughs, Richard Brautigan, Joseph Heller, and Kurt Von-
negut. These and other authors told, or more accurately seemed at the
time to tell, their readers what they wanted to hear—that authority is
corrupt and should be ignored or resisted, that pleasure can be an ultimate good and self-indulgence is fine, that freedom is something that
can be exercised without responsibility, that lives lived according to the
traditional values of self-sacrifice, courage, and self-discipline are wasted
and spent foolishly. In resisting all of this, Wallace Stegner was a rebel
against the pervasive rebellion, out of step with time and tide. He has
never been a celebrity among America's youth. He has more often
spoken as a parent than as a child, about struggle and responsibility
rather than freedom and desire. Our world is upside down: we may be
inclined to think that there is something wrong with a man who has
been married to the same woman for almost sixty years.

To paraphrase what Robert Stone said in a recent novel about one of
his characters, Wallace Stegner believed in all those things we used to
believe in. He was a remarkable man, not the least remarkable in
making his life and work of one piece. His integrity shone forth equally
in both. He was not stern, self-righteous, or judgmental, but was a person
who could be the life of the party, someone who knew how to have fun
and who had a ready sense of humor. Yet he was unbending in his belief
in right conduct. He was kind, thoughtful, and generous, a person who
was easy to talk to, yet he was held almost in awe by many who knew
him as being somewhat larger than life, in the expectations he had for
himself and in his superhuman capacity for hard work.

In his pursuit of living a worthy life and in expressing that pursuit in
his writings, he passed beyond the modernist rebellion against Victori-
anism—its emphasis on respectability and conformity—by the writers
of a previous generation. He did not see it as his task to tear down the
taboos of a shopworn Puritanism, but rather to search through the
cultural ruins produced by rampant individualism for a solid foundation from which to live a good life in the good society. He found that
foundation in responsibility and concern—responsibility for our own
actions and concern for the welfare of others and the welfare of our
environment. These in turn might lead, he hoped, to a recovery of
our sense of community and a realization once again of the importance
of cooperation.

Although he has become known primarily through his prizewinning novels and championing of environmental causes, his name most recently came into the news, in May 1992, when he turned down the opportunity to receive the National Medal of the Arts with seven others in a White House ceremony. Stegner was protesting politically motivated censorship of the arts by the acting head of the National Endowment for the Arts. In his letter to the endowment, he wrote that he was "distressed by what has been done to the Endowment for the Arts by its congressional and administrative enemies." While supporting such subsidies, he wrote, "I also believe that support is meaningless, even harmful, if it restricts the imaginative freedom of those to whom it is given." This stand has been typical of Stegner and defines him rather well: he had never been a fan of erotic art, but he had never been able to give way on matters of principle.

In recent decades, he was a white, older male writing against the grain of our constant emphasis on youth and the promotion of multicultural diversity, the valuing—sometimes for their own sake—of other voices from other rooms. Youth and diversity are cultural forces which tended to shunt him aside, and his position was somewhat akin to the liberal who has fought hard for equal rights who finds himself or herself passed over by affirmative action. He felt ambivalent. It certainly isn't that he opposed these voices; on the contrary, I can think of no other recent male American writer who has shown as much sympathy for the condition of woman or who has so often taken the woman's point of view in his fiction.

Furthermore, he wrote a book (*One Nation*, written with the editors of *Look*) back in 1945, when it could have been dangerous to an academic career to do so, about the problems of various minorities in various localities around the United States—not just African-Americans, but Hispanics, Asians, Native Americans, Catholics, and Jews. One of the short stories he wrote while doing research for this nonfiction book is called "Pop Goes the Alley Cat." It is about a white photographer who accompanies a social worker on her rounds in the Mexican barrio of Los Angeles. In the experiences and reactions of the photographer, Charlie Prescott, we see the ambivalence of the white liberal as his sympathy is pushed to the breaking point. As in so many of Stegner's stories and novels, the problem posed by this story is one of "getting one's head straight," which usually involves reexamining one's thinking processes and feelings. Stegner picked out precisely the difficulty of race relations, a difficulty that most whites are incapable of seeing. Middle-class whites, with the best of intentions, want dispossessed blacks to participate and achieve in society on *white terms:* everything, including compassion and understanding, is strictly limited, defined by white expectations.

Wallace Stegner was in the strange position of having been constantly cast in the role of outsider, often for reasons that might seem to be contradictory. Some people have resented him as an outspoken liberal; others, for having been too often critical of liberalism (which he was when it lapsed into irrationality and radicalism—he hated extremism of any sort). He has been ignored, even belittled as a Westerner, but has earned the enmity of Western fans who resent his refutations of the Western mystique. And then late in life, as a lifelong liberal in the best sense of the word—open-minded, tolerant, and compassionate—he was once again outside the artistic, intellectual vanguard as someone too much in the mainstream, too straight, too traditional.

He wrote about his dilemma in a 1964 essay, "Born a Square," in which he describes the Western writer (not the writer of Westerns) as "in a box with booby traps at both ends . . . at one end by an inadequate artistic and intellectual tradition, and at the other end by the coercive dominance of attitudes, beliefs, and intellectual fads and manners destructive of his own." Writers in the West, he laments, are likely to find themselves "so unfashionable" that they feel practically voiceless. Most of the writers of this region are likely not to feel very much "at home in a literary generation that appears to specialize in despair, hostility, hypersexuality, and disgust." In an age when so many people are trying so desperately to assume the mantle of victim, these "unfashionable" writers find it difficult to believe themselves either victim or victimizer. And when one of these writers

tries to write like people who are admired for their "honest" and "compassionate" demoralization, he hears the snickers from the wings. The society in which he got his conditioning has known no such demoralization, real or faked. . . . The literature that seems important, the literature that gave his crowd in Boise or Spokane its wicked thrill of being Inside with the Outsiders, now shuts him out. It is being written mainly by members of minority groups either wronged by his sort of middle-class world or angrily at odds with it, contemptuous of its limitations.

The question about Wallace Stegner remains: can a middle-class white male who wrote not about victimization, but about the facing down of adversity, and who, through example both in his life and work, extols the old verities of love, friendship, sacrifice, compassion, and forgiveness—can this writer find a place in the literature of the 1990s? Or are these aspects of the human condition, once considered to be at the foundation of the best we can become and the best that our society can become, now irrelevant along with those who write about them? Has separateness, hatred, envy, fear, and the need to control others with religious doctrine, or guilt for past wrongs, or the fear of being different, become the norm? Will there never be forgiveness, a coming together? Wallace Stegner believed that there can be, that there must be, and made that belief a cornerstone of his work.

There are other ways in which Wallace Stegner's career can be thought of as against the grain. Unlike most writers of fiction, he wrote nearly as much nonfiction. He wrote several histories, several biographies, and numerous essays and articles about the environment, the landscape, geography, writing, and history; he also wrote literary history and criticism. The breadth of his attention is astonishing, as is his knowledge. He is a throwback to the time in which it was thought important that an individual have a general education in the arts and sciences and that that education should continue throughout a lifetime.

In an age of specialization and an age that has sanctified separateness, he worked all his life to know more about peoples, places, and cultures. A country boy who was suddenly exposed to a larger world, he eagerly sought to learn all those things about art, literature, and history that were left out of his early, provincial experience. Even at the time of graduation from college, he recalled, "I knew nothing, literally nothing. I had a million books to read to catch up with my country and my generation and my classmates." Because he was always curious, terribly culturally ambitious, and eager to learn, the direction of his attention was always outward, in effort to learn his inner dimensions—to find out about the world so that he could confront and understand himself and his own life and pass on those discoveries to others. This need to grow is reflected directly in his career: unlike many novelists who write their best books at the beginning of their careers, Stegner's novels have gotten better and better. He has defied the cult of youth and triumphed with age.

"To pass on to others" has been a unifying theme in a multifaceted career. This was a man who at heart was a teacher in everything he did; as writer, as environmentalist, as historian, he lived to discover the truth and to help others in their own search. Such a man could have nothing but contempt and perhaps a touch of pity for those who claim that art has nothing to do with truth or experience, and in this Stegner operated once again against the grain, against those currently popular poststructuralist doctrines which deny that texts have any experiential meaning.

Not only out of step in his identity, in his experiences, and in his very values, Stegner seemed very much out of step with the current vogue in fictional approaches, a vogue that all too often seems to value experimentation for its own sake. He was a realist and met some contempt for being a realist. At one point there was a small group at Stanford that was agitating in favor of getting rid of him as head of the creative writing program because it thought him hopelessly old-fashioned. If he has been old-fashioned, he has been so in that he had something to say and was willing to submerge the self in the process of trying to say it well. He felt very strongly that writing should be the expression of belief. And "any work of art," he has said, "is the product of a total human being."

What he has had to say has always been concerned with tearing down barriers between people, building trust, encouraging love, concern, and cooperation. If, as Robert Frost suggests in "Mending Wall," there are two kinds of people—those who build and repair a wall and those who question its need—Wallace Stegner was someone who "doesn't love a wall ... [and] wants it down." But Stegner's world is more complicated than that. It is true that if there are villains in his work, they are the selfish, the self-centered, and the greedy. But more often the fault is on the part of those with the best intentions, as they reach out to understand but fail. Like Joe Allston in *All the Little Live Things*, they try to reach across a barrier, but they are unable to reach quite far enough. As a realist, Stegner saw the complexities of life, and like Henry James, as he grew older his fiction became more and more filled with ambiguities.

In *All the Little Live Things* Joe Allston finds it easy enough to love and to understand the lovely Marian, the almost saintly cancer victim, but the real challenge, the hippie biker, Jim Peck—unlikable, arrogant, self-centered—is beyond him. And his failure hurts, since Jim reminds him of his dead son, a probable suicide, whom he was never able to reach. Larry Morgan in *Crossing to Safety* is confronted with a similar challenge, a more complicated one that is presented in the two sides of a single character. Charity is beautiful, loving, and generous—but she is also domineering, manipulative, and willful. Larry is somewhat more successful in reaching out, forgiving the fault in order to embrace the good, than his predecessors in other novels. But it is not easy, nor is it without misgivings.

First in *The Big Rock Candy Mountain* and then in its sequel, *Recapitulation*, Bruce Mason's problem of forgiveness is similar to Larry Morgan's in its ambiguity. On the one hand, he wants to win his father's approval; on the other, he is oppressed by his father's callousness and dishonesty. His father makes life difficult and unpleasant not only for him, but for his mother—and it is the latter that the son cannot forgive. His mother, a simple, hardworking woman with a taste for books, only wants the opportunity to settle down somewhere and make a home for the family. But her husband's boom-or-bust temperament makes them permanent migrants, first as he tries one get-rich scheme after another and finally as a bootlegger, always just one step ahead of the law. It is an archetypical conflict between man and woman in the West as it really was.

But Bruce's father, Bo, is not an evil man. His worst quality is a bad temper, and this, and a rather flexible sense of right and wrong, is balanced against courage, a fun-loving nature, and enormous capacity for hard work. The reader is likely to find Bo somewhat attractive, but Bruce, the artist-as-young-man and by temperament the opposite of his father, grows increasingly resentful and finds, by the end of *The Big*

Rock Candy Mountain, that he hates him. In this, the most autobiographical of Stegner's novels, the situation is one that closely reflects his own experience, as he admitted on a number of occasions. He was haunted all his life by his relationship with a father very much like Bo Mason, and in listening to him talk about his father, one couldn't help but feeling that for him, personally, forgiveness was a difficult battle. That was why, perhaps, it came to have such a central place in his work.

Just how much it haunted him may be indicated by Stegner's return to the Bo-Bruce relationship more than thirty-five years after the publication of *The Big Rock Candy Mountain* in *Recapitulation*, an apparent effort to put the ghost of the first novel to rest. And this same struggle is one, as we realize later in *Angle of Repose*, that motivates Lyman Ward's compulsive historical research into the lives of his grandparents: his recreation of the story of their relationship is an effort to come to terms with the wrong done to him by his wife, who ran off with her doctor, abandoning Lyman to crippling disease. Once again, in this novel as with the long journey of Bruce Mason toward expiation of his hatred and resentment, one feels that Lyman Ward is a lost soul, wandering, mentally, not only the face of the earth, but through time as well in an effort to find some formula, some mechanism by which to make his spirit, if not his body, whole once again.

Forgiveness. The coming together of fallible human beings. In Stegner's work there is always struggle; in novel after novel we suffer through the strivings of human beings to be better. Following the pattern set in the Nobel Prize acceptance speeches of Faulkner and Steinbeck, Stegner also believed in the possible perfectibility of man. Here, too, he ran against the grain of current opinion, which declares that individuals do not need to strive to be better—all they need to do is sit down and recognize how wonderful they already are.

As one might imagine, Stegner was not in favor of the American Dream, or at least not the materialistic dream of status and possessions. And, indeed, when we see the damage done by such a seeker of the dream as Bo Mason and a dozen other Stegner characters looking to find the "Big Rock Candy Mountain," we realize that for this author, as for so many other American writers (one can't help but think of another mountain, the one in F. Scott Fitzgerald's "The Diamond as Big as the Ritz"), the dream is seen as having led to moral and physical catastrophe. It has brought us a land despoiled and a people largely exploited and disheartened. A few have gained their yachts, while the old growth forests are clear-cut, poisonous heavy metals run down into the rivers of the Rockies, and thousands have lost their retirements in corporate "restructurings" and savings-and-loan scams. Not much has changed since Upton Sinclair wrote *The Jungle*; not much has changed since Steinbeck wrote *The Grapes of Wrath*.

Stegner found the American Dream far more damaging than does Dreiser in *An American Tragedy* or Fitzgerald in *The Great Gatsby*. Almost alone among major writers of our time, he realized that the dream has not only twisted our lives and corroded our values, it has despoiled the very land that has given us such hope. And that hope, as represented by the frontier, is what has given the West such a symbolic role in representing the dream, has made the perpetuation of the mythic West possible. What motivates Bo Mason in *The Big Rock Candy Mountain* is what motivates poor people, dreaming the impossible dream of sudden riches, to hate unions and vote Republican. Like Willie Loman in Arthur Miller's *Death of a Salesman*, they wait for Uncle Ben to pass on the secret of wealth, while at the same time, the land and air are so polluted they cannot plant seeds that will grow in their own backyards. For Stegner, who was concerned with cooperation, empathy, and mutual support in basic relationships, the American Dream very often spelled disaster, not only for individuals, but for our society and our land.

When Stegner depicts in his writings someone who is successful, it is not for his material possessions or status due to wealth or fame, but for what he has made of himself morally and spiritually and what he has accomplished. Most of Stegner's heroic figures appear in his nonfiction: John Wesley Powell, who took on the nearly impossible job of surveying the Colorado River; Ansel Adams, who, working often in the most awkward and inhospitable circumstances, became gradually, picture by picture, our preeminent landscape photographer; and Bernard DeVoto, who for many years, like a voice in a wilderness of exploitation and greed, fought for our public lands and the preservation and expansion of our

National Parks system. In every case these people not only faced terrific odds with courage and persistence, but their motives went beyond themselves, serving others through science or art or journalism.

For the most part, Stegner's fictional protagonists are neither hero nor antihero, neither conqueror nor victim (in a time in which the hero figure dominates popular culture and the antihero, high culture). They are usually relatively ordinary people who are trying to find their better selves. They do good things, if not heroic things, but they also fail, betray themselves in some way, and try to recover. In the early novel *Fire and Ice*, Paul Condon wants to improve the world by his activities in the Young Communist League, but realizes at last that he is essentially motivated by revenge, a hatred generated out of the mistreatment of his parents by an uncaring society. He ends up at least in part cleansed of his hatred and becomes a less self-centered individual.

At the opposite end of the social scale from the impoverished Paul Condon is the socialite Sabrina Castro, who, in *A Shooting Star*, realizes she is leading a useless life, a life without goals, achievements, or satisfactions. She feels trapped by her wealth and position and is baffled by the need to somehow escape, going through a number of hideous and demeaning experiences before at last finding a true path out of her frustration and selfishness. With neither Paul nor Sabrina is there a happy ending—there is only the sense that the internal struggle is worth it, that one can, with courage and persistence and goodwill, find a path that might lead to a productive and meaningful life.

In *All the Little Live Things*, Joe Allston, formerly a literary agent and now retired to California suburbia, is seen as having gained some success by the kind of person he is, rather than by his comfortable retirement circumstances. He has rubbed shoulders with the high and mighty in the heady atmosphere of New York media circles and never lost his integrity or sense of what is really important—the inner man. And to the end of his life, he is trying to find the right thing to do, worrying not only about his actions, but about his attitude. Attitude is important to many of Stegner's characters—and one's motives. The battle is nearly always an internal one, the attempt to triumph over the meaner self, ignoble thoughts and reactions, and this conflict is very often externalized through interaction with another character.

In the case of Allston, it is his wife, Ruth, who resists his tendencies to categorize, to be dogmatic, to be less than generous in his reactions to activities and people that don't match his expectations. Larry Morgan's wife, in *Crossing to Safety*, performs the same function, applying common sense and a generous spirit to the foibles, weaknesses, and irritations of others, things that drive Larry to the edge of explosion. But conscience is not always played by the women. In *A Shooting Star* that function is performed by Leonard MacDonald, the schoolteacher husband of Sabrina's best friend. Leonard, like the two wives just mentioned, provides the common sense, the optimism, the standard of caring for others, the lack of prejudice and dogmatism that helps Sabrina in her inner struggle to achieve self-esteem. At a climactic point in the novel near the end, he tells her, "I'll tell you what I believe in. I believe in human love and human kindness and human responsibility, and that's just about all I believe in." And one can say that that is close to being true for Stegner as well.

Responsibility is one thing Stegner insists on that is often ignored or slighted by his writer contemporaries, and it is the one thing above all that for him defines the function of the individual. In an essay, "That New Man, the American," he has written:

> We are all likely to blame the system, the military-industrial complex, the multiversity, or something else for what is weak or wrong in ourselves. The aim of our lives, so far as I can see, is conduct, not behavior; and conduct is not a galvanic twitch in response to stimuli, but activity guided by a code of personal ethics and an obligation of personal integrity. There are some things too dishonest or self-indulgent or socially harmful for a good man to do.

Wallace Stegner was a man who lived under the obligation of trying his best to be "a good man," and his writing was part and parcel of that effort. For him, the individual, insofar as his or her capabilities allow, must not only take charge of his or her own destiny, but take on the responsibility of contributing to the welfare of others in family, community, and society.

Quietly modest in behavior and gentle on the outside, Stegner was a very confident, competent, tough man. There is nothing in his works that by any stretch of the imagination could be called sentimental. He has been hard on himself and in equal measure has been hard on his fictional protagonists, and in this regard can be seen once again to be out of step with his times. For several decades the most common leading characters in our fictions have been victims, the host of antiheroes who are the descendants of Stephen Crane's Maggie and Salinger's helpless and unhappy Holden Caulfield. But while Stegner's characters live in an equally harsh and unjust world, their role has been to cope, rather than complain.

Having grown up in the difficult circumstances of the frontier, and subject to the harsh code of frontier culture and to the discipline of a father intolerant of any show of weakness, Stegner had understandably been at odds with those of his contemporaries who have celebrated suffering and made victimization a virtue. Writing of the effects of these circumstances, he has said:

> Little as I want to acknowledge them, the effects of those years remain in me like the beach terraces of a dead lake. Having been weak, and having hated my weakness, I am as impatient with the weakness of others as my father ever was. Pity embarrasses me for the person I am pitying, for I know how it feels to be pitied. Incompetence exasperates me, a big show of pain or grief or any other feeling makes me uneasy, affectations still inspire in me mirth I have grown too mannerly to show. I cannot sympathize with the self-pitiers, for I have been there, or with the braggarts, for I have been there too.

Nothing could be more against the grain of a society in which groups compete with each other in their claims to be the most victimized, and responsibility is more often than not abandoned in favor of self-pity.

As a writer, Stegner's primary concern in regard to the role of the individual was to define the difference between the reality of individual responsibility and the myth of total independence and larger-than-life achievement. This concern is anchored to his own role as truth-seeker, to his conviction that literature can mirror life, and to his devotion to the realistic mode of storytelling as the best way to get at and communicate truth. His realism can be seen as a natural outgrowth of his toughness. There are several strands of Realism in twentieth-century American fiction, and of these, probably the most persistent and enduring is that which attempts to refute the illusions we attempt to live by, both as individuals and as a society. In this mode, Realism is essentially moralistic, for it suggests that the illusions we hold so dear are the sources of many of our social ills, allowing us to avoid problems and to become self-righteously judgmental. We are great avoiders (revenue enhancement is all right, but taxes are forbidden), and we are great pretenders: we have found it far more convenient and pleasant to live our lives according to a mythology ("It is morning again in America") and to follow maps that have little to do with the actual territory.

The role of a realist such as Stegner is to tell us disagreeable truths, to pull away the masks and tear down the attractive facades that allow us to pretend and cover the reality. This is not an activity that is likely to endear the writer to a wide audience. His role as a moralist in his fictions has been to challenge us, not only to participate in difficult decisions in an often ambiguous world, but to participate in the even more difficult task of adjusting our attitudes toward our roles, our relationships, and the earth we have inherited, once the myths have been exposed for what they are and the masks and facades have been torn away.

Roger Tory Peterson, the eminent naturalist, speaking of how one develops an environmental conscience, has said, "First comes awareness. Once one becomes aware, one becomes concerned." In everything he wrote, whether fiction or nonfiction, Wallace Stegner strove to make us aware, to make us look at life as it is and thereby discover what is important. The writer's task, a task that Stegner took up as his own, was defined well by Ernest Hemingway when he said:

> I was trying to write then [speaking of his apprenticeship] and I found the greatest difficulty, aside from knowing truly what you really felt, rather than what you were supposed to feel, and had been taught to feel, was to put down what really happened.

Discovering what one really feels, rather than what one is supposed to feel, and learning to see things as they really are—that has been Stegner's realism, his challenge to himself, and that has been his challenge to us, his readers.

1

THE LAST HOMESTEAD
FRONTIER:
A Prairie Childhood

One way of describing Wallace Stegner's career is as a process of confrontation. He has often described fiction as basically coming out of two motives—the desire to entertain and the desire to confront and make some sense of the author's own experience. It has been Stegner's pattern to emphasize the latter, to hope to bring some enjoyment and enlightenment to the reader while he tries through the process of writing and confronting old ghosts to understand who he is.

Stegner came back again and again in fiction and nonfiction to a childhood that marked him deeply, one that was not terrible in all its aspects, but certainly one more dramatic, in retrospect, than most spent in rural America at the turn of the century. He was born on February 18, 1909, on a farm near Lake Mills, Iowa, the second son of George and Hilda Paulson Stegner. The birth came during a visit to Hilda's parents. George was employed as the manager of a hotel in Grand Forks, North Dakota. Stegner's mother was a warm, loving person who, as a farmer's daughter in the West of that time, was denied the education her intelligence deserved. She was the one who encouraged Wallace's interest in books, who praised him for his accomplishments at school. He developed an abiding love and respect for her, since not only was she kind and fair-minded, she was the one who stood up for him against the wrath or scorn of a father who favored the stronger, more athletically inclined older brother. Her hopes, based on her limited horizons, were modest: she was, as her son has described her, "a nest builder" who simply wanted to make a good home for her family. To her sorrow and much to the regret of her younger son, who wished for her the one thing she most wanted, she never was able to do so. She led a hard, often lonely, and largely unfulfilled life.

Wallace's father was another matter—unfulfilled, certainly, but for very different reasons. He had all the frontier virtues—tough-minded, courageous, physically strong—but no real frontier to go to. He was a man who came fifty years after his time—the time just before or after the Civil War when a fortune in gold or land or lumber might have more easily been made by a man, armed only with grit and ambition, who got there first. He became a vagabond looking for the main chance, a risk-taker by nature whose risks seldom paid off. Always too late, always disappointed, George Stegner reached out, but each time the rainbow disappeared and the pot of gold was gone. It was a style of living that took a terrific emotional toll on his family.

It seems almost inevitable that one of the first places Stegner's father looked toward was Alaska. When Wallace was three, the family moved from North Dakota to Washington in preparation for relocating to Alaska, and the author's first memories are of living in a tent in what would become the little logging town of Redmond. His father's dreams of digging up baseball-size nuggets in the Far North were stymied when Wallace got scarlet fever and the short summer season was lost. The family moved from one small town in Washington to another until in frustration George went off by himself to seek his fortune in Saskatchewan, Canada, leaving Hilda behind to take care of their two young sons as best she could in Seattle.

It turned out that the only job Hilda could get, at a department store, paid so little that she could not support herself and her children, so she was forced to assign the boys to the care of an orphanage. It was, as Wallace remembered, an old-fashioned asylum right out of Dickens. When the orphans were fed, a dishpan of crusts and food scraps was brought out, and it was a test of the fitness to survive. Four-year-old Wallace was weak and rather sickly, but fortunately his older brother, Cecil, was big for his age and tough. It was an early lesson in the importance of cooperation in the face of "every man for himself."

When Hilda found out just how bad conditions were, she somehow scraped together enough money to get them all back to the sanctuary of her father's Iowa farm—a move that must have been humiliating for her, since she had left home to escape her father's tyranny and her father's disapproval of her marriage. Her father was "a tough old Lutheran [and] there's nobody tougher and stiffer and more inflexible than an American Lutheran—somebody who came from the old country to this country and then froze." Wallace was left to the care of the old ladies of the household, with its strange smells and foreign sounds, and he remembered wanting very much to be able to go to school.

In the meantime, George Stegner was working to get established in Saskatchewan, where the coming of the railroad had opened up a large area of the prairie to homesteading. After spending the fall and winter of 1913 in Iowa, Hilda and her two sons went north to join her husband in the early summer of the following year. Wallace Stegner arrived in Saskatchewan much as the young Jim Burden, in Willa Cather's *My Ántonia*, arrived in Nebraska—by horse and wagon—and the first impressions of the two boys in response to their surroundings must have been similar: the land flowed on forever and the sky was as wide as you could see. George Stegner had settled in Eastend in the Whitemud River Valley, a streak of green vegetation in an undulating sea of brown. Not yet a town, Eastend was a scrubby collection of shacks and tents, a construction camp, and for a time the family lived in a derailed dining car on Main Street.

It is not clear what George was doing at this point to earn a living, but he was a jack-of-all-trades and in this boomtown he had plenty of opportunities. Although the accommodations were makeshift for a while, the family was back together. "Saskatchewan is the richest page in my memory," Stegner has written, "for that was where . . . for a half dozen years, we had . . . a house of our own, a united family, and a living, however hard." At last Wallace got the opportunity to go to school, the first year in a room over the pool hall, then in a shack next to the butcher shop, and finally in permanent quarters in a brick schoolhouse. The new brick building was a testament to the faith of a raw frontier town in its future.

Stegner has written in several places about the nature of his education here. Well-meaning teachers tried to make a "European" of him—the focus was on European history and English literature. In looking back, the author has mourned the lack of any information given to the youngsters about the history or geography of their own region, a lack which he felt deprived him of roots, a sense of a meaningful past, and a sense of identity. His early schooling was not a total loss, however. There was a great emphasis in those days on reading, memorizing, and reciting poetry, a process that gave the author early in life an ear for language. Learning poems was reinforced by his father's love of rhymes, folk songs, and verse. George was a treasure house of such lore, which usually surfaced when things were going well and he was in a good mood. One of Wallace's first memories as a very young child was of being taught a song about Whistling Rufus, the one-man band.

Part of George Stegner's plan in Eastend was to combine what he could earn in town during the winter with what he could earn from homesteading a farm. During World War I there was a great demand for wheat, and one could, with luck and good weather—and a lot of backbreaking labor—make a considerable amount of money. The Stegner farm was south of Eastend; the Montana line was its southern border. Stegner filed his papers, and then in the early summer of 1915 he and the two boys, Cecil and Wallace, went out to 'prove it and, if there was time, plow, seed, and harvest the first crop. Hilda stayed in town. They traveled the fifty miles from Eastend across unplowed grass and burnouts—there were no roads—in a lumber wagon. When they found the stakes and located their half section, there was nothing to distinguish it from its surroundings. What they saw was a stretch of gently sloping dry land, treeless and virtually without feature, out in the middle of nowhere. Its only advantage was that it did have a spring that ran most of the year. Much later, looking back on the homestead, Stegner decided that they were not real farmers. Their improvements were largely primitive and temporary: "What we did ... was written in the wind." What they were, really, was "wheat miners." In George's mind, they were there to make a killing while the time was right.

That first summer, with only the occasional help of the two young boys, George got an enormous amount of work done. He built a shack, a corral for the workhorses, a dam to create a reservoir at the end of the coulee, and then planted a crop, which he harvested before they left for the summer. In describing the shack, Stegner recalled that it "had a seven-foot ceiling, with one room and a sleeping porch, so the breeze could come through the screen. No ice box, no power, no anything. There was a hole under the floor to keep milk and stuff cool or reasonably preserved—maybe half a day. And no shade." He also recalled how uneventful and lonesome the homestead was for two boys who increasingly become tired of each other's company, who

had read everything in the shack ten times, had studied the Sears Roebuck catalog into shreds, had trapped gophers in increasing circles out from the house until the gopher population was down to bare survivors, had stoned to death the one badger they caught in a gopher trap, had lost in a big night windstorm their three captive weasels and two burrowing owls, and had played to boredom every two-man game they knew.

The following years on the homestead Wallace became expert in hunting gophers. In town a prize was given every fall to the farm boy who killed the most during the summer—evidenced by presenting the tails—and he won several years in a row. This may have been a small triumph, but it suggests just how competitive he was at an early age: give him something to aim for, and he would go for it with all his will and energy. It became a ritual, after the day's kill, for him to come back to the shack, get out his cache of tails, and recount all of them with the new additions. He was proud of his hunting prowess and his business-like, unsqueamish contribution to the farm economy. Looking back later in life, Stegner was appalled at the time and effort he spent on the homestead killing things.

Wallace's life in Saskatchewan was divided between prairie for three to four months and a frontier town for eight or nine. For the summers that followed the first one, Wallace's older brother stayed in town working at the grocery store, while the rest of the family went out to the homestead. The author learned early on how it felt to be isolated:

You don't get out of the wind but learn to lean and squint against it. You don't escape sky and sun, but wear them in your eyeballs and on your back. You become acutely aware of yourself. The world is very large, the sky even larger, and you are very small.

Around them there were no other buildings, no works of man in sight. Ten miles away they might run into another homestead, the plowed land standing out as an odd patch on the face of the prairie. If the Stegner horses broke loose, they could wander day and night and never run into a fence. Almost all the homesteaders camped out for the summer; few braved the winter furies of those plains to stay year around. It wasn't just the bitter cold that drove them back to town, temperatures that got down to forty, even fifty degrees below zero, but the total isolation.

Stegner was probably the only important writer living into the 1990s who actually experienced the pioneering period of North American history, on the last unsettled frontier. Something happens to the psyche when one is alone a great deal in such an overwhelmingly large environment. Perhaps a permanent sort of modesty sets in, a sense of helplessness in the face of forces quite beyond the power of human muscle or spirit. It is in such circumstances that we realize that only by helping each other can we be saved from the oppression of a harsh environment and omnipresent emptiness.

Stegner's first important story, "Bugle Song" (1938), reflects the isolation he felt during the long summers on the homestead. The story deals with a boy on a prairie farm who, far from town and without friends, looks to a routine of chores and invents fantasies to pass the time, such a boy as Robert Frost would like to bend his birch trees. But here there are no trees, no shade except from the shack that takes the place of a farmhouse to block out the insistent sun and its terrible heat. The boy leads a dual life, representing a conflict in roles that he does not yet recognize. Alone, except for the occasional company of his mother (his father is presumably out on the farm working), he divides his time between trapping and killing gophers on the one hand, and reading lyric poetry and dreaming of distant places on the other.

Hard and insensitive to the suffering of animals, he seems to perform his grisly task of ridding the farm of pests as part of the process of growing up into the masculine frontier role. His mother protests his cruelty and he ignores her, yet he does follow her wishes in preparing for school in the fall by reading his poetry book, and in this and the romantic daydreams generated by the poems, reflects her softer, more civilized approach to life. Similar contrasts between male and female roles, between insensitive and sensitive, caring and uncaring, are carried on as themes in a series of short stories and later in the semi-autobiographical novel, *The Big Rock Candy Mountain*, which incorporated most of the stories.

Stegner was not only often physically alone—without friends and left by his parents to his own devices—he was often emotionally cut off as well. His older brother, Cecil, tough and strong, outshone him, and his father favored Cecil, on occasion mocking Wallace for his lack of "manhood" and urging him to be more like his brother. Although he didn't know it at the time, Wallace had a circulation deficiency in his hands, and in the severe Saskatchewan winters, his hands always hurt. No one knew that there was a medical problem, so that as far as his father was concerned, he was simply the "baby" of the family, always complaining about the cold that everyone else was "man enough" to bear in silence. Wallace's emotional isolation and feelings of deficiency and failure early in life had a profound effect in the formation of the outlook and values held later in life and in the selection of the subjects and themes for his writing.

Both the nonfictional and the fictional accounts of his growing up (which in outline match each other almost verbatim) make it clear that a dichotomy developed early in his consciousness between the proud, tough, intolerant rugged individualism represented by his father and the friendly, tolerant, neighborly tendencies toward caring and cooperation represented by his mother—and it was his mother whom he learned to admire. Later, as a writer, he came to see the conflict between his father and mother as a synecdoche for the Western clash between the forces of rugged individualism on the one side and the forces of cooperation and community on the other. The metaphor extends to society as a whole, its pervasive conflicts of conservative versus liberal, know-nothing versus intellectual, the doctrine of getting-rich-quick versus the belief in service to others. It may seem like a gigantic jump from childhood unhappiness to adult environmentalist, but the very ethic espoused by his mother of charity and concern for all is at the root of Stegner's concern for the earth, and his hatred of his father's opportunism and greed is at the root of his resistance to the forces of exploitation.

In the fall, Wallace returned with his family from the homestead to spend the winter in town. He has recalled that it was always a moment of pure excitement, after a long hot day on the wagon track, their joints sore from fifty miles of jolting, to come to the rim of the South Bench and look down on Eastend, snug in its valley with the river cutting through the banks of green shrubs and willows. Winter meant school, where he could shine, as well as friends, opportunities for mischief and adventure; winter replaced the sameness of the summer with possibility.

Eastend changed over the years that the Stegners were there. At the beginning, it was nothing more than the Z-X Ranch house—the one remaining cattle operation that had survived the blizzards and droughts that over the years had driven off the rest—and a boardinghouse for Canadian Pacific crews building the grade for a branch line down from Swift Current. Later, there was a Main Street, with plank sidewalks, and a drugstore, hardware store, grocery, hotel, and bank. The Pastime Theater; a "Millionaire Row," with its modestly affluent bungalows; and "Poverty Flat," with its shacks housing Chinese and half-Indians, made it an almost typical western town of the period during and just after World War I.

Wallace's first year in Eastend, 1914–15, was a chaos of experiences, both good and bad. Although he was a runt and thought of as the baby of the family, he was by no means a goody-goody, and the environment offered many opportunities for play and adventure, as well as for getting into trouble. He recalled that during his first year in Eastend,

I caught lice from the half-Indian kids I played with and was fiercely shampooed with kerosene. I learned dirty words and dirty songs from the children of railroad construction workers and from Z-X cowpunchers. With other boys, I was induced to ride calves and lured into "shit fights" with wet cow manure in the Z-X corrals. . . . We put .22 cartridges or blasting caps on the tracks ahead of approaching handcars or speeders, and once we got satisfactorily chased by the gandy dancers of the section crew.

He remembered, too, the licking he got when he was caught playing with his father's loaded .30-30, and another time when his father was so furious at something he had done that he whacked him with a chunk of firewood, knocking him over the woodbox and breaking his collarbone. On this occasion, his mother, who tried to shield him from his father's temper, was too late. Nevertheless, he and the other boys in town tended to roam freely with very little supervision and engage in activities that, if their parents knew about them, would certainly have led to further lickings.

The frontier culture was hard, often mean, and frequently intolerant. It "sponsored every sort of crude practical joke, as it permitted the cruelest and ugliest prejudices and persecutions." When Wallace was ten or eleven, he became friends with a Chinese cook by the name of Mah Li, who was constantly being victimized by having his pigtail pulled or his shirttails set on fire. Although Wallace considered him a friend, the boy was still under great pressure to conform to the general climate of intolerance and toughness—particularly since he was fighting the label of weakling and crybaby—and "would have been ashamed not to take part in the teasing, baiting, and candy-stealing that made . . . [Mah Li's] life miserable."

Having given way to peer pressure, Wallace came later to regret the betrayal of his friendship, his behavior haunting him until he exorcised it in a story called "The Chink." The opening lines are telling: "After almost a quarter of a century I still remember Mah Li better than I can remember anyone else in that town." In the story, Mah Li (Stegner uses the man's real name) is a Chinese laundryman and truck gardener who delivers vegetables to the boy's family and who befriends the boy. He is cheerful and agreeable, a hard worker, but a lonely outsider who never really becomes acclimated to the white man's world. As time goes by, the boy becomes more and more friendly with the Chinese, although they communicate more with gestures than by language. But the boy still shares the community prejudice to some extent and doesn't really think of Mah Li and his brother, Mah Jim, as people. Then one day the boy hangs around the brothers' garden, and Mah Li gives him a vine-ripened tomato:

> I remember how heavy and sun-warmed the tomato was, and how I had to jump backward and stick out my face because the juice spurted and ran down my chin when I bit into it. We stood in the plant-smelling garden, under the yellow summer hills, with the sun heavy and hot on our heads, and laughed at each other, and I think that's where I first found out that Mah Li was human.

But despite the growing affection between the two, on Halloween the boy is part of a gang that turns over the Chinese brothers' outhouse, with one of the brothers in it. The boy thinks it is Mah Jim, but it is Mah Li. Finally, after several opportunities to stop the prank, to report the problem to the authorities, the boy discovers his friend in the outhouse, unconscious. In part the boy has been delayed by the outbreak of the 1918 flu, but primarily by his hesitation to go against the group. Mah Li is dead and Mah Jim will go back to China.

The story is heartbreaking without resorting to sentimentality. It follows very closely what Stegner has reported happened in life—Mah Li did in fact die—and we can infer that a hard lesson had to be learned: the pain of being scorned by the group is neither as deep nor as long-lasting as the realization that one has done the wrong thing by going along with the group. And in looking back, the author could see that he was led astray by what he later was able to identify as the callous frontier values of that time and place. "It was," he has said, "the cowboy tradition, the horseback culture that impressed itself as image, as romance, and as ethical system upon boys like me." He had participated in his own "Oxbow Incident" as a child and lived to regret it, a regret that would contribute to one of his major preoccupations as a writer.

Another matter of regret that came out of those values was his frequent occupation of killing. In a slight exaggeration he has claimed to have shot at anything that moved within sight during those years. "Nothing," he has written, "could have prevented us from hunting, fishing, trapping, and generally fulfilling ourselves as predators. I think there was not a boy who did not have a .22 by the time he was ten or

eleven." Whereas he trapped record numbers of gophers and killed a
miscellany of other prairie animals out on the homestead, his efforts in
town concentrated on trying to trap animals along the river for their
fur—weasel/ermine and mink—partly for the challenge but also in an
effort to make some money.

The exorcism of this regret of wholesale killing comes much later in
his life in the novel *All the Little Live Things*, in which Joe Allston,
retired to the suburbia of the San Francisco peninsula, spends part of his
time trying to raise a garden. Like a man obsessed, he pursues a blood-
thirsty eradication program against pests. These include gophers, which
he shoots with a shotgun, poisons, traps, or drowns. But a new neighbor,
Marian Catlin, who discovers him with a shotgun blasting a gopher,
objects, and we feel that the author's sympathy has come around to her
side of the question:

> I should think you'd have a nice natural garden where things are in
> balance and you don't have to kill anything. Is it fair to plant a lot
> of plants that were never intended to grow here, and then blame
> the gophers for liking them?

All the Little Live Things was published in 1967, some fifty years after
Wallace's childhood killing sprees. His guilt lingered—prodding the
writer to write, as well as contributing to his motivation to adopt a
conservation-environmentalist ethic. "My adult contrition for all the
killing we did made an environmentalist of me later," he has said.

Not all of Wallace's activities in Eastend were destructive or mischievous. Another element in the making of a future conservationist was his
participation in the Boy Scouts. "A man named Briscoe," he recalls, "was
the scout master. We were all too young to be boy scouts, but he organized us anyway." With the scouts and also as part of his schooling, he
was involved early in life in nature study, a process that evolved into the
lifelong habits of observing nature closely and of reading in various disciplines related to nature: "I can remember little tours down into the
brush with a grade school teacher in the second or third grade, identifying plants and flowers and berries."

School was the one place where he could achieve, but his success there
seemed of dubious value at the time:

School, and success therein, never fully compensated for the lacks I felt in myself. I found early that I could shine in class, and I always had a piece to speak in school entertainments, and the teachers found me reliable at cleaning blackboards, but teachers were women, and school was a woman's world, the booby prize for those not capable of being men. The worst of it was that I liked school, and liked a good many things about the womanish world, but I wouldn't have dared admit it, and I could not respect the praise of my teachers any more than I could that of my music teacher or my mother.

In the Eastend school the children were in class from eight to four, five days a week, and, depending on the crops, as much as nine months a year. The teachers, on the whole, were at least average in performance and often "made up in enthusiasm and dedication whatever they may have lacked in training." As Wallace advanced through the grades, the curriculum became more and more rigorous: geography, English, arithmetic, and history—mostly of Europe, although some of Canada. They read, and he memorized and recited, a great deal of poetry, mostly Longfellow, Tennyson, and a lot of "Tom Moore-ish kind of poetry." At recess there was usually a bare-knuckle fight between two boys (Wallace's brother was often a participant), and at lunchtime they played games—mainly "run, sheep, run"—and often the kids would go down to the river to see if they could find a muskrat swimming in the water to throw stones at from above.

In 1916, two years after Wallace and his mother came to Eastend, George began work on a house on the west end of town, near a bend of the river. He may have bought the lot, but the family always understood that he won it in a poker game. In his youth, George had apprenticed as a carpenter, so the house was well-built and a bit fancier than many of the others in town: two stories, with four gables—each a bedroom—and downstairs, a front hall, dining room, living room, and kitchen. He also put up a small barn, where the family kept a cow, pigs, and chickens; the horses were just turned loose to roam in the hills up behind town. After almost a year of work, in 1917 the house was finished.

Hilda kept a kitchen garden and, having been raised on a farm, was used to canning and preserving, so that all in all the family was nearly self-sufficient. When groceries were needed, the boys would be sent to the store with their wagon to haul the supplies back. Wallace's chores included feeding the chickens, and despite the nausea his fictional counterpart feels in response to such activities in his story "In the Twilight," he regularly cut off the heads of chickens at the old chopping block. He also was assigned to dashing the churn, gathering eggs, milking the cow, bringing in the kindling, and running errands.

Like other children in those days who spent a lot of time alone and who, at the same time, were shut in for long periods due to bad weather and northern darkness, Wallace became an avid reader. The first year on the homestead there wasn't much to read, so the following summers he brought schoolbooks with him and the occasional book that he was able to buy for himself: "I can remember my brother and me, on our muskrat-pelt money, buying books for ourselves for Christmas. I remember buying Owen Wister's *Red Men and White*. Here's the beginning of the western myth." Once the Stegners were settled in their own home and began to acquire furniture and housewares, they even began to accumulate some books:

[We had] some novels of George Barr McCutcheon and Gene Stratton-Porter, a set of Shakespeare in marbled bindings with red leather spines and corners, and a massive set of Ridpath's *History of the World*. I handled them all, and I suppose read in them some, uncomprehendingly, from the time I was five. Their exteriors are still vivid to me; their contents have not always stuck. . . . Until I began to get a few books of my own—Tarzan books, or the Bar-Twenty novels of B. M. Bower, principally—my favorite volumes were the Ridpath histories, because I liked the spidery steel engravings with which they were illustrated.

Wallace's mother told it around town with some pride that her son had read through the history volumes before he was six—which, as he has declared, was not true; he like the pictures. It was part of her campaign to defend him in the intolerant frontier culture as sensitive and talented. He did have a precocious sense of a need for a family history, a need for connection with the past that would seem to be the seed from which a later love of history would develop. Wanting to have a past to which he could be committed and having some desire, even as a child, for a sense of tribal continuity, he found himself forced to turn to Norway, from which his maternal grandfather and grandmother had emigrated. All throughout his childhood, he signed his books and most personal documents with the Norwegian name, Hardanger, that his grandfather had given up in coming to America. "It seems to me now an absurdity that I should have felt it necessary to go as far as the Hardanger Fjord for a sense of belonging," he wrote many years later.

Although Wallace spent at least two months every summer with only his parents, and spent many a dark winter day reading, we should not get the impression that he was always solitary. Besides his brother, Wallace had several close friends among the boys his age, and sometimes they roamed as a gang, playing games or getting into trouble. He recalled that when it came time for them to move from Eastend, it was his friends he missed most. His closest friend was Neville Huffman. Wallace remembered that "they lived two doors from one another and were right there if there was sleighing or skating or swimming, and all the kinds of after school or after dinner and before dark kinds of games. . . . It was very much a block playing kind of thing." When a family with a horse and sleigh would come out for a pleasure ride, the word was passed quickly. Wallace, Neville, and friends would gather with their sleds, one kid hooking up to the sleigh and each in turn to the ankles of a kid in front of him, so that there might be a train of a dozen children being hauled behind the sleigh.

When the ice on the river was right—when it wasn't snowing and the wind had calmed down—families would gather for skating parties with a big bonfire on the ice. It would be four or five feet thick and clear, so you could see the bottom, with air bubbles the size of silver dollars. And on Saturday nights, the Pastime Theater, which served as a curling rink during the week, would put in chairs and show movies. The whole town would turn out, women sitting on one side, men on the other, while the projector whirred and the piano player accompanied the action.

There were several major events that impressed themselves forcefully on the young boy's mind: the time when the Canadian Pacific bridge was brought down by an ice jam, and the town celebrated by collecting enough firewood at the edge of the river to last for a year; the blizzard of 1916—fifty-one below zero and eighty-mile-an-hour wind—which marooned the children and their teachers in the schoolhouse for a day and a night and part of the next day before George Stegner and others could beat their way to the rescue. But the event that seems to have made the most impression, appearing a half-dozen times in Stegner's writings, was the ordeal of the 1918 flu, which in two days filled the four rooms of the schoolhouse with beds for the sick and dying. "Everyone in town had been enlisted, either as patient or victim or helper. A tenth of the town died, beside a lot of farmers who had crowded in to be near help. The cemetery was a less lonesome place thereafter, and the bonds between the survivors were stronger." These and other such trials that helped to make the town a community impressed themselves on the boy's mind not only because of their drama, but because he shared a sense of exhilaration in the spirit of cooperation that they called forth. He never forgot that feeling. For him, this was the West at its best.

Despite being a runt and classified as a crybaby, Wallace felt Eastend was a good place to grow up—or, as Wallace has said in looking back, a good place to be a boy, but not so good to be a man. It was very disappointing for his father. The very first summer on the homestead, 1915, brought in a big crop of wheat, "forty bushels to the acre at nearly three dollars a bushel," a rate that over several years would have made them "rich." The demand for wheat during the war was high and the price was good. But in 1916 George plowed a hundred acres and lost the crop—the weather had been too wet and the wheat developed rust. In 1917 the family's crops were burned out by hot winds, and the following year, with still more acres, they were burned out again. Doubling his acres for one last try in 1919, George faced a summer with almost no rain at all and "the fields were dust before mid-July." Like the gambler he was, George upped the stakes each following year, and every year he lost. Hedging his bet one year, he also rented some bottomland near town and grew several hundred bushels of potatoes, which he stored in the basement of the hotel waiting for the right price. But the hotel burned down. That winter he supported the family by playing poker. All in all he made more money playing poker during those years than by farming.

Even before the last crop died, George was out and around in Montana scouting for new prospects. His reaction to the accumulated failure was not discouragement but anger. He was, his son recalled, furious and determined to leave "this dung-heeled sagebrush town on the disappearing edge of nowhere." When Wallace had come to Eastend, he was five; he would be eleven when they left. He had seen it change from tiny village to a substantial town, from horse and wagon to automobile, a town that now had telephones and electricity. These were the most impressionable years of his life, he has declared. "I wouldn't have missed the experience of childhood in Saskatchewan for anything. I drew more from that than from anywhere else. I was marked by the space and geography of the plains."

When the family left town in 1920, Wallace recalled, "I was desolate at leaving my friends, my town, my life. In the back seat I pulled a blanket over my head so that the others would not see my tears." Years later, in 1943, the writer would use this moment to end a short story, "The Colt" (a story that is also part of chapter five of *The Big Rock Candy Mountain*), combining it with another emotional blow that had come to him as a boy the year before leaving town.

In life it was a traumatic moment of horror and sadness: he had seen the colt he had loved, which had broken forelegs and which he thought might heal with steel braces, skinned and rotting in the town dump. His father had secretly arranged with a neighbor to put the animal out of its misery, and the neighbor had carelessly tossed the carcass out with the garbage to rot. In the story Stegner's fictional counterpart, Bruce, spots the colt with its "bloated, skinned body . . . the chestnut hair left a little way above the hooves, the iron braces still on the broken front legs," and buries his head in the blankets under him, sobbing. In thinking back in his life on that discovery, Stegner has said, "I think I might eventually have accepted the colt's death, and forgiven his killer, if it had not been for that dirty little two-dollar meanness that skinned him."

Leaving Saskatchewan was difficult for Wallace. He mourned what he was leaving behind—everything he had intimately known, everything he was. And he was anxious about what might be ahead. He could tell, just by looking at her, that his mother felt the same way, but his father and brother were leaning out of the car, exhilarated by the motion, by the fence posts flying by, anxious only that they not somehow miss their destination: Great Falls, Montana, a sizable mining and cattle town of some twenty-five thousand. The family would live there fifteen months, from the spring of 1920 to June 1921, and then move on again.

Just as he had in the months before they left Eastend, Wallace's father ran whiskey. In Saskatchewan he carried it across the border into dry Canada; by the time the family moved to Montana, the Volstead Act had been passed and George began a long career of bootlegging liquor from Canada, which was gradually becoming wet, into the United States. In *The Big Rock Candy Mountain*, there is a long section that details George's adventures on a whiskey run over back roads into Saskatchewan. In life, one of the first things George did with his profits was sell the Ford and buy a big, powerful Essex, which could carry a heavy load, maneuver through mud and snow, and be fast enough to get away, if chased. There weren't any closed cars at the time, so he drove with the side curtains on, making it difficult to see inside. Since anyone driving alone in a fast car in border territory was under suspicion, he set up a dummy in the passenger side of the front seat.

Wallace's initial reaction to his new home was one of amazement:

In my first days there I made the acquaintances of things I had read about but never seen: lawns, cement sidewalks, streetcars, streets with names, homes with numbers. I had never known anybody with a street address. Now I had one myself: 448 Fourth Avenue North. And in the house on Fourth Avenue North were other things I had never seen: hardwood floors that were wonderful to skate around on in stocking feet, a bathroom with a tub and running water, a flush toilet. It was incredible that only the day before, we had lived in a world of privies and wash basins and slop buckets.

He had to practice with the toilet a bit to realize that it would not repeat its act immediately and that "it had a little folding saddle and did not have to be ridden bareback." But the most traumatic experience within the new civilization was the discovery of electrical outlets in the baseboards of the new house. Finding one that had the insides missing,

leaving a hole about an inch in diameter and an inch deep, he decided
that this would be a perfect little wall safe in which to store his nickels
and pennies. As he shoved a stack of coins into the hole ... the world
exploded in his face and he was knocked silly. The whole environment
was intimidating. He didn't know what he would face outside; he was
afraid of meeting strange kids on the street.

His initial experiences at school were in their own way equally traumatic. He had left Eastend having finished sixth grade and with a letter
from his teacher saying that he was ready for the eighth grade. When he
went to junior high school, he was not only the smallest child in
the class, but at least two years younger than the others. He had daydreams of entering his new school a sensation—dressed as a frontiersman out of the wilderness—but as he entered the classroom late, the
class erupted into laughter. Worse, the teacher, Miss Temby, picking up
on his vulnerability as small, frightened, and different, made him her
scapegoat and thereafter led the laughter at his expense. He learned the
lesson that tyrants find scapegoats necessary to divert hostility away
from themselves.

As autocratic as Miss Temby was, he still tried to please her. Success
in school was his only possible success. He was too little for sports or for
the Boy Scouts (the group in Eastend had not been an official troop), too
little to get a job like his brother did. For a long time he stayed in his
room as much as possible; he even reverted to baby talk, which drove his
father crazy. When Miss Temby assigned the class ten lines of Joaquin
Miller's "Columbus" to memorize, Wallace memorized the whole poem
and recited it, to his teacher's delight, without a mistake. She was probably the first to indicate to him that he might have a literary career
when she read aloud and praised a theme of his about getting half-
buried in a cave-in near Eastend. "But I never forgave her, even when
she praised me, for when it mattered, she had laughed, and invited the
class to laugh; and laughter is the bitterest of all disparagements."

By spring he had made some friends. Among them was the boy next
door, an entrepreneur who sold ice-cream cones in the park during the
summer. He was able to hire Wallace as his assistant—for nothing. "I
thought," Wallace recalled, "he was pretty hot stuff ... he was about my
age, but he was savvy and I was not." He was also able finally to join the

Boy Scouts and belong to something, and it was as if by joining with this group and engaging once again in outdoor activities he was saved. With the scouts he spent weekends hiking to the Giant Spring or to Black Eagle Falls and on one occasion up the Missouri, where they swam a channel and camped on Third Island. Given time he might have felt as much at home in Montana as he had in Saskatchewan, but by the beginning of summer 1921 the Stegners were on the road again, now in a Hudson Supersix, seeing the West, with "our camp beds and Stoll autotent on the running boards and a big grub box on the rear bumper."

This was a family camping trip but also a reconnaissance for Wallace's father, who once again was looking for a new opportunity. The family spent several weeks on the road, first touring Yellowstone, then camping out alongside Henry's Fork of the Snake River, and finally setting up camp in a canyon east of Salt Lake in the Wasatch Mountains. They were captivated by the area, and since George was determined to relocate, they went back to Great Falls, cleaned out the house, and moved to Salt Lake City. For Wallace and his mother it was less of a wrench than leaving Eastend, but it was still an uprooting, again facing uncertainty.

Although it had a population of a hundred thousand, much of Salt Lake was more reminiscent of a large, well-laid-out Midwestern town than what we think of today as a city. A neat, relatively compact downtown of stores and offices was surrounded by imposing homes of brick and stone, which in turn gave way to Victorian frame houses, progressively smaller as one moved away from the city center. The houses bordered on clean, broad streets, and throughout the more affluent residential areas there were trees, lawns, and flower beds. Dominating the center of the city were the Mormon Tabernacle and Temple; half a mile north, on a hill, the State Capitol overlooked the city; to the east, at the foot of the mountains, was the University of Utah. What seems to have stuck in Stegner's mind was a sort of wonder at the city's general atmosphere, its quality of light and feeling of space: "How it lies under a bright clarity of light and how its outlines are clean and spacious, how it is dignified with monuments and steeped in sun tempered with shade, and how it lies protected behind its rampart mountains."

Wallace would spend his twelfth through twenty-first years in Salt

Lake City and would come to consider it his hometown. "The Mormons who built it and lived in it," he has written, "had a strong sense of family and community, something the Stegners and the people they had lived among were notably short of." In fact George was still bootlegging and running a "blind pig," an illegal saloon, in his house; in order to avoid the law, the family would change houses every few months, more than twenty times in nine years. For Wallace it was once again a lonely life, and he was driven back into himself, into schoolwork and reading.

During the decade that he was in Salt Lake City, the Mormons would have a profound effect on Wallace's life, his philosophy, and his career. Although never embracing the religion itself, he would end up writing two histories of the Mormon movement west and the development of their territory. He would make many close friends among their members, and through church organizations that were open to members and nonmembers alike, he was able to grow and develop socially. What appealed to him most was that the Mormons seemed to stand for everything that was the opposite of his father's life and goals. The church emphasized cooperation rather than rugged individualism and endorsed a solid family life of the sort that he had not known. Indeed, although a liberal, politically and in regard to most social issues, through his life Stegner has demonstrated also a conservative streak in regard to family issues and personal morality that would seem to have at least in part come out of his Mormon associations.

Out of the loneliness, Wallace found himself "always volunteering to do something," trying to ingratiate himself with others in the neighborhood or at school. "What I most wanted," he has reflected, "was to belong to something." Throughout the next ten years, high school and college, this painful need to belong demonstrated itself in his joining one group after another, and it would become one of the motivations for the later emphasis in his writings on the need for cooperation. The Mormons of Salt Lake City were nothing if not collective and cooperative, and Mormon institutions were "made to order for belongers." Wallace recalled:

> I suppose one of the things that made me feel friendly to the Mormons all my life is the fact that, in Utah, again a waif and torn up

again from any kind of association and friendship, somebody took
me down to the Ward House one Tuesday night and here was all
this going on and everybody belonging to something, you know....
So I spent all my Tuesday nights in the Ward House.

There, he found dances, sports, scout meetings—friendly and welcoming
people enjoying themselves.

Wallace had been an unofficial Boy Scout in Eastend, part of a troop
in Great Falls, and now he entered into the activities of his new troop
with a vengeance. He "went up through the ranks to Eagle like smoke
through a chimney." Some measure of his desperation to belong and be
admired for something was demonstrated in his admission later in life
that he cheated in getting two merit badges on his way to Eagle Scout.
That cheating stuck in his craw for decades, and that regret is probably
in part responsible for producing a grown man who clearly would rather
die than lie or cheat anyone for any reason.

But with the new scout troop he was once again lucky enough to be
with a group that had a lot of outdoor activities. There were weekend
camping trips up in the Wasatch Mountains just beyond the city, both
sponsored and informal. Just east of his backyard, seven canyons opened
up, accessible for hiking. To go farther, the boys would snatch rides on
the D&RG Railroad freight cars as they labored up the grade into the
mountains. Up there was another climate, another world from the city, a
world of climbing, fishing, and hunting; of orchards and forests, pastures
and meadows, rocky cliffs and waterfalls. Then, two years after his
family moved to Salt Lake, he went on a two-week trip with his scoutmaster and the scoutmaster's son to the Grand Canyon, Zion, and Bryce.
He had a very early taste, while these places were still just National
Monuments, of the country he later would become so attached to, help to
preserve, and treat in several works of nonfiction.

Whether by his father's design or by accident, most of the houses that
the Stegners occupied during these years were in the east or southeast
part of town so that Wallace never had to leave East High School, but he
did find himself beating his way to school "across lots from many different directions." It was a good school that, in looking back, he feels
gave him better training in fundamentals than his grandchildren
received in much more sophisticated places. But during his first year he

had to face rejection and isolation yet again. ROTC was compulsory in those days, but he didn't meet the minimum weight, and he found himself the only boy in school who wasn't in uniform. In desperation he began a program of overeating and lifting bricks. Since he had grown up with a rifle, he was a good enough shot to make the rifle team, thinking to use that as leverage to get into the ROTC. But it backfired—he wasn't allowed to compete with the team since he was not in the officers training program. The muscle-building regimen worked, however, and by his junior year he was accepted, and by applying himself in his usually intense way, he shot up through the ranks from file-closer to sergeant, to first sergeant, to second, and then to first lieutenant. He recalled, "I had my moment of glory when, in Sam Browne belt, leather puttees, shoulder pips, and sword, I led a platoon down Main Street in the Decoration Day parade."

Also while in high school he began to pursue sports. His father had been a club baseball player, and his brother was a star pitcher on the high school team and played varsity football, so that there was pressure here, too, for Wallace to succeed, to define himself in masculine terms as something other than just a good student. At first he was too small to compete on school teams, but he played a lot of sandlot baseball and football, and through the Ward House he joined basketball club teams that played in gyms throughout the city. But it was tennis that really would become his sport.

One day his mother was passing one of the municipal tennis courts and saw her son intently watching the play through the fence. After seeing him a second time, evidently entranced by the game, she bought him a secondhand racket. Again with his typically intense application, he became a very good player, making the high school tennis team. He was doing something he was proud of, something that made him stand out from the crowd, something that brought him friends, and something that allowed him to feel, more than any other activity he had engaged in, that he really belonged. Later in life he would look back and declare that it was tennis that really saved him from the army of the estranged and disaffected. By the time he got through college, he reckoned that he had played on just about every public and private court in and around the city, and tennis would remain a lifelong passion.

His habit of reading nearly anything he could get his hands on con-

tinued through high school. The summer after his high school sophomore year he worked for the Utah News Company, which was a wholesale distributor of magazines, but also carried books, so that the
basement was full of sets of boys' books—like the Tom Swift and Hardy
Boys series. He was able to take these home and read them. He became a
"library freak." He recalls that "I was always down at the library taking
books out four and six at a time." At the same time in the various houses
that the family rented there were often books or sets of books left behind
in bookcases. In one house the previous tenants had left behind a yard or
so of Joseph Conrad's works, and suddenly Wallace's tastes graduated
from adventure novels and boys' books to include works of literature.
Near the end of his life, he still remembered his excitement while
reading *Almayer's Folly* and "Typhoon." He credited his love of Conrad
for first directing him toward becoming a writer and claimed Conrad's
works, along with the stories of Chekhov, to have been the most important influences on his own writing.

2

FROM PRIMITIVE
TO INTELLECTUAL:
The Education of
Wallace Stegner

Out of Wallace's high school years emerges a picture of a boy with incredible energy, determination, and ambition. His life was a living testament to the virtues extolled by the boys' books that he devoured. He was indeed "Ragged Wally" (after the Horatio Alger hero Ragged Dick), who came out of a childhood of social and cultural deprivation to climb the ladder of success. He was the runt scorned by his father and often by his peers—sometimes he felt by the whole world—who made good.

But unlike Alger's heroes, his goal was never wealth so much as acceptance and belonging, never acquisition of material goods so much as the gaining of some recognition, some status beyond scorn. He seemed to rise to the top of or conquer everything he tackled. He combined constant reading, a heavy schedule of schoolwork (which gave him superior grades throughout), participation in sports, and achievement in scouts and ROTC with frequent outings and camping trips. In addition, he always had a summer job and often worked after school or on weekends. An extremely intelligent, capable boy who had been hurt, frustrated, and embarrassed was not defeated, did not withdraw totally into himself or give up and go wrong, but instead took his problems as a challenge, and in a sense his whole life story became an answer to the insecurities he had felt and the pain he had endured.

Insofar as it may have pushed him to fight and endure, his frontier childhood had been a blessing, despite its disadvantages; and despite the pain, his anger toward his father and his general discomfort with his family's circumstances no doubt contributed to his energy, determination, and fiery ambition. He seems to have recognized this himself when at the end of his autobiographical novel *The Big Rock Candy Mountain*, Bruce, his fictional counterpart, is depicted by the narrator as adding up his gains and losses while meditating about the past, standing over his father's grave:

> Perhaps that was what it meant, all of it. It was good to have been along and to have shared it. There were things he had learned that could not be taken away from him. Perhaps it took several generations to make a man, perhaps it took several combinations and re-creations of his mother's gentleness and resilience, his father's enormous energy and appetite for the new, a subtle blending of masculine and feminine, selfish and selfless, stubborn and yielding, before a proper man could be fashioned. He was the only one left to fulfill that contrast and try to justify the labor and the harshness and the mistakes of his parents' lives.

He was born weak, but became tough; he grew up in a family with no history of schooling beyond grade school and he would go on to get a Ph.D.; he was raised a rough, uncultured Westerner and he would go on to teach at Harvard.

In his senior year, between the ages of fifteen and sixteen, a miracle happened which would change his life: he suddenly grew six inches. "It was," he recalled, "like a second graduation, more important to me than graduation from high school and the beginning of the happiest years I ever knew or will know. Suddenly, I was big enough to hold my own in sports. Suddenly I had friends who looked on me as an equal and not as a maggot." Suddenly, he found that he could compete to get dates with the girls that he had only been able to admire and lust after from afar.

In his senior year he carried on his heavy load of activities and added work on the yearbook, which was the first time he had written for publication. With his increase of height, he devoted more energy to his tennis game, and within a short time ranked second on the high school varsity.

He met one of his best friends during this period, Jack Irvine, while playing tennis, and he and Jack representing East High, in turn, became friends with Milton Cowan and Lyn Crone, the two top players of West High School.

The one negative trait that Wallace displayed during these years, especially when disappointed on the court, was a terrible temper. When he missed a shot he should have made, he would become furious. He would have to fight to control that temper throughout the rest of his life. He was tough on himself in nearly everything he did, as one might expect from someone as competitive as he became. Nevertheless, despite the drive that pushed him constantly, because of his sudden growth and because of his involvement in tennis he was a much happier person leaving high school than he was entering it.

Stegner's autobiographical novel dealing with his high school and college years, *Recapitulation* (1979), looks back forty-five years, written when he was in his late sixties. Strictly speaking, it is not really a sequel to his novel of growing up, *The Big Rock Candy Mountain*; rather, it parallels the latter part of it by going back to retell the story of Bruce Mason's life in Salt Lake City in a more penetrating way. *Recapitulation* is a book about memory that contains the author's real memories. It fictionally processes them, giving them dramatic form and thematic relevance, while at the same time adding "memories" that are invented. It is also a novel about time—one might say it is a meditation on the nature of time, memory, and the processes of remembering.

As such it is a book of flashbacks, constantly switching and playing with point of view and perspective. At the center of this complexity of technique is Stegner's concern with identity—who are we, as we look back on ourselves, and what is real in the present as it has come out of the past. At one point the narrator describes older Bruce thinking:

> Simultaneously aware of where he is, and how familiar it is . . . he feels how the whole disorderly unchronological past hovers just beyond the curtain of the present, attaching itself to any scent, sound, touch, or random word that will let it get back in.

But the technique is not simply flashbacks, in that these memories are triggered by a variety of circumstances in several different ways, and many of them take on the aura of dream, of nightmare, or of short fiction (self-consciously presented as fictitious adaptation). What we have in this latter situation is a fiction within a fiction about a real life. By wrapping the past in a package of fiction—laden with doubts and possibilities for the reader—the author/narrator, and Bruce, pretend to exercise a control they really cannot exercise totally:

> What he liked about the past he could coat with clear plastic, and preserve it from scratching, fading, and dust. What he did not like, he could either black out or revise. Memory, sometimes a preservative, sometimes a censor's stamp, could also be an art form.

However, beyond the fictitious version of a life, for the older Bruce (and behind him the author), the pain is real, the dismay is real. The self-conscious use of the conventions of fiction become not only a mask to hide behind, but an anesthetic. In the words Malcolm Cowley used to describe Hemingway's "Big Two-Hearted River," Stegner's novel is not just an exorcism of the painful memories of embarrassment, loss, and rejection, it is also, as a whole, a "spell to banish evil spirits."

As ritual drama, the novel begins in painful recollection and ends in reconciliation. The "reconciliation" is not only emotional and figurative, it is also literal. By bringing the past into the present, the older Bruce brings to life a younger Bruce as a sort of doppelgänger throughout, and at the end of the novel the doppelgänger is not banished back to the past, but joins the older version to form a complete person—at last.

Early in the novel, Bruce thinks of his younger self, recreating an earlier version of himself to be his companion for the duration of the novel. But the author is also, one might presume, providing a wonderfully insightful, frank appraisal of the young Stegner's emotional condition. As the older Bruce walks down South Temple Street, he

> walked double. Inside him, moving with the same muscles and feeling with the same nerves and sweating through the same pores, went a thin brown youth, volatile, impulsive, never at rest, not so much a person as a possibility, or a bundle of possibilities: subject to enthusiasm and elation and exuberance and occasional great black

moods, stubborn, capable of scheming but often astonished by consequences, a boy vulnerable to wonder, awe, worship, devotion,
hatred, guilt, vanity, shame, ambition, dreams, treachery; a boy
avid for acceptance and distinction, secretive and a blabbermouth,
life-crazy and hence girl-crazy, a show-off who could be withered
by a contemptuous word or look, a creature overflowing with brash
self-confidence one minute and oppressed by its own worthlessness
the next; a vessel of primary sensations undiluted by experience,
wisdom or fatigue.

Asked if this was an accurate picture of him early in his college career,
Stegner replied, "Yes, absolutely."

The older Bruce goes on to think that he would like himself and his
younger double to be able "to see without being seen, as if they looked
through one-way glass," and that is precisely the position of the author
here. He wants confession and the release of confession (the narrative
has much in common with St. Augustine's famous work) without paying
the price. In this meditation on the past, what are the sins that Bruce
Mason, Wallace Stegner's persona, confesses? Pride (while inferior in
size and status, he feels he is better than everyone else, that they are
"inferior to him in brains and potential"); envy (he "coveted the kind of
notice he saw given to football heroes, sheiks, slickers, and campus politicians with glib tongues"); cowardice (he repeatedly fails to face up to
physical and moral challenges, particularly those presented to him by
women); hatred (he hates his father, with whom he feels he is in competition—that "harsh judge who must be appeased"—and hates Jack
Bailey—whose memory is "unpleasant and troubling" and who is his
rival for Nola, the first real love of his life). And he confesses to lust. In
its blundering discoveries and mournful epiphanies and in the tensions
between virtue and vice, between Puritanism and liberation, the novel
also is very reminiscent, particularly in its tone, of Joyce's *The Dubliners*
and *Portrait of the Artist as a Young Man*. We don't usually think of
Stegner as a religious writer, but while he may not concern himself with
the metaphysical, he does reflect the ethical concerns of Christianity.

Because he had skipped years in his schooling, Wallace was a very
young freshman at the University of Utah at age sixteen. When he

entered he was slightly over six feet tall and weighed a hundred twenty-five pounds—a classic case of stringbean, a callow youth anxious to make his mark. He made most of his friends while playing high school tennis, and they all planned to make the university team. Among them was Milton Cowan, who recalls that he and several others drove over to pick up Wallace so they could all go over to the campus and pay their registration fees: "The humiliation was very painful when he was getting the twenty-five dollars. The old man, in our presence, wanted everybody to know that for crying out loud it was just a bunch of God-damned nonsense for every kid to want to go to college. It was all very embarrassing to Wally. It more or less endeared him to us, but it also added to our dislike of the old man." This kind of response by his father—not at all atypical of him—led Wallace to want to get as much financial independence as possible, as soon as possible, while still going to school.

The university in the fall of 1925 was a streetcar school of barely three thousand students. It was safe, friendly, comfortable, and, like the city itself, bathed in light and cheerfully landscaped. It was a happy and relaxed place that exuded a spirit of optimism—Western optimism, Mormon optimism, youthful optimism. Stegner remembered his experience there as "good . . . because that was the first chance any of us had to see minds at work at all. They weren't great minds, but they were at work, and I think there was a lot of good teaching that went on. . . . My teachers . . . were very kind to me, and they opened up a lot of doors."

Several things happened in his first year that would influence the course of his career in college and, in a couple of instances, his life thereafter. A crucial test was passed (because it was the lynchpin of his confidence and self-esteem) when he made the freshman tennis team; he was accepted into a fraternity, Sigma Nu; he took his freshman composition class from the writer and poet Vardis Fisher (who had not yet published a book when Stegner studied under him); and his continuing friendship with Jack Irvine and his family led to a job with the I & M (Irvine and Miller) Rug and Linoleum Company, a job he kept all through college and which gave him the money to buy his own clothes and pay his own way (although until his parents moved from Salt Lake, he still lived at home).

Jack Irvine's counterpart in *Recapitulation*, Joe Mulder, befriends Bruce and helps to change his life:

> He [Bruce] would have played five sets barefoot on broken glass for him. He rescued his summer and perhaps his life. He taught Bruce not only tennis but confidence, and not only confidence but friendship. Simply by accepting that outcast, he made him over. If Bruce Mason knew anything at all about magnanimity, he learned it from Joe Mulder.

Eventually Joe brings him home and Bruce becomes gradually part of his family, entering normal family life for the first time. Then Joe's father, J.J., offers him the job that enables him to gain the financial independence that would carry him all the way through four years at the university.

In the novel, the job is at the Mulder nursery; in life, the job was at the Irvine flooring company, where Wallace worked from one to six every day and all day Saturday. ("Sunday was the day you would go out and play five sets [of tennis], but the rest of the week you had a hard time working it in.") His work consisted primarily of selling rugs, but he also worked on stock and inventory, and often delivered. In addition to working for the rug company, he occasionally took on other jobs, such as taking care of the clay courts at the Salt Lake Tennis Club.

One of the advantages of working at the rug company was that Jack's father was very supportive of the tennis playing of several of his young employees (he had to be, since his son was on the team) and would allow them to adjust their work hours so that they could play the varsity schedule and participate in tournaments during the summer. Wallace continued to sharpen his game and as a sophomore made the varsity, eventually ranking fourth on the team. One member of the team recalls that Wallace "was very competitive. Didn't like to lose. He wasn't a great player—but a good player." Wallace remembered that the summer after his freshman year he entered into a tennis tournament and caught Ellsworth Vines in the first round. Two years later Vines was the national champion.

Another significant event in Wallace's development was the encounter with Vardis Fisher as his freshman writing instructor. Extremely bright himself, Fisher was not overly impressed with his young student. That was not his style. But at the end of the first quarter he did take Wallace out of the beginning class and put him in his advanced class. He gave Wallace good grades, but he made him earn them; one of Fisher's main contributions to Wallace's education was to make him work at writing. As a teacher Fisher was critical, sometimes sarcastic, and not easily satisfied by simplistic answers or clichés. Wallace remembered Fisher as

> one of those teachers who liked to take can openers to unopened minds. He had the notion we were all Mormon provincials, that we'd never seen anything, and that a real idea would shock the pants off us. It was thrilling, in a way, to be treated almost like an adult.

Fisher started a group called the Radical Club, which Wallace was part of during the latter part of his freshman year and for his sophomore year. They discussed such heretical topics as methods of birth control and the historicity of Jesus Christ.

Certainly Fisher's encouragement was one factor in leading Wallace toward becoming an English major—it was in his English classes that he found the most challenge to his thinking and the most stimulation in his reading. There may have also been an unconscious influence on the young man in his eventual career choice, since Fisher's example exposed him early to a professional writer with professional ambitions and standards. But Wallace had no idea at this point of becoming a writer, or a professor, for that matter. Until nearly the end of his time at the university, if he thought about his future at all, he thought vaguely in terms of going on to work at the store and making it a career.

He began his academic career with a vengeance, getting A's, working hard in response to a new challenge. But by the time he reached his second year he was in a fraternity, dating and having a wonderful time, hanging out with the jocks in various beer joints near campus. He and his tennis friends joined together in an informal club called the "Tillicums" ("the common people of an Indian tribe as distinguished from the chiefs"), which gave the group an identity through which they could enter intermural sports teams in university competition. Wallace and Jack Irvine, Milton "Red" Cowan, and the others even adopted a uniform: in an "I-am-a-camera" vision of the past in *Recapitulation*, confirmed as true-to-life by Cowan ("That's the way we dressed"), Bruce sees himself among

> three sunburned boys of sixteen or seventeen or eighteen, one of them very tall, with red hair, one dark and curly-headed, one thin and blond [Bruce/Wallace], all of them in white shirts whose sleeves were rolled nearly to the shoulder, and in white Navy-surplus bell-bottomed ducks with laces at the back of the waist. Slim-hipped identicals, walking with a spring that could at any moment break into a run, they grin back over their shoulders at the camera.

Wallace Stegner was having a hell of a good time. His grades during his sophomore year fell from straight A's to B's.

By the time he was a junior and senior, and had become an English major, Wallace began to gain control of himself academically again, although as he learned the ropes, he was never under such pressure as he was his first year. Nevertheless, he and his friends found the university "pretty abstract and remote and airless" so that the things they looked forward to were the coming of the most recent Jolson movie and the traveling shows that came to the old Salt Lake Theater. Through the influence of Fisher and other campus radicals, Wallace had begun to realize just how provincial and limited his situation was in respect to the world of culture and ideas. Being a Mormon institution, the university gave him "a good bone to chew on ... a great deal of contempt of authority, that kind of authority." And while he came to admire Mormon friendliness, neighborliness, and cooperation, and many of his closest friends were Latter-Day Saints, it was this authoritarian aspect of the church, along with its doctrine (which he found preposterous), that kept him from joining.

During his last two years, Peg Foster (she is fictionalized as Holly in *Recapitulation*) took over the shepherding of Wallace's rebellion where Fisher left off. Foster ran a literary salon for the brighter young professors of English literature and their most promising students. Wallace recalled that despite the airless quality of the university, "I don't think we all felt starved for culture. I don't think we had any capacity for culture. That's where . . . Peg Foster came in because she wrote poetry and she knew a lot of poetry. It was kind of nice, off the university grounds as it were, to run into somebody who took poetry seriously." Red Cowan remembers her as a "rather exotic creature" with slinky dresses, figured shawls, and dangling earrings. Like the Radical Club, Peg Foster's group loved to poke fun at what it considered narrow-minded, bourgeois Salt Lake.

Again, *Recapitulation* is as true a description of Wallace as it is of Bruce when it summarizes his busy life as a senior:

> He was making nearly straight A's—and if he felt that he didn't deserve his grades, considering the amount of studying he did, he carefully kept that opinion to himself. He worked a forty-hour week while going to school and a sixty-hour week during vacations. He bought his own clothes and had bought his own car. He had a bank account that approached a thousand dollars. In that last year of school, he was editing the literary magazine and reading papers for Bill Bennion and another professor friend—how, and during what free time, only God knew. . . . He said and believed that the more he asked himself to do, the more he could do.

Actually, he was reading for three professors his senior year—strike out Bennion, and put in Syd Angleman, Ed Chapman, and L. A. Quivey. All, but particularly Angleman, became friends as well as teachers and employers. Angleman would have patio parties for a circle of professors and students on a regular basis, and in addition to attending those, Wallace felt free simply to drop by Angleman's house to talk.

Although Stegner claimed later that he had no idea while he was an undergraduate of becoming a writer and indeed has said "I didn't know you *could* be a writer," there must have been something, some seed of intention, in the back of his mind. He took fiction writing courses from Quivey, "who was sort of odd, but excited about writing and able to communicate his excitement." Wallace contributed to and edited the university literary magazine, *PEN*. And when Quivey had a writing contest, Wallace entered and won. Art Deck, the editor of the *Salt Lake Telegram*, had agreed to pay the winner of the contest $25 and publish the story. Not only did Wallace gain his first paid publication, he began work as a freelancer for the *Telegram* when the sports editor, an old tennis friend, saw his piece and started giving him assignments— covering tennis matches, amateur boxing, university wrestling matches. Then he started getting assignments from the city editor to review shows when they came into town. Of course, this work did not take the place of other jobs Wallace had. He simply added it to his repertoire.

In his senior year, Wallace dropped out of school for winter and spring quarters. By this time he was living on his own in a dorm and simply ran out of money; he needed to work full-time at the flooring company for a few months in order to get caught up. He would have graduated in 1929, but now graduated in 1930 with what was, in effect, two senior years at the university. In addition to giving up his classes, which for the most part he enjoyed, he had to give up the tennis team for that season.

He still had no specific plan for the future but was simply "going to college." He enjoyed working at the store, where he was given more and more responsibility, and he liked the Irvine family and felt a certain loyalty to them. He probably would have gone on working there after graduation if the chair of the psychology department, Professor Barlow, had not one day asked him, "Why don't you go to graduate school?" Wallace said he didn't know. Barlow asked him, "What if I got you a fellowship in psychology? Would you like to come to graduate school?" Wallace replied, "Sure . . . fine. Great." Later, he related his good fortune to Professor Neff in the English department, who reacted with dismay, "You're an English major. What are you doing in psychology?" He said he would try to get Wallace a fellowship somewhere. Surprised and pleased, Wallace agreed, and shortly afterward found himself looking forward to a teaching assistantship at the University of Iowa.

This was probably *the* major turning point in his career and it had come, as such things so often do, without any deliberate thought, nearly by accident. In response to this and two or three other such accidentally presented opportunities, changes of direction that had profound consequences, Stegner has paraphrased that familiar verse by his friend Robert Frost, "Two roads diverged in a wood, and I—I took the one I was pushed into." So, in the fall of 1930, off he went, not knowing exactly why or comprehending what he was in for, "just like poor old Maurice, the campus moron, given a nickel to buy a root beer." He was off to Iowa, "which I then thought of as the East." Once there, he encountered two people who dramatically affected the course of his life: one was a fellow student, who became a dear friend, and the other a teacher, who would lead him into the studies that would become the basis for his life's work.

One would have to say that Wallace Stegner was very lucky in his friends. In Salt Lake he had been befriended by Jack Irvine and his family, and that had brought him tennis, confidence, and a good job that got him through school. In Iowa City he met Wilbur Schramm. Schramm had just finished his M.A. at Harvard, and he came to Iowa with a background in languages, art, music, and world literature. He was as sophisticated as Wallace was innocent: "I [was an] . . . incomparably green and ill-prepared first-year graduate student from the wild west. . . . [whereas Wilbur] had been seasoned for a year in the intellectual life in the place that called itself headquarters." The contrast between the two was emphasized when they became roommates and Wallace put a .38 in a gunfighter's holster and cartridge belt on his dresser, and Wilbur decorated his with his flute.

In September 1930 Wallace arrived in Iowa City by bus. All that fall it was wet, dark, and gloomy, and Wallace, who was away from home for the first time, began to yearn for Salt Lake:

> Homesickness is a great teacher. It taught me, during an endless rainy fall, that I came from the arid lands, and liked where I came from. I was used to a dry clarity, a sharpness in the air. I was used to horizons that either lifted into jagged ranges or rimmed the geometrical circle of the flat world. I was used to seeing a long way. I was used to earth colors—tan, rusty red, toned white—and the endless green of Iowa offended me. I was used to a sun that came up over mountains and went down behind other mountains. I missed the color and smell of sagebrush, and the sight of bare ground.

But his attacks of homesickness were gradually replaced by a nearly overwhelming burden of work (as if a burden of work could ever really overwhelm him). He has said, in looking back, that he probably learned more, and faster, during those two years in Iowa City than during any other two-year period in his life.

The University of Iowa is one of the great Midwestern land-grant institutions. Its graduate-level creative writing program, since its begin nings at about the time Stegner arrived, has become generally recognized as the best in the country. Wallace's multifaceted career as writer, professor of American literature, and teacher of creative writing had its origins in the emphases provided by his Iowa experience. Most influential on him was a professor, Norman Foerster, who had arrived only a few months before from North Carolina, to become director of the new School of Letters. Foerster was an unusual teacher of literature in those days—he specialized in the not entirely legitimate discipline of American literature (most teachers of English literature doubted there was any such thing until well into this century), having written such books as *Nature in American Literature* (1923), *American Criticism* (1928), and *The American Scholar* (1929) and having in 1934 edited *American Poetry and Prose*, which was one of the most influential college textbook anthologies for several decades. He was also unusual in that he was interested in pushing forward a graduate program in literature that permitted a creative writing master's thesis or Ph.D. dissertation. Something of a pioneer, even a radical, in these areas, he was, however, best known in academic circles for his philosophical conservatism as a leading voice of the New Humanism—a philosophy that was concerned with the history of ideas, the evolution of ideals, and the expression of values and beliefs in literature.

Foerster, and others associated with the movement, such as Irving Babbitt and Paul Elmer More, fought the social realism, radical experimentation, and liberation of the individual from traditional morality that were major components of European and American literature of the 1920s and 1930s, and instead emphasized the importance of control and discipline in the creation and criticism of literature. Wilbur Schramm recalled that while the dozen or so students who joined the School of Letters all admired Foerster for his learning, which was deep and profound, and his critical acumen, they tended to disagree almost entirely with his philosophical position. They all considered themselves Naturalists, admired Hemingway, Huxley, and Frost, and read Joyce, Havelock Ellis, and Freud.

This disagreement between Foerster and his students, which kept the seminars lively, in no way seemed to inhibit his effectiveness as a teacher of literature and writing, nor did it limit his generosity toward his students, whom he invariably supported in their career aspirations. It was Foerster who suggested to Wallace that he go on for his Ph.D. in an academic discipline, namely American literature, since his chances of getting a job with an M.A. with a creative writing thesis would be dim, and it was Foerster who suggested later that Wallace do his dissertation on a Western nature writer, a suggestion that also had an enormous impact on the course of his career.

When Wallace got to Iowa City, he had no intention of becoming a writer, but he still considered himself "literary." The M.A. program with a creative thesis required separate application with samples of writing. Wallace gave Foerster two samples, including the one that the *Salt Lake Telegram* had paid him for, but after reading them, the professor did not think that he was good enough. "That made me mad," Wallace has recalled. "That hurt my pride. I was literary. Of course I was good enough. So I wheedled around and talked to a lot of people and finally got myself into the program with my confidence somewhat dashed."

Wallace found himself embarked on a sixteen-hour-a-day regimen of reading, writing, thinking, discussing, and teaching. He felt that he was "hopelessly chasing other students whom [he] saw as better prepared, better disciplined, and with sharper minds," feeling, as he has said, that "every class, even the freshman classes I taught, opened my eyes to things I should have known but didn't." Schramm, who found his roommate quiet and likable, thought that Wallace engaged himself more fully and tirelessly than he might have needed to, but that he was prompted to make up for the deficit he felt and invariably "he wanted to know more about nearly anything that might come up." They took courses together, several from Foerster, who began calling them "Simon and Schuster" and who occasionally assigned them papers to write jointly. One course that impressed them was his "History of Criticism," which began with Aristotle, and it was at that point that Wallace discovered his roommate knew both Latin and Greek. He prevailed upon Wilbur Schramm to teach him ancient Greek. The idea expanded so that his roommate was conducting an informal seminar every afternoon for a half-dozen of his fellow students.

And Greek was not all. When Wilbur found out that at the age of twenty-one, Wallace had never heard a symphony orchestra, he began making suggestions for radio listening and took him off to concerts. In none of his tutelage was there ever a sense of condescension or officiousness. Wilbur was simply generous and out of friendship wanted to share what he knew or had experienced and enjoyed. And of course he had a student hungry to make up for lost ground—Wallace's eagerness and openness were both amusing and gratifying. Even travel was for Wilbur an opportunity for education, and the two hitchhiked together during vacations, seeking out museums and concerts (or baseball games and jazz sessions) wherever they went. On one occasion at the beginning of their second year, they hitchhiked separately, meeting in Chicago, the farthest east that Wallace had ever been. On campus they had rooms that adjoined in an old, brick dormitory called the Quadrangle, and shortly after getting to know each other, they opened the connecting door, creating a suite of a bedroom on one side and a study on the other. This arrangement also gave them space so that they could play catch for a few minutes in between study sessions.

His two years at Iowa gave Wallace the best of times and the worst: on the one hand there was the constant excitement of intellectual challenge and a new arena in which to prove himself, and he would meet the beautiful young woman who would become his wife. On the other hand, he would suffer illness, the oppression of severe financial difficulty, and the emotional distress of deaths in his family.

3

FROM STUDENT
TO PROFESSOR:
The Further Education
of Wallace Stegner

Shortly after arriving at Iowa, Wallace felt the effects of the Great Depression. All his savings, so laboriously gathered over the years of work in Salt Lake, disappeared in a bank failure. When he awoke one morning to find that every bank in Johnson County, Iowa, had been closed, he and other graduate students were able to survive only by borrowing money from each other and by barter. He and Wilbur Schramm made do. They pooled their meager funds to buy a carton of Shredded Wheat, which gave them at least the certainty of breakfast for the rest of the year.

Then, just after Christmas that first year, Wallace got word that his brother had suddenly died. That big, strong athlete, the one in the family who had seemed beyond illness or disability, had contracted pneumonia while helping to rescue a motorist in the snow. He was only twenty-three. It was a terrible blow to the Stegner family. Wallace recalled that his father, who had put so much hope in the athletic achievements of Cecil, was nearly broken, never quite recovering. "That first reduction of our family," Wallace has written, "made me realize how tight a cluster we were, knotted against respectable society, our own sole resource, our own prison." Wilbur loaned him money for a ticket so that he could go back to Salt Lake City for the funeral, and as Wallace boarded the train, Wilbur put his overcoat over his friend's shoulders.

Wallace's father was jolted into changing the pattern of his life, taking Wallace's mother off to Reno, where he purchased a half interest in a gambling casino. His son's reaction was "at least it was legal." The summer after his first year at Iowa, Wallace took the train once again, this time to meet his mother in Salt Lake. In a gesture typical of her and expressing her pride in her only remaining son, she presented him with a used Model A. Then, with Juanita Crawford, the girl who had been waiting a year for Wallace to return from Iowa, they drove to Reno. Wallace, who had been so involved in his own plans and so concerned about seeing his girl again, felt guilty when he found out that his mother was still suffering some effects from the radical mastectomy she had had two years earlier. The car seemed now a desperate effort to pass on to him something of value before it was too late.

During Wallace's second year at Iowa, the Depression came down on him and Wilbur hard. They seldom ate anywhere but in their rooms, and with milk at two cents a quart and eggs a nickel a dozen, they set records for economy. In looking back, Wallace has commented that in these tough times "in certain curious ways there was more security then than later. You couldn't fall any further, and then you demonstrated to yourself pretty early that you could live." For his master's thesis Wallace wrote a series of three short stories (two of which were published later in newspapers), and he had completed his degree requirements by midyear. Nevertheless, he decided to stay in school:

I looked outside and saw the Depression so deep and black that it was frivolous to think of going out into it and making a living. It was safer in school, where I could live on the $700 I made as a graduate assistant; and besides, my old friend inertia now had me in a rut headed toward the teaching profession. Without a real vocation for scholarship and with imperfect training (my own fault) I decided to go on for the Ph.D.

When he returned to Salt Lake in June 1932, he found that his two years away had cost him his girl. Juanita Crawford was his first serious love affair, an affair that had developed during his last year in Utah. She was a beautiful dark-haired Mormon, but aside from physical attraction they had almost nothing in common: he was becoming an academic and wrote her enthusiastic letters filled with literary allusions; she had little interest in books. What she wanted was marriage and children; he promised marriage, but put her off while he pursued his education. Losing her to another man during his long absence was an event that with common sense he could have predicted but that nevertheless sent him into a tailspin of anger and depression.

Driving on to Los Angeles, where his parents were now living, he was given a second blow when he learned that his mother's cancer had recurred. Rather than go as far away as Iowa, he decided to join his old friend Red Cowan, who, back from his Mormon mission, was taking his Ph.D. in German at the University of California, Berkeley. Wallace has looked back on that year as "a strange interlude, an underwater period." For one thing, the rather stodgy graduate curriculum in English with its emphasis on philology—on Latin, Old French, Anglo-Saxon, and Middle English—was not really his cup of tea. For another, he was haunted by the specter of his mother's poor health.

Nevertheless, Cowan and Stegner, who were living on Cowan's $75-a-month fellowship and Stegner's meager savings, did find some fun. They scraped up enough money to buy a beat-up old sailboat and somehow found the time to refurbish it and then sail it out on the bay. They made regular tours of the ten-cent bargain bins at the many used bookstores in Berkeley—one of the very few hardbound books he bought during these years, Wallace recalled, was Hemingway's *Death in the Afternoon*. And there were plenty of readings, lectures, and musical performances to attend that were free of charge. Cowan remembered one occasion when they went together to hear Aldous Huxley speak.

By the end of the year both of the young men had had enough of Berkeley. It seemed to Wallace that the university, unable to get jobs for its Ph.D.s, simply continued to add requirements for its candidates to limit the number. The prospect of having to take Old Norse was the last straw. Cowan, equally pressured in German and unhappy with his major professor, was beginning to babble the *Niebelungenlied* in his sleep, much to his roommate's dismay. As they left, that June 1933, they decided together to go to Iowa in the fall. Wallace drove first to Salt Lake, dropping off his roommate, and then south to Fish Lake in southern Utah, where his parents had a vacation cabin.

When he arrived, it was clear that his mother was dying. She suffered without complaint, but the pain became so great that on one occasion Wallace, who couldn't stand by and watch her intense suffering any longer, had to go to a nearby Civilian Conservation Corps camp to bring back a doctor to give her a shot. By July, Wallace and his father realized that Hilda needed the more constant medical attention she could only receive in the city, and so, despite her desire to remain, they moved to an apartment in Salt Lake. Shortly afterward, George, the big, burly man who had been so impatient with what he perceived to have been his son's childhood weakness, decided he couldn't take it anymore and disappeared. For this, his son was never able to forgive him.

Summer faded into fall as Hilda gradually declined. In addition to Wallace's attention, she had the frequent company of Red Cowan's mother—Red's parents had the apartment across the hall. On November 1 she finally achieved relief. It had been a very depressing and draining experience for her son, who would carry the emotional burden of her death throughout his life. This experience would reinforce the pain of other, similar experiences much later, as four of Stegner's women friends, in the space of a few months, would die of cancer (and some years later his wife would undergo a radical mastectomy of her own, from which she would recover). The cumulated trauma of these illnesses and deaths would form the background for his novel *All the Little Live Things* (1967), and his last novel, *Crossing to Safety* (1987)—both are stories of remarkable women defeated by cancer.

Hilda's moment of death is very poignantly recorded in a "Letter, Much Too Late," in which he addresses his mother to tell her what she meant to him when she was alive, but somehow never got around to telling her directly: "Somehow I should have been able to say how strong and resilient you were, what a patient and abiding and bonding force, the softness that proved in the long run stronger than what it seemed to yield to." She, he writes, lives on in his head, speaking to him when he faces some "crisis of feeling or sympathy or consideration for others." And she is still with him as a curb on his "natural impatience and competitiveness and arrogance." He recalls sitting up with her that fateful night, after midnight, while the nurse rested, watching her take her last breath. Just before that she had raised her head and asked,

" 'Which ... way?' I understood that: you were at a dark, unmarked crossing. Then a minute later you said, 'You're a good ... boy ... Wallace,' and died.... I knew how far from true your last words were."

After his mother died and his father had returned for the funeral, Wallace found himself stuck in Salt Lake without a job and without money, rooming with a father with whom he had never gotten along and whom he now hated. It was a dreary fall and winter as he struggled with his sense of loss and with his antagonism: "I was," he has written, "never lower in my life." It is this time and this emotional struggle that became the subjects of one of his best-known short stories, "The Blue-Winged Teal" (later incorporated into *Recapitulation* as Chapter 2 of Part IV). It is a story not so much of forgiveness—a frequent Stegner theme—as of something short of that and more ambiguous: the process of working though one's own emotions to achieve some kind of emotional equilibrium.

In February 1934 Wallace hooked up with Red Cowan again, and the two drove in Wallace's Model A to Iowa City to continue their doctoral studies. Shortly he was back in the old dormitory and renewing his friendship with Wilbur Schramm and others and conferring with Norman Foerster about his doctoral program. He enrolled for the second semester and began to attack his first order of business—preparing for his exams. He had no money at all, but within a couple of weeks, Wilbur, who had become director of the university writing program, had found a fill-in job for him at a Lutheran college, Augustana, in Rock Island, Illinois:

> At Augustana I lived in the theological seminary among people training to be Lutheran preachers, and on Thursday evening, when my classes were over, I escaped to Iowa City for a three-day weekend of reading for my Ph.D. exams.

He had a half-time load, which at Augustana involved teaching four classes: he became, in effect, the entire English department at $900 a year. Included in his load was a course on *Beowulf*, in Anglo-Saxon, and he found himself struggling to keep two lines ahead of the class the entire term. The Model A had been put up on blocks in storage for the winter, so he hitchhiked the fifty miles to and from Iowa City every week.

When at Iowa he roomed with Wilbur Schramm, while Red Cowan along with two friends became caretakers for an abandoned fraternity house—"a great place," Cowan recalled, "to party." This would seem to have been the original model for the setting of the story "The View from the Balcony" (1948), which focuses on a character based on Vardis Fisher. Cowan recalled that another mutual friend, Don Lewis, invited Fisher and his wife out from Idaho, and they stayed in the fraternity house: "Fisher immediately dubbed it Eagle Heights. He was a heavy drinker, a loud, violent man and very caustic in his comments about everybody. All of this proved too much for Mary. She didn't like it, so Wally and Mary didn't associate very much with the crowd."

Mary was Mary Page, the woman who would become Wallace's wife. She was diminutive, lively, and very attractive. Unlike Juanita, the girl he had been engaged to in Utah, Mary was an intellectual—knowledgeable about literature and an accomplished musician. Her interests and her values matched those of Wallace very closely, while at the same time she was her own person, self-contained and confident, with opinions of her own. They could talk and did, for hours at a time; he came to not only love her, but admire her. Born and raised in Dubuque, she was a graduate student at the university, working in the library. She had been introduced to Wally by Wilbur Schramm, who continued to have a profound effect on the direction of his friend's life. Mary recalled that first meeting:

> I had gone with Wilbur some, and I was down in his office one afternoon and Wally came in. And Wilbur introduced me and then I remembered that I had read his graduate student's thesis which was a thesis of three short stories. I had been very much impressed with it. So I was very interested and pleased when I met him. That afternoon he called and asked me for a date. . . . He said that Red Cowan was with him and could I get him a date, and so I got him a date with Teddy [Theodora] Romaine, my roommate, and we went out.

Not only did Mary Page become Wallace's wife, but her roommate would become Red Cowan's wife.

Mary fell for Wallace, and he fell deeply in love with her, so deeply that the love they had for each other would sustain and nourish him for the rest of his life. He was tall, handsome, and well-built; she was short, slight, and beautiful, with light hair cut in a pageboy, and a pixie smile. Her intelligence and ready wit engaged him; her Ariel sprightliness delighted him. Throughout the spring, mostly on weekends, he courted her, hitchhiking back and forth from his job at Augustana, impatient to get to Iowa City and dreading the trip back.

Nearly every day while he was gone, he would write to her, even though some of the letters might arrive after he returned and saw her in person. An excerpt from one of those many letters reveals the tender, loving, very private side of him that would always be, in its direct expression, hidden from the world:

My Dear,
 . . . Having japed a little to vent my embarrassment at talking about anything that touches me closely, I can now sit down seri- ously and tell you what loving you means to me. . . . I've told you before that it means a chance at mental health, for one thing, so that you become not only the woman I love but a sort of Messiah. I hope you don't mind being invested with super-mundane qualities. I will grant you faults, if you wish, but I still insist that you are an angel, although perhaps with a slight limp. And I love you because you are fine and clean and youthful and high-hearted and honest and loving and dozens and dozens of other adjectives that don't mean anything in the abstract, but mean such when applied to you. I love you also because of a certain Puckish, Peter-Panish quality in you that doesn't let anyone take you seriously—you belong in Mid- summer Night's Dream, somehow. You should live on nectar and play with butterflies. But in spite of that quality you are not a but- terfly and not a doll. . . .

It was a courtship that went on intensely, but without much money. They took a German class together, studied together, occasionally ate out together, and did a lot of walking and talking. Alongside of him, Mary was so diminutive and young-looking that once while walking along, they were approached by children wanting to know if his little girl could come out and play with them sometime.

Wallace had intended to continue teaching at Augustana the following year, but suddenly the evangelicals who had hired him were thrown out of power at the school by the fundamentalists, and they wrote him a letter demanding to know if it was true that he was an agnostic and atheist, a disbeliever in the Augsburg Confession. He wrote back that he didn't see how he could be an agnostic and an atheist at the same time—which seemed to him philosophically difficult—and that as far as the Augsburg Confession was concerned, he couldn't remember ever having read it. They demanded an affirmation of the principles of higher Christian education over his signature. Although the confrontation sounds silly in retrospect, it was really an early manifestation of what would become more common in the 1950s, a request for a declaration of political purity, a loyalty oath, and Wallace declined to subscribe to a set of beliefs with which he disagreed or that he felt were irrelevant, just to keep his job.

Jobless for the moment, he enrolled in summer school at Iowa, while at the same time managing to drive periodically to Dubuque to visit Mary, who was home for the summer. He was able, through old friends at Utah, to arrange an instructorship at the university for the fall. But Mary, arranging her own career plans, had obtained a job with Dawson's Bookstore in Los Angeles. He was going to Utah; she, to Los Angeles. So they decided to get married—on the first of September, 1934, six months from the time they had met. They had a small wedding in her home in Dubuque, where she had lived all her life, in the company of her parents and a few childhood friends. Looking back on a marriage of more than fifty years, Wallace has said, "My wife was the best thing that had happened to me since I first knew my mother. She was a musician, a reader, an eager and curious searcher of the world. She gave me new eyes to see the West with, for she really saw what I took for granted." She was extremely bright, very well read, and would become over the years a true partner in his writing career, his severest critic, editorial collaborator, and unflagging supporter during those dark periods of rejection or failing inspiration faced by every writer.

After the wedding they drove west through the Badlands, the Black Hills, Yellowstone, Jackson Hole, and the Grand Tetons to Salt Lake City. Arriving in the city late one evening, they drove directly to Syd Angleman's house. The Anglemans weren't home, so the Stegners "broke in" and stayed two nights until they could find a place to live.

Once they found an apartment, the newlyweds settled down and prepared to make themselves a life on $1,700 a year. They had many friends almost immediately—the Irvines, the Anglemans (Syd had become a dean), and several old-time members of the English department, including the chairman, Dr. Neff, whom Wallace had known as a student and who welcomed him back. But there were several in the English department, especially among the newer members, who were suspicious, even hostile: in the best of times, let alone the Depression, college teaching can be a very competitive business, and in those days, many more were hired than would ever be retained and granted tenure. Wallace's job was not secure, but at least he had one, and he had the luxury, for the first time in recent memory, to relax a bit and enjoy life among friends and in familiar surroundings. He felt that he had been ground down by the drudgery of getting through his degree program, and he had plenty to do with teaching four classes, so that for the present, he had no desire to do any writing on his own. He recalled:

> I was back in Salt Lake, and we were a young married couple. There was a lot of partying going on, and lots of hikes and picnics, and so on, up in the mountains. Salt Lake is an easy town to get out into the country from, and I had grown up doing that. So what I remember about those years in Salt Lake is how many times we were up picking dog-tooth violets in the mouth of Hughes Canyon, instead of being down on the campus interviewing students.

Throughout his college career there had been a number of events that would influence the direction of his future. He still did not think in terms of being a writer, although it is clear in retrospect that his talents and inclinations were pushing him in that direction—he simply didn't recognize the push at the time. He had done some writing: for his college literary magazine, for the *Salt Lake Tribune*, for the University of Iowa newspaper (two articles), and for his master's thesis (three stories). That winter of 1934–35, one of those stories, "Pete and Emil," was published in the *Salt Lake Tribune*, and the following June, another, "Saskatchewan Idyll," was published in the *Monterey Beacon*. Both of these stories came out of his Eastend childhood: they point out the direction that much of Stegner's apprenticeship and early fiction would take.

Not until the spring of his second year at the University of Utah as an instructor did Wallace get the urge to write again (following his work on his thesis stories nearly three years earlier):

Then I sat down one idle afternoon and wrote a story in three hours. About what? Saskatchewan, naturally—the homestead, the loneliness and savagery and poetry of the prairie. *Virginia Quarterly* bought it, and shortly *Story* bought another. Something in me began to wake up. Never having known any writers, I thought of them as distant in both time and space, perhaps as mythical as gryphons. Now my psyche began to hint to me that I could be one.

"Something in me began to wake up": his first conscious acknowledgment of his vocation suggests that he, like so many other writers, was on his way to becoming a writer before he knew it, in a sense sleepwalking into a role he could not think of as relevant to him.

Other patterns that developed into major interests and would lead to later accomplishments can be seen in his college career. Wilbur Schramm remembers him reading in graduate school—outside of his assignments—Western history and fiction, and it was about this time that he read Frederick Jackson Turner, who is best known for his argument that the proper perspective of American history must be based on "a connected and unified account of the progress of civilization across the continent" and our national consciousness of that moving frontier and its changing character. For quite some time Turner's thesis, perhaps most succinctly stated in his essay "The Significance of the Frontier in American History," has come under attack as overstated and oversimplified, while in more recent years it has been attacked by Native Americans as Eurocentric. But these objections are not entirely relevant to Stegner's interest, which was primarily in the historian's concern with changes in frontier life and social organization and development, sequences, as Turner put it, of "evolution." What Turner gave to Stegner was a way of understanding his own background on one of the last American frontiers, a need, lasting nearly all his life, to explore and understand his roots—a need that he has claimed was intensified by his association in Salt Lake with Mormons who were preoccupied with family history.

"Turner," Wallace has acknowledged, "had a great influence on my thinking, certainly, and therefore on my writing." Turner's appeal to him was one of the factors that led him to become a historian, as well as writer of fiction. It contributed direction and motive to his search for understanding of himself, his early life, and his relationship to place which was expressed in his first major novel, *The Big Rock Candy Mountain*; and the Turner thesis and its impact on him led to a long period of reading and thinking about the evolution of communities from prehistoric times to the present, not only in this country but abroad. Along the way Wallace read extensively in social anthropology and cultural history and got a grant for an anthropological project having to do with the evolution of communities. It also led to fieldwork and writing about minority communities in the United States during World War II, and all of this work culminated in that minor masterpiece, the search for his own personal cultural and historical context, *Wolf Willow* (1962). This work, a mixture of history, anthropology, geology, memoir, and fiction, reflects as well as anything Wallace ever wrote his multifaceted interests and his driving impulse toward self-discovery.

In connection with this strand of development, Wallace has recalled in graduate school going to listen to Stephen Vincent Benet speak and rushing to the platform to catch his ear and tell him about a three-decker peasant novel that he planned to write. Stegner has said of this plan,

> It turned out that the peasant novel I wanted to write was a peasant novel about the ending of the frontier, and it was right straight out of Frederick Jackson Turner. I didn't realize at the time that I had simply borrowed his ideas and transplanted them into a lot of my own experience, which was the experience of growing up on the tail end of that frontier—the very last demoralized end when it was quite impossible way out in the dry country—when the homesteading and small farm, free-land frontier came to a kind of dribbling end, not with a bang, but a whimper.

Benet (author of *John Brown's Body, The Devil and Daniel Webster, Listen to the People*) was interested in native materials and the importance of bringing forth (as Emerson had advocated a century earlier) a uniquely national literature divorced from the influences of Europe. These interests matched those of many of Foerster's Iowa students at that time (Foerster was interested in the West and native materials himself and endorsed this enthusiasm), and they had all read and were entranced by the work of Öle Rölvaag, who had just finished his own peasant trilogy, the best known volume of which is *Giants in the Earth* (1927 in this country). As for Stegner, this entire emphasis was part of the drive toward *The Big Rock Candy Mountain*, the embryonic origins of which were in his plans for a "three-deck peasant novel."

Yet another strand that came out of Wallace's college years and that would influence his future career began when he was a freshman at Utah. He had been taking a course in geology from Frederick J. Pack. A friend of his on examination day smashed his thumb in his car door, and so Wallace had to take him to the hospital and missed his final. Instead of giving him a make-up exam, the professor had him read Clarence Edward Dutton's *The Geology of the High Plateaus of Utah* (1880), one of the early geologic reports. "By pure accident," he recalled, "we had a cottage down on the Fishlake Plateau, right in the middle of the high plateaus, and all of a sudden history crossed my trail. I found that when I went up Seven Mile I found I knew what had happened there sixty, seventy years before."

Once again touching on Wallace's lifetime concern for the history of places, this experience extended his view from history to the science of places, their evolution and composition. It was a discovery of a related interest that would come back again and again in his career, most notably, first, when he came to write his Ph.D. dissertation. Dutton was not just a scientist and engineer, but a literary naturalist whose quality of prose went far beyond the necessities of scientific reporting. When it came time for Wallace to select a subject for his dissertation, it was Foerster, who had some interest in the many journals, diaries, and reports of literary quality that had come out of the westward movement and that had been neglected by literary historians, who persuaded his student to pick up that strand of investigation from the past. The result was a year of work that produced, by the summer of 1935, a dissertation (Stegner has called it a "very bad dissertation"), "Clarence Edward Dutton: Geologist and Man of Letters," later revised and published by the University of Utah Press as *Clarence Edward Dutton: An Appraisal* (1936) and excerpted in *The Scientific Monthly* (July 1937).

As a dissertation, it was not really such a bad piece of work, but it certainly was a most unusual topic for a Ph.D. in literature. The dissertation shows its author, a young man of twenty-five who, in the mid-1930s before environmentalism became the movement it is today, was concerned about preserving the beauties of the national parks and conserving our land heritage. In the author's view, Dutton is memorable because, for one thing, his work led him, from 1875 to 1887, to five different spots that would later become national parks: "Six . . . parks . . . owe something of their history to Major Dutton. All of them, except Mount Lassen, owe him more: the basic geological explanations which are now commonplaces aired by park rangers and guides for the edification of tourists." Dutton also gave the place names to many of the features of the Grand Canyon and its environs. And finally, "People recognize in him a great geologist and important explorer, but they recognize even more immediately a great nature writer. . . . One thinks of Muir and Burroughs as comparisons. Dutton was more limited in his field than they, but as fine a writer within his limits and a greater scientist than either."

Wallace had an early familiarity with three of the parks connected to Dutton—Zion, Bryce, and Grand Canyon—plus Yellowstone and Yosemite, and these national parks would come to be of special concern to him. He would later fight to defend several of them against incursion or destruction and would serve the Department of Interior in reporting on their problems. His study of Dutton led to his interest in other geologists, engineers, and explorers of that same period: Clarence King, who figures prominently in the novel *Angle of Repose*, and more importantly, John Wesley Powell, about whom Wallace would write a biography.

Not only was the seed for *The Big Rock Candy Mountain* planted early in his graduate career, but later, just after finishing his dissertation, the seed for the Powell biography was put into the earth to remain dormant for nearly twenty years. In the back of Wallace's mind he wanted to continue the work he had begun in his study of Dutton, particularly in finding out more about Dutton's colleague Powell, who, belonging to a time and place overrun with myths, was a true hero—courageous, constructive, and, perhaps of greatest interest to the young instructor, extremely energetic, very determined, and highly intelligent. These were qualities Wallace could identify with, and Powell was a man he could admire.

Wallace remembered the occasion when he first spoke about his thoughts regarding this project. He and Mary looked forward every semester to the visit of a textbook salesman who invariably took them to a fancy dinner, a rare event in those Depression days. The salesman always inquired about the possibility that Wallace or his friends might be interested in writing a text, and Wallace recalled telling him, in late 1935 or early 1936, that what he wanted to write was not a text, but a biography of Powell. He did—*Beyond the Hundredth Meridian: John Wesley Powell and the Second Opening of the West*—but not until 1952–53 (published in 1954). Twenty years later, in 1974, he published his biography of Bernard DeVoto, *The Uneasy Chair*. Leaving aside a lifetime of conservation activities—with the publication of these two books alone, bringing to the fore and preserving the ideas of men who have become, largely through his efforts, two of our greatest environmental heroes—Wallace Stegner has well earned a place in our pantheon of those who have cared for the earth and have worked to protect it.

4

BECOMING
A NOVELIST:
Write a Novel and
Win a Prize

One day in the fall of 1936, Stegner saw, among the book reviews in a magazine he was reading, a notice announcing a contest for the best short novel submitted to the Little, Brown Publishing Company in Boston. The prize was $2,500. As an instructor he was now making $1,800 a year. He thought, *I can do that—I can write a novelette,* and perhaps he would win and his and Mary's money problems would be eased. With Mary pregnant, money had become such a worry that he had returned to work in the flooring store during the summer to supplement his income. The official start of his writing career was not carried out for the most noble of artistic motives—self-expression and literary achievement had little to do with it. Entering the contest was more like an act of desperation, like poor people everywhere hoping for the lottery to somehow save them and give them a little cash for comfort.

Wallace didn't have any classes until ten in the morning, so he sat down every morning at eight, in their apartment on 12th East, and wrote until he had to grab his coat and books and race up the hill the two blocks to his first classroom. Thus began a lifetime habit of writing the first few hours of every morning. After six weeks of this, he finished his manuscript, "Remembering Laughter," and sent it off to the contest and all but forgot about it. The manuscript was based on a story that his wife had told him about a skeleton in her family closet, and the characters were relatives who had lived in her grandfather's small town in Iowa.

In their book on Stegner, Forrest and Margaret Robinson have commented that "in hands less skillful than Stegner's, *Remembering Laughter* might have become implausible melodrama." Yet, ironically in light of this impression of skill, Wallace found that the story almost told itself and has recalled, "I just sort of happened to have this story ready made, and it came pretty easily, actually. I don't remember having the slightest trouble with it. It was like one of those births you know when you hardly notice you've dropped a child." What the book shows more than anything else is his sheer, raw talent. It remains the best of his early novels, although it may seem a bit old-fashioned in today's permissive moral climate.

Remembering Laughter is a somber little tale of adultery within a family at the turn of the century. The adultery has been kept secret among the affected family members for eighteen years in an atmosphere of failed hope, bitterness, and silent despair. Margaret Stuart, her husband, Alec, and her younger sister, Elspeth (with whom Alec has had a brief affair) have reached a state of suspended animation; life goes on as only a routine, a joyless standoff.

In a prologue and epilogue the novel begins and ends in the "present," grimly framing the story with the same scene of a funeral. The prologue, filled with foreboding, raises a number of questions, chief among them, what is the relationship between these two stiff-backed sisters who have aged so preternaturally? The two are described meeting in the formal parlor, waiting for the funeral to begin:

> Their eyes met briefly, ice-blue and ice-blue, but it was not a cold or hostile look. There was something in it that struggled toward warmth, as if sympathy and affection were fighting to the surface through crusted years of repression and control.

"There was something in it that struggled toward warmth" is a wonderfully ambiguous line, suggesting a delicate, yet mysterious emotional balance—tension, from an unknown cause, and the possible relief from tension, from an unknown cause. Other hints in the prologue raise fur-

ther questions: Who is Malcolm? What role does Margaret's dead husband have in all this?

In the subsequent flashback, Stegner gradually reveals the answers in
the unfolding story of a love affair and its tragic consequences. At the
heart of the emerging conflict is Margaret's character, which is stern and
inflexible, just the opposite of her husband's. Alec, a successful farmer,
likes to joke and play, and worst of all, he likes to have a few drinks now
and then—activities that his wife disapproves of. In one of the very
few times in his fiction where a female character is viewed with less
admiration than the male, Stegner here takes a more traditional western
view of the male as freedom-loving and the female as restrictive and
civilizing.

When Margaret's younger sister, Elspeth, comes from Norway to live
with them, she finds Alec a kindred spirit, fun-loving and gay. Her sister,
however, is clearly another matter. As Elspeth sits with her in the formal
parlor, which she perceives as gloomy and unlivable, she reflects:

There is something in this cold room that matches something in
her—it's almost prim, but prim's hardly the word. Prim, starched,
stiff, formal, dignified, haughty—none of those.

But all of these do apply to her sister, who frowns on Elspeth's friendliness and high spirits. Throughout, Elspeth is associated with nature, the
animals, the creek, the warm seasons, whereas the parlor becomes
emblematic of her proper sister—and it is the parlor, as we see in the
epilogue, that wins out. At the end Elspeth's pallor suggests that she has,
over the years after the affair, hardly gone outside at all.

The product of Alec and Elspeth's impulsive love and betrayal is a
son, Malcolm, whom the family misleads the community to think was
born of Elspeth and a farmhand, Ahlquest, who suddenly returns to his
home in Norway. Raised in an atmosphere of silence and contained emotion, Malcolm's only release is, tellingly enough, outside the house in the
company of Alec, whom he considers his "uncle." As they tramp across
the fields and as Alec tends to the animals, he regales his "nephew" with
Western tall tales, and overhearing them one day—Malcolm has never
laughed so heartily out loud in the company of the two sisters—Elspeth

wants to let him know that she remembers her own laughter years earlier in response to Alec's joking. But she cannot break her silence. The title of the novel thus becomes a bitter irony.

There are several things that stamp *Remembering Laughter* as different from Stegner's later work. As I have just noted, the roles of the sexes are not typical of Stegner—usually it is the woman who is wise, and frequently it is she who represents the life force. The characterizations are less realistic than usual. In looking back on the book, Wallace has commented that "we're dealing there with figures who are not real figures from life. They stand a little taller and a little more distant; they're like stage figures, in shrouds and cloaks." But while there are differences, there are also techniques and themes that make their first appearance here that become common in his work.

The heavy foreshadowing of bad things to come in the prologue of this novel has become almost a Stegner signature. In *The Big Rock Candy Mountain* (1943), for example, the reader encounters one signal after another that disaster is coming. Never does a Stegner novel lead the reader forward promising a pleasant resolution. Instead, novels such as *Fire and Ice* (1941), *The Preacher and the Slave* (1950), *A Shooting Star* (1961), *All the Little Live Things* (1967), and *Angle of Repose* (1971) are filled with warnings, often likely to provoke a sense of dread.

There are a number of themes in this first novel that figure in the author's later fiction: Identity is one. Not only who am I, but how do I relate to the people around me? What should my role be? How am I a product of the land and culture around me and its history? This, too, is a theme that is particularly appropriate to fiction dealing with the raw West, and even, as here, the relatively civilized Midwest of 1910. Emotional repression, so overwhelming in *Remembering Laughter*, is another common theme in Stegner's work, and, once again, a fitting one for the stiff-upper-lip culture inherited from the frontier. Sometimes, as in *On a Darkling Plain* (1940), it comes out of or is a reaction to experience— Vickers has been emotionally scarred by the war; in other situations, as in *Crossing to Safety*, it is a repression imposed by the control of a strong-willed character. In *Remembering Laughter* the repression seems to come from both directions. Closely connected to emotional repression is Stegner's frequently expressed antagonism for emotional extremes, or fanaticism. Margaret is inflexible and fanatical in her properness and Puritanism, just as Vickers is a fanatic in his hatred of people in general. Paul Condon, in *Fire and Ice*, is a fanatic in his hatred of people with money, while Joe Hill, in *The Preacher and the Slave*, is a fanatic in his hatred of bosses and Jim Peck, in *All the Little Live Things*, is a fanatic in his pursuit of pleasure and his attempt to escape all responsibility.

In bed in their Salt Lake City apartment, the Stegners were awakened in the middle of the night of January 30, 1937, with a telegram. They had won the prize, the $2,500, which later was doubled by the magazine publication. They were rich. A new Chevrolet in 1937 cost $777. Wallace recalled:

> We had a party, quite a party. At the end, Mary went into labor, and after a couple of hard days produced a son. My new family responsibilities and my new literary life began together. All of that, too, in my frugal way (I learned frugality by watching my mother make jelly out of the peelings of apples she had just made pies of) I eventually used. Fifty years later, with changes of personnel and location, I wrote that episode into *Crossing to Safety*.

Now that he was "famous," Wallace thought he should be promoted out of the slave-labor camp of temporary instructors, to the more distinguished position of assistant professor, where he could make a bit more money and hope for tenure. He even took his case to the university president, who turned him down, explaining that mired in the Depression the university simply could not afford to promote him. Thus, in June 1937, Wallace resigned his position and he and Mary determined that they would take their money and go to someplace exotic. They decided on the Virgin Islands, where they would live on the beach, eat bananas and coconuts, and he would write great books.

Unfortunately, the birth of the child had been a very difficult one—a breech birth at the end of a very long labor—and their baby son, Page, had come out of it with an injured leg. Furious at what he considered the doctor's incompetence, Wallace would refer to him ever after as "that butcher." When the family stopped off at Dubuque, Mary's mother exclaimed, "Take that little injured *baby* to the Virgin Islands? Oh, you can't." She made them a proposition: she would take care of the baby while Wallace and Mary could go on vacation somewhere and get the wanderlust out of their system. So they ended up doing the more conventional thing, going to Europe for a month, bicycling in England and France. Mary found it amusing that her husband had never learned to ride a bicycle—he had never been given one as a child—and was amazed when, with luggage on the back of his bike and riding over cobblestones, he still took off from the dock at Boulogne-sur-Mer with only a bit of a wobble as if he had been riding all his life. They took the student route, economizing as much as possible, living off bread and cheese and staying in youth hostels, but managed, nevertheless, to spend most of their money. Back home, with the help of Foerster, whom Wallace had written to earlier about his dissatisfaction with the University of Utah, he got a job, again as a lowly instructor, but a step upward in institutions—at the University of Wisconsin in Madison, a well-regarded university with several nationally recognized scholars on its English faculty.

At Wisconsin Wallace was once again lucky in his friends, for it was in Madison that he and his wife met Phil and Peg Gray, a couple who for years would be counted among their closest friends. The story of their friendship is the basis for Stegner's final novel, *Crossing to Safety*, which he wrote after the couple's death. The Grays were a different breed than Wallace was used to—they were wealthy, sophisticated, and Ivy League. Phil had inherited money from a banker father who had made a fortune by loaning money to Henry Ford. The son, who had degrees from Yale, had no interest in making more money, nor did he really want to be a professor, although he enjoyed teaching. It was his wife, who came from a family of Ivy League professors, who pushed him in that direction, even though he had little aptitude for scholarship. What he really aspired to be was a poet, but Peg thought that this was a waste of time and something he should do, if he had to, on the side. It is this conflict that is at the center of *Crossing to Safety*.

At Madison, Stegner ran into a whole group of well-educated and very intelligent young instructors, including Stuart Brown, Curtis Bradford,

S. I. Hayakawa, and Claude Simpson—all of whom became well-known in their fields:

> We were all interested in the same things, and the quality of the conversation at parties and so on, as between Salt Lake City and Madison, was—whew!—up like that. It was like the first year in graduate school. You had a feeling you were learning at four times the normal pace.

Several of these young instructors, particularly Simpson, would become lifelong friends. At the same time, Wallace was continually renewing his ties to friends in Iowa. Norman Foerster had written to him to congratulate him on the publication of his dissertation, and then in a long letter praising *Remembering Laughter* and quoting Emerson's salutation to Whitman after reading *Leaves of Grass*, Foerster concluded: "I greet you at the beginning of a great career" (10/8/37). He wrote letters of recommendation for Wallace to various institutions, telling the people at Wisconsin that "my guess is that Stegner is not likely to produce much 'research,' though he will always handle his courses in a scholarly manner. What he will produce—as things look now—is fiction" (5/4/37). The Iowa professor also recommended to his protégé that he apply for a fellowship, perhaps a Guggenheim, or a scholarship at the Bread Loaf Writers Conference, and advised him with whom to get in touch.

Wallace also kept up his correspondence with Wilbur Schramm, who not only was making a name as a scholar and editor, but was working his way up the administrative ladder and making connections throughout the academic-literary world. Wilbur's journal would publish a couple of Wallace's early stories, he would arrange lectures for Wallace at Iowa and elsewhere, and he would be instrumental in helping his friend get several jobs during his career. In the meantime, Wallace was himself developing a network of contacts, a network that would be invaluable in his continuing search for academic jobs and for financial support for his writing.

One connection he made at this time that would turn out to play a significant part in his life was with the agents Brandt and Brandt, who would end up representing him throughout his career. Although he seemed doubtful about the success of *Remembering Laughter* prior to publication (he thought it might be too "experimental"), Alfred R. McIntyre, the president of Little, Brown and Company, nevertheless recommended Wallace to the agency, and in response to that recommendation, Wallace received a very cordial letter from Bernice Baumgarten telling him that she would like to see some of his stories. The relationship with Baumgarten that evolved would become important not only to the growth of his career, but in the refinement of his work. Bernice did not just sell stories and novels—and she had an excellent marketing sense, as well as admirable persistence—she had taste, a knowledge of quality fiction, and the eagle eye of a good editor. She, as much as anyone aside from Mary, Stegner's wife, was responsible for helping to develop, extend, and encourage the writer's talent.

Another connection that would have deep and long-term consequences in his life and career was the one with Bernard DeVoto—conservationist, columnist, fiction writer, editor, and, later, Pulitzer Prize–winning historian. DeVoto had been one of the judges on the panel that had awarded the Little, Brown prize to Stegner, and it was clear to the young writer that it had been DeVoto's influence that had given him the award. So Wallace wrote him a letter thanking him, and DeVoto was, in Stegner's words, "very kind in answering a letter from a young, brash upstart." As part of his effort to advance in his college teaching profession, Wallace agreed to participate on a panel at the Modern Language Association annual meeting held that year in Chicago, and he recalled that "Benny was making a speech, one of those thunderous, tub-thumping speeches, offending everybody in sight and standing hair on end. That was when I first met him."

Wallace would become a close friend of DeVoto and his wife, Avis, when a couple of years later he moved to Cambridge, and DeVoto would introduce him to many of the leading lights of Cambridge intellectual society and encourage him in his writing. It also was probably his association with DeVoto that more than any other single factor led Wallace, already inclined in that direction by interest and background, toward a more explicit commitment to environmentalism and, eventually, a life of environmental activism. Stegner was not only attracted to

DeVoto as a successful writer and engaging intellectual gladfly, but also as a fellow Westerner, an ex-Mormon who grew up as Wallace did, in Utah. He saw in this rude and bumptious, but terribly kind, Westerner who aspired to the gentility of the East a paradigm for his own life and more generally the lives of so many young, raw Westerners who, going to the East, tried to overcome the shortcomings of their background to grow culturally and to gain intellectual status. Wallace had striven all his life to belong, and here was a man who as an academic strove to belong to the most elite club of all—the Harvard faculty. It was this paradigm that later, along with his friendship for Avis, would lead Wallace to write the DeVoto biography and edit his letters.

During the months prior to his leaving for Wisconsin, Stegner had wrestled with the dual role of writer and teacher that he would be forced to follow until such time as he might be able to make a living by writing alone. It was an eventuality he hardly dared hope for. In doubt about which role he should emphasize and which might give him the best means to support a young family, he continued to write regularly, although after finishing *Remembering Laughter* he did not know yet whether he could get the novelette published, let alone win the prize. Three stories did get published the following summer (1937) before he went on to his new teaching job. "Pete and Emil," his first short story, had been published while he was an instructor at Utah in the *Salt Lake Tribune* (1934) and had been revised for inclusion in his M.A. thesis along with "Bloodstain" and "The Dam Builder." Now, in 1937, the latter two stories had been rewritten for publication in little magazines, and a new story, "Fish," also was published—all were stories about his experiences in Saskatchewan.

Earlier, at the beginning of 1937 while still struggling with his career decision, he published a short article in the *Intermountain Review of English and Speech* called "Can Teachers Be Writers?" which reflected his thinking at the time. In it he staked out a position that he would hold later as a teacher of creative writing, which was that teaching English was essentially a negative task—the teacher can point out errors, but he cannot "actually help the artist write one phrase." Furthermore, for the teacher who wants also to be a writer, teaching can be a positive hindrance in that it leads him into a negative attitude and "makes him so cautious of errors that he dares nothing." He recognizes here something that many beginning writers fail to see: to be more than a writer, to be an artist, one must take risks. He seems to be clearly thinking of his own position, at the threshold of a possible literary career, when he concludes:

> And if, in the first five or six years of teaching, nothing of artistic merit emerges from the close struggle with creation, the English teacher always has a door open. It is not an attractive door, and he shrinks from entering it, but he knows in the back of his mind that if his artistic labors are abortive and ineffectual, he can always fall back upon the solid phalanx of his profession, contribute to the educational reviews, write a rhetoric, and pretend that he can teach what he cannot do.

Ironically, it was the day before this article appeared that he had heard from Little, Brown and found that he had at least one success to go forward with.

It was this news that pushed him into a conscious recognition of which path his life was going to follow. By the time he had arrived at Wisconsin, he had made the key decision: his teaching would be secondary to his writing. No one taught more conscientiously, but he was now a writer who was supporting himself with teaching, rather than writing in the hope he could supplement his salary as a professor. Once he was settled in his new position, he went on a writing binge:

> In two years, besides collaborating on a textbook and writing a dozen essays and book reviews, I wrote four short stories, a novelette called "One Last Wilderness" that killed *Scribner's Magazine*, a novel called *On a Darkling Plain*, another called *Fire and Ice*, and the first few chapters of *The Big Rock Candy Mountain*. This while teaching four undergraduate classes.

As one can see from this list, he was still hedging his bet, producing a significant amount of scholarship in addition to his fiction in an effort to qualify for professional advancement.

A major reason for this hedge was that English departments in those days not only gave very little credit for creative writing of any sort, but often had a positive antipathy for those who were considered "mere journalists," faculty members who published in general-audience magazines or wrote nonacademic books. Wisconsin, which considered itself something of an elite school, had a good measure of that kind of snobbery, as well as a protectiveness that set the older generation of faculty against the younger, the "barbarians." Adding fuel to these emotions was a competitive atmosphere made almost cutthroat by the exigencies of the Depression. The sense of being something of an outsider (again) and of not being quite scholarly enough (again) rankled, and prompted Stegner toward doing more scholarship than he really wanted to spend his time on. Faculty prejudice against writers would follow him throughout his academic career.

All the young instructors got along well together, however, ignoring the competition and instead cooperating in their teaching and sometimes in their publications. Although all of Wallace's group had several years of teaching experience, the department insisted that each of them teach under the supervision of a more senior professor. One professor who had this duty for Wallace recalled visiting his classroom and being surprised to find that he was teaching his freshmen and sophomores using the Socratic dialogue method most commonly employed at that time with graduate seminars. Wallace would single out a student and for some time question him or her, probing, agreeing, disagreeing, and then would suddenly turn to another student across the room and ask, "What do *you* think?" It was a technique—stimulating a train of thought, tracing the consequences, and moving around the room challenging the students to think critically—that he would refine and employ throughout his career.

He was a lanky but good-looking young man, who had, on the one hand, the appearance of a gentle academic in his clothes—rep-stripe tie, dark tweed jacket, and khaki pants—his glasses, and his wavy brown hair parted just to the left of middle. But on the other hand there was something resilient and very Western, very Scandinavian, something almost "this was once a farm boy" look about him that he would never lose, no matter how sophisticated his surroundings. Students remember him as modest and soft-spoken, friendly, and very engaged with his classes. He didn't lecture as much as some professors, but when he did, he is remembered as an eloquent and expressive speaker, a man of wit and humor. He worked hard at speaking well, maintaining eye contact with his audience rather than burying his nose in his notes. As busy as he was—and one can see from his publications list just how busy—he was the kind of teacher who always had time for student conferences in his office. Wallace Stegner always performed above and beyond the call of duty.

Not only were the young instructors closely supervised, they were all required to teach the same text and give the same assignments. This was extremely difficult for young people who were experimental by nature and bursting with creative ideas and energy. S. I. Hayakawa's *Language in Thought and Action*, begun as a freshman composition text, was written in part as a protest to this enforced conformity, and the same lack of imagination on the part of the department motivated Wallace to join Stuart Brown and Claude Simpson to produce *An Exposition Workshop: Readings in Modern Controversy* (1939), published by Little, Brown. A committee of young instructors managed to push through a proposal that materials from both texts, while still in the process of being written and compiled, could be used by the composition staff. Stuart Brown remembers Wallace challenging his classes with parts of Hayakawa's work-in-progress, a somewhat revolutionary view of language and communication at that time.

What brought Wallace into a sense of himself as a writer, as a professional, more than any other influence was probably his connection with the Bread Loaf Writers' Conference. It would provide a number of very close and rewarding friendships, enlarge his network of acquaintances in the academic and publishing arenas, and provide the opportunity for him to polish his techniques for teaching the writing of fiction. He would go on to spend the bulk of his career as the founder and director of a creative writing program, and his experiences at Bread Loaf provided the guidance and the contacts that would enable him to do the job.

Bread Loaf was the first of the summer writers' conferences. Founded in 1926 on a farm on Bread Loaf Mountain in Vermont and administered by Middlebury College, it has, especially in recent decades, spawned innumerable imitations all over the country. The idea was to provide a setting where accomplished writers could instruct and inspire would-be writers in an informal atmosphere, mixing lectures by staff and by visiting dignitaries with workshop sessions in which writing was read aloud and discussed, and with one-on-one tutoring. The latter was felt to be very important—to give everyone admitted to the conference a chance to have his or her work read and critiqued by a professional. The idea of professionalism in writing would take on particular significance at Bread Loaf, which tried, on the one hand, to avoid the preciousness too often associated with schools of the arts, and on the other, the English-teacher mentality too often associated with writing instruction.

Wallace, feeling overwhelmed by the workload that he had undertaken at Wisconsin, began to look for a way to get some time off for his writing. He applied for a Guggenheim, for a stay at the Yaddo artists' colony in upstate New York, and for a fellowship at the Bread Loaf Writers' Conference. He was turned down for all three, but then the following summer, of 1938, he was invited to Yaddo, a place that gave aspiring artists the time and peace and quiet to pursue their art (he was working the manuscript that became *The Big Rock Candy Mountain*), and while he was there, he got a call from Wilbur Schramm, who knew the Bread Loaf director, Ted Morrison. There was a sudden vacancy on the conference staff, he told Wallace, and "I have been talking you up. . . . There won't be much work. . . . Your chief occupation will probably be to play tennis in the afternoons . . . and to drink constantly." He would have to associate with the likes of Robert Frost, Bernard DeVoto, and Louis Untermeyer.

But it was not all tennis and strong drink. The day often started with a keynote lecture, followed by workshops and seminars in the late morning and early afternoons. Until Ted Morrison had taken over as director, there had been a tradition of serving primarily schoolteachers in their aspirations to become writers or poets, and as a result the conference became, in Morrison's view, too much like a summer school refresher for English teachers (even though no credits were offered). He decided to put much more emphasis on the practical business of writing for publication and began getting publishers, agents, and editors, in addition to successful writers, on the staff. As a result the conference, in

Morrison's words, "emphasized work, application to craft, as against self-expression, indulgence, or faith in ... 'inspiration.' " DeVoto, who headed the fiction part of the faculty for several summers, was particularly insistent on adopting a professional attitude. This approach rubbed off strongly on Stegner, giving him a self-image he could adopt and giving him his best defense against the academic snobbery, with its antipathy to commercial writing.

After nearly a full day of work, in the late afternoon there were opportunities for tennis and swimming and strolls through the surrounding countryside. In the evenings there were get-togethers, sometimes with the students, often just the staff. Usually the evenings went on until late, and the fiction staff, in particular, were hard-pressed to read a number of long manuscripts, squeezing out the time somehow in the late night or early morning hours. After two weeks of this, everyone was thoroughly exhausted and many gave thanks, as they nursed a hangover and packed their clothes on the final morning, that the conference did not last a day longer. In his biography of DeVoto, Stegner describes the activities in the Treman Cottage parlor, which over the years of the conference had evolved into a club lounge and refuge for the staff:

Evenings were a fitting completion of the days. If there was an evening lecture, either by a regular or a visitor, most [of the staff] attended, if not out of interest then out of sheer solidarity. But afterward they found themselves again sprawling in Treman's worn wicker arguing the lecturer's points or rehashing theory or trading notes on the Conference madwoman (there always was one), or with astonishing generosity and unselfishness promoting some newly discovered talent among the Fellows or the customers. Or they played poker, or made a game of throwing ice picks at the pocked kitchen door, or settled down to soul-searching with highballs in hand. I can remember vignettes from those evenings as clearly as I can remember anything: Eudora Welty sitting worshipfully at the feet of Katherine Anne Porter after a reading, Truman Capote holding himself conspicuously aloof from Louis Untermeyer after Untermeyer had lectured on contemporary poetry and called T. S. Eliot a writer of society verse, Carson McCullers in her starched, white, boy's shirt deep in talk with W. H. Auden—and deep in my last bottle of bourbon, which I had been saving for Sunday, when the liquor store in Brandon would be closed. . . .

Sometimes, while the conscientious tried to read manuscripts in their rooms upstairs, to which every word and laugh penetrated, and while the snakebit lay down to recover, others stood with their arms around one another in the hall and sang barbershop under the baton of Louis Untermeyer. . . . I do not take seriously DeVoto's complaint about the glee-clubbers. Often I was one of them, and they were magnificent.

So much for the drinking. As for the tennis, Wallace found that there were few at Bread Loaf who played to his level, and in order not to hurt feelings, he had to take his game in a relaxed, and, untypical for him, noncompetitive manner. Robert Frost—perhaps as a reflection of his basic philosophy—would plant his feet firmly in the middle of his side of the court and, unmoving, would chop at everything that came over the net. Untermeyer—perhaps as a reflection of his personality—would scurry, suddenly, from one side of the court to the other, like a squirrel that had just discovered the onset of winter.

5

ACCOMPLISHED WRITER,
HARVARD TEACHER,
AND FRIEND TO
THE FAMOUS:
What More Do You Need?

Stegner's next three book-length fictions, after *Remembering Laughter,* were in one way or another experiments, and they were all to some extent failures. Although he had already had one major writing success, such an early success can be disastrous for the career of a fledgling writer, unable to repeat it, no matter how hard he tries. One lesson Wallace had to learn is that it is not enough to be a skillful writer of prose; you have to have a story to which you have a strong connection, a connection that will give your work depth and substance.

For the most part these early works are artificial, well-made but contrived. *The Potter's House* (1938), *On a Darkling Plain* (1940), and *Fire and Ice* (1941) are each based on an idea for a story, rather than a dramatic situation as in *Remembering Laughter.* The idea is then carried out by characters, for the most part, about whom the author does not know or care much, resulting in a weak story, told in a thin way that does not compel the reader's involvement. In part, Stegner seems to have been searching during this period for his own milieu and a story he could get his teeth into. But he also seems to have been writing just to exercise his craft and get something published while he pursued his major project, *The Big Rock Candy Mountain.* To some extent Stegner's early career paralleled that of Willa Cather, who, before she discovered her milieu in her own pioneer childhood, wrote about artists in the East and the socialites of Boston drawing rooms. Stegner, too, had to escape from the peripheral in order to embrace the organic.

Although listed among his publications as a book, *The Potter's House* is really a long short story. It was written in the winter of his first year at Madison (1937–38) and published not only by the Prairie Press on fine paper, but by his friend Wilbur Schramm in *American Prefaces,* which had become the publication organ of the writing program at Iowa. The idea for it came the previous winter when Wallace and Mary indulged themselves and went to Laguna Beach to escape the Salt Lake cold. In Laguna they were pulled eventually, as every tourist was in those days, to the Pottery Shack, which stood in a large lot on the corner of the main street in town and sold everything from garden pots to dinnerware, much of it made at that time by local artisans. Wallace has speculated that "the image of that lot . . . in the sunshine of Laguna . . . I suppose was something bright and vivid in my head." It was the beauty of that seaside scene and the warmth of its sun, as it contrasted with the cold and darkness of Salt Lake, that led him to think of writing a story that depended almost entirely on visual imagery.

What also seems to have struck him was the idea of someone working and living largely through sight, a deaf person who would be unaware of the activity around him except through visual clues, such as shadows, and the vibrations he might feel. And in turn this led to the idea of focusing on the life of someone who worked largely by feel—a potter, who, because he is handicapped, is isolated, defensive against prejudice and afraid of ridicule. So it was as a conscious experiment that Stegner wrote a story about a deaf couple with three deaf children and one hearing child, in which he limits the reader's senses, as his main character, the potter, is limited—there are no auditory images in the story. The plot is a strange one, a bit reminiscent of Victorian melodrama, but it is the wife and mother, in this instance, who falls into drunkenness and depravity, leaving the potter at the end to wonder how he is going to survive without her and keep his family together. It makes interesting, if mournful, reading, but fails in its intensity because the author does not feel the drama of the situation very deeply and because he is dealing with locales and situations he knows little about.

The summer that "The Potter's House" was published, 1938, was a busy one. While Mary went to Vermont to stay with the Grays at their summer home, Wallace went to Yaddo, where he struggled with *The Big Rock Candy Mountain.* His start was with his memories of his life on the homestead in Saskatchewan, which included that piece of the manuscript which became the story "Bugle Song," about a lonely boy's activities on the prairie. He sent the story off to Brandt and Brandt, they sold it to the *Virginia Quarterly Review,* and sent him a check for $40.50 in June. These were almost the first words he had written for his novel, and this was the third story in a row that he had sold through his agents, cementing a relationship that would last a lifetime. The story, along with "The Potter's House" and "The Two Wives," were all published in July just before he went to Bread Loaf, quite a string of publications, and he went feeling that now, at last, he was on the road to becoming a professional.

At Yaddo he decided to change course and go back in time in his manuscript, before his own childhood, starting instead with his parents. He wanted to make it more the saga of a family, rather than a personal history. At the writer's retreat he had little he could do except write, eat, and sleep. He ended up writing two hundred pages about Bo and Elsa Mason's backgrounds, about their courtship in South Dakota, and about the family's life in Washington. (Much of this material became a false start which he later decided he had to scrap.) Then in August he went up to Greensboro, Vermont, picked up Mary, and they went on over to Bread Loaf at Middlebury, Vermont, for two very intense weeks, the first of eight summers he would either be on the staff or lecture at the conference.

The intensity came in part from a busy schedule, but also from conflicting emotions and the excitement for Wallace of meeting and being able to talk intimately with literary stars he admired. There was also the pressure on the new boy to perform well in a high-powered environment at a job new to him. He had never really taught creative writing on this level before. He made friends with important people who both helped and inspired him, chief among them Bernard DeVoto.

DeVoto may be the one person who influenced Stegner the most. In Stegner's words, "He sort of became my father figure to grow up to. He used to take me under his wing at Bread Loaf." As he is described in Stegner's biography of him, *The Uneasy Chair,* he was of average height, bookish-looking, with a round head, round glasses over almost bulging round eyes, and short dark hair, parted a bit to the right of center. He had grown up a Mormon in Utah with Catholic father and Mormon mother, a precocious boy, a ferocious achiever, and finally a rebel against the culture, religion, and environment in which he grew up. He went to the University of Utah for a year, and then, unable to breathe in the smug provinciality he felt was choking him, he transferred to Harvard.

Sensitive about his looks and sensitive about his provincial origins, he developed in his youth a prickly, sarcastic, bumptious personality. He had, in Stegner's words, the "incomparable knack of infuriating people," and one of the things he never did learn, all his life, was

> the social sense of how much was enough—how far to go in colloquialism among those, who spoke only the stiffest king's English, how far to go in profanity among those whose mouths had early been sterilized with soap, how far to go in familiarity with reserved strangers or friendly women, when to stop tomahawking the body his intelligence and eloquence had slain, how much to resent an apparent slight, how not to turn simple disagreement into insult, how to state his opinions, which were quick, powerful, and sure, without stating them at someone's expense.

At the same time, if one learned the trick of discounting ten to twenty percent of what he said for showmanship and indignation, there remained "one of the sanest, most acute, most rooted-in-the-ground observers of American life that we have had." And if DeVoto caught himself in an exaggeration or mistake, he would cheerfully make corrections, "for despite a reputation as a wild man or an ogre, he was open always to the persuasion of facts." He has sometimes been compared in his love of invective and insult and his strong opinions to H. L. Mencken (whom he knew and wrote for), but in looking back, Mencken often seems merely aggressively bigoted, whereas most of DeVoto's causes—attacking the stubborn blindness of liberal Eastern establishment criticism and the pompous wrongheadedness of literary stuffed shirts; attacking the myths and discovering the West as it actually was; attacking the exploiters and exposing the West as it actually is; and defending our land heritage and preserving our public lands—are of continuing concern and most of his targets today seem justified. In fact many of his targets would later become Wallace Stegner's as well.

DeVoto taught as a lecturer at Harvard. But he could not get a regular appointment, much to his disappointment; for most of his life he supported himself as an editor, columnist, and freelance writer, which meant that he lived constantly with insecurity. Much of his income for the first half of his career came from slick, formula stories he wrote under the pen name of John August, and he wrote these, very successfully, to support his serious work, his novels.

It may be because Wallace and DeVoto shared such a similar background that they got along so well, and as a fellow Westerner it may have been easier for Wallace to take the older man's wildness with a grain of salt. They came out of the West to Cambridge, Massachusetts, from rural to urban America, and from a nineteenth-century style of living into the twentieth century. Both were born on a frontier, as the frontier was passing, and both grew up as outsiders. Wallace could be just as well writing of himself when he wrote about his longtime friend, "Brilliance, especially when associated with insecurity and assertiveness, can isolate a child as effectively as if the disapproving community had shut him in the closet of his mind" and when he wrote, "It is entirely possible that like many lonely children young Bernard DeVoto didn't recognize his trouble as loneliness, but I am sure it was."

Both as children were something of the show-off, "before girls, teachers, and God," and both read furiously, beyond their years, and used their reading to impress people. And both early in their careers read, beyond the curriculum of their schooling, "western history, geography, exploration, travel," and read them avidly all their lives. Both men were concerned throughout much of their careers with deflating such myths of the West as rugged individualism and discovering the multifaceted Western experience as it really was lived. They faced similar prejudice against writers who had commercial success as they tried to make their way through the halls of academe, and both were late bloomers who started off in the wrong direction in their work and only found the path that brought them to greatness as writers after midcareer. Stegner, of course, had a very different personality from DeVoto's; while the older man was an actor, even just in words, and seemed always to go to extremes, the younger was an observer and was moderate in most everything he did or said. Nevertheless, they had so much in common that one has the feeling in reading *The Uneasy Chair* that the author on occasion is really writing as much about himself as about his subject.

At the time Wallace got to know him, during the summer of 1938, DeVoto had been going through a year of rough waters emotionally. Not once but twice he had been turned away from the job he most aspired to, permanent appointment to the Harvard faculty. After the first refusal he went into a dark depression, suffering migraines and an inability to write and suffering from worry about money. His ace in the hole was that he had been offered the editorship of *The Saturday Review of Literature*, but he hated having to move from Cambridge. Furthermore, he was not welcomed at the magazine, which was in financial trouble, with a staff that was demoralized. His stay in New York was something under a year. At the same time, Robert Frost, the other major personality at Bread Loaf, also had had a bad year. His wife, Elinor, had died in March and he seemed to be unable to adjust to life without her steadying influence. He suffered also from the criticism of his children, who in the wake of the death of their mother blamed Frost for spending too much time on his poetry and not enough on the family. While Wallace came to look up to DeVoto as a father figure, DeVoto, in turn, had had that same relationship with Frost.

In person, Frost could be witty, funny, even profound, but he was also a terrible egomaniac who could not stand to share the limelight with anyone else. Stegner has pointed to the Lawrence Thompson biography, which "demonstrates, in a hundred contexts, how much irritable self-love lay behind the rumpled white thatch and the rumpled clothes, behind the piercing blue eyes, back of the teasing smile." The role of mentor or father figure suited Frost's ego, and he cultivated that relationship with a number of younger men, DeVoto for several years and now, beginning in the summer of 1938, with Stegner. As a youngster just getting started, Stegner offered no challenge, and Frost took an immediate liking to the modest but obviously promising young man, who in turn was flattered by the attention of the great poet. It was Frost's habit to invite his young protégés

> to walk and talk and count stars with him along the midnight road to Middlebury Gap. More than one Fellow or junior staff member crawled into bed at two or three o'clock after such an expedition, his mind dizzy with the altitudes it had been in and every cell in his body convinced that Robert Frost was the wisest and sanest man alive.

As one such junior staff member, Stegner could have been recording here his own reactions that summer, having accompanied the poet on several such walks. At the same time Wallace was also getting to know DeVoto, whom he had only met once, at the Modern Language Association meeting in Chicago the previous December. It was ironic that just as he was making friends that summer with the two men who would have such a profound effect on him, those men who had themselves been so close should have a quarrel that would split them apart permanently, leaving the younger man with divided loyalties.

Wallace tells of the events leading to the breakup—which must have been painful for him to witness—in his DeVoto biography. Frost, who one must remember had been snubbed by many of the most prominent American critics of the time, had found a place in Bread Loaf where he could shine as the main luminary among other luminaries, and he loved the idea of having a writer's conference on his home turf, out in the country on a New England farm. That summer, however, Archibald MacLeish came as a visiting lecturer: "He was a friend of most of the staff, an old Bread Loafer, and warmly welcomed. Of all the poets who had been on the mountain that summer, he was the only one who could have been said to rival Frost."

As MacLeish was reading his poems to the assembly on the evening in question, Frost sat near the back. He found some mimeographed notices on a chair nearby and sat folding and rolling them in his hands. As the reading went on, to the obvious pleasure of the audience, the sound from the rattling papers became louder, more disturbing, so that finally, unbelievably, Frost set a match to a pile of papers. The attention of everyone in the room was diverted as he stomped out the flames and waved the smoke away. Later, at Treman Cottage that night, as MacLeish was again reading, Frost repeatedly interrupted with comments and wise-cracks. As Stegner recalled, "What began as the ordinary give and take of literary conversation turned into a clear intention of frustrating and humiliating Archie MacLeish, and the situation became increasingly painful to those who comprehended it."

Among those who did was DeVoto, who became more and more agi-tated in response to Frost's behavior, getting up once to go outside and walk circles around the house. He went back in and listened restlessly until he could endure the baiting no more and burst out, "For God's sake, Robert, let him read!" Stegner speculated that it is possible that his rebuke was motivated by generosity of spirit—that "he was too mag-nanimous himself to sit quiet while the man he worshiped picked on a man he liked." But in the background there had been other causes for friction between the two men, and Stegner has felt in retrospect that considering their personalities, a clash between them was inevitable. But it took this incident to bring on the rift, a rift that was never healed. At the end of the Bread Loaf session, shaking Frost's hand as he departed, DeVoto is reported to have looked him in the eye and said, "You're a good poet, Robert, but a bad man."

Escaping from the emotional turmoil of the conference, the Stegners drove back to Greensboro to stay for a few days with the Grays. They had fallen in love with the area and ended up buying an old farm—two hundred acres, with a dilapidated farmhouse and a broken-down barn—for $600, most of the money coming from recent sales of stories to maga-zines. The barn was destroyed and the house somewhat damaged by the hurricane of '38 that winter, but the Stegners were in the area to stay, returning nearly every summer for the rest of their lives. Considering Wallace's earlier negative reaction to the lushness of Iowa, it is hard to think that he would feel at home in an area that was so green and, in recent years, so overgrown.

But in a way it would take the place of a West that was disappearing, or a West that never was. Here was a part of the country that was uncrowded, with room to walk and roam, with trees—there was so much moisture that you couldn't stop the trees and brush from growing, from replacing themselves rapidly when they had been cut back. It was also a place that displayed the best of Western virtues, a spirit of community and strong connection to the land. In speaking of Greensboro, he said:

> Everybody who grows up here grows up working hard, and at all kinds of jobs. They're all jacks-of-all-trades. They can fix things, toggle them up. That's a characteristic of any frontier, and that's the kind of West that I grew up in.

In recent years while he became more and more pessimistic about the fate of the West, Stegner felt that the old-fashioned insistence on hard work and integrity and the emphasis on personal responsibility he encountered in Vermont might very well save it from the population pressures that threatened it. Certainly the presence of the Grays increased the area's attraction, but it is also probable that his encounter with Frost at Bread Loaf, the author of all those Vermont poems that Stegner taught and knew so well, gave the country for him a special glow. At Iowa Wallace had been immersed in Americana and became convinced of the importance for writers to explore all that was native to the American experience, and certainly there was nothing more "Americana" than Robert Frost's New England.

That glow, that sense of Vermont as a special place, is reflected in a story, "The Sweetness of the Twisted Apples," that Wallace wrote after having experienced the country for ten years. He and Mary often took walks or got in the car and drove around, exploring, more or less aimlessly, in an effort to learn about the area. The story is about such a couple, also summer people, who drive down a track, hardly a road anymore, on a voyage of discovery, although their ostensible purpose is to find suitable landscapes for the husband's painting. He is the artist, but it is his wife, Margaret, who is sensitive and open to experience. As they travel farther and farther away from the paved road, it seems as if they are also traveling back in time. Margaret spots an old stone wall that

> within a few feet bent off to the right and was swallowed in impenetrable brush.

Margaret turned and stared back, but the wall did not appear again. It was lost in the woods, still carefully enclosing some obliterated and overgrown meadow, and all the labor that had built it was gone for the greater comfort of woodchucks and foxes. "It doesn't seem as if anything in America could be this old," she said.

"It doesn't seem as if" is typical Frost syntax, and the passage as a whole, with its perception of nature reclaiming what man has built, may remind us of Frost poems like "The Last Mowing," in which the trees, in a shadowy march, threaten to take over a meadow that will no longer be mowed, or to "The Wood-Pile," in which vines and decay threaten to obliterate a cord of firewood left by someone in the woods. The couple go along the road and encounter a mother and daughter—strange country people isolated from the world who may remind us of the mother and son in Frost's "Witch of Coos," also isolated by place and time, whom he calls "two old believers."

Then, too, there is that sense of "haunting," so common to Frost's poetry. While her husband paints, the wife strolls up the road through a deserted village to a burying ground where she stops and sits on a gravestone. She thinks about the gradual abandonment of the area over the years so that at last "there would be a day when you would come to your door and see nothing alive, hear no human sound, in your whole village." Unlike her unseeing husband—ironically, a painter—she is attuned to the vibrations behind appearances:

She stood up uneasily. A hawk was methodically coursing the meadow beyond the graveyard. It was very still. She felt oppressed by the wide silent sky and afraid of the somehow threatening edge where meadow met woods, where not a leaf stirred but where something watched.

It is an apprehension familiar to Frost readers; we see it, among many places, in "The Fear," "An Old Man's Winter Night," and "The Hill Wife," where something threatening lies just beyond the familiar, where some tenor of the environment strikes terror in the heart of the sensitive observer.

When the wife discovers the deformed apples hanging from the trees in an old orchard, she picks one, tries it, and exclaims in joy at her discovery—they're absolutely delicious. Her husband dismisses her enthusiasm and jokes about the Garden of Eden, but she decides to gather as many applies as she can to fill the whole back of their car and take them home for cider. The metaphor here, so similar to Frost's in "After Apple-Picking," of apples gathered as tokens of experience, suggests once again that the woman is open, able to get beyond surface appearances, and, unlike her husband, can gather experience unto herself and savor it.

Whereas Bernard DeVoto's influence on Stegner was overt, providing for him an example of taking a public stand on environmental issues, as well as validating his already held interests in Western history and geography, Robert Frost's influence was more subtle, creeping into the younger man's diction, his philosophy, and his values. Frost was able to formulate and give intellectual authority to such values as individual effort and responsibility that Stegner, out of his frontier past, already felt, but had not fully articulated. But perhaps even more important to Stegner's writing, Frost seemed to imbue his protégé with an ironic stance in regard to human nature and a more tolerant, yet distanced view of human fallibility. He seems to have reinforced Stegner's own lack of sentimentality and to have given further validation to Stegner's tendency to find drama and meaningful conflict in ordinary lives. The Frost-like language, imagery, and characters of "The Sweetness of Twisted Apples" are not so common in other Stegner fictions, but they come forth frequently enough to suggest that the poems were often on his mind. And, of course, two of his novels have titles taken from Frost poems, *Fire and Ice* and *Crossing to Safety*—one near the beginning and the other at the end of a career.

For most of his life, Stegner would have two homes, one in the West and one in Vermont, and his two friends, DeVoto and Frost, would seem to have acted as emblems of those two poles that he would bring together in his thought and work. In this regard he would become a national writer rather than a Western writer alone, for in his heart and mind the West would always be joined to rural New England, and DeVoto moderated by Frost. At the same time it should be said that Stegner, even at a comparatively young age and even though somewhat awed by such stellar company, still was his own man, a man not easily influenced in directions contrary to his own basic beliefs. He did not, for example, let Frost's devotion to individualism persuade him when it moved beyond a simple valuing of individual effort to become a sort of ultraconservative political doctrine. Stegner believed strongly in the importance of group effort and cooperation, and he supported the New Deal programs that Frost scorned with such vehemence. Nor did he allow DeVoto's tactics of exaggeration and denunciation to influence his own manner, which was courteous and moderate. DeVoto had a habit of going off half-cocked, with a Quixote-like gleam in his eye; Stegner thought through issues, balancing the claims of one side against the other, before he took a stand—a habit that would rankle in the hearts of his more extremist environmentalist colleagues over the years, although it never seemed to bother his relationship with DeVoto. Indeed, Wallace could be a friend to both Frost and DeVoto without allowing their character flaws to sidetrack his relationships with them, and while at the same time taking from each the best that was offered.

A third person Wally met that summer who would play an important part in his life was Theodore Morrison, the director of Bread Loaf in the summer, and for the rest of the year the head of the writing program at Harvard. Tall, thin, with sandy brown hair and even features, he looked like a tennis player. Morrison was a fine administrator, a gracious gentleman who could be firm, but was also expert in conciliation, soothing the hurt feelings of students (or "customers," as they were called), and massaging the egos of some of the more temperamental visiting lecturers. His wife, Kay, who had many of the same skills, became Robert Frost's secretary and, as he referred to her occasionally, his "keeper."

Wallace's budding friendship with Morrison would provide the opportunity for his next step up the professional ladder. As had been the case at Utah, his career at Wisconsin seemed stalled. When he had moved there, he had done so thinking that he would have more opportunity for creative writing, especially since he had won an important prize. But Mark Ecoles, a colleague who was an assistant professor, recalled a feeling in the department that it couldn't afford two writers, and it already had Helen White. Furthermore, there had not been a promotion in the English department for twelve years. So Stegner was pleased that Morrison, backed by recommendations from DeVoto and Wilbur Schramm, offered him a job, which eventually became a Briggs-Copeland Fellowship, at Harvard.

The Briggs-Copeland Fellowships had been the outgrowth of an idea forwarded by Morrison that the writing program he was in charge of could be much improved by attracting a staff of promising writers who were also teachers, while at the same time the careers of young writers could be forwarded by their association with Harvard. Technically, the fellows were lecturers, not on tenure track for the English department, but to receive such a fellowship was an honor. Wallace received a letter from Morrison in November 1938 just as he had decided that he would have no future at Wisconsin and would have to move on once again. He was gratified by the turn of events, although the note from Morrison was somewhat tentative about the job and didn't mention the possibility of the fellowship. But there was nothing tentative about Wilbur Schramm's reactions to his friend's good fortune:

Stegner of Harvard! Someday he will be silvery haired and mellow, and will walk around the yard in his bedroom slippers, and students will point him out in the same awed whispers they used to say "Copey" or "Kittredge" or "Palmer." Just another tradition. (1/4/39)

Wallace wrote to Morrison that if he was looking for anyone else, he could highly recommend one of his colleagues, Claude Simpson, and Morrison took Simpson on as well, but as an instructor of writing. Looking back, Stegner has commented that it was "brute luck that Claude Simpson and I got to Harvard. ... We got out just in time. It wasn't the school's fault [Wisconsin's]. It was the time's fault. And the war." His luck held, also, in regard to the war and the onset of the draft: "I had the highest draft number in history—a crippled child and I was on the upper edge of the age limit. I was 30 in 1939, and they were taking 18 to 25."

Although constantly going back during this period to his long-range work in progress, *The Big Rock Candy Mountain*, Wallace started on another novel, *On a Darkling Plain*, in the fall of 1938, finished the manuscript that winter, and submitted it to Little, Brown in the spring of 1938. Although the publisher had an option for his next book after *Remembering Laughter,* it promptly turned the book down, but *Redbook,* through the efforts of Bernice Baumgarten, accepted it for serial publication. Wallace took some time that summer and fall revising it for possible book publication, and it was eventually accepted by Harcourt, Brace and published in April 1940. It was in that way that he made his first change of publishers. Harcourt, Brace was not optimistic about the book, hoping that its sale would somehow make up for publication expenses, but was willing to take a chance to get a promising writer on its list. Once again the novelette prize had come to Wallace's aid to push his career forward. Wallace has referred to *On a Darkling Plain* in recent years as "a little jejune novel" in which he was "trying out fictionally the textures of my Saskatchewan childhood." It sold two thousand out of a printing of twenty-five hundred, and he has refused to allow it to be reprinted.

The novel describes the isolated life on the prairie of a disillusioned Canadian World War I veteran. In exposing once again Stegner's antagonism toward rugged individualism, it acts indirectly to endorse the importance of community and cooperative activity. Perhaps the main problem with the novel is its basic premise—a man who has been driven to strong antisocial feelings by his war experiences strives to live as totally apart from society as possible. Inevitably, not much happens in the novel, as we focus on the protagonist, Edwin Vickers, alone, and the author seems much more interested in Vickers's feelings and experiences in that lonely Saskatchewan landscape, and the qualities of that landscape, than in Vickers's fate or in the somewhat lame love story that seems tacked on to give the novel some form and direction.

But despite Stegner's later rejection of the book, it does have its themes and virtues, and it did play its part in the evolution of the writer and his art. In a way, it can be considered a parable for the author's own search (which, we should never forget, would last a lifetime) to understand himself and his own experience. By placing Vickers out in the middle of nowhere, creating a modern version of the Robinson Crusoe story, life is reduced to its basics and there is both time and need to contemplate large questions of purpose: What is fundamental to being human—can a human being live without love, companionship, and interaction or help from others? Is there any purpose to life other than serving others? And courage—how do we summon it when we need it? These are very large questions that can be found in the background of much of Stegner's work, both fiction and nonfiction.

In early June 1939, as the Stegners gathered up their belongings for the move east, they marveled at how little stuff they had. They bought a station wagon and packed it with whatever they could use in Vermont— the typewriter, some boxes of books, some dishes and pans, and a few chairs. It was their intention to spend the summer working on the damaged house on their farm and to try to make it livable. They brought with them a graduate student from the University of Wisconsin to help with the rebuilding and as a baby-sitter for Page. Although he, unlike Wallace, had no skills as a carpenter, Earl North was big and strong and willing. His body was so beautiful that he earned much of his living while going to school modeling for art classes, and he was pleased to work for just board and room as long as he had some time to himself to lie out in the sun and get a tan in preparing for modeling during the winter.

The small farmhouse was out some fifteen miles from town and a mile or so from the nearest neighbor, without electricity or inside plumbing. While Wallace was burdened with the problems of reconditioning a house a hundred years old made with hand-hewn beams and rough-sawn planks—none of the measurements matched new lumber— Mary was impressed with the loneliness and darkness. How very dark it was! It was frightening. One evening, she remembered, they had left Earl with the baby while they went to the Grays' for dinner. When they returned, they found Earl sitting in an overstuffed chair with a large club at his side, "standing" guard—but fast asleep. But it turned out that he had only intended to watch for porcupines who were invading the house at night.

Near the end of August 1939, the Stegners closed up the house and drove over to Middlebury, where Wallace would be a "visiting speaker" at Bread Loaf. The slots on the staff for handling the fiction were taken by DeVoto in the novel and Edith Mirrielees in the short story. Mirrielees had been a staple of the staff since the second year of the confer-

ence's inception, was on the Stanford faculty, and had been John Steinbeck's teacher there. She was "a maiden lady," as the term went in those
days, and in her quiet, incisive, totally competent way, made an enormous impression on those who worked with her. Wallace's acquaintance
with her would, as with so many of his friendships, work to his advantage in later years. She and Stegner and DeVoto formed what they
thought of as the "Western contingent" at Bread Loaf.

Although he was not "staff" officially, his duties were pretty much
what they had been the year before. He wrote to Phil and Peg Gray,

> Breadloaf about as I expected: a pile of mss. a foot high (three
> novels, fifty short stories) to read this week and have conferences
> about next; much drinking and gabbing with Hershel Brickel,
> Gorham Munson, DeVoto, Helen Everitt, and Frost. Frost is
> undoubtedly one of the few great men in the world—certainly the
> greatest I ever met, the most integrated, the one who fuses man
> and poet most fully. And DeVoto is clever as hell, even though a
> little loud. Munson is a cultist of sorts, but pleasant. Brickel is a
> prince from Mississippi. The tennis is good, the climate fine, the
> cottage pleasant. Viola[*sic*], the Stegners are having fun. (8/20/39)

At the end of the summer they packed up the station wagon once again
and were off for Harvard. They were in a state of considerable excitement, for, as Stegner has said, "Cambridge was our Athens and our
Rome."

6

HARD WORK
AT HARVARD:
Climbing the Big Rock
Candy Mountain

Each time Wallace moved, went to a new school or got a new job, he seemed to move into faster company, a situation more intellectually challenging. His life followed a pattern of continuous growth—almost as if it were following a script, giving his progress a far more planned aspect than it actually had. But if he was dazzled by the company at Bread Loaf, that was merely the moon. The sun was at Harvard.

In September the Stegners moved into a house in Newtonville, near Boston, which had been vacated by a Harvard faculty member on leave. Wallace recalled that they were made to feel at home almost at once:

If you are on the Harvard faculty, you have a kind of welcome that rather astonishes me as I think back on it because I don't think we were as open in any sense to new junior faculty in the department here [at Stanford]. . . . And I had, you know, I suppose some notion in my head of Harvard as a very snooty place, which in some ways intellectually it is, but socially it is not and certainly wasn't for us.

In addition to the welcome by the department, the Stegners were made to feel at home by a number of Bread Loaf regulars who lived in Cambridge and by several Harvard faculty, in various departments, who had summer homes near Greensboro. I mention "in various departments" because the Stegners, wherever they were, because they had varied interests and activities, always made friends among faculty other than in English or writing (at Harvard, these included Gordon Allport and his wife in psychology and Sprague Coolidge and his wife in science), as well as friends among townsfolk and neighbors. There was to some extent a side benefit to a wider acquaintance—Wallace, like all writers, needed to observe life and find material, and he would often use bits and pieces of friends and neighbors in his novels (sometimes much to their dismay). One of the activities that spread their acquaintance was Mary's membership in the Socialist Party. At one of their dinners, Wallace heard them sing "I Dreamed I Saw Joe Hill Last Night"—the first time he had heard it—and at home that night, Mary recalled, he was singing it over and over. From this small seed sprouted the idea that led to the writing of *The Preacher and the Slave*. After a year in Newtonville, they took over an apartment in Cambridge vacated by Henry Nash Smith.

In the first group of Briggs-Copeland Fellows, besides Wallace and Claude Simpson (who was not a Briggs-Copeland, but part of this group of young writing instructors), there were Mark Schorer, Bob Davis, Delmore Schwartz, and Howard Baker. Of these Simpson became a well-known professor of American literature at Stanford and Schorer a writer of fiction and critic at Berkeley. Schwartz became a much-respected poet, winning the Bollingen Prize, and also was a well-known eccentric, becoming the model for Von Humboldt Fleisher in Saul Bellow's novel *Humboldt's Gift*. "Nobody," Wallace commented, "got to know Delmore. . . . He was strange." He not only had an odd, quirky personality, but he was paranoid, convinced that the students all hated him. Nevertheless, the Stegners recalled going to his place several times, on one occasion renewing acquaintance there with W. H. Auden, whom they had met at Bread Loaf.

There was a good deal of camaraderie among the younger writing staff during these years. They worked hard on their teaching, reading and correcting "tons of papers" and having frequent student conferences, but in addition they all had their own writing projects which weighed heavily on them and which they had to find time for one way or another. But they also played hard. Mary remembered the late evenings at many parties where Claude Simpson and her husband teamed up, Claude with his shirtsleeves rolled up and the butt of a cigar clenched in his teeth, sitting at a piano, and Wallace standing by, also coatless, glass in hand. Wallace was a great singer of folk ballads, as well as knowing most of the old favorites that someone in the group might suggest, and Claude, a genius at the keyboard, could play anything. Wallace could also delight the crowd with a great soft-shoe routine.

When Wallace got to Harvard, he had asked for a half-time teaching load so that he could put most of his energy into his writing. But halfway through the first semester he was thrust back into a full load when he was called on to teach an advanced writing class, replacing a professor who died suddenly. Walter Rideout, who with some irony would later become one of the mainstays of the Wisconsin faculty that Wallace had just left, became Wally's reader at Harvard for that advanced course. He recalled:

When he [Wally] knew what the roster was, he said 'Well, the best way to do this is simply to divide the papers in half. You take, say "A" to "O," and I'll take all the rest, and that's just about half for each of us. But there's a kid named Norman Mailer who's in the class, and I want his papers because I think he looks good.' And I remember that vividly because he obviously had spotted Mailer [through a writing sample].

Mailer, for some reason, did not wind up in Stegner's class but in Bob Davis's, but Mailer does remember that his fellow students all spoke highly of Stegner. Wallace felt he was under the gun and did work hard on his classes. He insisted that Rideout make full comments on student work, as Wallace did himself, not just putting down a grade, and insisted that each of them must give every one of their students a conference after every paper.

Rideout remembered that during the fall of 1939 he was invited to the Stegners', along with a couple of other graduate students, to meet Robert Frost. Frost became a frequent guest of theirs, often just dropping in for dinner. He might "pay" for it by dropping an aphorism or two into the conversation, like one that Wallace was fond of recalling: "Tell other people's stories as if they happened to you and your own as if they happened to other people." Ted Morrison, who with his wife, Kay, might also be at the Stegners', remembered Frost as a pleasant and comfortable guest, a man with a keen sense of humor and irony often expressed in understated ways: "Just an enjoyment of comic situations, contradictions and oddities in people." Over these months, Mary Stegner would become good friends with both Kay Morrison and Avis DeVoto, as well as with Peg Coolidge and Ada Allport. Mary and Wallace were busy with Page, whom they had taken to a specialist in Boston; Wallace was required to massage his legs daily and exercise him without his brace so that the injured leg would not atrophy.

The company the Stegners were keeping was high-powered indeed. Some of the best-known scholars in the study of American literature were at the parties that they attended—F. O. Matthiessen, Perry Miller, Howard Mumford Jones. Wallace remembered Jones as a "very lively character" and his wife as a good hostess: "They entertained quite a lot." Even the provost, Paul Buck, who was running the university while President Conant was off at the Manhattan Project, was "one of the boys," went on drinking parties with Wallace and his friends, and was often at the DeVotos' gatherings on Sunday afternoons. Wallace reflected back, "I had a sense of, of being 'in,' " of belonging. The Stegners were often included in the DeVotos' famous "Sunday Evening Hour," which began in the afternoon and often stretched into a late evening dinner that Avis would somehow put together. It was in the DeVoto parlor that Kenneth Murdock, Arthur Schlesinger, and John Kenneth Galbraith had the discussions that led to the birth of Americans for Democratic Action. At the university, Wallace recalled:

> DeVoto, Frost, Conrad Aiken and others made up a little commu-
> nity which hadn't existed anywhere that I had lived up to that
> point.... T. S. Eliot would come lecturing, and we would all go
> together. The poetry room was a gathering place where all kinds of
> people from Ted Roethke to John Malcolm Brennen would be
> coming through to read their poems.

It was a happy but hectic life, and in an effort to squeeze out as much time as possible for his writing, Wallace began to write in the evenings, from eight to ten, as well as taking what early mornings he could. Mary began to worry about him as he wore down, with a chronic case of sinus infection accompanied by frequent splitting headaches. Despite nagging minor health problems, he, Mary, colleague Carvel Collins and his wife, Mary, went up to stay with the Grays in Vermont over Christmas and had wonderful skiing. However, Wallace still had a fever when he went through the ordeal that later inspired the writing of the story "The Traveler": the old station wagon got stuck in a drift on the road to town. Weak and feverish, he tried to push it out through the snow; then he tried waiting for someone to come by, but the cold was more than he could abide just waiting and stomping his feet. So he took off down the road with the car blanket over his shoulders to try to find a farmhouse.

After returning to Cambridge he wrote in January 1940 to his agents that he felt his work was going poorly and that he was "trying to keep three balls in the air at once, with drastic results. Novel has stopped temporarily, novelette is bogged at the end of two chapters, short story causes daily pain" (1/25/40). The novel he is referring to here is a manuscript of the first part of *The Big Rock Candy Mountain*, which seemed to go forward in fits and starts.

For one thing, it was too close to him; for another, he still thought of it in epic terms, as three volumes, which must certainly have been intimidating. His agent, Bernice, did not care for the first volume, suggesting that he revise it further, but submitting it that spring for publication anyway to get another opinion. That opinion came from Frank Morley, an editor with Wallace's new publisher, Harcourt, Brace, who described well where Wally was with the book at this time and the trouble he was having:

You are attempting in this trilogy something which can't yet be done ... because I think your attitude towards the story is still, inevitably, tangled. It has one kind of importance for you, and that is private; and it has another kind of importance as the material for a novel. . . . The two main characters *don't* come alive, because your vision is divided. What you express about them is not adequate to carry what you yourself feel about them. . . . Damned if I know what you can do about it, except to wait. If you wait, I wouldn't be surprised to find the vehicle for *those* characters (Saint and Sinners, or Puritan and Pioneer) something very much simpler than the scaffolding you set up—which isn't so much *their* scaffolding as an extension of your own boyhood notions of their scaffolding. (6/28/40)

He went on to say that by contrast he found "Bugle Song" very moving, but in "The Still, Sad Music," the name Wallace had given to the manuscript of this first volume, nothing of the same intensity was evoked. The editor wound up by suggesting that Wallace pursue his other projects and publish other books first before going back to this one.

The novelette Wallace spoke of in his January letter to his agents was what eventually was extended to become his next published novel, *Fire and Ice*, the last of what might be called his apprenticeship fiction. As with *On a Darkling Plain*, this novel did not sell out its printing and has not been reprinted. As he was writing it in 1940, the author was not sure that it could be printed in the first place or that he wanted it sold. He wrote Bernice:

You ask where the novelette is. Where, oh, where, echo I. If you must know, it's on page 65, after having got to page 90 twice. And if you want further information, it's utterly unsaleable. It makes me weep to say it, but I know it is, unless for book publication, and I am not sure in any case I'd ever want to see it in print. It's full of four-letter words, it's about a neurotic communist who's about the angriest man you ever heard of, and it ends in an attempted rape. Try that on Redbook. (9/20/40)

In later years, the author, although by no means ashamed of it, was happy to let the novel fade into obscurity.

The novel's materials came largely out of the author's experiences at Wisconsin. Wallace, along with several other junior faculty, went to some meetings of the Young Communist League, which in 1937–39 were largely concerned with supporting the Loyalists in the Spanish Civil War. His observations supported his previous antipathy for Marxism (an antipathy shared by Frost, by DeVoto, and by the liberals DeVoto surrounded himself with at his Sunday gatherings), and for the calculating mechanisms such groups as the YCL used to increase their membership and political clout. For them, the end always justified the means, a doctrine that Stegner had never been able to tolerate, let alone endorse.

Yet, the viability of a free-enterprise, participatory democracy was a major topic of conversation and contention during these last years of the Great Depression, as intellectuals watched our society still stagnating, still mired in heated debate over New Deal programs, and at the same time observed what seemed to be the increased power and efficiency of communist and fascist governments abroad. At least, the argument went, in Russia, as unpleasant as a totalitarian regime might be on a temporary basis, there were no unemployed, no people, as in this country, starving.

Fire and Ice was Stegner's contribution to this ongoing debate. In his novel, he focuses on a young man, a student at a midwestern university—presumably Wisconsin, since its geography matches—who is an active leader in the student Communist movement. Paul Condon is the archetypal angry young man, angry at nearly everyone in the world except his landlady and a fellow student, Zoe Milstein, who works with him for the cause. His bitterness increases during the course of the book, and it gets to the point that, prompted by his hatred, he takes unilateral actions not part of the party's plan.

Paul is a figure composed of a number of ingredients. He is, of course, related to his creator, having much the same parentage, but also as a poor boy who must work at several jobs in order to get through college. Wallace, like Paul, occasionally felt the sting of class snobbery, of being condescended to by wealthy students from prominent families. But Paul is also, like many of the negative male characters in Stegner's work, partly a reflection of the author's father.

Paul's Big Rock Candy Mountain is not wealth so much as revenge against the wealthy, an effort to bring down those whose power or prestige have allowed them to lord it over him. And finally, it should be added, since it shows a bit how Stegner worked, one of Paul's jobs, posing for art classes in the nude, is an ingredient taken from the Wisconsin graduate student, Earl North, who worked for the Stegners during the summers of 1939 and 1940.

Regardless of the ingredients that make up Paul, he is essentially a disagreeable and unsavory character. Despite his poverty and the injustice he has faced, it is very difficult to have much sympathy for him. Of course, other novels have been successful despite having an unhappy, unlikable central character headed for disaster—Jim Nolan in John Steinbeck's *In Dubious Battle* or Bigger Thomas in Richard Wright's *Native Son*. But the rich texture of the prose and the interplay of timely and engaging ideas in these two novels provide rewards to the reader that take the place of vicarious experience. By contrast with Wallace's more successful works, both the background and foreground of the action in *Fire and Ice* are relatively thin.

At the climax of the novel, Paul's anger and resentment lead him to attempt the rape of a snotty sorority girl. The scene does illustrate the contemporary understanding of rape as more a crime of violence than of sexual passion, but Paul gets off too easily (the young woman's wealthy parents pull her out of school to her home in another state and exert political pressure to have the charges dropped) for today's sensibilities. Our present view, shaped by a justified feminist revolt against abuse of the female and insensitivity to the plight of rape victims, would be that Paul should serve a term in jail. Instead, we see him at the end, leaving college himself to hit the road on a journey of self-discovery. On the novel's own terms, this does not ring true. We have witnessed, as we would watch an experiment, his behavior as a determined product of the conditioning given to him by his environment, a "rat," like the metaphor used for Bigger Thomas in *Native Son,* caught in the trap of his own hostility. That he should be turned loose with any expectation that he will be able to overcome his own history and the emotions produced by that history is unrealistic.

Stegner seems betrayed here in part by his own experience, wherein he was able, through will and determination, to transcend his own impoverished and often unhappy history. But his anger was directed primarily at his father, not at society as a whole, and he was never as crippled by bitterness as is Paul. Although a naturalist and therefore largely a determinist in his general belief, Stegner had to believe personally in free will in order to strive for success. In his writing he seems to be haunted by this contradiction, as during his career his novels move back and forth from one position to the other.

*   *   *

There was at Harvard considerable pressure, both inner and outer, on Stegner to succeed. Several years had gone by since his success with *Remembering Laughter*, and he needed to demonstrate to himself, and others around him, that he could go forward with the novel. He was surrounded by writers, which was good and bad: bad because there was an implicit competition and an implicit expectation that he would progress; good because he felt accepted, was part of something, a feeling he never had at Wisconsin. Perhaps because of his problems with the novel form, he began giving more attention to the short story, many of the stories dealing with the same Saskatchewan subject matter as the early chapters of *The Big Rock Candy Mountain*.

His correspondence with his agents during the years 1940–42, nearly all of which deals with Bernice's efforts to sell stories to various magazines, reflects an increasing amount of work in that form and an increasing success with it. In 1940 he received fourteen letters from the agency; in 1941, thirty-two letters; and in 1942, forty-eight letters. Most of the stories dealing with childhood were written during this period: in addition to "Bugle Song," his agent placed "In the Twilight," "The Volunteer," "Butcher Bird," "The Chink," "The Colt," "Goin' to Town," "Two Rivers," and "Chip Off the Old Block." Of these nine, only "The Chink" and "In the Twilight" would not be incorporated into *The Big Rock Candy Mountain*.

"Goin' to Town" is a delicate story without much plot but which depends instead on mood and atmosphere. It is a bit reminiscent of Steinbeck's "Breakfast," in which a migrant family, in the joy of the morning before a day of work, invite a passerby to join them for breakfast. The poignancy comes not only from the sweet and welcoming dispositions of the family, but from our knowledge that such mornings of joy are probably rare in their lives: in the background looms the dark sufferings of the dispossessed in our society, but the contrast is implicit. The contrast in "Goin' to Town," as we shall see, is explicit.

Stegner is at his best in such descriptions as that which opens the story, setting a mood of joyful expectation:

After the night's rain the yard was spongy and soft under the boy's bare feet. He stood at the edge of the packed dooryard in the flat thrust of sunrise, looking at the ground washed clean and smooth and trackless, feeling the cool firm mud under his toes. Experimentally he lifted his right foot and put it down in a new place, pressed, picked it up again to look at the neat imprint of straight edge and curling instep and the five round dots of toes. The air was so fresh that he sniffed at it as he would have sniffed at the smell of cinnamon.

And in just two sentences he lets us know, in case we were born and bred in the city, just what the prairie *feels* like to a child on a glorious morning filled with expectation:

Standing in the yard above his one clean sharp footprint, feeling his own verticality in all that spread of horizontal land, he sensed how the prairie shrank on this morning and how he himself grew. He was immense. A little jump would crack his head on the sky; a few strides would take him to any horizon.

The boy has "hungered" for weeks in anticipation of going to town on this Fourth of July—he can envision the band, lemonade stands, the crowds, the parade, the ball game, and the fireworks.

But the situation changes, as the family's long-hoped-for outing is spoiled by a balky car that won't start, and the joy, hope, joking, eagerness, and affection of the morning gradually dissipate in the face of intense frustration and turn to hopelessness, anger, blame, defeat, churlishness, and even violence. Once again, as in many of these childhood stories, the conflict between father and mother—the Western rugged individual with his macho code versus the more civilized, softening influence of the frontier woman—is played out, putting pressure on the boy, who weeps at his disappointment but knows he shouldn't show weakness.

"Two Rivers" is a companion piece to "Goin' to Town." It takes place on the day after, on the same homestead farm, and the boy is still smarting from the slap his father gave him in response to his "blubbering." It is even clearer in this story how the patriarchal father serves as thermostat of the family's emotional situation: they must "read" him to know where they stand and how to relate to him and to each other. On this day, the reading is well into the comfort zone. The boy learns that they are going to go on a picnic into the mountains, to make up for the failure of the day before, and finds that the car is already packed and ready to go:

> All his sullenness gone now, the boy said, "When did you get all this ready?"
>
> His father grinned. "While you slept like a sluggard we worked like a buggard," he said. Then the boy knew that everything was perfect, nothing could go wrong. When his father started rhyming things he was in his very best mood, and not even breakdowns and flat tires could make him do more than puff and blow and play-act.

If in the first story everything goes wrong, now, for this trip, everything goes right.

This story is not just about mood and how our emotions can affect the emotions and well-being of those around us, but turns to other, related themes—the emotions we invest in places, the individuality of memory, and a favorite Stegner topic, identity and whether we really can know other people. As in "The Berry Patch" and "The Sweetness of Twisted Apples," we see how places come to have emotional values. Their picnic spot leads Brucie to a half-buried memory of a picnic day in the past, when he was nearly an infant. But his memories of that day come in conflict with those of his parents, each of whose, in turn, differs. His mother remembers a bear, but "there wasn't any bear in what he remembered. Just feelings, and things that made his skin prickle." His mother looks at him, puzzled:

> "It's funny you should remember such different things than we remember," she said. "Everything means something different to everybody, I guess." She laughed, and the boy thought her eyes looked very odd and bright. "It makes me feel as if I didn't know you at all," she said. She brushed her face with the handful of leaves and looked at the father, gathering up odds and ends and putting them in the picnic box. "I wonder what each of us will remember about today?"

What a wonderful detail, that gesture—"She brushed her face with the handful of leaves."

Despite the upbeat nature of the story on its surface, the story is one, like many of Stegner's stories, with sinister overtones that the reader is clearly meant to feel. All this happiness and joy comes out of the male patriarch who sets the emotional agenda; neither the boy nor the mother have much to say about whether it is going to be a good day or bad. Indeed, the mother is reduced to her traditional role of intermediary in these stories.

Also sinister is the boy's memory of another excursion years earlier, a sketchy remembrance accompanied by "things that made his skin prickle," things unnamed and certainly ominous. The boy can't quite recall what happened on that other day, but it was "something bothersome and a little scary," and looking out from a ledge in the mountains

over the whole canyon, like a haze in the clear air, was that other thing, that memory or ghost of a memory, a swing he had fallen out of, a feel of his hands sticky with crushed blackberries, his skin drinking cool shade, and his father's anger—the reflection of ecstasy and the shadow of tears.

"Chip Off the Old Block," the last of these Saskatchewan stories, switches the central character from Bruce to his older brother Chet. The setting is one that Stegner has used on several occasions in his fiction— the 1918 flu, which hits the small town with a heavy hand. In contrast to the Bruce we see in other stories (here he and his parents are hospitalized in the schoolhouse), Chet is "a chip off the old block," displaying the survival skills and frontier toughness of the father.

Left alone, Chet holds the fort, feeding himself, stoking the fire, and taking care of the house, and then, when the opportunity arises, selling his father's bootlegged whiskey. When the father returns, he is impatient, even angry with the boy until he learns how well the boy has managed things. The father, however, can only express his approval indirectly: "Okay," he said. "Okay, kid, you're a man. I wouldn't take it away from you."

The model for this father, George Stegner, had over recent years come into hard times, and his son, still resentful of a battered childhood and the way his father had treated his mother, abandoning her during her final illness, had parted from his father forever, only remaining in touch with him by mail out of duty. Emotionally, it was another angle of repose. George had run through all his money, still looking for his big strike and investing in a run of failed claims and mining possibilities in Nevada. A series of letters from him to Wallace in early 1939 begged for money, told of one lost opportunity after another, and expressed a pathetic desperation. George had no pension and wasn't old enough yet to qualify for social security. Wallace sent him as much money as he could, even though he was barely able to make ends meet himself—and he did so with a certain cynical fatalism, since he knew his father was a "sucker." It was a harsh term, but one that, Wallace felt, applied perfectly. He has described the kind of gambling fever his father was caught up in:

> Mining men have been immemorial players of hunches. In any mining town, anywhere, it is still possible to run into excited men with new jiggers and devices and doodle-bugs, descendants of the forked hazel sticks with which their ancestors witched for water in New England. With those doodle-bugs it is a cinch to discover ore bodies. Just walk around, with this little magnetic dingus held before you, and if there's a metal in the ground the dingus will click or whistle or bend downward or make a noise like a cash register.

Wallace's father was a believer in doodle-bugs and men with hunches who needed partners. Now that he was growing old, it was his last chance to find that Big Rock Candy Mountain and live on Easy Street for a time before he died.

But the money Wallace sent him at such sacrifice was not enough to revive his father's optimism. That summer of 1939, Wallace was giving a speech at the University of Iowa, at the invitation of his old friend Wilbur Schramm. He recalled how similar the situation was to when his brother died:

> As if wheels had ground around to some starting point, he [Wilbur] was there to come to the lecture platform to halt the questioning

after my talk and tell me that word had just come of my father's death. He didn't need, this time, to lend me train fare or an overcoat, but he showed me all over again the meaning of sympathy.

George had shot himself in a squalid room in a cheap hotel in Salt Lake City. He felt full of self-pity—old, defeated, and weak, without any promise for the future. His condition had brought him into direct conflict with the code of strength and intolerance of weakness and complaint that he had lived by during those years that Wallace was growing up. For Wallace there was bitter irony in this act, which he considered the ultimate display of weakness. What made the situation worse, more emotionally taxing for Wallace by adding shame to the hatred, guilt, and distaste, was that his father had shot and killed the woman he was going with, before taking his own life. This was the end of Wallace's immediate family. There was no one left but him.

The mixture of strong emotions that followed his father's death remained to haunt Wallace for the rest of his life. There was only a partial confrontation with them in his novel *Recapitulation*, written forty years after the event. The narrator's dead aunt, the corpse in the mortuary, his old friend, Joe Mulder, whom he cannot bring himself to look up, and even the villainous, macho Jack Bailey all seem to be stand-ins for the father whose memory appears to be constantly pushed to the back of the narrator's mind. On reflection, one realizes that it is not as much about memories of growing up in Salt Lake as it is about a father who is seldom even mentioned in the text until the end.

One remedy for the sadness, shame, and anger that nearly overwhelmed Wallace was work. He strove during the months that followed to fill his life with one project or another, often several at the same time. In addition to the stories he was writing and the two novels he was struggling with, he was also writing and publishing nonfiction articles during these first two years at Harvard. These he placed himself, not wanting to clutter Bernice's desk with what generally were low- or nonpaying pieces. One of his steadiest customers was the *Delphian Quarterly*, a publishing opportunity that came to him through the wife of colleague, Willard Thorp. He had met Thorp (who became a well-known professor of American literature at Princeton) at Yaddo and became acquainted again with him at Harvard:

Willard's wife, Margaret, used to edit a little magazine called the *Delphian Quarterly*.... Willard got me involved in *The Literary History of the United States* because he was one of the general editors. [The other editors were Robert E. Spiller, Thomas H. Johnson, Henry Seidel Canby, and Richard M. Ludwig. This reference work, first published in 1947, became extremely influential in setting the "canon" for the decades following World War II. Stegner was the author of the section "Western Record and Romance."] But Margaret was my meal ticket for awhile there in Cambridge because ... when I couldn't find a dollar in the till, I could always write an article for the *Delphian Quarterly* and get $30 or $40.

In an interview in his later years, Stegner claimed that he never did know what the Delphian Society was—he had the vague idea that it was "kind of a literary ladies' literary society."

In addition to the *Delphian Quarterly*, he published pieces in *Publishers Weekly* (which paid him $15), *The Writer*, and, more profitably, in the *Saturday Evening Post* and *Harper's*. His topics ranged from regional publishing to writing technique, language, and topical subjects, such as "Colleges in Wartime," the advantages of co-ops, and "Care and Feeding of Ration Hogs." It would appear that he had the skill to take any idea that came to him, about his job or about current affairs, and turn it into an article. And while he never gave up publication in little magazines, quarterlies, regional journals, or professional journals that paid little or nothing, a pattern developed, over these years, of his work appearing more and more in large-circulation magazines. However, throughout his career, he seemed more willing to have something published in an academic journal or a low-paying quarterly than not at all.

He seemed to use some of these articles as a sounding board for thoughts about writing problems he had had or was having, and two of these articles are in this regard particularly revealing. One, " 'Truth' and 'Faking' in Fiction," (*The Writer*, February 1940) seems to be something of a confession as well as an exploration of a problem of technique. After *On a Darkling Plain* came out in its magazine version, Stegner got letters from two Saskatchewan farmers telling him that obviously he had never been on a farm and asking why he would want to write about something he didn't know anything about. The letters hurt his pride—he *had* been a farm boy. But at one point in the novel he is describing the harvesting of wheat and has the threshing machine pouring the wheat into sacks. Wrong—it was harvested in bulk and allowed to cure. He was faking the details that he didn't know and got caught.

This got him to thinking about some kind of general rule for writers, who can't always be sure of every detail they include in their story in order to be convincing. One method would be to look everything up, but such busywork leads inevitably to more busywork, and "the story gets lost in the multitude of its undeniably accurate facts." He decides that

the safe system to follow, it seems to me, is self-evident: spend most of your time, most of your thought, on the people, the psychological rightness, the ultimate implications of your story. Look up your details when they are important and must be exact, but fake them where hunting them down would be tedious and unnecessary labor. I was not writing a thesis on wheat farming; I was not writing for farmers, but for fiction readers irrespective of class or occupation. I faked badly, and got caught, but I should feel much worse about it if readers had objected to the motivation of the characters or the truth of the theme.

A second article in *The Writer* (April 1942), called "The Shaping of Experience," reveals Stegner's thoughts about his novel in progress, *The Big Rock Candy Mountain,* although he never mentions the novel by name. The article shows his thinking about his struggle with the problem of the autobiographical novel, but here he puts it in terms of writing a story based on experience:

The technical problems involved in translating experience into fictional truth are the basic problems of form, and form is the most difficult and at the same time the most essential problem of writing. . . . The transcription of life is not a transcription at all, but a re-making, and that re-making implies taking many liberties with fact.

He then goes on to describe as the basis for his argument, without revealing their personal application, the facts and the emotional situation that in his own life would become the foundation for his novel: an unhappy childhood with a father who had been irritable and unhappy and "whose disappointment emerges in heavy-handed domination of his family" and a mother who tried to act as intermediary between her husband and her children and make up to them for their father's neglect and harshness. As a writer, the article continues, you have a long record in your mind of the family quarrels and recriminations. You have more than twenty years of reality—how can you make it into a story? That, of course, was Stegner's own question.

In retrospect, the article seems to go on as if he is instructing himself as he describes, in terms of his example, how one can select incidents, eliminate unnecessary characters, invent scenes, and alter chronology. When you, the writer, finish your story, he tells his audience, you may even have the impression that it has reproduced your own experience, faithfully, but you have made changes, "changes dictated by the needs and the logic of fiction." He paraphrases Robert Frost as once saying, "Nothing in Nature ... ever quite achieves form by itself. It takes the imaginative eye, the imaginative mind, to put the form on the experience."

It is clear from this article that he knew what to do, that he didn't need Frank Morley to spell it out for him, but that knowing and being able to do it successfully were two entirely different matters. What he doesn't tell the reader of the article is that when it is a story from your own life you are trying to use, it can be very difficult to escape being captured by its emotions, to stand back from it far enough to be able to make the necessary changes that transform experience into a work of art. There are those who simply can't—Thomas Wolfe, without the help of Charles Scribner, could not. He wanted to tell everything—and so, apparently, did Wallace Stegner.

7

LOOKING BACK
AT THE WEST
FROM CAMBRIDGE

The first day of the advanced writing class, the students filed in, one and two at a time, and sat down around the long table in the seminar room. Like the tall, bespectacled professor, each student wore coat and tie and carried a briefcase. After calling the roll, the professor looked up and asked if any of them was seriously interested in writing. They all raised their hands. The professor then said:

> "Well, I suggest that all of you get the hell out of here, get back to your rooms, and start bending over your typewriters and get to work, because the best way, the only way, to learn writing is by writing, and there probably isn't a great deal that I can teach you about it."

The students sat stunned. He went on to add:

> "You need to write what you know about . . . and the next thing you need to understand is that all of you sitting there are somewhere between 19 and 22 years of age, and you really don't know enough about what it is you want to say until you are at least 30."

They should still write, write as much as they could, but they shouldn't expect to write well until they reached thirty.

That was Wallace Stegner's message to his Harvard writing class at the beginning of a new school year, 1940. Not very encouraging. Nor were the conditions of Wallace's own life particularly encouraging. He was at Harvard, true, but elite universities in those days seemed to feel that the honor of teaching there was enough—you shouldn't expect also to get a living wage. Traditionally, professors were expected to have family money to supplement what the university gave them (they were *gentlemen*, after all), and the university seemed pleased that first the Depression and then the war gave it the excuse not to promote its faculty. Stegner had sold some stories and had received a modest fee for going to Bread Loaf during the summer, but this income was more than offset by ongoing doctor bills and the trip west to bury his father and settle his affairs.

The shock of his father's death was still with him, along with guilt in regard to its circumstances. A shabby room, a shabby woman, and a shabby man—paunchy, worn out, and threadbare even in death. Then in October, he was with Robert Frost the day Frost got the news that his son, Carol, had committed suicide. It was the second family death in a row that Frost had suffered and once again he was filled with guilt and remorse. He wrote to Louis Untermeyer: "I took the wrong way with him. I tried many ways and every single one of them was wrong. Something in me is still asking for the chance to try one more. There's where the greatest pain is located." Having just suffered suicide in his own family, Wallace may have been the best possible companion for Frost at that moment. They walked together a long distance that day.

Throwing himself into his work, Wallace found some discouragement there, as well. Harcourt, Brace had turned down the first volume of his trilogy, and during the summer he got word that the company had also turned down *Fire and Ice*. Wallace's unhappiness was not just wounded professional pride; hope had been dashed for an advance that could help to bail them out financially.

But the *Fire and Ice* manuscript Bernice turned back to Duell, Sloan and Pearce, who had made it clear that they had been sorry to lose Stegner with Harcourt's publication of *On a Darkling Plain*. Sam Sloan decided he wanted Wallace back and made a very modest offer for the book, an advance of $250 to be paid when the manuscript had been revised and copyedited. Wallace wrote Bernice to accept the offer. He was, he wrote on December 18, glad to be back with Sam, but there was something he would like Bernice to do for him:

> Take Sam aside and whisper in his ear that the Stegners are stony broke, and that Santa Claus will not come to Trowbridge Street unless something drastic is done. In short, see if you can get that advance now, immediately, pronto, rush, instead of when the manuscript is finally delivered to the printers. I think maybe Sam will trust me to get it in. I never missed a deadline in my life. Failing that, maybe you could fudge on Harcourt's second royalty check. Could you? Some money's got to come from somewhere or my credit rating's ruined.

There was a bit of exaggeration here, but only a bit. Stegner was old-fashioned and pessimistic in his management of finances. He hated to owe money to anyone and was never comfortable without at least a slight cushion against further disaster. He worried about money, and to understand that, one has to remember that he had lost years of savings accumulated slowly and painfully to a bank failure while he was in graduate school and that he had a very tough time making ends meet throughout the Depression. Throughout their relationship, he pushed Bernice on sales and payments, usually jokingly, but sometimes seriously pleading for action. Brandt and Brandt made very little on magazine sales, and they had made very little, so far, on Stegner books, so that Bernice's patience and persistence during these years, in the face of frequent editorial rejections on the one hand and Stegner's requests and suggestions on the other, has to be thought of as a great act of faith by her in her author's promise.

While the summer of 1940 was spent almost routinely in Vermont, at the summer house and then Bread Loaf, the next summer took a new direction—the Stegners went west. Wallace had taken up the suggestion of his publisher Sam Sloan that he write a book for the American Folkways Series, a volume that would deal with the history, geography, and social patterns in an area with which he was quite familiar—the Great Basin, which had its geographic center in Utah and its cultural center in the Mormons. It was a suggestion that hit home. He had need to turn to another project, putting off work on his novel as his agent and his former editor had suggested. And he was getting homesick for the West.

He and Mary enjoyed Boston, took advantage as much as their means would allow of its cultural opportunities—particularly its music—but it had become clear to them that even if he got tenure (which he did) they would never feel entirely at ease in Cambridge. They loved the people, and Wallace took the challenge that Harvard offered, but the couple had a somewhat empty feeling, as if they were in a foreign country and needed eventually to go home.

The West was frequently on Wallace's mind. He had planned to do a biography of John Wesley Powell, but felt he would have to take more time than was available to him—a year or two off from teaching—in order to complete the research. Nevertheless, whenever the absence of student papers and small writing jobs would allow, he read everything he could get hold of about Powell, Powell's colleagues, exploration of the West in the plateau area of southern Utah and northern Arizona, and the history of various government departments, such as the Geological Survey, which Powell had founded. At the same time Wallace's relation-ship to DeVoto became closer and closer; their research projects often touched each other, and now that Wallace set off, in the winter of 1941–42, to write history, there was much discussion between them about how history should be written and who had done it right and why.

Wallace and Bernard DeVoto spent more and more time together, not only at social gatherings and at each other's homes, but they also began about this time to play badminton together regularly (Wallace's tennis partner was Ted Morrison). The two of them constituted an assertive western contingent among a faculty that tended to be very Eastern Establishment in its perspective and very Eurocentric in its values. It was a gesture meant both to hold the fort and tease his friends that Wallace, with DeVoto's boisterous support, would at parties launch into such unsophisticated Western ballads as "The Cowboy's Lament."

A point of disagreement between them, of course, was the Mormons. Wallace had grown up admiring them, feeling that they had welcomed and saved him from loneliness and alienation; DeVoto had grown up scorning their ingrown provinciality, feeling that the Mormons had driven him into isolation and rebellion. Considering DeVoto's reputation for stubbornly held views, it sheds some light on Wallace's character and powers of persuasion that he was largely responsible for gradually modifying the older man's opinion. Much of this change came out of their discussions of Wallace's new project, in which the focus would be on the Mormons, defining the boundaries of his book by culture, rather than by geography. The book would be called *Mormon Country*—probably not a good title, since non-Mormon readers around the country would be all too likely to think of desert, authoritarianism, polygamy, and missionaries. The negative echoes of the title for many are particularly unfortunate since this was by far Stegner's best book up to that time, a delight to read. If it is history, it is very entertaining and engaging history.

Stegner's concept of how history should be written would seem to be almost entirely formed in his discussions with DeVoto. While Stegner was working on *Mormon Country*, DeVoto was working on his landmark history, *The Year of Decision: 1846.* The historian whose method both writers admired the most was Francis Parkman, "who dealt with sweeping events in which a continent was at stake and re-created them as vividly as fiction." DeVoto's aim was readable history, a readability that irritated a few traditional historians, but they could not attack him on the soundness of his material: he was extremely careful of his facts, checking and double-checking. As Stegner himself assessed his friend's achievement and influence:

I admired more than just professionalism in Benny. I guess I admired his honesty. I sometimes shrunk from his pugnacity, but he was an absolutely honest man and he knew a great deal—he was loaded, he was a great mine of information. And he did get his facts straight, though he thumped an awful lot of heads. . . . But he was never content to be dull, and that I think is one of the abiding sins of some academic historians who think that in order to be factual and responsible they have to be dull.

Mormon Country is anything but dull, even if one is not particularly interested in Mormonism. In one of the very few critical assessments of the book, Forrest and Margaret Robinson take Stegner to task for the very qualities that make it exceptional: "What is admissible as point of view in fiction turns up as bias in social history. Strong personal prepossessions are an asset in the novel but a weakness in ostensibly objective non-fiction." But the Robinsons are off the track here in two ways. First, the book does make judgments, but they are carefully balanced, and second, the Robinsons seem to have no idea what the author's goals are, what kind of history he is trying to write. That is best laid out in Stegner's description of DeVoto's goals and methods, which very closely matched his own:

> His kind of history not only permitted the selection and dramatization of striking actions, it also allowed the historian to pass judgment on both events and people, and it permitted the elaboration of large, umbrella theses to contain and explain events, so long as the theses were developed inductively and not imposed from without. Furthermore it permitted symbolic selection—history by synecdoche, the illumination of whole areas and periods through concentration upon one brief time, one single sequence, a few representative characters.

"History by synecdoche" was the essence of the method adopted by both writers, and it could not have been a method so very contrary to the historian's creed—DeVoto won the Pulitzer Prize for *Across the Wide Missouri* and for Stegner's second Mormon history, *The Gathering of Zion*, he received the Award of Merit of the American Association for State and Local History.

Wallace prepared for his stint as historian by a regimen of reading, partly guided by a spreading net of correspondence with those, like Dale Morgan of the Utah writer's project, who he had heard might be able to help him. But he was unwilling to start on the manuscript itself until he had renewed acquaintance in person with the territory. So, that summer of 1941, he and Mary drove to Dubuque, Iowa, where they left Page with Mary's mother and father; across the country to Ellensburg, Washington, where they visited old friends from graduate school; down to Salt Lake City, where they took side trips into the countryside; and over to Boulder, Colorado, where Wallace had arranged to be group leader for the short story at the Writer's Conference in the Rocky Mountains. They still managed almost a month in Greensboro, giving Wallace the opportunity to start his manuscript.

Stegner has said that he wrote *Mormon Country* in Cambridge out of "nostalgia" for the West, passing it off rather lightly. But the book really stands at a crossroads in the author's career. His earlier interest in Clarence Edward Dutton had been one of the first markers in this direction, followed by his work on John Wesley Powell. He also had traveled many times throughout the territory and camped out in so many places and knew them so well that he thought of Mormon country as his own. Several years before this project, he had become interested in the life of Earl Douglass, a remarkable man and pioneer paleontologist in the region, and wrote an account of him for the *Southwest Review* called "A Pioneer Record" (1939), which he included in *Mormon Country*. And finally, there was an urge in him to right a wrong, to bring some justice to the Mormons, who had done so much for him, and who had such a bad reputation among Americans generally.

Out of this book would emerge roads to several other future projects. His continuing interest in religious and ethnic differences and in cultural groupings would provide a foundation for his research and writing about various minority communities in the United States and the prejudice and discrimination that they faced in *One Nation* (1945). The chapter on Powell would lead to his biography-history, *Beyond the Hundredth Meridian: John Wesley Powell and the Second Opening of the West* (1954). The chapter on Douglass would form the basis for his editing *This Is Dinosaur* (1955), a collection of essays that was put together in order to help prevent the construction of dams at Echo Park. His research on the history of the Mormon Church and the migration westward would form the basis of his more detailed telling of the Mormon pioneer story in *The Gathering of Zion: The Story of the Mormon Trail* (1964). And his general knowledge of the exploration, exploitation, and topography of our land, the Great Basin and beyond, gave him the basis for those chapters he contributed to one of the finest books on our complex and generally destructive relationship to our continent, *American Places* (written with his son Page and published in 1983).

Mormon Country is by no means your usual, chronologically told history, but instead is organized as a series of vignettes, a few taking a large view (as in the brief history of the Mormon migration west), but most acting as synecdoche, a small scene representing the whole. Just as large is mixed with small, so also are the odd mixed with the typical, and ordinary people considered alongside the famous. Narratives in *Mormon Country* are intertwined with biographical sketches, nonfiction stories with descriptive sketches, myth and legend with factual surveys. Social history is the main strand in the book, but there is considerable attention paid to geography, topography, and geology. Overall, what might at first appear to be an impromptu patchwork, on second glance turns out to be a cleverly designed tapestry in which many small figures and bits of color come together in a total effect of breadth and depth.

The book is divided into two parts: Part I, the larger part deals with the Mormons, their country and history; Part II, with the gentiles in the same country. Stegner begins with what he remembered best and loved best about his years living among the Mormons: the weekly recreational and faith-promoting meeting at the Ward House, the "Mutual." As a teenager, he took advantage of the recreation—the Boy Scout groups, the basketball leagues, and the dances—although here, in a narrative that follows the activities of a young woman going to Mutual in a country Ward House, he focuses more on the community meeting and its religious overtones.

Stegner tries very hard to find a balance between the positive and the negative aspects of Mormon life and history, but in their critique of the book, the Robinsons see no balance: "In general, he expands upon what is attractive in Mormons, but he ignores or makes light of what is less agreeable." They seem particularly incensed about what today might be called Stegner's lack of political correctness:

There is some discussion of polygamy, but Stegner's tendency is to dismiss it as a calculated response to the population shortage. . . . We hear nothing of the Saint's racism, and too little of the luster less drudgery that was the portion of most Mormon women. It may be that Stegner's version of Mormon despotism is a trifle on the benevolent side.

This commentary would seem to be more than a little unfair as a description of what Stegner says and what is implied about his motives:

he deals with polygamy in several places in his text and devotes a chapter to a community of adherents to the practice—nowhere does he "dismiss it as a calculated response to the population shortage." He deals briefly with its history, the conflict with U. S. law, and describes a band of polygamous holdouts, disapproved of by the church. What he doesn't do is express outrage. Nor is Stegner's "version of Mormon despotism" in any sense benevolent. The book is filled with condemnations of it, such as this: "Within the United States, almost a hundred years ago, existed a dictatorship as complete in its power as any in contemporary Europe." And this was written in 1941.

Perhaps the best summary of Stegner's attitude toward the church and its culture, its treatment of women and its authoritarianism, comes in his introduction to a chapter in which he presents biographical sketches of two Mormon leaders, J. Golden Kimball and Jesse Knight, whom he admires:

> It would be fatal to generalize. Mormonism has created its share of bigots, parochial intolerants, and authoritarians; the very patriarchal structure of the Mormon family and the Mormon church assures that. The Church has fostered rigidity of belief, even a branch of theocratic state-ism, has consistently kept women in their place as cooks, housekeepers, and breeding machines, and has subjugated the individual small-fry Mormon to the authority of the priesthood. . . . It is just as true to say that among garden-variety Saints one finds rather more human kindness, more neighborliness, more willingness to devote time and trouble to the assistance of their fellows, than one will find in most sections of the United States.

While he praises both Kimball and Knight for their humanity and generosity, he cannot express much admiration for either Joseph Smith or Brigham Young. Although he tries to be fair to them, to their leadership and courage, he has a systemic dislike for fanaticism of any stripe. One of the reviewers of the book, George R. Stewart, takes him to task for not recognizing that Young "seems to loom taller with the years, among the really great Americans"—a sentiment that very few non-Mormons would agree with then or now. Nevertheless, the review was favorable, and it was the first of his books to be reviewed in *The New York Times Book Review*.

But despite the Robinsons' assertion that "he expands upon what is attractive in Mormons . . . [and] just the opposite is the case in his treatment of the Gentiles," Stegner's greatest admiration is reserved for several of the Gentiles of Mormon country: Jedediah Smith, John Wesley Powell, and Earl Douglass. Smith, a mountain man, trapper, and explorer, was unusual in his religiosity, education, and his great intellectual curiosity. Though suffering incredible hardship and facing nearly constant danger, he brought the first Anglo-American tracks to a large part of the Mormon country. Stegner notes that he "could endure hunger and thirst and fatigue better than most of his wild companions" and "he could be painfully kicked by a mule and still go on the next day without even a complaint to his journal."

And then there was Powell, who would become the greatest hero in Stegner's pantheon. He had been a soldier who had lost an arm in the Civil War, a loss that did not for a moment slow him down, even when climbing the sheer cliffs of the Grand Canyon to survey them or taking his wooden boats down the fiercest river in America. To him belongs the credit for the first exploration of Colorado:

He was one of the big men of the West, one of its foremost explorers, and in addition the father of half the scientific government bureaus. . . . Three [of these] government departments have had an incalculable influence in shaping the intermountain West, and through his sponsorship of them, Powell affected more people's lives than all but our greatest presidents have. . . . He was a bright and polished intelligence, a hotbed of ideas, an organizer, a martinet, a man of cool courage and the ability to plan.

Another of Wallace's heroes was Earl Douglass, field geologist, paleontologist, and fossil hunter. Like Smith and Powell, Douglass had an enormous appetite for knowledge and a huge, driving curiosity about his physical surroundings which led him, at his camp on the Green River, to learn everything he could about the birds, animals, plants, and geology of the region, collecting and classifying them. He became one of the most prominent experts on dinosaur bones of his time, and spent years unearthing magnificent specimens in the most difficult and primitive of circumstances and then shipping them to museums in the East. When it came time for him to withdraw a bit from the harshness of living entirely in the field, he hoped, on the basis of an international reputation, to gain a responsible position at the University of Utah. But in this hope

> he had been betrayed for a reason that probably never entered his head. The professorship of geology at Utah is a chair, its incumbent subject to Church approval. That system kept certain sciences dangerous to fundamentalist belief under the thumb of the priesthood. . . . Still, Douglass did not himself feel the failure of his life. He did not waste time thinking how abused he was, did not complain any more than Mormon settlers in an unfriendly location complained.

Just as Stegner had striven in his own life to become resilient and steadfast, he admired toughness in others, but of a particular kind—people with moral backbone, people who were tough in pursuit of constructive ends, people who took what fate had dealt them and made the best of it. He had been taught as a child not to complain, and he grew up hating complainers and people who felt sorry for themselves. The difference between these three Westerners and so many others was that they had no lust for easy riches, no obsession with the Big Rock Candy Mountain, but instead they had a greed for knowledge.

Mormon Country sold better than anything of Stegner's since *Remembering Laughter* and has remained in print over the years. It was reviewed more widely than anything else Wallace had written up to this time, getting good notices, even raves, in *The New York Times Book Review*, the *New York Herald Tribune Books*, the *Boston Herald Annual Book Fair Section*, the *Chicago Sun Book Week*, *The Boston Globe*, and *The Salt Lake Tribune*. This last one was a triumph, a rave notice ("Onetime Utah Educator Writes Superb 'Biography' of Region and People of 'Mormon Country' ") in the leading paper of the region he had written about and the paper to which he had sold his first story. Two church papers, as one might expect, did not care for the book, but *The Educational Forum* concluded, "Sympathetic yet at times critical in its treatment, the book affords an understanding of this virile people who are the dominating factor in the Great Basin." Not a bad assessment from a church organ, and it was an opinion that would be carried on over the years: most Mormons who have read the book would seem to look upon Wallace Stegner, despite his criticism—certainly very severe at times— as a friend who tried to be fair.

It took him only a few months to write the actual manuscript, and the book came out in September 1942. In the meantime he continued to write and regularly publish articles and short stories, and he was becoming known as an important short story writer. One of his stories appeared in each of the successive years 1941, 1942, and 1943, in the annual *The Best American Short Stories*, and "Two Rivers" won second prize in the 1942 O. Henry competition. Over the next three decades one of his stories would be included in the *Best* series on four more occasions, and he would make three more appearances in the *O. Henry Memorial Award Prize Stories*, including another second prize, for "Beyond the Glass Mountain" (1948), and a first prize, for "The Blue-Winged Teal" (1954).

In May 1942 the Stegners went to the little farmhouse in Vermont, where Wallace once again took up the task of finishing *The Big Rock Candy Mountain*. He had received a small grant from Harvard so that he could take a year off, and the summer was only broken by his return to Bread Loaf. Frost was there, along with Untermeyer, Edith Mirrielees, and John Marquand (who had won the Pulitzer Prize for *The Late George Apley* in 1937). Page started school in Greensboro in the fall, and the Stegners moved out of their house into the Grays' "Children's House"—it was on the lake, closer to town, and was "winterized." How winterized it was, however, might have been a matter of debate. That winter the temperature dropped as low as 40 degrees below zero. The Stegners had purchased two sides of beef that they hung in one of the bedrooms where the meat froze and did not thaw out during the entire winter. In an effort to stay warm, they hung blankets over doorways and on the ceiling to block the flow of heat up the stairs.

Wallace had planned to supply his own wood, and that fall had joined one of the local farmers, George Hill, in a wood-sawing project. On a number of occasions in previous years, Wallace had helped out with house repairs, barn-raisings, and hay mowing when asked by neighbors, including Hill. Every day for several weeks in the early fall, Wallace went up into the woods on the Hill farm and manned one end of a cross-cut saw or swung a double-edged ax from noon until dark. It was tough work for a man who sat at a desk most of the time, but it was also satis-fying to keep up with Hill and show him that he had as much country in him as Hill had. It was a good fall. He wrote the Grays:

For two months I've been thinking of nothing but wood, cabbages, carrots, potatoes, apples, and home-canned vegetables. I write my three hours in a dream, eat lunch in a fog, saw wood all afternoon in a sun that's like May, in weather so perfect the air is like wine, it really is, and now I believe the novels. Then I read a book for a couple hours while Mary darns socks, and we fall into bed exhausted at nine-thirty. It's a marvelous life, only it's like living in a badger hole. I guess I'm Frost's "Drumlin Woodchuck." (10/14/42)

That feeling of satisfaction of hard work well done, is at the center of a story that he wrote based on the experience, "Saw Gang" (1945). The story is concerned with the happiness that can come out of simple things, the courage to keep going when the situation gets hard, and the ethic of not complaining. The story has virtually no plot, but it does have "wholeness, harmony and radiance," in the words of Stephen Dedalus, quoting Aquinas in *A Portrait of the Artist as a Young Man*, a radiance that convinces us, as in many Stegner stories, that although not much seems to have happened, a whole lot has.

The Stegners stayed in Greensboro from May 1942 to early 1943, while Wallace worked on the final version of *The Big Rock Candy Mountain*. It was not the best of conditions for writing: typing while sit-ting at a table in the living room, wearing a wool shirt and two sweaters, sitting surrounded by a kerosene lamp and enough candles to read by, and having to get up every few minutes to stir or stoke the fire. Much of the time in midwinter the road into town was unplowed, and Mary and Wallace would have to ski into the village to get supplies. In the evening they entertained themselves by taking turns reading aloud from Joseph Conrad's *Lord Jim* by candlelight. The primitive conditions were just the thing to bring back the memories and emotions of living on a homestead farm in the turn-of-the-century West.

Many of Stegner's readers still consider *The Big Rock Candy Mountain* his best book. It does have a vitality, a sense of authenticity that he would never surpass in his later work, and he deals with certain aspects of the Western experience—its mobility, its gambling spirit of optimism, its boom-and-bust mentality, its rugged individualism as opposed to family obligations—that no one has treated with more power and conviction. Over the years it has found its place alongside such other works as *The Big Sky*, *The Ox-Bow Incident*, *My Ántonia*, and *Giants in the Earth* as a classic novel of Western experience, particularly as it describes and follows a mind-set—the "boomer," as Stegner has called it—so common to the West.

It is a book that takes the pioneering West into the twentieth century and the 1930s. The semiautobiographical character in the novel, Bruce Mason, realizes that as dysfunctional and peculiar as his family may be, it is also in some ways typical. As one critic has commented:

> Contemplating the influence of the growing Great Depression upon his family, Bruce admits that they are insignificant in the pattern of the nation's historic events. But he also realizes that his family's identity is molded by American history—that, although isolated, the family and each of its members are expressions of forces which have resulted in making the modern West.... He understood that his family was not unique in its rootlessness. "The whole nation had been footloose too long. Heaven had been just over the next range for too many generations."

In contrast to Stegner's previous books, which were either novelettes or short novels, this is a big book of epic scope, full of characters and incidents. Howard Mumford Jones in *Saturday Review* called it a "vast, living, untidy book." The problems that had plagued the composition of the book in its earlier stages, such as narrative voice and overly personal involvement in the characterizations, have not been overcome entirely, but they are so overshadowed by the power of the narrative, they hardly seemed to matter. Unlike Stegner's previous works, which by and large are almost classical in their unity and proportions—and perhaps a bit tame by comparison—this novel has, to cite the same reviewer, a "quality of vitality, of generous strength, of something pressed down and running over." That last phrase seems perfect in describing the novel's effect.

However, on successive readings the novel may strike the reader quite differently. At first one is carried away by the strong personalities of the characters and their emotional interactions as a family (and the family, like Steinbeck's Joads, is all they have), while at the same time one is carried along by what seems like the constant change of scene as the family moves from one place to another. It is from this point of view an exciting, involving book even though there is not much of a conventional plot line, a book that does seem to overflow. But on further readings, it may strike us just how sad this novel is. On reflection it would seem to have been written through a veil of pain and loss, by someone lost—an author-narrator who has experienced the deaths of all his immediate family and who is trying to sort out his feelings and at the same time discover who he is and where he belongs. Bereavement, sadness, guilt, love, and anger—all make themselves felt here, but there is also a sense of bewilderment, as if there are too many questions to ask and not enough answers to be found. The book is certainly a journey forward, but it is also a search backward for answers, answers that come only reluctantly and incompletely.

Like Stegner's first book, this is a book about remembering, and it is his most autobiographical work of long fiction. On those bases, it has several times been compared to Thomas Wolfe's *Look Homeward, Angel*, but it is superior to that work in at least two ways: Stegner can be poetic without being self-consciously poetic, and he can remember without becoming sentimental. The work is so closely based on Stegner's own life that it is difficult even for the biographer to find those few differences that mark the book as fiction, and it is difficult not to talk about the events in the book as if they happened to the author, since almost all of them did. Most fictitious, of course, are those early episodes that describe Elsa and Bo's (the fictional counterparts of Hilda and George Stegner) meeting and courtship, which are outside the author's direct knowledge, as are the reports of Bo's bootlegging adventures. But even here the facts of place, time, and event, as much as they might be known to the author, match life very closely.

Least fictitious are those experiences reported through the eyes of Bruce, the author's self-character, which are usually exact down to the precise speech of the characters on a particular occasion. When Bo Mason tells his son he doesn't want to see him again, those were the words used by George Stegner; when Elsa Mason tells Bruce as she dies, "You're a good boy, Bruce," and later, "Which . . . way?" those were the words of Hilda Stegner, words that broke her son's heart, a breaking that he never fully recovered from. "Which way?" burned in his mind, was a phrase that led him to find special meaning in Robert Frost's poem "I Could Give All to Time":

> I could give all to Time except—except
> What I myself have held. But why declare
> The things forbidden that while the Customs slept
> I have crossed to Safety with? For I am There
> And what I would not part with I have kept.

The metaphor of crossing a border, escaping customs with forbidden things, was a telling one for Stegner, considering his father's occupation for so many years. The connection between his mother's words and death and the poem prefigures his last novel, *Crossing to Safety*, wherein the central character, Charity, also dies of cancer.

8

FROM THE FIGHT AGAINST RUGGED INDIVIDUALISM TO THE FIGHT AGAINST PREJUDICE AND RACISM

Such an expansive novel as *The Big Rock Candy Mountain* is difficult to summarize, but in brief it can be said to deal with Bruce Mason's family history, from the courtship of his parents, through his childhood and high school years, to the deaths of his parents while he is going to law school. But since most readers have seen the father, Bo Mason, as the central character, one could say that the book deals with Bo's background, his courtship of Elsa, the early years of their marriage as he tries to get to Alaska but ends up in Washington state, his failure to make a fortune with wheat on the Saskatchewan homestead, his years as a bootlegger in Salt Lake, his attempt to strike it rich with a Reno gambling house, his decline as an investor in dubious mining prospects in Nevada, and his death in Salt Lake.

The main alteration from the actual Stegner chronology is that the father, as we have seen, did not commit suicide until almost a decade after his wife's death (instead of two years after), and as an alteration of circumstances, Wallace did not go to law school at the University of Minnesota, but to graduate school in literature at the University of Iowa. Bruce's college years at the University of Utah and Bo's bootlegging enterprises in Salt Lake are not dealt with in any detail in the book, a gap in the autobiographical chronology that Stegner filled in later with his novel *Recapitulation.*

The Big Rock Candy Mountain has ten chapters, each composed of several subchapters. On an informal basis, one can divide the book into four parts, each part distinguished by its settings and its dominant point of view (technically, the center of consciousness, since the book is told by the same voice in the third person). The first part (chapters one, two, and three), the longest, takes place in Minnesota, North Dakota, and Washington state, and Elsa Mason is the primary focus. Part two (chapters four and five) takes place in Saskatchewan and takes Bruce's point of view. It is this section that contains all of the short stories about Bruce in childhood ("Buglesong," "Goin' to Town," "Butcher Bird," and so on) plus that story that features Chet (Bruce's older brother), "Chip Off the Old Block." Part three (chapters six and seven) takes place in Great Falls, Montana, and Salt Lake City and is almost evenly divided between Bo's point of view and Chet's. The final section (chapters eight, nine, and ten) is set in Minneapolis, Salt Lake, and Lake Tahoe and returns to Bruce as the center of consciousness. In each part, a chapter or segment of a chapter may move temporarily to focus on one of the other four major characters, and the chronology is occasionally broken by flashback or flashforward.

So many perspectives in the telling can lead us to view the novel in several different ways: as a novel about a family, a novel about the life and death of Bo Mason, or a novel about son Bruce, whose sensibility dominates the latter part of the novel. Perhaps a compromise is most accurate—to see it as a book about parents and how they influence the lives of their children. To focus on Bo alone tends to ignore his wife, who has an important, although passive role, and to downplay the *effects* of Bo's values and behavior which would seem to be the concern uppermost in the author's mind, according to his own statements about the novel.

No writer has been more preoccupied by the memory of his parents than Stegner—their roles, their relationship to each other and to him, and their archetypal qualities and experiences as Westerners. He has written about them not only in many short stories and in *The Big Rock Candy Mountain* but in *Recapitulation* and in his memoir, *Wolf Willow.* He has also talked about them extensively in several published interviews and dealt with them, in greater or lesser detail, in several essays. One essay, "Letter, Much Too Late" (1989), is a letter to his mother long after her death, remembering her loving, giving character and expressing regret that he had not expressed his appreciation for her at the time. He also expresses regret that he has not represented her virtues fully in his fiction:

> In the more than fifty years that I have been writing books and stories, I have tried several times to do you justice, and have never been satisfied with what I did. The character who represents you in *The Big Rock Candy Mountain* ... is a sort of passive victim. I am afraid I let your selfish and violent husband, my father, steal the scene from you and push you into the background in the novels as he did in life. Somehow I should have been able to say how strong and resilient you were, what a patient and abiding and bonding force, the softness that proved in the long run stronger than what it seemed to yield to.

But, he adds, her character is the hardest sort to make credible on paper, since we tend to be skeptical of such unfailing kindness. Furthermore, "saintly and long-suffering women tend to infuriate" feminists who look upon them as masculine inventions.

It is true that Bo Mason tends to take over the novel, especially if one reads it as commercial fiction, an adventure story. He, as the patriarch, tends to set the emotional agenda and lead the action. With this character Stegner has not only created a metaphor for the West—specifically, a West that continued to believe in the frontier and tried to live by frontier values as the frontier was disappearing and then long after it was gone—but more specifically he has created a metaphor for the rugged individualism we still believe in. Bo Mason is a frontiersman trying to succeed in a settled society with pioneering skills:

> He was not a lazy man; his activities had been various and strenuous since he was fourteen.... Obstacles raised by nature—cold, heat, drouth, the solid resistance of great trees, he could clog through with almost fierce joy, but obstacles raised by institu-

tions and the habits of a civilized community left him prowling and baffled.

But Bo Mason taps into a deeper vein than this. He is not just a Westerner—he is an American, with an American faith in the New World and the possibility of making it. He was Gatsby before Gatsby was born. He, too, invented himself; he, too, turned to Gatsby's means to wealth—rum running—and we can just as well ask about Bo what Nick Carraway asks about Gatsby: What foul dust did he leave in his wake? Or we might note how very much Bo Mason is like another seeker of the American dream, Arthur Miller's Willie Loman, in a play set far from the West, in New York City, *Death of a Salesman* (1949).

Willie is also cut off from his own family at a young age; he, like Bo, dominates a wife who nevertheless defends him to his children; and both men show that they belong to an earlier time by being most content when they are building something with their hands—Willie is a happy man with a bag of cement and Bo sings and jokes while building the homestead shack. Both men have the wrong dreams; both have sons that cannot communicate with them; both have older sons who blame them for the wrecks of their lives. Both scorn schooling in favor of athletic achievement for their sons, both commit suicide in despair over the failure of their dreams, but neither understands what it is that went wrong.

Easy Street is just around the corner, but they can't find it. In a recurrent hallucination in the play, Willie asks the vision of his Uncle Ben, whom he believes struck it rich somewhere, in Alaska or the African jungle (he is vague about the details): How did you do it? What's the secret? As for Bo, he is certain that he will hit the Big Rock Candy Mountain just over the next horizon. When Bo hears about the gold rush in Alaska from a drifter in his bar, his wife realizes that

he was born with the itch in his bones. . . . He was always telling stories of men who had gone over the hills to some new place and found a land of Canaan, made their pile, got to be big men in the communities they fathered. But the Canaans toward which Bo's feet had turned had not lived up to their promise. People had been before him. The cream, he said, was gone. He should have lived a hundred years earlier.

With all his faults he nevertheless comes off larger than life, a suitable protagonist for a Western novel, big, strong, dynamic, and emotional, and his wife and children are left to react to him, rather than acting on their own. With his violence and his stubborn insistence on wrong-headed goals and ideas, he destroys his family as he is destroying himself—his older son and his wife suffer at his hands and perish, and his younger son, while surviving physically, is marked forever, just as the author is marked and must go over the same emotional territory again and again. Regardless of what feminists might think of Elsa, the nester who only wants a home where she can be a real wife and mother, it would be impossible to say that this is a book that endorses the ruggedly masculine elements in Western experience. At the end of the novel, in trying to reach some synthesis of the best in both his parents, Stegner writes:

There were things he had learned that could not be taken away from him. Perhaps it took several generations to make a man, perhaps it took several combinations and re-creations of his mother's gentleness and resilience, his father's enormous energy and appetite for the new, a subtle blending of masculine and feminine, selfish and selfless, stubborn and yielding, before a proper man could be fashioned.

He was the only one left to fulfill that contract and try to justify the labor and the harshness and the mistakes of his parents' lives.

As a novel about Bruce, *The Big Rock Candy Mountain* has many of the typical elements of the "growing up" or initiation story. Bruce is sensitive, misunderstood by his father and nearly everyone else but his mother, and tries desperately to "belong." The gender conflict between his parents, the rootlessness of the life chosen by his father, and his own physical weakness lead him to low self-esteem and a constant questioning of his own identity. He comes to think of his family as an outlaw family, always secretive, always on the run, and never in tune with neighbors or community, except for a time in Saskatchewan.

Like his creator, Bruce becomes a super-achiever in an effort to over-come his shame and enforced separation from ordinary society. He is an A student, and he works his way through college and graduate school, even though neither of his parents went beyond the eighth grade. He is given many of the drives and yearnings of his creator: he wants to belong to a place; he yearns to be a part of some kind of community, particularly for his mother's sake; and he is driven to hate his father and to try to pro-tect his mother. But unlike the author's choice of becoming a professor, Bruce chooses the "cosmically ironic" profession of the law. It is his answer to the outlaw status that he was forced to assume for so many years.

Bruce's musing at the end of the novel about the meaning of his expe-riences suggest that the author, in writing the novel, is involved in the same process. Two questions seem to guide his search: Who am I? Where do I belong? As banal as they may sound, these have been the key ques-tions for Americans, who are not assigned roles as they may be in other, more settled societies, but must find them for themselves. These ques-tions are even more relevant to the Westerner, who typically, like Natty Bumppo, Huck Finn, Boone Caudill, or Tom Joad, is orphaned or cut off from family roots, from ordinary society, and constantly on the move. At one point, driving day and night back to Salt Lake City for his father's funeral, Bruce is viewed thinking:

It was all familiar. It seemed to him, yawning, scratchy-eyed, that there was the whole rhythm of his life in it, that all through his remembered life the days had gone under him like miles, that he and his whole family had always been moving on toward some-thing that was hidden beyond where the road bent between the hills.

The vast spaces of the West seem to lie as an underlayment for the entire novel, from the endless prairie of the homestead in Saskatchewan to the endless highway that Bruce must travel three times from Min-nesota to Utah and Nevada, once to go "home" to Reno (he has never spent more than six hours at a time in Reno) during a summer vacation and then after the deaths of each of his parents. Constantly on the move; never to "love and know a single place." As the Masons arrive in Salt

Lake City (from Great Falls, from Whitemud, from Richmond, from Hardanger), the narrator focuses on Bruce:

> Long afterward, Bruce looked back on the life of his family with half-amused wonder at its rootlessness. . . . Twelve houses in four years, in every part of the city. They moved in, circled around like a dog preparing to drop its haunches, and moved out again, without any chance of every infusing any house with the quality of their own lives.

Thinking this over, he decides that "it was not permanence alone that made what the Anglo-Saxons called home ... it was continuity"— change, but change over time "always within the framework of the established and recognizable outline." What makes Bruce's search the more poignant is not only that there is no continuity to his life, but that he has to live it nearly alone and nearly invisibly, to never even admit to a father, an occupation for his father, or a location.

A little beyond halfway through the novel, it becomes clear that while there may be a technical distinction between character and narrator, this is a story told in retrospect by Bruce in an effort to make some sense of his experience. It is told, although the narrative is not overtly structured that way, as a review of experiences and realizations that have formed and changed a life, much as Frederic Henry, in *A Farewell to Arms*, tells of the war and his love and loss of Catherine after the events—he is now the distillation of what has happened to him. As Bruce goes back to his early life, shuffling through his memories, he realizes that he is

> a childhood hunter, a searcher for old forgotten far-off things and battles long ago, a maunderer. He knew it. Yet the words of life were in those songs and those smells and the green dreams of childhood; in his life there had been the death of too many things.

In this statement of the search for life in the midst of death, Stegner seems to state the overriding theme of the novel and its purpose—to sift out from the pain those memories that will help him live, that tell him at the end, "It was good to have been along and to have shared it."

*　　*　　*

The Big Rock Candy Mountain was published in September the same
year that the manuscript was finished—1943. From the end of January
when he sent in the manuscript and through the following spring, both
Bernice and Sam Sloan tried to get him to make changes. They felt the
eight-hundred-page manuscript was too long and needed cutting. They
suggested cutting the last part, which deals largely with Bruce's reactions, keeping the focus on Bo. Bernice also suggested that the end
should come after one of Bo's escapades and as he looks forward to
another, so that the ending should be more "up." But although he usually followed Bernice's advice on his short stories, in this case Wallace
resisted. On March 1 he wrote to Bernice, "I can't see how to avoid going
to the bitter end. Bo's running from wife's death seems the single most
important detail about his character." And then again in the middle of
the month he wrote:

> Not convinced cutting is necessarily good. Will consider. Main
> objection to suggestion to end earlier: leaving Bo at high spot
> weakens the inevitability of his slide down—also, I'm interested in
> how he goes down. Not writing book about pioneer fulfillment but
> about pioneer in post-pioneer world, about the homelessness of
> much of America—about talents and energies going in wrong/lost
> causes—about the millennial dream that no longer pays off.
> Ending early might make Bo a hero rather than a victim-villain.
> (3/16/43)

He decided to remain firm about no cuts and just as firmly insisted on "a
fat advance and guarantee of publicity and advertising."

The book came out in the middle of the war, and because of paper
shortages, publication was difficult. But the first printing, according to
Stegner's bibliographer, was at least fifteen thousand. Duell, Sloan and
Pearce obviously knew they had a big book on their hands. According to
the author, initial sales through the early printings were from twenty-six
thousand to twenty-eight thousand, and succeeding editions, reprint and
paperback, have boosted the total sales to several hundred thousand
copies.

The reception was generally warm and the reviews numerous. One gets a sense that many reviewers, having followed Stegner's career from its beginnings with *Remembering Laughter*, had been waiting for such a substantial novel in order to justify their good opinions of him. The book was featured on the front cover of the August 23 *Publishers Weekly*. Orville Prescott reviewed the book for the daily *New York Times* and found it to be "a novel that commands respect.... One of the most impressive novels of the year." He particularly was impressed by the author's ability to make Bo Mason a little more than life size, "always vibrantly dynamic and always thoroughly reprehensible and without inner integrity, and yet to keep him human and even sympathetic." In reacting to the critics of his manuscript, this was perhaps the main change that Stegner had made, creating with Bo Mason a believable, several-sided fictional character, one that the reader can identify with and sympathize with at times, rather than simply reproducing George Stegner and transferring his own dislike to the fictional Bruce.

The other problem, encompassing point of view, voice, and tone, he was less successful in handling. As Prescott, among other reviewers, pointed out, the book "is written in a jog-trot, homespun prose that is pedestrian and monotonous without grace or bite or evidence of a particular personality." Joseph Warren Beach in *The New York Times Book Review* noted that in the book

> the patient, realistic method is adequate to the plain truth of the situation, but the point of view is indeterminate. It is not sharply objective, as in pure naturalism; and at the same time the impressions of the several characters, through which the action is interpreted, are not nicely individualized in tone. They are all presented in a uniform soft middle style, a trifle hesitant and apologetic, and not remarkable for either beauty or precision.

This is a bit harsh, since Stegner proves in this novel, more convincingly than ever before, that he is a master of description. There are many beautiful passages throughout the book, such as the opening sentence of the section that was also the story "Buglesong": "There had been a wind during the night, and all the loneliness of the world had swept up out of the southwest. The boy had heard it wailing through the screens of the sleeping porch where he lay." But to give his prose an individualized voice, to give it "bite" and strong "evidence of a particular personality" would be a problem that would haunt the author until later in his career. Solving it would bring a good writer into greatness.

It would be a long, long process, however, and one with ironic overtones, since Wallace all through these years was a teacher of writing. Among the several stories and articles he was writing or revising during the months just after finishing the novel was an essay that he would publish in *The Writer* called "Get Out of That Story!" dealing with the problems of point of view in fiction. It shows his thinking at this stage of his career about his own most pressing writing problem. He warns about mixing the external and internal points of view in the same story or in the same scene in a novel—"they are oil and water; they will not mix." If the writer conceives a story omnisciently in his own person, apart from the action, he is liable to slip back and forth in his point of view, from outside to inside, and he is liable to assume that remote relationship to his work best left to the essayist. But if

he approaches the material as if he were one of the characters, if he lives the story before he writes, and lived it as he would have had to live it if these things had happened to him in life, he has imposed upon himself a limitation which is likely to pay dividends in credibility.

This certainly underlines the basis on which *Big Rock* succeeds, that is, in its emotional truth as a result of the author's participation, but it doesn't deal with the stylistic aspects of point of view that were targeted by the reviewers: establishing a distinctive tone and voice.

Other articles he wrote during this period had to do with another interest, one that he and Mary shared—cooperatives. For Wallace, this would seem, considering his background among the Mormons and antipathy to rugged individualism, a natural idea, and for Mary, who was a socialist, working with cooperatives had been an important part of her life for several years. They both strongly believed that cooperatives were the solution to a more equitable distribution of goods in our society, a form of economic democracy to match our political democracy. Both were alarmed that America was "growing increasingly individualist and predatory." In a series of four articles, published from summer 1942 to spring 1943 in the *Delphian Quarterly*, Wallace traced the history of the cooperative, starting in England, spreading to northern Europe, and then finding its way to this country. It was a movement that seemed to flourish in hard times and had grown to become an important factor in our economy during the decade of the depression.

In an early example of a career-long opposition to censorship by the government or self-imposed by the media, one of his articles takes to task the NBC and CBS radio networks for refusing to broadcast a series of programs to be paid for by the Cooperative League of the United States. The programs, called by the networks too "controversial," were to be informational, explaining what cooperatives were to an audience largely ignorant of them except for the vague perception, sown by the mass media with the backing of corporate advertisers, that there was something foreign and subversive about them. The network ban was praised by *Variety*, which stated that "this is a nation of shopkeepers and traders, not of Communists and theorists." Stegner replied in his article that this was an unfortunate remark since "one half of Britain's population, shopkeepers or traders or whatever, are members of cooperatives."

Co-ops for him were the wave of the future. They operated on the principle that "the *consumer* is the person most intimately concerned with the production of distribution of goods, that it is his needs and not the profits of the manufacturer which should control production." This doctrine, of course, did not sit well with such organizations as the National Association of Manufacturers and the U.S. Chamber of Commerce, which encouraged those who would label the co-op movement "communistic," an opposition that would lead in the early 1950s to the placing of such organizations as Consumers Union on the attorney general's list of subversive organizations.

In his final article, "The Cooperatives and the Peace," Stegner advocates a plan for the postwar world that is not just political, but economic: "If we don't produce such a new order on democratic terms, open to every people of whatever color and creed, this war may well, as somebody said, last longer than the duration." Many of the postwar blueprints that were already in 1943 being circulated seemed to him "unim-pressive" because either they "approach world problems as purely polit-ical problems, or they assume that world economic problems can be cured from the top down instead of from the bottom up." When one thinks in the 1990s of the situation in Russia or, closer to home, in West Los Angeles after the riots, one can appreciate the profundity of this simple statement born of a firm faith in democracy and the power of the people.

Out of these articles one gets a sense of how idealistic, how committed to social justice, and how thoughtful the Stegners were in response to ongoing events. It may be that Mary was somewhat more aware and committed than her husband and was the engine that drove him further, in directions he was already inclined. In a letter to the Grays in 1942, just before Wallace's first article on the co-ops would appear, Mary wrote:

> We are much interested in the work the coops are doing in the Japanese concentration camps. In fact I would like Wally to give up teaching at least for the duration and go into that work. We could both work together then. However, that is not my decision to make and all I can do is influence him a little. He really doesn't have much of a social conscience I am afraid. Maybe it is a good thing for his writing that he doesn't. At least if he did he probably wouldn't have any time to write. (5/12/42)

This says much about their relationship and mutual concerns at the time, although the casual comment about her husband's lack of social conscience is one that Mary in later years would probably withdraw. It was this thinking, however, that they shared about the importance of cooperatives, about the injustice to the Japanese Americans, and about the crucial need to do something about race relations in the postwar period in America that would lead to Wallace's taking on the job of researching for and writing *One Nation*, his next big project. In tackling the problems of working on the book, he could embrace the values he and Mary both shared and do some public good, while remaining with his profession.

The Stegners had planned on staying in Greensboro for the year, until September, but not long after Wallace sent off his novel manuscript, Mary became ill and had to be rushed to the hospital. The bills for the operation that followed were too much for them to handle, and so they decided to return to Cambridge. Harvard had largely been taken over by the Army by this time, and Wallace went to work teaching writing in the Army Specialized Training Program. Then in a desperate bid to make some money between royalty checks, he spent the summer of 1943 with George Stewart preparing indexes for books in page proof. He returned to Harvard for the next school year and found the teaching in the ASTP depressing:

> It was a melancholy job to see these eager guys from Philadelphia ghettos and so on, who had been drafted into the army. They found themselves in Harvard, wide-eyed and lapping it up and loving it, but it would only last a quarter, a semester, and they would be gone to lose the top of their heads.

Aside from his personal feelings, he was worried, on a broader front, about the role that colleges were taking in wartime. Such functions as training servicemen were not only legitimate but very necessary, but the use of the colleges and universities in this country as vehicles of propaganda worried him. It was a role, as he wrote in "The Colleges in Wartime," that was "most likely to obstruct the traditional circulation of open inquiry and opinion," and one need only look at what happened in Germany when the universities were perfectly willing to let the government tell them what to do, how to think, and what to teach.

In the fall of 1943 Bernice wrote from the agency that a number of magazine editors were clamoring for stories, but Wallace wrote back that he didn't have anything in his file that had not already been rejected many times. Furthermore, his duties teaching for the Army didn't give him any time to write new ones. The normal load of writing classes at Harvard had been three, but now that the Army had taken over it had extended it to four. At the February break, Paul Buck, who was the acting provost of the university, told the faculty that it had done its work for the year and let it go early for the summer. The Stegners went to Mexico for a two-week vacation at the beginning of March 1944, and when they came back, Wallace went to work on a new writing assignment.

He had been offered a job with *Look* magazine to write a series of articles on prejudice in America, primarily as resulting from racial differences, but also religious. Despite the war, which had not yet turned the corner in favor of the Allies, there was a sense of optimism about the possibilities of building a better nation and a better world when peace came. It was a time of enormous patriotism and cooperation, and within this spirit Harlan Logan and the other editors of *Look* thought it might be a good time to address "one of the gravest social problems facing our country at this critical time: to present an objective treatment of individual minorities in picture-text."

Wallace would travel with various *Look* photographers to several sections of the country—the Northeast, South, Southwest, and Pacific Coast—and investigate the lives and situations of minorities who have had to struggle with hatred and discrimination. Then each piece as it was written would be published in *Look*, and all the pieces would be gathered into a book to be called *One Nation*.

Wallace jumped at the opportunity. Not only would it triple his salary, but would give him the chance to write about those things that were of deep concern to him and his wife. He took a leave of absence from Harvard, but he also had some doubt whether he would ever return, despite his promotion. He was interested in getting a teaching position that paid more, allowing him to teach only half-time on a more or less permanent basis and a position where he would have more opportunity to teach dedicated creative writers. He was also looking to see if he and Mary couldn't return to the West. He put out feelers with many of his old contacts, including Wilbur Schramm, and began responding to notices of job openings, including an opening at Mills College in Oakland, California.

When they got back from Mexico, they took a cottage in Martha's Vineyard and Wallace began to read "all the sociology books that [he] ... probably should have read in college and never had." Martha's Vineyard would become home base for the summer, as Wallace took off to one place or another to do his research. His first focus was on discrimination and its resulting violence in his own backyard—South Boston. Catching up on his reading as time permitted, he spent some of his days walking about and talking to people in the area and at night "messing around," as he put it, in various South Boston pubs to get the talk and a feel for the territory.

What he was aiming at was discovering the basis of incidents of Jew-baiting and violence against Jews that had been increasing in recent months, particularly in Dorchester, where Jewish boys had been set upon and beaten by gangs of Irish youths. Neither the police, who seemed reluctant to act against their fellow Irish (on occasion arresting the victims and letting the perpetrators go free), nor the Catholic Church, which seemed determined to look the other way, had done anything to stem the problem. Stegner, along with Ted Weeks and other editors at *The Atlantic*, got together and decided to expose the situation, and Stegner wrote an article, "Who Persecutes Boston?" In it he reviews the history of the Irish in Boston, a history of being "snubbed, bought and sold in the labor market, segregated, and disliked." But now that they were in the majority and had political power, the Irish youths at the bottom of the ladder, as a reaction to their own group's long history of having been discriminated against, had felt free to turn on the Jews in their community as scapegoats, encouraged, it would seem, by Nazi propaganda and the Christian Front with its anti-Semitism as preached by such priests as Father Edward Lodge Curran.

And while Stegner declares that there is no evidence that the Catholic Church itself had been responsible for these anti-Semitic outbreaks, he concludes that "it could do more than any other single agency or institution to stop them, if it would." The response to the article was immediate and startling. Unknown to Ted Weeks, *The Atlantic* was owned by Irish Catholics, who took great offense and called Weeks on the carpet. Weeks's much-valued secretary turned out to be Irish Catholic, and she quit her job. And Stegner himself was denounced from the pulpit throughout the area and attacked by the archbishop over the Yankee Radio Network. Nevertheless, the violence stopped cold, and *The Atlantic* forces felt that they had achieved a great victory, not just for the Boston area, but for the country at large in its fight against fascism.

But it may be that the controversy set off by the article led *Look* to

reconsider its project. To its credit, it stuck with Stegner and the book—
he would continue to do research for it. However, the editors decided
that individual articles on various forms of discrimination throughout
the country would be too hot for the popular magazine to handle
without serious risk to its circulation. Instead, they published a summary
of pictures and text out of the book in a single, totally innocuous article.
Distressed by this lack of courage and social conscience, Stegner found
himself in the position of wanting to protest, but wanting nevertheless to
keep his job and go on to do what good he could with the book.

The *Look* articles were out, but at least the writer would be free to
publish the results of his investigations in other magazines, providing
that the articles did not duplicate those written for *One Nation*. As a
result, his publication record for the years 1944–46 is made up primarily
of nearly a dozen articles exposing prejudice and the mistreatment of
minorities, as well as articles that came out of his travels, such as the
four-part essay for the *Saturday Review* on "Rediscovering America."
One of the less important reasons for having taken the *Look* job was that
it enabled him to travel around the country at a time, during the war,
when travel was restricted.

One Nation remains a testament to the depth and passion of Stegner's
social commitment and provides a clear picture of his vision of what this
society should be and could become. The book expresses throughout a
concern for the survival and improvement of democracy and dismay at
the continuing intolerance, and the ignorance that spawns it, in our
society. It reflects the hope that our experience of the war against fascism might prompt us to reexamine our attitudes and that the postwar
period might provide an opportunity to rid ourselves of prejudice and
discrimination at home.

During the summer of 1944, while Mary and Page stayed at Martha's
Vineyard, Wallace took several trips to North Carolina to get a firsthand
view of the effects of the Jim Crow laws and then, again with a photographer, to Chicago to observe the results of the African-American migration northward. In August he went once again to Bread Loaf, spent
several frantic days of work at the *Look* offices in New York, and then he
and his family gathered all the gas ration stamps they could and drove
out to the West Coast. They stopped on the way and spent some time in

Santa Fe, New Mexico, where Wallace interviewed Hispanics and where he was given a tour of the pueblos by an official from the Bureau of American Indian Affairs. In Santa Fe, also, they became acquainted with the colony of artists and writers there and met Oliver La Farge and Ansel Adams. They went on to the coast and established their western head-quarters in Santa Barbara, where they rented the guest house on a large estate.

From Santa Barbara, Wallace wrote to DeVoto:

> For plain unadulterated good looks, they don't make many towns better than this one. We perch in a royal palm grove up from the beach, and clear days, which are few, the view is fine of both mountains and ocean and Channel Islands. The public schools are good, the ration board fairly liberal, the place full of refugee writers and publishers, with whom we have so far avoided contact. . . . Our host, formerly of Boston, Falmouth, and Squibnocket, is an old lady named Mrs. Gardiner Hammond, a kind of sweet old girl who has just joined the socialist party, belongs to a dozen pacifist groups, writes weekly to her ex-gardeners in the Relocation Centers. (10/26/44)

Mrs. Gardiner Hammond would become one of the models, some fifteen years later, for Mrs. Deborah Barber Hutchins, the matriarch in *A Shooting Star*.

During the next few months Wallace followed a hectic schedule of travel. From Santa Barbara, he went to a number of pickers' camps in California's Central Valley, to two of the Japanese relocation centers in the desert near the Nevada border, to Chinatown in San Francisco, and to Los Angeles, where he talked to the pachucos, the young Mexican-Americans of that generation. Of these experiences he has said, "I cannot say that [they] made a man of me, but they cured me of seeing America from the monastic distance of the campus." He also gathered material in Stockton and the Central Valley on the Filipinos in this country and went to the Midwest and New York to do research on the history of prejudice against Catholics and Jews.

While in the Midwest, he visited Mary's parents in Dubuque and then spent some time with the Trappist monks at an abbey in Peosta,

Iowa. In between trips he worked in the Hollywood offices of *Look*. It was not a good time for him to be traveling so much and working so hard. Both he and Mary were terribly worried about his health. He had been diagnosed as having a serious heart infection, but without the antibiotics we have today, there was little the doctors could do.

In the meantime, he and Mary had been hired as "West Coast editors" for Houghton Mifflin, a job that was primarily carried out by Mary while he was on the road. They picked up a publishable book here and there, most notably *Mister Roberts*, which Wallace's cousin, Tom Heggen, sent to them chapter by chapter from the South Pacific. Then at the beginning of the year, Wallace and Mary went to New York, so that Wallace could work at the *Look* headquarters to finish up the book, the editing and layout. They were there for almost four months, their longest stay in New York, living in the Beekman Tower Hotel. Mary's parents came to Santa Barbara to vacation from the cold of Iowa and to take care of Page.

Published in September 1945, just after the war ended, *One Nation* won the Life-in-America Award and shared the *Saturday Review* Anisfield-Wolf Award for the year's best book on race relations. Stegner had used many of the techniques he had used in *Mormon Country*, short narratives to make a point dramatic and believable, maps, charts, short historical reviews, and sketches—he clearly had done his homework both on the street and in the library.

One difference between Stegner's views and those of many others who made similar arguments for tolerance and equality was that Stegner was very much concerned about groups maintaining their heritage and traditions, while at the same time becoming also part of that larger group we call Americans. "Cultural diversity" is not a phrase he uses in the book, but it is a condition and remedy he argues for. He points to education, specifically the kind of education demonstrated in the "Springfield Plan" in Massachusetts as an important part of the solution:

> The schools not only give students an effective, practical experience in working together, but encourage their pride in their backgrounds. The Negro, Jewish or Polish child is not allowed to feel that his being what he is something shameful.... And since democracy is a task, not a fact, students are not spoonfed with

mythical tales about its wonders. They learn about it by studying its faults and break-downs and failures as much as its successes.

One group in particular to which Stegner gives attention, a group that was made to feel ashamed of its identity and was deprived of its traditions, was the American Indians. The "Americanizing" programs of missionaries and reservation boarding schools were aimed at eradicating stubborn Indian adherence to their own heritage. In the book Stegner has hope for a new program based on the clear recognition of "the Indian's right to personal dignity *as an Indian.*" He adds that "we already owe the Indian so much that we might well consider learning more instead of trying to make a white man of him."

What is sad about the book is not so much its dated material but its hope—hope that, despite some advances, has largely dissipated in the fifty years since the book came out. Unfortunately, the promise that Stegner saw in 1945 has only partially been fulfilled—Jim Crow is gone, written housing covenants against Jews and blacks are gone, school integration is an ongoing and sometimes successful process, and Native Americans have often found a new independence and pride in their heritage. But on an overall basis, there would seem to be more fear, more conflict and violence, more antagonism and friction between groups than ever before. Stegner, despite some hope for a general and gradual elimination of discrimination in our society, was wise enough to know that it would not be easy, nor would it be immediate:

None of us is so different from the classic Southerner, the unreconstructed Johnny Reb. The germs of prejudice are as common as those of tuberculosis: most of us under the x-ray would show the tubercles of old infection. . . . So long as the average American permits himself the apparently harmless indulgence of cussing the Jews or damning the Catholics or feeling superior to the Negroes or taking out his hatred and fear of Japan on Americans of Japanese parentage, the hard and durable spore of all the worst kinds of bigotry is preserved, and can be watered and tended and fertilized by fanatics and lunatics and politicians willing to build up a clique by any method.

9

BACK TO FICTION,
ON TO STANFORD

Wallace did not get the job at Mills College. Although he came highly recommended and the president of the college wanted him badly, he was vetoed by the board of trustees. Several of its members considered *The Big Rock Candy Mountain* "too pornographic."

Meanwhile, an old friend from Bread Loaf, Edith Mirrielees, who was retiring from her job as creative writing teacher at Stanford, put in a good word for him there. The result was a far more satisfactory offer from a far more prestigious school. He was offered a full professorship, with tenure after a year as "acting professor," and would teach on the half-time basis that he had hoped for. He preferred teaching creative writing, but he agreed to teach some American literature as well, since the department had a shortage of professors trained in that area. Usually the course was "The Rise of Realism," American fiction from the Civil War until after the turn of the century, which required four lectures a week, a schedule, as he has admitted, that made "the business of writing on the side a bit tiring." He had become an expert on the Realistic period—in the weeks after he came to Stanford, he was writing a chapter on literature in the West after the Civil War for *Literary History of the United States.*

He would be in charge of the creative writing program, and he was told that the department and university wanted the program to be expanded and given more stature. As someone who had witnessed the birthing of the program at Iowa (which had become the most prestigious in the country), who had been part of Morrison's pioneering work with the writing program at Harvard, and who had been a regular at Bread Loaf, he was uniquely qualified to do just that. Even before he arrived in Palo Alto, he was bursting with ideas he wanted to try.

His feelings when he arrived at Stanford were quite different from those he had had in taking up other jobs. Almost always before, and especially at Harvard, he had felt, as he has said, "beyond my depth and [I] was treading water desperately to keep up." But when he got to his new post, he recalled that

> I came out pretty confident, actually. Because I had been promoted at Harvard, and that was the first time anyone had promoted me. And then I had done that year and a half job for *Look* and that book was out just about the time we arrived here and made a kind of big splash and made a lot of front page headlines because of the interest here in race relations.

For more than a year after coming to Stanford, as a result of *One Nation*, he was in demand as a speaker on race relations and spoke to groups in San Francisco and the Bay Area. He also served a term on the board of the local ACLU.

The reaction to his coming to Stanford was mixed. By and large he was accepted with open arms as a well-qualified colleague. But there were several among the English faculty who, with some justification, resented his hiring as full professor. The department was undergoing a sea change. A number of distinguished people had been hired during the Depression who, like Stegner earlier at Utah and Wisconsin, had not advanced. They had had a department chairman who bragged that he had never asked for a raise for anyone in his department, and none of these people had been promoted. A new chairman, R. F. Jones, had come in and in a few years promoted all those who had been waiting so long, and it was with Jones's backing that Stegner was able to make the cre-

ative writing program so successful from nearly the beginning. But
when he was hired in at full professor, he was the same age as those who
had been waiting in line, and "as things went on, he didn't have too
many friends from that generation."

When Wallace and Mary arrived in June 1945, they found that there
was a terrific housing shortage at Stanford, and for some years the Stegners' ability to get a house of their own was in doubt. Aside from the
farm house in Greensboro, this would be the first time they would own
their own home, and they looked forward to it with great anticipation.
During the summer they lived in a women's convalescent home, then
moved to a rental on Waverly Street for the school year, and after that to
a house on campus for two years. It was during that period on campus
that they worked on plans to buy some property and build their own
home. First, they joined a cooperative, the Peninsula Housing Association, that planned a community behind the campus in Ladera. (The first
name that had been adopted was "Lark Hills," but that was so corny that
Wallace suggested *Ladera*, or "hillside" in Spanish, instead.) He wrote
an article about the association called "Four Hundred Families Plan a
House" when he was still enthusiastic about this housing cooperative,
but delays and disagreements discouraged the Stegners.

They finally left the association when it was discovered that the organization could not get any loans from the FHA because it did not have
any exclusionary rules. The Stegners, along with the other members,
stood firm that they would accept any member regardless of race or religion. Without the FHA loans, building was impossible even though the
houses were to range in cost from $5,000 to $12,000. The plan fell
through, the association was abandoned, and the land was eventually
sold to a developer. The Stegners ended up buying property on a hilltop,
with a magnificent view of the peninsula foothills between Stanford and
the ocean in what later became Los Altos Hills.

The difficulties they faced in building there were formidable, however. There was no nearby electricity, no road, no water, and no sewer
hookup available. In order to afford the house, Wallace had to commit
himself to doing much of the finishing work and all the landscaping.
The son of a sometime carpenter ended up doing quite a bit of building
over these years in both California and Vermont. There has been, in fact,

a tradition of carpentry in the family: son Page has built several houses, doing most of the work himself, and Page's son, Wallace Page—Wallace's grandson—is a building contractor in northern California. Page remembers as a child helping his father plant eight thousand Norway pines on their logged-over two hundred acres in Vermont, and just a year or two before his father died, Page cut down some of those trees, some eighty feet high, to mill and use to build a house. He now has the almost unique pleasure of looking at a house made out of trees he himself planted.

As soon as Wallace had finished his work on *One Nation* earlier in 1945, he had started working on his fiction again, as well as spending some time with his long-term Powell project. The story "The Volcano," which came out of his and Mary's vacation in Mexico, had been published in September 1944, and two stories that had been previously rejected, "The House on Cherry Creek" and "Balance His, Swing Yours," were slightly revised and finally found publication in the summer and fall of 1945, along with a new story, "Saw Gang."

But perhaps Stegner's most important story of the period was "The Women on the Wall," published in *Harper's* in April 1946. In retrospect, we can see that this story was the first tentative step—unrecognized by the author at the time—toward the persona that he would develop for the prizewinning novels of the late period of his work, a persona that was largely responsible for the novels' success.

"The Women on the Wall" is a story that features a Mr. Palmer, a retired man of late middle age, who is writing his memoirs in a house near the Pacific Ocean (the setting and central situation came to Stegner during his year in Santa Barbara). He is courtly in manner and, even in 1945, seems out of his time in a present more violent, full of conflict, less genteel, less polite than he seems to expect. Rather than writing, he spends much of his time looking out the window—a habit that reminds us of Joe Allston, his successor in the second of these germinal stories, "Field Guide to Western Birds." (Stegner arranged his desk in his study in Los Altos Hills so that as he typed he looked at a blank wall, rather than in front of a window with a fine view on the other wall.)

Mr. Palmer is the earliest appearance of what might be called the elderly, writer-observer figure in Stegner's fiction. He is experienced, sensitive to his environment, an observer of people, a bit skeptical and self-doubting, and despite a somewhat hardened shell, vulnerable to emotion—all qualities that would be carried over, although in somewhat different proportions, to Joe Allston in "Field Guide," *All the Little Live Things*, and *Spectator Bird*; Lyman Ward in *Angle of Repose*; and Larry Morgan in *Crossing to Safety*. And while these latter characters have a romantic streak, Palmer's romanticism is so extreme it carries him into fundamental errors about the people he observes. This is a harsh, almost shocking story about the discovery of what is real.

Palmer looks out his study window at the women who line up along the wall every day, Navy wives who during World War II wait at their mailboxes for word of their husbands, and out of his bookishness he is reminded of Homer's Penelope "on the rocky isle of Ithaca above the wine-dark sea," and he finds himself getting "a little sentimental about these women." Of course, the point of the story depends on the unreliability of his perceptual framework—the women turn out, on closer acquaintance, to be very unromantic figures indeed. One of his Penelopes turns out to be a dope addict who is willing to neglect her young daughter in favor of a fix; another smothers her child with overprotectiveness; another, unmarried, has become pregnant and worries that her lover may not come back and "make a decent woman" of her. They are backbiting, self-involved, and in conflict with one another—not at all the placid, patient, heroic figures Palmer has imagined them to be and has admired.

To a lesser extent the narrators of the later novels—Joe Allston, Lyman Ward, and Larry Morgan—are unreliable in their perceptions, and they, too, want to place the people around them as players in their personally scripted dramas, dramas that reflect their preconceptions, prejudices, and desires. This tendency contributes to a theme related to the discovery of reality behind appearances—identity, our own (that is, the self-discovery of the narrator or center of consciousness) and others' (that is, the characters observed by the narrator). Each novel carried by these first-person narrators has as its central concern an effort to understand and make a judgment about a major character in that novel, a pattern prefigured not only in "The Women on the Wall" but in "Field Guide to Western Birds" as well. Each of these narrators in the late novels finds himself in a position where he is not only unsure of precisely what judgment to make, but unsure about his own ability or qualifica-

tions to make that judgment. Mr. Palmer, by contrast, seems so certain of
his own vision that both he and the reader are startled by his mistake,
and the thought that sticks with us from "The Women on the Wall" is
the complete failure of the center of consciousness to see things as they
really are.

Wallace did not go to Bread Loaf or Greensboro during the summer
of 1945, but stayed in Palo Alto to settle into his new job and get some
writing done. At the end of the summer, however, the family took off for
King's River, and Grant and Sequoia National Parks. This was the
beginning of a series of trips in the West nearly every summer during
the late 1940s and early 1950s, most of them lasting for several weeks.
Both Wallace and Mary had the itch to travel. Two years earlier they
had driven across country, "but that trip," Wallace has noted, "was
clouded by scarcities, rationing, and the pressure of business." Both of
them enjoyed exploring, hiking, and camping out. And, finally, Wallace
needed to traverse the ground (and water) associated with the surveying,
map-making, and exploring of John Wesley Powell.

Their travels were not necessarily confined to Powell country, however. In the summer of 1946, they spent the first part of the summer on a
desert trip with Page and another faculty couple on a loop down through
Bakersfield, across the Mojave into the Nevada desert, and up to Lake
Mead, where, as guests of the Park Service, they were given a tour of
the lake. At Virgin Basin, where Powell ended his passage, the first
of the Colorado River by boat, Stegner looked around with interest and
then disappointment as he saw that "where Powell saw low shores
and placid muddy river and muddy banks, there is now an even spread
of blue sweeping northward. . . . I curse myself that I never got down
here when the lake went deep into the cliffs, or when the river ran
unimpeded."

Page was eight, nine, ten years old when he went with his parents on
these trips, and looking back he has recalled:

My father . . . could never just *look* at scenery. If we happened to be
driving across the Colorado Plateau through southern Utah, say

from Cisco to Price along the Book Cliffs, he'd offer up an anecdote about Powell being rescued by Bradley in Desolation Canyon, and then explain to his slightly annoyed eight-year-old boy (me), who was trying to concentrate on his Batman comic, who Powell was and why he was important. Then he'd point out the La Sals and Abajos to the south and tell that boy something about laccolithic domes, betting him he couldn't spell laccolithic.... Crossing over the Wasatch Plateau and heading south through the Spanish Fork canyon would remind him of the specific dates of the Escalante/ Dominguez expedition through the region (September 23, 1776) and that it was exactly fifty years before Jedediah Smith came through following essentially the same route. He had a kind of holistic relationship with the land, and he couldn't look at it without remembering its geological history, its exploration, its social development, its contemporary problems, and its prognosis for the future.

On their 1946 excursion, after leaving Lake Mead they headed through Las Vegas, up Death Valley, the Owens Valley, and over the Sierras at Tahoe, and then through the Motherlode country to home. Avoiding as much as possible prepared campgrounds and paved roads, they slept on the ground and whenever they could took back roads. On one occasion they tried a jeep track up Greenwater Canyon and had to dig out of the sand seven times and deal with a repeatedly boiling radiator, vapor lock, a broken fuel pump, and two sidewinders. After two days of struggle over fourteen miles and with only two miles to go, they found the track impassable and had to turn back.

Wallace wrote up the story of this trip as "Rediscovering America," published in 1946 in four parts in *Saturday Review*. Succeeding years saw the publication of the accounts of other trips: 1947, "Packhorse Paradise," an account of a trip down into Havasu Canyon, a tributary canyon to the Grand Canyon; 1948, a river trip down the San Juan and the Colorado into Glen Canyon as recorded in "Backroads River"; 1949, a trip through Navajo country and attending a rodeo, depicted in "Navajo Rodeo." (All of these are included in *The Sound of Mountain Water* [1980], although some of the titles have been changed.) A journey through the desert and up into Utah by auto on the way to Greensboro in the early summer of 1950 led to two articles published in *Tomorrow* in 1950, a seriocomic reflection on the nature and meaning of West in "Why I Like the West" and a journal-like account of the trip itself in "Backroads of the American West."

In this series of articles over several years, the essential flavor is that of the travel piece designed to entertain. The observations of a sharp and sometimes critical observer are interspersed with humorous asides, personal notes, and historical reflections. They were written to make more immediate use of impressions that were being gathered as background for the Powell book, but also to help pay for the research. Mostly innocuous, the articles do sound a serious note now and then, and increasingly so. Beginning with the first articles, "Rediscovering America," there is a sense of regret (although he often treats these encounters humorously) over what some call "progress," what seemed to be the gradual paving over of everything, the overly civilized facilities provided by the national parks, the multiplication of tourist traps— junky signs, amusement parks, and phony museums. And even in 1946 he bemoans the trashing of the desert by careless travelers and campers and the loss of the Colorado through dams and the creation of lakes. Years later he would play an important part in stopping the attempt to put more dams on the river.

In "Packhorse Paradise" he addresses the serious problem of the Havasupai Indians in Havasu Canyon, as civilization encroaches farther and farther into their isolation:

> There is something to be said for the policy that urges keeping the barrier canyons around this tribe unbridged, for according to the enthnologist Leslie Spier, the Havasupai retain their native culture in purer form than any other American Indians. Other Indians, losing their hold on their native culture, have ceased to exist.
>
> I doubt if there is a clear-cut answer to the problems the Havasupai face. Inevitably there will be more and more intrusion on their isolation, and inevitably they must proceed through the phase of falling between two cultures, of being neither Indian nor white American.

A similar concern for the fate of the Indians, in their mixed status as both citizen and government ward, is expressed in "Navajo Rodeo." While acknowledging that they have an enduring and wonderful capacity to enjoy themselves—as witnessed in the rodeo—Stegner points out that they lead "a bad life and hard one, a life dirty, ridden with tuberculosis and trachoma and ringworm, a life always close to the edge of real danger."

By the time he gets to his articles for *Tomorrow*, in 1950, one can see that his Powell research is making a strong impression on him. In "Why I Like the West" he takes the opportunity to educate his readers, first that "there is no such thing as the West. There are only Wests, as different from one another as New Hampshire from South Carolina," and second, in the Powell doctrine of the importance of aridity, "for upon the lack of sufficient rain depends practically all the things that make the Wests western." In "Backroads of the American West" we encounter once again two themes that Stegner returns to over and over in the articles of this period—the dangers of overdevelopment and the excellent job that the Park Service has been doing. On another desert-mountain trip, they encounter the little Mormon town of Fruita, Utah:

> All around us, in every direction, is country that so far has never taken its pay or paid its penalty for being beautiful. But we are told that a super-highway has already been surveyed down this wash and through this village. . . . We are all a little sad to think that the oasis of Fruita, whose charm is less durable than that of the red ledges, may be gutted and spoiled. . . . Indiscriminate development would ruin this little paradise. The rocks and canyons are pretty well beyond harm barring people with paint cans, but the village of Fruita could be made unrecognizable in a few years.

After arriving at camp at Mesa Verde, they give thanks for a clean campground, a stove and table and benches, free wood, and showers. Then at lunch they "reflect almost with awe that in all our camping excursions we have never had an unpleasant word or a surly look from a single member of the Park Service. Despite facing on occasion unreasonable demands and various provocations, the staff shows an unfailing willingness to be helpful." When a campground was not available, the Stegners would look for what Wallace called the "local knowledge box," as they drove over the endless miles of high desert and ranch country, and they would pitch their tent in the schoolyard for the night.

In 1951–52, by which time Wallace had been at work on the manuscript of *Beyond the Hundredth Meridian: John Wesley Powell and the Second Opening of the West* for several years, his articles took an even harder line, his first overtly environmentalist article published in 1953. Here the influence of Bernard DeVoto comes to bear, both in terms of the example of his writings—his "Easy Chair" editorials for *Harper's*— and in his explicit encouragement of his protégé to join in the fray:

> Benny was very early in that line and in the 1940s and the beginning of the '50s, he was practically the stalwart single champion. I made some remark in a letter . . . some angry remark about something that was happening to public lands, and he telephoned me and said, "If you feel like that, write it." And I suppose the first magazine article that I wrote of the environmental kind was sometime about then, and it was all Benny's doing.

The article was "One-Fourth of a Nation: Public Lands and Itching Fingers," published in *Reporter* on December 5, 1953, and was provoked by his realization that the same battles John Wesley Powell had fought to preserve public lands from exploitation were still being fought, and that the battle was joined with the same kinds of people. Once again, the leader of the opposition was a senator from Nevada, Pat McCarran, using the same old time-worn arguments that had been employed by Senator William M. Stewart in 1890 against Powell. It would seem that little had changed over the intervening decades. It was as depressing as it was outrageous. "There is," Stegner wrote, "a brand of states-rightsism that is more Western than Southern, more Republican than Democratic, and based not on history or sentiment but on natural resources of enormous value."

But the real struggle, as he points out, is not between the states and the federal government, but between public interest and powerful private interests "who for years have tried to corral the West's land, water, timber, and water power." The author then traces the beginnings of the conservation movement to Powell's *Report on the Lands of the Arid Region* in 1878, and he points out that if Congress had acted on the report, many troubles such as the Dust Bowl would have been in large part prevented, and the United States would be further along with a coherent program of reclamation for the West and would certainly have simpler, more workable water laws. Nevertheless, despite his defeats at the hands of Congress, many of Powell's proposals have over time been put into law or practice, and with the exceptions of the Republican Taft and Hoover administrations, the government has generally acted—not always soon enough or strongly enough—on the side of conservation.

However, in 1953 the nation had once again a Republican administration under President Eisenhower and the signals from his Secretary of Interior, Douglas McKay, and the Republicans in Congress were not encouraging. Once again the Sagebrush Rebellion seemed to be under way. In his article for the *Reporter*, the author warns that

> it may be taken as gospel that the strongest antagonism to govern-ment ownership and management will be found among those who would profit most from their elimination. Whatever the diver-sionary tactics and political smoke screens, the issue is public interest vs. private profit. If stockmen or landowners grow wrathful about Federal absentee landlords and call for the "return" of Fed-eral lands to state tax rolls (where they have never been), they do so because a powerful local group can dominate a state government more easily than it can a Federal bureau.

It seems ironic now, in retrospect, that Stegner and the conservationists were so worried about Eisenhower—they had no idea how bad things could get until President Ronald Reagan and his Secretary of Interior, James Watt, would try to give away the store during the 1980s.

It is worthwhile noting that in this article, as elsewhere, it was a common practice for Stegner to trace the history of a situation or problem. Here, he gives us a brief history of the conservation movement going back to John Wesley Powell, just as earlier he had given us the his-tory of co-ops in an article recommending them and the history of the

Irish in Boston in an article recommending that the Catholic Church take action against anti-Semitism. This practice underlines the importance of history, always, in Stegner's consciousness. Above all it is for him a key to self-discovery. But also, on a larger stage, conflicts between humans, and between humans and their environments, have historical contexts that are essential for us to know in order to understand them, adjust our attitudes, and take proper social or political action.

This pattern suggests a further parallel with Wallace's two prizewinning novels, *The Spectator Bird* and *Angle of Repose*, in which the past is discovered and used to understand the present. In the latter novel, Lyman Ward, a historian, works through letters and other materials in order to discover his grandmother's life and her relationship with his grandfather in the hope that he might better understand himself, as well as his wife and his relationship with her. Stegner spoke often of a condition he felt was all too characteristic of our society: "a present amputated from the past." He himself had been cut off from his past by the circumstances of his early schooling and the alienation of his parents from their parents, and so he was more conscious of this amputation than most and spent his life trying to point out and remedy this failure of continuity and connection in our social consciousness.

Meanwhile, Stegner was finding his way at Stanford, starting in the fall of 1945. He began by teaching half-time through the year, and that was a disaster. He recalled, "I was supposed to be on half-time, but I never worked harder in my life," so he changed over the following year to two quarters on and two quarters off. That second year he adopted a schedule he would keep throughout his career during the quarters he taught. He would get up, make breakfast, and then bring it into the bedroom. He and Mary would talk or sometimes practice Italian together. In later years they had a radio and would listen to the news, and later still, when they finally were able to get a newspaper delivered to their hilltop home, they would read it together. Wallace was a sports fan, followed baseball closely in the papers (and when TV came, spent time watching it and football on the weekends), and knew all the batting averages. After breakfast, from about eight o'clock to eleven-fifteen or so, he would be in his study and as much as possible devote his time to writing, though sometimes he had to prepare lectures for his literature class.

Then, as his wife remembered, "He would shower and shave and dress and . . . [go to campus] for a one o'clock. . . . In the afternoon I suppose he had a writing class too, and he had office hours, and then he would come home and we would have dinner. I would see him every night sitting in that chair [in the living room] grading papers." During the quarters when he wasn't teaching and in Greensboro during the summer, he would follow a similar pattern of writing every morning and then doing work around the house or garden in the afternoon. It was understood by his friends in both in California and Vermont that he should not be disturbed in the mornings.

The very first manuscript he read for his very first creative writing class was "Rest Camp on Maui," a short story by a student named Eugene Burdick. Burdick was just out of the Navy and still wearing his uniform grays. It was a "jolting and powerful story," as Stegner remembered the experience, and was later published in *Harper's* (arranged by Stegner) and won second prize in the O. Henry Memorial Awards. Burdick later went on to a Houghton Mifflin Fellowship (which came out of the joint sponsorship of Wallace and Mary in their capacity as West Coast editors) and a Rhodes Scholarship, eventually publishing *The Ugly American* (with William Lederer, another Navy veteran) and *Fail Safe*.

To Wallace's sponsorship of Burdick, it should be added that Stegner was extremely generous to all his students not only in time and support while they were enrolled, but after they had gone out on their own. He was constantly reading manuscripts of ex-students who had requested his help even long after he had quit teaching, making suggestions, helping to find publishers, and writing blurbs. Ex-students have testified that it was common for him to take the time to type out three-, four-, or five-page critiques, single-spaced, of their work. No writer ever took more pains to help other writers.

But Burdick was not the only outstanding student. A whole generation who might not have gone on to college were enabled to do so through a generous GI Bill passed by Congress, and beginning with the fall of 1945, veterans were flooding into colleges around the country. Burdick was only the most energetic and noticeable of a dozen nearly or equally talented in Stegner's writing class, and he felt "it was impossible

not to give encouragement and support to students of that caliber."
He found these years, from 1945 through the early 1950s, to be an
exciting time in the classroom. "Instead of green nineteen and twenty-
year-olds," he recalled, "my classes were full of mature, experienced,
highly-motivated men and women with hard experience, serious minds,
and an urge to catch up lost time. . . . Teaching had never been, and has
not been since, the pure pleasure that it was in those years."

The many ideas that he had gathered over the years for developing a
successful creative writing program came flooding back to consciousness
now as he realized, "We have to do something; this is too good to be
coasting along just like an old dull college class." One idea that he had
was that in order to provide further incentive to students to do their best
work, prizes should be offered for the best manuscripts of each year, but
that first year, 1945–46, he was able to scrape up only a few small
awards. He was prompted by the excitement generated by teaching such
able and motivated students to go further: he drew up a "rather
grandiose" proposal of a half-dozen pages that outlined a program of
undergraduate and graduate creative writing education, including a
hierarchy of increasingly demanding classes—all classes to be taught by
writers—and a mix of "fellowships, prizes, publication in annual collections, an M. A. program for those who needed a teaching certificate, and
a fund for literary visitors."

Stegner felt the latter was necessary because Palo Alto was forty miles
from anything that might be considered a center of literary activity, and
he felt that it was important that the students be exposed to accomplished writers of various stripes in order, for one thing, to show the students that a writing life was possible. He recalled,

> when we moved back West, I knew that literary careers cut off
> from New York tend to wither over the years. But we never felt iso-
> lated, because we could bring people in, and did—Katherine Anne
> Porter, Walter van Tilburg Clark, Hortense Calisher, May Sarton,
> Elizabeth Bowen, C. P. Snow, Frank O'Connor, Malcolm Cowley,
> William Styron, Saul Bellow, and from the old Bread Loaf clan
> Robert Frost, Bernard DeVoto, Ted Morrison, Catherine Drinker
> Bowen, John Ciardi. They enriched our personal lives while they

were doing for the young and unaffiliated what Bread Loaf had done for me in the summer of 1938.

That spring of 1947 he took his plan to the department chairman, R. F. Jones, to approve before handing it on to the university administration. It just so happened that Jones's brother, E. H. Jones, was visiting at the time. E. H., an M.D. who had never practiced medicine because oil had been discovered on his property in Texas, took his brother and Stegner to lunch, where Stegner explained his plan in some detail. E. H. offered to fund the program for five years and later made the offer permanent, his loyal family coming through with the remainder of the endowment even after his death. Richard Scowcroft, who later became Wallace's partner in running the fiction part of the program, feels in looking back on these events that Jones "wished he'd been a writer instead of rich oil man."

The plan went into effect in the fall of 1947. Scowcroft, who had been a student of Stegner's at Utah before doing his graduate work at Harvard, has summed up the program's success in saying:

For years almost every prominent writer applied for a Stegner fellowship. Stanford was the place where you could be paid to starve to death for a year with no responsibilities. My guess is that fewer than half the Fellows got degrees. [But] you had to attend the writing class; you had to be part of the writing group. And of course this is what made it a workable and successful plan—that it was more like a congregation of talented young people than an academic situation.

Having these three or four Fellows who were almost professional was a great help in raising the standard of a class. It was rare—almost unheard of—when you didn't have a high standard of expectation and achievement. Students wouldn't do less than their best because they were being judged by people whose talents and judgments they respected.

Over the years the program was altered in light of experience. After four years the prizes were dropped because although they engendered intense competition, they also generated some bad feeling. Also, the out-side judges were hard to recruit (Wallace had the unhappy task of sending begging and apologetic letters out to friends who hardly had time for their own work), and not everybody was satisfied with the judges' decisions. The drama fellowships were dropped because "the stage apparatus as well as the courses in dramatic writing were over in Speech and Drama, while the rest of us were in English." If the drama fellows stayed to work in their home environment, they missed out on the comradeship and interplay of ideas provided by close association with the other fellows. The number of fellowships increased over the years with the addition of eight more designed just for the support of M.A. candidates. After several years, those who were awarded the fel-lowships were called "Stegner Fellows," and it was decided that they need not be regularly matriculated students or candidates for degrees.

In addition to his work designing the program, writing both articles and short fiction, and doing research for his Powell biography, he began a new novel during the summer of 1946 that would be called *Second Growth*. It is not as good as *The Big Rock Candy Mountain*, nor is it nearly as ambitious, but it is an improvement over his other early novels. Unlike *On a Darkling Plain* and *Fire and Ice*, Stegner allowed *Second Growth* to be reprinted in recent years and at the end of his life was still pleased with it as a modest contribution to his oeuvre. It is a quiet little book with a tangled web of distinct personalities and emotional prob-lems, almost a collection of stories, almost a *Winesburg, Ohio*, in the sense that many of the characters are boiling on the inside but repressed by social pressure. It is a book in the American tradition of exposing the reality behind appearances, the Freudian underbelly of the puritanical respectability of small-town USA.

The setting of the novel is the town of Westwick in northern New Hampshire, a fictional place obviously patterned after Greensboro. The lake as a center of activity, the record concerts of classical music broad-cast over the water, the professors and their little "think houses" where they study and write while their families play, and the sharp division between the summer people and the natives—all were from the Steg-ners' summer-home town. Less tangible but also carried over from life is the stultifying environment, especially during winter, of narrow-mindedness, gossip, prejudice, pious judgmentalism, and lack of cultural resources. (One character cannot even listen to music on her radio because of her neighbor's dial-twisting between one loud and strident religious service and another.) It is a place where the young people (the "second growth" of the title) are stunted from lack of stimulus or forced out to find room to grow. For those who choose to stay, it is a difficult life, especially to keep a farm going and paying enough to live on. Stegner may criticize this small-town farm community, but he also admires the gumption of its people. He has said about Vermont that he was drawn to people who, under difficult circumstances of relative poverty, could "make do," and he admired their ability to "cobble together" repairs—all this reminded him of his own experiences on the Saskatchewan frontier.

Despite the spiritual and cultural stultification, Westwick is a beautiful place, wooded and tranquil, a place where the summers are delightful and where neighbor helps neighbor. In the summer there is life everywhere—nature is bountiful and the summer folk take over. The summer concerts, *The New York Times* in the mail, the dinner parties, and the golf games bring a different atmosphere to the town. But the summer people, largely made up of Ivy League professors, do bring a social elitism with them, a clannishness and snobbery that is often brutal, and this, in turn, is matched by an exclusiveness on the part of the natives, who refuse to let anyone feel he or she belongs unless he or she is born there.

There are three plot lines in the novel: one deals with the growing up of Andy Mount; another deals with the destruction of Helen Barlow; and a third deals with the assimilation of a refugee from the city, Abe Kaplan. The story of Andy Mount brings an autobiographical strain into the novel, since there are several parallels with Stegner's life. Both men come out of a family with a loving but subordinated mother and a ne'er-do-well father; both grow up with family shame; both decide to break away from the past by going to college despite the fact that no one in their families has gone to college before. Both have a strong connection to their natural surroundings as they grow up; both lose fingers in an accident; both do hard physical work although they are very attached to books.

Andy has a hard life. His stepfather is a fugitive from an arson charge (he burns down the barn for the insurance, a major incident in the novel, which was also published separately as the short story "Hostage"), and his mother goes to jail as an accomplice. Andy is taken in by Mr. Richie, not so much because Richie is fond of the boy, but for the work the boy can do without pay to earn his keep. Years later Andy is offered an opportunity to go to college, to escape Westwick and advance himself, by one of the summer people, Stephen Dow, headmaster of a prep academy for Ivy League colleges. Dow, in an exception to the aloofness shown by many of the summer residents, takes an interest in the boy and sees promise in his hard work and bookishness. But Andy, who has had some harsh experiences with educated people, has to live down his fear of the outside world, which he sees as possibly cruel, certainly impersonal. Mr. Richie, reflecting his own self-interest and the judgmentalism of the town, advises him to stay to "live down" the shame of his mother and father. But John Mills, the town carpenter and old-time craftsman whom Andy thinks of as a sort of god, advises him to go—there is nothing left in that place for him to stay for. The pattern is very similar to George Willard's escape from Winesburg in Sherwood Anderson's novel.

The second plot has to do with Helen Barlow, a "second growth" who is stunted and destroyed. Her mother is a pious, heavyset, hardworking drudge with little imagination, hope, or liveliness. Helen's father is crippled from a stroke and sits all day in the living room, hardly communicating. His wife says "he takes things too hard" and is unable to accept the difficulties of life that God gives us. Helen has an active inner life; a romantic, she has a melancholy imagination, writes poetry, and prefers to be alone. Again, she reminds us of an Anderson character, perhaps Kate Swift, also a schoolteacher. Helen leads a dreary, dead-end existence, although she has graduated from college—she has come home because of her father's illness and is trapped. She is too shy and, like her father, "takes things too hard" to leave. She is pretty but mouselike, a born victim, who falls into the clutches of the aggressive Flo Barnes. Helen tries to avoid her, but Flo tracks her down. The impression given is that Helen, who has been told from childhood what "God wants for her," is so stricken by guilt from the resulting lesbian relationship that she commits suicide. This is a story that would outrage readers from the religious right, who would be incensed by the portrait of the mother, and from gay activist readers, many of whom have insisted that such a seduction is not possible.

The third major plot has to do with Abe Kaplan, a refugee from the city, having come out of city tenements because of tuberculosis to live in the country on his doctor's advice. He is the complete outsider, a Marxist and union member. Although nearly uneducated, he is a reader and talker who can meet the intellectual level of the various professor visitors he encounters, arguing history, religion (he is adamant atheist), and politics with them. He is a liberal in the best sense of the word, in his acceptance of social difference in Westwick and in his tolerance even in the face of intolerance. Although the local minister has denounced Kaplan as an "unbeliever," Kaplan still feels that there are "fine" people in the village. However, after he meets Ruth Liebowitz, also from New York, a visitor, he resents very much the treatment at the local inn that she receives, being seated at meals separately.

Nevertheless, Abe talks Ruth into the virtues of the country and they find that they are compatible—both are orphans, both nonreligious Jews—and so they get married. On the marriage night they wait for a chivaree, the local custom, but three nights later they still have not been serenaded and that becomes a signal that they have not been accepted. Ruth has a lonely life with almost no one willing to talk to her, and as winter approaches, she wonders whether she'll be able to stay. At the last evening concert on the lake, however, Abe hears a noise like something going into the water. It is dark, and shining a light over the lake, they see an empty boat. Abe dives, trying to help whomever has fallen into the lake (it turns out to be Helen, committing suicide), and he winds up in the hospital with pneumonia. Ruth receives a hospitality basket of food from the women of the town, a signal, at last, of acceptance and appreciation.

Abe and Ruth were patterned after a Jewish couple in Greensboro, the characters in the novel most closely modeled on actual people, and were good friends of the Stegners. Wallace thought of them as his heroes in the book and was writing about their difficulties as Jews in a small, tightly knit Yankee town, doing so out of the perspective brought to him from his experiences in writing about anti-Semitism in *One Nation*. Also, having published "Jews Are the Most Misunderstood Minority" in July of 1946, this was a topic that obviously was still much on his mind. Working close to life in this novel, Wallace ran into the sort of problem he would encounter with several of his books, in which characters were developed on the basis of people who could be recognized as models. Gossip in Greensboro developed from the book's publication, grew beyond Stegner's actual use of people and situations in the town, and became somewhat sensational, leading to resentment and charges of scandal-mongering and disloyalty. There was a period during which Wallace felt that he and his family might not be able to summer in Greensboro again.

10

ABANDONING THE NOVEL AND EMBRACING THE SHORT STORY

Throughout his career, Stegner was caught in a trap. He was a writer who, even when he was dealing with historical materials (as in *Angle of Repose*), usually worked very close to his own experience and the life he observed around him. Many writers do, of course, but he was more concerned than most about possibly causing distress to those who provided inspiration to him. If he stayed too close to the original models, they might easily be identified and resent his use of them; if he altered either people or situations through his imagination—which he usually did—then people might object to the way they had been changed or, if he combined several people into one character, the role they had contributed to. He felt that people did not understand the difference between fact and fiction or how a fictional character must be created. But at the same time, it must be said that like many other novelists, he was a bit ingenuous about his use of people, wondering why, since he had fictionalized them, they or their relatives should resent it. He first encountered this problem in a serious way with *Second Growth*.

By the end of 1946 he had finished the novel, and already, months before publication, he was worried about the real-life consequences. He wrote to Phil and Peg Gray:

Us, we envy you, naturally. Greensboro, white or green, is a pretty homesick place for us. Especially since, having committed a book, and having committed the indiscretion of telling a couple of people that there were some things in it based upon Greensboro life, we probably will never dare go back. Like Stegner himself, Stegner's friends talk too much, and with a hint to go on, delight to read-in Greensboro people and Greensboro events whether they're there or not. In fact, the whole thing was a complete mixture of little facts and big imaginations, but I doubt if any Greensboroite would ever believe that now. Do me a favor and say naught about it. It's an inconsequential little book, but I thought it was a fairly readable one, until people began worrying me about too-close local applications. Now I am pretty sour on the whole business. The one thing which is pretty straight out of Greensboro is Louis and Esther [Abe and Ruth], and I told them what I was going to do to them. In a way, they're the among the heroes of the book, but maybe even they won't like what I've done to them. (1/19/47)

When he heard that people were upset, he first withdrew the novel entirely. Then he let his publishers talk him into revising and altering. But a month before publication he was still worried about the trouble the book might cause, even though he had added "A Note on Fictional Character" to the novel that began by stating:

The making of fiction entails the creation of places and persons with all the seeming of reality, and these places and persons, no matter how a writer tries to invent them, must be made up piecemeal from sublimations of his own experience and his own acquaintance. There is no other material out of which fiction can be made.

   In that sense, and in that sense only, the people and the village of this story are taken from life.

He had sent a copy of the proofs to the Grays, who wrote back praise for the novel, but also added that they thought he had made his village a rather sinister place. Still worried about the reaction, Wallace objected to the characterization, saying in his reply that "I certainly never thought I was making it sinister. I was only trying to make it complex, which it is." He had not lost his sense of humor about it all, however, and added,

> I guess I'm like the colonial colonel who was finally brought to court for improper relations with an ostrich. If I had known people were going to be so dashed excited and make such a ruddy row I should have married the damned bird. (7/24/47)

Second Growth was published in August 1947. While the previous year he had gone to Bread Loaf (his last year on the staff) and Greensboro, this summer he did not go east and wrote the Grays that he and Mary might not go east ever again except to harvest their Norway pines. As we have seen, not only was he worried about the reaction in Greensboro, he was also deeply involved in his Powell research and had fallen in love all over again with the back roads of the West. Another big change in his life that he contemplated after moving to Stanford was to cut himself loose from his agents. He wrote to them he had been selling so little in recent years that he felt he had become a "poor relation" rather than an asset to them and probably could do just as well on his own. Another factor that contributed to this decision was that after going to Houghton Mifflin, as well as acting as West Coast editor, he thought he would never again be moving to another publisher and need an agent to negotiate for him. But he turned out, over the next few years, to be wrong on all counts: he and his family did return to Vermont on a regular basis; he did need Brandt and Brandt and would return to them in 1951; and he did change publishers, several times.

As head of the evolving writing center, Stegner had to struggle to get any writing done at all. But he was a workaholic, and no period in his life demonstrated that more than these early years at Stanford. Students who were in his literature class remember him delivering lively, witty lectures, and they were amazed that he usually did so without notes. He had a beautiful voice and a fine, understated delivery. In addition to his effective manner of speaking, he was a strikingly handsome man—one is tempted to add that he "glittered when he walked." As a Realist himself, he seemed to have a special connection with the American Realists—Stephen Crane, W. D. Howells, Hamlin Garland, Edith Wharton, Henry James, and, especially, Mark Twain. His students felt that he must have reread the literature the night before, it was so fresh in every detail in his mind. And in fact he had—rereading at least a novel or story collection a week along with going through all the student papers and stories he had to read and comment on.

But his literature class was usually over a hundred students; his most personal and direct contact with students came in his advanced writing classes (later graduate seminars) with limited enrollment. He tried to foster an atmosphere of congeniality and noncompetitiveness in these workshops—tried to create a good, positive feeling. Early in the quarter, he would have all the writing students over to his house for dinner along with some of the writing faculty. On those occasions he would often end the evening by taking groups of students in to show them his study, the inner sanctum. Once in a while the writing group would meet for the workshop at his house, and, especially in the early years, there were potlucks or barbecues at the Stegners'. And whenever a guest lecturer came to campus to speak to the creative writing students at Wallace's invitation, the seminar students, along with English department faculty, were invariably invited to a dinner or reception honoring the visitor.

On the one hand, Stegner could be very human with his students, admitting to them his doubts and problems as he worked on a project, occasionally reading to them something of his own to try it out and ask for suggestions. "Despite his reserved nature," recalled writer Jim Houston, "he had a way of letting you into his life." There was also in his approach a certain amount of humility. In looking back, Wallace has reflected, "I think I got more understanding of technical possibilities after I began to teach the Advanced Writing Seminar here. People were very good and were doing interesting things. I learned from my students." On the other hand, although he wanted to connect with his students and lead them to understand he, too, faced writing problems, at a certain point he would draw back from too much familiarity. He did not feel comfortable with the role of father-confessor that some professors are willing to undertake, and while he was concerned about such things as his students' finances, he did not want to hear about their deeply personal problems. One former student remembered seeing him, during a conference with a writing student who was always complaining about one thing or another and giving excuses for work that had not been turned in, pulling a sign out of his desk drawer that read, WHY NOT TRY JESUS?

In the early years of the workshops, Wallace would pick out two manuscripts to read aloud himself and then ask for comment; later, he assigned specific meetings for the students to read their own work aloud and he did the reading only occasionally. He always made it clear to his classes that he could not teach them to write; all he could do was create the circumstances and atmosphere in which their learning was possible. Boris Ilyn, who was in Stegner's first few classes at Stanford, remembered that there was nothing exceptional about his method—it was a rather standard creative writing pattern. "But it was simply his personality and character" that made the class exceptional. He would read a student's story aloud, but "it was the way that he read it. He reads very well, without too much tonal inflection, just enough to get it right. . . . a very controlled manner of presentation, so that you get the feeling. . . . It comes out in a very dramatic way." And then he would ask questions, no leading questions whatsoever, just "What do you think?" and if someone would say, "Well, I don't think that the ending comes off very well," he would say, "Why not?" "It was," in Ilyn's view, "a very democratic way of teaching. He wasn't telling anything. He was drawing it out of us." Stegner had a great knack for drawing people out, getting the best out of everybody and "carrying the discussion in such a way that it was creative. He invisibly pressed [the class session] into a certain shape and then at the end or somewhere along the line, he would make his point or he would have led us to make the point he had in mind."

There were many reasons for Stegner's success as a teacher, and certainly a lot of hard work was at the bottom of it all. Many teachers of creative writing today let their classes run themselves, so that the teacher is not required to put in any preparation—not at all the Stegner method. He read everything and commented in detail in writing on everything and carefully prepared so that each workshop session would deal with a writing problem in such a way that all the students might learn from the discussion. Also his success was due in part to the fact that he had thought a lot about writing technique and had written much about it, and he had the confidence provided by his own success to create a nonauthoritarian, noncompetitive atmosphere. But his teaching was not always totally inductive and Socratic. James D. Houston, who attended the workshop a decade after Ilyn in the late 1950s, recalled that after each student in turn responded to the manuscript that he had been read aloud, Stegner himself would comment on the comments and on the manuscript, and "in his comments, he had a storehouse of maxims, of writerly wisdom that he could draw on to apply to nearly any particular writing problem." Then, too, much of his success might be attributed to the example he provided. On one occasion a student complimented him on his prose in a story he had published, and Stegner replied, "You should have seen the first draft"—the lesson was clear.

However, he wasn't callous to the problems, particularly problems of time and finances, faced by most of his students. Throughout his years at Stanford he went out of his way to find teaching jobs for his students while they were at the university and after they left. If teaching jobs were not available for students, he often managed to arrange something else—as reader or research assistant or to work around his house to help with building or landscaping. Boris Ilyn recalls that he and two other students were given jobs of last resort, to dig a hole for the Stegner water tank. The adobe was so hard that after a day with pick and shovel they had only penetrated a couple of inches below the surface. Wallace gave up on the idea of putting the tank below ground, and the three young men pooled their pay, bought a bottle of champagne, and went back to the Stegners' to have a party.

Wallace did everything possible to promote the students he believed in, not only getting them jobs, but getting them scholarships and grants, and finding them markets for their stories and publishers for their novels. After his first year at Stanford, he was so impressed with Eugene Burdick and another student, Jean Byers, that he took them to Bread Loaf with him as fellows during the summer of 1946, and when he came back, he brought with him to Stanford two fellows that had impressed him at Bread Loaf. Another boost to students was the inauguration of the *Stanford Short Stories*, which Stegner arranged to have published annually by the university press. Publication in this volume (there were fifteen volumes, from 1946 to 1964) became a prize awarded to outstanding students, an actual publication that each one could aim for. Stories by both Burdick and Byers were included in the first volume.

Needless to say, Stegner was very relieved when the much-needed Stanford fellowships were established for the fall of 1947. That spring Mary Stegner called Boris Ilyn and his wife, Edda, to ask if she and Wallace could drop by for a few minutes. This was very unusual, Edda recalled, and somewhat surprised, she said, "Well yes, of course." When they arrived:

> Boris came out from his little room where he was working and Wally, and Mary came in, and we all sat down on the pretend divan, which was really a double bed with slip covers. We made conversation, and then after awhile, Wally said, "Oh, Yes ..." We were all standing up, and he said, "Sit down, because I am about to tell you something, and when Mary heard this when we were your age, she immediately had a baby ... so you had better sit down!" And so he told Boris that he had received one of the fellowships.

Boris got the very first fellowship for a novel—a novel, when it was completed, that was published because of Stegner's recommendation.

Wallace started on research for a new novel of his own, beginning with letters of inquiry in the spring of 1946 (about the same time that he started on the manuscript of *Second Growth*) and continuing with library- and fieldwork through 1948. This research was for *The Preacher and the Slave*, a fictional treatment of the life of Joe Hill, the IWW (Industrial Workers of the World) labor martyr, a project in which Stegner was able to use his skills as an academic researcher and historian, as well as novelist. The song "The Ballad of Joe Hill" was apparently much on his mind during this period, since many remember him singing it at parties. The first stanza runs:

> I dreamed I saw Joe Hill last night
> Alive as you and me.
> Says I "But Joe, you're ten years dead—"
> "I never died," says he.
> "I never died," says he.

(The ballad was sung, for the first time, at the IWW memorial service for Hill in Chicago on November 25, 1915.) Another factor that may have drawn Stegner to the story was that at the end of his life Hill lived in Salt Lake City, Wallace's "hometown," and the family of a close friend of Stegner's had a store very near the store in which Hill had committed the crimes for which he was finally executed.

The story of Joseph Hillstrom seems to have been ready-made for someone of Stegner's background and interests. Hillstrom was in several ways like Wallace's father—an outlaw who was self-centered, manipulative of others, hot-tempered, and most of all, a rugged individualist—in the extreme. And beyond that, Hillstrom seems to have stood in Stegner's mind as a symbol of all the Western bad men, gunslingers, and holdup artists who had been glorified and immortalized in story and song. All his life and in much that he wrote, he pursued the theme of demythologizing the West, of exposing the reality of its history and its people, as well as the reality of the land itself. The gunslinger was usually a despicable person, sometimes even a coward, who killed from ambush and victimized others who were weaker and vulnerable—hardly a hero. He was another variety of the "lone horseman" who, Stegner assures us over and over again, was not at the heart of the Western experience. This, of course, was not a message most readers wanted to hear, nor was a debunking of the Joe Hill myth. In this regard, the novel was ill-fated from the start. Wallace doesn't seem to have been as aware of the unpopular nature of his theme at this point in his career as he would become later. Toward the end of his life he was asked by an interviewer what the difference was between his West and the West of Louis L'Amour. He chuckled and replied, "About two or three million dollars."

His research took him to various locations around the country to interview the few remaining people who had known Hillstrom. Stegner got photostat copies of the trial transcript; he got copies of all of the articles in the *Salt Lake Tribune* and *Deseret News* dealing with the trial. He interviewed the ex-sheriff who had executed Hillstrom and the warden of the Utah Penitentiary, who walked Wallace through a mock execution "so that I would know imaginatively how a condemned and blindfolded man might feel in the very soles of his feet during his progress toward death." The experience, he recalled, "was kind of hair raising. He was a humane and touching man that warden. He hated capital punishment. [But] Utah ... that's a tough place. They like to hang or shoot people. . . . Anyway it curdled my blood for awhile." He revisited the scene of the crime, talked with the family of the two men Hill was accused of murdering during a holdup, and interviewed the Wobbly (IWW) editor who arranged Hill's public funeral in Chicago.

The novel did not begin in a spirit of debunking a myth. Since Stegner had great sympathy for the union movement and detested the red-baiting that had already started in Congress and around the country in the late 1940s, he began his project with great sympathy for Hill, trying to prove that he was indeed a martyr and, in the spirit of the song Wallace was so fond of, that his message lives on for all of us. But the further Wallace went with his research,

> the less I thought of him as a legitimate martyr, you know? . . . I thought at least that he was probably guilty of the crime he was executed for. I thought probably if I had been on the jury, I wouldn't have voted to execute him, but I would have thought privately in my heart that he was guilty.

After the novel was published in 1950, "The Ballad of Joe Hill" had disappeared from his repertory of songs to be sung around a campfire. Even when he was requested to sing it, he would refuse.

The most notice his project received came not in response to the novel, but to the second of two articles he wrote before getting to the manuscript. In the first article, "I Dreamed I Saw Joe Hill Last Night," published in the spring 1947 issue of *Pacific Spectator*, he takes on details of the legend, first developed by Ralph Chaplin in an article for the *New Masses* shortly after Hill's execution. For example, Chaplin's source describes Hill as "soft-spoken, generous, mild, gentlemanly. He neither smoked, drank, nor chased women." Stegner's sources refute this idealized picture, stating that Hill drank and got at least one woman "into trouble," as they used to say, and one witness, who roomed with Hill during the summer of 1911, remembered Joe "as resembling a certain type of Western badman, with a pleasant manner, an immaculate exterior, and a lot of cold nerve." It is this description, with the weight on

"Western badman," that may well have tipped the scales in Stegner's mind.

But the furor, such as it was, came as a result of Wallace's second article, which appeared the following year in the *New Republic*: "Joe Hill: The Wobblies' Troubadour." Letters of protest flooded in, a selection of which were printed in the magazine, typically beginning, "Sir: I wish to protest the inclusion of Wallace Stegner's compilation of guess-work, imagination and outright falsehood in the *New Republic*." There is no fury like that of the adherent to a myth, scorned. The IWW organized a picket line of protest that marched back and forth in the snow on the sidewalk outside the offices of *The New Republic* in New York.

But the angry letters and picketing did not stir enough interest to produce large sales for the novel, and there were somewhat fewer reviews than Stegner had received for recent novels. It may be that the media thought the material was too limited by sectional interest, or it may be that the novel's somber subject and predictably unhappy ending did not inspire much enthusiasm among book editors. Stegner himself felt in retrospect that a "proletarian novel published in 1950 was way out of date," but readers interested in the labor movement would hardly have cheered even if the novel had come out in the thirties. He has said that the response discouraged him from writing novels again for almost a decade, but that may overdramatize his reaction, and there were probably other reasons as well.

He seems to have been discouraged about his novel publication record as a whole for more than a year following *The Preacher and the Slave*. He wrote his agents in 1951, summarizing the sales figures for his career, and concluding:

What depresses me about these figures is not Remembering Laughter, which has certainly had all the success it deserved, or The Big Rock Candy Mountain, which did as well as I ever expected anything of mine to do. It is the decline and fall that bothers me. Of all the books I ever wrote, only two have sold ten thousand copies in the original edition. The last two novels have gone 8 and 6, in that order, though the last one [*The Preacher and the Slave*] was a major effort and I think a good book. . . . I have got some critical attention for short stories, not very much for novels. Neither has made me a living. On the Montgomery [British World War II Field Marshal Bernard Law Montgomery] theory that a commander should reinforce success, I have only the short stories to reinforce. I am tempted to say the hell with writing any more novels, and concentrate on trying to write a dozen stories in a year. Should I? . . . I wonder if I'm not just pounding sand down a rat hole writing novels. (9/17/51)

Another contributing factor may be, as Boris Ilyn has speculated, that Stegner put so much energy into his teaching that he was simply drained. Still, the decade of the fifties would see the publication of his long-in-progress Powell biography, as well as a number of short stories.

As a short story writer, Stegner's career can be seen as having two bursts of activity: from 1938 to 1943, during which he published eighteen stories; and 1947 to 1958, during which he published fifteen. With one exception, "The Women on the Wall" (1946), there was a hiatus for the last two years of the war and the year after while he struggled with the increased teaching load at Harvard, went to work for *Look*, and started his job at Stanford. By the mid-1950s, he had become known as a major practitioner of the form. As mentioned earlier, he had a string of inclusions in the annual *The Best American Short Stories* and several appearances in the *O. Henry Memorial Award Prize Stories*.

This was a period also when his stories were regularly included in general anthologies and in collections of stories aimed at schools and colleges. And it should be noted that these years also saw the publication of the first collection of his own short stories, *The Women on the Wall*, all of which had seen previous periodical publication and several of which had been incorporated into *The Big Rock Candy Mountain*.

One of the most revealing publications during Stegner's second burst of short story activity was an article titled "A Problem in Fiction," which appeared as the third in a series of essays on how writers write, in *The Pacific Spectator* in the fall of 1949. Usually, writers are loath to discuss their own creative processes in any detail. There may be some element of the magician unwilling to reveal his secrets, but there is also the problem of reconstructing a series of experiences that may not be very clear in the writer's own mind, so that the insights given in this article are not only rare for Stegner, but rare for writers in general.

In this article the story in question, "The Women on the Wall," was not one that mysteriously seemed to write itself, but one that had to be hewn out step by step by main force, thus fixing its progress in the writer's memory. The scene viewed by Mr. Palmer across a point overlooking the Pacific Ocean, of the Army and Navy wives lined up against a wall every day waiting for their mail, was a scene the author saw out his own study window. He had returned from New York to Santa Barbara to recover from an illness (the heart infection) and to rest up after his frantic days in the *Look* office finishing *One Nation*. Just out of habit he would go to his desk every morning, with no particular task in mind, and, he remembered,

> before two mornings had passed, what I really did in my study was watch that most beautiful, lulled, enchanted place above the blue and violet sea, with the frieze of bright, still women along the wall.
>
> I have no idea at what point I began to think of them as a story. It was simply apparent after awhile that I felt them with the clarity and force of a symbol, and that I wanted to write them. But you do not write a picture. You do not even write a "situation."

He was on his way to writing a story—he had a place, a group of people, a situation, even a classical parallel (Penelope waiting for Ulysses)—but he had no idea what the story was going to be about.

He tried to force action on the women, but that didn't work; he tried bringing in some invented suitors, following *Ulysses*, but they were out of place; and then he tried a kind of Grand Hotel scheme, following each woman and her husband to a conclusion, but that got to be too long and complicated. Then it became clear to him "that these women fascinated me precisely because they did nothing but wait" and that he should concentrate on the effects of waiting on them and that there should not be a single line of action, but a series of uncoverings:

> The problem, I finally began to see, was not to make action out of this picture, but by moving the picture slightly to reveal what was

hidden behind it. This story would develop, certainly, not as a complication resolved but as what Henry James called a "situation revealed."

And if revealed, it must be revealed to someone. I had already tried, with a dismal sense of failure, to get at these women from the inside. In the end I adopted the point of view that was at once easiest and most natural—my own, the viewpoint of the external observer.

This persona, Mr. Palmer, tries to make acquaintance with the women and is rebuffed. The author needed something to bring him close to them again, and fate provided him with a real-life incident in the form of a cocker spaniel that appeared one day tied to a tree, barked and howled, and then at sunset mysteriously disappeared. Stegner brought the dog into the story and used it not only as a means to bring Palmer into the company of the women, but to lead to a characterization of one of the women, Mrs. Kendall, and to symbolically represent "the way everybody in the story, adult, child, or dog, was tied down helplessly and no relief for it." Through another woman, Mrs. Corson, who gets high on marijuana and becomes talkative, the conditions of the other women are exposed to Palmer, and the "idyllic and wistful picture [he] started with has been violently shoved aside and the turmoil of suffering and frustrated humanity it has covered is revealed."

What is most interesting in this description is the interplay of experience and imagination to the creative process, how the original scene—the smell of pine and eucalyptus and wood smoke and kelp; the sound of the surf on the beach; and the sight of the women, waiting quietly and patiently for the mail—stimulated the writer. First, he was reminded of literary parallels, Keats's "Ode on a Grecian Urn" and then Penelope on the rocky isle of Ithaca above the wine-dark sea. In both cases a situation very dramatic was encapsulated, waiting to be revealed by the poet's imagination. Second, he was led to realize that he, too, must stay with the picture and by moving it slightly, "reveal what was hidden behind it."

Many details came to him out of ongoing (the barking dog) or recent experience (Mrs. Corson smokes marijuana because having just interviewed Mexican youths in Los Angeles, he "had marijuana on [his] mind"). In regard to such details, he notes that

> so much of what attaches itself or insinuates itself when one is making a story is purest accident; the story growing in the mind becomes a kind of flypaper that catches everything light, everything loose.

As readers or critics, we are all too likely to think of the essence of a story and its details as the result of a much more conscious and deliberate process than is actually the case. We see connections, an underlying pattern, and we just assume that in writing a particular text, the author does the same—consciously seeking to apply "his theme" to a particular occasion.

It never seems to have occurred to Stegner in looking back on the composition of this story that his theme here, the revelation of stark reality behind romantic appearances, was a very common one in his work. He didn't start with that as a goal, but came to it after a struggle, unconsciously, just as he didn't start out to expose the real Joseph Hillstrom behind the myth. What seems to be fundamental to his process was an attitude—a skepticism, a suspicion of smooth exteriors, and conviction that there is always more to a situation than appears on the surface, and indeed he says at one point in his essay, "I thought that their [the women's] quiet could not possibly be more than skin-deep, that beneath their muted surface must be a seethe and dart of emotion like a school of small fish just under the unbroken surface of water." It was a similar conviction that of course tied together such disparate authors of the Realistic Period as Henry James and Mark Twain, Edith Wharton and Theodore Dreiser. In this respect, one can see "The Women on the Wall" as a clear precursor to *Angle of Repose* and *The Spectator Bird*. Both of his prizewinning novels are novels of discovery.

What is more common for the writer than laboriously carving a story out of a still picture is going through an experience that in itself is the basis for a story. The difficulty in this case is recognizing it as such. Two of his best stories of this period, from the late forties through the fifties, depict dramatic moments in his own life: "The City of the Living"

(1954) and "The Traveler" (1951). Both took an approach unusual for Stegner up to this time—the dramas were essentially internal, tracing the emotions and thoughts of a "self" character to external circumstances.

"The City of the Living," which won an O. Henry Award in 1955, is a powerful account of a father's worry and dread during a night of vigil over a critically ill young son in a foreign country. It is based on an incident that happened in Luxor, Egypt, while the Stegners were on a seven-month trip around the world for the Rockefeller Foundation, beginning in September 1950. The purpose of the trip was to establish a postwar connection between the writers of the East—particularly Japan, India, and the Philippines—and the West, and to encourage the mutual exchange of literatures. Stegner has summarized the trip by saying that they spent

> six weeks in England, Germany, France, Italy, and Egypt [which] gave us a look at the wreckage of the war. That was followed by five months, as strenuous as if I had been an American politician running hard for office, in India, Thailand, the Philippines, and Japan. Sometimes I lectured five or six times a day. We spent a week at Rabindranath Tagore's ashram at Santiniketan, in Bengal; we talked to writers in Bombay, Hyderabad, Bangalore, Mysore, Delhi, Calcutta, Bangkok, Manila, Tokyo. I wrote articles for *The Reporter* and other magazines, and I got . . . several short stories out of the trip. For two years after our return I was involved in a program to introduce Asian writers to American readers.

When the Rockfeller Foundation asked him to go to Asia, he told them he would be glad to, but only if his wife could go with him, so in order to pay for her ticket, the foundation appointed Mary as well. This left Page. The Stegners had a piece of property that they had purchased years earlier when they lived in Salt Lake, and they managed to sell it for $1,500, which was enough to buy a ticket for Page. After traveling through Europe and Egypt, they spent nearly two months in India, which, as Mary recalled, was "interesting, but very, very saddening." They were not able to make any serious literary contacts there, however, nor in Thailand. In Japan, however, a number of contacts were already in place. Their friend Ben Page and other Stanford people were there in connection with the postwar rebuilding effort, and the Stegners were lucky enough to get as their guide a professor from prestigious Keio University, a school with strong ties to Stanford.

Among the writers they met was Yasunari Kawabata, who would later win the Nobel Prize. He invited them to dinner at his home, where they sat on cushions around a sunken charcoal fire. It was winter, with no heating, so they sat with their feet near the charcoal and were given comforters to wrap around their upper bodies. Their guide, Professor Hiramatso, took them to the Kabuki Theater and then backstage to meet some of the actors, and he also arranged for the Stegners, along with Virginia Page, to have luncheon at the home of Mikimoto, overlooking the Sea of Japan. Mikimoto was the one who had developed the cultured pearl industry, and because of his wealth and entrepreneurial acumen, he had become a revered national hero. Since Stanford's first president, David Starr Jordan, who was a marine biologist, had done some of the background investigation leading to the cultured pearl process, Mikimoto was particularly gracious and welcoming to the Stegners. At the luncheon he had placed a favor on Mary's plate of a pearl necklace, which Wallace found amusing, thinking back on the legend of old Mr. Rockefeller passing out dimes. After returning to the States, Stegner arranged for Kawabata to be published in *The Atlantic*, and he remained in contact with him for many years, but their correspondence was broken off by Kawabata's tragic suicide in 1972.

On his return Wallace continued his work in behalf of Asian writers. Just as he spent nearly two years, unpaid and simply prompted by his conscience, giving speeches about racism in America after he finished *One Nation*, so once again, prompted by his sense that we needed in the postwar world to build bridges to other cultures overseas, he spent a considerable amount of time giving speeches and arranging exchanges, trying to enlarge our awareness of Asian literature. Of the six articles he published the year after he returned, 1951, all six came out of his trip and half of those were part of his effort to spread the word about the writers and their works that he had encountered in the Far East.

Aside from the hectic schedule of speeches and meetings during much of their journey, it had been a marvelous experience for the Stegners, "the first trip," Mary has said, "that opened up the world to us." But the counterbalance to this was their son Page's unhappy life much of the time while accompanying them. He had, according to his own testimony, "from the age of 13 or 14 ... just decided to be rebellious and silent—a non-speaking, non-reactive son, and whatever they wanted me to do I did the opposite." Wallace did his best to become a different father to his son than his own father had been for him, to exercise patience and understanding. But the one thing he did feel was important was that his son learn the value of hard work, and inevitably there were scenes of a sullen lack of cooperation and an angry response. Part of the problem was that Wallace set a standard of work and behavior so high that his son felt always insufficient. And another part of the problem may have been loneliness, something the father, who looked back on his own childhood summers alone on the homestead as a valuable experience, might not have had enough sympathy for.

On the many trips the Stegners took throughout the West, Page was often the only child among several adults, and the months that the Stegners traveled around the world were difficult for him. Because he could not be taken to many of the dinners and receptions his parents were invited to, he was often left behind in a hotel room to eat room-service food and find amusement as he could. One night, in a hotel room at the Taj in Bombay, he was lying on his bed, idly throwing small objects at the overhead fan that was circulating on a hot night, when he hit one of the blades and broke it. It flew out the window and down onto the terrace outside—fortunately, it hit no one, but it created quite a stir among the hotel staff, several of whom stormed up to confront him in his room. One of the reasons Page was left behind more than usual, presumably to rest, was that he had become very ill with typhoid in Egypt near the beginning of their trip, and although the fever had broken and he was on the road to recovery, weakness and episodes of nausea had stayed with him.

The night the fever came to a climax and broke is the basis for his father's story "The City of the Living." Wallace wrote to Phil and Peg Gray from Egypt to report the actual events:

All through Europe, when we're fooling around, we stay healthy. The minute it comes time to work, Page comes down with typhoid, and here we stick. Fortunately, thanks to Chloromycetin, typhoid is no longer its old self.... All last night, while I was sitting up ladling pills into poor Page, the muezzin kept howling from his minaret and every dog and jackal in upper Egypt howled back, and about dawn a baboon or some goddam thing climbed on the balcony and yelled bloody murder. But what a fine river is the Nile and what a picturesque character is the fellaheen. (11/6/50)

Reported so matter-of-factly, these were the events out of which the story, written three years later, would grow. Always the reticent and uncomplaining Westerner, Stegner never in his letters—or conversation, for that matter—reveals the true depth of his emotions. These he saves for his stories, and even there they are often stowed in inconspicuous suitcases that await unpacking by the reader.

Although it is one of Stegner's most personal stories, the central character, Robert Chapman, has little in common with the author. One change is particularly significant: he is divorced and therefore must face this crisis alone. The illness of his son, the outside crisis, is only the beginning, the occasion that forces a crisis internally wherein Chapman must acknowledge his past sins and his present aloneness and helplessness. This is a frequent process in Stegner fiction—self-examination, which leads to self-acknowledgment, which in turn leads to a revelation promising possible change. Often in his fiction, as here, it is not what the central character does that counts, but the experience that he undergoes and the actions by others that he observes that become the catalyst for enlightenment.

In this short story we undergo with Chapman a long night of the soul, a vigil during which he must confront the choices he has made and the self he has created. While there are only a few overt references to religion, there are overtones that suggest this is a religious experience—the night of prayer and fasting that a novitiate must endure before the priesthood or a squire must pass through before being knighted. One such overtone is the sense that although the father puts his faith in antibiotics (if he had to pray to something, that is what, he decides, he would have to pray to), he is haunted by a primitive fear of the unknown and comes to a realization that the struggle between life and death takes place in a zone beyond his control, beyond even his understanding, something that as a person who has always striven to control his circumstances makes him profoundly uneasy.

The boy's life and death are balanced on a knife blade, leading to new definitions for the father of both life and living, death and dying. The story is framed in such fundamental contrasts throughout—light and dark, American and foreign, familiar and strange, safe and risky, modern and ancient, clean and dirty—until both the external (the illness of the boy) and internal (the fear and dread of the father) conflicts are resolved, and with the dawn, the "city of the dead" turns into the "city of the living."

Chapman is a wealthy, self-centered, worldly San Francisco attorney, a member of exclusive clubs, a play-it-safe conservative who takes out plenty of insurance—he not only has insurance, he *likes* insurance—and who, along the same lines, has packed a special bag for medical emergencies overseas. He is a man who doesn't want to take the smallest emotional risks—he was even glad when his wife left him. He may remind us of a Stegner character, Mr. Burns, in another story that came out of the Rockefeller trip, "Something Spurious from the Mindanao Deep." Burns, too, considers anything foreign as possibly dangerous—will not, for instance, eat the Filipino food—and his unwillingness to take risks seems to rob him of life. But unlike Chapman, Burns does not show the promise of change but ends where he began, as we see in the final metaphor with its potent imagery:

When the gimlet was on the table before him and its penetrating lime odor was rising to his nostrils as clean as the sniff of Benzedrine from an inhaler, he fished from his shirt pocket the envelope he carried there, and out its assortment of pills and capsules selected an iron pill, a multi-vitamin capsule, and a concentrated capsule of vitamin C.

It is clear that in the author's mind, this is not living. And it may be that since both these stories deal with the risks, physical and emotional, that these travelers in a foreign country are loath to take, a conflict in Stegner's mind over his own touristlike timidity would seem to have bothered him during his year abroad. More important, however, was his ability to make of this conflict, so common to Americans overseas, a complex metaphor for the risks one must take and the commitment one must make in order for love—and living—to become possible.

In "The City of the Living" the father is seen in the lit bathroom of a hotel with his son lying sick in the adjoining bedroom. The opening time is the oncoming of darkness, and the night signals a time of crisis in his son's fever. All around him seems threatening—the dark, the foreign city, and the noises that suggest that something is looking into the room from the trees outside. He looks with horror at the way the disease had wasted his son in little more than a day, and "he drew into his lungs the inhuman, poisonous stench of the sickness. That was the moment when it first occurred to him that the boy could die." He tries to keep busy and occupy his mind by writing bills and postcards—but he realizes there is no one to whom he can write a letter, not about his real feelings at this moment. "I am just beginning to realize that here or anywhere else I am almost completely alone. I have spent my life avoiding entanglements."

Early in the morning he dozes off and then awakes with a start at five-thirty, feeling guilty. His arm aches from a booster shot, and as he takes a drink of water from the carafe, "the chlorine bite of the halazone tablets gagged him. The effort, the steady, unrelieved, incessant effort that it took in this place to stay alive! He looked at his haggard, smudged face in the mirror and he hated Egypt with a kind of ecstasy." But when he checks on his son, he finds the crisis is over, and it is almost dawn. He is greatly relieved—exultant. Suddenly his perceptions change. Everything looks better. He looks out across the river at the City of the Dead, which the night before seemed so threatening, and sees that it "was innocent and clean now, and the river that when they first came had seemed to him a dirty, mud-banked sewer looked different too."

It is at this point, near the end of the story, that Chapman has a vision that brings to him a realization, joining life and death. Safe now, and relieved of anxiety, he looks down out his window as "all the Nile's creatures, as inexhaustible as the creatures of the sea, began to creep and crawl and fly," watching them from "his little cell of sanitary plumbing, and on his hands as he held the binoculars to his eyes he smelled the persistent odor of antiseptic." He looks out, receptive for the first time to that which is outside his antiseptic circle—a metaphor that extends from the physical to the emotional. He looks down and sees one of the ragged boys who takes care of the garden paths and sees him wash and pray:

> Yet the praying boy was not pathetic or repulsive or ridiculous. His every move was assured, completely natural. His touching of the earth with his forehead made Chapman want somehow to lay a hand on his bent back.
>
> They have more death than we do, Chapman thought. Whatever he is praying to has more death in it than anything we know.
>
> Maybe it had more life too.

This boy, of course, is also his boy—as well as all mankind—as we face the darkness of our limitations and the forces of nature, forces that a ring of antiseptic can hardly begin to forestall. We know that Chapman will not change his entire lifestyle, revise all his beliefs, such as they are, or values, but we do believe at the end that he becomes a little more connected to other men and to the earth, that in some way he is better for his experience. The gradual movement in this story toward enlightenment and self-knowledge may well have been a technique that Stegner learned from the story writer he admired most: "Chekhov had a way of turning up the rheostat, little by little . . . Joyce called it an epiphany. Katherine Mansfield called it a nuance."

"The City of the Living" is a very complex, rich, and moving story that would seem to have been generated out of the very depths of its author's soul, out of a terror that he could not report directly even to his closest friends. It seems to be able, like tragedy, to inspire pity and fear, as we become aware along with Chapman of being surrounded by the omnipresent threat of fate.

11

FROM SHORT STORY WRITER TO ENVIRONMENTALIST

"The City of the Living" underlines a theme common to much of Stegner's fiction and that can be found from his first full-length novel, *On a Darkling Plain*, to his last, *Crossing to Safety*: life is hard and unpredictable, and in order to survive, people need the support, physically and emotionally, of others. Stegner's *Collected Stories* (1990) closes with "The City of the Living" and opens with another story that came out of his experience, "The Traveler" (1951), which also deals with the need to reach out to others within a threatening environment. It concerns a pharmaceutical salesman whose car breaks down at night out in the country, in the snow. At first he waits for a passing car, but none comes, and he decides to walk and look for a farmhouse. But having set out to find help for himself, he is the one who must give help when he finally reaches a farm and finds a boy, anxious and desperate, whose grandfather has fallen ill.

The situations in the two stories are roughly parallel, as both protagonists find themselves thrust by fate into fearful life-or-death situations that they find difficult to believe. Chapman is "overcome by a feeling almost like terror at how strange this all was.... The darkened room next door was real to him, and this bathroom with its iron shutters open to night and the mosquitoes, but their reality was an imprecise reality of nightmare." In "The Traveler" the salesman thinks of where he should be—comfortably bathed, fed, and in his warm hotel room. He thinks, "For all of this to be torn away suddenly, for him to be stumbling up a deserted road in danger of freezing to death, just because some simple mechanical part that had functioned for thirty thousand miles refused to function any longer, this was outrage, and he hated it."

But just as Chapman has a transformation of attitude with the breaking of dawn and looks out, feeling a kinship with the boy in the garden below, so does the salesman experience a change from terror to radiance with the appearance of the moon. This is a moment of enlightenment, of "warmth"—he is about to be taken out of his need to be rescued into the role of rescuer. In a moment the entire perspective is changed; both stories are in part about perception—how we see things and why. As he approaches the farmhouse, he encounters the boy stumbling out of a barn, where he had been hitching a horse to a sleigh to get help. In this meeting with the boy, Chapman seems to meet himself at the same age. The kitchen is familiar in all its smells: "The ways a man fitted in with himself and with other human beings were curious and complex." As he takes the sleigh to get help at the Hill farm, two miles down the road, he "looked back once, to fix forever the picture of himself standing silently watching himself go. . . . For from the most chronic and incurable of ills, identity, he had looked outward and for one unmistakable instant recognized himself."

Identity—that prison that locks us away from others, and the only key, as T. S. Eliot has said, is sympathy. Nowadays we would be more likely to use "empathy," a quality that suddenly emerges out of darkness into radiance in both stories to draw each central character out of himself and self-concern to embrace a stranger. The quality that both men achieve in small measure is most fully expressed by a character in Stegner's later fiction, Marian Catlin in *All the Little Live Things*. She is nearly saintly, a difficult character for any realistic writer to present credibly, as he points out in his "Letter, Much Too Late" to his mother after her death. Marian is a nurturer, a person closely connected to all the little live things, always concerned about others, always tolerant of the foibles and mistakes of her neighbors. It is her spirit that Stegner seems to cling to, as he clings always to the spirit of his mother, a spirit that can give us some hope for the future of mankind and of the earth. For, as he says in his essay "The Book and the Great Community":

> No risk, as Josiah Royce once said, is ever private or individual, and no accomplishment is merely personal. What saves us at any level of human life is union, mutual responsibility, what St. Paul called charity.

The experience that triggered "The Traveler" came to him a decade before the writing while he was staying with the Grays in Vermont on a Christmas skiing trip. "It was," he recalled, "about 20 below, everyone had the flu, the car wouldn't start, and I had to walk about two miles to town . . . to get some help." As he walked through "a magical kind of moonlight," he was reminded of his own childhood in Saskatchewan—suddenly he was transported back in time. He felt he had done this before and he had been "here" before. In the story as he walks in the starlight, "Something long buried and forgotten tugged in him, and a shiver not entirely from cold prickled his whole body with gooseflesh. There had been times in his childhood when he had walked home alone and had been temporarily lost in nights like this. . . . He felt spooked." In discussing the story in front of a group shortly after *Collected Stories* was published, he explained that this and his other stories "are places where I have paused more or less to understand something that happened." How could his experience of recognizing a feeling from childhood be translated into a story about a medicine supply salesman whose car breaks down on a lonely country road? "Don't trust the details," he replied, "trust the feeling."

A longtime friend from graduate school, Stuart Brown, once described Stegner as a man who "loved books, loved parties, and loved to laugh." By the time of his forties in the 1950s, Wallace had sobered a bit, perhaps, but still loved all of those things, and despite a certain reserve by both husband and wife, the Stegners were very active socially and politically. They were activists in one neighborhood group after another dedicated to maintaining or improving the local environment. The earliest was the Peninsula Housing Association, with Mary serving on its board; and when the planned community in Ladera failed, they worked for the Page Mill Road Association, a group that tried to limit and shape development in their area of Los Altos Hills. Wallace was elected president and went door to door with petitions to the county supervisors. This was followed by the Committee for Green Foothills, which he helped found and which made him its honorary president, a group that over several decades fought to maintain open space and limit development in the region. In looking back on the group's activities, he has said:

> We were trying to save them [the foothills] from county carelessness. . . . The county seat was down in San Jose, a long way off, and nobody gave a damn about the foothills down there. The developers were doing pretty much as they pleased. We operated primarily to keep a sharp citizen's watch on planning commissions and town council meetings.

The group, often with Stegner's help, won some battles over the years, preserving enough areas of green so that, as he was able to put it in his speech on the twenty-fifth anniversary of the organization, even "your enemies . . . have benefited from your work."

Wallace not only gave his name to be used by Green Foothills and to Hidden Villa, a nature preserve and camp for underprivileged and disabled children, he gave of his time, serving on boards, speaking or writing when called on. At community meetings he did not speak often, but when he did, he always had mastered the facts. Friends remember him speaking with a very deliberate voice, the essence of reasonableness, never any table-pounding or shouting, but sometimes giving his listeners a sense that behind his calm was a good deal of emotion, controlled and suppressed. He could be very convincing. Once, however, his emotions did almost get the best of him when Mary along with the rest of the board for the Peninsula Housing Association were being pushed around by one member who wanted to run everything. In a firmer voice than usual, and with some heat, Wallace got up and told him off—but indirectly and with the courtesy he would not abandon even when he was upset.

Many of Wallace and Mary's friends were from these community groups. And while they had friends from the English faculty—in particular, the Scowcrofts, Simpsons, and later, Nancy Packer—several of their closest friends came from other Stanford departments as a result of associations formed in groups like the Palo Alto Building Association. Unlike those professors who tend to stick with their own immediate colleagues, Wallace enjoyed associating with faculty out of various disciplines. Two such friends were the Chodorows, Marvin and Leah. Marvin's appointment to the university was in applied physics and electrical engineering. Two others were Kenneth and Selma Arrow—Kenneth became a Nobel Prize winner in economics.

They all worked together on local issues, worked for the campaign of Adlai Stevenson in 1952, and belonged to the Sierra Club together. Early in their acquaintance, they began playing badminton together, first at the Arrows' house in Ladera and then, when the Chodorows moved nearby and had built a badminton court, they played there. It became a customary get-together that began with Sunday lunch and went on to a series of doubles games. Wallace and Mary often would not show up until he had put in some time at the typewriter, even on a Sunday morning. The tradition lasted for more than twenty years. Once Wallace had transferred his allegiance from tennis to badminton, he became the spark plug of the group and was largely responsible for keeping it going.

Another activity that this group had—not always together at the same time—was to go up to tour the High Sierra Camps in upper Yosemite. There are a series of a half-dozen tent-platform camps, about six or seven miles apart, in the high country that required only that you bring a change of clothes and a toothbrush. Nearly everything else—food, showers, and bed—were supplied, a perfect setup for those, like the Chodorows, who were basically city people. Wallace took it upon himself to make the reservations (a year in advance) and then lead the party. He was, when called upon, a reservoir of information—it was like having your own park ranger, a ranger with wit and humor. It was always he who would get up in the morning to light a fire, and in the evening he might contribute to the entertainment with a recitation of "The Face on the Bar Room Floor" or "The Cremation of Sam McGee."

Another activity that brought the Stegners friends was Mary's music. She played violin with several groups, but most particularly with the

Stanford Orchestra. The Stegners became quite close to the director, Sandor Salgo, professor of music and conductor of the Stanford and San Jose symphonies, and his wife, Priscilla. The music department had numerous recitals, and friends can remember occasions, after they had attended such a recital with the Stegners on an afternoon, when they would go up to the Stegner house in the hills for supper. It was common for the Stegners to attend concerts in San Francisco. At first they went regularly to North Beach for dinner before the symphony, but neither of them liked going out to dinner, dealing with the problems of parking and getting a table, so Mary began packing picnic dinners. They would park the car at Land's End overlooking the Golden Gate, or in the Golden Gate Park overlooking Stow Lake, or at the Palace of the Legion of Honor and eat their dinner in the car, watching the sunset. If it was Wilbur Schramm in graduate school at Iowa who began Wallace's education in serious music, it was Mary who continued and refined it. Not only did she play herself, first on the violin and then, after a shoulder operation, on the piano, but they had a good record collection from which she would select works of classical music to play for them before bed. Wallace's education in the arts extended in other directions as well. Since he felt it was important to illustrate the Powell book (he felt that the changing styles and approaches of the artists well illustrated our changing perceptions of the West), he became an expert on the early painters of Western landscapes.

The Stegners' was a wonderful house for entertaining. As one observer put it,

> the house ... blended quietly into its surroundings with a low-slung, Frank Lloyd Wright sensibility. A broad wooden deck has been cut in the middle to embrace a live oak, and the house's enormous windows open in every direction, bringing bright sunlight.

It was not an overly large house, but had a spacious living room with an open-beam ceiling and easy access through glass doors to a long brick terrace, adjoining the wooden deck, which could take the overflow of guests. It was here that the Stegners often served drinks to their guests before dinner parties, where they could, in the early years, sit and enjoy an unimpeded view of the nearly wild foothills beyond. Wallace was

proud of his terrace, writing to the Grays in the fall of 1949, just after the
house had been finished:

> We have had a lot of unseasonable warm weather, beautiful late
> September weather, and one good rain, so that the hills are all get-
> ting misty green and beginning to look like Vermont again outside
> our front window, and the scars of bulldozers around our house are
> beginning to heal over with weeds. We're sitting here now just at
> sunset with all the doors open, and right outside the window . . . the
> hundred beautiful bricks I laid in the terrace this afternoon. That
> makes about 4,375, and only three thousand to go. (11/20/49)

Still another activity that brought them friends and brought their
family closer together was horseback riding. They ended up belonging to
the Los Altos Trail Club. It all started with Page. He wanted a horse, and
so, hoping to encourage any kind of positive activity on his part, they
bought him one, which they kept at the stables on campus—expensive
and not very convenient, but the only choice they had at the time. This,
in turn, added another reason to their decision to build out in the
country. They wanted enough land so they could keep a horse. Then the
whole family got involved during the summer of 1948 when they stayed
a month and a half at a dude ranch in Wyoming owned by Struthers
Burt, rancher, novelist, a conservation activist. Wallace wrote to Phil
Gray from the Three Rivers Ranch:

> A month . . . in this place has incapacitated us for habitation else-
> where. Apart from the quiet, which is profound, and the thinking
> which goes on, which is profounder, there are the Tetons, in sight
> from our windows and very beautiful indeed, and the horse trails
> which we ride six days a week up through the Grand Teton monu-
> ment and the back lakes. . . . We have been so stimulated by this
> environment that first we bought another horse, a dainty mare
> name of Trinket, for Mary to ride back in Palo Alto, and then . . .
> the forlorn Huckleberry Finn son of a somewhat dissolute cow-
> puncher, and lo we are taking him back to live with us, and maybe
> adopting him. Age seven, name Conrad.

Conrad was a bright and affable boy, pretty much left to his own devices, whom Page had befriended, and with the agreement of both the boy and his father, the Stegners brought him home with them as a companion for Page. They had thought of adopting him and giving Page a brother, but Conrad seemed to take over in the relationship and the Stegners decided after a year that he was not a good influence and, reluctantly and with regret, sent him back.

Mary remembered, during these years, the early fifties, Wallace coming home from the university, going down to the pasture, and catching Babe and Trinket (they ended up with three horses). Then they would ride off together. "All these hills were free then," she recalled somewhat wistfully, and "we had a key to the Lee property which is now the Palo Alto Park." All during their marriage, they were also great walkers. Virginia Page, whom the Stegners got to know in Japan on their Far Eastern trip, can remember that on many occasions either she or her husband would call the Stegners, or vice versa, on the spur of the moment, and they would hike out through the hills.

The period from the early fifties to the early sixties was not only one in which many short stories were published, it was also the period in which Stegner became fully dedicated to the environmental movement and helped define its goals. The crowning achievement of this dedication was *Beyond the Hundredth Meridian* (1954), a book that many have compared in its importance to Rachel Carson's *Silent Spring*. Although he began the project in the early forties while he was still at Harvard, the "big push," as one might call it, began in 1948 when he spent much of the year on research. During the summer the Stegners went on from Struthers Burt's ranch to Colorado, "to get some more Powell dope, and follow some Powell tracks around" (WS to Gray, 7/8/48). Stegner, earlier in his career, had expressed some admiration for Boulder Dam as "one of the world's wonders," but that summer, at Struthers Burt's, and while he was working on the book, he was also

listening attentively as Burt, Arthur Carhart of the Izaak Walton League, and DeVoto poured out their vigorous conviction that either dam [proposed at Split Mountain and at Echo Park] would flood significant portions of the monument [Dinosaur National Monument] to no good end whatsoever. By the end of the summer, he says, "I was pretty well back into the thick of things." [Since DeVoto was not there at the time, his preachment against the dams must have come to Wallace by letter.]

A grant gave him the time to spend part of the spring and the fall of the same year at the Huntington Library in San Marino (near Pasadena), where he wrote to the Grays in November:

The Huntington is a kind of scholarly paradise of a dull sort— beautiful and quiet and without incident, a lotus land. I write on Joe Hill till ten thirty, work at the library on Powell till four thirty, come home and write letters till dinner time, and read 19th century novels against the day when I have to teach them, in January. (11/20/48)

Research at the Huntington was supplemented by work at the Bancroft in Berkeley and by material sent to him from the Library of Congress, the National Archives, and the Geological Survey. He also corresponded extensively with other historians. Although he had done a great deal of research for *The Preacher and the Slave*, he had doubled or tripled that time and effort by the time *Beyond the Hundredth Meridian* was published in 1954. He knew he was writing an important book, and since he was not formally trained as a historian, he became very nervous about the job he was doing. As time went on, he began to fret about all the different related fields he had to master, all the things he should know that he didn't.

The historian he was most able to express his doubts to and ask questions of was his old friend Bernard DeVoto. In 1947 Stegner discovered that another writer had been working on Powell for several years, and he wrote in some alarm to DeVoto who replied:

I will find out what I can about your Mr._____and let you know what I find out. But you are a damsite sillier than you have given me any previous reason to believe if you let anybody or anybody's book stand between you and a subject which you chose yourself and for which God's providence obviously designed you. Suppose ten books in a row on Powell come out? We still want Stegner and Stegner still wants to write Powell. You can be quite sure that this bird will never get within sight of your coattails in either public performance or private estimation. (10/28/47)

By the end of 1951, Stegner was halfway through the manuscript when he wrote DeVoto about the problem of researching the illustrators of the time and about the maps that had been made on early expeditions to the West. In regard to the latter, he felt he had to make some sort of appraisal of Powell's job of organizing and extending the official mapping of the continental United States and needed to know something about the chaos that had preceded him: "If you can give me a few tips you can save me a hell of a lot of time and anguish, I suspect, and earn my enormous gratitude, for what it's worth" (12/31/51).

In a two-page single-spaced answer, DeVoto gave him leads to the illustrators, and then told him:

Most of your map problem will be easy too. The rest will be so God damned hard you'll wish you had stuck to fiction. . . . What makes it easy is that the Pacific RR *Reports* are studded with historical and analytical essays on the existing and earlier situation, and with lovely, lovely reproductions of maps it would take you forever to find by yourself. You simply sit on your can, make notes, and thank God for a time when West Point was an educational institution. . . . But beyond that and to fill in the chinks and to render the authoritative Stegner judgment, well, son, those are tears of pity you see on my cheeks. You're going to wish you'd paid your tithes. You are going to live for a long time in the best collection of maps you can handily reach. The Bancroft, I guess. Nobody has done this work for you, you've got to do it map by map, hypothesis by hypothesis, correction by correction. . . . Don't permit yourself to go chasing off in misconceptions beyond the thing immediately at hand. They fascinated me, I lost months on them, and they distort my book. Stick to your job and just say, hell, most of what they thought they knew was screwy.

It's easy, my boy, it's just looking at maps for ten years.

Oh, and being wrong about them. (1/13/52)

By the middle of May, Wallace was going back to put in footnotes (and cursing himself that he had not done so as he had been writing) and promised to send on a copy of the first part of the manuscript to DeVoto as soon as he could put together a readable version. But he would do so with misgivings:

I really am scared to death to let anybody see this, for some reason. Maybe I know the thing stinks. Maybe I'm scared of falling between two stools, not quite sure whether I'm writing for the twelve experts on Colorado River explorations, or for the great unwashed, or for the academic historians, or for you and Dale Morgan. Ah, well. (5/17/52)

After receiving and reading the first section of the book in manuscript, DeVoto replied to Stegner's letter, again at length, typically salting his encouragement with mock insult, while at the same time providing detailed suggestions:

You must be going through some previously undramatized part of your adolescence. I don't know that I ever saw a worse attack of literary megrims. Why, you God-damned idiot, this is a distinguished book, a fascinating book, and a very much needed book. For Christ's sweet sake! Stop beating your breast and earn some writer's cramp.... From my point of view, you are just now getting round to the guts of the book. We want every damned inch of them. And I charge you by the maidenhead of the sainted Brigham's seventeenth wife to give us the Report on the Lands of the Arid Region in full. The expression I have just used is, in full.... One principle: when you've got a climax, make it a climax. No point in putting a silencer on the gun when you shoot a sheriff. (7/7/52)

He went on to advise that Wallace must help the reader more by locating the ongoing event on the map whenever possible and constantly locating it in time "by heaving dates at him every couple of minutes." Also, he advised Wallace to tie his narrative to other people, places, and events the reader may be aware of. Then he concluded, "Don't be a damn fool, Wally. This is a fine book. Write it without qualms. If you want some qualms, go have a baby."

By May the following year, Stegner was more confident in the book, but angry at what he felt were stupid criticisms by his editor at Houghton Mifflin, who had suggested writing whole new chapters and reorganizing the others to bring a stricter chronology to the narrative. He had also suggested that Stegner include more personal biographical details about Powell. Wallace decided that he would rather someone like the Smithsonian publish the book for nothing than let it remain in hands that had treated it so doubtfully. He told DeVoto,

> my historical fears, at least, are reasonably allayed, first by you and since by Dale Morgan, who is lyrical, and Henry [Nash] Smith, who is soberly enthusiastic. Now I know who I was writing the damn book for: you and Henry and Dale. . . . I'll try to follow your urgings to the letter. . . . I will write in dates and more dates and make concrete the allusive. I will wrench chronology as much as seems necessary, and I will continue to ignore the home life, bathroom habits, and other minutiae of Major Powell. (5/3/53)

By summer he was largely through with the manuscript and his revisions, but would be struggling for months, off and on, with Houghton Mifflin in an effort to get the maps and illustrations done right. After all his research on illustrators of the western landscape, he hoped to be able to publish an article, perhaps a series of articles on "Thomas Moran and Other Early Recorders of Western Scenery" in *Life* or *Holiday*, but although his agents peddled the idea around to several publications, it went nowhere. A similar fate came to a little article related to the book, "Powell and the Names on the Plateau," that his agents tried to place but failed, so that he finally gave it to *Western Humanities Review*.

Writing the last chapters of the Powell book led him to think more and more about conservation, and with the urging of DeVoto, he expressed his fear of what the new Republican administration might permit to be done to public lands in "One-Fourth of a Nation: Public Lands and Itching Fingers" (1953) in *Reporter*. A few months later, early in 1954, he published "Battle for Wilderness" in *The New Republic*, which expressed many of the same fears about the administration, specifically in regard to plans for the proposed Echo Park dam, which would destroy Dinosaur Monument. He argued that

> the fact that Reclamation has picked these sites within the Monument, and plugged for them, suggests that perhaps it *wants* to infringe the sanctity of the parks. . . . It could build dams with a much freer hand and have to compromise less with other interests if it could break down the national park immunity. Something similar might be guessed of Secretary McKay: one who ponders the evidence might well conclude not only that Secretary McKay is willing to violate park territory, but he would like nothing better.

The year following *The New Republic* article, he published what turned out to be in effect the last of a series, "We Are Destroying Our National Parks" (1955), in the large-circulation *Sports Illustrated*, in which he makes many of the same arguments about the Echo Park dam. His main concern was that invasion of Dinosaur National Monument could be the first step in the destruction of the park system as a whole. The first of these articles convinced David Brower of the Sierra Club that Stegner was the right person to edit *This Is Dinosaur* (1955), the book which, distributed to every member of Congress, was, in Stegner's retrospective view in 1985, "an effective weapon in the first great conservation battle of recent times." It was certainly the first time that all the major conservation organizations had come together in one cause to show their muscle in a matter of pending legislation.

While waiting for the details and editing of the Powell book to be completed, Stegner not only wrote conservation articles and short stories, including "The City of the Living," but he started off on a new phase of a project he had been thinking about for some time, a sociological, historical, and anthropological study of small communities, how they evolve and how they shape their inhabitants. He had in mind investigating several villages in his own background as part of his long-standing campaign of self-discovery. His novel *Second Growth* had come

out of this interest—he thought of it as a fictionalized, informal sociological study of Greensboro. He would begin a new phase in the summer
of 1953 with a trip to his boyhood town of Eastend in Saskatchewan.
This would lead eventually to *Wolf Willow* (1962). He would follow this
the next year, 1954, with a trip to his maternal family's place of origin in
Norway, and an extended stay in Denmark, where he hoped to find a village that had been nearly unchanged over the centuries and see how that
lack of change may have affected the character of the inhabitants. He
gave up on his sociological-anthropological study of village life, but his
experiences in Denmark would lead eventually to *Spectator Bird* (1976).
There were hardly any of his experiences that did not lead to at least an
article or story, and sometimes to a book, although the meaning of his
experience as he would use it in a book might have to germinate and
develop in the back of his mind for a decade.

Wallace's problems with *Second Growth* convinced him that he
should return to Saskatchewan incognito. Before the trip, he had written
a two-page statement to his agents laying out his reasons for going and
what he hoped to learn, as a prospectus for their getting a commission
for one or more articles:

> I want to go back and spend a month or so seeing what forty years
> of the town's life have come to, and incidentally examining ...
> what the education it gave me amounts to now, in 1953. I want to
> see how a boyhood like that in a town like that fits a man for the
> twentieth century; I also want to see how a town on the bald-assed
> frontier, which was hit by the automotive revolution in its second
> year and whose patterns have had to change constantly to match a
> changing world, develops.... The changes wrought in half a
> lifetime in a frontier town seem to me interesting in themselves,
> because they put in a capsule much of the western, or even the
> American, experience. (5/53)

He thought that his article might be approached from several possible
angles: a "Nostalgic Native's Return to Boyhood," an examination of
how the institutions of village democracy have developed, or a look at
the country's importance, if any, in the future economy of Canada.

After the Stegner family spent a week in Glacier Park, Page went on by train to Vermont, where he would work for the summer for a farmer neighbor, and Wallace and Mary went on up to Eastend, where they would spend three weeks in June in a little house trailer they had purchased for the trip. From Eastend Wallace reported to the Grays:

> Revisiting the childhood home, especially incognito, has its interesting points. There is a moment when what—especially since it's never been revisited—has always seemed unreal, or like an especially vivid but unbelieved-in dream, has to be accepted as real, and that's an astonishing thing, almost as astonishing as the syntax of this sentence. (6/22/53)

He expected change, but as always when we go home again, there were some surprises. The river was there, going around the same bends, but smaller than he remembered, and smaller, too, were the swimming hole and footbridge. The old Bank of Montreal had become the post office; the Chinese restaurant, a tavern. Most of all, he was surprised at the dense crop of trees that now covered much of the town and the disappearance of the windswept flats that as a boy he cut across. "This," he told the Grays, "is all very strange because I've written about this town until I think I imagined it. Now I have to imagine it over" (6/22/53). The Norwegian woman from whom they were getting their electricity for their trailer told them that if they were interested in the history of the place, they should read *The Big Rock Candy Mountain.*

At the end of June the Stegners drove with their trailer to Vermont to stay with the Grays for several weeks. Returning for the first time in several years, they fell in love with the area all over again. The Grays had urged, even begged the Stegners to let them sell to them, at a minimal price, a piece of property closer than their farm to the pond and to the village. At first the Stegners thought of building a new cottage, but then a friend asked for one of the beams from the old farmhouse, they changed their plans. While getting the beam for Froehlich Rainey (curator for the University of Pennsylvania Museum), the Stegners found that the old house was basically just as sound and square as when it was built in 1860, and so they decided to move it to the new property and rebuild it there. Rainey recalled:

When I was rebuilding the Old Sugar House on Baker Hill in Greensboro, Wally also built a house nearby. We both did much of the carpentry. I remember Wally working with me to shingle the roof of the Sugar House—he was always much the better carpenter, much more skilled. But he never failed to spend each morning writing ... and manual labor for him was always in the afternoons.

The writing Wallace was doing that summer was an article on Saskatchewan, as it was and as it is, and what it meant to him, based on the extensive notes he had taken while he was there. It turned out to be one of the best essays of its kind that he ever wrote, but it failed to find a publisher among mass-circulation magazines despite the energetic efforts of his agents. After many months he finally was able to place it in *American Heritage* with the title "Quiet Earth, Big Sky." He had always been very good at descriptions, but the return to his boyhood home seemed to trigger a lyric dimension in his prose that enabled him to surpass anything he had done previously. This is the prairie:

Across its empty miles pours the pushing and shouldering wind, a thing you tighten into as a trout holds himself in fast water. It is a grassy, clean, exciting wind, with the smell of distance in it, and in its search for whatever it is looking for it turns over every wheat blade and head, every pale primrose, even the ground-hugging grass. It blows yellow-headed blackbirds and hawks and prairie sparrows around the air and ruffles the short tails of meadow larks on fence posts. In collaboration with the light it makes lovely and changeful what might otherwise be characterless.

The summer and early fall of 1953, in addition to the Saskatchewan article, he also finished a long story, "Field Guide to the Western Birds," which his agents placed in a collection of short novels, which included a novelette by Norman Mailer. The collection would be published by Ballantine, but not until 1956. The following January Wallace wrote to his agents that "I think maybe I have me another novelette of the same general kind as the Birds. This is a funny world I live in: eventually I may have a book of things about it, maybe to be called Indoor Outdoor

Living" (1/31/54). This would become a full-length novel, stimulated by observation of his neighbors, *All the Little Live Things*, published in 1967—bringing to our attention once again that thinking for a book usually began in Stegner's mind at least a decade prior to publication.

Also during January of 1954, he was reading proof of *Beyond the Hundredth Meridian: John Wesley Powell and the Second Opening of the West* and making the index for it. The plates for the maps and illustrations were still lagging behind so that publication was delayed until September 1954. The first printing was relatively small, six thousand copies (plus a second printing of three thousand at nearly the same time), but that it was a relatively small initial sale did not hurt—Stegner did not write this one for fame or money. It was a book he had wanted to write since graduate school, one that said a lot of things he felt needed saying. There are books that need to be judged not by their sales, their popularity, or their reviews, but by their impact on the thinking and perceptions of the society that is their context, and particularly their influence on leaders and opinion makers.

When Stewart Udall was appointed interior secretary under President Kennedy, Stegner recalled:

> I was sufficiently aware of what the situation was so that I cheered. I thought it was time we *had* a good Secretary of the Interior; so I sent Udall a copy of *Beyond the Hundredth Meridian*, with a little note saying, "Horray, I'm glad to see you in there." This was not very characteristic of me, but I was enthusiastic.

But Udall had already read the Powell book and had been, in his words, "educated by it." Then, after Bruce Babbitt was appointed to the same position under President Clinton, he testified that

> when I first read "Beyond the Hundredth Meridian," shortly after it was published in 1954, it was as though someone had thrown a rock through the window. Stegner showed us the limitations of aridity and the need for human institutions to respond in a cooperative way. He provided me in that moment with a way of thinking about the American West, the importance of finding true partnership between human beings and the land.

Unlike Rachel Carson's *Silent Spring* or Paul Ehrlich's *The Population Bomb*, Stegner's book was not a best-seller. Its impact has been felt less dramatically, but on a steady and spreading basis. (About twelve hundred copies a year have been sold every year since the initial sale, for a total of about forty thousand.) It has become a basic book for many in the earth sciences and for those historians who have had some concern for the West, but has been of even more importance to the American environmental movement that has developed since the book's publication. It has contributed substantially to the basic philosophy that has led the movement to challenge the conventional thinking regarding "progress" and "development" and to challenge the agendas of the Corps of Engineers, the Bureau of Reclamation, the Bureau of Land Management, and the Forest Service.

Some projects require the right person at the right time. John Wesley Powell, although known, had been overlooked, his full contribution not even perceived by most historians of the westward movement. DeVoto wrote in his preface for the book that

the reason historians have ignored Powell is that the *preconceptions* with which they have approached the area Powell figures in correspond exactly to the *misconceptions* with which the American people and their government approached the West.

Powell's biography was long overdue, and Stegner was just the man to write it. He had for years been reading about the Great Basin and Plateau areas, about Powell, about Clarence King, and of course his dissertation had been about Dutton. He knew much of the area personally from earlier experiences, and in preparation for the biography, he made it his business to experience the areas that remained. As we have seen, he made river trips so that he would become familiar with the problems, needs, and dangers of such journeys. He did research in all the relevant documents that he could find and that others might helpfully point to—journals, contemporary accounts, maps, and reports. It was in his nature to do his homework fully and carefully, and he did.

But all this ignores the fact that the book is eminently readable—a good part of it a rip-roaring adventure and the remainder a high drama of political conflict. It is perhaps not only the impact of the book's themes that has given the book such a long life, but Stegner's skill as a novelist, selecting and organizing the material in such a way that what might in other hands be pedestrian is made interesting and even moving. Not only was the region as a setting for the book made to order for Stegner, his central character expresses all those qualities that he admired in human beings and aspired to himself. Like Stegner, Powell came out of a culturally impoverished background, off of a subsistence farm in Illinois, with no connections to the rich and famous of the Eastern Seaboard. Like Stegner, Powell engaged in a process of lifelong learning—he was fascinated both by theory and by facts. Like Stegner also, Powell eventually left the West to go east to encounter elitist judgment, and just as Stegner succeeded at Harvard, so did Powell succeed, by and large, in the corridors of power in Washington.

In nearly every way, Powell was the antithesis to the George Stegner–Bo Mason figure that looms so large in Stegner's work and thought, the figure and its values that he would try to escape all his life. Powell had almost no interest in personal gain; his whole life was dedicated to serving others—his country and the ordinary citizens of his country. He was hero in the sense that he displayed extraordinary courage and persistence in the face of terrible odds, not only physical but political. But he was in no sense a rugged individualist. In all of his endeavors— exploration, scientific research, and bureaucratic service—he depended on others and always delegated responsibility. What always attracted him, like his biographer, were ideas—both were intellectuals in the best sense of the word. Both were very ambitious, but not so much for fame as for achievement; both were workaholics—steady, dependable, courteous, considerate of others, and totally moral. There was nothing in the Boy Scout code (except perhaps a belief in God—neither was very religious) that they did not adhere to—a matter of congratulation or of disparagement, depending on one's own values looking back from the 1990s.

12

TO THE BARRICADES
FOR THE ENVIRONMENT

Wallace Stegner was very thoroughly taught as a child, with a backhand or mockery, not to cry, not to complain. It was no wonder, then, that John Wesley Powell was a man he could admire. While fighting in the Civil War, Major Powell was wounded at Shiloh, and Stegner notes:

> Losing one's right arm is a misfortune; to some it would be a disaster, to others an excuse. It affected Wes Powell's life about as much as a stone fallen into a swift stream affects the course of the river. With a velocity like his, he simply foamed over it.

This once again brings us to Stegner's theme: the land in the Plateau Province, like that faced by his family in Saskatchewan, is not just a setting, but a testing ground for character. Powell met that challenge through courage, leadership, and cooperation, rather than a rugged individualism, and what drove him forward was a thirst for knowledge, rather than a desire for riches. He respected the land, wanting to know it, rather than conquer or own it.

John Wesley Powell's character was formed by growing up with the West and dealing with its challenges. In discussing his education, Stegner shows how much he identifies with Powell, both of them having grown up with an "education of a special kind," one that to the Easterner would have seemed a deprivation. How was Powell (and to a large extent, Stegner) formed?

> He was made by wandering, by hard labor, by the Bible, by an outdoor life in small towns and on farms, by the optimism and practicality and democracy of the frontier, by the occasional man of learning and the occasional books he met, by country schools and the ill-equipped cubs or worn-out misfits who taught them.

Both men had advanced formal education—Stegner certainly more than Powell—but despite his Ph.D. Stegner thought of himself as largely self-educated, constantly reading, exploring, and trying to make up for what he felt were the large gaps in his educational background. Each had the experience of having one person who helped him early in life with his informal education—for Stegner it was Wilbur Schramm, and for Powell, it was a self-taught farmer by the name of George Crookham, who had a library of scientific works and a museum filled with Indian relics and natural history specimens. When Wesley Powell began to develop adult interests, they were for the most part Crookham's interests. Of Powell's development, Stegner has said, "What distinguishes this early career of Powell's is not its unusualness, but its intensity. He did the things that many of his contemporaries were doing, but did them with a kind of ferocity." In focusing on this quality of intensity or "ferocity," Stegner seems to have inadvertently located an important key to his own character as well, for he, too, had a "driving will to completeness and perfection" that raised him above those around him. Both Stegner and Powell taught (Powell for only a short time), but in a more general sense they were teachers who spent their lives trying to get their contemporaries to see the world as it is, rather than as their contemporaries would like it to be.

But more revealing, perhaps, than a recounting of Powell's early life toward understanding him is to see him in action. The upper Colorado was probably the roughest, fastest, most dangerous stretch of river in North America, often running between sheer cliffs impossible to climb.

There was good reason why up to the time of Powell's exploration the area had remained a blank on the maps. Time and time again we see him acting coolly, deliberately under the most intense pressure of circumstances—something that he may well have learned in battle—and at other times, with sudden daring. Every day presented a series of seemingly impossible challenges—holes and whirlpools, looming rocks, white-water rapids through canyon walls with no place to land, each rapid, with its terrifying, thunderous roar, seeming to be the worst they had encountered. When dangerous rapids threatened, sometimes they could portage, hauling with great difficulty the heavy oak boats across the shoreline rocks. At other times, they lined, letting the boats go with the current and controlling their movement with ropes.

On one occasion a current was so fierce that it pulled a boat away from its stern post, which had been lined to the shore. A man who had been working in the boat, Bradley, jumped to the steering oar, fighting to head downstream, for to go broadside over the falls looming ahead would mean certain wreck. He managed to turn the boat just as he hit the fall and "went clear under in a welter of white, came up on a huge crest, went down again and out of sight beyond some rocks." Helplessly, Powell watched, knowing that what happened to that man and that boat might well determine the life or death of all on the expedition, for they could not turn back. Then suddenly the boat shot into the open and swung into an eddy, and Bradley, still on his feet, looking back at Powell and his companions, waved his hat in triumph.

There are many such vignettes during the course of the journey given to us by Stegner, each emphasizing the enormous courage and endurance of the men involved. One unforgettable picture is that of Powell climbing with one hand up a nearly sheer, ledgy wall in blistering sun. Early in the voyage, he made it a practice to climb the steep walls of the canyon, whenever it was possible, to learn as much as he could about the unexplored land back from the river. Somewhere on this cliff he made the mistake of jumping to a ledge where he found himself unable to go forward or back. Standing on tiptoe, his legs shaking from the effort to hold on to a knob above him, he shouted to his companion, Bradley, above. But Bradley could not reach him with his hand. "As a last desperate measure," Stegner writes, "Bradley sat down on his ledge and yanked off his long drawers, which he lowered to Powell. With nice timing, Powell let go the knob, and half falling away from the cliff, grabbed the dangling underwear."

But as the difficult journey continued, it was not just the danger of the river which pressed down on them, but the constant discomfort, which had been increased by losing food and equipment in various disasters. We know that Stegner had been there in body, as well as in spirit, when we read such descriptions as this:

> There are characteristic discomforts on a river voyage. Not the least is the incessant wetting and the sharp alternation of heat and cold. On a bright day a boatman swiftly sunburns the backs of his hands, the insteps of his feet if they are bare, every unexpected spot exposed by long sitting in one position. In the shade, in soaked clothes, the wind is often icy. And worse than either sun or wind is the irritation of sitting long hours on a hard wet board in sopping pants or drawers. . . .
>
> Their clothes, even in the valises and carpetbags stowed under the cabin decks, were soaked. Their flour was wet and souring, their bacon gritting with silt, their coffee damp, their beans sprouting. Their muscles were sore and their bodies bruised and their tempers tried.

And with all of that, they had to constantly screw up their courage to go forward into rapids that looked impossible to navigate, that at their worst seemed to promise not only shipwreck, but certain death.

It is no wonder that there were times when the men grumbled and came close to mutiny, when they came to heartily dislike the man who kept them going come hell or high water—and it was mostly both. But Powell was resolute, and as an ex-officer the habit of command stuck with him. His devotion to science, which sometimes delayed them while he probed and measured, and his cautious approach to dangerous situations often irritated his men, but all the same they had to admire him: "He had nerve, and he had a variety of interests that excited him, and he participated fully in camp life. Actually he was a commander more likely than most to hold so centrifugal a crew in hand." At Separation

Rapid, near the end of their journey, three of the men, dispirited by lack of food and facing a stretch of river that seemed to them an impossible run, decided to take their chances by climbing out of the canyon toward a Mormon settlement. Unfortunately, they were ambushed and killed by Indians who apparently misunderstood their intentions, since no one had ever come out of the river at that point. The original ten were now six (one had perished during the journey), four boats reduced to two, and what had been rations for ten months was now rations for five days. But they made it through the last of the fearsome rapids and back to civilization:

> Nine men had plunged into the unknown from the last outpost of civilization in the Uinta Valley on the sixth of July, 1869. On August 30 six came out. . . . Only the loyalty of five men and Powell's own resolution had kept it from ending in failure on the very brink of success.

In writing his biography, Stegner was interested in character rather than personality, career rather than intimate details of a private life. Stegner not only defines his protagonist by showing him in action, his character tested against the challenges of nature under the most extreme circumstances, but defines him further, as well as locating him in his culture and providing him stature, by a series of contrasts with other characters.

First there is William Gilpin, whom Stegner sets up at the beginning of his book as the ultimate advocate of romance and myth, who joined the politicians and railroads, eager for settlers, "in finding most of the plains exuberantly arable" and could quote everything from folklore to government geologists to support the theory that "rain follows the plow." Gilpin's antithesis was the realist Powell, a man "who before he was through would challenge almost every fact and discourage every attitude that William Gilpin asserted or held about the West—challenge and attack them coolly and on evidence. He brought science to the argument, where Gilpin brought rhetoric."

The contrast between Gilpin and Powell sets up a duality pervasive throughout the book—the romantic versus the realistic. To this conflict

Stegner brings in his knowledge of the Realistic Period in American literature by pointing out that Powell was part of the inevitable but slow movement toward realism whose literary beginnings in the work of John Hay and Edward Eggleston were almost precisely contemporary with his own beginnings as a scientist. And Stegner seems to be thinking of his own method as used in *Mormon Country* when he says, "Both Powell and Twain, realists and even factualists, might on occasion be led to follow Twain's own advice to Kipling: Young man, first get your facts and then do with them what you will"—a quotation that had been brought to his attention by Bernard DeVoto.

The facts, as Powell discovered them over a career of two decades, put him in a position where

almost alone among his contemporaries he looked at the Arid Region and saw neither desert nor garden. What he saw was the single compelling unity that the region possessed: except in local islanded areas its rainfall was less than twenty inches a year, and twenty inches he took . . . to be the minimum needed to support agriculture without irrigation.

That is the central realistic axiom of *Beyond the Hundredth Meridian*, and the "Second Opening of the West" was not so much an opening of territory as it was an attempt to open eyes. For the romanticizing of the West had led to

acute political and economic and agricultural blunders, to the sour failure of projects and lives, to the vast and avoidable waste of some resources and the monopolization of others, and to a long delay in the reconciling of institutions to realities.

Powell was acutely aware of the suffering that had been caused by the myth and ballyhoo, and a good part of his motivation in establishing the facts about the Western lands was an attempt to bring rationality to land policy and avoid such suffering in the future. Stegner had, of course, experienced the very disasters that saddened Powell. He had witnessed the disappointment, despair, and rage that had come from the attempt to work a homestead in a country that five out of seven years would not grow wheat. All the investment of hope, money, and hard, hard labor had come to nothing but a harvest of bitterness.

A related contrast to that with Gilpin is set up between Sam Adams, a con man and faker, and Powell. Adams, whom Stegner sees as a "lunatic counterpoint" to Powell, tries to achieve fame and fortune by selling the romance of the Gilpin doctrine and by a foolish attempt to top Powell's exploration with his own river trip. He sets out from Breckenridge, Colorado, to go down the Blue to its junction with the Grand "and from there float on down this unobstructed waterway to California" in four boats built on the spot out of green lumber and with no air compartments. He is the scheming buffoon, the "Duke and Dauphin" figure in the background of the Powell river journey. "His career," Stegner notes, "is a demonstration of how far a man could get in a new country on nothing but gall and the gift of gab, so long as what he said was what people wanted to believe."

Other contrasts with other characters come into play as Stegner moves beyond the river trips to the years that Powell spent sometimes in the field, but mostly in Washington trying to push forward government science and organize it. One such that the author develops is with Henry Adams. In this and in the contrast between Powell and Henry Adams's friend Clarence King, we move from the antithesis of romanticism versus realism to other antitheses—of East versus West, wealthy elite versus ordinary citizen, privilege versus democracy of opportunity, and, in the case of Powell and King, disinterested public service versus private gain.

Henry Adams was the very model of the Eastern intellectual whose attention, when not focused on the Northeast, went to Europe, or even to the Orient, but seldom to the western United States. Early in life he decided that of the careers open to him and of all the possibilities, the West offered him the least. Stegner observes that he was right in not going west to grow up with the country, since

whatever his education had prepared him for, it had not prepared him for that. That took an education of a special kind. To grow up with the West, or to grow with and through it into national prominence, you had to have the West bred in your bones, you needed it facing you like a dare.

Adams may loom as one of the wisest men of his time, but Stegner finds Powell to be "in most things . . . quite as clear-sighted as Adams; in some he saw even clearer." The basic differences between the two men, Stegner suggests, have to do with Adams's elitist sympathies and his growing pessimism about our government and our future. By contrast Powell had faith in our form of government and shrewdly worked to improve those aspects of policy he was concerned with, even though he was every bit as realistic as Adams about bureaucratic infighting and about the corrupt nature of some congressmen—that "criminal class," as Twain labeled them. Time after time in hearings before committees of Congress, he expressed the same competence, coolness under pressure, and faith in his own vision as he had on the Colorado. He learned to play the political game well, while never sacrificing his integrity, and was finally able to get a bill passed bringing the competing surveys of the West together in one bureau, the Geological Survey.

At first the new bureau was given to Clarence King—almost always described as the "brilliant" Clarence King, since he was not only well-educated in the East, talented, and capable, he was also handsome and witty. (Stegner later makes him a character in his *Angle of Repose*.) But King served only briefly, going off to seek riches in the gold mines of Mexico, and Powell was appointed by President Garfield in his place, although he was already at the head of the Bureau of Ethnology. Stegner once again shows his identification with Powell, as well as his antagonism to the Eastern establishment when he points out that Henry Adams might have given the study of geology or of the tribal cultures of America to

> his friends Agassiz or King, superbly equipped and with the wealth and social standing that made them better companions at dinner.
>
> But who in fact undertook it was a one-armed little man with a bristly beard, a homemade education, and an intense concentration of purpose.

Unlike King, he had no ambition to get rich. "If he had any single ambition," Stegner points out, "it was the remarkable one of being of service to science, and through science to mankind."

As head of the Bureau of American Ethnology, Powell brought rare qualifications of attitude—concern that the Indians be able to retain their dignity and that their traditions be treated with respect. Even before being appointed to his post he was deeply committed to discovering and preserving Native American cultures, languages, and traditions. It was very important to him that no more of the Indian inheritance be lost, since so much of it by that time had been. Stegner notes in regard to his relations with the Indians during his years of exploration when they were not yet subdued, that

> Powell respected them, and earned their respect, because he accepted without question their right to be what they were, to hold to the beliefs and institutions natural to them. To approach a strange culture and a strange people without prejudice, suspicion, condescension, or fear is common enough among students now; it was not too common in 1870.

During these years in his contacts with the Indians, Powell never carried a gun and never was threatened. His study of them became one of the two great works of his life, as he labored with unremitting purpose for three decades to put aside the misinformation that had been attached to Native Americans over the years, "substituting knowledge for the hatred, fear, sentimentality, hearsay, rumor, and legend by which we knew the tribes of America."

The other great work of Powell's life, of course, was the survey of western lands and, on the basis of that survey, the development of a rational federal land policy. Embodied in his *Report on the Lands of the Arid Region*, 1879, was

> a complete revolution in the system of land surveys, land policy, land tenure, and farming methods in the West, and a denial of almost every cherished fantasy and myth associated with the Westward migration and the American dream of the Garden of the World.

Here he was not only challenging political forces who used the popular myths about the West as a screen, but challenging also the myths themselves, which had become "as rooted as the beliefs of religion." Bringing this material into print was as brave an act as Major Powell had ever performed.

In his report Powell recommended that eighty acres be the homestead unit for irrigatable farms, but that pasture farms have a unit of 2,560 acres. He proposed that surveys be based on the topography, and that farms be as irregular as was necessary to give everyone water frontage and a piece of irrigatable soil. With such a system not only could monopoly of water be prevented, but it would permit the maximum number of freeholds to be carved out of any usable parts of the public lands. Further, on the basis of what he had learned from the Mormons of Kanab and the Sevier Valley, he proposed cooperative unions to control pasture lands and the organization of settlers into irrigation districts capable of self-government. If Powell's way had been adopted, Stegner notes, "it might have changed the history of a great part of the West." It would certainly have avoided the pattern of land and water monopoly by a few families and large corporations that have traditionally held much of the economic and political power throughout the region.

Powell had a vision of the future based on a faith in science and a belief in human equality. He was a utopian who believed in the evolutionary force of democracy. Enlightenment brought by science would be largely responsible for bringing humankind into a civilization in which power would not come out of magic, kinship, raw force, or property, but from ethics and conscience. All the world must eventually come to republican institutions and social conscience, for what science has revealed to us is this: "Every generation in life is a step in progress to a higher and fuller life; science has discovered hope. . . . Man was no mere organism at the mercy of forces." His vision and his optimism may well have been the secret of his ability to survive for years and act constructively in a Washington surrounded by a web of political intrigue and the sticky opposition of those with vested interests.

As head of the Bureau of American Ethnology he worked under the aegis of the Smithsonian and thereby was sheltered from political pressure. But as head of the survey and advocate for new public lands legislation, he often had to do battle with political opponents. His enemies tended to be of two sorts: those members of Congress, often representing the far West, who were motivated by personal gain or the profit of influential constituents; and other scientists who were jealous of Powell's successes and who were guarding their turf. Powell was one of the leading scientists not only in this country, but in the world, but he did not fit the usual pattern. In post–Civil War America, science was largely a wealthy man's game, divided up into fiefdoms that were protected and fought over. As might be supposed, Powell was totally opposed to the notion of private property in science, stating that "the learning of one man does not subtract from the learning of another, as if there were a limited quantity to be divided into exclusive holdings." In the broadest sense it was Powell's efforts to establish the principle of government science, as essential to our form of government and prerequisite to our cultural advancement and physical well-being, that was his greatest contribution. Government science today is still under attack from vested interests, but we have to a great extent lost this consciousness of how very important such science is in preserving the democratic foundations of our republic.

When *Beyond the Hundredth Meridian* came out in 1954, several reviewers complained that while the trips downriver were exciting, the latter half of the book was rather dull. But as Stegner tells of Powell's confrontations with Congress, there is plenty of drama. Toward the end of Powell's career, both types of enemies, congressmen and scientists, ganged up together in order to strip him of his powers and defeat his programs. "Enemy" may sound too strong, but there were those who were definitely out to get him, one way or another. One major foe, for example, was Professor E. D. Cope, whom Stegner describes as "a character out of fiction, a distinguished scientist with an emotional life like that of the villain of a Jacobean tragedy." He was totally corroded by vanity and hatred, doing his best to cause trouble for Powell by beating the bushes for disgruntled former employees who might talk against him and trying to suborn current employees from loyalty to the survey. Another foe was Representative Hilary Herbert of Alabama who was a member of a joint committee set up by the 1884 authorization bill that provided the funding for the survey. The committee was instructed to investigate the organization, accomplishments, and efficiency of Powell's agency, among others, and Herbert was determined to use the hearings to embarrass Powell or impeach his integrity. This latter would be difficult, since Powell kept scrupulous books and records and was known to be totally honest and selfless in his service.

Nevertheless, Professor Cope with some help was able to scrape up bits and pieces of gossip, enough to make up a twenty-three-thousand-word document that blasted Powell and was circulated among members of Congress, providing Herbert with the ammunition he needed for his attack in the hearings. In addition, Herbert wrote to Alexander Agassiz asking him to give specific criticisms of Powell's work. A rich man and member of the elite socially and scientifically, Agassiz was against government science in general. Powell answered Agassiz's criticisms:

> He had one central question to ask of Agassiz and those who honestly held Agassiz's views: Was knowledge the private possession of an elite, or was it something broader? "Shall the work of scientific research and the progress of American civilization wait until the contagion of [Agassiz's] example shall inspire a hundred millionaires to engage in like good works? Before that time comes scientific research will be well endowed by the people of the United States in the exercise of their wisdom and in the confident belief that knowledge is for the welfare of all the people."

It was a dramatic statement of liberation and of faith in the egalitarian ideal of our form of government, a sort of Gettysburg Address for American science, one that probably could have come only from a Westerner.

Powell survived this test in 1884, but nearly every year there were challenges to his work and his authority by Congress. Cope and his cohorts kept up a steady fire of defamation and innuendo from the scientific sidelines and launched a particularly vicious attack in the newspapers in anticipation of the hearings of 1890. At the same time Herbert was joined in his crusade against Powell by several other members of Congress, including Senator Big Bill Stewart from Nevada, who was, in Stegner's words, "in his way, a man of faith: he believed in Western 'development,' and he believed in the right of men—himself among them—to get rich by this 'development.' "

When Powell came before the Senate Appropriations Committee, and as he faced Stewart and a half-dozen other senators from the arid region, he may well have felt as if he were facing a hanging jury. Congress had given Powell the job of doing an irrigation survey as a preliminary to development of a general plan for the continued settlement of the West, but Congress now was impatient, Powell was taking too long, and the senators made it clear that they "did not want individual initiative interfered with, they wanted the West taken care of by means of 'natural conditions and natural enterprise.' " Two years later, in 1892, Herbert once again pushed hard and was able to rally enough support so that sufficient cuts were made to bring the house down and "with it much of the structure of government science that Powell had labored with for more than twenty years." In 1894 Powell resigned from the survey and settled into the relative obscurity of the Bureau of American Ethnology.

It may be that Powell's end—a good man who towered above those around him brought down by the wolves of self-interest—smacks of tragedy, but he was not a tragic, beaten figure. Although he wore the scars of two dozen years in Washington, he did not end up defeated, a victim like Clarence King, who had suffered a complete breakdown, nor was he ever touched in the slightest by the cynicism and bitterness that poisoned Henry Adams's long later life. Powell was an explorer of note, an acclaimed scientist of world renown, and founder of the Geological Survey and organizer of several other bureaus, including Ethnology, where he systemized the study of anthropology. He was the person who made a substantial start on a consistent mapping of the entire United States, the one who more accurately than anyone else at the time defined the nature of the West, and perhaps, most important of all, the person who championed government science, insisting that scientific study in a democracy must not be confined to a wealthy elite and that knowledge derived from science belonged to the people. None of this could be taken away by vote of the Senate Appropriations Committee.

In writing this biography-history, Wallace Stegner did more than bring to American consciousness the contributions that had been made by a great man who had been largely overlooked by historians, he had established his own credentials on a firm basis as a writer about the West and environmental issues. It was a landmark in Wallace's career as environmentalist, just as the publication of *The Big Rock Candy Mountain* gave him credibility as an important writer of fiction. And as we have seen, the two works came together in theme in several ways—opposition to rugged individualism, advocacy of cooperation, antagonism to Western myth, and emphasis on a realistic approach to life.

Before he had read Powell, Stegner had only looked at the West around him; he never saw it, understood its essential nature. It was Powell who educated him, involved him, it had been DeVoto who prodded him forward to express his fears in print about damage the Republicans were threatening to do to the park system, and it was DeVoto who cheered him up and supported him when he thought that the Powell book might be too much for him. But it may be also that DeVoto's acerbic introduction to that book, which praised Stegner but attacked academic historians, caused him to lose the Pulitzer Prize for history. The story, as Stegner heard it later, is that the decision came down to his book and another, and his book lost in the deliberations because DeVoto had used the introduction to mock a distinguished historian who was a previous winner. As much as Stegner admired DeVoto and was swayed by him to fight many of the same battles, this was a lesson in moderation to a man already inclined toward moderation, a lesson that he would carry over to his environmental work, including his next project.

That next project was one that he got involved in only reluctantly. He was very busy, as usual, with his own work, having fallen behind because he had just spent six months in Denmark, when David Brower, executive director of the Sierra Club, came down from Berkeley to ask him to edit a book. Brower, who would figure a good deal in Stegner's life over the next few years, was a man of incredible energy, in those days lean and hard, a leaf spring—the type who could hike with a pack for four hours, climb a mountain that afternoon, and then that same night dance the evening away. His single-mindedness and fanatical devotion to conservation (he could never understand why Stegner should waste his time writing stories) was made palatable by a sense of humor and a talent for having fun. Loquacious, inspired, and determined, he thrived on political battles.

What he had in mind was a collection of essays about Dinosaur National Monument that could be used to alert the public and persuade Congress that the scheduled building of dams at Echo Park and Split Mountain would destroy the monument and that the monument was worth saving. Brower wanted Stegner to edit the collection—gather the contributions, arrange them, edit them, and come up with appropriate illustrations—as well as contribute an essay of his own (later, they would decide that he should do an introduction as well). The idea for the book had been conceived by Brower, who then brought on board publisher Alfred A. Knopf, who would put out the book and also contribute an essay. Wallace didn't want to take on what promised to be a time-consuming and onerous chore, but Brower was nothing if not insistent, and he finally gave in.

While Brower was in a fighting mood and thought in terms of firing a broadside, Wallace was able to convince him that a more temperate approach would win more votes in Congress. They decided together that the book should be informative and beautiful—a coffee-table-type book with color photos that would sell the area's features. "We only wanted," Stegner has written in a new foreword, "to describe the treasures of natural beauty, history, archaeology, and peace of mind that lay in Dinosaur, and what the Echo Park and Split Mountain dams would destroy." One of the main problems that they faced was that the whole thing had to be put together with great speed in order that copies be put in the hands of congressmen before the matter came up for action at the beginning of the 1955 session. In a November 1, 1954, letter to the contributors, Wallace asked for their essays by the end of the month. Packages came and went by air express, and because of the rush, Wallace took on a lot of the burdens of revising the contributions and selecting and captioning photos himself. Brower remembered on one visit that illustrations were spread all over the floors of the Stegner house so that you could hardly walk. He recalled complimenting Wallace on his essay, on his wonderful way with words, only to have him smile and say that "words are a form of black magic."

Another problem was that though Alfred Knopf admired Brower, he resented his bossiness, especially since Brower refused to guarantee any sales of the book through the Sierra Club. At that point as far as Knopf was concerned, Brower should be out of it. Stegner found himself in the middle, even more so when he and Brower decided to tone down Knopf's essay, taking out the personal attacks, and Knopf blamed Brower for not letting him know what the tone of the book was supposed to be. At the same time Knopf raised Wallace's hackles when he wrote in a letter, "assuming there *is* going to be a book." Stegner wrote back:

If I hadn't thought that was settled for sure I wouldn't ever have started working on it, because though my enthusiasm for Dinosaur is great, my need to earn a living is also great, and I can't waste time on good works that turn out not to be works but idle speculations. (11/30/54)

The dispute about the fighting tone that Knopf wanted was settled when the three decided to include a pamphlet in the book that would attack the motives and arguments of the dam boosters, while maintaining the "air of probity" of the book itself.

This Is Dinosaur: Echo Park Country and Its Magic Rivers (as the book was finally titled after weeks of dispute and indecision) turned out to be a great success. Because of the book, which was distributed to every congressman, and through the efforts of the Sierra Club, Wilderness Society, Izaak Walton League, and other conservation groups—seventeen in all—the dams were not built and the monument was preserved. It was the first time these organizations had tasted victory in such a major political battle, and it led them to take a more political, activist stance in the future. Michael P. Cohen in his history of the Sierra Club has written that "it . . . constituted a crucial turning point in the nature of the Club's organizational structure and aims." In effect, the experience politicized the club, for as Stegner has said, and as most conservationists have come to agree, nothing can be done to preserve the environment without laws and the enforcement of those laws. The law that was used to protect Dinosaur was the National Park Act of 1916, which stated that the purpose of the national parks was "to conserve the scenery and the natural and historic objects and the wildlife therein and to provide for the enjoyment of the same in such manner and by such means as will leave them unimpaired for the enjoyment of future generations."

As Stegner had indicated earlier in his articles for *Reporter* and *The New Republic*, the words of the new administration suggested that it would like nothing better than to break through the barrier of the law so that the parks could be developed, and in that sense, the dams had been a test case, a way of opening the door that the conservationist victory pulled firmly shut. In his essay for *Dinosaur*, looking forward to the battles for the preservation of wilderness that were ahead, Stegner ends with an eloquent appeal:

> It is legitimate to hope that there may [be] left in Dinosaur the special kind of human mark, the special record of human passage, that distinguishes man from all other species. It is rare enough among men, impossible to any other form of life. *It is simply the deliberate and chosen refusal to make any marks at all....* It is a better world with some buffalo left in it, a richer world with some gorgeous canyons unmarred by signboards, hot-dog stands, super highways, or high-tension lines, undrowned by power or irrigation reservoirs. If we preserved as parks only those places that have no economic possibilities, we would have no parks. And in the decades to come, it will not be only the buffalo and the trumpeter swan who need sanctuaries. Our own species is going to need them too.
>
> It needs them now.

The effectiveness of the book reinforced an idea that David Brower had in the back of his mind for a series of Sierra Club books, large format and full color, that could be used to bring environmental issues right into the living rooms of possible supporters and sway them emotionally. Over the next fourteen years, until Brower was replaced as executive director, the Sierra Club would produce nineteen more such books.

There was a serious downside to the victory over Dinosaur, however. In winning there, the conservationists lost Glen Canyon, and the pity was they didn't have to. Both Stegner and Brower blamed themselves. Stegner told Richard Etulain for his book, *Conversations*:

> We really whipped the Upper Colorado River project. We could have strangled it to death. We had it down completely. They took the dams out of Dinosaur in a desperate conviction that if they didn't they were going to lose the whole thing. Maybe we should have been harder-nosed than we were, but that's hindsight. Having saved Dinosaur, we accepted the ruin of Glen Canyon, which was not very smart of us. Dave has regretted that all his life. Nobody knew Glen Canyon then except me; I'd been down it a couple of

times, and I told him it was better than Echo Park. He didn't
believe it, and I didn't push it.

It wasn't that Brower didn't believe him, it was simply that he hadn't
seen Glen Canyon and by that experience been inspired enough for
extraordinary action. Brower recalled:

> We did have the thing stopped, and the Sierra Club executive com-
> mittee sent a wire to me when I was back at the Cosmos Club lob-
> bying against the project. And the wire came that if Echo Park and
> Split Mountain dams were taken out, the Sierra Club would drop
> its opposition. But that opposition was keystone to the whole struc-
> ture! If that came out the whole structure fell, and what I didn't do
> is grab the next airplane west for a meeting of the board and talk
> them out of retreat. . . . It was consistent for the Sierra Club to hang
> in there. We had voted to block the whole thing. Senator Paul
> Douglas wondered why we had given up. And Senator Cliff
> Anderson said if it hadn't passed that year, it would never have
> passed, and I have asked myself again and again, why didn't I
> move?

In hindsight, it would seem that Stegner should have in this instance
shaken off his moderation and more vociferously acted as advocate for
Glen Canyon. If he had, maybe Brower would not have failed to act in
the clutch. Years later, after the dam was built and the fill-up was begun,
the two of them went together down through the canyon to get one last
glimpse of what they had irretrievably lost. It was an incredibly sad
occasion—a wake that the environmental movement will never forget.

At the same time as there was a concerted effort to protect the
national parks and monuments, there was a rising tide of sentiment
among many conservation groups, the Wilderness Society and Sierra
Club in particular, for a congressionally passed program to formally
establish a wilderness set-aside and protection program. Stegner has
written, "If the national park idea is, as Lord Bryce suggested, the best
idea America ever had, wilderness preservation is the highest refinement
of that idea." Concern for wilderness has had a long history in the
United States, and where it begins is hard to pinpoint. Perhaps we

should go back to Henry David Thoreau, for whom wildness was a passion and who wrote, "In wildness is the preservation of the world"; and to George Perkins Marsh, who in 1864 articulated the concept of the interrelatedness of all life. " 'Man,' Marsh wrote, 'is everywhere a disturbing agent. Wherever he plants his foot, the harmonies of nature are turned to discords.' " Through the late nineteenth and early twentieth centuries, the preservation of wild areas was carried on in the effort to establish national parks and forests, during which the most notable contributions were probably those of Theodore Roosevelt and his chief forester, Gifford Pinchot, and, of course, John Muir, who was largely responsible for establishing Yosemite and Sequoia and who formed the Sierra Club.

In the 1930s Robert Marshall and others formed the Wilderness Society, an organization dedicated to saving as much of the remaining wild as possible. At that point certain areas of federal land had administratively been put aside as wilderness, but the society wanted areas set aside by law so as to protect them forever against encroachment. As Stegner points out in his essay "A Capsule History of Conservation," it was Marshall who developed much of the program, but "the philosophical justifications, the statement of first principles, appeared in 1949 in Aldo Leopold's posthumous *A Sand County Almanac*." In this, in his essay "The Land Ethic," Leopold argued for the same consideration for the land as civilized persons should show in their human relations. "He wanted," Stegner writes, "a portion of the land left wild, for ultimately all human endeavor has to come back to the wilderness for its justification and its new beginnings." This was a sentiment that Wallace was perfectly in tune with. In an autobiographical article he has said, "Like Aldo Leopold, I had grown up in wild places. Like Leopold, I could not bear to think what the world would be like without such places to grow up in."

In the decades after World War II it became clear that the situation in the national parks and national forests was changing rapidly as our population grew, acquired cars, and became more and more mobile. Because of the "multiple use" philosophy of the Forest Service and the tendency of the National Park Service to create more and more civilized environments in the parks, even the "near wild" was disappearing and the parks were becoming overwhelmed with visitors. The effort to get

wilderness legislation passed was inspired by a new urgency. In that
struggle, the work of Howard Zahniser, the executive director of the
Wilderness Society, was especially notable. He drafted a wilderness bill
in 1956, and over the next eight years he had to revise it sixty-six times.
Again, as Stegner writes in his "Capsule History":

> When, after innumerable hearings and thousands of pages of testi-
> mony, it [the Wilderness Act] was finally passed, it still contained
> Zahniser's definition of wilderness as "an area where the earth and
> its community of life are untrammeled by man, where man him-
> self is a visitor who does not remain."

It was during the period leading up to the passage of the bill that
Stegner played his part. His was not the major part that had been played
by those such as Zahniser and Dave Brower, but it was significant nevertheless. As Brower was fond of saying, Stegner had indeed "a way with
words," and especially was he able to create brilliant conclusions in
which he was able to encapsulate the essence of his argument along with
a strong emotional charge. We have already noted his conclusion to his
essay "The Marks of Human Passage" in *Dinosaur* where he said, "In
the decades to come, it will not be only the buffalo and the trumpeter
swan who need sanctuaries. Our own species is going to need them
too. . . . It needs them now." In 1959 he wrote an article for the *Sierra
Club Bulletin* called "The War Between the Rough Riders and the Bird
Watchers" in which he reviews the status of the wilderness bill (stalled
through two sessions of Congress) and the arguments for and against it
in some detail. It is in large part a satiric attack on those self-interest
groups and their representatives who had made fun of the "bird
watchers," as they derisively called them, who had supported wilderness legislation. The basis of the pro-exploitation argument had been,
Stegner points out, pretty much the same for fifty years; the typical
opponent as he testifies before a congressional committee always begins
by claiming to be a friend of wilderness, but

> this bill [he would go on to say] would reserve far too much of it.
> And why does it all have to be set aside in the West, thereby
> locking up the resources on which the West must depend for its

payrolls and its growth? And is there justice in a bill that would restrict the livelihood of present permittees and permittees as yet unborn?

At one point in his article Stegner quotes at length from a speech by Senator Watkins of Utah who made the rather astounding statement that he wondered why, since there was so much unoccupied land in the East, Midwest, and South, these lands couldn't be put into wilderness reserves. That is, not having the slightest idea of what a wilderness was, he wanted other sections of the country to get busy and create some of their own. Stegner uses this abysmal ignorance on the part of one of his most prominent opponents as a springboard for another supercharged conclusion with its memorable last line:

In spite of former Senator Watkins's feeling that we ought to help establish a few wildernesses in other parts of the country and let the West get on with its lumbering and mining, it has never been man's gift to make wildernesses. But he can make deserts, and has.

But the most memorable last line of all in support of wilderness came in another document whose words would ring throughout much of the world. In 1960, at the urging of David Brower and other environmentalist friends, Stegner sat down one December afternoon to write to David E. Pesonen, who was consultant to the Outdoor Recreation Resources Review Commission, which at that point was reviewing for Congress the need for wilderness legislation. Wilderness "had plenty of supporters (and plenty of enemies)," writes T. H. Watkins in an essay summarizing Stegner's conservation career, "in and out of Congress; what it lacked was a manifesto, a central document, what Stegner himself would come to call a coda." In his letter he "elicited the wonder contained not only in the nation's forests and mountains, but in its prairies and deserts as well," and using Robbers' Roost country in Wayne County, Utah, as an example, he wrote:

It is a lovely and terrible wilderness, such a wilderness as Christ and the prophets went out into; harshly and beautifully colored, broken and worn until its bones are exposed, its great sky without a smudge of taint from Technocracy, and in hidden corners and pockets under its cliffs the sudden poetry of springs. Save a piece of country like that intact, and it does not matter in the slightest that only a few people every year will go into it.

He goes on to say that this is precisely its value—roads would desecrate it and crowds would ruin it. Those who haven't the strength to hike into it can simply sit and look—and they can look for two hundred miles and look as deeply into themselves in response to what they see as anywhere he knows. He concludes:

> These are some of the things wilderness can do for us. That is the reason we need to put into effect, for its preservation, some other principle than the principles of exploitation or "usefulness" or even recreation. We simply need that wild country available to us, even if we never do more than drive to its edge and look in. For it can be a means of reassuring ourselves of our sanity as creatures, a part of the geography of hope.

Even before the letter was published as part of the Recreation Commission's 1962 report, it was used by Interior Secretary Stewart Udall at a wilderness convention. It had just come into his hands, and he was so moved by it, he put aside his prepared speech and simply read from Stegner's letter. Over the years since, Stegner had many requests to quote from it and said that "it's been made into posters in half-a-dozen countries. It's in the Canadian parks, the Australian parks; it's in South Africa . . . in the Sinai Desert . . . [and] in a tree house in Kenya, with the animals running down below." Even just the last four words, "the geography of hope," which perfectly countered the constant emphasis by the exploiters on "use," had enough magic to help sway a nation toward a course that would have been unimaginable fifty years ago.

The Wilderness Act was passed and signed into law by President Lyndon Johnson in September 1964.

13

TRAVEL,
TRAVEL LITERATURE,
AND THE SEARCH
FOR NARRATIVE VOICE

Like John Wesley Powell, Wallace Stegner led a life of constant activity and one that had many different strands to it. While the fifties was the decade that brought him firmly into the conservation movement, it was also a decade of travel and writing about his travels, as well as a period during which he made significant progress in the development of his fiction. The period began with a trip around the world, most of the time being spent in Asia—India, Japan, and the Philippines—carrying out a program of the Rockefeller Foundation to bring Asian and American literature to some postwar mutual recognition. The trip led to a number of articles, including "Cairo, 1950," "Asian Literary Articles," and "Literary Lessons Out of Asia" (all 1951). In 1953, Stegner returned to Eastend, in Saskatchewan, the scene of his childhood, which led to "Quiet Earth, Big Sky" (1955), the first piece of what would become *Wolf Willow* (1962). Then, in March 1954 he and Mary departed on a ship to Copenhagen to spend nearly six months in Denmark, with side trips to France, Norway, and Germany. In this trip were the origins of *Spectator Bird* (1976).

On the boat the Stegners met the daughter of Mrs. Niels Bohr, who, after they arrived in Copenhagen, invited them to a cocktail party and introduced them to a number of notable residents of the city, including the brother-in-law of a countess who was looking for someone to share her flat. The countess had been reduced in circumstances because her husband had been a quisling, cooperating with the Nazis during the war. She, however, was a charming, attractive woman in her early fifties, very cultured and fluent in several languages, and she was very happy to have an American author and his wife rent from her. They really became members of her household, for they would share both a kitchen and bathroom with her, and over the weeks she and the Stegners would become very good friends (she not knowing, perhaps, how dangerous it can be to befriend an author). She took them around to show them the art and architecture of her city and also helped Wallace with his Danish, gave him several ideas for articles, and introduced the Stegners to a number of influential Danes. On one occasion she took them out to her family estate, but as they drove through the village and in through the gates, she hid herself under a blanket in the backseat of the car because the people of the area were so bitter about the role her husband had played during the war. Beautiful, wistful, a bit mysterious, and damned by her past, she would stick in Stegner's mind.

He wrote to his agents from Copenhagen about his first impressions two weeks after they arrived:

> Copenhagen is an interesting town, the beer is very superior, the women smoke cigars, the cuisine, at least at this season, is not as marvelous as the travel writers crack it up to be, the weather is beginning to warm up a little, and I can now say, slowly and with emphasis, about two hundred words of Danish unintelligible to a Dane. Hard liquor and schnapps are taxed astronomically so that no petit bourgeois like me can afford them, but beer, once you find out what to ask for, comes at 45 ore a bottle, which is about 6 or 7 cents. Music is good and plentiful and balcony tickets come about sixty cents. The ballet is one of the best. And the number of drunken sailors on Friday night, which is paynight, would astonish the Anti-Saloon League. (4/23/54)

While many writers might give up their work while traveling, to relax, and then take it up again on return, Stegner never seemed to stop writing or planning new writing projects. For a man who seemed to be self-contained and at peace with himself, he was still driven in a quiet, determined, self-disciplined way. It was his steadiness one would have to admire, along with consistent quality of performance, even in the face of those events throughout his life that were discouraging or depressing.

He wrote his agents that it may seem "a little peculiar to be sitting on the bank of the harbor in Copenhagen and writing a story about Kyoto, but that's the way it turns out" (4/23/54). This story was "Garden Made for Snow," which along with three other stories remained on the shelf unsold despite the energetic efforts of his agents. This difficulty in finding a market for his stories was a considerable setback for a writer whose stories had regularly appeared in the *O. Henry* and *Best Short Stories* collections. A good part of the reason for the difficulty was that the magazine market was changing, as several of the fiction editors reported to him with regret—what was taking over the women's magazines, even those like *Cosmopolitan* and *Redbook* that had a tradition of quality fiction, was romance, which was not Stegner's genre. General magazines that published fiction were beginning to disappear or were cutting back severely on the amount of fiction they were publishing. Although Stegner would write several more stories, including some of his best, such as "Volunteer," "Genesis," and "The Wolfer," by 1958 he was almost through with the form and found that many of his ideas for stories, like "All the Little Live Things," were leading him into novels. Later, as another reason for gradually giving up on the form, he would declare that short fiction was a young man's game and that as he got older, he found himself running out of beginnings and endings.

In Copenhagen, as usual, he found ideas for articles. Like many another author, he found that such articles were a two-way street: travel brought articles, which helped fund the traveling, and commissioned articles led to travel in the first place. One idea came from his landlady, whose sister was a baroness who, after her husband's death, took on the job of prioress at a home for elderly noblewomen. The Stegners, with camera, went to visit and interview the prioress and some of her charges, but inquiries by Wallace's agents could not dig up a customer willing to commit to an article. Wallace also worked up a prospectus that he sent to his agents for an article on the first painters of the Grand Canyon, an idea that came out of his work on the Powell book and that he had been trying to sell for some time. Another idea he forwarded to his agents,

which once again came out of the willingness of the Stegners' countess
landlady to help out, was to write up a house party given for the nobility
for an annual shoot of partridge and pheasant. Then he came up with a
plan that his agents were able to sell, finally—to do an article on sport
fishing for salmon in Norway. A third of the way through their stay in
Scandinavia, Stegner complained that they were almost broke (a frequent lament and nearly always untrue), and so he was pleased when
Sports Illustrated was willing to provide an advance against expenses for
the fishing story.

The trip to Norway allowed him to find the hotel on the edge of the
Hardangerfjord that had been founded by his maternal grandfather's
brother in the 1880s and was still owned by distant cousins, but the
fishing trip itself was a near disaster, a comedy of errors. For the article,
which would be titled "Queen of the Salmon Rivers," the editor at *Sports
Illustrated* wanted some pictures of royalty fishing, and Stegner, through
connections provided by the countess, made arrangements to get some
pictures of the prince. Although they got photos of the prince's residence,
the grounds, and the servants, they found "at the last minute, Prince
Harald [*sic*]—the little prince!—decided he was on his vacation and
didn't want to be photographed" (8/14/54). Then while driving down
the Laerdal, looking for rivers to fish, a passing bus put their rented car
into a ditch. They had hired a fishing guide to pose for pictures, and in
the accident his prize rod and reel were completely busted on a fence.
Wallace wrote Carl Brandt, Sr., who at Brandt and Brandt was gradually
taking over from Bernice as Wallace's agent:

> I couldn't do anything but replace it—which I couldn't quite do,
> because the rod was a present from Lord Portman. But I got him a
> duplicate from another gillie for 550 Kroner, and left him 100
> Kroner to get himself a new reel. Since all this happened in the line
> of duty, I am adding it to the expense bill. It ran me so low I had to
> telephone Oslo and a get a couple hundred dollars telegraphed up
> to the bank in Stryn. (8/27/54)

He reported that all in all, however, their mission was successful—they
got a lot of good pictures. "The only thing we're short on," he added, "is

*The Stegner house in Eastend
(c. 1952)*

*WS (second from right) and
playmates, on the bank of the
Whitemud River (Eastend,
Saskatchewan, c. 1923)*

Clockwise from lower left:
*Wallace Stegner, age three;
his mother, Hilda Stegner; his
aunt, Mina, and brother, Cecil
(Seattle, c. 1912)*

George Stegner, WS, unidentified
man (Fish Lake, Utah, c. 1929)

Jack Irvine and WS on
the varsity tennis team
(University of Utah, c. 1929)

WS at age twenty
(Fish Lake, Utah, c. 1929)

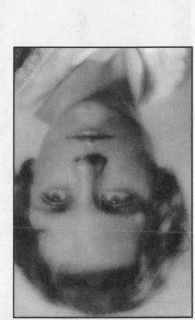

Mary, WS, Page, and Koofna (Greensboro, Vermont, 1942)

WS and Page Stegner (Salt Lake City, 1937)

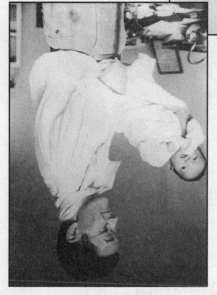

Mary Page (1931)

*Packed for their walking trip:
Mary, Peg Gray, WS, Phil
Gray, unidentified woman
(Greensboro, Vermont, c. 1939)*

*Robert Penn Warren, Wilbur Schramm,
Eric Knight, and WS (Iowa City, Iowa, c. 1941)*

*Bread Loaf faculty and fellows, 1946: (rear) Robert Frost, Robert Bordner, Graeme
Lorimer, Andrew Glaze, WS, Rudolph Kieve, Theodore Morrison, Eugene Burdick,
William Sloane; (front) Mrs. Burdick, Kay Morrison, Helen Everitt, Mary Stegner*

Group photo taken in Glen Canyon's Hidden Passage
in 1947: WS (rear, fifth from left), Mary (front, fifth from left)

WS and Page
playing cribbage
(Stanford, 1947)

A. B. Guthrie, Jr., and
Bernard DeVoto at Bread Loaf
(Middlebury, Vermont, 1948)

WS in first study (1951)

Page, WS, Mary
(Los Altos Hills, c. 1953)

Malcolm Cowley,
WS, Frank O'Connor
(Palo Alto, c. 1955)

Seminar meeting in Stegner home, c. 1960:
Ed McClanahan (far left), WS (center),
Larry McMurtry (right of Stegner),
Mort Grosser (far right)

WS, Dean Brimhold, Bates Wilson
(Canyonlands, Utah, 1962)

The Gray clan on Barr Hill at the picnic just before Peg Gray's death: (front, left to right) Margo Gray, Ellen Gray; (second row) Hazel Burton holding Bruce, Burr Gray, Peg Gray (seated), Phil Gray, Jr.; (middle) Sherry Gray, Clive Gray, Harold Gray, Phil Gray, Sr. (standing, far right); (back row) Nancy Gray Keyes, Lanny Keyes, Ronna Gray

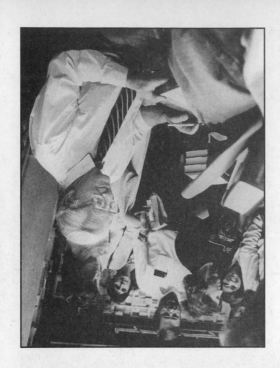

Bookstore signing for
Collected Stories *(1990)*

WS in his Los Altos Hills office (1986)

fish. Otherwise we can make a very pretty layout" (8/27/54). He was the only one to catch anything, and he caught it by accident. He was posing for a photo on someone's private stretch of river when a thirteen-pound salmon attached itself to his spinner. The woman—an irate American—who owned the riverbank in that area came running down from her house to confront him. Before she was placated, it cost him a lengthy apology, thirty dollars—and the fish.

In all of this activity Wallace's original reason for coming to Denmark had been set aside and then after investigation was abandoned. He had come to study village life in a European country where that life had remained rather steady, evolving over several centuries, and compare that with Eastend, a village that only recently had been established on the frontier. But he also wanted to carry forward his interest in the cooperative movement that had taken root early and still flourished in Scandinavia. Thus, the comparison he envisioned would be of the rugged individualism that characterized the frontier and was basic to American culture, and the cooperation he thought he would find as a foundation for society in European small towns in rural areas where, as in isolated areas of Denmark, World War II had had only minimal impact. After inquiries, the Stegners went to a little village on the southern Danish island of Taasinge, where they spent two weeks. They left and Wallace gave up his project after he found that the research would be too difficult without a better knowledge of Danish and that there didn't seem to be enough substance to his theory to make it worthwhile to study it further.

As Stegner's production of short stories slowed during the late fifties and by 1962 had ended, his production of articles increased in order to fit a new market, so that he averaged about six a year after 1956, reaching heights of eleven items in 1967 and fourteen in 1981. A significant number of these publications could be categorized as travel articles (others could be categorized under the topics of history; conservation; writers, writing, and the teaching of writing; and a relatively new genre for him, autobiography). In the spring of 1955 he began a relationship with *Holiday* that would bring him commissions to write three articles over the next three years, beginning with one on the Sierra Nevada high country that would be called "America's Mightiest Playground" (1956). He and Mary spent part of August in the Sierras, where they took in several areas that they had not seen before and touched bases with Page, who had taken a job working as a packer. In his article, besides describing the topography, scenery, folklore, and history, Wallace gives the reader of a popular magazine a good dose of environmentalism—but gently:

> In some ways the Sierra is a 14,000-foot monument to conserva-tion—a philosophy that all but began here, in the mind of John Muir, and has been fostered ever since by the Sierra Club, which Muir founded in 1892 to save at least some of the mountains from exploitation.

He had planned on going back to the Sierras in the late fall snows, but he became involved in yet another project that involved travel, this time to the Near East. He had been awarded a fellowship at Stanford for a year's stay (1955–56) at the Center for Advanced Studies. The fellowships were based on a scheme to bring together prominent or very promising scholars in various disciplines to pursue their own projects, but to do so in the proximity of the others, so that very bright people with different interests would have offices near each other, eat together, and socialize, and presumably be enriched and stimulated by the interac-tion. The project that Stegner would be engaged in was the one that would result in *Wolf Willow*, but he also had in mind that he would try a novel again. At the beginning of his tenure in September 1955, however, his agents contacted him in behalf of *Colliers* about an article for a series on "great events in the American past" which he had half agreed to do, and it was settled that he would write about the Mormon trek ("Ordeal by Handcart: the Mormon Trek," 1956) which would, in turn, lead him to *The Gathering of Zion* (1964).

Then in October of 1955 a former student at Bread Loaf who had become a public relations man for Aramco got in touch with him. The former student had become involved in setting up a project to write down the history of the oil company before the people who had made it—who were getting old—had passed from the scene. He called on Stegner because he had read something of his that gave him the notion that Stegner had some knowledge of deserts and frontiers and also because a lot of the people who had made Aramco in Saudi Arabia were Standard Oil of California people who had come out of Stanford. The project was attractive to Stegner because Saudi Arabia before oil development was a true frontier with few roads and almost no amenities—you couldn't even buy a paper clip or safety pin anywhere in the country. In addition, he had had a longtime interest in geology and geological exploration.

But as Mary remembered it, she talked him into taking the assignment because she had had dreams of Arabian Nights and had always wanted to see that country. So, in November, Stegner took a leave from the center and Aramco flew the Stegners on the company airplane, the *Flying Camel*, first to Amsterdam, where the corporation offices were, and on to Beirut for a few days of conferences. In between business sessions they were able to get to Damascus, down the Lebanese coast to Sidon, and up to Baalbek in the Bekaa. They took another plane to Dhahran, where they would be headquartered while in Arabia. Mary recalled:

> When we arrived there, it was no Arabian Nights at all. It was just a kind of shack, it seemed to me. Air conditioned shacks with a great big swimming pool in the middle with a canvas over the top. And that's where all the wives spent the days, because we were not allowed to go out with our husbands or out into the countryside to see anything.

Wallace added, "I got to go out into the deserts quite a lot with geologists and drillers and other kinds of people, but Mary got stuck in the compound where Musak played endlessly over the radio ... and by the pool you sat and disconsolately drank your jungle juice." He went out by truck and occasionally by small aircraft around the country, interviewing all the old-timers who were still left, checking out distances and the topography (which looked pretty much the same everywhere), and looking over the fields of the earliest wells (which looked pretty much the same everywhere).

One evening before leaving Saudi Arabia, the Stegners got the sad news over the radio that Bernard DeVoto had died.

When they got back to Stanford, Stegner was writing *Wolf Willow* with one hand and trying to assemble the Aramco history with the other.

There were a number of people in this country also that had to be talked to because they knew some of the history—a few had recorded their experiences in diaries or journals—and the company spared no expense in paying for Stegner's travel or sending people to him. Everything for him was first class, and as he has commented, "It was kind of nice for an old English professor to operate in terms like that." At the same time, he would run into a great deal of trouble in regard to publication. Aramco was paying him as a "consultant," and he would get no royalties (he counted on a lump sum on publication to give him a "stake" to take time off from teaching and do more writing). The manuscript would be published privately and distributed by Aramco. This didn't bother him. What was upsetting was that the company top executives decided that they didn't want to publish, although they had originally approved the project, and simply sat on the material for years, apparently afraid of a negative reaction from the Saudi royal family. Eventually, the material was published, but in a severely edited version, first, as "DISCOVERY!" in fourteen consecutive issues of *Aramco World Magazine*, from 1968 through early 1970, and then as a paperback book with the same title in 1971.

Although *DISCOVERY!* has never been available to the general public except as a relatively rare used book, we should note that the book tied in to Stegner's career and themes in several ways. It is a book whose heroes are often men like John Wesley Powell, men of science who have guts and integrity. One such is the American geologist Max Steineke, who was the first man on the scene to understand the stratigraphy and the structure under eastern Arabia's nearly featureless surface. Frequently, Stegner makes comparisons with the American frontier, as when he is talking about the difficulties of flying a plane over Arabia and the worry of the pilots about having to make a forced landing out in the empty desert. But they realized they need not fear, since the Bedouins had the habit of seeing everything that went on. "Even in a region apparently empty of humanity," he writes, "they had the knack that some of the Americans had observed among the Navajo. Beside a broken car or a stranger afoot or mounted, they could appear out of the ground."

And finally, one is aware throughout the book of his admiration for the cooperative effort that these engineers, mechanics, and construction workers had to make in order to overcome obstacles of climate, terrain, lack of proper materials and equipment, untrained workers, and the restrictions of Saudi Arabian laws, religious customs, and tribal traditions. They seemed to him to demonstrate what pioneering cooperation can accomplish, as versus the individualism so often practiced on our frontier. But on a more subtle level, one becomes aware of certain implicit conflicts in the author: he admires progress, while he is suspicious of it; likes the can-do, cobble-it-together enthusiasm of the oil field pioneers, but displays an underlying unease at a project so motivated by exploitation of the land for money, even though the land is largely barren. It is the same conflict in the author that one can trace back to his early, initial enthusiasm for the engineering accomplishment of Hoover Dam which later turned to antagonism for such projects, and his enthusiasm for Powell's engineering, land and water planning, and survey skills, but unease concerning his reclamation program, particularly as carried out long after his death in huge projects by the Bureau of Reclamation.

Although in part coming out of travel, the "Discovery!" series is best labeled as history. However, frequently Stegner's travel articles are framed by history, as are his conservation pieces; he was, as we have noted, a writer who was shaped in large part by a personal sense of the importance of history. When he traveled, he didn't just move across the surface of the earth; with knowing eyes he traveled through a panorama of historical events, as well as through geological and anthropological time. Typical of his essays that bring meaning to the present landscape through constant associations with the past are the second and third of his series for *Holiday*, "The World's Strangest Sea" (1957) and "California's Gold Rush Country" (1958).

Like all of his articles of this type, these are incredibly rich in detail and lore. They surpass in nearly every way the typical travel article in a popular magazine—in their arresting descriptions, in the detailed recall of historical events that give meaning to the landscape, and in a geographical and topographical placement that gives his area of focus texture and context. He always made sure that he read or reread all the relevant background material first and then took a physical tour of the area he would be writing about, no matter how familiar it might be to him, in order to get fresh impressions.

During this period of the late 1950s, he would publish several other travel articles beyond those already mentioned, including "A Love Affair with the Heber Valley, U.S.A.," which takes him back to Utah and is framed by the changes he has observed during several visits over several decades, and a thirty-page (including photos) extensive survey of "The Rocky Mountain West" that was published as a chapter in a book called *The Romance of North America*. In this latter piece, Stegner once again preaches the doctrine of Powell and DeVoto, along with his history, geography, geology, and sociology: "Those who live by the myth, or pretend to, have never yet admitted that they live in a land of little rain and big consequences."

On the fiction front, it was for Stegner a time of progress, but progress made in spite of discouragement. Several stories of the fifties never did reach publication, and several others, among his best, found homes only with difficulty. He very much wanted his first collection of stories, *The Women on the Wall*, back in print. It had come out in 1950, and Houghton Mifflin, despite earlier assurances to the contrary and despite the fact that Wallace and Mary had been working as "West Coast editors" for the firm, had let it drop off its list. This was one of the factors that would lead Stegner to search for a new publisher at the end of the decade. Houghton Mifflin did, however, bring out a second collection, *The City of the Living*, in 1956. A couple of months before publication, Wallace wrote to his editor, Austin Olney, in order to build up some enthusiasm for the book:

Actually these eight stories are ones I like, or I wouldn't be putting them into a collection. I write stories pretty slowly, one or two or three a year, and I have to mean one pretty seriously before I can make myself stay with it clear to the polishing stage. These are distillations—I suppose that's the best word—of experiences that have insisted on being remembered, or themes that have insisted on coming back into my head. One of them ["Pop Goes the Alley Cat"] is a reflection of the days when I was writing *One Nation* with *Look*. Two of them are reincarnations of my Oedipus complex, which seems to need periodic therapy ["The Blue-Winged Teal" and "The Volunteer"]. "The City of the Living" and "Impasse" utilize scenes, and the first one utilizes experiences as well, from the trip we took around the world in 1950–51. "The Traveler" is a survivor from our Vermont days, "Field Guide to the Western Birds" a kind of distorted reflection of our present exurbian existence—a commentary on the position of the artist in society as Henry James would *not* have written it, and a half-humorous half-defense of the American Philistine as a man of feeling. "Maiden in a Tower" is a nostalgic crying-back to the days of innocence. (4/6/56)

Of all of these, "Field Guide to Western Birds" is by far the most important, a milestone in his development as a writer of fiction. Written in 1952, it was a long story, nearly a novelette, and had had no success getting magazine publication. As it turned out, it finally gained publication in two books at nearly the same time—his own collection and a collection in paperback of short novels by various authors (*New Short Novels*, 1956).

In "Field Guide" Stegner creates Joe Allston, retired from an active life as a New York literary agent to a California suburb, spending much of his time looking out his study window, bird-watching, rather than writing his memoirs. This is a complicated metaphor that stretches on from the story into the two novels, *All the Little Live Things* and *Spectator Bird*, that also use him as narrator. First of all, of course, there is the declaration in the metaphor that this character is, above all, an observer. He looks out, away from himself, giving up the more self-centered occupation of writing memoirs, explaining (with some irony) at one point in the story, "I am beginning to understand the temptation to be literary and indulge the senses. It is a full-time job just watching and listening here."

Second, his looking involves identification and classification, a process that extends from real birds to those "Western birds" or people that he encounters in his neighborhood and at social gatherings. At the party that takes up most of the story, he looks at the various guests and thinks, "It is all out of some bird book, how the species cling together, and the juncoes and the linnets and the seedeaters hop around in one place, and the robins raid the toyon berries *en masse*, and the jaybirds yak away together in the almond trees." His story is a modified version of Mr.

Palmer's story in "The Women on the Wall": despite long experience with various kinds of people, he learns, in the instance of making judgments about the guest of honor at the party, that classifying people is not always so certain or easy as classifying birds. Life, like literature, is not a science.

Joe and his wife, Ruth, have been invited by neighbors Bill and Sue Casement to a concert party—cocktails, a gourmet catered dinner, and after, outside near the pool, a recital by a down-on-his-luck young pianist, Kaminski, whom the hostess hopes to promote toward a concert at Carnegie Hall. Kaminski turns out to be an arrogant and unhappy artist who does his best to insult everyone and to make Sue Casement, his benefactress, as uncomfortable as possible. At one point, the pianist throws a public tantrum about the guests eating and drinking so much before his performance. Standing in the buffet line, Joe and his wife see him stalk off, apparently threatening not to play, pursued by Sue, and Ruth comments:

"If she weren't so nice it would be almost funny."

"But she *is* so nice."

"Yes," she says. "Poor Sue."

As I circle my nose above the heaped and delectable trencher, the thought of Kaminski's bald scorn of food and drink boils over my insides. Is he opposed to nourishment? "A pituitary monster," I say, "straight out of Dostoevsky."

"Your distaste was a little obvious."

"I can't help it. He curdled my adrenal glands."

"You make everything so endocrine," she says. "He wasn't that bad. In fact, he had a point. It *is* a little alcoholic for a musicale."

"It's the only kind of party they know how to give."

"But it still isn't quite the best way to show off a pianist."

"All right," I say. "Suppose you're right. Is it his proper place to act as if he'd been captured and dragged here? He's the beneficiary, after all."

"I expect he has to humiliate her," Ruth says.

Sometimes she can surprise me. I remark that without an M.D. she is not entitled to practice psychiatry. So maybe he does have to humiliate her. That is exactly one of the seven thousand two hundred and fourteen things in him that irritate the hell out of me.

"But it'll be ghastly," says Ruth in her whisper, "if she can't manage to get him to play."

I address myself to the trencher.... But Ruth's remark of a minute before continues to go around in me like an auger, and I burst out again: "Humiliate her, uh? How to achieve power.... Did it ever strike you how much attention a difficult cross-grained bastard gets, just by being difficult?"

Here, unlike in Stegner's early fiction, often so flat, the dialogue crackles and snaps like a free wire dangling from a power pole. One of the main things Stegner achieves through this voice is interest. Joe—not to mention his wife—is intelligent, intensely observant, and above all, witty. The power of the personalities of these late narrators—Lyman Ward and Larry Morgan, as well as Joe—forces us to read on.

Although Joe, as we have just seen, takes an immediate dislike to this "Glandular Genius," as he calls Kaminski, he also begins to feel somewhat uncomfortable himself at the surfeit of food and drink on "this movie set where the standard of everything is excess." The contradiction here to his objection to Kaminski's saying pretty much the same thing underlines the ambiguity of Allston's position—he is both right and wrong in his reactions to the pianist. As the performance begins, Joe listens carefully in order to hear how good Kaminski is, but typically backtracks in his mind, wondering if, after all, he is capable of any final judgment. Nevertheless, he almost gloats when he thinks he hears "a fat, naked, staring discord" during Kaminski's performance of a difficult Bach piece.

The reader, who by now shares Allston's intense dislike of Kaminski, finds the pianist's disintegration after the recital almost predictable, almost enjoyable. He begins to drink heavily and shortly after makes a long, drunken, public confession in which he proclaims his need to fail and his fraudulent identity as a Polish Jew victimized by the Nazis. Finally, when the host tries to pull him off to bed, Kaminski drunkenly stumbles over a chair and falls into the swimming pool. The harmony, or the "niceness" as it might be called, of the occasion has been thoroughly shattered.

But things are not as they seem. As Joe and Ruth drive home, Joe discovers that Ruth, whose judgment in such matters he respects more than his own, thinks that Kaminski is, indeed, very good, exceptional—worth helping toward a concert in New York. But, of course, this chance, which might have been his only chance, is now gone. Joe wonders, "Why would he? . . . Where in God's name does he belong?" and "How shall a nest of robins deal with a cuckoo chick? And how should a cuckoo chick, which has no natural home except the one he usurps, behave himself in a robin's nest? And what if the cuckoo is sensitive, or Spiritual, or insecure? Christ." The epiphany here is ambiguous—the moral escapes him, and life remains as obscure as the fog that they drive through on the way back from the party. Joe can only be grateful to Ruth "for the forty years during which she has stood between me and myself."

A complicated narrator—a fallible wise man, as he might be called—has led us down the garden path into a complex of emotions difficult for the reader to sort out. It is a pattern repeated over and over again in the final novels. Kaminski is brimming over with self-pity; he is a phony, a pretender; he is arrogant and cruel and filled with self-importance—so that Joe Allston's dislike, and ours, is certainly justified. But Kaminski is also a poor Jewish young man, with feelings of inferiority and a compulsion to self-destruction, who nevertheless has a very real talent. He is thrust into a scene of upscale opulence dominated by a wealthy society that is with few exceptions largely populated by pretenders and philistines—the entire party is a kind of charade of artistic appreciation. Isn't the artist's discomfort, posturing, and anger justified? Just because he makes a social stink, are we justified in hating him, gloating over his downfall?

Even Joe Allston, who knows something about art and music, is wrong and comes to admit it, realizing that the identification of the human species can be a lot more difficult and fraught with possible error than he earlier in the story thinks it to be. At the end, the narrator is mired in doubt: "I don't know whether I'm tired, or sad, or confused. Or, maybe just irritated that they don't give you enough time in a single life to figure anything out." If there is a lesson, it is not so much about the nature of life as it is about the problem of discovering the reality behind appearances, which involves here the process of observing and judging others, a process that needs to be performed with humility and openness, with conclusions always subject to revision.

Such is the nature of this narrator as he evolved through "The Women on the Wall" and "Field Guide to Western Birds" to become the voice, the "fallible wise man" of the later novels. Stegner has remarked that "any work of art is the product of a total human being," but it is only with these late works that he was able to bring himself totally to his art. With the evolution of the Joe Allston voice and stance, Wallace was able to create a narrator that is a fiction, someone other than himself, and yet bring to that fiction all his faculties, all the force of his personality. By doing so, his storyteller is made near and real, and through the author's investment of himself, his deep participation, the complexities and ambiguities of living are made manifest.

These narrators make use of Wallace Stegner's personal assets—his dry sense of humor and wit (which make these later novels so entertaining); his willingness to laugh at himself and to examine himself; his skepticism; his search for the truths behind cultural and historical myth; and his concern for the preservation of the earth. Over time the narrators get closer and closer to the inner man, his concerns and values, as the man sheds his reluctance to risk and reveal himself. As he grew older, Stegner began to think he was getting wiser, but the last two decades of his life he threw out that notion, wondering if over time he had gained any wisdom at all.

One of the things that draws to Stegner's later storytellers—Joe Allston, Lyman Ward, and Larry Morgan—is that their wisdom is certified by their uncertainty, by inner debate and self-examination, by their consciousness that although they have had long lives and a variety of experiences, they don't know everything. All of them, at a late stage of life, like Stegner, are trying to learn more about themselves, as well as about other people and the world around them. While having strong values and carefully nurtured, strong characters, they nevertheless remain open to experience, and it is often in the conflict between their strength and their doubt that we find the central tension of these novels. With these traits, like their creator, they often seem younger than the young people around them who are often so very sure of themselves, so frozen in their opinions, so terribly closed-minded.

14

AN
ALL-STAR CAST

"It was like playing football under Vince Lombardi." So said novelist Ken Kesey a few years ago on a talk show when asked about taking Wallace Stegner's writing seminar. The spring before Kesey enrolled for the first time in the seminar in the fall of 1958, Stegner wrote to Avis DeVoto, Bernard's widow, "Every year this teaching business gets more like being broken on the wheel. It seems to me the kids get progressively brighter and worse-educated, so that they need to be told more, and give you more hell while you're telling them" (3/27/58). In the thirteen years since he had begun the new writing program, there was no doubt that the students had changed and that the teaching had grown increasingly more burdensome. Wallace's early delight with the classes of returning veterans, eager to learn and about his own age, had by now dissipated. Kesey was a student with an "attitude," a marker pointing to the rebellious students of the late sixties to come.

Seldom has Stegner been written about or the Stanford creative writing program written about that Kesey isn't mentioned, often leading the list of successful former students. And just as Stegner was invariably asked about Kesey, Kesey has almost as often been dogged by the question of Stegner's influence. Over the years both became thoroughly sick of being linked together, and each has had very mixed feelings about the other. The constant linking has no doubt come from the fact that they have been so very different, in lifestyles, values, and writing, that they have formed a natural pairing, a built-in center of drama, a fundamental conflict between generations, which has excited the journalist. In later years Stegner summed up his relationship to the younger writer by saying:

> I think they all make more of my antagonism to Kesey than there was there. Personally, I was never sympathetic to any of his ideas because I thought many of his ideas were half-baked. . . . [But] we got along in class perfectly well. I liked his writing most of the time very well. It was his extracurricular activities after he left the class and after he left Malcolm's [Cowley] class that kind of teed me off.

The tendency on the part of many has been to see these two authors in Miltonic terms, as a conflict between the forces of God and Satan, a representation reinforced by biblical metaphors used on occasion by the authors themselves. Which person represents good and which evil, or what kinds of good or evil, depends on the perspective of each author and the values of the observer. Kesey has depicted himself as a sort of imp of the perverse—his collection of stories is called *Demon Box*—a troublemaker for those in authority or who take themselves too seriously. Ordinary, middle-class values and behavior are shown in his work as empty, false, and hypocritical. He sees himself (and central characters like McMurphy in *Cuckoo's Nest*) as heroic in his rebellion, as, of course, did Satan. And from the Stegner point of view, like Satan, Kesey tried to make what is good—morality in the service of others—evil, and what is evil—self-indulgence—good. Stegner, in turn, refers to a fictional character, Jim Peck in *All the Little Live Things*, who espouses Kesey's values and lifestyle, as a Caliban, joined to the forces that are corrupting and destructive of life. Stegner's own nearly impeccable personal behavior from a conventional point of view would, for some observers, place him on the side of the heavenly host (he was not self-righteous, but he was judgmental), whereas for Kesey such adherence to convention made Stegner not only a failure, but a danger to all those who seek to discover an inner truth apart from what they have been told they should be. The conflict would become the essence of the youth revolt of the sixties, a conflict of generations, of goals, of artistic vision and methods—one that continues to this day and that has in part defined Stegner's audience and reputation.

Ken Kesey went to the University of Oregon as an undergraduate, where he took some creative writing courses from James Hall and where he was on the football and wrestling teams. Malcolm Cowley, who taught him writing for a quarter at Stanford when Stegner was on leave, described Kesey as having "the build of a plunging halfback, with big shoulders and a neck like the stump of a Douglas fir." It is important in understanding the Kesey persona to understand that he likes to talk of himself as a "jock," part of an anti-intellectual, blue-collar, "I am just an ordinary working guy" stance that he has taken throughout his life. Despite his later antipathy toward everything connected to academics and academic life, he was an outstanding student at Oregon—not so much through disciplined application to his studies, however, as a result of being extremely bright. He was recommended by his professors for a Woodrow Wilson Fellowship, and receiving it, he decided to enroll in the creative writing program at Stanford.

What seems to have been one of the most important factors influencing his personal and professional life was his reading, three times, of Kerouac's *On the Road* before coming to Stanford, "hoping to sign on in some way, to join that joyous voyage, like thousands of other volunteers inspired by the same book, and its vision, and, of course, its incomparable hero." In looking back, he has said that Kerouac influenced him primarily in showing him "that the best reason for being a writer is doing what you *like* to do." Coming to Stanford with that vision of the writer's life set him on a collision course with Stegner before they even met, since, as we have seen, Stegner believed in discipline, hard work, and revision as the basis for good writing. Upon arriving in the Bay Area, Kesey looked for the Kerouac version of the writing life in San Francisco's North Beach, where remnants of the beat generation still hung out.

While he enjoyed the interaction with the seminar students, he seemed to have developed an antipathy to Stegner almost immediately. When asked later what he learned from Stegner, he replied, "Just never to teach in college." He added, referring to the writing teacher:

A man becomes *accustomed* to having two hundred people gather every day at one o'clock giving him all of their attention—because he's clever, good-looking, famous, and has a beautiful voice. That can't happen without affecting a man's writing—the wrong way.

Kesey came to feel, about the time he went to Stanford, that reading and gaining knowledge from books and teachers was a poor substitute for the kind of experiences recommended by Kerouac.

His interaction with the professor in the seminar would seem to be best summarized as a polite sullenness. Publicly, there was never a harsh word exchanged. However, early in their relationship, Kesey submitted a paper for a story assignment with a title familiar to all teachers: "On Why I Am Not Writing My Last Term Paper." It was the usual sophomoric attempt to justify not completing an assignment because the student judged it not meaningful or challenging enough. Kesey told his teacher that he should be writing a novel, not engaging in academic exercises. Kesey critic Stephen Tanner describes the response:

> Stegner would have none of that. His annotation chides Kesey by saying the paper is merely self-expression, which is really self-indulgence. "Now go write that novel, but don't for God's sake let it turn into self-expression."

What Stegner didn't know until later was that Kesey had nothing at all against self-indulgence. He also showed some arrogance. Another student, Nancy Packer, recalled a time when Kesey did submit some fiction, reading it aloud to the seminar. The class discussed it, missing something that Kesey thought that it should have seen, and "he said, 'Yeah, I didn't think you'd get it,' with a very proud tone to his voice that somehow showed a superiority over all of us because we hadn't been able to understand what he was driving at."

Judged by the amount that each has said about the other publicly, Kesey would seem to have been much more preoccupied with Stegner than the other way around. And a good proportion of Kesey's reactions to his former teacher, mostly negative, seem based on false impressions or inadequate information. No one else seems to have thought of the older man as an elitist or as snobbish—just the opposite, as friendly, democratic in attitude, generous. Furthermore, as a creative writing teacher, Stegner had been throughout his career, despite his scholarly credentials, constantly under pressure of being cast as a second-class citizen and had been himself the target of snobbery. In objecting to Stegner's fame and position, Kesey seems to have had no conception of how hard Wallace had worked to get where he was, that he had come out of a working-class background and worked his way through college and on to support himself while he got his university degrees. There is also the suggestion in Kesey's comments that he thought of the Stanford professor as effete and his fiction ingrown, precious, and directed toward an academic audience. In an interview he said,

> You go back and read his early stuff, *On a Darkling Plain*, maybe. Fine work. Then you try his later stuff and you find he's not writing to people any longer, not to the people he knows and loves, anyway. He's writing to a classroom and to his colleagues.

Kesey reacted to his creative writing teachers not on the basis of what they had to offer, but on a more personal basis in terms of how they reacted to him and his work. He finished his Woodrow Wilson Fellowship year with Stegner and then applied for a Stegner Fellowship the following year and the year after and was turned down both times and felt snubbed. After Stegner went on leave in the fall of 1960, the seminar was taken over by Malcolm Cowley, who was excited by Kesey's originality, and the two of them had a number of private sessions discussing the manuscript that would become *One Flew Over the Cuckoo's Nest* (1962). Cowley has claimed not to have contributed anything material to the novel, but did ask questions and pointed out passages that he thought didn't work. Cowley had singled him out for attention and praise, and Kesey would thereafter give him credit for teaching him how good a writer he could be, while giving Stegner none. It may be also that the two got along so well because Cowley was not a writer of fiction and Kesey had no reason to feel competitive.

The following quarter the class was taken over by Frank O'Connor, and, according to Cowley, Kesey did not like the way he was running the class and dropped out. Kesey had rented a bungalow on Perry Lane, an area near the Stanford golf course notorious for its bohemian lifestyle, and invited other members of the seminar to meet at his home for readings and discussion. What he was doing, in effect, was setting up a competing group, with him at the center. It might be termed the "anti-seminar," since, as it developed over several years into the drug experimentation of the "electric kool-aid acid test" as described by Tom Wolfe and into the Merry Pranksters, its essence was countercultural rebellion. Kesey would during these years of the early and mid-sixties become a prominent guru of the "youth-cult movement, a psychedelic impresario in the transition from Beats to Hippies." In looking back, Kesey has said:

> As soon as I took LSD, and he drank Jack Daniel's, we drew the line between us right there. That was, as far as he was concerned, the edge of the continent and you're supposed to stop there. Well, I was younger than he was and I didn't see any reason to stop, so I kept tooling along forward, as did a lot of my friends. Ever since then, I have felt kind of impelled into the future by Wally, by his dislike of what I was doing, what we were doing. That was the kiss of approval in some way. When we got together and headed off on a bus to deal with the future of our synapses, we knew that Wally wasn't liking what we were doing and that was good enough for us.

Some of the seminar students were torn between Wallace, his values and teaching, and Kesey, his values and example. Some, like Ken Babbs, became solely devoted to Kesey's doctrine of freedom, but others, like Robert Stone, refused the choice:

> Stegner saw Kesey and what he represented as a threat to civilization and intellectualism and sobriety. And Ken was a threat to all those values. But for those of us who were there, what was going on around Ken was so exciting, and just plain fun, that we were not about to line up against each other on ideological grounds.

In any case, having at least some of his students seduced down the path of fun and games was somewhat troubling for Stegner during these years, especially since he was aware that Kesey was making him the symbol of everything that a young, vital person should rebel against. But in Stegner's life and career, there was so much going on that on a personal basis Kesey's activities were little more than an annoyance to shake one's head over (although the values he stood for as adopted by a significant portion of the younger generation a decade later would trouble Wallace a great deal). For Kesey, however, the Stegner that he had created in his mind would seem, according to his testimony, a lifelong impetus toward rebellion: "I have felt kind of impelled into the future by Wally." He also stated in 1993, several months after Stegner's death, that "he [Wally] was able to put together a power that ruled literature in California—and in some ways the rest of this nation—for awhile." This would have been news to Stegner, the man who had been so often discounted as a mere "Western realist" and ignored by the Eastern media.

In the long run what irritated Stegner about Kesey were the values that his life and work endorsed, which in many instances were diametrically opposed to his own. For a man dedicated to the ideal of cooperation, the advocacy of anarchy was outrageous. Much of his life, as we have seen, Stegner fought a battle to dispute the Western myth of rugged individualism, particularly as it has been embodied in the lone horseman. Kesey fondly embraces that myth, which Stegner found so destructive of the people and the land, and uses it in his work, modeling his central character in *Cuckoo's Nest* in part after the gunslinger figure, not out of history, but out of TV Westerns and movies. When McMurphy arrives at the electrotherapy ward of the mental hospital, he announces his arrival: " 'McMurphy's the name, pardners,' he said in his drawling cowboy actor's voice, 'an' the thing I want to *know* is who's the peckerwood runs the poker game in this establishment?' " This is a joke, of course, but a characterization that is used in admiration and one that Kesey obviously thinks provides his character with stature. His use of the TV cowboy and the comic book hero as "the honest American myths" suggest his disdain for traditional literary sources, as well as for history.

One contemporary of Kesey's remembered that the seminar seemed to be divided between the intellectuals and the barbarians, "the intellectuals who had read some stuff and the barbarians who had never read anything . . . [and] were proud of it, thought you sullied your style if you read anybody else." By contrast, as we have seen, Stegner found it important to learn from other writers and felt that history was an all-important context by which to discover the self, and within which contemporary society and the contemporary landscape could be understood. Stegner's answer to Kesey's know-nothing stance and gang of Merry Pranksters is well stated in his essay "The Book and the Great Community," in which he says:

> Thought is neither instant nor noisy. . . . It thrives best in solitude, in quiet, and in the company of the past, the great community of recorded human experience. That recorded experience is essential whether one hopes to re-assert some aspect of it, or attack it.

And elsewhere in the same essay:

> No young person respects history as much as do people who have lived a little of it. "Why do you care where you came from or what your ancestors did?" a girl asked me when I was trying to explain to a group of students my reason for writing a somewhat personal history book, *Wolf Willow*. "Isn't it what you *are* that matters? *Now?*"
>
> Now. It is a big word with the young, almost as big a word as wow. Between them, those two words seem sometimes to comprehend the responses of a whole generation. . . . Iconoclasm can become as compulsive as any other form of conventional behavior, and the voice of the young hormone is sometimes mistaken for the voice of God.

In addition to a great difference in regard to the importance of the cultural tradition, there was also between Stegner and Kesey conflicting visions of woman. There is macho edge to Kesey's use of hero types out of popular culture. Again, to go back to *Cuckoo's Nest*, which most directly speaks of the writer's values during the time he knew Stegner, Big Nurse is a caricature of one kind of Hemingway female—the woman with power, as in Mrs. Adams in the Nick Adams stories or, more to the point, the head nurse, Miss Van Campen, in *A Farewell to Arms*. They are castrators all. The other kind of woman most commonly found in Kesey's work is another Hemingway variety, the woman who frankly enjoys sex—the good females in *Cuckoo's Nest* are the prostitutes. Both kinds of women characters are also part of the Western myth: in the myth it was the gentlewomen (puritanical and straitlaced) who brought rules and civilization to the frontier (established and enforced the System), and it was the prostitute (with heart of gold) who frequented the cow towns and mining camps before they got law and religion. Stegner's works, by contrast, show women of whole characters who often demonstrate the worthwhile values of compassion, sympathy, and tolerance; they may be victimized in a man's world, but they maintain their strength of character, like Elisa Mason in *The Big Rock Candy Mountain*, who endures and remains caring despite hardship. Stegner's women, created out of admiration, are complex and live in a complex world. Take, for example, Susan Burling Ward in *Angle of Repose*—one finds no easy answers to life or relationships in that book. Rather than caricatures, women in Stegner's fiction are richly endowed individuals, like Ruth, Joe Allston's wise and forbearing wife, or Marion Catlin, who loves all the little live things. Charity, in *Crossing to Safety*, is a woman with power, a castrator of her husband, but also a person who empowers others through her love and generosity.

Although he has not admitted to it publicly—writers are often unable or unwilling to admit to the influence of others—Kesey does seem to have learned some valuable lessons from Stegner. By demanding careful writing and a readable manuscript, Stegner might share some of the credit with Cowley for converting Kesey to a writing process that involved extensive revision. John C. Pratt, by reproducing sample manuscript pages of *Cuckoo's Nest*, demonstrates just how extensive the revisions were. Furthermore, in a letter from Kesey to his close friend Ken Babbs (also reproduced by Pratt) while Kesey was writing *Cuckoo's Nest*, he refers to Stegner in a way that suggests the teacher did make a major contribution to the novel's success:

> I am beginning to agree with Stegner that it [point of view] truely [*sic*] is the most important problem in writing. The book I have been doing on the lane is a third person work, but something was lacking; I was not free to impose my perception and bizarre eye on

the god-author who is supposed to be viewing the scene, so I tried something that will be extremely difficult to pull off, and, to my knowledge, had never been tried before—the narrator is going to be a character. He will not take part in the action, or ever speak as I, but he will be a character to be influenced by the events that take place, he will have a position and personality and a character that is not essentially mine.

This is a reference to the brilliant creation of what became the narration of Chief Broom, the schizophrenic Indian, who, because he has become a deaf mute as a refuge from the power of the "Combine" (organized society), is both part of the scene and yet removed from it. There is a Hemingway-like irony in the emotion that comes out of a narrative that is so dreamlike, silent, and passive. The only close antecedent for this narration is the first-person narration of the idiot Benjy in Faulkner's *The Sound and the Fury*, which may or may not have inspired Kesey. (Malcolm Cowley was well known for regenerating the reputations of both Faulkner and Hemingway.) Benjy becomes a symbol for the degenerated South; Broom, for the emasculated and dehumanized condition of the contemporary male. Point of view, the way a story is told, was not only something that Stegner himself had struggled with through much of his career, it was, according to his former students, something that he discussed over and over again in class: that they needed to find the right voice in order to make their narrative work.

The period from the mid-fifties to the mid-sixties was a particularly rich time in terms of major talent going through the Stanford creative writing program. There have been many students from that period who in their writing careers have achieved as much as or more than Kesey, and because of this Stegner resented journalists giving so much attention to someone he disagreed with so thoroughly. To name but a few of the best-known such students in fiction, there was Tillie Olsen, Edward Abbey, Wendell Berry, Nancy Packer, Ernest Gaines, Peter Beagle, Larry McMurtry, Robert Stone, Thomas McGuane, Al Young, James Houston, Pat Zelver, and Evan Connell. Almost without exception, their perceptions of teacher and class differ markedly from those of the guru of Perry Lane.

During these years of the late 1950s and early 1960s, Wallace stood tall and loose, well but not expensively dressed, with broad shoulders, his thick hair just beginning to gray, and with what one writer has called "Robert Mitchum eyes." Son Page recalled that his father "was the kind of guy who always put on a necktie." Judith Rascoe, a former student who did the screenplay for *Dog Soldiers* (Robert Stone's book), has said, "I have a mental image of him sitting back in his chair. Someone physically at ease, in control, and very attractive." Wallace's schedule, when he was teaching, was nearly always the same: writing in the morning at home, and a literature class or the writing seminar in the afternoons, with a lot of time before and after classes devoted to student office hours. He was, according to Nancy Packer, who shared an office with him for two years, "about the most responsible person I had ever met, someone who didn't shirk his duty in any way . . . he was utterly open and accessible to students. . . . He'd never turn them away."

Once at the end of an office hour, Wallace turned to Nancy, who was sitting at her desk across the room. "Who's your favorite writer?" he asked. "Anton Chekhov," she said. "Mine too," he said. "The world," he added, "is divided into those for whom Tolstoy is the greatest or Anton Chekhov, and short story writers always prefer Chekhov." Nancy then asked, "You're such a great short story writer—why haven't you continued to write stories?" "Because you can't have a major reputation on the short story," he answered.

Kay House, who was in the workshop at the same time as Packer, Ernest Gaines, Ken Kesey, and Larry McMurtry, took notes during the class. Here is a sample from over the quarter:

A representative from Houghton Mifflin was coming to campus. *Esquire* has some fellowships that Stegner says are better deal than most. He says look at some good dramatic writing in Ehrlich's *God's Angry Man*. A novel should be integrated structure; no Los Trancos Woods novels are great architecture. Motion necessary— revery not dramatic—beginning ought to give a hint of the crux in the first chapter. (I remember his writing on one of my papers, "You're going a mile and a furlong. Break!") Stegner on symbols— critics get on a coon trail of symbols. Discovering them is like discovering a story is written in words. A symbol is supposed to extend the wall, but you need the wall. He quoted Norman Foerster—all symbols are not correlated specifically, but suggest—

When she was revising her dissertation, in which she had said that the Dutch's only sins were sins of excess, he had written, "All sins are sins of excess." She was tempted, writing the acknowledgments later, to say, "Thanks to Wallace Stegner who taught me the nature of sin," but decided against it.

Ed McClanahan (*The Natural Man*), who, like Robert Stone, found himself split between Kesey and Stegner, recalled what he believed to be the most important lesson that Stegner gave him, one that he invariably uses himself when teaching. Wallace was talking one time about the importance of keeping a narrative moving, and he said, "You must strive for a balance of scene and summary." What he meant by scene was dialogue and action in real time, as if the characters are standing in front of you on a stage, and what he meant by summary was the authorial voice or narrator summarizing the action, expository passages that condense time—these must be balanced. Al Young (*Snakes*), who was a fellow in 1966, felt that

Wally was very businesslike. He would tell you exactly what he thought, and he would be considerate of your feelings, but he would not pull punches. He had a manner, a style, that was gentle. And he would give you bad news in a gentle way.

Young tried a number of different styles and approaches in his stories for the class, and finally turned in a story that he had written in the vernacular. Wallace liked it and encouraged him to go on with it, telling him that he had tapped into a voice and a whole vein of characterization that was wonderful. Then, later, when Young wrote *Sitting Pretty*, which was all in the vernacular, "Wally wrote an incredible blurb for it ["Huckleberry Finn in Black English"] and then sent me a letter saying, 'I am now a fan.' "

Wallace worked hard to bring as much diversity of students into the program as possible. Ernest Gaines (*The Autobiography of Miss Jane*

Pitman), who was there at the same time as Kesey and Packer, remembered how there was often opposition to certain people being admitted, but he recalled how Stegner would say:

"We're not going to have only the Ivy Leaguers coming in here! . . . We have other writers who have something to say." We had [all kinds of people] . . . Southerners, Blacks, Europeans. "We're going to get anybody who can submit work that we think is the kind of work that we want to deal with—[it has to be] based on his work . . . regardless of whether he is a Martian or Communist or whatever!" And I think that's the kind of guy he is, and that's the kind of teacher you should have.

Stegner tried to make the workshop/seminar sessions as open and relaxed as possible, encouraging an atmosphere of help and support, rather than a sense of competitiveness. Jim Houston (*Continental Drift*), a student of this same era, recalled that all of them learned a lesson of humility and mutual support when Wallace came in one day and told the class that they would not be working on their manuscripts that day, but that he was going to read from his own manuscript. He said that he was stuck, that he and his editors at Viking had gone around and around on it and couldn't find a solution. He had lost his way, he told them, and needed their help and suggestions to get out of the bind. That class session taught them, a workshop "full of gung-ho, full-of-ourselves writers," in Houston's words, that *even he* could get lost, that writing remains always a struggle. According to Houston, also, what Stegner gave them was the example of the professional writer, how he conducted himself, disciplined himself, and still was able to give to others.

The main thing a fellowship gave him, Ernest Gaines has said, was time. For the first time in his life he had the opportunity to do nothing else but write—and so it was for so many of the other students. Even those in the workshop who were not fellows were often given a light teaching load of undergraduate creative writing classes (there was an E. H. Jones Visiting Lectureship that required only one class), enough to support them while also providing time to write and the companionship of other writers. Through his experiences with the Iowa program, the one at Harvard, and at Bread Loaf, Wallace had discovered how important companionship, mutual stimulation, and peer criticism and support could be to a developing writer. Many discovered for the first time that the difficulties they faced and fears they had were shared by others. Wallace sought to make the experience of being at Stanford a total one, and through his parties and socializing with the students attempted to build a camaraderie among the students that would extend beyond the classroom. While he was not buddy-buddy, the kind to go out to have a beer with his students after class, he knew that for his students the discussions at a party, a barbecue, or at the local pub after class might be the most valuable after all. It was the sense that the fragile ties of fellowship might be destroyed, the workshop fragmented into factions, and some students led away from the discipline and hard work that he thought absolutely required for success, that was at the bottom of his disapproval of the Kesey distractions.

Ernest Gaines recalled that at first in the class there was some tension between him and Wendell Berry (*A Place on Earth*). They felt some reluctance to criticize each other's work, until one afternoon they were at a party:

> He just called me into the backyard like a cowboy shootout, saying, "Okay, now we have to talk this over—we have to get this out of our way." And I thought it was just the greatest thing that could have happened because after talking we realized that we probably had more in common than he had with many of the other students in the class. White students outnumber the Black anyway, and I probably had more in common with him than I had with any of the white students because of the land. We were both Southerners loving the land, and after that we became close friends, and I have been back to his house [in Kentucky] several times.

Many of Stegner's students ended up as writers concerned with the land, with a strong sense of place, and perhaps it was in part his example that led them in that direction. One thinks, in this regard, of Jim Houston and California, Larry McMurtry and Texas, Edward Abbey and the Southwest, Ernest Gaines and Louisiana, and even Ken Kesey and Oregon.

But of his students perhaps the strongest adherent to place and defender of the land may be Wendell Berry, and because his stand has been so principled, his connection to family and tradition so strong, he may have turned out to have been the writer his teacher most admired. Born and raised on a farm which had been in his family for generations, Berry had the dream of so many country boys of leaving dreary farm work, getting an education, and making his way in the world—"his way" became gradually clear to him as becoming a writer. He had no idea of ever returning to the land. After getting an M.A. at the University of Kentucky, he submitted a novella to the Creative Writing Program at Stanford. He was notified in the spring of 1958 that he had won a fellowship for the following school year. The good news was so exhilarating, he spent the summer before moving to California reading as much of Stegner fiction as he could find. First, he read *Remembering Laughter* and thought, "As the would-be author of a first novel myself, I envied it and was intimidated by it. I saw plainly that this man, when he was perhaps my age, had known how to write, and that he had known how much better than I did." He then went on to read the two collections of Stegner stories, *The Women on the Wall* and *The City of the Living*, reading them dispassionately, since he was not interested in writing short stories, and for the first time looking to see how works of fiction were made, "seeing how an able workman made use of a form." Thus, Stegner became his teacher, he felt, even before he ever laid eyes on him, teaching him in a way that he has since come to realize as characteristic of him: "By bestowing a kindness that implied an expectation, and by setting an example."

In recent years, thinking back on Stegner the teacher, Berry recalled that he did indeed feel a great burden of expectation from Stegner:

> I'd describe him as . . . well, his performance was like a really good foreman. . . . He gave you good technical criticism and good technical criticism comes from somewhere. I think you always know that. He would get down to the nuts and bolts of it. . . . [For example] he made me see that an ending I'd made on my novel was phony. He didn't say that it was phony, but when he'd finished his comment on it, I knew that that's what it was—not genuine, unauthorized by the things that went before it.

Berry eventually realized that his place was not teaching on some college campus in California or Massachusetts but on his native soil. He was able to buy a farm next to his family's farm on the banks of the Kentucky River near Port Royal. He is a working farmer, operating with the minimum of machinery, and his sense of the land and its history, his farm and his work on it, his childhood growing up nearby, and his family and neighbors have given him much to think and write about—poetry, fiction, and essays. What part Stegner's example, his concern for place and history, may have had in this decision to go back to the land is problematic. But Berry does feel a sense of his influence that came to him after returning to Kentucky, and in thinking back on it, he said:

> I don't think he was the kind of teacher who tried to make his students into followers, but the outcome of my acquaintance with him is that I've become his follower in lots of ways. And it didn't happen at Stanford, but when I came away, when I came back and settled here and began to read his non-fiction books—*Wolf Willow*, *Beyond the Hundredth Meridian*, the DeVoto biography, and the conservation essays. His very painstaking attempt to understand himself in terms of his own regional sources has been extremely important and confirming to me. . . . I think he's probably the first American fiction writer to be a conservationist. . . . I'd like to understand better exactly what the lineage is. . . . Stegner becomes the ancestor or predecessor of the next generation of people like Edward Abbey and Gary Snyder.

And Wendell Berry, it should be added.

Wendell Berry is the only student whose life and work Stegner has ever written about at length. He does so in an essay called "A Letter to Wendell Berry," which was reprinted in his final collection of essays, *Where the Bluebird Sings to the Lemonade Springs*. But in another essay in that same collection, "The Sense of Place," he provides this considerable tribute:

> If you don't know where you are, says Wendell Berry, you don't know *who* you are. Berry is a writer, one of our best, who after some

circling has settled on the bank of the Kentucky River, where he grew up and where his family has lived for many generations. He conducts his literary explorations inward, toward the core of what supports him physically and spiritually. He belongs to an honorable tradition, one that even in America includes some great names: Thoreau, Burroughs, Frost, Faulkner, Steinbeck—lovers of known earth, known weathers, and known neighbors both human and nonhuman. He calls himself a "placed" person.

In his "Letter" Stegner praises Berry's sincerity, his total involvement in his work, and his values. He cannot look upon Berry's books as simply books, but as substantial chunks of Berry himself, "the expression of qualities and beliefs that are fundamental, profound, and rare." And when he quotes Berry, he says he does so not just to pay tribute to his exstudent's verbal felicity, but also for those qualities of character—thoughtfulness, integrity, and responsibility—to which he responds. It is comforting to have Berry's success, which has illustrated that one doesn't have to be crazy, alcoholic, or suicidal to write well and have something valuable to pass on to the world. Furthermore, those who read Berry devoutly—and Stegner said that he was proud to be one of them—find in his work something too often lacking in this world today—"the value, the real physical and spiritual satisfaction, of hard human work."

Student after student will tell you of the many kindnesses that their teacher performed for them. Berry remembered the occasion when Wallace drove up to San Francisco to appear on a radio show with him, an act "far beyond the call of duty." Kay House, a student who eventually became a literature professor, recalled being given the opportunity to write one of the essays, along with several of the most distinguished scholars and critics in the country, in a critical survey of American literature. It gave an invaluable early boost to her career. Nancy Packer remembered the long, moving letter he wrote to her on the occasion of her mother's death. And Al Young told of Wallace's offer of his house to Young and his wife. The Youngs had come down from Berkeley, had no car or anyplace to stay, and Al would not get his first check until the fall, and Stegner offered his house for the summer while he and Mary were in Vermont: " 'Just take care of the yard and flowers.' I was very moved by that."

The list of such examples is long, but one more is worth mentioning. Robert Stone has not talked about this, but his close friend Ed McClanahan recalled the time when Stone, who was a heavy drinker, began to become very worried about his health. He had stayed on in the Stanford area after his fellowship year to finish his novel, although he had very little money. He began to have terrible, splitting headaches that wouldn't go away and was having trouble with his eyesight, constantly aware of something on the periphery of his vision. He was a tormented soul anyway, as Ed thought back on him, and these developments really began to worry him deeply. He finally went to the Stanford Medical Center, where they gave him a battery of tests and concluded that he may have an inoperable brain tumor. They said that they couldn't be sure until they did an exploratory, boring holes in his skull. It turned out that he didn't, that the cause was probably mental and emotional, and in fact, after they told him he didn't have a tumor, the symptoms went away.

However, Stone could not possibly cover the medical bills. Stanford students at that time got all the medical attention they needed essentially free, but he was no longer a student. As Ed told it:

Mr. Stegner for the first time in the whole history of the Stegner fellowship program extended Bob's fellowship after the fact. The term had already begun when Bob got sick, and Bob was not the kind of guy who would go around and ask for that. In fact, I don't think he ever wanted anybody to know that Mr. Stegner was doing it. . . . The whole reason for his doing it was to help Bob through this crisis. When Mr. Stegner extended the fellowship to him, he not only got his medical bills covered, but it gave him $1250 for the quarter's worth of the fellowship—the cash. And Mr. Stegner didn't even ask him to do so much as come to the class after he got back on his feet, which everybody else was automatically expected to do.

Ed also remembered when Mr. Stegner—as he invariably referred to him—read to the class from the first chapters of *All the Little Live Things*, and "everybody was really knocked out by it." Everyone was in awe by the quality of the prose, and one student was really lavish in his praise: "Oh, it's a great book. This obviously is a Pulitzer Prize winning book. What would it mean to you if you were to win the Pulitzer Prize with this? What changes would you make in your life if you were to win it?" Mr. Stegner thought about it for moment, and he said, "I'd drink a better brand of bourbon."

15

THE
STRUGGLE TO
LOCATE ONESELF

A Shooting Star was a mistake. Early on he knew it. Stegner, unlike many other writers, was a good judge of his own work, and when the manuscript was two-thirds completed, he told Nancy Packer that he was very uneasy about it. He brought it to class and read parts aloud, hoping for some insight from his students into what he could do with it. As early as 1956 he had written to Frank O'Connor, despairing of his lack of progress:

> We live in our mild dusk or twilight. I am stuck cold and dead in the novel I'm working on, and have wasted three weeks, and I am tempted every day to take out in bricklaying the energy I should apply to the god damned typewriter and the god damned problem of how to say an expository section without seeming expository. This morning I am warming up the typing finger on you, and I hope for results by associative magic, because the O'Connor story flows so inevitably that I cannot imagine that one was ever stuck. (4/18/56)

He kept revising and trying different approaches, but he felt like he was in a sand trap: he kept hitting the ball, and it would hit the lip and roll back into the deep sand again. The basic problem was that he had created a character, Sabrina, but he didn't know where she was going. He took the manuscript with him as he and Mary took off for the year to Europe in the early summer of 1959.

On his third try, he finally was awarded a Guggenheim Fellowship, which had given him the year off from teaching. He planned to spend that year abroad, using it to finish *A Shooting Star* and go on to another project—probably, he thought, another novel. Although he was also in progress on *Wolf Willow*, he would wait on it until he got back to a good library, since the parts that remained to be written required historical research. Before they could leave, Mary had to finish her work as editor of the *O. Henry Memorial Award Prize Stories* and Wallace had to write an introduction to the volume. He was also in the middle of changing publishers and wanted to make a decision before he left. He was disappointed with Houghton Mifflin on the grounds that they had not really promoted his books and they had refused to put several of his books, now out of print, into paperback. After much consultation with his agents, Carol and Carl Brandt, he decided on Viking. He liked the idea of Marshall Best becoming his personal editor, and wrote to him, "I can't tell you how I am looking forward to working with you and your staff. I shall sit in Florence and Rome and write you letters like Fitzgerald to Max Perkins" (4/23/69).

In June the Stegners took off, stopping at Hudson, Ohio, for Page's marriage (he had met Marion McKenzie in Greensboro, where her family had a summer home), and then went on to take an apartment in London for the summer. While they were there, C. P. Snow, whom they had met when he had been a visitor at Stanford and who admired Wallace's work, invited all the London writers of his acquaintance to a reception to meet them. They also took a side trip to Dublin to visit Frank O'Connor. In the fall they bought a car, a little Hillman convertible, and drove down through the Low Countries and France and over the Alps into Italy, where they were joined by the Grays and spent the following four months with them in Florence.

Much of Wallace's time, aside from a couple of breaks for sightseeing in France and Germany, was devoted to his writing, often seven days a week. But although he was working hard, he also was enjoying the atmosphere of Florence—the streets and shops, the river and its bridges, and, of course, the incomparable museums. They often went to the galleries with Phil Gray, who was very knowledgeable about Italian art, and Mary recalled that they learned a great deal from just going to see the pictures and having him talk about them. All in all, the year, first in Florence and then in Rome, was in Mary's estimation the best year they'd had abroad together. In Florence they were fortunate to get a large, comfortable room at the pensione, with bath and access to a big balcony with a view of the Arno River. They soon found that the pensione had a marvelous cook, so good that they seldom ate out. They met several other people who were staying there, and many evenings after dinner they would have a most pleasant hour or two together, sitting in a room off the balcony and talking over coffee and brandy.

Ben Page, the Stanford geologist, and his wife, Virginia, were in Florence also and became good friends of the Grays, and the couples often went out together on trips into the countryside. In the Hillman with the Pages, they went off to Pisa, Siena, and Urbino. Mary and Wallace were particularly interested in Piero della Francesca, so they went to Borgo san Sepolcro to see his *Resurrection*, to Monterchi, for the Madonna del Porto, and to Arezzo, where they marveled at the magnificent frescoes in the church. Wallace had learned a good deal of Italian and felt at ease in Florence—it became his favorite European city. He wrote to his agents in September:

I have been going through Book II reorganizing it, writing in some Sabrina chapters to change the emphasis [not only the name of the central character, but also an early title for the novel], writing new exits and entrances, shifting chapters around, and all that. It's a nasty job because I hate to plot things, and this has to be plotted. . . . We'll be here till Christmas. What is more, I think this must be the best hotel room [actually, a room at the Pensione Consiglia] in Florence, with an immense balcony terrace and a view both ways up and down the Arno, and the food is superb. So it looks like a happy place to have alighted. I write five or six hours every day and walk the rest—when I'm not eating. Mary walks most of the time, and soaks her corns the rest. It is really very good here. And I feel like working. (9/23/59)

By early December, he had finished revising the first three hundred pages of his rough draft, with two hundred to go. Then in January they left the Grays and Pages to go to Rome, where Wallace had been appointed writer in residence at the American Academy, following Elizabeth Bowen. Through December and January the weather had been cold and wet and Mary's sciatica had kicked up, making it impossible for them to spend Christmas in Vienna as they had planned, and Wallace had three colds in six weeks. Nevertheless, they were able to entertain a number of visitors from the States and were entertained in turn, having become part of a group of writers and their wives in Rome at the time, including the William Styrons and the Philip Roths.

Stegner was able to finish his revisions and send the manuscript off to Marshall Best from Rome in mid-February. He was still doubtful about the book, however, and looked forward to Best's comments. But he wasn't prepared for the onslaught. Through winter, spring, and summer he received letters of criticism and suggestions from his agents, from Best, from Harold and Tom Guinzburg (Harold owned Viking and Tom was his son), from Malcolm Cowley, and from two other Viking editors. On one occasion he received a six-page, single-spaced letter of suggested revisions. During the first three months of 1960, he sat down and again rewrote the entire book. Then in May he rewrote it yet once more "as we were driving north again from Rome through Provence and the Dordogne, sitting out in the courtyards of old country inns, with weeds up to my knees, [typing the manuscript] on a card table." Finally, during the summer in California, he went through the manuscript one last time, cutting and pasting and rewriting segments. That there was so much correspondence, so much revision is evidence not only that he was unsure of his direction with this particular novel, but that after a ten-year hiatus from novel writing he still was searching for a voice, a novel form that would supplant the autobiographical mode.

The current project had been percolating in his mind since their year in Santa Barbara when Mrs. Gardiner Hammond, who had arranged for the Stegners to rent her guest house, showed Wallace her mother's diaries. Knowing that he was a writer, she suggested that the diaries might be the basis for a book, and after reading through them, he agreed, and Mrs. Hammond loaned the diaries to him. What came to him as the basis for a novel were the thoughts of a woman who had everything, but who was distraught because she came to realize that she lacked a purpose in life. He also found himself entranced by Mrs. Hammond herself, a woman who in wartime was a member of pacifist organizations and who, although wealthy, was interested in socialism. So he began with two characters, Mrs. Hammond and a projected daughter, who would face the problems confessed in the diary, and a moral question—but no thesis, no setting, no plot. Over fourteen years from the receipt of the diary to beginning of the manuscript, his sense of his projected central character, the fictional daughter, grew, enriched by acquaintance with a dozen people who out of a clear blue sky found themselves in similar straits. In looking back on the germination of the novel, he has said that these people were then joined to the woman of the diary to become a composite portrait in his mind. These acquaintances,

> without any preliminary symptoms, [found] their stabilizers ... suddenly quit; lives which have appeared fortunate, even enviable, reveal themselves as arid and empty; people who have seemed, to themselves and others, normally contented human beings discover that for years they have had no responsible reason for existing— have been spiritually starving when every single desire seemed to have been gratified.

His use of the diaries as a basis for his novel may remind us of his use of historical materials, such as the trial transcripts for *The Preacher and the Slave*, or even more of his use of Mary Hallock Foote's letters as a basis for *Angle of Repose*. Like many other writers, when he didn't write out of his own experience, he seemed to need some kind of outside narrative to provide a scaffold from which to build his long fiction.

During the long process of revision, he became concerned at one point that his agents and Viking be aware that "a good many of the details of this family, both contemporary and historical, are modified and paraphrased out of a real family," since out of that might come some legal problems. But, he explained, the woman who loaned him the diaries enthusiastically concurred in the book he intended to write. In addition, she was now dead and so was everyone else from the family papers, and there is nobody in the family like Sabrina, nobody like Oliver, and the secretary was very different in every way.... The prototype of Leonard MacDonald is here in Rome and just sold his second novel to Viking; he knows what I have done to him, which includes making him a triple father, and is resigned. As for the family diaries ... I do not quote them exactly; I use incidents from them, freely re-written. (3/15/60)

The novel as completed focuses on the consciousness of its female central character. Thirty-five, beautiful, wealthy, the spoiled daughter of a prominent San Francisco Peninsula family, Sabrina Hutchins Castro is a woman undergoing a severe identity crisis. At the beginning of the novel, fed up with her cold, society doctor husband in Pasadena, she storms out into the night to drive the four hundred miles north to her mother's estate in Hillsborough, where she decides to stay and sort things out. But she has no clue as to what she should do. She betrays her bewilderment to her friends, Leonard and Barbara MacDonald early in the novel: "Give me the formula. What can you suggest for the girl who has everything—too much of everything, a bellyful of everything?"

She is lost, feeling "solitary and excluded and defiant." Her mother, weak and indecisive, is of little help. Lost in the past, Mrs. Hutchins has a good heart, but is baffled by her grown-up daughter's rebellion against a loveless marriage and a sterile life. Sabrina's brother, Oliver, is not only indifferent to her plight (except that her behavior might lead to scandal), he becomes her antagonist when she attempts to do something constructive by getting her mother to donate land for a community park. Oliver is domineering, self-indulgent, and arrogant, and although he has money, he wants the land for development to make more money. Without family support, Sabrina depends on her childhood friend, Barbara MacDonald, and Barbara's husband Leonard, who, although they are barely getting by financially, have a stable, loving family life with two small children in a tract house nearby. Sabrina is envious, but also wonders how they can stand to live such a stereotypical life.

As she more and more questions her purpose in life and can find no answers, she finds herself unraveling. She goes with her brother to Carson City for the auto races, decides not to go back with him, and ends up in a nightmare of dissipation, a lost weekend with a stranger. At home again, after being rescued by Oliver and her estranged husband, she manages to arrange a deal with her mother so that her brother will give up some of the land for the park. She volunteers to take care of the kids while Barbara is at the hospital giving birth to her third child. When Leonard returns after the birth, they talk once again about what gives life meaning and what a person can believe in. He declares in words that would seem to have come directly from the author:

> "I'll tell you what I believe in. I believe in human love and human kindness and human responsibility, and that's just about all I believe in. . . . The political revolutions will blow us all up at last, probably, but I'm not working for any. The only revolution that interests me is one that will give more people more comprehension of their human possibilities and their human obligations."

Sabrina tells him that she is pregnant, that she told her husband that she is ready to come back, but that the child was not his. He turns her away. In an act of desperation she drops her dress and tries to seduce Leonard, but he turns her away. In the early morning at home, filled with shame and despair, she finds a gun and is determined to commit suicide, but, looking at herself in a mirror, fires at the image instead. Later she tells Leonard, and when he asks why she didn't go through with it, she says, "I guess I decided at the last minute that I'm not a tragic heroine." The novel ends with Sabrina deciding to have her baby and to stay, letting air into "the old crypt of a house" and becoming a real daughter to her mother.

The plot of *A Shooting Star* is somewhat more tangled than I've just outlined, but enough of it is presented that the author's problems with it can be made apparent. One such was that of proportion—he cut back on the space given to such minor characters as the husband, whom we see only briefly in the final version, and gave more to Sabrina herself and her interaction with the MacDonalds. Another was the ending. Best and others complained that the early version wasn't cathartic enough. Wallace struggled with this, and by the end of the second total revision had decided that Sabrina should commit suicide and so informed his publisher and agent. Marshall Best rushed to send a cable to him in Rome on May 2, "Don't kill off Sabrina!"

Also in later drafts her brother, Oliver, is given more attention as the conflict over donating the family land for a park is made more central, and it is by means of that conflict, Sabrina taking a conservationist stance, that Stegner promises his heroine's eventual salvation. This would be the first time he would include a conservationist argument in his fiction—something he would do again in his next novel, *All the Little Live Things*. At one point late in the novel, Sabrina describes Oliver in terms that certainly reflect the antagonism the author was feeling toward what was happening all around him in California:

> His kind never anticipated consequences. His was the kind that left eroded gulches and cutover timberlands and manmade deserts and jerry-built tracts that would turn into slums in less than a generation. They got awards from service clubs and resolutions of commendation from chambers of commerce. They denuded and uglified the earth in the name of progress, and when they lay on their deathbeds—or dropped from the massive coronary that the pace of their lives prepared for them—they were buried full of honors and rolling in wealth, and it never occurred to themselves, that they nearly always left the earth poorer and drearier for their having lived in it.

A Shooting Star was published in May 1961 to generally good reviews and was a Literary Guild selection, guaranteeing a sales of at least twenty-five thousand. Up until the early 1980s, it had been translated into more languages and had more success abroad than any of Stegner's other novels. Nevertheless, Stegner did not look back on the book with fondness, never asked that it be reprinted, and has spoken of it in mild disparagement as tending toward soap opera. It would seem in retrospect that what he was trying to do was walk a very fine line between quality and popular fiction, an all-too-conscious attempt to break through previous barriers to achieve the best-seller he had never had. Confirming this, he has said he was "walking a tightwire all the way, knowing the dangers but hoping I could get by them." But on a deeper level the relative failure of the book would seem to rest again on the author's failure to carry the work with a convincing narrative voice, and Stegner seems almost as out of his element in taking Sabrina's part as taking Vickers's in *On a Darkling Plain* or Condon's in *Fire and Ice*. By comparison to his best work, this novel feels artificial; it lacks that Stegner quality of total conviction. His next novel, *All the Little Live Things*, is just as dramatic as *A Shooting Star*, but Joe Allston's voice carries the day. Albert J. Guerard has located this phenomenon in *The Triumph of the Novel*, in which he says:

> The concept is of a "personal voice" discoverable in the work of every truly original writer: a voice that is the intimate and often unconscious expression of his temperament and unborrowed personality, a voice that in its structures and rhythms reflects the way his mind moves, and reflects too the particular needs and resistances of his spirit.

Stegner has often spoken of his role as author as that of a ventriloquist, but when he was not playing himself, as in the autobiographical novels, it would seem he could only fully succeed when he projected a voice close to his own. *A Shooting Star* was a "comeback" book that did not take him in the right direction.

As Sabrina's description of her brother, outlined earlier, clearly indicates, Stegner's thoughts continued to dwell on environmental matters. What is remarkable about Sabrina's characterization of Oliver as one of those who "denuded and uglified the earth in the name of progress" is that it suggests a level of anger the author had not reached before. During the 1960s he would become more and more involved politically on behalf of conservation both on the local and the national levels, working within environmental groups and within political parties for candidates who were friendly to the cause. Shortly after *Dinosaur* had been published, he was made an honorary life member of the Sierra Club, and he was a leading voice in the club for the next decade and a half during a period of controversy and contention as various factions tried to influence the organization's direction. Another leading figure in the club, Ansel Adams, the famous landscape photographer, talked Wallace into running for election to the board, and he won, serving for two years. Also during the 1960s he served on the Sierra Club Publications

Board and on the National Parks Advisory Board. After returning from
Europe in 1960, Stegner and several other activist neighbors formed the
Committee for Green Foothills.

Then, after John Kennedy was elected president and appointed
Stewart Udall early in 1961 as his secretary of interior, Stegner sent, as
mentioned earlier, the new secretary a copy of *Beyond the Hundredth
Meridian* with a note of congratulations. "He seemed to me," Stegner
recalled, "precisely the kind of Secretary we needed—a Westerner with
an intimate knowledge of the dry country but with a distaste for the economics of liquidation that was killing it." Thereafter Wallace received
several phone calls during which Udall tried to talk him into becoming a
special assistant. Wallace resisted, however, since he didn't want to give
up his own plans, namely, finishing the *Wolf Willow* manuscript. Nevertheless, Udall persisted.

Wallace had been appointed as a Phi Beta Kappa lecturer for the
spring of 1961 and was giving speeches all around the country at various
college campuses when Udall caught up with him in person at Pullman,
Washington. Stegner finally agreed to go to Washington, D.C., as Udall's
assistant for the last few months of the year. In his acceptance letter, he
wrote, "I am very happy to be on my way into this, and I shall be
keeping my hand very close to the conservation pot this summer by
editing Powell's Arid Lands report of 1878 for the John Harvard Library,
and by finishing up my book on the Saskatchewan finale to the Plains
frontier" (6/11/61).

Udall, for his part, had read a lot of Stegner's work and had admired
him. He had decided that once he was appointed secretary he would
create a position on his staff that he called "artist in residence," someone
to radiate ideas. Udall wanted appointees like Stegner to participate:

I didn't just bring people in and stick them off in a corner and tell
them to write speeches or something. I would let them be involved
in meetings and let them do memos and let them throw out
ideas. . . . I'd have a lunch every day for my top people and I'd have
him to the lunch. And he would talk along about issues and things
that were happening. . . . Stegner is not a bashful person! . . . He
had pungent opinions about people.

Udall also was aware of Stegner's long affair with Utah and the Mormons (about which Udall himself had knowledge out of a rich Mormon family history of his own), and aware also that Stegner had a great interest in the Colorado Plateau. "I knew that," he recalled, "because of the Powell book. I remember I used to send him out on trips as sort of eyes and ears, and I remember he went to look at the Canyonlands and spent several days and then reported on it."

His four months in Washington were, Stegner remembered, "another learning period." Although there only briefly, he got an inside look at parts of the Kennedy administration during its first energetic year. Washington gave Stegner

> a quick, deep look into the politics of conservation as it might operate when friends of conservation were in power, as well as a good lesson in how long ideas that on their face seemed to me self-evident and self-justifying could take to be translated into law.

It seemed to Wallace that Washington had been staffed from Harvard, and several of his and Mary's Harvard friends, including Arthur Schlesinger and Kenneth Galbraith, were in high places. Also, the Stegners were reunited with Robert Frost, who had read a poem at the inauguration (which came out of a suggestion by Udall) and had been subsequently appointed as a consultant to the Library of Congress. Nevertheless, this was not Cambridge. Even though the Udalls went out of their way to introduce them to their Washington crowd, Mary found the city cold and unattractive, a lonely place, not a place where when you arrive everyone goes out of his way to entertain you. Wallace was on the Washington bureaucratic schedule, leaving in the morning at eight and coming home at six in the evening, and she had the whole long day to herself. She missed her piano and friends with whom she could do things, and even more distressing, Marion had given birth to a son, Wallace Page, and she and Wallace were missing the early babyhood of their grandson. At least, she recalled, she had her dog, and they walked a lot.

What Wallace was busy doing was helping to work up an agenda for what they fully expected to be an eight-year Kennedy presidency, essentially a program of land acquisition for parks. New parks—Canyonlands,

Glacier Peak, Arches—were all on the agenda. Wallace remembered that one of the things Udall did

> was to send me out to the Escalante Basin, which was the part of the country we had been talking about the first time we met, to see what was going to be drowned by the Glen Canyon Dam, and what should be done about the things like the Cathedral in the Desert and some of those Arches and so on. So I made an expedition out there along with a number of other people. I picked up a couple of superintendents from Arches and Capital Reef and they provided the expedition. And what we did really was to design some upgrading for a lot of those things that were National Monuments and have since become National Parks. Capital Reef for one, and Arches for another.

When he got back to Washington from his trip, he wrote to his agents:

> The desert, in case you haven't been there lately, is totally superb. We met one jeep in five days, but a great many deer, coyotes, foxes, bobcats, tarantulas, lizards, and other of God's creatures, and we saw a hell of a lot of big cool stars. (10/18/61)

During the last few weeks of his stay in Washington, Wallace's energies were given another direction. Udall had had a difficult year. When a new administration comes in, the press tends to put it under close scrutiny, looking for mistakes, and Udall had made more than his share of bloopers that the press had trumpeted, declaring with each new discovery that he had embarrassed the president once again. He asked Wallace, "How do you shake this sort of thing?" And Stegner said:

> Well, I'm not an expert on public relations, but I think maybe you could do it like the old outlaws used to do when they put their horses in a stream and went up stream for several miles and lose the trackers.... Just lower your profile, disappear for awhile, and write a book.

Udall asked, "About what?" And Wallace said, "About what you are doing here and what you think needs to be done." So Udall put Wallace to work researching the particulars and looking up the facts, figures, and background material in the Library of Congress. Before he left Washington, Stegner had completed an outline for the book, notes suggesting various possibilities for development, and a sample chapter. Two of his former students took over his work on the book when he left Washington, first Harold Gilliam, who would write nature books and become an environmental columnist for the *San Francisco Chronicle*, and then Don Moser, who would become editor of *Smithsonian*. When *The Quiet Crisis* came out in 1963 after two years of work by Udall, it became a best-seller. Udall has said, "It was the best thing I ever did [during his tenure as secretary] because I was studying my job."

Wallace returned to Stanford in late December and was back in the classroom at the beginning of January 1962 and back also to his manuscript, *Wolf Willow*. "The Saskatchewan book," as it was called until shortly before publication, had begun with his idea in the late 1940s of a comparative study of village life, which in turn had led him to return to Eastend, Saskatchewan, in 1953. The idea of a comparative study was abandoned during his trip to Denmark the following year, but a new concept, that of a book about the discovery of his own history and the history of the country where he spent his childhood, took its place. The book's form gradually came together as an eclectic mixture of materials as indicated by its subtitle, "A History, a Story, and a Memory of the Last Plains Frontier." But the main thrust of it is made clear in a comment by the author in an interview: "This is fiction and autobiography being used for historical purposes. I intended to write a historical work in *Wolf Willow* not a fictional one."

The title, as the book explains, comes from a sensory experience that more than anything else arouses his memory and brings him back across the years to his childhood:

It is with me all at once, what I came hoping to reestablish, an ancient, unbearable recognition, and it comes partly from the children and the footbridge and the river's quiet curve, but much more from the smell. For here, pungent and pervasive, is the smell that

has always meant my childhood. I have never smelled it anywhere
else, and it is as evocative as Proust's madeleine and tea.

But he cannot, search as he will, find the source. In an interview, Stegner
recalled that search:

> My wife and I drove up through from Medicine Hat, driving east,
> and I hunted around that old hometown incognito, trying to find
> out how it felt, and I smelled that smell at once. It all came back. I
> couldn't figure out what the smell was. It took me two days to find
> out. I ate leaves of every shrub in the valley, I think, before I found
> the right one.

The smell was from a native shrub they called wolf willow, a small gray-
leafed bush with small yellow flowers.

The book is composed of four sections. The first is "The Question
Mark in the Circle," which is largely memoir, set up by the journey of
a middle-aged pilgrim back to the village he last saw in 1920. The
second is "Preparation for a Civilization," which traces the history of
the Cypress Hills region (which contains "Whitemud," the name he
gives to Eastend) from the early explorers, through the roles of the
Indians, the half-breed *metis,* the Hudson's Bay Company, the surveyors
that established the 49th parallel, to a history of the Mounties who
brought the law to the Cypress Hills. The third part contains an autobiographical segment about the frontier code the author learned while
growing up, "Specifications for a Hero," which introduces the two
works of fiction that follow—"Genesis" and "Carrion Spring." The
final section, Part IV, "Town and Country," combines both history
and autobiography as it deals with the founding of the town and the
author's experiences in Whitemud and at the homestead. An epilogue
closes the circle and brings us back to the pilgrim who has returned to
his early home and to some final thoughts about growing up in such
a place.

Of the twenty chapters or segments, eight were previously published
in magazines. Not only do we find memoir, fiction, and history in the
book, but also elements of anthropology, sociology, geography, and

geology. Although Stegner was concerned about the book holding together, in the final version we find every approach supporting every other to give the book a richness and fullness not often achieved in either history or autobiography. Such a return to the place of one's childhood is inevitably nostalgic, and his uses of both the harsh lessons of history and the tough battle against the elements in the fiction easily counteracts any tendency toward sentimentality. However, such a mixture of materials was difficult to categorize, and Stegner found that reviewers sometimes didn't quite know what to make of the book and that bookstores and libraries had trouble placing it.

The plan to combine various genres came to him in rough form during his year at the Center for Advanced Studies, 1954–55, when he wrote the novella *Genesis* but then was stuck and the manuscript of the book as a whole stalled when he couldn't find an ending to the story. When he took up the reins again in the summer of 1961, he realized that "the reason I hadn't been able to finish 'Genesis' was that it was already finished—done." He didn't need to carry the story of Rusty, the young Englishman who becomes a cowboy, through the entire miserable winter of 1906–7, but just through that one week-long blizzard. With that problem out of the way, he went on to complete the historical research for Part II, "Preparation for a Civilization," which he had postponed while abroad. After his stint as special assistant to Stuart Udall, he went on to Part IV, "Town and Country," which is largely about the founding (in 1914) and development of Whitemud. He depended on notes that he had taken from interviewing old-timers, particularly Corky Jones, who had become the town historian, and from the town newspaper, *The Eastend Enterprise*, during the period 1914 to 1918. A few items from his newspaper notes gives the flavor of the material he was working with:

Jan. 10, 1917—Worst storm in years lasted for two days with four lives lost and considerable damage done.

Accidental death of D. N. R. Stewart. Drank wood alcohol on a wager that he could drink it and it not kill him. The doctor with whom he bet also met his death.

Jan. 7, 1918—Board of Trade wrote Dr. Seymour at Regina

asking assistance to combat small pox and that vaccine be forwarded.

Jan. 12, 1918—Joseph Stauber, farmer, found frozen to death in shack. Relative in U.S. notified. Believed death of self and dog found under bed due to suffocation from coal gas.

After writing about the early days of his hometown, he turned to revising and smoothing out the manuscript. One major change he made was to omit the story "The Wolfer," which he had originally planned as a companion piece to "Genesis." "The Wolfer," while connected in subject matter and character to the other story, simply did not follow in the spirit of the book's frontier theme of building toward the future despite adversity, and so he wrote a new follow-up story, "Carrion Spring." It takes the heroic ranch foreman and his wife into the period following the disastrous winter. The foreman wants to buy what is left of the ranch—dead, bloated bodies of cattle litter the landscape—and his wife, somewhat reluctantly, agrees. Their willingness to "stick" (in Stegner terminology) despite extreme hardship is testimony to the best in the frontier spirit.

But after sending a preliminary manuscript to Viking in the spring of 1962, Wallace was still concerned about the parts coming together as a whole. He wrote Marshall Best,

My uneasiness meant I was pretty sure the parts didn't all hang together. Now I've talked with Malcolm [Cowley] twice, and gone over the manuscript with him, and had some suggestions of a structural kind that I think are highly intelligent. One of my difficulties, I think, was that I had not much rewritten the several magazine articles that went into the book, with the result that each new article had a sense of beginning over. I can fix this, now that I know what it is, but it will take a little while. . . . I . . . hope you'll like the thing—I have always, myself, liked it piecemeal, and with Malcolm's help I may eventually like it whole. (4/1/62)

He went back to the manuscript and altered several of the chapter beginnings, giving them transitions and linking them back to the autobiographical opening of the book. And in order to do that for Part III, the fiction section, he had to add more than the paragraph or two he had added elsewhere and ended up with a new autobiographical chapter, "Specifications for a Hero."

After *A Shooting Star*, he obviously felt a good deal more at home in Saskatchewan than he had in Hillsborough. Published in October 1962, *Wolf Willow* is a return to the autobiographical mode he had found so successful in the past and to his lifelong effort to "locate" himself. He has said about the book that

> I found the writing of non-fiction easier in that mangled decade [the 1960s]. . . . It was a book as personal to me as *The Big Rock Candy Mountain*, for though I was dealing with events that were largely historical, I permitted myself the luxury of a historian's omniscience and right to judge.

The writing is so deeply felt and often so beautifully evocative, one might be excused for thinking that this, nonfiction history and nature writing, was really this writer's forte. Yet, the fiction is wonderful. "Genesis," by any measure, is one of the author's finest stories. As Larry McMurtry put it in his review of the book, the story "is as good a short novel as anybody has done about the West or any part of it." As testified to by the liberal use of quotations earlier in this book, one may find oneself underlining memorable passages all the way through *Wolf Willow* either for the prose, which is often very close to poetry, or its insights into an archetypal American story. Claude Simpson wrote in his review that the book was as "keenly observant as 'Walden.' It expresses more knowingly than Thoreau could have expressed it, the twentieth-century problem of individuality as each must try to define it."

By blending elements from several forms, Stegner, long before *Roots*, really invented a new kind of history, a history of self-discovery, history "as it relates to me and places me." And, one might add, what gives it such power is that it is scrupulously real, nothing is faked, fiction is labled "fiction." His description of the landscape of Saskatchewan and of his place in it in the opening pages of the book is a synecdoche for the relationship of the author to his book:

On that monotonous surface with its occasional ship-like farm, its atolls of shelter-belt trees, its level ring of horizon, there is little to interrupt the eye. Roads run straight between parallel lines of fence until they intersect the circle of the horizon. It is a landscape of circles, radii, perspective exercises—a country of geometry.... The world is very large, the sky even larger, and you are very small. But also the world is flat, empty, nearly abstract, and in its flatness you are a challenging upright thing, as sudden as an exclamation mark, as enigmatic as a question mark.

His position in regard to the land around him—"The Question Mark in the Circle" is the title of his opening segment—is a metaphor for his search, his need to have a history of his own. It was a need that he had felt all his life, one shared by so many other Westerners. After publication, Walter Van Tilburg Clark wrote to him, "A beautiful book, a memorable one, and, needless to say, it reaches out and touches so many memories and concerns of mine" (8/8/62). And A. B. Guthrie, Jr., sent him a note saying,

Damn it! You've beat me to the punch—to a lot of punches. The manuscript I'm just completing has much in it about my old home town of Choteau, Montana. A good many of our experience were similar, as are a good many now, of our reflections. I was particularly interested, since it's a point I've hammered, in your observations about the isolation of minds from the surrounding history. (7/1/62)

Stewart Udall, who also shared a similar childhood, sent him a letter of appreciation for the book, and Stegner replied,

After a slow start, it seems to be beginning to move—not big, but pretty steady. And if it doesn't fulfill your prediction about being around a while, I'll haunt somebody. I felt this one the way old Robert feels some of his poems: I wanted to put it out there where they couldn't overlook it even if they wanted to. So if they overlook it in spite of me, I'll begin introducing cobras into the drains of critics and booksellers. (12/9/62)

His next undertaking was waiting in the wings and followed on the heels of the Saskatchewan book almost immediately. Once again it was a project connected to his own background and interests. It would be a history of the Mormon pioneers in their movement to the West, reaching out for the New Jerusalem, rather than the Big Rock Candy Mountain, and succeeding by prodigious feats of endurance and cooperation, rather than by a dog-eat-dog competition among rugged individuals. As far as Stegner was concerned, the Mormon pioneers

> were the most systematic, organized, disciplined, and successful pioneers in our history; and their advantage over the random individualists who preceded them and paralleled them and followed them up the valley of the Platte came directly from their "un-American" social and religious organization. Where Oregon emigrants and argonauts bound for the gold fields lost practically all their social cohesion en route, the Mormons moved like the Host of Israel they thought themselves.

He was pursuing the diametrically opposite story to his father's boom-and-bust life. But in many ways it was a story close to home. As he has said, "If I have a home town, a place where a part of my heart is, it is Salt Lake City, and the part of western history that seems most personal and real to me is Mormon history."

But the project didn't start out by having anything to do with the Mormons. It began with an invitation from A. B. Guthrie, Jr., an old friend, to contribute a volume to the American Trail Series which he was editing for McGraw-Hill. The initial proposal in February of 1959 was for Stegner to do a book on the Spanish Trail in the Southwest. In the middle of *Shooting Star* and working on and off on *Wolf Willow*, his first inclination was to say no, but he began with maybe and ended up a month later saying, "I am definitely interested in the Spanish Trail, which would take me back to country and a period of history that I know and like" (3/19/59).

However, during the final stretch on *A Shooting Star*, he changed his mind and decided to write about the Mormon Trail instead, primarily because he was pushed for time. He knew the Mormon story better and felt because of *Mormon Country* and his connections with the University of Utah, he would have easier access to the research materials. Before he left for Europe in 1959, he employed a graduate student to work up a bibliography for him that would be waiting for him when he got home. He also wanted to save time because he could not think of a book for a series as a major contribution to his career, and he wanted to get back to novel writing as soon as possible. At age fifty, he was hearing the winged chariot somewhere up above and behind him and wondering how many books he had left in him.

In March and April while making final revisions to *Wolf Willow*, he was already working on his new manuscript. By June he had completed two hundred pages, dealing primarily with the Mormon background prior to the establishment of the trail west, and had sent them for review to a friend, Juanita Brooks, a Mormon historian who had published *The Mountain Meadow Massacre* (1950), much to the discomfort of the church elders. (For help with his work, Stegner picked out those few exceptions to his belief that most Mormon historians were incapable of objectivity.) Early that same month he had received the *Wolf Willow* proofs and was getting ready to spend part of the summer following the Mormon Trail eastward, and the remainder in Vermont. He wrote his agents:

> As soon as I get these galleys off tomorrow, I have to spend a solid week of hard reading on the Mormon Trail—meantime packing up and getting the house ready for renting. Akh. I think I have never been so bushed in my life. Driving across the continent will be a pure dream. (6/14/62)

In Vermont he divided his time between trying to finish his and Mary's house, which was still in progress, and research. In September he told Carol Brandt:

> Next summer, when we've got plumbin' and other amenities in, I hope you'll come up. This is unfashionable as anything, except for

John Gunther, but we like it and think we can defend it against all advocates of glamor. We haven't stripped a starlet and thrown her in the pool for ten days, but we're alive to our opportunities, just the same.

Lovell and Kay Thompson were up last evening, talking about a biography of Benny DeVoto. I suggested Kitty Bowen, and shall continue to. . . .

And what I say, there's nothing like a September cold wave to make a 'ouse a 'ell. We moved out of our sugar-house after a week of 45 degree internal temperatures. I was spraining my numb wrists typing notes. So we're in oil heat for a few days [at the Grays' "children's house"], getting ready to leave. (9/27/62)

In the fall, back in Los Altos, Wally moved to get more material on the details of life on the trail. He went back to many of the sources of Mormon information he had used before, most particularly to historian Dale Morgan (*The Great Salt Lake*, 1947), who in 1962 was working at the Bancroft and who was able to supply a number of Mormon pioneer diaries and journals and direct Wallace to others. The most logical source of this kind of material was the Church of Jesus Christ of Latter-Day Saints library, but his request to use the manuscript materials in the library was turned down. (Years later he commented that "the Mormons get defensive and the non-Mormons blow it [the history of the church] up into something more than it is, and controversy and dull prose are magnified again. The only way to get away from attack-and-defense history, it seems to me, is to throw the archives open to everybody.") In December he wrote to Udall, "I've been doing nothing but read Mormon history for five months, and I haven't yet started to write [the story of the migration]. Saturation, they tell me, is the historian's ideal. But it's hard to manage when you have another job or two in hand" (12/9/62).

Teaching through the winter and spring quarters, he found progress on *The Gathering of Zion: The Story of the Mormon Trail* to be frustratingly slow. Finally, after working most of the summer on the manuscript, he told his agents in August 1963, "The Mormons are in the last chapter. I do not especially cheer what I have done, but at least it's close to *done*. For all McGraw Hill knows, I am head over heels with excitement about it. But I've been corrupted. Mormons are getting too *wholesome* for me." (8/10/63) He promised to send the manuscript shortly. He wanted to get it off his mind so that he and Mary could get ready to go abroad—he had accepted a Fulbright Fellowship appointment to Greece for the fall.

In September, from Athens, he wrote his agents:

We just got back from a three-day excursion, full of beans and octopus and ready to go to work. We have an apartment at Athens College, very pleasant, complete with typewriter, thank God. It's been so long since I used one I have almost forgotten how. . . .

Mrs. Kennedy has been stealing all the headlines here, but as soon as I can get downtown and reveal myself we'll fix all that.

All our best,

Wally

P.S. Speaking of Bests, we ran into Marshall and his son John in the streets of Toledo. I almost wrote a ballad. (9/?/63)

Looking back on his time in Athens, Wallace has said that no day on that or any other journey had more impact on him than one when he was giving a talk to a meeting of the Association of Greek Writers. He told them about "growing up without an extended family or a definable culture in a place with no history, about a childhood in which everything was to be made anew." He intended to express his embarrassment at appearing to think that he was bringing culture back to Athens. But instead, his audience expressed envy of his situation, and every newspaper in the city printed the speech as "a revelation from the New World, where it seemed talents were not shriveled in the competitive glare of a great past. I did not quite accept their view, but I had to realize how different my problems were from theirs."

One evening in late November, he and Mary were at a dinner party at the house of the man who was the headmaster of the American School for Boys. A maid came in and whispered something to the host, who then turned to his American guests and told them, "A message has just come for Mr. Stegner that President Kennedy has been shot." A few minutes later, the maid came back to say that the president was dead. Wallace said immediately, "I'm going home." The next day the Stegners encountered people crying in the street, and some of them, identifying Mary and Wallace as Americans, came up to them and tried to express their grief and dismay. The Stegners, sick at heart, left for the States early, canceling plans to stop in Yucatan and flying straight home.

16

HISTORIAN AND
"CONTEMPORARY"

Wallace Stegner might well become known as the writer whose fiction often crossed over into history and whose histories often crossed over into the use of fictional techniques. This, of course, was a reflection of his own need for history and tendency to view people, events, and even landscape in historical perspective on the one hand, and his penchant for storytelling on the other. And what a story the gathering of Zion and the Mormon trail made! His telling was the first time that it had been told from a friendly, but relatively neutral point of view, motivated neither to propagandize for the Mormon faith nor to blacken the Mormon reputation. "I write," he says in his introduction to his bibliography, "as a non-Mormon but not a Mormon-hater. Except as it affected the actions of the people I write of, I do not deal with the Mormon faith: I do not believe it, but I do not quarrel with it either."

The story beings in 1846, when the Mormons were driven out of Nauvoo, Illinois, and ends in 1868, when the transcontinental railroad supplanted the need for wagon trains. During those twenty-two years, some eighty thousand souls passed some fourteen hundred miles from the banks of the Missouri, along the Platte River Valley, across the plains, and over mountain ranges, many enduring incredible hardship, until they reached the Great Salt Lake. Some six thousand did not make it, but lie buried along the way. This was the exodus of a whole people, a people of extraordinary faith, who, subjected to the prejudices of the gentiles around them first in Missouri and then in Illinois, escaped westward with a discipline and coherence unknown to the ordinary immigrants to the open lands of Oregon or the gold fields of California. "They traveled," the author tells us, "on the road like villages already developed, organized humanity instead of disorganized." At first, they weren't sure of exactly where they were going—it might have been to the Southwest or to Southern California—just as long as it was away from the United States, away from the persecuting and violent mobs of those who called themselves Christians. They didn't know where—they counted on the Lord to tell them when they got there.

The author himself has said of the book:

> What I was trying to do in *The Gathering of Zion* was something very close to the Parkmanesque, Benny DeVoto thing—narrative history plus judgment. Well, I guess it was Bancroft who said it first, "Present a man in his own terms and judge him in yours." But I did want these people to present *themselves*.

But one reviewer who apparently felt that Stegner was biased *against* the Mormons in *The Gathering of Zion* counters the author's assertion by insisting that

> the novelist does not really present actual people in their own terms. If he wished to do that, he would write history and not novels. . . . What I am most disturbed about is the complete absence of an objective study of the 19th Century Mormons. Stegner will never give it to us—not while he places Fawn Brodie and Bernard DeVoto in the quartet of the best Utah historians.

By aligning himself with DeVoto, Stegner put himself in the line of fire for those who still resented DeVoto and disliked his method of selective narrative framed by commentary. But this antagonism was not shared by the majority of Western historians; published in 1964, the book won the 1965 Award of Merit of the American Association for State and Local History.

Zion is superior to *Mormon Country* on several counts, but the comparison is of two different kinds of books: the latter is a survey made up of many stories, something like a short story collection; the former is one continuous story, more like a novel—the drama builds throughout. In addition, having written *Mormon Country, Beyond the Hundredth Meridian,* and *The Preacher and the Slave,* Stegner was far more experienced in dealing with history and shows a firmer hand in managing his materials and maintaining his objectivity: if *Mormon Country* was written in Cambridge out of nostalgia for the West, *Zion* was written by a professional whose research had a solid foundation in previous work and who had, with his usual conscientiousness, mastered all the documents available to him.

The result is a complex, yet readable and moving narration woven together out of many different strands selected from extant histories and biographies, but also, most frequently, from original trail journals. It is the material based on the journals, sometimes summarized and sometimes quoted at length, that allows the participants to present themselves and their experiences. Above all, this is a story of people, not of an undifferentiated mass but of many individuals of various stripes, although almost all are Mormons. As Stegner writes in his introduction:

> Suffering, endurance, discipline, faith, brotherly and sisterly charity, the qualities so thoroughly celebrated by Mormon writers, were surely well distributed among them, but theirs also was a normal amount of human cussedness, vengefulness, masochism, backbiting, violence, ignorance, selfishness, and gullibility.... That I do not accept the faith that possessed them does not mean I doubt their frequent devotion and heroism in its service. Especially their women. Their women were incredible.

We might take a look at a sampling of these women and their stories as a way of getting a taste of Stegner's treatment and technique. And we have to think that it was characteristic of Stegner and his values that he would concentrate on the women participants of this journey.

Among them was an unnamed woman that Eliza Snow wrote about in her journal. The woman gave birth

"in the rude shelter of a hut—the sides formed of blankets fastened to poles stuck in the ground—a bark roof, through which the rain was dripping. Kind sisters held dishes and caught the water—thus protecting the mother and her little darling from a shower-bath on its entrance to the stage of human existence."

Then there was Ursulia Hascall, "a complacent, gossipy, lively woman with a cornpopper mind, an interest in anything that moved." She was lucky enough to be looked after by a very competent son-in-law and could look forward to her stay at Winter Quarters on the Missouri with more equanimity than some. But, Stegner tells us,

one feels that she would have managed equanimity under any circumstances. She had a knack for making the best of things. If it had hailed stones as big as baseballs she would have come out from shelter wondering if it wasn't a good time to make up a nice freezer of ice cream.

Not all women need to be "looked after," by any means. Mary Phelps Rich found that hard physical work and moving into higher, drier air improved her health:

Working like a man, yoking up, outspanning, walking fifteen or twenty miles a day through brush and sand beside the slow churn of the wheels, hunting up strayed oxen on mornings when the sun stretched everything incredibly long up the Platte's long valley and meadowlarks whistled sharp and pure, she began to feel whole again, began to feel that it was "a pleasure to take hold and do something."

People, yes, a concentration in this book on the experiences of individuals, but nearly always Wallace's portraits, as here, are given a context of a place vividly described, a scene we can see and hear. We should interrupt our roll call of heroic women for a moment to once again make note of that other Stegner forte—scene and setting.

After reading Stegner in *Zion*, one may get the feeling that the cliché "a sense of place" not only has here some real meaning, but that it is so apropos it may have even been coined in response to this particular writer and his work. Whether novelist or historian, Stegner dealt with people *and* their environment. Just as he had walked Joe Hill's last steps, ridden down John Wesley Powell's Colorado, he had driven over and walked down the Mormon Trail. He had to feel the territory in his pores in order to tell his story. He writes in an essay called "Fiction: A Lens on Life":

> The fiction writer is an incorrigible lover of concrete *things*....
> By his very profession a serious fiction writer is a vendor of the
> sensuous particulars of life.... His most valuable tools are his
> senses and his memory; what happens in his mind is primarily
> pictures.... Any good piece of serious fiction is collected out
> of reality, and its parts ought to be vivid and true to fact and to
> observation.

He speaks here of fiction, but he could just as well be talking about the Stegner brand of history, which indeed was built out of "the sensuous particulars of life." And in his history, as in his fiction, it is out of the particulars that the reader should be able to draw conclusions. "The ideas, the generalizations, ought to be implicit in the selection and arrangement of the people and places and actions. They ought to haunt a piece of fiction as a ghost flits past an attic window after dark." Regardless of the genre, Stegner respects and depends on his reader, and his reader, more likely than not, finds himself or herself forming a strong bond with the writer.

Again, a major component of Stegner's story in *Zion*, as we have seen, are the Mormon women, who were incredible—whether in their spirit, in their capability, or in their capacity for endurance. Once more a powerful characterization is joined to an unforgettable scene in the book when during one horrendous trip, on a bitter cold October night with snow flurries, no shelter, not enough clothing to keep warm, and the valley still three hundred miles away, a camp guard stumbled across a man whose legs were stiff. The guard reached down and found the man was dead, with his wife, still alive, alongside him. He did not wake her. Later, not hearing her husband breathing, she reached over and touched him, crying out at her discovery, but realizing that there was no help:

> Until morning she lay beside the stiff corpse, and in the morning helped wrap it in a blanket for burial in the snow—and the giving up of that blanket was a concession that only love would have made. The ground was frozen too hard for the digging of a grave, and she wanted him to have *some* covering.

This incident occurred during the journey of one of the handcart companies. These companies made up a cross-country procession that is the climax of both the exodus itself and the book, which has built toward this, "the harshest testing of both people and organization," in Stegner's words. "The story of the 1856 emigration," he continues, "is a story of hardship and horror crowned with heroism." There are many stories of hardship and horror in the book—for example, one wagon company, starving, found the frozen heads of a donkey and mule that a previous group had killed for food, and they cracked them open and ate the brains. But no story out of the western migration as a whole, except for that of the Donner Party, is as dramatic as that of the passage by handcart.

By 1855 most of the Mormons from Nauvoo and elsewhere in this country who wanted to go had made their way to Salt Lake, and the church began to concentrate more and more on bringing in its converts from abroad, largely from England, Scotland, and Wales. For the most part, these were poverty-stricken people at the bottom of the social ladder who barely made it across the Atlantic on crowded immigrant ships and landed with no resources, and so it was up to the church to somehow get them across the country. But despite Mormon tithing and resourcefulness, cash in the Perpetual Emigrating Fund had been already stretched beyond the limit. It was Brigham Young's idea to have these people walk the hundreds of miles to Salt Lake by hauling their meager possessions and supplies behind them in carts manufactured at the staging area on the banks of the Iowa River at Iowa City. They started off to the West like Chinese rickshaw drivers, except the wheels of their carts were not nearly as good and those who pulled them did not have nearly the strength or endurance. As a result of years of unhealthy work and poor diets, they were thin and pale, many in poor health or well along in years; none had ever slept on the ground, camped out, or pitched a tent. Their carts were quickly constructed out of green wood that shrunk and cracked in the dry air of the Platte Valley. In ignorance they greased their axles, which then attracted sand and wore down the wood so that the wheels wobbled and then collapsed. In these carts they tried to haul as much as four hundred pounds across the plains, through rivers, and over the mountains.

In the year of the experiment, 1856, the handcart immigrants got a late start from Liverpool because Atlantic storms delayed departures, so that in early June when all of them should have been setting out from the Missouri, they were anywhere from three hundred to six thousand miles short of Iowa City, depending on which ship they had taken. Then departure to the West was delayed further while the carts, which should have been waiting for them and weren't, were hastily thrown together. As shiploads of converts from Europe arrived in New York and then were taken by train to the frontier, they were formed into companies— in all, five companies of several hundred immigrants each. The first three were able to leave early enough to make it to Salt Lake with only moderate suffering from exhaustion, hunger, and fever, if you could call a day hauling four hundred pounds in a cart behind you twenty-eight miles uphill on short rations only moderate.

As bad as it was for them, the last two companies of tenderfeet departing the Missouri in late summer encountered in the fall terrible weather on the trail and, lacking sufficient food or warm clothing, went through a freezing, starving, exhausting hell. There was much loss of life, and many, through frostbite, lost fingers, toes, and even their lower legs. They should never have been allowed to depart. But there was a sort of blind stubbornness on the part of the leaders, a need to make Brigham Young's plan work, regardless of the cost in human life and suffering, mixed with a blind faith that God would clear the way and provide, no matter what the obstacles. And the pilgrims themselves followed blindly, enduring the agony, feeling, as they had often been told, that they were being tested in their faith by God.

One of these two companies, Willie Company (named after its leader), first had to cut the flour ration (and flour was all they had) when it was found that a waystation, Fort Laramie, had none to sell. Then as the pilgrims crossed over the North Platte and climbed toward the Sweetwater, they found themselves in higher and colder altitudes, and the nights that had been chilly on the Platte were now freezing cold. At Independence Rock, Captain Willie had to cut the ration yet again. Now, at this point,

> fatigue, malnutrition, cold, failure of faith, wore them down, and now those who wore out were as often as not their strongest, the men who had labored all the way to protect their families and the weaker members. These days, they stumbled into camp with their faces drawn and set, and sometimes if they rested a few minutes before putting up the tents they lay down and died without ever knowing how completely exhausted they were.... [As one of the company wrote in his journal,] "We traveled on in misery and sorrow."

Things got worse as they were caught in a heavy October snowfall. One day a man, Brother Stone, had dropped behind, and when they went back to look for him, they found that he had been half eaten by wolves. At the last crossing of the North Platte, they bypassed the bridge (probably to avoid the toll), and most of them had to wade across through the freezing water, up to their necks, many just escaping from drowning. Then they stumbled forward along the trail toward camp in their wet clothes, which froze on them, and, reaching camp, found they had no dry clothing to put on and it was too late to find wood for a fire.

Every day the situation got worse as supplies ran out, the snow continued, and several people each day died. Finally, relief came gradually when rescuers and wagonloads of supplies were sent eastward along the trail out from Salt Lake, too late for some, although the acts of courage by the rescuers were many. Stegner writes:

> It is hard to feel how hope that has been crushed little by little, day by day, can come back like feeling returning to a numbed limb. It

is hard even to imagine the hardship that rescue entailed—the jolting, racking, freezing, grief-numbed, drained and exhausted three hundred miles through snow to sanctuary.

It is hard to read this vivid account of such terrible suffering without weeping for those who so long ago suffered or without some anger toward the stubbornness of the church elders who long ago went to their accounting.

The first part of the Willie Company was brought into the valley on November 9, but until the end of the month, stragglers were still coming in, some in wagons but others still grimly hauling their own carts. Another remarkable woman, Margaret Dalglish,

a gaunt image of Scottish fortitude, dragged her handful of belongings to the very rim of the valley, but when she looked down and saw the end of it she did something extraordinary. She tugged the cart to the edge of the road and gave it a push and watched it roll and crash and burst apart, scattering into Emigration Canyon the last things she owned on earth. Then she went on into Salt Lake to start the new life with nothing but her gaunt bones, her empty hands, her stout heart.

The Gathering of Zion: The Story of the Mormon Trail is a remarkable book that tells an unforgettable story. It could only have been told with such force by a Wallace Stegner, a historian who had knowledge of the Mormons, who admired them but who could also show them at their worst as part of the truth that should be told, and who had the novelistic skills to make the people and their environments come alive for us. The book is a major contribution to the literature of the movement west, but the story lives and breathes with such vividness that it would seem to have interest for any reader, whether the reader cares about the West and the Western Movement or not. Although Stegner was unhappy that he got involved in the project and impatient with the time it took away from his writing of fiction, the book will be recognized as one of his best as long as his work is remembered.

Zion may not be as significant a work as the Powell book, but the

writing has more zest and bite, and because it comes to a climax toward
the end, rather than in the middle as *Hundredth Meridian* does, it is,
overall, more dramatic. Stegner was a writer whose writing improved
with nearly every book up to and including the last one—following his
pattern of constant learning and never being satisfied. But he was determined to expend his energies in the future on fiction, and as his concern
grew for what time he had left to write, he began to think more seriously
about retiring from teaching early, whenever his financial situation
would permit it. After finishing the manuscript of *Zion* in the late
summer of 1963 and after he returned in the fall of 1964 to teaching
after his trip abroad, he wanted to give all the time he could to his next
novel. In fact, he had two in mind. One idea was for what turned out to
be *The Spectator Bird*, the writing of which for various reasons
was delayed until the early 1970s. In a letter to Carol Brandt, Marshall
Best told her that he had received from Wallace "the good news that
he is really thinking hard about a novel with Danish material"
(1/25/63). But a few weeks later Wallace wrote Marshall again, having
changed his mind:

> I have thought of a way to make that novelette "Field Guide to the
> Western Birds," along with a story Carol likes called "All the Little
> Live Things," into a novel that could be a good one. The hell with
> Denmark; I'll do that one when I'm old. The beauty of this one is
> that it's already nearly half written. Maybe I'll call it Indoor-
> Outdoor Living. And maybe, for once, I'll look like a contemporary.
> (3/10/63)

He intended to set to work at once on what would become *All the Little
Live Things*, the first and most underrated of the works of his great
period.

But with one thing or another, the writing was delayed. In June 1962
he had received an official invitation from Secretary Udall to serve as a
member of the Advisory Board on National Parks, Historic Sites, Buildings and Monuments. It was not something Wallace was crazy about
doing, but it was an invitation he thought he couldn't refuse, considering
all that he had said and written—and he did care very much about the

national parks. But it would take precious time, traveling to sites to assess their appropriateness and going across country to meetings, and he had little enough to spare after fulfilling his teaching obligations. A writer becomes obsessed with time, tending to resent anything or anybody who takes it. Stegner, however, was blessed, or cursed, with a social conscience and a highly developed sense of duty. Throughout the rest of his life there was an internal conflict between that sense of duty to causes he so firmly endorsed and his drive to achieve more as a novelist. He sometimes felt in his work for the environment a tinge of guilt for not doing more—it was a raw nerve that would be touched more than once in the years ahead.

Harold Gilliam, the ex-student who had taken Wallace's place as Udall's special assistant, was also a member of the advisory board and recalled Stegner's participation. He observed him in one aspect as someone who would say just what he thought whether it was diplomatic or polite or not. Early in his tenure on the board, at a meeting in Salt Lake, Wallace got into a heated discussion over dinner with the chairman of the board, who was a Mormon elder, over the character and activities of Brigham Young. Wallace did not have a very high opinion of Young and said so. It was not a politic thing to do, but according to Gilliam, "It just mattered [to him] that he was telling the truth as he saw it." Fortunately for harmonious relations among the board members, the Mormon elder had a sense of humor and did not take the argument too seriously.

In whatever environmental organization he may have held office, Wallace could be very persuasive and nonconfrontational when he wanted to be. While he was on the advisory board, it was considering including the Allagash River Valley in Maine as part of the national parks system. Udall, familiar with the river and concerned that the national parks and monuments include areas other than those just in the West, had proposed it, and Gilliam, who was still working for Udall, presented and argued for it. The purists were saying, no, what we want in the national park system is pristine areas; we don't want to take any of these butchered territories into the system. (A lot of logging had taken place there.) Stegner came to the defense of the proposal, saying, in effect, "O.K., these areas are in bad shape now, but they will grow back in time, and if we get them now, we'll be able to set them aside and let them grow back. It doesn't matter that they have been butchered, because we have to think of the future." Gilliam remembered that Wallace

> gave a very eloquent defense ... which swung the board around then to that viewpoint, and I think it had an influence on what the board recommended from thereafter, as well as the National Park Service itself, which had done a lot of work in holding out for the pristine areas.

Wallace's years in Vermont had taught him a good deal about the flora and fauna of northern New England, and he saw in the second growth of the trees on his farm a resilience and strength that, as a Westerner, surprised him. Whereas in much of the West, when the trees were gone, particularly if they were clear-cut, it might take decades for the hillsides to even start to recover—if ever—the wetness of the East made regrowth not only certain, but relatively quick for some species.

There was another episode that took place involving the National Parks Board, this time regarding a place of local significance in Illinois. One member of the board wanted the home of a historical figure to be declared a national historical site. The Park Service was recommending very strongly against it, since the man was not nationally known and the house was not of national importance. The service made a very strong case and the board seemed to be going along with it. However, Wallace spoke up and said he had just finished reading a book on what it is like to grow up without history. (He had not too long before written such a book himself, *Wolf Willow*.) He continued by saying that he knew what the history of a region can mean to someone growing up there. He told the board what it would have meant to him to have known what had happened in his area of Saskatchewan. He felt cheated of his heritage, of "Fort Walsh, and all that story of buffalo hunter, Indian and half-breed, Mounted Policeman and wolfer" that had come to a climax in the Cypress Hills and that he had really needed to know about when he was a child. It is, he argued to the board, so vitally important for us to take every opportunity we can to help the younger generation remember what has happened in their area because it gives them a sense of roots and passage that they wouldn't have otherwise. Gilliam recalled that once again

> he was very eloquent, especially with this subject. . . . And he swung the board around again in this case. They decided to go with it. . . . He was quite a persuader—all the more so because he was low key. Wally spoke very calmly and quietly and saying what he felt very deeply. . . . His very literary choice of words as they came, his similes and metaphors swung the board around . . . and it happened on more than one occasion.

Gilliam is just one of many who knew him and read his work who has remarked on Wallace's constant use of figurative language and his effective manner of speaking. His frequent use of such figures to express himself, even in casual conversation, would seem to reflect what had become a habit of thought. David Levin, who joined the Stanford faculty in the early 1950s, has recorded his first impressions of Wallace Stegner:

> Everyone spoke affectionately of him, and here he was, a handsome, athletic-looking man with hooded eyes like John Wayne's and a musical baritone voice. He had obviously cultivated his talent for metaphors, not only in writing but in conversation. His speech . . . often showed you that he observed details acutely and that he remembered them. His disarmingly youthful delivery and the aptness of his choices made this artful speech seem as natural as the poems of his old friend Robert Frost or the deceptively simple monologues of Mark Twain.

Stegner used his facility for colorful comparison and witty juxtaposition to powerful effect in his writings about the environment, which, despite his resolution to concentrate on novel writing, multiplied during the 1960s.

During this period, in his introduction to a Sierra Club book about the Olympic Peninsula by ex-student Don Moser (who also had worked for Udall), he wrote:

This book is like a holding of hands, like a looking into eyes. A quiet book and a gentle one, it is also absolutely clear-eyed, and the fact that it is clear-eyed never reduces for an instant its respect, even awe, in the presence of natural things. The Olympic Peninsula, it means to say, is not merely a topography and an ecology, a natural and delicate balance among all the interacting life forces, plant and animal, bacteria and mold, moss and tree and man. It is a miracle as well, and worthy of wonder.

In an editorial for *Saturday Review* dealing with the urgent need to establish a redwood national park before it was too late, a park of great enough extent that it would be able to survive as an ecological unit, he wrote:

In no sense ... can any tree-farm forest, even an honest one, replace the depth and silence, the druidical green peace, of the ancient groves. To reproduce what is now being cut off would take at least a thousand years, assuming that the ravaged and eroded soil could do a second time what it has done over the last thousand or two thousand years.

In a way, the redwood lumber companies are like slave owners before the Civil War: they are engaged in a bad but legal business.

And writing once again in *Saturday Review*, this time about "the real conservation problem," which is the problem of population, he notes that the projected world population for A.D. 2150 is 150 billion. *Fifty* times as many people and problems we now have is simply inconceivable. "It will no longer be human life," he writes, "it will be a termite life." Already, he adds, the national parks are being badly battered: "You cannot turn well over a hundred million annual visitors into a park system and expect them to leave no marks, even if they are well-intentioned, well-educated, and well-policed." Then, in referring to the constant tension between the industrial on one side and the pastoral or primitive on the other, a dialectic of forces within our lives and even in our individual minds, we need not think of the pastoral or primitive as necessarily nostalgic and sentimental. For, he writes, they are the indispensable opposite to industrial regimentation and dehumanization; in our haste to become something new, termites or otherwise, we need constantly to be reminded of who we are: creatures, made of water and chemicals but the children of sun and grass, and cousin by warm blood to birds and mammals. Though it is necessary for our survival to husband resources, it is necessary for our emotional health to husband natural things, and places where they may be known.

One reason for the increase in article activity was that in November 1962, William Patterson, associate publisher of the *Saturday Review,* had asked Wallace to become a contributing editor, sending in a minimum of four pieces a year. Wallace considered the offer carefully, since it would give him a bully pulpit for the causes he believed in. Almost no other general magazines were interested in publishing articles on conservation, and to a certain extent, he would be following in the footsteps of his mentor, Bernard DeVoto, who had pioneered speaking out about public lands and the national parks to a popular audience in the same magazine. As it turned out, Wallace decided he couldn't accept the editorship—he didn't want to be pinned down—but he did accept the invitation to contribute, sending in nine essays, two printed as editorials and one as a review, over the six years from 1964 to 1970. These were almost entirely on subjects related to conservation, dealing with the population threat and the need for further national parks, as we have seen, but also the need to protect the Everglades, the beautification of highways, and, in several essays, the need to protect the Grand Canyon from the proposed dams at Marble Gorge and Bridge Canyon.

He felt deeply about trying to prevent the building of the proposed dams. His feelings were generated in large part out of his regret for the loss of Glen Canyon to Lake Powell, a regret tinged with a bit of guilt that he had not done more to try to save it. He came up with the idea of an article that would contrast the present lake with the canyon that had been lost, based on a tour of the lake he planned to take (in December 1964) and on his previous trips through the canyon before it had been covered over. He had Carol Brandt try to sell the idea, and she got a commission from *Holiday.* Once the article had been submitted, it became clear that Wallace and the editor of the magazine, Don Gold, had two different ideas, although Gold in commissioning him had imposed no conditions. Gold wanted a travel piece, a voyage through pretty scenery punctuated by nostalgic flashbacks to the canyon as it had been. He didn't like the geological and geographical detail Wallace had typically used throughout the article, nor did he like Wallace's "editorializing." However, the author, in his turn, seems a little disingenuous in his dismay at Gold's reaction, since he was using the article to propagandize a point of view: he wanted to use what ostensibly was a travel article to make a point about what dams can do to beautiful canyons (without mentioning the damage that would be done at Marble Gorge and Bridge Canyon), and he wanted to make a further point that the Escalante Basin, back from the lake, should be set aside as wilderness.

Wallace did some revision, but Gold gave in on nearly every objection he had made. In his article Wallace admits that Lake Powell has a certain beauty and its recreational facilities—boating, fishing, waterskiing, swimming—will be used by hundreds of thousands of people each year, but pleads for setting aside a different kind of area in the adjoining Escalante Basin. He refers back to a camping trip he made there in 1961 when he saw no vehicles, no people outside of their own party, and hardly any animals. This is country that provides another kind of experience, country "that does not challenge our identity as creatures, but . . . shows us our true size." Pressing home the value of preserving such places, he uses all his descriptive powers:

From every evening camp, when the sun was gone behind the Kaiparowits, and the wind hung in suspension like a held breath, and the Henry's northeastward and Navajo Mountain southward floated light as bubbles on the distance, we watched the eastern sky flush a pure, cloudless rose, darker at the horizon, paler above; and minute by minute the horizon's darkness defined itself as the blue, domed shadow of the earth cast on the sky, thinning at its upward arc to violet, lavender, pale lilac, but clearly defined, steadily darkening upward until it swallowed all the sky's light, and the stars pierced through it. Every night we watched the earth-shadow climb the hollow sky, and every dawn we watched the same blue

shadow sink down toward the Kaiparowits, to disappear at the
instant when the sun splintered sparks off the rim.

To read this description is in itself an experience. Stegner makes his final
plea by saying, "Save this tributary and the desert back from it as wilderness, and there will be something at Lake Powell for everybody."

In many of his articles, he talks about the interconnectedness of life,
and of life to its environment, often quoting such forebears as George
Perkins Marsh and Aldo Leopold. This ecological sensibility was always
there in his conservation writings, but it becomes more and more
emphasized in his work as a philosophical basis for his advocacy, and
becomes one of the themes of his next novel, *All the Little Live Things*,
which is perhaps the most ecologically grounded of his works of fiction.
He recalled that during the time he was writing the novel, he had been
reading Teilhard de Chardin and "was interested in his particular version of immortality, which is just an exchange of protein. That's the ecological point of view too—that you give your pound and a half of
minerals ... back to the earth, and you've paid your debt to Nature."
And of course he had taught Walt Whitman's *Leaves of Grass* for many
years:

I bequethe myself to the dirt, to grow from the grass I love;
If you want me again, look for me under your boot-soles.

The background to the novel is complex, and its focus changed several
times. It began with Wallace's fascination with his neighbors, their conflicts, idiosyncrasies, and their California modes of living (which at the
beginning were very strange to him) in his semi-rural area of Los Altos
Hills. This led to two stories in the late fifties, "All the Little Live
Things" and "Indoor-Outdoor Living," and some of the characters of
these are carried over into the novel. But an even more important contribution was made by Stegner's discovery of Joe Allston as narrator in
"Field Guide to Western Birds," which has the same setting as the novel
but whose characters, aside from Joe and his wife, are either gone or
barely present. Then the most important contribution of all, which gave
the novel central characters and the direction for a plot, came as a series
of events in Stegner's life during the early 1960s. First, four of his

women friends died, one after another, of breast cancer—Wallace and Mary were devastated. (The novel is dedicated, "For Trudy, Franny, Judy, Peg.") But out of his grief the idea for a protagonist for the book came to him—Marian Catlin.

At about this same time, a young man, ostensibly a student, came on his motorcycle and without asking permission began camping out on the Stegner property in a canyon near their house. The Stegners simply tolerated it until they found out that he was tapping into their water and electricity and began having "come-one, come-all" parties. Presumably to stir up some action and meet some new girls, he would put his party invitations up on the bulletin board in the basement of the Stanford Union—with a map showing anyone interested how to get to the Stegner property. Then their tenant in the little house below them, which had been Wallace's original office, was discovered to be growing marijuana on their property. Stegner's observation of the activities of these two obnoxious characters suggested an antagonist, Jim Peck.

As with many of his novels, he began with characters and a setting and then struggled over several years to let his characters find a plot for him. After finishing during the summer of 1964 a preface and an essay on Willa Cather for a volume he was editing called *American Novel from James Fenimore Cooper to William Faulkner,* and essays on Theodore Dreiser and Thomas Wolfe for another critical collection, *American Literary Masters*, he started work on *All the Little Live Things* in the fall, and by the end of the year he had four chapters. He may have been a bit overconfident, since at this point he thought that much of the novel would come out of the stories that he had already written, and he told his agents, "If I ever find the right handle, the novel will almost pump itself" (11/7/64). But he couldn't find the handle, and he wrestled with the manuscript all the following year, the writing made even more difficult by his Sierra Club responsibilities and his assuming the chairmanship of the Secretary of Interior's Advisory Board on National Parks. He was also teaching and wrote to his agents, "Do you know anybody who would like to endow me for approximately my Stanford salary so that posterity will not be deprived?" (1/27/65).

In mid-July of 1965, he wrote to his agents in regard to an offer by

Harper & Row to write a book about the history/geography/ecology of California. He found the offer tempting, but after thinking about it, he decided that he just couldn't do it:

> I'm moving slowly with this novel, but I'm moving, and I don't want to stop. So far as I can see, teaching shouldn't stop me until New Year, since I'll be teaching only one course in the fall. But I'll be up to my neck from New Year to the end of March, and then we go to Austria, to the Stanford campus at Semmering, until June, then we come back, fairly leisurely, to Vermont and a sabbatical year and—I hope—that Danish story I once threatened to write.... It seems to me that I can always get commission books of this kind, but as long as I have any energy left for fiction I had better use it for that. (7/16/65)

In August he got back from an advisory board trip to Alaska to find that Harper & Row was still after him. He told his agents, "I'm not sympathetic enough with California culture to do it justice" (8/13/65). Nevertheless, he wrote the first of several articles he would write on California over the next two years—one that lamented all the things, such as overcrowding and the disappearance of prime farmland to housing tracts, that he saw as warning signs to the country as a whole: "The Clouded Skies of Lotus Land," which appeared, for some mysterious reason, in the *St. Louis Post-Dispatch*.

It is really with the assumption of the first-person narrator—Joe Allston and variations of his voice in the late novels—that Stegner's fiction, aside from *The Big Rock Candy Mountain*, really became first-rate. Stegner has said that he "got onto the Joe Allston business . . . [because] I was just looking for a tone of voice which had to be light and flippant. As it developed, it began to develop undercurrents of seriousness, but the tone stayed light." He felt he had to maintain a light tone in order to balance the somber nature of the material and in order to maintain his own equilibrium while dealing with material that was so personally distressing. And as we have also noted, it was the creation of a fictional character close to Stegner's own personality that made that voice effective. In an interview, when told that the interviewer saw much of him in Joe, he replied:

> Oh, yes, but ... don't read him intact. He goes further than I would. Anybody is likely to make characters to some extent in his own image, but if he's at all self-protective, he'll make them also *out* of his own image, just to throw people off the scent.

"He goes further ..." appears to be a key here. Joe does and says things, perhaps, that Wallace, as frank and direct as he could be at times, would like to do and say but was prevented from doing because of a tight lid on his emotions and old-fashioned politeness. Almost everyone who has known Wallace well has felt that Joe Allston is a sort of an "extreme Stegner." Richard Scowcroft, who worked as Wally's assistant and partner in the creative writing program for decades before he took it over himself, has commented that "knowing him ... made it hard for me to read his books because I've heard his voice in every line."

All the Little Live Things is a more emotional book than anything Stegner had written since his autobiographical fiction, and he seemed to have learned, whether he acknowledged it consciously or not, that a powerful book requires the input of powerful emotions, for all of his remaining novels would have that same impact. In *All the Little Live Things* there is much love, tenderly expressed by Joe for his wife but also, more especially, for Marian, the young woman dying of cancer who is his neighbor. Of the four women who died of cancer to whom Wallace had dedicated the book, one was Peg Gray, who, as we have seen, had been a very close friend for decades and whose dying would become the subject of his last novel, *Crossing to Safety*. Another was Franny Fisher, who had been a part-time secretary with the creative writing section of the English Department for several years until she married Joe Houghteling. Joe and Wallace met early on, only a year after the Stegners had moved to Palo Alto, when the two of them were working for the Committee to Save the Two Party System, part of the Truman campaign and a response to the candidacy of Henry Wallace. Once Joe and Franny met and were married, they saw the Stegners socially frequently.

There were several models for Marian, but Franny Houghteling probably contributed the most to her. Like Marian, Franny was a warm, loving person, generous to a fault, and kind to all creatures, great and small; she differed from the character created by Stegner in that she could be very funny. Nor did she have the totally ecological point of view that he gives Marian. However, she does have the same plan as Marian, which is at the center of the novel. Joe Houghteling recalled:

> In essence it [the novel] is about the woman detaching her daughter from herself and trying to get the links moved over to the father. And Franny did that. We had three children then and she tried to, but it didn't work. It [just] doesn't work. It cannot prevent the traumatic experience of the children.

Increasing the emotional burden that the author was carrying into this project was the fact that not only had four dear friends died, but his mother, whom he had nursed through her last painful days, had also died of cancer. He seemed to be haunted by a dark angel of death, surrounded by a malignant atmosphere that tested his will to face life with optimism and tested his ability to acquiesce to the principle of the ecological cycling of life and death, a principle that he accepted intellectually but that he found difficult to handle emotionally. The novel was his way of working through this dark night of the soul. There would seem to be no doubt that Marian is in part a stand-in for Wallace's mother, expressing many of the same qualities of courage and gentleness, as well as a spirited love and concern for others even at the worst of times.

Wallace talked to Joe about using his wife in a general sort of way in his novel, and after it was published, he gave Joe a copy, writing a note to him on the flyleaf:

> Dear Joe—
> Some of this will pain you—it pained *me*. But I hope you will recognize in it the tribute to Franny that I intended; though I took liberties with fact and circumstance, I wanted more than anything to get a little of Franny's spirit to shine through this story.
>
> Wally

17

TROUBLE IN
THE SIXTIES

There is much love in *All the Little Live Things*, but also much that is somber and distressing, as well as a great deal of anger. Events may conspire to make us believe, as they evidently did to Stegner, that the good die young while the rotten among us seem to persist forever. Or, as his alter ego Joe Allston puts it in the novel, "I was pondering the vanity of human wishes and the desperation of human hope, the tooth of time, the vulnerability of good and the unseen omnipresence of evil." In a way, that is what this novel is about—a consciousness of the reality and endurance of evil and feelings of helpless anger and frustration in response to the ironies of fate. And these are precisely the same feelings at the end of *The Big Rock Candy Mountain* when Bruce's mother dies and his father lives on. We know that writers such as Mark Twain and Ernest Hemingway have become Realists, embittered and satiric in their writings, as a result of having had an earlier, youthful romanticism shattered by painful experiences. This would seem to be at least partly true for Wallace Stegner as well, as his realism, always dark and Twain-like, in *All the Little Live Things* becomes bitter with a layer of satire only partly masked by comedy. As Joe says about himself, "I am a tea bag left too long in the cup, and my steepings grow darker and bitterer."

But there is much, much more. Stegner was feeling his age, deeply, for the first time (in 1967 he was only fifty-eight), and connected to that was a growing sense of separation from his students. It had started during the Kesey years and had only gotten worse over time. Not that he lacked during the early and mid-sixties good relationships with his classes as a whole and with many of his students. It was a minority who had embraced hippie values or thought of themselves as the shock troops of a new age that caused him at least perplexity and occasionally distress. He simply could not for the life of him understand that which was being called the "youth culture of the sixties." It contradicted everything he had done with his own life, the growing and learning, the hard work and sacrifice, and the values he believed in and lived by. In personal values he was very conservative and he found any kind of extremism upsetting; he was a rationalist, in the tradition of Western civilization, and the extreme romanticism and the Eastern mysticism of many of the young he tended to consider a self-centered indulgence, a cop-out from the difficult jobs of getting things done. In an essay written at just about the time he was finishing revisions on his novel, assessing the current "far-out young" and whether they were passivists on a "Zen-love-pot-LSD course" or "activists strident for . . . reform," he writes that

> as a group they are reckless, they stampede toward the emanci-
> pated future like dry cattle scenting a water hole; and they are all
> the less regardful of consequences because their faith leads them to
> disparage tradition, convention, organization, discipline, the past
> and all forms of authority. To a puzzled elder, they often seem to
> throb rather than think.

Since they (the upper-middle-class children that characteristically make up the activist and passivist branches of the youth revolution) have known no Depression, no World War II, and have lived in almost uninterrupted prosperity, they look for adventure, not security. Since they have not suffered to build, it costs them nothing to destroy.

Stegner was particularly irritated with the gurus of the young, men such as Alan Watts, Allen Ginsberg, and Gary Snyder. At the beginning of his essay in *The Nation*, he flatly states that "the hippie poet Gary

Snyder, declaring that the revolution now being made by young people will leave not one value of the old America standing, is not fooling." He used almost the same line in an editorial for *Saturday Review* called "California: The Experimental Society." Within a month, Snyder, who was in Japan, heard about the blast and wrote an angry letter with a copy to *Saturday Review*. He told Stegner that his paraphrase from a speech given at Stanford was "irresponsible," but he didn't really deny saying it. And he briefly laid out a philosophy that confirms the spirit, if not the words that Stegner had cited:

> The "real values" of course have nothing to do with social orders, new or old. They are somewhere in nature, and human nature. . . . the old order is destroying itself, good and bad; while some of us— using history, prehistory, archeology, cultural anthropology, the experiences of our friends and families, and our own deepest intuitions, are trying to find the few threads in that old order that are still alive, that DO go all the way to the Real Values. In the process—and here's where California's young sometimes appear bizarre—a lot has to be put to the test to find if it works or not. . . .
>
> Does Jesus Save Redwoods? If not we'd better figure out why and do something about it. The Buddha is a twin brother to the Christ—both Divine Sons of the Goddess, and if his mythology and practice helps save Redwoods (respect for ALL creatures) then the Buddha is not irrelevant to us. The Gary Snyders and their ilk are, I do most deeply believe, not destroyers but preservers. (11/24/67)

Stegner, who had been in Europe when Snyder had written to him, answered with a long letter at the end of January the following year. It was clear that the two men were talking very different languages and coming at such topics as saving the environment from entirely different directions. Stegner was polite and conciliatory ("We may have more in common than you think"), but although he apologized if he had misrepresented Snyder, he had gotten the quotation from three different people who had been at the Stanford speech—two who thought that leaving nothing of the old order standing was a "swell idea," and one who was appalled. After that, he takes up each of the poet's arguments in turn:

Real values. You say they have nothing to do with social orders, but exist in nature, in human nature. It is a strange faith for a student of cultural anthropology. I would say that values aren't values at all until some social order, some social agreement or consensus or acknowledgment, makes them so. Until then, they're only human possibilities, alternatives in the genes and the meat and the mind. What gives them any value they have—what makes them conduct instead of merely behavior—is a social agreement on what constitutes legitimate, desirable, or undesirable behavior. . . .

I would say your experimental search through the mystical and the Eastern, however admirable as a sign of intellectual unrest and curiosity, is unlikely to turn up anything very substantial for the saving or rejuvenating western civilization. . . . You ask if Jesus saves redwoods? Christians, or pseudo-Christians, cut down all that have been cut. But they also saved all that have been saved. The Old Order that you say is destroying itself has elements, segments, that I respect at least as much as I respect Coyote or even the Buddha. I have spent a lot of days and weeks at the desks and in the meetings that ultimately save redwoods, and I have to say that I never saw there on the firing line any of the mystical drop-outs or meditators. (1/27/68)

He ends his letter suggesting, when Snyder gets back to the States, that they try to get together and talk out their differences. The correspondence ended with a letter from Snyder that begins with an apparently sarcastic response (he says he did not intend it be taken that way) to Stegner's concluding sarcasm, "I am happy to hear you've been at work on conservation problems"—this, which would have appeared to Stegner so condescending, to the man who had become one of the foremost leaders of the conservationist charge, who had written the "Wilderness Letter," *Beyond the Hundredth Meridian*, numerous essays on conservation, and edited *This Is Dinosaur*; a man who had served on the boards and as an officer of several environmental organizations, who had worked for and given speeches for many local candidates, as well as for Congressman Don Edwards, Senator Alan Cranston, and other politicians he thought were friends of the environment. None of this sacrifice of time and energy, so important to him at this point in his career, would seem to be of much importance or ultimate value to Snyder, who thought that the environmental movement up to that time had been "remarkably genteel." Instead, one should be one of those who was "at this very moment, deeply feeling the great sighing life of a redwood tree, almost hearing it breathe and speak, [this] is what gives meaning to 'saving the redwoods.' Though they may never attend meetings, I think that's where the ultimate firing line is" (2/1/68).

The poet, who had been in Japan since 1956 and who appears to have never read Stegner (who had defined wilderness in deeply spiritual terms), seems to imply here that anyone like Stegner, people who work and act rather than meditate, is incapable of an aesthetic response to nature. Snyder does make a good point, however, when he reminds Stegner that "John Muir (to speak of redwoods) was a drop-out and meditator for a good spell of years." Stegner and Snyder seemed to see things from diametrically opposite points of view. Not only did they represent different generations with different values, but Stegner's particular experience—a lack of a stable home life, a felt lack of history, and an enormous effort over years to haul himself up into the cultural mainstream by his own bootstraps—pushed his perceptions even further away from Snyder's. His revolt had been in the opposite direction:

> I had no tradition to declare myself independent of, and had never felt the dead hand of the past. . . . I was always hungry to belong to some socially or intellectually or historically or literarily cohesive group, some culture, some offshoot of western civilization. . . . I had to revolt in the direction of tradition, cultural memory, shared experience, agreed-upon grammar and synatx.

East never did meet West during that period. It was twenty-five years later, only after Stegner had moderated his reactions to hippies and gained appreciation for Snyder's environmentalism and some of his poetry, that they finally got together. Snyder recalled, "He was grumpy for a number of years, but a year ago [just before Stegner's death in 1993] when I invited him to come speak at [University of California at] Davis, he responded most graciously—and we became friends."

All of this Zen Buddhism, nature mysticism, primitivism, glorifica-
tion of instinctual behavior, and rejection of history or authority of any
kind was particularly connected, in Stegner's mind, to California. On the
one hand you had the hippievilles, which despite the expressions of
nature reverence by people like Snyder, were generally dotted with dis-
carded beer cans, strewn with garbage, and puddled with open sewers,
the runoff from overloaded outhouses. The trashing of America. On the
other, you had the developers, driven by greed and totally unconscious of
the values of the nature they were carelessly destroying, who were
rapidly clearing off all vegetation and terracing the green foothills,
building mansions out in what had been "country," and wiping out the
Stegners' way of life. Bulldozers and chain saws ran day and night, so not
only was their peaceful view gone, their peace itself was shattered.
Stegner began to hate California and nearly everything about it—from
Ronald Reagan to the Free Speech students at Berkeley who also hated
Reagan; from the smog and traffic on the Peninsula caused by an inva-
sion from the new rich, to the drug- and disease-ridden ghetto of
Haight-Ashbury. In his *Saturday Review* essay in which he quotes
Snyder, he says,

> Like the rest of America, California is unformed, innovative,
> ahistorical, hedonistic, acquisitive, and energetic—only more so.
> Its version of the Good Life, its sports, pleasure, and comforts, are
> increasingly copied by the envious elsewhere. It creates an art and
> literature as nervous, permissive, and superficial as itself. . . . Cali-
> fornia is a state in which it is at times almost intolerable to live. . . .
> Yet . . . this is indeed where the future will be made—is already
> being made, with all the noise, smog, greed, energy, frequent
> wrong-headedness, and occasional greatness of spirit that are so
> American and so quintessentially Californian.

It is on this pessimistic note of California as the bellwether for the
future of the country as a whole that he began to fear for the future of
Vermont. By comparison to California, Vermont seemed to be on the
whole sane and, as he says in a letter to Carol Brandt, " 'unspoiled' in
ways that make it a peculiarly desirable haven and hideout—why else

would we come all the way from California every summer? Why else would Paul Goodman in *Ramparts* suggest it as a haven for Hippies?" (9/18/67). Out of a sense of dread, perhaps, that he would lose Vermont as well to the dual threat of hippie trashing and developer greed, he wanted to write an article warning rural New Englanders of the coming growth problems.

To that end he spent an afternoon talking to Governor Phil Hoff of Vermont and his aides about future pressures both from the New York–Boston axis and from Montreal sprawl in connection with the new interstate highways system. He told Carol that he wanted to write an article for a general magazine like *Look* or the *Saturday Evening Post*, with pictorial coverage, and asked her to query these magazines for a possible commission. The commission, from *Life*, didn't come for three years and the photo-article, "We Have Met the Enemy, and He Is Us," had a more general and less severe message than the wake-up call he had in mind, but he was still grateful for the opportunity. The only article that focused on the possible destruction of Vermont was one that, adapted from a speech to the Vermont Historical Society, was published as "The People Against the American Continent," in *Vermont History*. After reviewing the grim situation throughout the country, Stegner focuses on California, which "is in the midst of a vast, frantic boom that has left it with a lapful of almost insoluble problems: pollution of air and water, abusive uses of land, wild speculation, strains on the budget, and impossible needs for schools."

We have to take the time to think about what is happening to us, and there is no time, the problems are already upon us in all their frightening force even before we are aware that they exist. And what does all of this have to do with Vermont,

> this green sanctuary of peaceful meadows and painted woods, off the main line of the Progress which has swept most of the other states like a fire? I will tell you what you already know. It is coming here, and you can't escape it.

The twin threats of hippie and developer are dramatically represented in *All the Little Live Things* by Jim Peck, in the first instance, and

Tom Weld, in the second. Of the two, Peck is far more sinister. Weld, a transplanted country boy from Texas, owned the land from which the Allston parcel in the California coastal foothills was purchased. A bumbler, seemingly well-intentioned, he is unconscious of the damage he is doing in his roughshod treatment of the land. His plan to subdivide and make money is in the American tradition of subduing nature and acting in the spirit of free enterprise. When Joe complains about Weld's horses getting loose and ruining his garden, Tom puts on an agreeable face, seems not quite to understand the problem or what needs to be done (build a fence), and does as little as possible. His constant compliant non-compliance is maddening—he manipulates Joe as the hick outfoxes the city slicker. So there is much that is comic in Joe's small defeats at the hands of Weld, but the larger picture is another matter, and Joe finds Weld's landscape mutilations extremely upsetting. He looks out over the spoiled view from his house with bitterness:

> The hill that once swelled into view across the ravine like an opulent woman lazily turning was mutilated and ruined.... Only an amateur planning commission unable to read a contour map could ever have approved that site plan; only a land butcher could have proposed and carried it out.... There would be no restoring what he had ruined.... It made me sick to look.

As destructive as he is, Tom Weld is not deliberate in it and is a villain only as a reflection of the values of the majority culture.

The villain of the minority culture is another matter. Jim Peck is more than just a "bad boy," a mischievous trickster, as his namesake from a popular children's book of the late 1800s (*Peck's Bad Boy and His Pa*) would suggest. The irony of the comparison is carried out further in that the allusion to the earlier book suggests the conflict of generations we see in the later book, and Peck tries to ingratiate himself with the Allstons (whenever he wants something) as a sort of stand-in for their own son, who was also a hippie, lost in drugs and an apparent suicide. Peck, not knowing the facts but sensing the couple's sorrow and guilt, plays upon those skillfully—he is above all things a manipulator of others. He uses their middle-class politeness and their reticence to engage in confrontation. "Oh, he was alert," Joe tells us with drip-ping irony, "he was as sharp as a pin, he missed nothing in fact or by implication."

Joe Allston first discovers him sitting uninvited under a tree on his property, ostensibly meditating (just as he is ostensibly a student). What he is really doing is casing the joint, already planning to camp out on the property if he can worm himself into getting the older couple's permis-sion. Joe, worldly and cynical, sees him for what he is—a con man—while Ruth, his wife, is more tolerant and wants to give him a chance. (She thinks of him as a poor student who needs a place to sleep.) Working on Peck's behalf by appealing to Joe's sense of fairness, Ruth gets her husband reluctantly to go along. They are very nearly acting out the same parental roles they played while their son was alive. In giving permission, Joe sets down a few commonsense rules, all of which Peck blissfully ignores (just as Joe's son always ignored his rules). Rather than burying his trash and garbage, he throws it on the ground all around his tent-tree house; asked not to, in a dangerous brushy area, he constantly lights campfires; having assured Joe he will use a chemical toilet, he and his gang defecate on the ground; and having promised to clean out the poison oak as a sort of payment for the use of the area, he reneges; he steals water from Joe (runs a pipeline—without permission—rather than using a bucket as he says he will) and electricity from PG&E.

In short, he turns out to be a liar, a cheat, a thief, and a hypocrite. Worst of all, perhaps, Peck lures innocent teenagers into his nest of drugs and sexual abandon while spouting pious platitudes about natural living and self-discovery. He demonstrates a self-righteousness and arrogance that Joe finds unbearable, qualities that Stegner has always had at the top of his list of hated human attributes. Furthermore, the doctrine according to Peck and those like him runs right across the grain of Stegner's belief in cooperation and his antagonism for rugged individu-alism. In the writer's mind, Peck would seem to be a not-too-distant cousin of the sociopathic Western holdup man of years past. As Joe says (and Wallace could be speaking here just as well):

It's his *temperament* I don't like—that True-Believer stance, and his faith in the emancipated individual. The whole history of mankind is social, not individual. We've learned little by little to turn human energy into social order. . . . The free individual is an untutored animal. Society even teaches him the patterns of his revolt.

There is much in Jim Peck's arrogance and behavior that might remind the reader of Ken Kesey, and that association has been made, but Wallace has said that he did not have Kesey specifically in mind, only the type. Instead, Peck would seem to be the generic hippie guru. When asked sixteen years after the novel's publication about the view that it was essentially a rather grumpy criticism of the hippie generation, Stegner answered:

> The hippie just wandered into it by accident and became a rather half-witted Principle of Evil. The book is about "little live things" and the relations one has to life. . . . The hippie is only a kind of dumb bystander. That was my feeling about hippies in general at that point. I've changed to some extent since, but the ones that I knew then were dumb bystanders who didn't have any notion of what went on but thought they did.

Although Tom Weld, the other source of "evil" in the book, is from Texas, he is your generic California Okie entrepreneur, modeled in part after one of Stegner's neighbors in California and with some qualities imported from another "country" neighbor, George Hill, in Vermont. Marian, as we have already seen, was patterned in large part after a good friend, Franny Houghteling. Beyond these characters, we have something close to a fictionalized autobiography, this time depending on con- temporary scenes and events, rather than, as in *The Big Rock Candy Mountain*, depending on childhood and adolescent memories. Taking on the Joe Allston persona seems to have led Wallace to work very near the bone, using the materials around him with very little alteration. He worked closer here than any other novel except for *Crossing to Safety*. Not only do Joe and Ruth Allston resemble Wallace and Mary Stegner as individuals, their relationship is close to the actual one as well. Like Ruth, Mary tried to restrain her husband's tendencies toward anger and

sarcasm—a restraint that, as in the novel, did not always work. The Allston house, garden, surroundings, and neighbors are patterned after the
Stegners', so that it is no wonder the people in the Los Altos Hills area
have looked upon the novel as a roman à clef and for years talked about
who matched whom. A doctor friend of Wallace said to him after the
book came out, "I don't mind you putting me in your book, but why did
you have to give me bad breath?" Mrs. R. E. Cameron, longtime friend,
has said that the novel "was taken completely from our circle of
friends." When she asked Stegner about this, he smiled and replied,
"Never have a writer for a friend."

All the Little Live Things in several respects goes beyond previous
Stegner novels. As pointed out earlier, it deals extensively with the subject matter of both ecology and conservation without preachiness. And in
addition to breaking new ground in a novel with his use of the first-
person narrator and in his use of contemporary experience, the novel is
also his most entertaining, primarily because it is so witty. The assumption of the Allston personality allows the author full rein to express his
own personality and even, using his fictive identity as cover, to go
beyond and say that which in life he would repress. Stegner has
admitted that

> it's self-indulgent. You let yourself blow off in a way you wouldn't
> blow off in real life. I think there is something, too, about the cur-
> mudgeon. He's a useful kind of person if at the same time his cur-
> mudgeonness is funny. I was trying to make Joe Allston sort of
> funny and soft-hearted at the same time.

In creating Allston, Stegner does make good use of his own sense of
humor, as well as his skepticism and an exceptional ability to see connections and likenesses. For example, the Allstons have a cat that has a habit
of bringing little gifts "which he composes on the door mat with an
imagination that transcends his homely materials," parts of the rats
and gophers it has killed during the night. One morning Joe gets up and
finds at the front door what must be considered his cat's masterpiece, and
the cat nearby waiting for compliments. The cat makes no objection
when Joe lifts the mat to dispose of the animal entrails, teeth, and tail:

"He understands," Joe thinks, "that his art, like a Navaho sand painting, should not survive the hour of its creation." Or, contemplating the Coast Range beyond the foothills where he lives, he tells us,

> It used to comfort me to know that these little mountains, like everything else around, are very lively, very Californian. The range grows, they say, a half inch or so a year, and in the same time moves about that distance northward. It is a parable for the retired. Sit still and let the world do the moving.

As further examples, shortly after the Allstons have met the Catlins, they are in the car and have stopped to chat with Marian and Debby. As they go to leave, Joe starts the engine, "mother and daughter stepped back, we were a rotating lighthouse of smiles." At one point Ruth is described looking at Marian, who comes to the Allstons looking very drawn and tired: "Ruth was staring at her with the absolutely expressionless expression she wears when she is concentrating on something that bothers her." On a very hot day, the Allstons and Catlins walk down a trail through burrs and foxtails on their way to a neighbor's party, and Joe describes them as "a tiny procession between brass earth and brass sky, little coolies in straw garden hats." Above them is a redtail hawk, which is "riding the thermals, looking not as if he were up there hunting, but as if he had gone up in search of a breeze." As they come to the party, they hear the sounds from it "as volubly unintelligible as an Italian traffic argument." As the bartender lifts a glass to pass it to a guest, "the ice cubes caught the sun and threw me a brilliant blue wink." In an essay called "Sensibility and Intelligence," Stegner has written, "There ought to be a poet submerged in every novelist." Furthermore, "he needs a memory that spills easily, a memory with a loose top, so that any chance can tip it and send rolling the vast and invaluable supply of what the writer did not know he knew."

Besides wit, usually expressed in metaphor or simile, the reader is entertained by a narrative rich in literary allusion, and these allusions carry a subtext of warring polarities—good versus evil, order versus disorder, life versus death, health and growth versus disease and destruction. One such context for conflict is the frequent references to the Garden of Eden. Joe and Ruth have moved from New York City to retire in the supposed paradise of the California coastal foothills. Joe wants to establish and maintain an Eden, cut off from the rough edges of the world, a carefully planned, manicured, and sanitized one. But their garden is invaded by innumerable pests that seek to destroy it—the grubs, snails, mildew, aphids, and gophers—and that Joe battles with spray, traps, and even his shotgun. He views the pests as evil—but it is not that simple, for in seeking to preserve the life of his artificial garden, he finds he himself is destroying life, something that is pointed out to him forcefully by Marian, who tells him:

> "I should think you'd have a nice natural garden where things are in balance and you don't have to kill anything. Is it fair to plant a lot of plants that were never intended to grow here, and then blame the gophers for liking them?"

While Joe tries to create an appearance of naturalness through artful planting, constant care, and an ongoing battle against pests, a garden fit to human desires, Marian presents the ideal of a different kind of garden, one that is left natural, with native plants, native animals, without pesticides, manicuring, or interfering with natural processes. This contrast of gardens provides the basis for what is essentially an ecological argument over man's relations with nature, and even beyond that to one over what is nature or natural—an argument in the novel that resonates with the continuing debates in contemporary society over the agricultural uses of chemicals, the economic and ethical rationale for eating meat, and the killing of animals for the use of their fur. This argument between Joe and Marian would also seem to relate to our continuing debate over preserving wilderness as versus "managed" forests.

A third pattern of allusion involving conflict—in addition to the Garden of Eden and the neoclassical versus romantic ideal of garden—is the connected use of Shakespeare's *The Tempest*. This is brought to our attention early in the novel when Joe spots Jim Peck for the first time sitting on his motorcycle down in the Allston creek bottom, dressed in orange helicopter coveralls, and Joe identifies him immediately:

> The suit was unzipped clear to his navel, and his hairy chest rose out of it and merged with a dark, dense beard.

Caliban. . . .

Teetering, tiptoeing his padded boots to balance the cycle (surely
the feet inside those boots were cloven), he sat and looked at us. . . .
His hair was long and tousled, even matted . . . it crawled over his
collar, and was pushed forward on his forehead, hiding his horns.

The suggested parallel with Shakespeare's play underlines Joe's attempt
to create an "island" apart from the influences of a corrupt world. As in
the play, we have a wise man, who has been active in worldly affairs and
has turned his back on that world with both scorn and relief, a wise man
who is not always wise, but even sometimes a fool, marooned on a hilltop
"island" that should be paradise. Like Prospero, Joe is led gradually to
grudging forgiveness of those who sin against him and to give up power
in favor of the principle of love, a powerful and all-encompassing love as
embodied in Marian (who takes the part of Miranda and whom Joe
thinks of as a daughter). And as in the play, there are the themes of the
conflict between generations, the conflict between experience and innocence, and the conflict between the natural and man's control of nature.
Even the environment in the novel reflects the play, as nature has its
way: "Each new storm arrives with a pounce, and our house anchored on
its hilltop shakes to the padded blows of the wind, and the trees heave
and creak, and our terrace is littered with twigs and berries."

On the one hand it is a contemplative, philosophical book that exam-
ines our relations with life and how we tend to impose our cultural
bipolar values on nature, as well as on people. Joe as narrator tells us:

Where you find the greatest Good, there you will also find the
greatest Evil, for Evil likes Paradise every bit as much as Good
does. What makes the best environment for *Clematis armandi*
makes a lovely home for leaf hoppers. A place where Joe Allston
hopes to enjoy his retirement turns out to be Tom Weld's ancestral
acres and a place attractive to Caliban.

But on the other hand, this is also a stormy book, a tempestuous book.
It is energized emotionally by the many conflicts of extremes—the
extreme hippie, the extreme lover of nature, the extreme rationalist, the

extremely innocent, and the extremely worldly. Wallace Stegner in life would agree totally with neither Joe nor Marian, but take a middle position (although admiring Marian's spirit, he would not in his own life give up his hatred of poison oak and gophers). In a remembrance of Stegner, John Daniel—who rented the little house below the main house that had been Wallace's first study and that was later lived in by Page and his wife—has described the Stegner garden in such a way as to suggest that it was somewhere in between that desired by Joe and advocated by Marian:

> In nearly fifty years of living there, he and Mary created a humanized landscape in which the wild is welcomed and loved. There is an easeful order to their beds and hedges and trees—nothing regimented, nothing cropped in hard lines. The place is cultivated and natural, like its stewards.

Cultivated, yes, but there was still something of the "sensuous little savage," as Stegner calls the boy he had been, in him even in old age. Daniel recalled the reappearance of that boy, who excelled in killing pests on the Saskatchewan prairie, in strange combination with the retired English professor: "Once I found him gleefully declaiming a version of Milton about a gopher he'd trapped. 'Which way he flies is hell,' Stegner chortled, tossing the rodent in the field. '*Himself* is hell....' " To reverse matters—one must say that there is more than a little of Joe Allston here.

Taking a moderate position between developing extremes in the growing environmental movement during the sixties became more and more difficult as the decade wore on. Stegner became involved in the Sierra Club in the 1950s as a result of being recruited by the sincerity and drive of David Brower. But it was Ansel Adams, the preeminent landscape photographer, who during the next decade would have the most influence on him. He talked Wallace into running for the board, serving from 1964 to 1968. Affected in part by the social upheavals of the period, the club experienced more turbulence than at any other time in its history as it divided and redivided into factions over several major conservation issues, over the board's power over chapters, and over the role of Brower as executive director. In trying to maintain a moderate, reasonable posture in the midst of conflict, Wallace found himself following Ansel Adams's lead more often than not.

Stegner met Adams at Witter Bynner's house in Santa Fe back in 1945 when he was doing research on the Hispanics of New Mexico for *One Nation*. Adams was a bundle of energy, with a sense of humor that bubbled to the surface constantly and an integrity that was uncompromising. Mary Stegner has called him "the most interesting, funny man I had ever met." He had trained to be a pianist, but in his late twenties switched over to photography, and by 1932 had had his first one-man show. In his essay "Ansel Adams and the Search for Perfection," Stegner tells us that with Edward Weston, Imogen Cunningham, and others, Ansel founded *f*/64, "whose inaugural exhibit at the De Young Museum, in San Francisco, was a benchmark in the establishment of photography as a legitimate and distinct art in which the camera is not a substitute brush but a way of seeing." Adams began his connection with the Sierra Club in his youth as a caretaker of one of its lodges and leader of mountaineering expeditions in the early 1920s, and after his marriage to Virginia Best, he and his wife moved to Yosemite Valley in 1937, where they maintained a home for more than forty years.

Although he did portraits, Adams is best known, of course, for his landscapes of Yosemite, other areas of the Sierras, and the Southwestern desert. Stegner has said of him that as an artist, he has been "unfailingly open to the experience of seeing" and that he has seen "not only the shapes and brightnesses and beauties of the world but 'something intrinsic,' " below the surface. Furthermore, as artist, Adams

feels deeply about what he sees, he has a reverence for the earth in all its variety, delicacy, and strength, but he is the absolute reverse of effusive. He sees with such austerity, even severity, that some have mistakenly called him cold. He has an incomparable technical expertness in communicating what he sees and feels.... [His photographs] have taught thousands how to see; they have become household images; and when much art has been retreating into denial or crying out in pain and anger, they have steadily affirmed life.

There was hardly anything about Adams that Stegner did not admire, and he particularly admired the way that the photographer's art and his efforts to save the environment came together as all of one piece. In dedicating Mt. Ansel Adams after Adams's death, before a gathering in Tuolumne Meadows in upper Yosemite, Stegner said that the news media, discovering Adams as a "character," referred to him in his outspokenness as "fiesty." But Wallace said that made him sound like a public scold. It was not scolding that the press heard in Adams's public utterances,

> it was the sound of a great heart beating. It was the sound of a great artist speaking his mind on a subject that meant more to him than fame, money, or anything in the world except his art and his family. That subject was the integrity and beauty and health of the earth, and the respect that should accompany our use and enjoyment of them.

Stegner served on the board really out of his respect and love for Ansel. Despite his service on several boards during the decade, Wallace was not an organization man and didn't like doing it. "It was a mistake," he has said, referring to his service for the Sierra Club, "because I don't have the kind of life that can make meetings. . . . So I was never an effective or a good board member. I found it interesting, but difficult." What made it difficult was not only that it was always a problem to get away from his work to attend meetings, but that the issues split friends, and Wallace found himself having to choose. He could rail at President Reagan from the pages of a magazine, but he did not like bitter confrontation on a personal basis.

The first major issue to come up was Mineral King, an alpine valley in the Sierras near Sequoia National Park that some have declared more beautiful than Yosemite. When Disney Corporation proposed to make it a ski resort in the late forties, the club had decided not to oppose development that seemed inevitable. However, in a stormy meeting in May 1965, the board, at the behest of Martin Litton, reconsidered the previous decision, finally voting to oppose recreational development and ask that no action be taken until after public hearings. Litton was a tough-minded environmental journalist who began his career with the *Los Angeles Times* and went on to be the travel editor of *Sunset* magazine for many years. Stegner has called him an "unswerving partisan"; he is "sometimes abrasive and unyielding, but he is never soft, and is generally very effective. In addition, he knows the terrain of California and the West by the square inch—I don't know anyone who knows it better." As a hobby Litton organized and led river trips down through the Marble and upper Grand Canyon, and shortly after he started running the river, Wallace and Mary, along with Nat and Margaret Owings, Harold Gilliam, and others took the journey with him. Litton had picked up some oarsmen who didn't have much experience, and almost all the boats flipped over at one point or another, heaving the passengers into the drink. Litton used Mackenzie River dories rather than the "pontoons" of the commercial expeditions, which Wallace claimed "wallow down the rapids like dinosaurs." The party went down the Colorado from Lee's Ferry to Phantom Ranch, where all but Gilliam (who went on to the wilderness park) got out and hiked up the trail out of the canyon. They met several expeditions on the river, and all of them had copies of *Beyond the Hundredth Meridian* with them.

Wallace attended a meeting where the Mineral King issue was discussed but missed the crucial May 1965 one when the vote was taken. He did not know Mineral King, but came to agree with Litton's arguments and with Adams, who voted for the proposal (although Adams strongly disapproved of Litton's pugnaciousness), but disappointed another friend, Edgar Wayburn, who voted against it. Wayburn felt that there was a strong moral obligation to preserve a policy already set by the club, although he later changed his mind about Mineral King. Over the course of his tenure on the board, Wallace was torn by this argument of "moral obligation" to abide by previous agreements. Dinosaur had been saved, but the agreement, a compromise, had given up Glen Canyon; in a more recent compromise Marble and Bridge Canyon dams were defeated in 1966–67, but the agreement allowed instead for the coal-burning power stations at Four Corners that belched out enough smoke to cover Grand Canyon with haze. It seemed like every time the conservationists compromised with development, they lost as much as they gained. With this in the background, Wallace was of two minds—he was inclined to agree with the tougher stand taken on the board by Litton and by Brower as executive director, but while he admired their spirit, at the same time their uncompromising militancy bothered him more and more. One must remember also that during these years he was encountering abso-lutist rhetoric, sometimes condescending and nasty, on campus. In the department on campus and in the club, civility was lost along with the "gentlemen's club" atmosphere as the young made it clear that they considered those of the elder generation as sell-outs—pimps for the military-industrial establishment. (Litton and his allies were not all that young, actually, but they adopted that confrontational style.) Ansel Adams, who had been a young Turk himself, the most militant member of the board for years during the fifties, was bothered by the confronta-tional posture and sixties rhetoric of the club radicals. He became more conservative, particularly in regard to money matters and in the power of the board versus the executive director to set policy as the decade wore on, and took Wallace with him.

After Mineral King the next major issue also involved a decision about possibly going back on a previous agreement. The longtime club policy in regard to dams and power plants was to suggest alternative sites in order to appear reasonable. But as far as Litton was concerned, why should the club do the thinking for Pacific Gas and Electric? In 1962 PG&E bought a site on the Nipomo Dunes, south of San Luis Obispo, for the building of a nuclear power plant, but the area was of recognized scenic value and had been recommended several times for park status. The Sierra Club stepped in in June 1963 by recommending preservation of the dunes, and Edgar Wayburn and other members of the board exec-utive committee negotiated with the power company over alternatives, a negotiation that lasted over two years. Ultimately, in conference with the club president, William Siri, PG&E offered to build the plant "up the coast in Diablo Canyon, at the mouth of an isolated, undeveloped canyon just south of Montana de Oro State Park." In May 1966 the board voted that Nipomo Dunes should be preserved and that Diablo Canyon should be accepted as a satisfactory alternate. Martin Litton was out of the country and missed the meeting.

Although the vote was overwhelmingly in favor, Litton came back and blasted the reasoning behind it as "either false, irrelevant, or con-

trary to Sierra Club ideals," and along with Fred Eissler, began to push
for a reconsideration. Those who opposed reconsideration felt that Siri
had made a commitment in good faith, "and whether the decision was
right or wrong, the board members of the Club felt they were 'honor
bound to support Siri.' " Ansel Adams thought that if the club was going
to be adult about the issue, it had to recognize the utility's mandate to
supply power and the public's need for power. Litton felt that expanding
the power capacity to meet future needs was a self-fulfilling prophecy: if
you didn't supply it, population growth would not be encouraged and the
state's scenic values might be preserved. Stegner, along with Adams and
others, agreed that a deal was a deal and that the club's public integrity
depended on consistency. Stegner said in later years:

> I wasn't very pleased about the Diablo Canyon plant. And all of the
> later evidence is that nobody should have been pleased with it. . . . I
> wasn't an authoritative vote. . . . All I did know was that the club
> had in the past made a deal with PG&E, and now it was reneging
> on the deal, which I thought was unfortunate. I still do. You
> shouldn't make deals until you're absolutely sure.

Diablo Canyon became a much larger issue as the dissension it caused
began to snowball. The issue was presented to the membership as a ref-
erendum—the first time such an action had been taken. As the club
more often took political stands externally, it became more and more
politicized internally. There was what Michael Cohen, the historian of
the club, has called "open warfare," not only between factions on the
board, "but also between the board and the staff, which supported the
Eissler-Litton faction on Diablo and supported Brower in his bid for
more executive discretion." The board felt that it should set policies and
that the executive director and his staff should carry them out, not act on
their own. Brower felt hamstrung by what he felt was organizational
gridlock; always enthusiastic and pushing for new initiatives, he felt that
the board was too conservative, too much behind the times. Stegner
recalled:

> Some members of the board were violently opposed to Dave and
> thought he was trying to be Captain Ahab, you know, and run the

ship in spite of the board, in despite of the board. . . . Those were conflicts that, as I say, I didn't fully understand, but I talked with Ansel a lot about it and with some other people. Martin was with Dave; Ansel was against him. You had to take your choice.

One reason Ansel turned against Brower was his worry about the club's finances. During this period, the IRS seemed bent on taking away the club's tax-exempt status, and at the same time, Brower was heavily committing the club's resources to his publication program of expensive display books. Many members of the board believed that not all the books were relevant to the club's mission. But that was the point—Brower was determined to expand that mission, despite the opposition of the board and the local chapters. There was worry that if a book turned out to be a real dud, and they ended up with a warehouse full of books, the club's finances would be all tied up in dead books. But, Stegner remembered, "that didn't scare Dave at all. He was absolutely unscarable, and most of his stuff paid off, because he was so energetic."

Not only was Stegner turned away from full support of Brower by Adams's concerns over Brower's attempts to expand his power and what seemed to Adams a reckless expenditure of money, but he began to become irritated by Brower's increasingly radical political posture. Brower had become an environmentalist guru to the young. In fact Stewart Udall believed that Brower was behind the idea that led to the bumper sticker "Question Authority." Brower had begun to express a distrust of government and an advocacy of government by conscience, which some in the club heard as a strident echo of the youth revolutionaries around him in Berkeley. Stegner has said about Brower in an interview that

> he was taking the club on a confrontationist course which probably was not the most productive course it could take. Those were the years when you saw bumper stickers up in the Sierra, you know, "Fuck the Sierra Club," and he was making the club into something which the moment its name was mentioned would raise hackles. He was on the right side, we all agree; it was just a question of tactics. . . . I didn't, I guess, agree with Dave on the confrontation business, because it didn't seem to me to be productive.

It seemed to me to be productive of strife, but not of resolutions of any kind.

Feelings ran so high in the controversy, as Harold Gilliam remembered, that when he walked into a cocktail party-reception that was given at a conference about this time, each faction was gathered in separate groups on each side of the room. Not only did they refuse to talk to each other, but each group pretended the other didn't exist. And, as Gilliam recalled, it was a rather small room. The controversy came to a head in the board election of 1969 when pro- and anti-Brower factions each put up candidate slates. On one side was the ABC, which their opponents said stood for "Aggressive Berserk Conservationists," and on the other, the CMC, which their opponents claimed meant "Conservatives for Minimum Conservation." Because he was so respected, especially among individual club members, Stegner played a particularly important role in the campaign for this crucial Sierra Club election.

18

A NEW
LIFE

Right up to the election, Dave Brower went ahead, ignoring the board, with a self-righteous zeal that his opponents found maddening. On his own, as if it were solely up to him to set the club's direction, he began to set out an international policy for the club by publishing a special October 1968 issue of the *Sierra Club Explorer* that announced a campaign called "Toward an Earth International Park." The following January, again on his own initiative, he placed an expensive page-and-a-half advertisement in *The New York Times* calling for a program to preserve the Earth as a "conservation district"—"a sort of ... EARTH NATIONAL PARK." In the meantime, Ansel Adams had become one of the two or three leaders of the campaign to get rid of Brower, whom Adams believed had become a loose cannon. Adams's views alone might have been enough to sway Stegner, but then the Brower camp announced that Stegner would be a participant in a press conference called to defend Brower's policies and that he would be one of the writers of television programs in a new series being promoted by Brower—both of these announcements being made without consulting Stegner. Brower, with the license of his cause, seemed to feel free not only to use other people's money as he wished, but to preempt other people's lives.

When Brower called, after the announcement, to get Stegner on board as a TV writer, he got Mary on the phone. When Mary explained that Wallace had started work on a new novel and wouldn't possibly have time to write for him, Brower told her, as he had told Wallace on other occasions, that novel writing was really rather unimportant when considering the fate of the planet. His tone was, perhaps, inadvertently more strident than he intended, and Mary was upset. When Wallace heard about the conversation from his wife, he was furious. For him, this was the final straw. The dispute had already gone public as the allegations brought by Adams and others at a special board meeting in October had been widely reported in the press, along with countercharges that the allegations were libelous and slanderous. For the first time, the board had allowed electioneering for a campaign, and charges flowed back and forth not only in material sent to the members, but in the newspapers as well.

In his anger, Stegner decided to write a letter to the editor (which was printed as an editorial) in reply to a UPI story in the *Palo Alto Times* that reported the formation of a committee to back David Brower in his effort to gain complete control of the Sierra Club. He particularly resented the characterizations presented by Brower and those connected to him that those who opposed him were old and out of date—senile fuddy-duddies. As far as Stegner was concerned, the struggle was not, "as Brower insists, between those 'progressives,' who favor vigorous action and certain 'traditionalists' who want to keep the club's old image as a hiking organization." The charges against Brower were very real, he insisted, and not "hysterical" as his supporters have claimed. In announcing the formation of his pro-Brower committee, Donald Aitken made it a point to put the conflict in generational terms, touching on a sore spot with Stegner, declaring that the new, young members of the Sierra Club would be more activist, "a new breed of conservationist." As far as Stegner was concerned, these newcomers fell into the same camp as the hippie activists on campus—they were not a new breed, but rather simply "uniformed." They thought they knew everything but knew almost nothing. He had fought alongside Brower for many years in numerous conservation battles, but "Brower has ceased to be what he was. He has been bitten by some worm of power."

"Some worm of power" was a phrase that shocked Brower, and he has never quite forgiven it. It was used over and over again by his opponents during the election campaign, and he and his slate lost by a wide margin. Subsequently, Brower resigned as the club's executive director and then started his own organization, Friends of the Earth. In looking back, he has said:

> I notice in a film that has just been made, a documentary about me, that he [Stegner] commented that I was the sort of person you would like to have on your side in a fight, but I was a bit confrontational, a bit shrill. I guess that defines what he didn't want to be and what I thought I had to be to get attention and get things done.

He seemed to be unaware at the time and even in retrospect of the pain that his own rhetoric and name-calling, as well as that of his supporters, had caused Adams, Stegner, and others. Stegner has said that he was "pretty upset at the time," and as a consequence, didn't express himself very well in the editorial. "Later," he recalled, "I regretted in many ways having written it, because I liked Dave and I like him yet. I thought he was the most effective partisan that the conservation cause ever had, and he still is." He also, in the same interview, referred to Brower's importance when defending environmentalism against charges of elitism:

> It does seem to me that the world progresses only through its special people, and that instead of resenting them, it's time we acknowledged them. An Ansel Adams is worth ten thousand of us. We ought to admit that. Dave Brower is worth ten thousand of us, just because he is a very special person.

Throughout the crisis in the Sierra Club, Stegner had been caught between his admiration for two men on the opposite sides of the issue. His natural tendency to avoid extremes came into play, but the situation at the end no longer allowed for compromise, and he had to fall back on his sense of what was right or wrong conduct—and Brower, he deeply felt, was wrong.

*   *   *

While the battles in the Sierra Club were going on, skirmishes in the English department at Stanford were leading to ever more serious confrontations. Stegner's discomfort with the department can be located, to begin with, in his complex relations with two complex colleagues: Yvor Winters and Albert Guerard. Winters was thrust into a closer proximity to Stegner than he would have desired, in part because they had several things in common: they were at that time the only two on the faculty who taught modern American literature. They were both scholars and critics, but known in those days primarily for their creative writing—Winters for his poetry. There was ongoing friction between the two men because Stegner was in charge of the Stegner Fellowships and Winters was in charge of the creative writing program in poetry. A smaller number of fellowships were assigned to Winters to administer than were kept for students in fiction. This would seem sensible, since, after all, Stegner had gotten the money and it was his program, and there were usually only half as many applicants for the poetry awards as for those in fiction. But Winters resented this and fought against it constantly. The faculty knew that a battle was going on, but it was conducted almost entirely in private. Since both men were known for their stubbornness, their arguments must have been fierce—certainly their notes and memos to each other, still in department files, were often very sharp. Relations got so bad that they were hardly talking to each other.

Winters was a brilliant poet and teacher, but like so many geniuses was a dogmatic egotist who expressed the two qualities in a colleague that Stegner had come to hate—arrogance and condescension. For his part, Winters had achieved a national reputation relatively young in life, but while Stegner came in as a full professor at the age of thirty-seven, Winters had to wait until he was fifty, three years after Stegner arrived, to get his promotion. While the novelist was philosophically opposed to creating disciples, the poet became notorious for turning out students who spoke and wrote like their master, even adopting the same mannerisms. While Winters and Stegner in public said little about each other or each other's work, Stegner was heard one day by colleague David Levin, when the condescension of one of Winters's students became insufferable, to say, comparing Winters to the famous Harvard professor, that "Kittredge was tolerable. . . . What people couldn't stand was all those little Kattredges."

Some measure of the man can be taken by his favorite dogs—the poet raised Airedales so fierce they had to be locked away before he could answer the front door. Besides being a constant irritant in regard to the creative writing program, Winters also offended Stegner in his strong criticism of the novelist's friend Robert Frost. Winters had written an essay, "Robert Frost, or the Spiritual Drifter as Poet," that attacked the poet's romantic tendencies, his lack of precision in thinking and language. But he does not just disagree or condemn. There is often a edge of snideness and superiority in his criticism, as when he speaks of Frost as "a poet of the minor theme, the casual approach, and the discreetly eccentric attitude." For Stegner, Winters's critical opinions, even expressed as they were, were something he certainly had a right to—but his personal behavior was another matter. When Wallace invited his friend to come to Stanford to talk, Winters opposed the invitation. Then when the Stegners had a reception for Frost after his speech on campus, Winters refused to attend. Although one can understand in retrospect why Winters would not want to face a possible confrontation with Frost, Stegner looked on this as a personal affront to him and to Frost. After all, Winters represented the poetry section of the creative writing program at Stanford, and his rebuff had more than personal implications. It was a matter, once again, of right conduct.

But Stegner and Winters did agree on one thing—their opposition to the curriculum innovations proposed by Albert J. Guerard. Guerard was the son of a highly regarded professor at Stanford and had been raised on campus. After getting his degrees, he taught writing with Stegner at Harvard, and although the two were not close, they did have a mutual respect and a number of friends in common. Guerard came back to Stanford as a professor in 1961, and almost immediately wanted to change the department, pushing hard to bring more of the modern into the study of literature and the experimental into creative writing. Invited to sit in on freshman writing classes to see how they were conducted, he was struck by how old-fashioned the approaches were and volunteered to take over the directorship of the freshman English program, a difficult and thankless job.

Guerard was a professor who enjoyed the give-and-take of department politics, who liked to work through committees to accomplish things, and who enjoyed the challenges of administering programs. Stegner, on the other hand, disliked the time-consuming task of serving on committees, hated departmental politics (although he could be good at it), and was only an administrator because it gave him the freedom to do what he wanted to do and the ability to protect what he had built— and protective he was. At bottom he did not think that his or any creative writing program should be part of an English department and subject to its control.

At first Guerard and Stegner got along well, but as Guerard, always outspoken, began to assert himself more and more, relations between the two became strained and a sense of rivalry took over. Several of Guerard's colleagues had the impression that he thought of himself as *the* Stanford writer, and he seems to have been the person on campus that first applied with some scorn the label "Western realist" to Stegner, who absolutely detested the label and the limitations of his work that it implied.

Guerard was a man of enthusiasms and interesting ideas about how to improve undergraduate and graduate education, who, although ambitious, still had the welfare of the students on his mind. The one of several programs instituted by him that caused the most controversy and which brought Stegner's hostility to the surface was called the "Voice Project." This was an attempt to bring some life and excitement into the freshman writing program by helping, in various ways, each student find an authentic expository voice of his or her own. The main thrust was to follow the Briggs-Copeland Fellowships example from Harvard and bring in writer-teachers who would teach small classes and encourage their students on an individual basis to experiment in order to find their voices. The final quarter of freshman English was made a creative writing course (which would not be under Stegner's aegis). Guerard got a government grant which enabled him to bring in a squad of writers from the East Coast, beginning with his former student, the avant-garde writer John Hawkes.

Guerard has said that "Wally did not like the idea of writers coming to Stanford who were not his writers," but that explanation for Stegner's hostility to the program seems disingenuous since the uniformly Eastern orientation and avant-garde nature of the visitors were bound to be taken by him as a personal affront. Furthermore, Guerard was another one of those professors whom Wallace believed liked to create disciples: he would have access to prospective majors in creative writing at the beginning of their college careers and would be molding them to be antagonistic to Stegner and his program before they even got to him in the advanced courses. At the same time, Stegner, Winters, and others on the faculty objected to the "Voice Program" on the basis that it involved a lowering of standards—writing of nearly any quality, they thought, was being rewarded with high grades as long as it was "interesting." At one point during the rivalry, Stegner felt threatened enough to go to the department chair and warn him that the fellowships were given to him personally to administer, and that if he went elsewhere, forming a separate department, he would take them with him.

That which was behind all the furor, the conflict of personalities and beliefs, and which would seem to have caused Wallace the most pain was the sense, rightly or wrongly, that Guerard was trying to use Eastern elitist attitudes and values to undermine the perceived value of both his teaching and his writing. This hostility to Eastern arrogance was made apparent again in Stegner's relations with another colleague, Irving Howe. He also came in 1961 and was involved in a controversy before he even arrived at Stanford. He had been appointed William Robertson Coe Professor of American Literature, but at the last minute the university administration lawyers declared him ineligible and wanted him to be appointed simply a professor of English. Howe had described himself as co-editor of *Dissent: A Journal of Socialist Opinion*, and the Coe bequest had specified that the money be used to combat the threat of communism, socialism, and other ideologies opposed to our system of free enterprise. The teachers of American literature—Stegner, Winters, and David Levin—agreed that the administration's request violated Howe's academic freedom, and they endorsed a letter drafted by Levin to be sent to the university president, saying that they "would not teach in a program designed to accomplish political ends." With the backing of both Stegner and Winters, a compromise was worked out by the vice-provost which gave the money to buy books in American studies for the library and there would be no Coe professor.

Stegner predicted that Howe would not stay very long, and he was right. He knew that like other New York Jewish intellectuals—Leslie Fiedler, who made fun of the cowboys he encountered at the University of Montana, and Bernard Malamud, who made fun of his colleagues at Oregon State University who spent much of their time fly-fishing— Howe would bring an attitude of contempt for everything Western and endure his time at Stanford with a feeling of being in exile. Not long after his arrival, he came up in a panic to Wilfred Stone, a colleague, and asked, "Where is Palo Alto?" And Stone replied, "Well, you just go down under the underpass . . ." Howe looked at him in astonishment and said, "That street—that's Palo Alto?" Stone said, "There's a little more to it than that—people live in it." "My God," Howe moaned, shaking his head, "I can't live here. I can't live here."

Nevertheless, nearly everyone in the department went out of his or her way to try to make him feel at home. Wallace and Mary had him over twice, with rather disastrous results. Stone recalled that he

> was the rudest guy I've ever known. He'd come into a room . . . he'd be invited to a cocktail party, and he'd sort of look around and decide there was nobody there to talk to. Or maybe he'd sort of tap in on what's going on, and then he'd walk out—wouldn't say goodbye. . . . It was like "if the world isn't going to make it interesting to me, the hell with it."

A stickler for courtesy in his own behavior and always irritated by arrogance, Stegner did not find Howe a very congenial colleague. However, it was only when Howe was leaving California and in a speech said something about how he couldn't wait to get away from the "dead West" that Wallace became furious. In his autobiography, Howe writes, "Something about California, a softening of the mind, makes it finally a second-rate culture, self-satisfied and self-adoring."

As the 1960s developed into a decade of protest and political conflict, many remember Wallace marching in demonstrations against the war in Vietnam. As a matter of fact, Wallace and other professors had "been protesting this thing from about 1965 on," as Wilfred Stone remembered, "but by the time the students began to get on the band wagon, a lot of us were burned out." Wallace supported the nonviolent sit-ins and strikes for causes he believed in, but for the life of him could not understand what breaking windows on the Stanford campus had to do with stopping a war a continent away. He could not tolerate the deliberate nastiness, the anti-intellectualism, and the destruction. He had worked long and hard, traveling, giving speeches, and serving on committees, to help President Wallace Sterling raise the money to help Stanford become one of the best universities in the country. Now these disruptive students, he felt, wanted to go around and carelessly, even joyfully, tear down what he had helped to build.

For about three years, from 1968 to 1971, teaching was nearly impossible, and the lives of most faculty were painful and difficult. In January 1968 Stegner returned from a sabbatical at the beginning of winter quarter and talked to Dick Scowcroft, who had taken over the fiction seminar during the summer and fall. As Dick recalled:

I told him what had been going on. They [the graduate students] didn't want to meet in the classroom; they wanted to meet somewhere else. They didn't want to sit around the table. They didn't even want chairs. They wanted me to move the furniture out so they could just stretch out on the floor. And he listened to these stories about this class, and he said, "I'm not going to teach it. If they want to come see me in my office, though, I'll talk to them individually. I'm not going to put up with this."

After he got over his anger, Stegner decided to fulfill his duty—as one might expect—and meet his classes, but according to those familiar with the seminars, the situation was actually worse than Scowcroft described it. The students, including those who had received Stegner Fellowships, were arrogant, know-it-all, contemptuous. Page Stegner, then a graduate student at Stanford, recalled that there was "a whole sense of an attitude of disrespect." Gradually during the late sixties, Stanford became a center of protest for the entire peninsula, bringing on campus students from other schools, including the local high schools, and some nonstudents. Some were Marxists, some Maoists, some anarchists, and some just wanted to raise hell. The campus was in nearly constant turmoil during these years with sit-ins, strikes, and marches. One of the firebrands who harangued the mobs was a young English professor, Bruce Franklin, who eventually became notorious as only the second tenured professor Stanford had ever fired. Franklin was brash, urbane, and handsome (he reminded one observer of a young John Garfield). He was an excellent teacher, certainly the most popular one in the department at the time. Franklin went to teach at the Stanford campus in France and was radicalized by his association with Vietnamese students there. Now a Maoist, he came back with a supply of little red books (*Quotations from Chairman Mao Tsetung*), which he sold and distributed to colleagues and students.

About the time he returned to Palo Alto, campus protests against the war were heating up, and by the end of the sixties, he was commonly mentioned by the student newspaper as one of the leaders. As the demonstrations became more and more violent and destructive, his part in them divided the department. A few of his colleagues backed him, but Wallace and other traditional liberals were outraged. Wallace hated the war as much as Franklin, but he did not think it was ethical to use the classroom to indoctrinate, to tell his classes at the beginning of the year, as Wallace was informed that he did, "My purpose in this class is to make Maoists out of all of you!"

Eventually, it all got to be too much for Stegner. Wilfred Stone, who was sharing an office with him at the time, early in 1971, remembered one day when Wallace was reading the *Daily*, and there was a letter in it that attacked him personally:

He said, "That ends it. I'm not going to do anything more. I'm washing my hands of this whole business." And I can remember arguing with him. I said, "Wally, that's just one hot head talking like that." But he said, "Nope, nope," and he was done with it and he was sort of done with the [whole] modern generation.

Years later, Wallace did not recall the specific incident of the *Daily* letter to the editor as being *the* turning point, but he did remember the time when he made the decision:

There was a real sense of letdown. A sense that I had wasted a lot of years of my life. I was really disgusted with the teaching business at that point. . . . It was not a time when teaching was any fun anymore, and why the hell didn't I get out?

A year earlier he had changed publishers. He felt that Viking had lied to him and that it had been penny-pinching at his expense. By moving to Doubleday, Stegner was able to get a contract that gave him $150,000 in advances over several years for six books: two reprintings (*Joe Hill* and *The Big Rock Candy Mountain*), a collection of previously published essays (*The Sound of Mountain Water*), a novel in progress (*Angle of Repose*), a biography of Bernard DeVoto (*The Uneasy Chair*), and another book, probably a novel, yet unplanned. These were the tasks he had lined up for himself for the years ahead. The payments from the publisher added substantially to his rather meager Stanford retirement salary and gave him the assurance that he could afford to leave teaching. Nevertheless, he found out after two years of retirement that augmenting his income by writing magazine articles, if not absolutely necessary, gave him a bit more room in his and Mary's budget and more freedom to travel.

19

THE PULITZER
AND BEYOND

All during the troubling years 1968–70, Stegner was working on his masterpiece, *Angle of Repose*. He started on the manuscript in the spring of 1968, and that summer wrote his agents that he thought he would have a manuscript in a year. Then in August after several months of struggle he wrote to them from Vermont:

> I'm back in my gloomy little shack, at work again on the novel. I wish I had some bright posters of Faulkner accepting the Nobel Prize, and Truman Capote vacationing at Marrakesh. Then I'd maybe *believe* in the literary life. (8/27/68)

The novel would follow a familiar formula, both in terms of what had inspired it and what gave it a basic outline—the use of historical materials, this time a collection of letters, rather than diaries, journals, or trial transcripts. The letters were those of Mary Hallock Foote, a nineteenth-century artist and writer who married a civil engineer who took her out of her genteel life in the East into the raw West. In May 1970, when the manuscript was three-quarters completed, Stegner wrote to his agent, "It's hard to believe in Mary Hallock Foote when I listen to the radio and television or pick my way to the office through the barricades and broken glass and the smell of tear gas" (5/8/70).

To a great extent *Angle of Repose* is a novel about perspective—how we see ourselves and the world around us through vision shaped by our circumstances and altered by our emotions. In this new work, with Lyman Ward he wanted to change the perspective from that of Joe Allston, limit it in some ways and expand it in others. Lyman has what Stegner has referred to as "tunnel vision"; that is, he finds the present painful, physically and emotionally, and tries instead to focus as much as possible on the past. Stegner found the physical model for his narrator in his old mentor from Iowa, Norman Foerster, who, crippled, had moved to Palo Alto to retire. Wallace, aghast to find him a shell of the man who had been such a vital influence on his life, visited Foerster, brought him books, and took him out as often as he could. In working out the perspective of the novel:

> I was creating a situation which involved tunnel vision of the wheel chair. I really wanted that, and I couldn't figure any other way to do it. But I had a perfectly clear example right in front of me because Norman Foerster, who had been my thesis director ended up exactly that way, with his spine frozen and his leg off at the knee and in the wheel chair—so I simply borrowed intact to create the sort of tunnel vision perspective that I wanted. . . . I think of polio particularly as being a kind of a saint maker. Most of the people I have known who have had polio have had their character enhanced. It's a hard way, but the ones who survive it at all survive it with a kind of triumphant grace, I think.

Lyman Ward is no saint, but there is something saintlike in his monastic confinement, his constant study, his contemplation of ultimate questions, his hair-shirt sufferings, and his temptations to the fleshly joys of sex and alcohol which he strives to resist. Like the polio victims that Stegner mentions, Lyman has had his character "enhanced" by his immobility and as a result is a far more complicated character than Joe Allston; his perspective creates a novel that is more complex and at the same time more subtle than *All the Little Live Things*.

Although Lyman spends much of his time doing research, re-creating his grandmother's life from her letters, he does so in order to understand his own; his future is on the line in a way that Joe Allston's never is. Furthermore, although Joe is educated and intelligent, Lyman is even more reflective—a retired academic, a professional historian—and what he sees and thinks is given a much deeper context, driven deeper by his pain, both physical and emotional. Because his body is shriveled, his mind is forced to expand; he must live through his reading and the contemplation of what he reads. Because his body is immobile, he derives pleasure from participating vicariously in the mobility typical of these nineteenth-century Westerners who are his ancestors.

Like Joe Allston, he is a "fallible wise man," a thoughtful man who often comes to doubt his own judgments, wondering about certain basic questions: How can I have a life or think it worth living when so much has been taken away? What do I have left that is worth living for? How have my ancestors influenced who I am? How can a marriage survive under the weight of conflicting personalities? The complexity of the novel comes not only out of its ambiguity, as Lyman struggles to answer such questions, but out of a constant imposition in the narrator's mind of one time frame against another. There is a comparison between three generations, focusing on values and conduct as reflected in the marriages: the grandmother's time (Susan Burling Ward's time), Lyman Ward's time, and the time of Lyman's housekeeper's daughter and her "husband." Marriage, as Lyman says, is the subject of the book he is ostensibly writing. Referring to his grandparents, Susan and Oliver, he tells his son Rodman:

> What really interests me is how two such unlike particles clung together, and under what strains, rolling downhill into their future until they reached the angle of repose where I knew them. That's where the interest is. That's where the meaning will be if I find any.

The comparison of the marriages of Susan and Oliver, Lyman, and the young hippies, moving from the nineteenth century to the present, is one that the author has called a "progressive decline." Lyman mourns the current generation's loss of the past, its fixation on the existential, its thin perspective of "now" and thus its lack of bearings for conduct:

In my mind I write letters to the newspapers saying Dear Editor, As a modern man and a one-legged man I can tell you that the conditions are similar. We have been cut off, the past has been ended and the family has broken up and the present is adrift in its wheelchair.

The ambiguity of a doubtful man, the imposing of one time frame on another, the reconstruction of a story from letters, which involves subjective interpretation—all these place a heavier burden on the reader than any other Stegner novel. It was complicated for the author as well. With the narration of Lyman Ward, Wallace has said,

> the first-person wasn't . . . clearly an eye witness to all kinds of stuff here—the first person was first guesser in many instances—so a lot of the story is something he is telling straight from his first person point of view and a lot of it is what he is inferring from his research or from his knowledge of the past. His remembrances of his grandmother and so on. So that the first person there began to get more and more complex on me. He was not only recorder, but he was guesser, interpreter, and he wasn't at the same time always a reliable witness. He was both reliable in some cases and unreliable in others, and I got fascinated, really, by the complexities.

Not only does Stegner have in Lyman Ward a narrator who somewhat resembles him in voice and values, his storyteller is working from letters to reconstruct history, just as the writer himself is reconstructing and elaborating on history. Out of this relationship, a process within a process, certain questions were bound to arise, questions that would bring forth issues that would become the source of controversy after publication, as we shall see: Is Lyman Ward using his research (and his imagination) to write a biography-history of his grandmother's life, or is he really as "first guesser" writing a novel? Shelly, his hippie secretary, asks him why he is being so inhibited about his grandmother's sex life. After all, she tells him, what you're writing isn't history—"you're making half of it up, and if you're going to make up some of it, why not go the whole way?"

If it is a novel (within a novel), does it in its interpretations reflect Lyman's own needs more than it does his grandmother's actual life? Similar questions can be asked about Stegner himself and his uses of Mary Hallock Foote and the history that her papers provide. Certainly the decline in civility and respect for knowledge and tradition in his own time was a major motivating force behind his writing of the novel. But for him, not only is history a means for telling a story and for making comparisons that illuminate our values, it is in itself a subject, a way of thinking, a necessary perspective.

The importance of history in shaping our lives and the need for our knowledge of history in finding our way was a primary Stegner concern throughout his career and more so in *Angle of Repose*, perhaps, than in any other of his works. No one else in the novel cares much about history—particularly Lyman's own son, Rodman—so that Lyman's activities may remind us of the Fisher King in T. S. Eliot's "The Waste Land," who is depicted at the end of the poem striving, morosely, to gather together the cultural fragments of a society no longer connected to its past, just as the young people in the novel may remind us of Eliot's shallow and self-involved characters who no longer can connect anything with anything else. They are the "ahistorical young" of whom the Stegner has said, "They didn't give a damn what happened up to two minutes ago and would have been totally unable to understand a Victorian lady."

The Foote letters gave Stegner the opportunity to write about nearly all those subjects that were dear to him—not only history, but the decline of traditional values, the importance of loyalty and steadfastness in relationships, the problem in a young and mobile society of establishing one's identity, the need for and difficulty of forgiveness, East versus West, the new West versus the old, the mythic Wests versus the actual Wests, and male versus female roles and values.

In his book of conversations with Stegner, Richard Etulain pointed out to the author the connection between the characters and themes of *The Big Rock Candy Mountain* and *Angle of Repose*. "It was," Stegner replied, "like *The Big Rock Candy Mountain* without my realizing it. It was the boomer husband and the nesting wife, although with variations in it and on a much higher social level." It never occurred to him that there was a relationship between the two books until after he had finished writing *Angle of Repose*, and he added, "It's perfectly clear that if every writer is born to write one story, that's my story."

One important difference between the two novels lies in their treatment of the husband-and-wife relationship. Both women are strong, but show their strength in nearly opposite ways. Susan Burling Ward dominates her husband, but cannot see or appreciate him for what he is; Elsa Mason is dominated, but sees her husband clearly and shows her strength in her endurance and in her steadfast holding on to her own values. Despite their strength of character, both women are trapped by their sex, their roles limited by the societies of their times. However, Elsa's aspirations for a home of her own and employment for her husband that she need not be ashamed of are much more modest than Susan's. She, like Elsa, comes from an established, but not wealthy, farm background. But out of her friendship with a fellow art student from an aristocratic New York family, Augusta Drake, and out of her talents, demonstrated first for illustration and later for writing, she is able to move upward into social circles of the prominent and wealthy.

The narrator, Lyman, sees in his grandmother "a sort of Isabel Archer ... half-acknowledged ... a spirit fresh, independent, adventurous, not really prudish in spite of the gentility. There was an ambitious woman under the Quaker modesty and the genteel conventions." Sensing her ambition and expectations, the man who would become her husband, Oliver Ward, works for five years trying to make his way in the world before he proposes in order to be worthy of her. But even though she accepts his proposal, she always looks down on him. "I think," Lyman says, "her love for my grandfather, however real, was always somewhat unwilling. She must unconsciously have agreed with his judgment that she was higher and finer than he." When they are in the company of prominent visitors, she compares her husband to them and finds that he lacks "some quality of elegance and ease, some fineness of perception" that the others possess. As a mining engineer, he must find work out beyond civilization, but where he goes and what he does, as already noted, is often dictated by her desires or his concern for her well-being (although her greatest desire would be to return to the East). She, for her part, goes with him not to join a new society, but to endure the situation as long as she must, as if she were in exile, making "not the slightest concession to the places where she lived."

Both Susan's and Elsa Mason's fates are largely dependent on their husbands' fortunes, but with Susan's heart tied to Augusta in the East and all that Augusta stands for, she would seem incapable of being satisfied with Oliver, whatever his accomplishments might have been. However, neither Oliver nor Bo Mason have good fortune; both novels are litanies of disaster and the repeated disasters become tests of character. Bo fails, while Oliver passes. In the nearly lawless West where greed triumphed constantly over the niceties of conscience or fair play, many businessmen were untroubled by giving in to temptation:

> There was no reason Oliver Ward should not have been, except character. Pioneer or not, resource-raider or not, afflicted or not with the frontier faith that exploitation is development, and development is good, he was simply an honest man. His gift was not for money-making and the main chance.

Like Bo Mason, "he had heard the clock of history strike, and counted the strokes wrong. Hope was always out ahead of fact, possibility obscured the outlines of reality," but unlike Bo Mason, who always looking for the main chance regards himself as forced by ill fortune into illegal activities, Oliver stubbornly remains "a builder, not a raider." But he was also a loser, primarily because he was trusting of others (Susan asks him at one point, "Why are you always having to take a stand that hurts us or loses you your job?") and, significantly, he was a loser because he was ahead of his time. He was an exceptional man, and in the end, Susan's "real mistake was that she never appreciated him enough until it was too late."

Wallace began with the idea that Susan would be his heroine, and indeed, she does dominate the book in the sense that we see more of her and hear more from her than anyone else (but we see her, we should remember, always through Lyman's perspective). But as Wallace worked, he began to see her "as a heroine with a foot of clay," and he finished the manuscript with the thought that Oliver, although he is the silent character who left behind neither letters nor writings to speak for him, was more the hero of the book, and in that, Stegner reverses the terms of *The Big Rock Candy Mountain*. Originally an Easterner also, Oliver becomes a Westerner to a degree his wife never does and throughout the novel expresses many of the traits that Stegner admired: steadfast love and loyalty, compassion, total honesty, modesty, and an application to hard, constructive work. There are many things about Susan that Wallace could admire, but her snobbery and her condescension toward all things Western, including her husband, which is really part of her snobbery, eventually put Stegner off. Here the model, who was implacably snobbish, would seem to have asserted a stubborn influence over creation of the fictional character.

In *Angle of Repose* Susan Burling and Oliver Ward not only reflect the conflict between the boomer man and nester woman, they reflect the disparity frequently displayed in the Western tale between the ruggedly individualistic man, strong, silent, and practical, and the woman to whom cultivated society is all important and who strives to bring culture to the most primitive Western surroundings. Seen in such broad brush strokes, Susan and Oliver are archetypal figures. Lyman calls them "a masculine and a feminine. A romantic and a realist. A woman who was more lady than woman, and a man who was more man than gentleman." They follow the pattern of Easterners who come West to find opportunity, moving from one place to another in their search, so that *Angle of Repose*, like many another classic novel of Western experience—*Huckleberry Finn*, *The Grapes of Wrath*, *The Big Sky*, *The Way to Rainy Mountain*, and, of course, *The Big Rock Candy Mountain*—is as much about movement as about place. But even more it is about what people search for as versus what they find and must settle for—making peace with oneself, making peace with those one loves or has loved, and making peace with one's lost dreams.

Stegner first came across Mary Hallock Foote in 1946 when he came to Stanford and was doing research for a chapter to be included in the *Literary History of the United States* called "Western Record and Romance." He read several of her novels and story collections, as well as uncollected stories in their original magazine publication. He judged her "one of the best, actually; she was good and hadn't been noticed." He took notes on her work and put one of her stories in his anthology *Selected American Prose: The Realistic Movement, 1841–1900*, and included one of her short novels on his reading list for his American literature class. George McMurray, a GI student in the class, enthusiastically reported to Stegner that he had come across Mary Hallock Foote's illustrations and writings about New Almaden (in the Coast Range foothills near San Jose, California) and said that he knew that she had a granddaughter living in Grass Valley, California. He was going to go up there and see if he couldn't get Foote's papers for the Stanford library, with the idea of possibly using them as the basis for a doctoral dissertation.

The Foote family gave McMurray the papers on the understanding that he was going to publish from them and that he would supply typed transcriptions of the letters to the family. McMurray planned to do the dissertation under Stegner's direction, but a decade went by with no progress and he finally gave up. During the mid-1960s, Stegner borrowed the transcriptions from the Stanford library and took them with him to Vermont one summer to read:

> Reading her quaintly 19th century letters, I thought her interesting but certainly not the subject of a novel. She lay around in my mind, an unfertilized egg. . . . What hatched, after three years, was a novel about time, about cultural transplantation and change, about the relations of a man with his ancestors and descendants.

He did not want to write a historical novel, but a contemporary one, and as he thought about the story in the letters, it occurred to him that perhaps he could link the two together in some way, so that the past was made part of the present. That, in turn, led him to look for the sort of narrator that had "tunnel vision," frequently thinking about the past and thinking about the present in terms of the past.

Angle of Repose can be roughly divided in two parts. The first third of the novel deals largely with Lyman Ward and his experiences and thoughts about his life. Lyman's story frames the remaining two-thirds, which deals with his grandmother, Susan Burling Ward, largely conveyed by her letters to her Eastern friend, Augusta. This Susan Burling Ward material, based on Mary Hallock Foote's papers, would bring accusations of plagiarism, charges of misuse of source materials, and even angry denunciation by feminists who claimed that a male writer had deliberately set out to destroy the reputation of an accomplished female artist. It was one of the terrible sadnesses of Stegner's life that his greatest triumph would cause his greatest controversy. And that controversy would come directly out of that combination that he had formed and used in so much of his work, novelist plus historian.

Stegner had gotten to know Janet Micoleau, one of Mary Hallock Foote's three granddaughters, in Grass Valley through the husband of his secretary, Alf Heller. He visited the Micoleaus on several occasions while he was thinking about using the papers, and Janet encouraged him to do something with them, since her grandmother had been largely forgotten. She hoped that through Stegner's work, interest in her grandmother's life and work would be revived. When Stegner decided to go ahead with a novel based on the papers, Janet told him to use the papers in whatever way he wished. Stegner assumed that she, who had had custody of the papers, spoke for the family.

There probably would not have been any trouble had Stegner and the Foote family agreed on what they meant by "novel." What the Footes meant was explained by Janet's sister, Evelyn Foote Gardiner, when she stated recently in an interview: "I thought he would write something like Irving Stone's biographical novels. That he would invent conversations and all of that, but that he would pretty much stick to the facts of their lives." Stegner did stick pretty much to the facts, but Mrs. Gardiner and those who have taken up her cause have complained that he used too much of Mary's life and too many of her letters, accusing him of "stealing" Mary's material in order to write a prizewinning book.

How much of the novel was "taken" from the papers? None of the modern material, almost none of the conversations, many, but certainly not all, of the historical descriptions of place, some of the characters and characterizations in the historical sections, and almost all of the overall movement and locations. The Foote family reaction to the novel, understandable but inaccurate, has seemed to express the view that Mary's letters composed a major portion of it. Stegner does quote (with some changes) from many of the letters (roughly thirty-five out of a total of five hundred). There are thirty-eight instances of letter quotation for a total of 61 pages in a book with 555 pages of text—that is, roughly ten percent of the whole.

When Janet asked him not to use real names, since he was writing a novel, Stegner used fictitious ones, and went further in protecting the identity of his sources in his acknowledgments, "My thanks to J.M. and her sister for the loan of their ancestors." In addition, in his acknowledgments he included the disclaimer "This is a novel which utilizes selected facts from their real lives. It is in no sense a family history." But Mrs. Gardiner has insisted that since he did not give specific credit to Mary Hallock Foote, as he should have, what he has taken from her was an unethical act, close to plagiarism.

The situation became more complicated when Rodman Paul got in touch with Stegner, while he was working on the manuscript, to tell him that he had obtained backing by the Huntington Library to publish Mary Hallock Foote's reminiscences. Wallace agreed to read Paul's introduction and offered to show him the letters. But the whole idea of protecting the Foote name through anonymity seemed to be in trouble. He wrote to Janet:

> As I warned you, the process of making a novel from real people has led me to bend them where I had to, and you may not recognize your ancestors when I get through with them. On the other hand, I have availed myself of your invitation to use the letters and reminiscences as I please, so there are passages from both in my novel—stolen outright. Not long passages, a paragraph at a time, at most. But even this selected theft raises some questions, especially since I had a call last week from Rodman Paul. . . .
>
> You suggested that I not use real names in any of my book, since what I am writing is not history or biography but fiction. I agree with that. But if the reminiscences are now to be published, it won't take much literary detective work to discover what family I am basing this story on. . . . The question arises, must I now unravel all those little threads I have so painstakingly raveled together— the real with the fiction—and replace all truth with fiction? Or

does it matter to you that an occasional reader or scholar can detect
a Foote behind my fictions? (1970)

He went on to offer to modify the language and change all the names,
asked her to let him know what to do about changes if she thought it
necessary, and offered to send the completed manuscript to her to read.
Janet replied that she didn't think changes necessary, nor did she feel it
necessary for her to read the manuscript.

In his letter Stegner warned Janet several times that the book would
not be true to all the details of the Footes' lives. "For reasons of drama, if
nothing else," he wrote, "I'm having to foreshorten, and I'm having to
throw in a domestic tragedy of an entirely fictional nature, but I think I
am not too far from their real characters." Despite his attempt to make
sure that the Foote family had some idea of what a novel was and what
he was writing, and despite his offer to make changes as dictated by
Janet and his offer to let her read the manuscript, the Foote family took
great offense to the book when it was published.

The strange idea that *Angle of Repose* is essentially the work of Mary
Hallock Foote is put forward by Mary Ellen Williams Walsh, a professor
at Idaho State University and coeditor of the Foote letters with Mrs. Gardiner. She has taken all the family's objections at face value, become
their spear carrier, and set out to slay the male dragon in an essay published in 1982 called "*Angle of Repose* and the Writings of Mary Hallock
Foote: A Source Study." It is a nasty piece of character assassination.
There was no attempt to get Stegner's side of the story, nor to give
him at any point the benefit of the doubt, no possibility that there may
have been a misunderstanding or that Janet and the other heirs may
have contributed to the misunderstanding—he is portrayed as a deliberate fraud, a thorough villain.

Walsh's assault found its target—her charges, essentially pointing to
Stegner's supposed unethical behavior, hurt. They were especially difficult for a man who had all his life held himself to the highest standards
of conduct and had judged others on the same basis. Some measure of
how deep was the wound can be found in his handling of his last novel,
Crossing to Safety, which was based on the relations between the Stegners and the Grays. After Stegner had finished the manuscript, written

after both Phil and Peg Gray died, he sent copies of it to each of their nine children for approval, insisting on approval from all of them before he would publish.

In retrospect Stegner thought he should have insisted that Janet read the manuscript and that he should have insisted he be able to go beyond Janet to get in touch with the other sisters directly. It was a great novel, but there was a high price to pay for it: it had caused a great deal of distress all around, distress that he felt himself keenly and deeply regretted causing others.

With *Angle of Repose* Stegner aimed high with his most complex work and his most experimental. As he wrote in an article published in *Literary Guild Magazine*:

> For years I have wondered why no western writer had been able to make a continuity between the past and the present, why so many are sunk in the mythic twilight of horse opera, why the various Wests seem to have produced no culture or literature comparable to those of New England, the South, and the Midwest, why no westerner had managed to do for his territory what Faulkner did for Yoknapatawpha County.

With his "tunnel vision" structure, he set out to do precisely that— create a continuity between the Wests of the past and present—and while there were many different historical Wests, Stegner in his novel reproduces one very real one, a reproduction that in many ways refutes the myths. Lyman, the historian, tells us that he is impressed with how much of his grandparents' life was dependent on "continuities, contacts, connections, friendships, and blood relationships. Contrary to the myth, the West was not made entirely by pioneers who had thrown everything away but an ax and a gun." Lyman points out, further, that his housekeeper's family had worked for his family for three generations, that the West is not so new as some think, and that although the myth is that the West was the home of "intractable self-reliance amounting to anarchy," actually, as we see in the novel, large parts of it were owned by capitalists from the East or from Europe who ran their domains with iron-fisted bosses. Furthermore, in concentrating on the subject of marriage, the marriage of genteel, educated people who come to build and civilize, the author through his narrator gives us a very different angle on the West than is provided in the oft-repeated myth of the lone horseman.

The first review Stegner received was a negative one from *Saturday Review*. The reviews that followed were often depressing, often damning with faint praise. Feeling bruised, he wrote to Avis DeVoto to tell her that he was going to write his congressman to propose "a plan for licensing book reviewers the way we do dentists and other mechanics" (3/26/71). Overall, the reviews turned out to be mixed, with a majority favorable. Only a minority of reviewers, however, saw immediately that with this novel they had encountered a classic. William Abrahams in *The Atlantic Monthly* wrote that Stegner had

> written a superb novel, with an amplitude of scale and richness of detail altogether uncommon in contemporary fiction. . . . Between art and life, past and present, the moment and its aftermath, Mr. Stegner reminds us, there are still connections to be made, and we are the richer for them.

But such recognition by a few periodicals was eclipsed by the failure of *The New York Times Book Review* even to review the novel. In a letter to his agents, Stegner blamed the lack of a *Times* review for the novel not making the best-seller lists and mourned that "this was probably my last chance to make it with a novel. After sixty the spirit doesn't rally so fast from these knockdowns" (6/26/71).

Six months after the novel's publication, a sort of retrospective review appeared in *The New York Times Book Review*. In it William DuBois calls the novel "well-made," indeed, "*too* well made." By a comparison with Browning's Andrea del Sarto, he suggests that Stegner, too, is the perfect craftsman, but lacking greatness of spirit. The critic continues:

> Had one of Mr. Stegner's pupils submitted this shrewdly planned manuscript at his Stanford writing seminar, it would have deserved at least an A-minus. As well-made novels go, "Angle of Repose"

fills an aching void. Just as Marquand once did—even the later Marquand, when his carbon had grown faint from use.

The next year, after the Pulitzer Prize had been awarded to the novel, *The New York Times Book Review*'s editor John Leonard blasted the judges' choice of it over John Updike's *Rabbit Redux*.

The reputation of *Angle of Repose* grew, to some extent by the publicity attendant to the prize but even more, gradually over the years, by word of mouth. Stegner felt that he was suddenly noticed, now, at last taken seriously. For the last quarter century he had a feeling that

having left Harvard in 1945, I more or less withdrew from American literature. I was much more in it there, even though I didn't live in New York. My name got mentioned, I was visible, I had lunch with people now and again, people knew I was there. Coming out here, I had the feeling that I gradually receded over the horizon and disappeared. The books came out and were often respectfully received, but I was no longer a *presence* in any way.

Moving back to the West had its penalty, but Stegner also paid a penalty for his unwillingness to seek cheap publicity. In his view it is unfortunate that a literary reputation in this country is all too often generated out of notoriety, notoriety that comes by gaining a sensational press—by stabbing your wife, getting your picture taken with Hollywood actors, or throwing a tantrum in a New York bistro.

The Pulitzer Prize was the only remedy, just what was needed to put him back on the map. And he was genuinely pleased, as he indicated in a letter to Phil Gray:

One of the nicest things about this Pulitzer Prize is all sorts of people call up, and wire, and write. It's bettern [*sic*] Christmas cards. And it touches us, it really does to see how many people seem genuinely to wish us well. When a TV man asked how I felt, I said I felt humble, and Mary briskly kicked my shins. (5/6/72)

From the late sixties, when he was occupied by campus disruptions, Sierra Club infighting, and the composition of *Angle of Repose*, to the early eighties, Stegner still pursued an active travel schedule, going to Vermont most summers, and then to various spots around the globe, ranging from Baja, California, to England, Italy, Saskatchewan, and other parts of Canada. His travels also took him to Central and South America, Iran (where he lectured), and then Japan and Africa. One of his most notable trips came in the summer of 1968, when the Stegners were invited by a summer neighbor in Vermont, Froehlich Rainey (who had become one of Wallace's closest friends), to join him where he would be working in Guatemala. Rainey was the curator of the museum at the University of Pennsylvania, and the Stegners joined the Raineys in Tikal (in the far north), where the museum had been excavating for fourteen years. They had been working in the Peten Rain Forest, which was even then being cut down to make pastures for beef cattle. Stegner was stunned by the pace of destruction and determined to do what he could to help save something of that unique type of tropical forest. Having served on the National Parks Service Board in the States, he offered his expertise in drawing up plans for laying out and protecting national parks, and, according to Rainey, "Through his efforts, the Guatemalan government was led to establish a 25 square mile park that now stands as a remnant of what once was a huge jungle."

Another notable trip came in the summer of 1973, when Wallace and Mary went down to Ecuador to visit their son and his family. After a difficult adolescence, during which he had decided to disagree with his parents on principle about nearly everything, and after getting kicked out of a private academy and remaining a discipline problem up through his senior year in high school, Page gradually straightened out his life. He went through college in Colorado, majoring in history, and then went on to graduate school at Stanford, switching over to literature. He became an outstanding scholar and got all A's—except in a course taught by his father, who gave him a B+. Page has written,

> My father was a teacher in the most conventional sense: he gave me books to read, endlessly corrected my grammar, gave me *detailed* instructions on the difference between lie and lay, read my school themes and essays and went through them with me laboriously, suggesting changes to both content and structure that might improve their substance and distinctiveness. He was not, I might

add, particularly liberal with praise. "Okay," he would say, when I came home from school, "five 'A's' and a 'B+,' but still room for improvement." That was as lavish as it got.

When Page took an American literature course from his father as a graduate student, Wallace was disconcerted—how could he be fair? "What would I do if he did badly? Protect him? Flunk him?" Page got the second-highest grade on the final, but Wally gave him a B+ in order not to appear to be playing favorites; Page protested loudly at this injustice. His father gave the matter over to his teaching assistants, who gladly overruled him—and he was pleased that they did.

Relations between father and son gradually improved during Page's college years. At a rather drunken English department party, one of Page's graduate student colleagues was prattling on in his fake British accent about how Wallace Stegner was plainly a minor figure on the American literary landscape. Page decked him, depositing him in the department chairman's fish pond. Years later, when Wallace dedicated *Angle of Repose* to his son, Page's wife, Marion, felt overwhelmed by the gesture and wanted to weep for the reconciliation and acceptance, never spoken, that had at last been signaled. After teaching at Ohio State University, Page served in the Peace Corps for three years, first in Venezuela and then in Ecuador.

After the Stegners arrived in Ecuador at the end of January 1973, Wallace, Page, and young Page all traveled to a branch of the Amazon, the Rio Napo, and rode in a dugout canoe down to the Hotel Jaguar, a tourist accommodation that thrust itself up right out of the middle of the jungle. Young Page, with a child's imagination and enthusiasm, could hardly wait to see the lions and tigers, but didn't see anything more than crocodiles and parrots. In an interview he noted that he still treasured as a keepsake "the magazine article in which he [his grandfather] talked about the jungle excursion and the guide with his rifle" ("The Great Amazonian Plain," published in *Travel and Leisure*).

The bond between Stegner and his grandson was close. Pagie, as his grandparents called him, spent a lot of time with his grandfather in both Los Altos and Greenboro. In California Wallace would take him to Stanford or professional football and basketball games; he would take him over to the campus to look at the stained glass in the chapel or to go bowling at the Union, which Wallace always called the "onion." He was, young Page recalls,

> always messing with words—the kind of joke like, "Why does an Indian stick a feather in his cap? To keep his wig wam." ... I remember when we were kids, we all heard that "One bright day, in the middle of the night, the barefoot boy with shoes on who stood sitting in the grass," and then he would add, "and threw some cow over the hay."

Young Page remembers his grandfather in "perpetual motion" in the afternoons, working in the yard. One summer while he was going to day camp and staying with the Stegners, he helped Wally weed out the star thistles in the field out by the house: "He hated those thistles. . . . He said, 'If we get these all, they'll never come back' . . . and they never have come back. To this day, it's all green grass there." Wallace would sit and cut up the trimmings from a tree, every piece of greenery, to dry out and be used in the little Malm fireplace-stove in his study to save on electricity.

In Vermont they would hike up on Bar Hill, behind their house, Wallace with his walking stick—good for whacking down thistles: he'd turn the cane upside down and take a big golf swing at them. They would go down to the Gray beach on the pond and go swimming, and young Page remembers him always swimming the backstroke and "spitting out a little stream of water." Sometimes he would sing songs, "The Cowboy's Lament," "Blood on the Saddle," and the one that Page most vividly remembers him singing, "The Frozen Logger." Two of the verses that stick in his mind go:

> I see you are a logger
> And not a common bum,
> For no one but a logger
> stirs his coffee with his thumb.

> He never shaved the whiskers
> From off his horny hide,
> But he drove them in with a hammer
> And bit 'em off inside.

During the three years that young Page was with his family in South America, he corresponded with his grandfather by sending audiocassettes back and forth. On the end of one tape, Wallace sang "The Ballad of Old Cy Hubbard"; on another he recited the Robert Service poem "The Cremation of Sam McGee," and on yet another, he read from Don Marquis's "The Scientific Note."

While composing *Angle of Repose*, Wallace put together those essays that were published in *The Sound of Mountain Water*, his first (or second, if you count *One Nation*) of seven collections of nonfiction (most of the essays in this anthology we have noted at the time of their original publication). Half of the essays are travel and environmental pieces about the West and the other half are autobiography, literary criticism (essays on Bret Harte, Willa Cather, and Bernard DeVoto), and discussions of writing in the West. In his "Introduction: Some Geography, Some History" he writes, reiterating a familiar Stegner theme:

> The entire history of the West, when we hold at arm's length the excitement, adventure, romance, and legendry, is a history of resources often mismanaged and of constraining conditions often misunderstood or disregarded. Here as elsewhere, settlement went by trial and error; only here the trials were sometimes terrible for those who suffered them, and the errors did permanent injury to the land. . . .
>
> The history of the West until recently has been a history of the importation of humid-land habits (and carelessnesses) into a dry land that will not tolerate them; and of the indulgence of an unprecedented personal liberty . . . in a country that experience says can only be successfully lived in by a high degree of cooperation.

At this point in the winter of 1969, Wallace was still guardedly optimistic about the ultimate fate of the West: despite what careless people have done "to a noble habitat, it is hard to be pessimistic about the West. This is the native home of hope." But as Tom Watkins of the Wilderness Society has noted, by 1985 Stegner was beginning to feel less certain about the West's chances for creating "a society to match its scenery." In the spring issue of *Wilderness* in that year, in an essay on Aldo Leopold's land ethic, he wrote, "The number of functional illiterates that our free public education produces does not make us sanguine about educating the majority of the public to respect the earth, a harder form of literacy." Two years later, in a conversation with Watkins, he added to these thoughts about creating an environmentally aware society:

> I'm going to sound hopeful again in a minute. But it's kind of like a stubborn child. Over a period of time he may leave home on account of what you tried to teach him, but when he finds himself married and raising kids of his own, he echoes what you told him. It's possible to educate a public in that way—sometimes you don't even know that it's been done.

As a child of the prairie, raised on flat, dry land, the sound of mountain water became an emblem to him of what an environment, beautiful, clean, and refreshing, can mean in elevating our spirits and cleansing the soul. Recalling his first experience of a roaring mountain stream, the Henry's Fork of the Snake, which his family camped alongside for several days when he was eleven, Stegner writes in his "Overture" to the collection:

> By such a river it is impossible to believe that one will ever be tired or old. Every sense applauds it. Taste it, feel its chill on the teeth: it is purity absolute. Watch its racing current, its steady renewal of force: it is transient and eternal.

20

BACK TO BIOGRAPHY
AND ANOTHER
PRIZEWINNING NOVEL

In 1987 in a chapter on Bernard DeVoto for *A Literary History of the American West*, Wallace Stegner wrote:

> When Bernard DeVoto died on November 13, 1955, he was one of the most visible and most controversial literary figures in America, and had been for thirty years.... Many respected and revered him and depended on him for their thinking and their courage in public issues. Some hated him with a passion.... The staff at *Harper's* loved him as a curmudgeon with a heart of mush; they said he collected underdogs the way a blue serge suit collects lint.

Writing for such volumes tends to be a young man's game, a way to build a reputation, and none of the other contributors of chapters to the history were nearly as distinguished as Stegner. So it is a good bet that the only reason he took on the job was to make sure that his old friend and mentor was not forgotten; certainly, no writer knew him better.

Because he was a reticent man who tended to hide his emotions, Stegner's feelings about people are often hard to fathom. But occasionally the depth of his emotions is revealed, bursting forth in something he has written in a way that's almost shocking. Such is the revelation that suddenly surfaces in a letter to Avis DeVoto, Bernard's widow, in 1963: "Wouldn't it be luvverly if we could have Benny and Edith back, if only for an hour's reunion that would break our hearts when it ended? Sometimes I feel like smashing my fist against some stone wall" (2/24/63). After his friend's death, Stegner made sure that his papers went to Stanford, where he could be relatively certain they were treated well, and for many years thereafter, Avis had been after him to do her husband's biography. Always looking toward the next novel, Wallace resisted, suggesting a series of other possible biographers, but then, in 1968, when he was planning for his retirement and lining up projects for the future in order to get an advance from Doubleday, a DeVoto biography seemed like something he would enjoy doing, and he added it to his list.

He wrote to Avis:

I have a question. Is anybody working on a biography of Benny? Have you authorized anyone to do so? . . . If not, are you still interested in having me do one? . . .

It would be, obviously the work of several years, especially since I have a novel [*Angle of Repose*] to deliver (and none of it yet written) before I could do more than occasional work on Benny's papers. (2/21/68)

With Avis's pleased "yes" to his proposal, Wallace went ahead to juggle three projects during his last couple of years of teaching and the year beyond: the novel, the essay collection, and the biography. Somehow, while working nearly all out on *Angle of Repose,* he was able to take a few hours here and there to begin reading through the DeVoto letters. Early in 1969, nearly overwhelmed with work and under pressure, he reported again, turning his depression into a Joe Allston joke: "It's rained six inches here in three days. My gutters are full of leaves, water is sloshing down from every eave, my road is washing out, my trees are blowing down. I shall attack" (1/21/69). That summer he wrote to Avis that "this coming winter I'll go carefully through all the rest of the papers, which are voluminous, did you know?" but when winter came he found himself still under the gun, sixty or seventy pages short of finishing the novel.

Angle of Repose was finished in the spring of 1970, and largely as a result of Mary's urging, Wallace took a break and went to England for the summer. They went to Vermont first, and he wrote his agents from there:

> Vermont is lovely—why in hell are we going to England? . . . The walks are across spaghnum moss four inches thick, with wild strawberries poking their red heads out. The mornings are full of choirs of thrushes and white-throats. I work two hours a day with some brutal machine such as a chain saw, and in the evenings we sit and listen to Schubert quintets by one candle, with ten million fireflies winking around the grove outside. We not only live with the Earth, we live in the dirt, and love it. And our . . . pup has become a different dog within six days. Formerly I would have protected her against chipmonks; now I would send her against bear. (6/22/70)

In the fall he flew back to Boston, where he interviewed Avis at some length and several others in Cambridge, including Kenneth Galbraith, and then went on to New York to talk to Arthur Schlesinger and the people who had worked with Bernard at *Saturday Review* and *Harper's*. Finally, he went to Washington, D.C., to check out DeVoto's service on the National Parks Advisory Board.

Back in Los Altos Hills in November he wrote to his agents that he was working eight hours a day on the papers and hoped to have a manuscript for the biography by the summer of 1972 (11/27/70). Then, going to Vermont during the summer of 1971, he stopped off in Philadelphia to see Kitty Bowen, George Stevens (editor), Bill Sloane (editor and publisher), and George Ball, and coming back from Vermont in October, he stopped by Cambridge to once again interview Avis. In the meantime, he was making arrangements to publish a volume of DeVoto's letters. Carol Brandt had reached agreement with Doubleday for publication before the biography (a plan that was changed over time) and on Stegner's instructions had secured an advance of $10,000 to be shared equally between him and Avis (5/3/71).

In writing the biography, Wallace faced several problems. One was that DeVoto had been his friend, and in the writing Stegner was worried first that he might be inclined to be too favorable, and then, after he finished the manuscript, that he had overreacted and emphasized DeVoto's flaws and problems too much. In an interview with James Hepworth, Stegner commented on that difficulty, as well as defining what kind of biography he had wanted to write:

> *The Uneasy Chair* was a pretty straightforward kind of biographi-
> cal investigation, complicated by the fact that I had known Benny
> DeVoto very well. It's always more difficult to write about some-
> body you know well. For one thing, it presents you with the prob-
> lems of how much to tell: things that are nobody's damn business,
> and you don't want to embarrass your friends or your friend's wife
> or your friend's family with something that has nothing to do with
> the main subject you're writing about. In my case, it was Benny's
> career, the way his head worked, and what he did with his head.
> He was kind of neurotic, and he did some silly things in his life, but
> it didn't seem to me it was essential to dwell on the silly things. I
> wanted to write about the great things this flawed man produced
> out of his personal turmoil. So in a sense I suppose I can be called a
> whitewasher.

There was a strong sense of privacy in Stegner, a sense of privacy that he held for both himself and those he was close to. He did not want a full biography written about himself, as he wrote his biographer, "until my ashes are spread over a Vermont hillside," and he objected to having the models for his characters identified except when they were obvious, as in *The Big Rock Candy Mountain.* He decided in writing his two biogra- phies that both would be

> biographies of *careers* [Stegner's emphasis]—I realized that I was
> not interested at all in Powell's private life, and that Benny
> DeVoto's private life, minimal at best or worst, struck me as some-
> thing that I, as both friend and biographer, didn't particularly want
> to publicize. (8/24/87)

However, in writing biography it is often difficult to separate the private life from the career, since the latter is in so many ways the product of the former, and in getting at what motivated and directed DeVoto, his various neuroses and phobias, Wallace may have delved more into DeVoto's private life than he realized.

But there were other problems beyond Wallace's own reluctance to probe too deeply into his subject's private life. Page Stegner has thought that his father found the writing uncomfortable and even at times difficult because his own experience so often paralleled his subject's, so that "when he created DeVoto's life, he created his own." Another concern involved DeVoto's widow, Avis, who was a close friend whom Wallace loved and admired, and he brought her in to become very much involved in the project. He had interviewed her at length several times, and she helped him with names of people to interview, helped to verify events and dates, and made all of the papers available to him. However, although she was quite aware of her husband's quirks and neuroses, she quite naturally wanted the most positive and laudatory account of her husband possible, and as Stegner worked on the manuscript, he worried constantly about her reactions.

There was a year's delay in publishing *The Uneasy Chair: A Biography of Bernard DeVoto* (the title comes from the *Harper's* column, "The Easy Chair," that DeVoto wrote for twenty years), primarily due to a change of editors at Doubleday. In the meantime, Stegner was busy with articles and starting a new novel, which would become *The Spectator Bird*. He probably gave more speeches and wrote more articles during these last years than he needed to, but he was a member of the Depression generation, who had lost his savings when the banks failed, and he was always concerned—even more so now that he had retired—about having enough money, a cushion against disaster. In the fall of 1972, while the last two hundred pages of the biography were being read by Avis and by Ted and Kay Morrison, he and Mary took a trip down the West Coast from Vancouver in order to do a travel piece for *Travel and Leisure*, "The Coast of Oregon." In addition over the winter and in the spring of 1973, he wrote an essay on Walter Van Tilburg Clark, one on DeVoto for *American Heritage* (to be "published just ahead of the book, to stir the waters with his name" [1/2/73]) and put together pieces of the biography to make an essay, "DeVoto's Western Adventures." At the same time, he gave several lectures, including one for a Library of Congress symposium in Washington, D.C. In May he went to Saskatchewan to get an honorary degree, give a speech, and "be certified an authentic

Canadian Author" (4/15/73). This almost hectic activity would be typical of his schedule for the rest of his life, except that there were periods when his speech-making would become even more frequent as he accumulated more and more honorary degrees and awards.

The Uneasy Chair was published at long last in February 1974. The book was widely noticed, as a great many reviewers seemed anxious to get in their two bits' worth about such a controversial literary figure. But the reviewers seemed to Stegner to be focused only on controversy and personality. What very few of the reviews seemed to notice was, first, that this was a book that once again treated the relationship between East and West, speaking to the Western cultural inferiority complex in particular, and second, even more importantly, that it was a solid, invaluable contribution to the literature of conservation. As Wallace put it in a letter to Phil Gray, "In the 1940s and 1950s Benny's 'Easy Chair' in Harper's was the most effective focus for conservation thinking and action in the country" (11/29/70). But conservation—or environmentalism, as it was beginning to be called—had not yet become a hot topic among the general public.

The publication of *The Letters of Bernard DeVoto* lagged behind. Working on the collection during the summer of 1971 in Vermont, Stegner wrote Avis that he was going to make the volume the *selected* letters ("with a vengeance") and was selecting on the basis of certain topics: letters that revealed basic ideas, and attitudes, that dealt with controversies, and that were expressive of Bernard's deep friendships and many kindnesses. He told her that Benny "wrote damned good letters, and they'll make a book full of cayenne and the voice of Tiresias" (8/18/71). By the end of the summer of 1974, the work had been done, Avis had gone over the selection and made some identifications of names, and the galleys had been proofread. The book was published by Doubleday in February, a year after the biography.

In the meantime, Stegner struggled mightily to get into the writing of his new novel. He told Avis at the beginning of January that he was "sweating blood trying to get a new novel started" (1/6/74), and wrote Carol Brandt that

the gathering clouds that a few weeks ago I thought might be the beginning of novel have broken up into cloudy with bright intervals, but there's a new storm approaching off the Oregon coast, and that may turn into something. I go daily to the temple to meditate, and the time ahead is all, for a change, clear. Maybe that's what jiggers me. I invite your prayers. (1/9/74)

Near the end of the month, he was telling her that "I've heard of *birth-pangs* in relation to novels, but what I've got is *conception* pangs. I feel like a husband who isn't sure whether he or his wife ought to see a gyne-cologist" (1/20/74). He had lots of notes, but no pages yet. By mid-spring he had three chapters, but progress was agonizingly slow. This was due in part to his method of composition:

> I'll type a single page so many times trying to get it right before I go on to the next one that there never is a proper first draft. But certainly one of the things that happens before going on from page one to page twenty of that preliminary draft is trying to get the feel and the emotion right.

By summer, however, he was well into what would be called *The Spectator Bird*, and in October he reported that "the novel creeps ahead like an oppossum on a moonlit limb" (10/23/74). As usual he com-plained almost constantly during the struggle to compose, but judged by the contents of the finished novel, he must have had some fun with the manuscript before he was through with it, in that it allowed him to do some things he hadn't done before. He was able, at long last, to use the experiences he and Mary had had in Denmark way back in 1954, mate-rial that he had played with in the back of his mind for two decades, knowing that eventually it would make a novel. The novel also depended a good deal more on plot than his books normally did, and he wrote for the first and only time a gothic novel, what might be called, with tongue in cheek, his version of the "gothic romance."

The novel is given shape, and the strange story is provided credibility, by a journal kept by Joe Allston twenty years earlier, which he reads aloud to his wife, Ruth—a device that may remind us of other gothic tales, such as Henry James's *The Turn of the Screw.* The use of the journal provides the occasion for bringing the past into the present and for the dialogue between the husband and wife in the present, about the past. Ruth urges her reluctant husband to read his journal aloud so that they might deal with those past events that up to now have been something of an unexamined barrier between them.

On their trip to Denmark years earlier, Joe and Ruth find lodging by sharing an apartment with a down-on-her-luck countess, Astrid Wredel-Kramp, whom they befriend. She is the beautiful, but tragic and mysterious woman of the tale, cursed by a family secret in her past. The Allstons are puzzled as they see her ostracized by society. The American interlopers—innocents abroad encountering the old world and its decadence—struggle with the mystery, which is only partly explained when the countess tells them of her quisling husband. Other mysteries accumulate. The countess takes them on an excursion to her country cottage, stopping by to see a relative and family friend, Karen Blixen. Blixen brings up the countess's strained relations with her brother—the reason is left unspoken—and the possibility that Joe's mother, who comes from the same village as the countess's family, may have emigrated to America to escape the clutches of the old count.

The visit in the novel is based on an actual event. The Stegners did share an apartment with a penurious Danish countess who had something of a mysterious past, but it was her brother-in-law who took the Stegners to see Blixen. As in the novel, just as the Stegners arrived, Blixen had been digging in the garden and had dug up a rune stone under an oak tree and showed it to her visitors. The discovery of the stone as brought into the novel would seem to say something symbolically about the importance of the past, its continuing presence, within this old world society.

Later in the novel, the countess arranges for the Allstons to visit the family estate. During their visit, there is a luncheon with the countess's sister-in-law, her grandmother, a young boy relative, and a pregnant peasant woman who is mysteriously privileged among the family. The gathering is stiff and there seems to be a conspiracy of silence about both present circumstances and the past.

When Joe takes a walk around the grounds, he bumps into Astrid's sinister brother. The count is a modern and realistic version of the mad scientist figure, the inheritor from his father of a tradition of genetic experimentation with Nazi implications. This is the evil in the background of this novel that poisons the atmosphere.

The gothic material, which seems to dominate the book, is, however, but a scaffold in front of a more substantial thematic structure. Using Joe Allston again as his first-person narrator gives Stegner the opportunity once more, as in *Angle of Repose*, to "syncopate" time. Bringing the past into the present, making it relevant, is a recurring theme in these final novels, and this theme is in turn joined to the related themes of aging and the relevance and importance of memory, individually and societally. Also as we have seen, these are themes that had their origins in Wallace's own emotions. On campus and in the Sierra Club, he had been considered by some to be old and out of touch, a relic of a past that no longer mattered. His experience and his achievements had been discounted, "past history" in the flippant and redundant phrase of the young. Partly as a result of that scorn, he had felt his age early—in 1974 he was only sixty-five and still sound in mind and largely sound in body—a feeling of age which his friends thought strange considering how young he looked despite his "white thatch." Largely sound in body—although as he had written to Phil Gray the previous year,

I seem to have turned up with gout. All that guzzling in my dissipated youth, I suppose. They tell me it's a very intellectual disease. It also makes you hobble around like a decayed carthorse with a permanent tennis elbow. I retain my sunny disposition, however, and smile cheerfully at all. Sometimes I have wondered if I am one of those doomed to go through life suffering minor, irrelevant, frivolous, vaguely humiliating ailments—ulcers, gout, piles, while others encounter the great dramatic and tragic germs and blowouts. We also serve who only take aspirin. (5/4/73)

In his last novels, starting with *All the Little Live Things*, Stegner becomes the poet laureate of old age to an aging population. In *The Spectator Bird* Joe gives us this definition: "Getting old is like standing in a long, slow line. You wake up out of the shuffle and torpor only at those moments when the line moves you one step closer to the window." As in *All the Little Live Things* and "Field Guide to Western Bids," Joe Allston is depicted as several years older than the author at the time of writing: Joe is nearly seventy in *The Spectator Bird*. Unlike his creator, he has lost much of his hair and is limited in his activity by painful arthritis in his joints. But with all his ailments, his grouchiness and skepticism born of hard experience and blunted expectations, he is still a wonderfully acute observer. As a sort of synecdoche for the aging process, he tells of a recent visit to the dentist, who told him that a molar he has been trying to save will have to come out:

> I can read the future in that direction without cards or tea leaves. First a bridge, if he can find anything to hitch it to. Then a partial plate. Finally a complete cleaning out of old snags in preparation for false teeth, on television called dentures. There will be a morning when I look in the mirror and see an old sunken-cheeked stranger with scared eyes and a mouth like a sea urchin's.

In another place in the novel, Joe tells us: "It is not arthritis and the other ailments. . . . It is just the general comprehension that nothing is building, everything is running down, there are no more chances for improvement." Not only does one feel as one ages that he or she is falling apart gradually—and irreversibly—there are the unpleasant reminders all around us that we live in a youth-dominated culture, a fact that is underlined for the elderly in their daily encounters with younger people.

The very young people, who may be serving you at a restaurant or at the checkout stand at the supermarket, all tend to either look through you or past you, as if you really didn't exist anymore. The automatic smile and "Have a nice day!" float by you into thin air as the young woman at the cash register checks the line to see if there are any young men waiting—real people, still in the game. As Joe says during a visit to the Stanford campus, "They are not hostile and contemptuous as they were a few years ago; they just don't see you. . . . They don't seem offended that you exist, only surprised." Anyone over fifty will know the symptoms and recognize the feelings. When Joe's wife, who wants him to get out more and be with people, suggests that he, the former literary agent, might come on campus occasionally to speak to a class about contemporary authors, he replies with an anthem that many American elderly would respond to,

> If you were black, sure. Since you're female, fine. If you were blind, deaf, crippled, absolutely. But if you're old, you're up against discrimination that doesn't even know it's discrimination. You'd just better stay out of it.

But the worst thing of all is to feel yourself becoming less liberal, less accepting, less tolerant, and unwilling to consider new ideas. You have the horrendous experience of becoming the sort of person that throughout your life you haven't liked; you feel helpless to resist as the change takes place right before your eyes. Joe thinks about his wife, Ruth, telling him at least once a day that

> old people, or people getting old, tend to disengage, back away, turn inward, listen only to themselves, and get self-righteous and censorious. And they *mustn't.* (I mustn't.) She hates to drive anywhere with me because I am inclined to cuss out drivers who don't please me. What *good* does it do? she cries. *They* can't hear you. All you do is upset *me.* It lets off steam, failing which I might explode, I tell her. What are you doing *now* but exploding? she asks.
>
> Right, absolutely right. Faultfinding doesn't let off pressure it only builds it up. It is only one of the many processes, none of which I like and most of which I can't seem to help.

But Stegner is not only the poet of growing old, who would directly contradict Browning's lines "Grow old along with me!/ The best is yet to be," he is also the balladeer of monogamy, a testifier to the experience of a marriage that has become exceedingly rare, a marriage—Joe's as well as Stegner's own—of nearly fifty years to the same person. "These days," Joe tells us, "people hesitate for a marriage license no longer than dogs in a vacant lot, and marriage vows, those quaint anachronisms, are about as binding as blue laws from the Code of Hammurabi." Stegner, himself, felt very strongly about these things, possibly because he loved his mother so much and saw her betrayed by his father who not only had been unfaithful, but who abandoned her during her final illness. But also, to Wallace, who adhered to a system of behavioral standards that now seemed to many to be out of date, a commitment was a commitment. Near the end of *The Spectator Bird*, when Joe Allston recalls having been tempted by the Countess twenty years earlier by falling in love with her, he thinks:

> It has seemed to me that my commitments are often more important than my impulses or my pleasures, and that even when my pleasures or desires are the principal issue, there are choices to be made between better and worse, bad and better, good and good.
>
> Then why cry over it, twenty years later? Because in every choice there is a component, maybe a big component, of pain.

It is clear that here, as in many other places in the novel, Joe speaks directly for the author. Nancy Packer has said, "I've always thought that that was Wally, the spectator bird in there. That person is Wally, for whom character is so much more important than emotion."

When Froel Rainey, who probably was Wallace's closest friend during these years, divorced his wife Penelope (of whom Wallace and Mary were very fond) to marry a younger woman, Wallace was disturbed by his friend's behavior. Although they continued to correspond, there was for a time a definite edge of coolness between them. And when his son, Page, was considering getting a divorce from his first wife, Marion, he stalled longer than he should have, afraid that the demise of his marriage would

> terminate my relationship with my father. The prospect of God's moral condemnation was a lot less formidable to me than my old man's. However, the truth of the matter is I sold him short. When I told him of my dilemma, he wrung his hands in anguish with me and said he would support me in whatever I decided to do. . . . And he did support me throughout, embraced my new wife with open arms, loved her, and at the same time managed in some incredible kind and gentlemanly way to always remain a "father-in-law" to my first wife.

In dealing with marriage in *The Spectator Bird*, the author once again deals perceptively with a very basic human condition, just as in other novels he deals with love, loss, friendship, the search for identity, and death. Joe tells us and describes what it is like to live with someone for forty or fifty years—the relations, the compromises, the mutual concern, the give and take, and the ability to predict the other person's responses to nearly any situation or event.

There are any number of ways that Joe and Ruth can be seen to be similar to Wallace and Mary, and Joe is certainly a mouthpiece for many of Wallace's opinions. But ultimately Joe and Ruth should be viewed by the reader as independent creatures, products of the writer's imagination based on his own experience. In an essay called "The Law of Nature and the Dream of Man: Ruminations on the Art of Fiction," Stegner has written:

> Writers are far more cunning than the credulous reader supposes. We are all practiced shape-shifters and ventriloquists; we can assume forms and speak in voices not our own. We all have to have in some degree what Keats called negative capability, the capacity to make ourselves at home in other skins.

In 1975 while the novel was copyedited and went into galleys, Ken McCormick at Doubleday was already pressing for a new novel which he hoped would be another historical novel, preferably about the West— presumably, another *Angle of Repose*. Stegner told his agents that he would like to ruminate awhile, and that though he might enjoy doing such a book, he "wouldn't want to try to be Irving Stone." He added that "I might even try to do some unlikely things with the historical material, so that if Doubleday's expectations would be for a straightforward costume drama, they shouldn't put money down on me" (3/2/75). During the spring and early summer, he and Mary traveled to Milan for a month at the Rockefeller Foundation's villa and on to London for two weeks. Then they went for a month on a Royal Viking cruise ship to the Baltic and up to North Cape, paying their way by his "giving cultural highbrow lectures to the passengers" (3/2/75). In the late summer he was reading biographies morning, noon, and night, having been appointed to the Pulitzer jury. He was in the middle of reading *Stein-*

beck: A Life in Letters when he wrote Carol Brandt that he thought that it was an impressive book, but "how do people get that personal? How do they express so freely what they feel? He makes my inverted Puritan hide crawl at times, maybe with envy, maybe with pity" (7/21/75).

The Spectator Bird was published in May 1976 and won the Commonwealth Club of California Gold Medal for Fiction and the National Book Award. Although it, like *Angle of Repose*, was not reviewed in *The New York Times Book Review*, it did receive a lot of favorable notice around the country. One reviewer called *The Spectator Bird* a "vigorously inventive and restlessly, seeking, probing work," adding that "Stegner's satisfying ability to limn our times is surely one of our most precious natural resources." However, there were a few reviewers, particularly in the West, who expressed some disappointment that the book had departed from Stegner's "usual" subject matter—he was escaping their category for him of "Western writer." He was already preoccupied with his next novel, planning its subject and location. He had rejected the idea of a historical novel. The previous November, he had written to Phil Gray, after coming back from a series of lectures on teaching writing in Dallas, "That's the last of that kind of junket, though, for a good while, because I've got to get down to organizing the random fragments of a new novel and starting to write them into scenes." Then two weeks later, he wrote to Avis:

> We both expect to stay here [in Los Altos Hills] at least till spring or early summer, when we'll probably have to go automobiling in search of material for the next novel, which at the moment is a dim shape in the mist but pretty clearly wants to make use of western scenery and western history and maybe a little blood on the Past [*sic*]. The current novel finally denominated *The Spectator Bird*, is in press, due on Mary's birthday, May 7. You will receive a copy. I hope you like it, though it involves some of the unpleasantness of growing old, and directs itself to the problem of how to live reduced and shrinking in all ways. (12/1/75)

The book that "wants to make use of western scenery and history" and will include "a little blood on the Past" would be *Recapitulation*, a "trailer," as Stegner would call it, to *The Big Rock Candy Mountain.* It would be a retrospective, again bringing the past into the present, by an older Bruce Mason thinking back on the period of the earlier book, which took in his high school and college years in Salt Lake. The "automobiling" would consist mainly of a return to what Wallace thought of as his hometown, Salt Lake City.

Wallace had been home on several occasions in the past, most notably in May 1968 when he gave the address "The Book and the Great Community," dedicating the new Marriott Library at the University of Utah, and receiving an honorary doctorate. In his speech (reprinted in *The Sound of Mountain Water*) he had enunciated once again his opposition to our overemphasis on the "new," especially as articulated by sixties youth:

> No society is healthy without both the will to create anew and the will to save the best of the old: it is not the triumph of either tendency, but the constant, elastic tension between the two that should be called our great tradition.

During the summer of 1976 he went alone to Salt Lake and stayed at the Utah Hotel, the setting in *Recapitulation* where Bruce Mason—now in his mid-sixties and successful, having served in the State Department as an ambassador to a Near Eastern country—establishes his headquarters.

Then, in the fall, Wallace and Mary went back to the area around the Salt Lake, to Brigham City and the Bear River Bay Bird Sanctuary, through the Utah mountains, through the Heber Valley and down toward Duchesne in the Ute Reservation, across the pass to Helper, and along the Roan Cliffs. He reported to Phil Gray:

> We wound up in Santa Fe, saw some of the local literary, went to Truman Capote's birthday party, visited an old friend in Taos. . . . Now we are home, ten days or so, and caught up in the rehearsals of the opera made from Angle of Repose, which the San Francisco Opera will world-premiere on November 6. Busynesses, too: I got involved in painting the goddamn house and re-laying the brick terraces, so that I flee out here every morning and labor like a South African black all afternoon. I would like to read a book

again, or even sit and contemplate something. The mockingbirds and golden crowned sparrows have started sing again, in their autumnal way, and apart from the smog, our terrace is marvelous. I work outside, Mary sits inside and practices Chopin. (10/22/76)

The opera he speaks of was San Francisco's contribution to the celebration of the Bicentennial of the United States. The General Director of the San Francisco Opera, Kurt Herbert Adler, chose Andrew Imbrie to be the composer of an opera "with an American theme, by preference, and a Western orientation." Imbrie thought immediately of the Stegner novel, a copy of which his wife had given him on publication in 1972. Stegner had met the composer on the Peninsula through old friend Sandor Salgo, conductor of the Stanford symphony, and had kept in touch at meetings of the National Institute of Arts and Letters. When Imbrie called Stegner, who was in Santa Fe at the time, to ask about making an opera of *Angle of Repose*, Stegner was taken aback—he couldn't believe that an opera could be made from a novel that was set in so many different locations, that depended so much on the first-person narrator and on bringing the past and present together. But at the same time, he was flattered and intrigued by the possibilities. He said yes—as long as he didn't have to write the libretto himself.

After five years' work on the novel itself, he "couldn't wade into it all, axe in hand, cut it back to suit, make it fluid." His 220,000-word novel would have to be trimmed down to something like 6,000 words. Several writers were considered before Oakley Hall, novelist and teacher of writing at the University of California at Irvine, agreed to take on the assignment.

Although the opera has only had its five premiere performances, Stegner was nevertheless very lucky in the talent and effort put into this production, and lucky in that the artists he worked with understood his ultimate themes. The composer, Imbrie, was a professor at Berkeley, and the point he had been trying to make to his own more radical students was in his view related to the point of the opera:

To cut yourself off from the past is madness. Continuity with tradition doesn't prevent you from doing something new, fresh, original, radical. You can't operate without a tradition, you *can't* get out of your past. That's what *allows* you to be a radical!

Ironically, the problem with the opera, the factor that has apparently prevented it from gaining further performances, was that the music on the whole was too radical, too atonal, even for a relatively sophisticated San Francisco opera audience.

21

THE PAST
THAT COMES BACK
TO HAUNT US

Although Wallace Stegner seldom kept a journal, he did jot down notes when ideas came to him about a novel in gestation. Even more in line with his academic training was his tendency to outline a novel in advance of writing it, not in outline form, but as a series of points similar to what he might use as the basis for a lecture to a literature class. In addition to a chronology of events, he might jot down a short description of each character; he might pose questions or raise alternative plot events or endings. He liked to work things out on paper, especially if he was stumped.

This was his situation in the fall of 1976: he had a pile of notes, pieces of the book that he had typed out when a note had inspired him, and an outline of points. He had thought about this new novel for years; he had gone back over the physical territory; and he had a stack of material that he was trying to put together into some coherent form. What followed were months of frustration as he tried to get the novel to jell.

With such frustration before, he had at least twice turned to the students in his writing seminar for suggestions, and on other occasions to a sympathetic critic like Malcolm Cowley for advice. Now he turned to his novelist son, who picked up the problem almost immediately after reading his father's one hundred pages. His father had tried to use a Joe

Allston narrator, a voice that simply didn't fit the material. So on his son's advice, Wallace turned to the idea of tying his western material more closely to characters and events of *The Big Rock Candy Mountain*, returning to Bruce Mason as the center of consciousness and a limited omniscient narrator to tell the story. It was as if Wallace had turned aside from his older mouthpiece or double, which had been so successful for him in recent years, and back to a younger self, which had been a successful central character for him in a much earlier period—in that sense, too, a "recapitulation." Nevertheless, the frame remained similar, that of the thoughts of a man close to Stegner's own age. Once again he was determined to bring the past into the present.

Published in February 1979, *Recapitulation* is a novel that is clearly built on an autobiographical structure, framed with the material of Stegner's Salt Lake City years, from ages twelve to twenty-two, as seen from the perspective of the protagonist late in what would be conventionally thought of as a successful life. The novel is truly a "recapitulation"; it is not actually a sequel, following after the chronology of *The Big Rock Candy Mountain*, but instead parallels the latter part of it by going back to retell the story of Bruce's life in Salt Lake, with more emphasis on the college years and his first big romance. What is important to Bruce Mason in looking back are his father and mother—his conflict with the one and love for the other—his friendship with Joe Mulder; his introduction to tennis, giving him a path to self-esteem; his introduction to the world of art through his association with Holly and her bohemian friends; his love affair with Nola and his hatred of Jack Bailey; and his choosing of law school and a career over Nola and marriage. All of these things have their counterparts in Stegner's own experience. Events, scenes, character traits have been added or filled in, but the outline is Stegner's life.

Don Crawford, Juanita Crawford's nephew, has written about the relationship of his family to the author:

The girl from Utah [Nola] was Juanita Crawford, born March 16, 1905 at Ferron, Utah, and who died September 9, 1974 in Salt Lake City and was buried in the Avenue Cemetery.... As a child I remember "Wally Stegner" at a family picnic at Fish Lake. As we left the picnic in our car, my father muttered "soda jerk." To my father anyone who did not follow the ranching life was a soda jerk. My sister Faye, who frequently stayed with her grandfather and grandmother, Nathaniel and Evelyn Crawford, can remember sweeping the back dooryard because Aunt Juanita and her boyfriend, Wally Stegner, were coming. In later years, we were never certain whether Juanita jilted Wally, or Wally jilted Juanita. . . .

The aunt in *Recapitulation* was obviously buried in the Avenue Cemetery. The Ferron marriage described in the book, we believe, was actually the marriage of Fawn Singleton, Juanita's cousin, and Robert Dahle. The character "Buck," based on the description of his clothing, is obviously my father, Carlyle Crawford. . . . Juanita subsequently married a friend of Stegner, Francis Marvin Broberg, who clerked with Stegner at I. & M. Rug and Linoleum on State Street. They had two children, Ann and Francis Marvin, Jr. Francis Marvin, Jr. was killed in an automobile accident in 1945, and Ann Rierdon teaches at the University of Utah.

Just as *All the Little Live Things* led Stegner's friends and neighbors in Los Altos Hills to speculate about models and to take the novel as a roman à clef, so, too, his friends in Salt Lake have looked upon *Recapitulation* as a book taken rather directly from life. Because of bad experiences in the aftermath of the publication of *Second Growth* and *Angle of Repose*, Stegner became very sensitive about such guessing games. In a letter, he protested the process:

When Red Cowan [said] that the "original" of Holly in *Recapitulation* was Helen Foster, and the original of Nola was Juanita Crawford, he was maybe 18% right, and the rest of the time he was jumping to a conclusion. Even when you assume that Bo Mason was my father and Elsa Mason my mother, you're on very boggy ground, like a floating island in the Okefenokee Swamp.

In all of those cases I took hints from reality. In all of them I so manipulated the reality that none of those people, except maybe my mother, would recognize the character on the page. And though it might be intriguing to the kind of reader who thinks that way to assume that *Recapitulation* is the record of my broken heart, smashed by a faithless babe, it would be dangerously inaccurate, and unjust both to those "originals" and to me. . . . My heart was not broken. My vanity was hurt when I came back from graduate school and found myself Dear John-ed. . . . There are very few episodes in *Recapitulation* that come from reality (including all the romantic scenes and the Mormon wedding), except the circumstances of how I happened to get sent off by pure accident to graduate school. The people in the novel are there because the novel demanded them, not because I so vividly remembered them that I had to put them in. . . .

What *Recapitulation* boils down to, ultimately, is the domination that a harsh and dominating father can exert even after his death upon a son. What is revealed in this novel is the incurable damage done to Bruce Mason, not by Nola, but by his father. Nola is an episode, an instance of his traumatized nature. His refusal to marry is likewise from his father, not Nola. Notice whom he is communing with at the end of the book. In one draft I kept Nola alive and had her show up at that auntie's funeral. No way would it work. It was the father, not the girl, that had to be dealt with.

This is a book, however, about many things, not just fathers and sons. Perhaps most of all, this is a book about the nature of memory and perspective. The vehicle of memory here is a series of flashbacks that are triggered by a variety of circumstances, many of the memories taking on the aura of dreams, of consciously stylized recountings. The mind of Bruce floats freely—he seems almost disembodied—as the memories keyed by some encounter or other take over, producing an "I am a camera" feeling in the text. In discussing his process of writing, Stegner would seem to support this reaction to *Recapitulation*:

You take something that is important to you, something you have brooded about. You try to see it as clearly as you can, and to fix it in words. All you want in the finished print is the *clean statement of the lens, which is yourself,* on the subject that has been absorbing your attention. Sure it's autobiography. Sure it's fiction. Either way, if you have done it right, it's true. [My emphasis.]

Another, connected way we might look at the text is as a meditation on the nature of memory, the processes of remembering, how and why we do so, and what it does to us. To remember, the novel suggests, can be to see ourselves from the outside, to see ourselves as another person in another time in other circumstances might see us, to be both artist and subject, to be both attached and detached at the same time.

As a semi-autobiographical work, the novel suggests the evolution of the writer (ostensibly the evolution of a successful lawyer-diplomat— Stegner did not want to repeat the formula of the sensitive writer as young man), and in a way the novel also defines what a writer does. Rediscovered joys of youthful exuberance and the pain of failure and loss—the sharp recall of these becomes the writing, a ritual of exorcism and atonement, for as Bruce Mason realizes, memory "could also be an art form." Moving away from his largely painful past—he has not returned to Salt Lake for forty-five years—Bruce Mason has lived abroad and traveled the world for the State Department; the young Wallace Stegner made his escape in books, his imagination, and his writing. Yet there is a score to be settled for both in Salt Lake; that is why Bruce Mason returns and why the novel is written.

To a certain extent this is Stegner's *The Sound and the Fury*. Like the Faulkner novel, *Recapitulation* is a book about time and its multiplicity of meanings in human experience, about the history of a family in its decline, and about the moving on from a rural past to an industrial present. Both the Faulkner and the Stegner works are imbued with sadness and regret and would seem to be attempts to exorcise ghosts, painful memories of loss, conflict, and rejection.

Bruce Mason is brought back to the scene of his teenage years by the death of an aunt whom he hardly knew but who was his last living relative. He is not married, so this is the end of the family. At the end of the novel, after Bruce has arranged for her funeral and attended it and decided, with some misgivings, to put a headstone on his father's grave, he takes his leave with the thoughts:

He felt like the last survivor of a star-crossed family. He felt like the puzzled son of a feckless father—boomer, dreamer, schemer, self-deceiver, bootlegger, eventually murderer and suicide, always burden, always enigma, always the harsh judge who must be appeased. He felt like the last remaining spectator at the last act of a play he had not understood.

Like Dilsey in the Faulkner novel, Bruce Mason has seen the beginning and the end, from pioneering days on the last frontier to a graveyard in Salt Lake City, from make-shift shacks on the prairie to stone temples in the modern metropolis.

Although Stegner's syntax is not as tortured as Faulkner's and he does not use the direct interior monologues Faulkner uses, the technique is somewhat similar. By switching from first to third person, he had to "fade in and fade out," as he put it when discussing the novel with Richard Etulain: "When Mason is having dinner at the Hotel Utah, he looks through the sunset over Saltair and thinks of when he was fourteen and selling hot dogs out there, and then we fade back in again to dinner." This is, as he has said, a very different process from moving back and forth in time in the first person, and it was something he had to learn how to do. "I certainly do take advantage," he added, "of any way of interpenetrating past and present—whatever way I can find." This sense of the need to bring forward the past was something he missed in much of Western literature but found in Faulkner and admired:

> I think that's what western novels too frequently don't do, and some modern novels that aren't western don't do. Hemingway, for instance, has no past in him at all.... Ordinarily we live a three-generational life. Hemingway is absolute present—present tense, people between twenty and thirty-five, no parents, no children.... Absolutely different from Faulkner. Faulkner is *rich* with associations from the past. All those hoofs that are thundering through his Sartoris stories.

Once again in *Recapitulation*, as in *All the Little Live Things* and *Spectator Bird*, Stegner is talking about our mortality and how a consciousness of that mortality can give life a different perspective, prompting a self-examination and a shift of values. Once again, as in *Angle of Repose* he wants to convince us that the past is always with us, whether we like it or not. And he wants to show us that while doing the right thing is seldom easy, in the end we must do it not for someone else, but for ourselves, to make ourselves whole.

When Wallace retired, he was very concerned that Dick Scowcroft assume the directorship of the program. Scowcroft was a couple of years younger than Stegner, but they had a great deal in common: they had both grown up in Salt Lake, and both had attended the same high school before going on to the University of Utah. Dick arrived at Harvard to attend graduate school at the same time that Wallace came to teach from Wisconsin. "Utah boys in the camps of the infidel," Wallace has said, "we made common cause."

A year after Wallace came to Stanford, when Dick already had his doctorate and was teaching writing as a Briggs-Copeland fellow, he invited Dick to come and join him. For a quarter of a century Dick and Wallace alternated in the directorship of the writing program, as Wallace either taught only two quarters out of the year or went on leave. He could take off periodically from his university duties without worry or regret because the two of them got along so well and because Dick supported Wallace generally in his philosophy of writing and teaching of writing.

However, after Dick himself had retired, in 1982 the directorship was given over to novelist John L'Heureux, who had been at Stanford earlier and knew Stegner, but was not close to him. L'Heureux headed a search committee for a new, "name" writing teacher, and it considered some two hundred candidates before settling on New York experimentalist Gilbert Sorrentino, author of the "modernist cult classic, *Mulligan Stew*." He was also known for editing two New York literary journals during the 1950s and 1960s.

Interviewed when the appointment was announced for the *Palo Alto Weekly*, Sorrentino was described as "a direct, virile sort who bristles with the certainty that for the last 30 years he's been writing the right stuff. He doesn't resent the philistines so much as pity them." He willingly flees the best-seller scene, we are told, in favor of masters like Irving Wallace, who, he says, "have a gift—you have to be born with it. They are attuned to the most debased aspects of our culture. In fact, they're part of it." The article goes on to say that "Sorrentino isn't any easier on supposed 'good writers' who he says cater to the demands of respectable literary taste by diluting techniques that were fresh 25 years ago."

Several faculty—mainly Joyce experts, postmodernists, and, of course, Albert Guerard—had been pushing for some time for an "updating" of the writing program orientation. In addition, experimentalism had become *de rigueur* in creative writing programs around the country, and Stanford was out of the postmodernist loop. The pressure to conform became so intense that by the early 1980s the drive for an experimentalist had become nearly department-wide. When a decision came from the department to hire Sorrentino, Nancy Packer and Ken Field, the two main creative writing people there at the time, tried to stop it. (Although he had been chair of the selection committee earlier, L'Heureux was not there at the time the decision was made.) "Over my dead body," Nancy said, but on a vote, they lost. She was sick about it, knowing that it would be seen as a repudiation of Stegner's approach to writing instruction and all that he had built. She called Stegner and Scowcroft to tell them: "I said, 'I'm sorry. I couldn't stop it. It's happened.' And Dick was furious, but philosophical. Wally was just furious."

Sorrentino's New York, avant-garde scorn for "supposed 'good writers' who cater to the demands of respectable literary taste" was not the only thing, not even the main thing that stung and angered Wallace. The department had taken over and the independence of the program that he had fought so hard for was lost. What was really upsetting was that Nancy, who in effect wore his mantle, had been overruled and that she, a woman, had been pushed aside. Besides making his objections clear to the administration, there seemed little he could do. Then he wrote a letter to Nancy, asking her to take his name off of the fellowships. Her heart fell, and she went to the house and talked to Wallace and Mary:

> You just can't do this. This is your baby. It's like your child has been in an accident and you're disowning it because it's been disfigured. You can't do this—these are your fellowships—this is your baby. Don't give up on it.

But he insisted on his removal. Nancy kept postponing the time when she would do it, and he would ask, "Have you done it yet?" and she would reply, "No, Wally, I haven't done it . . . I'm going to do it, but it's too late for next year—it's got to be the year after that." She talked to him and talked to Mary, who was on her side, and they both tried to get him to change his mind; she lied about the timing in order to put it off. She went to see the dean and told him that they were going to lose Wallace completely if he didn't do something. The dean wrote a letter to the department telling them that the creative writing teachers must have a veto over future faculty appointments; he wrote to Wallace, enclosing a copy of his letter to the department, and called him on the phone, assuring him that it would never happen again. Finally, he was appeased, but the actions of the department still festered in his heart and his feeling for Stanford was never quite the same, even though members of the department who had been on his side wrote to him to apologize and in subsequent years Stanford took several occasions to honor him.

In the meantime, Wallace and Mary had traveled to Japan in the spring of 1979, to Paris in May and June 1980, and to Africa in January 1981. He wrote to Avis that "Mary revs herself up for these things, and enjoys them tremendously, and then creeps home to recuperate. I find travel an expensive way to be uncomfortable, but I'm an obliging fellow, and go along" (12/16/80). He received in 1980 the first Robert Kirsh Award for Life Achievement from the *Los Angeles Times*, and at about this same time he had started yet again on a new novel (*Crossing to Safety*) and had, together with son Page, put together a collection of essays on the current status of the land, called *American Places*. He wrote to Avis in December 1981:

Page and I have a book out—a coffee table book with teeth, and with pictures by Eliot Porter . . . Page works on his biography of Jeffers, I work or pretend to, on a novel. Privately, I kaf-kaf and box my ankles and make apologetic noises, because I am too goddamn *old* to write a novel, and I have happily lost touch with the culture. Any novel of mine, from here on, will be pure nostalgia. (12/7/81)

The purpose of *American Places* is stated in the foreword as "an attempt by sampling, to say something about how the American people and the American land have interacted, how they have shaped one another."

Wallace and Page do not try to write about all the regions of the country—that is, this is not a survey—but about several places that each has been familiar with and cared about: in Wallace's case, Vermont, Great Salt Lake, the high plateaus of Utah. In addition, they both record trips of discovery to areas unfamiliar or for many years unseen: a trip across the midsection of the country on I-80, a trip down the Mississippi on a steamboat, and one to the Beartooth Mountains and "Crow Country," where Wallace talked to ranchers.

While there are many beautiful vistas and moments of joyful discovery or rediscovery, the overall impression is a disturbing one. There are pictures of place after place despoiled by thoughtless development or excessive exploitation. Freedom, as part of the American creed, has meant freedom to express greed without limits; even in the 1980s, when the book was published, there seems to be little sense of responsibility to the land and to future generations. Wallace and Page find that the myth of limitless resources, the frontier ethic, continues. As they sum up the situation in their preface:

> We are the unfinished product of a long becoming. In our ignorance and hunger and rapacity, in our dream of a better material life, we laid waste the continent and diminished ourselves before any substantial number of us began to feel, little and late, an affinity with it, a dependence on it, an obligation toward it as the indispensable source of everything we hope for. . . . Land *gave* Americans their freedom. It also gave them their egalitarianism, their democracy, their optimism, their free-enterprise capitalism, their greed, and their carelessness. It is an ambiguous and troubling legacy.

One of the most interesting aspects of this sampling of the American people's relationships to their environments is that Stegner finds himself having to admire most those habitats that have been able to turn aside or resist man's encroachments the most successfully—the Beartooth Mountains, which historically "have not been inviting—exploration, exploitation, and settlement all passed around them"; Vermont, where vegetation and animals have rebounded after the land was exploited and where man, despite his best efforts, has won only a standoff with nature; and surprisingly, the Great Salt Lake, which Stegner admires for having been so hostile to man that it remains largely unchanged except by its own cycles of rising and falling. In maintaining themselves against us, the "Great Salt Lake and the salt desert teach us to acknowledge limits. Another hundred years, and we may come to recognize this as a holy place."

The opening chapter, "Inheritance," is a short history of the American land and its misuse, but typical of Stegner there are dollops of history throughout, and since several of the pieces are really travel essays, there is also a good deal of personal experience included. One notable example of that is "The River," in which Mary Stegner makes a rare appearance as herself, joining her husband for the trip down the Mississippi. But by and large the book is a jeremiad on what has gone wrong in our uses of the land and how destructive our attitudes toward it have been, and as such this book is another significant contribution by Stegner (and of course Page) to the literature of conservation. We have always had, in contrast to the Native American, a strong need to possess and declare ownership of the land and a strong sense that nature is somehow subordinate to humankind, that it is something we should control. Stegner counters these attitudes by writing:

Like Aldo Leopold, I would hate to be young again without wild country to be young in; and if I were to give my grandchildren my patriarchal blessing, in the Mormon manner, I would tell them, Be as powerless as possible. Submit whenever you can. Don't try to control the earth beyond the absolute minimum. Work with the earth, not against it. For the earth does not belong to you. You belong to the earth.

In 1982 he was presented the John Muir Award by the Sierra Club for his service to the club and his environmental writings. And in 1982 also, in an effort to boost concern about conservation, he participated in an unusual event on the Stanford campus. The Friends of the Library had asked Ansel Adams to speak on the current state of the environment and the environmental movement, but Ansel at first declined, insisting that he was no speech maker. Eventually, however, through Stegner's intercession, he agreed to a format that was billed as a "conversation" between the two of them.

Wallace and Ansel were in many ways soulmates—artistically, both were ultra-realists and defined themselves by the effort to see clearly and reproduce cleanly, without trickery. When Wallace said of the photographer, "He does not feel the need of cunning double exposures, tricky lighting, dodging. He is simply, deeply, and respectfully attentive; he works by natural light; he finds his meanings in the things seen," he could have been speaking of himself, and speaking of himself in regard to the experimentalists. The experimentalists might be thought of as having their counterparts in photography, in the photographer, by contrast to Adams, who feels the need to photograph things "while standing on his head, or by multiplying the apparatus with which to record them." For Wally, writing a story was a matter of taking something that is important to you, trying "to see it as clearly as you can, and [fixing] it in a transferable equivalent. All you want in the finished print is the clean statement of the lens."

That evening of October 24, in his introduction of Ansel to a packed auditorium (the demand for seats was so great, they had to move the event to a larger auditorium), Wallace paid him the ultimate compliment:

We work in different media, different symbolic systems of transference; but if I have any validity as an artist, I would like to be an artist of Ansel's kind. If I have any choice about what sort of man to be, I would like to be a man of Ansel's kind. I cannot write out of hatred or disgust—those emotions silence me—and I don't think Ansel can photograph out of hatred and disgust either. "Earth's the right place for love," Robert Frost says. "I don't know where it's likely to go better." Life, according to Ansel, is for affirming, and art is its affirmation.

One of the topics discussed was how to get the environmental message out to the vast audience that has not yet been touched by that message. Another was the need to consider the environment in its totality, rather than concentrating, as organizations had in the past, on parks and wilderness. Both Adams and Stegner expressed their deep concern about the Reagan administration, and Adams said he was shocked that a government that should be serving the people should be so blind to "the fast approaching 'limits of source' for so many benefits of the earth. It must be obvious to everyone that pollution is increasing." Stegner reiterated what he on many occasions had written about Reagan, declaring him to be a president not just indifferent to environmental concerns, but actively hostile. Ansel agreed, saying:

Many of us agree that Secretary of the Interior James Watt is a dangerous influence in our present society. But the President is more dangerous as he supports and encourages Mr. Watt to express and implement the Administration's desires.... James Watt is doing the expected; Ronald Reagan and his staff are doing more than expected and are negatively affecting our lives and the lives of our descendents. As the environment disintegrates, so will the nation.

Because of the Reagan administration's efforts to "give away the store" and its hostility to the environmental movement, Stegner was in a fighting mood. His anxiety about developments would lead him to serve, despite resolutions that he had made to the contrary, on the Wilderness Society's Governing Council, and he would publish extensively on environmental subjects during the 1980s. He began with a piece for *The Washington Post* at the time of the inauguration, "Will Reagan Ride with the Raiders?"—a silly question, as it turned out and as Wallace knew even in asking it. He followed that with the publication in *Living Wilderness* of "If the Sagebrush Rebels Win, Everybody Loses," in which he pointed out that the ultimate aim of the Sagebrush Rebels was not, as they admitted, to put the public domain under state management, but instead to transfer the best parts of it into private or corporate hands. He added, "The ranchers are on the wrong side. They should be backing the federal land management bureaus which, exasperating or not, are their best chance for survival." In the same issue of *Living Wilderness*, in "Land: America's History Teacher," he went over the history of public land policy and states' rights, and he went back over the lessons of John Wesley Powell about the arid West in "Water Warnings, Water Futures" for *Plateau* and in "Ask the Dust" for *California*. All of these came in 1981.

Another publication for that year that was only in small part concerned with environmentalism was a Tanner Lecture on Human Values delivered at the University of Utah the year before: "The Twilight of Self-Reliance: Frontier Values and Contemporary America." It is perhaps the most complete exposition of Stegner's political-social beliefs that he ever published and is impossible to summarize except to say that he runs through just about all our ills as a people, tracing where many of these ills came from, and still finds hope for this imperfect society and this besieged republic, concluding:

> Let us not forget who we started out to be, or be surprised that we have not yet arrived. Robert Frost can again, as so often, be our spokesman. "The land was ours before we were the land's," he wrote. "Something we were withholding made us weak, until we found that it was ourselves we were withholding from our land of living." . . . Like the folk mind he was wiser than the intellectuals. No American was ever wiser. Listening to him, we can refresh ourselves with our own best image, and renew our vision of America: not as Perfection, not as Heaven on Earth, not as New Jerusalem, but as flawed glory and exhilarating task.

In 1983, 1984, and 1986 Wallace published four articles on Ansel Adams; the last, "A Tribute to Ansel Adams," was taken from a memorial address delivered following Adams's death in 1984, an article that summed up his artistic accomplishments and environmental activism. In a special issue of *Wilderness* in 1983 devoted to the national parks, Stegner contributed an essay, "The Best Idea We Ever Had"; and for another special issue in 1985, a tribute to Aldo Leopold and his concept of a "land ethic," Stegner wrote "Living On Our Principal" in which, after Reagan's reelection, he sounds discouraged:

> The only real success, the creation and spread of an environmental conscience which will be as angered by the abuse of land as most consciences would now be angered by the abuse of a child—that may have to wait a few hundred or a few thousand years, and we may not have that much time.
> The land ethic is not a widespread public conviction. If it were,

the Reagan administration would not have been given a second term. The lunch bucket argument, and the deification of greed as the American Way, re-elected by a landslide one of the most antienvironmental presidents in our history. Aldo Leopold would not be encouraged.

In 1985 Wallace was asked by the Wisconsin Humanities Committee to write an essay, "The Sense of Place," which was later published in his collection *Where the Bluebird Sings to the Lemonade Springs.* Also in that year he wrote a piece for the *Los Angeles Times* on a topic familiar to him, "Water in the West: Growing Beyond Nature's Limits." And 1987 saw two articles on topics he has written about numerous times before: "The Spoiling of the American West" in the *Michigan Quarterly Review* and "The Function of Aridity" in *Wilderness.*

During the last decade and a half of his life Stegner presented the most cogent arguments he could think of to convince us of what he knew to be true and inevitable. He had become a modern Paul Revere, riding his typewriter, over page after page in journal and newspaper, to warn us of the disastrous consequences of our stubborn adherence to the frontier myth of inexhaustible resources. In a letter to Tom Watkins of the Wilderness Society when Watkins was preparing to write about Stegner's environmental record, Wallace deprecated his own efforts:

> I have not been an effective or even eager activist. In all the issues that matter, there are dozens of people—Dave Brower, Ed Wayburn, Howard Zahniser, the hard-nosed, tough, and durable types who run the Trust for Public Land, the American Farmland Trust, and the big conservation organizations—who have had an immediate, practical, effective usefulness. I never have.... Actually I would like, and would always have liked, nothing better than to stay home and write novels and histories.... I am a paper tiger, Watkins, typewritten on both sides. Get that in somewhere.

Watkins refused to accept this self-characterization.

22

CROSSING TO
SAFETY

Throughout his career Wallace Stegner could be said to be almost obsessed with reality—in his fiction he tried to present the clearest, most honest picture of life possible; in his nonfiction he strove to uncover the facts and tried to get his readers to see things as they really are. He and his characters are truth-seekers. It was a lifelong pilgrimage. He was a tough man with a gentle manner—hard on himself and hard-nosed about what was right and what was wrong and what needed to be done. He was impatient with those who played with literature, who wrote self-indulgently to show off or as "self-expression." Writing was not a game; it was a challenge to the soundness of your character, a challenge to the clarity and depth of your perception, a challenge to your ability to write, in Hemingway's words, truly and well.

Wallace Stegner was, if nothing else, a moralist, and he was thoroughly convinced that the act of writing was an expression of belief, a moral act. He cared, and that is what has made his death so difficult for so many, even those who didn't even know him personally, to accept. There was a depth of caring, for people and for the land, that was so profound that once a reader had been touched by him, it created a special bond, and in a strange way, a very personal one. On this basis, his readers, as well as many critics, recognized a qualitative gap that raised Stegner above most other writers: he was simply different—more genuine, closer to his work somehow, and broader in outlook. He was an artist large in spirit who could see beyond his own shadow. He was willing to risk more of what he was and more of what he believed in.

In his final decades, particularly with his assumption of the Joe Allston–Lyman Ward–Larry Morgan persona, his writing seemed to become a natural expression of his integrity and his search for what was right and true. Stegner's friend Frank O'Connor once said about Hemingway's short stories that you get the feeling while reading them that here is a writer who would rather die than lie to you. That is the feeling that Stegner achieved in the fiction and nonfiction of the last decades of his life. Total honesty.

One of Stegner's most commonly expressed realistic themes can be found in his lifelong effort to bring forth the actual American West (or Wests) from behind the myths. It was an effort that began with one of his first stories, "Bugle Song," and is the subject of one of his last pieces of work, a little book called *The American West as Living Space* (1987). This came out of a series of three William W. Cook Lectures, which he was invited to deliver at the law school at the University of Michigan in October 1986.

The original lectures were only fifty minutes each, and as he admitted, a sensible way of dealing with the subject as large as "the West" would have been to pick out some narrow, manageable aspect of it. But Stegner decided to "risk superficiality and try to leave an impression of the region in all its manifestations." These three essays are in a sense Stegner's final and most eloquent words on what the West was, is, and should be—his last will and testament, so to speak, which he left to us to ponder. He begins by stating that "the West is a region of extraordinary variety within its abiding unity." He testifies to its extraordinary splendor, and he wills to us its special care as the most fragile of our regions. His first essay, "Living Dry," is about water, or the lack of it; the second essay, "Striking the Rock," is about the federal role in the West, particularly the Bureau of Reclamation; and the third, "Variations on a Theme by Crèvecoeur," talks about the results of Western aridity, that is, how it has affected Western culture, character, and society.

In "Living Dry" Stegner declares, "If there is such a thing as being conditioned by climate and geography, and I think there is, it is the West that has conditioned me." Referring to John Wesley Powell's 1878 *Report on the Lands of the Arid Region*, he delineates the territory: "the West is defined . . . by inadequate rainfall, which means a general deficiency of water" (and he lists the exceptions, the mountain snowsheds and the Pacific Northwest), and "aridity and aridity alone, makes the various Wests one." Stegner traces the effects of aridity in molding the West. It first brought the movement toward settlement to a halt at the edge of the dry country and then forced changes in the patterns of settlement.

"Two lessons all western travelers had to learn," he tells us, "were mobility and sparseness." Beyond the Missouri, mobility was a condition of life. After they acquired the horse, the plains Indians were as migrant as the buffalo they hunted; the mountain men working the beaver streams were "no more fixed than the clouds"; and after the fur trade died, the mountain men turned to guiding wagon trains, and the essential idea of those trains was to get an early start and get through the West as soon as possible. This migratoriness "has hindered us from becoming a people of communities and traditions. . . . Rarely do Westerners stay long enough at one stop to share much of anything." Our cherished Western freedom and individualism have developed without the essential corrective of belonging. If we stop to think about it,

> the principal invention of western American culture is the motel, the principal exhibit of that culture the automotive roadside. A principal western industry is tourism, which exploits the mobile and the seasonal. . . . The West is still primarily a series of brief visitations or a trail to somewhere else, and western literature . . . has largely been a literature not of place but of motion.

Even those who have settled in Western cities have found reason to move on yet again: the cities are growing beyond their access to water; they are like "bacterial cultures overflowing the edge of their agar dishes and beginning to sicken on their own wastes."

In "Striking the Rock" Stegner points out that instead of adapting to conditions as they are, Westerners have tried to make over the country and climate in order to match their own habits and desires. The unrestrained engineering of Western water was, in his view, "original sin," a sin exuberantly committed by the Bureau of Reclamation, which was and still is the creature of the boosters and developers. Involved in empire-building for their bureau and pursuing the glittering dream of the "Garden of the World," the water experts have allied themselves with landowners and politicians, and by making "land monopoly through water control immensely profitable for their backers, they have made it inevitable."

The other bureaus, by contrast, have as at least part of their purpose to keep "the West in a relatively natural, healthy, and sustainable condition ... [walking] a line somewhere between preservation and exploitation." Between the energy conglomerates, lumber companies, and stockmen and recreation public, the argument is over where this line should be. But beyond this argument, he asks, isn't there "a higher duty to protect these lands from everybody?" Can we not transcend that urge so basic to our culture, coming out of our Judeo-Christian heritage, to dominate nature?

In "Variations on a Theme by Crèvecoeur," Stegner writes of Western culture and tries to define, in broader brush strokes than ever before, Western character. Is there such a thing? In the course of the essay he brings to mind once again Crèvecoeur's two dominant American character types: the idealized "new man," the American farmer who is industrious, optimistic, family-oriented, and socially responsible; and the man of the raw frontier, who "lived alone or with a slattern woman and a litter of kids out in the woods ... had no fixed abode, tilled no ground or tilled it only fitfully, lived by killing, was footloose, uncouth, antisocial, impatient of responsibility and law." In this, of course, Crèvecoeur predicts the antithesis that would become one of the foundations for Western myth, except that the myth reverses the judgment. The wild man would become the type "who really fired our imaginations, and still does. . . . Our principal folk hero, in all his shapes ... is essentially antisocial." The ruggedly individualistic lone cowboy or mountain man we can identify with; the cooperating, stolid, dependable farmer—the settler or clod buster—is booed or scorned. The East has never gotten over its romantic notions of the West, and the West has never gotten over its romantic notions of itself. It is a tribute to the power of the media, from dime novels, through shoot-'em-up movies, to the marshals, outlaws, and cowpokes of TV:

> The Western culture and western character with which it is easiest to identify exist largely in the West of make-believe, where they can be kept simple.... The pronounced differences that some people see between the West and other parts of America [in culture] need to be examined. Except as they involve Spanish or Indian cultures, they could be mainly illusory, the result of the tendency to see the West in its mythic enlargement rather than as it is, and of the corollary tendency to take our cues from myths in the effort to enhance our lives.... There is a discrepancy between the real conditions of the West, which even among outlaws enforced cooperation and group effort, and the folklore of the West, which celebrated the dissidence of dissent, the most outrageous independence.

Once again Stegner hammers home the need for a realistic view of the West, a position taken by many of his realist predecessors—Edward Eggleston, Hamlin Garland, and certainly Mark Twain. Even Mary Hallock Foote should not be left off this list, for "her mining camps in California, Colorado, and Idaho are almost the only real ones in local color fiction."

Reality and the relationship between East and West are two concerns Stegner had in mind in the composition of his next, and last, novel, *Crossing to Safety*. In his edited textbook anthology of writings during the realistic period of American literature, Stegner notes in his introduction that the realists recognized the existence of an "external, objective, sensuously-perceptible world" and that they defined realism "as the literary method which proposed to present it without distortion." They made a cardinal virtue "not of cleverness or vividness, but of honesty." And honesty, above all, was Stegner's aim with his last novel. He commented in an interview:

Actually, I didn't even write it as a novel. I wrote it as a sort of memoir more for Mary and myself than for anything else, and I wasn't at all sure I was ever going to publish it. These people were our very close friends, and at the same time they had some problems which were very personal; and an honest portrait of them, as honest as I could make it, I thought might be offensive to the family. Before I ever sent it to any publisher I sent it around to all the children, and they all said, "Yes, publish it." So, if it wasn't offensive, I thought, okay. But it was, really, in a way that no book of mine ever has been, an attempt to tell the absolute, unvarnished truth about other people and myself.

The beginnings of the novel manuscript date from 1981. It had started as a California story, since Phil Gray and his wife had moved west. He had obtained a teaching job at Scripps College, and they had been living in Claremont for some years. Wallace was sitting in his office one morning, looking out his window at whatever wildlife was moving around, putting off wrestling with his first chapter. A phone call came announcing Phil Gray's death. He had remarried, and Stegner's original manuscript gropings dealt with Sid's (Phil's) very different relations with his second wife and recollections of his first—Charity (Peg Gray). Stegner never got very far with his manuscript before he realized that "the people I was writing about were so New England, rather than Californian, that they wouldn't ever be anything but remembered exotics in this setting." He started over, and the only thing left from his original tentative attempt was a little scene about a mouse drowning in the swimming pool, which he meant to be a metaphor for survival. Even this he moved from California to New Mexico.

Stegner recalled that

there was no "shape or form" to the original idea. I only knew I wanted to write about that couple, and I was trying to find the handle, starting close to home. Very shortly I moved the story way back in time, before Charity died and before Sid ever thought of dying, and thereby saved myself the few dramatic crumbs the story contained.

One shape that the novel takes as a result of moving the setting to New England is to create a more marked contrast between the two couples, the Morgans and the Langs, in regard to their native regions, creating an allegory of East versus West and much that was typical of each. It is a bit like the contrast in Fitzgerald's *The Great Gatsby* between Gatsby and the Buchanans, East Egg and West Egg.

Just as Gatsby moves east to pursue Daisy and status, so too Larry Morgan moves gradually eastward as he moves up in his job and social status—from the University of California in Berkeley to Wisconsin, then to Vermont, a reversal of Westering. The Langs, by contrast, are of the New England wealthy. On one side you have a pair that have come from the Harvard of Bliss Perry, from Cambridge society, from summer "cottages" on long lawns of lakefront. On the other side you have the Westerners—open, decent, ambitious, and full of character. Through the Langs, the Morgans are brought into one wing of New England aristocracy with its certainties of taste and manners and its exclusivity. Nevertheless, the Morgans bring a great deal, just by being who they are, to the relationship between the two couples. In an academic atmosphere too often sullied by pretentiousness and affectation, their genuineness and their battle against circumstance and poverty in order to succeed make them admirable, as Charity is quick to point out to them during their first extended conversation.

Just as he never seemed to have made up his mind about the primacy of free will or determination in guiding human life, Stegner seems to have been of two minds about the possibility of regional "character." In a conversation with Richard Etulain he said, "If there are such things as regional or national characteristics, you have to try to define them. They're always slippery. They may not exist at all. Maybe in the eye of the beholder." He hesitates to generalize, but he certainly expresses the feeling consistently that *individuals* belong to places, are defined by them, shaped by them. That is his message about himself in *Wolf Willow* and *Recapitulation* and the message of his essay "A Sense of Place."

The novel was finished in the late summer of 1986. In December, he wrote to Avis DeVoto:

Gotany [*sic*] good news back your way? Our own personal news is meager. Looking at the calendar and calculating our age by our best logarithmic tables, we decided we had better do it while we could, and last June took off for two and a half weeks in Bora Bora and Moorea—overage swingers. We survived it, too. Then we drove east to Vermont, where Mary spent her time on the piano and I finished up that novel that's been pestering me, and then wrote three lectures that I gave in Ann Arbor on the way home. . . . That will about do it for me. When that novel comes out it will be exactly fifty years since my first one. (12/18/86)

In writing *Crossing to Safety* Stegner was taking a number of chances. As usual, he really was not interested in plot. But not only did he lack a plot, he had very little else besides the idea of writing as honestly as possible about a relationship—very little that could be termed exciting and certainly nothing that could be called adventurous. Could he make a successful novel out of such materials? In looking back, he has said:

There was nothing very dramatic in those lives . . . so that I was taking risks, I was quite aware. The contemporary novel deals commonly in sensation, but there was not much sensation in this story to deal with. . . . I suppose the only reason it struck me as a potential something that I had to write was that I was puzzled about the relationships of those two very different personalities and the ambiguities within both of them. I loved them both and saw them breaking their hearts and their heads until they died. And also, I suppose, I had the muleheaded notion that it *ought* to be possible to make books out of something less than loud sensation.

What has made *Crossing to Safety* a success, both aesthetically and popularly—it has probably sold more than any other of Stegner's books except *Angle of Repose*—is the very quietness that he worried about. The reading public for books of literary quality seems to have been hungry for something that was not sensational, that was quiet and rang true. After the book came out, Wendell Berry wrote to Wallace, putting into words what would seem to have been a common reaction among its audience:

It is a masterful book—not the least in the way it walks serenely past "novelistic" opportunities that would, in fact, have diminished it. . . . We are so grateful for it here because it so steadfastly affirms the struggle of people to love each other. What else is there? And how much else we have had! (10/31/87)

In addition, there is no doubt the book has achieved its popularity because of the quality of the prose—it is not as epic in scale as *The Big Rock Candy Mountain*, nor as complex in structure and meaning as *Angle of Repose*, but every sentence seems to confirm that this is a writer who has mastered the art of writing well.

The descriptions are magnificent. Here, Larry is walking once again, after an eight-year hiatus, in his beloved Vermont woods:

It is a road I have walked hundreds of times, a lovely lost tunnel through the trees, busy this morning with birds and little shy rustling things, my favorite road anywhere.

Dew has soaked everything. I could wash my hands in the ferns and when I pick a leaf off a maple branch I get a shower on my head and shoulders. Through the hardwoods along the foot of the hill, through the belt of cedars where the ground is swampy with springs, through the spruce and balsam of the steep pitch, I go alertly, feasting my eyes. I see coon tracks, an adult and two young, in the mud, and maturing grasses bent like croquet wickets with wet, and spotted orange Amanitas, at this season flattened or even concave and holding water, and miniature forests of club moss and ground pine and ground cedar. There are brown caves of shelter, mouse and hare country, under the wide skirts of spruce.

It isn't just the beauty that makes his experience here so meaningful, but recollection of the people connected to it. It is a somber occasion—he and Sally have come back because Charity is dying—yet he "wonders if he [has] ever felt more alive," as he looks out over the lake and the surrounding countryside. "There it was," he says to himself, "there it is, the place where during the best time of our lives friendship had its home and happiness its headquarters."

This one day in Vermont near the end of Charity's life frames the memories that come flooding back to Larry Morgan. They are memories that trace the growth of the friendship between the two couples, from its beginnings at the University of Wisconsin, over the years in Vermont and abroad in Europe, to this last reunion. Some of the memories are not altogether pleasant. As in Joe Allston's garden in *All the Little Live Things*, this garden on Long Pond has its own serpent. No Eden, Larry tells us, is without a serpent:

> It was not a big serpent, nor very alarming. But once we noticed it, we realized that it had been there all along, that what we had thought only the wind in the grass, or the scraping of a dry leaf, was this thing sliding discreetly out of sight. Even when we recognized it for what it was, it did not seem dangerous. It just made us look before we sat down.

What "it" is, is that part of Charity's character that insists on total control.

Charity is an amazing creation. The conflict between her and her husband, which continues throughout their lives together, is representative of the conflict of two extremes in point of view and in approaches to life. Sid would seem to represent the emotional side of human experience—appreciation, love, care, connection with the earth. Charity seems to represent the almost totally rational—continually planning, forever making lists—and yet, she becomes irrational in her overplanning and scheduling of every activity, even relaxation. To paraphrase Emily Dickinson, she preaches rationality till it argues her irrational.

The split between the two is large and touches nearly everything in their lives, including Sid's choice of vocation. He is a poet, a passable one, but a romantic and out of step with his times. But no matter—he has inherited enough money so that he could pursue poetry, full-time, for the rest of his life. But Charity has other plans for him. Following the pattern of her own family, she wants him to pursue a career in academia, becoming a published scholar who teaches, preferably, at an Ivy League university. Although Sid is a good teacher, he is no scholar and finds scholarship a dreary occupation. His wife is so impatient with his attention to poetry rather than writing scholarly articles that he has to sneak around her constant surveillance to write his poems, like a secret drinker.

In this most poetic of Wallace Stegner's books (with the possible exception of *Wolf Willow*), poetry seems in one way or another to run through its fabric. There is the conflict between Sid and Charity over the importance and worth of poetry; Sid often quotes from poets on appropriate occasions; and the language with which the story is told, its imagery and carefully structured sound, reinforces a poetic sensibility at the heart of the novel. Furthermore, the ghost of Robert Frost seems in many ways to haunt this narrative about rural New England. There are paraphrases—unacknowledged in the text—of Frost lines, and the book's title is taken from "I Could Give All to Time." The final stanza appears as epigraph to the novel:

> I could give all to Time except
> What I myself have held. But why declare
> The things forbidden that while the Customs slept
> I have crossed to Safety with? For I am There,
> And what I would not part with I have kept.

The title of the novel may refer to those things, nonmaterial, that mean the most in life—family, friendship, generosity, love—that we might take with us into death. Perhaps it refers to Charity and her will to insist on the worthwhile things in life—as she sees them—and her insistence, in dying, to "do it right." Or the title may refer to what lasts, what turns out in the long run to be valuable.

Looking back on these last years of Stegner's career, one can see that the writing of *Crossing to Safety* was one of a series of closures to his life. He had written about Saskatchewan and childhood in *Wolf Willow* and *The Big Rock Candy Mountain*, about his teenage years in Salt Lake in *Recapitulation*, and about life in California in *All the Little Live Things*. But even though *Second Growth* was about Vermont, he had never really written about his own experience, the complex of emotions that the people and the landscape of Vermont had brought to him over the years.

Near the beginning of the novel, Larry Morgan, Stegner's literary counterpart, sits on the porch of the guest cottage in the Lang compound, looks around him in the early morning light, and thinks of the past:

From the high porch, the woods pitching down to the lake are more than a known and loved place. They are a habitat we were once fully adapted to, a sort of Peaceable Kingdom where species such as ours might evolve unchallenged and find their step on the staircase of being. Sitting with it all under my eye, I am struck once more, as I was up on the Wightman road, by its changelessness.

As Larry's thoughts go back, it is almost as if Stegner is reviewing his own life, a summing-up tinged with regret, and one can't help but wonder if, deep inside, the author himself may have felt this way at times near the end of his career:

> Though I have been busy, perhaps overbusy, all my life, it seems to me now that I have accomplished little that matters, that the books have never come up to what was in my head, and that the rewards—the comfortable income, the public notice, the literary prizes, and the honorary degrees—have been tinsel, not what a grown man should be content with.
>
> What ever happened to the passion we all had to improve ourselves, live up to our potential, leave a mark on the world? Our hottest arguments were always about how we could *contribute*. We did not care about rewards.

One of the main activities of the Grays and Stegners over the years during the summers they were together, one of the things they cared about most, was talk—serious talk, about politics, sometimes history or literature, occasionally music or the Greensboro environment. All four were engaged, opinionated, intense people, people who read a great deal and were interested in many things. Phil's son, young Phil, recalls his father as probably the best conversationalist he ever met, and neighbors in Greensboro recall how easy it was to talk to him and what a great variety of things he seemed to be interested in. Others remember how common it was for guests to search Wallace out at a gathering to talk to—it was always possible that you would learn something from him. Sherry Gray, another son, remembers an instance when Wallace's comment about a writer's need for self-discipline and what one needed to do to maintain it made such an impression on him, an aspiring writer, that he thought about it all winter. Wallace, in the words of Gray's daughter Nancy, "always took seriously being serious," and had an intensity about life and people that set him apart.

He brought that same intensity to his physical work or to his play. There was a right way to mow the lawn, the right way to cut wood, even a right way to square dance—Wallace, Nancy has noted, seemed to bring a moral dimension to everything. Sherry recalls that the first thing Wallace did after arriving for the summer was not to relax, but to get out his hoe and begin to clear out the scrub trees that had begun their yearly invasion around the house. The second thing he would do a few days later would be to cut wood and split it. It was an occupation he loved, like the narrator in Frost's "Two Tramps in Mud Time," who finds joy in feeling

> The weight of an ax-head poised aloft,
> The grip on earth of outspread feet.
> The life of muscles rocking soft
> And smooth and moist in vernal heat.

He stocked himself well with wood, and Mary might show up at a neighbor's house with a basket full of kindling. And one of the occupations that he and Phil senior shared together and enjoyed was clearing trails. Many of them were seldom used but Phil felt it a duty to keep them open anyway, and Wallace was glad to join him for the companionship and talk.

In the evenings at get-togethers, there might be charades or music, sometimes reading aloud. And when Arthur Perry was with them, he and Phil and Wallace could recite miles of poetry. One of the Stegners' main entertainments in Greensboro was square dancing, and when they built their second house on Baker Hill closer to the lake, they built it so that two squares could swing partners comfortably in the main room. Earlier, going to dances at the Grange in town, there would be musicians and a caller, but at the Stegners', there were records and Wally himself would call. He took it seriously. He tried to hide it, but he sometimes found it irritating when younger people, fooling around and not paying attention, would mess up and then collapse in laughter at their own confusion.

The four of them, the Grays and the Stegners, were very close, and when the Grays had a dinner or an excursion, the Stegners were always included. The sort of picnic we see in the novel might be put on, in the early years, several times a year, and the Pierce Arrow with its wicker baskets was kept up to perform for those occasions. A grill for cooking the steaks was loaded on, and someone almost always brought along a guitar. A list in Peg Gray's handwriting is still pinned up in the kitchen of her house which outlines in detail the supplies for the "Perfect Picnic." As Westerners who had seen cattle on the hoof, Wallace and Froel Rainey liked their meat well-done, but Phil had picked up the New York fashion of cooking steaks bloody rare. For twenty years Wallace went to these picnics, usually on Barr Hill, and never once said a word, suffering through eating his meat and telling his host how much he enjoyed it. Grilling steaks was the one accomplishment that Peg gave Phil credit for, and sensitive to his pride in this and in light of Peg's frequent criticism, Wallace said nothing.

Wallace never did like confrontation of any kind, and despite his love for both Peg and Phil, their flare-ups made him very uncomfortable. Peg's constant bossiness and criticism of her husband made her children, as they got older, angry with her. Nancy has felt, with perhaps more bitterness than the others, that Wallace could have, should have, intervened. Once, for example, after the couples had sat down to dinner, Mary took a bite. Peg gave her a look, and, much to Mary's discomfiture (she was "Molly" to her close friends), said in a stern voice that Peg would use only with her friends, "*Molly!* Don't eat before grace!" Observers thought Mary might burst into tears. According to Nancy, "Molly didn't do anything but wither and Wally, who could have said, 'Okay, come *on*,' said nothing. . . . Mother definitely had the power to hurt." In Nancy's view, *Crossing to Safety* presents a very mild depiction of what her mother was really like. Yet, for the most part, the Stegners were willing to overlook such incidents in light of Peg's constant generosity and thoughtfulness. She really did care about them, boosted their spirits, and became someone they could depend on, someone who was always there for them. Mary thought of Peg as her best friend.

One of the main reasons, as he has said, that Wallace wrote the book was to try to sort out his own, very complex feelings about these two people he was so fond of. And the relationships between him and Mary and the Grays were very complex, a tangled web of emotions. It was hard to know sometimes, in response to Peg's arrangements for you, whether to resent them or be grateful for them. After Page was born, Peg "just sort of took over." She decided it would be much better for the health of mother and child if they went to Vermont, and so they did, leaving Wallace in Madison, sitting at his desk working and, as described so vividly in the novel, enduring the Wisconsin summer:

> I rose at six and got in three hours on the typewriter before my first class. I tried writing in the late afternoon, too, but even stripped to the waist I sweltered in the midwestern heat, and my arm stuck to the varnished desk and my sweaty hands smudged the paper.

Wallace's feelings, in life, were mixed: he was grateful to Peg for getting Mary and the baby out of the heat, grateful for a house to stay in rent-free for the summer, but this was the first separation he had had from his wife since they had been married. And he worried about her and the baby's health and missed them terribly.

Nancy describes another time, recalled to her by Mary, during the summer in Vermont when Peg decided that Mary needed a rest. She

> hired baby-sitters for the kids including Page, and Page stayed in some other house while they were staying here, and basically they couldn't have access to their own child! This lasted all summer, and they put up with it because that was the way mother was, so powerful and assuming that you wanted her to be generous. Molly said once that Peg was somebody who did things for you whether you wanted it or not!

Peg was a beautiful, vivacious woman, and Wallace was attracted to her, even defended her to own family or to others who might criticize her. Wallace, as far as she was concerned, was the perfect specimen of what she would have wanted in a husband—gentlemanly, but at the same time highly motivated and an accomplished scholar. What made

Wallace uncomfortable was her tendency to hold him up to Phil as a model for what Phil should do with his life. Phil was not ambitious or driven. Both he and Wallace had a pattern of working in their studies in the mornings and then doing physical work with hoe, or chainsaw, or clippers outside in the afternoons. Just as Wallace had his "think house," patterned after the other little houses used as studies by academics in the Greensboro area, including Peg's father (as we see Charity's father in the novel withdrawing from the chaos of the family to go to his little sanctuary), Phil had his own place adjoining his shop. But where Wallace was disciplined and pretty much stayed glued to his seat all morning, Phil tended to get up to work at something in his shop or fiddle with one thing or another. He was an inveterate collector of odds and ends and spent a lot of time organizing them. According to his children, he saved everything; there was even a box in his shop labeled "strings too short to use." In making trails or cutting back brush or mending furniture or writing a long poem, Phil could be just as hardworking as Wallace. But he marched to a different drummer, and that was something that frustrated Peg, since she found, over and over again, that his stubbornly held patterns were largely out of her control, making her even more critical and demanding. Relations between the two became more and more bitter as time wore on.

Since they loved them both, the Stegners found the ongoing conflict between the Grays very sad to witness and hard to accept or even for the most part to understand. After all, when they had met them, they encountered a couple who seemed to have everything—attractiveness, wealth, family, intellect, and place. Peg and Phil were always willing to share what they had with the Stegners. They brought them into their family. And they gave them a place—Vermont. At the time of the novel's publication, Wallace wrote from Greensboro:

Life here is very mild and amiable—beautiful weather, plenty of thrushes in the woods, a rave review of the new book in Publishers Weekly, old friends, picnics, walks, even a conservation struggle into which we can stick our noses. (8/24/87)

23

GIVING ALL
TO TIME

After *Crossing to Safety* came out, an ailing eighty-nine-year-old Malcolm Cowley sat down at his desk and wrote out a note in longhand to a seventy-eight-year-old Wallace Stegner:

7 August 1987

Dear Wally,

Felicitations on having finished a novel in spite of interruptions, to be published before the 50th anniversary of your first novel. What a career, unequaled in this century. The new book contains some of your best writing. . . . Virtues have not been celebrated in recent prose fiction, but you make them persuasive: unshakable loyalty and all the others. Nobody else could do it. . . . Our love and admiration to Mary. If she were just here to play for me!

As always,
Malcolm

"A career unequaled in this century," and, indeed, it was a lifetime of incredible accomplishment by a man who, in his own quiet way, had led a life of heroic dimensions. It was an accomplishment all the more admirable when one realizes, in an age when so many have decided that the rules are irrelevant and that it is only the end result—money or fame—that counts, that this was a man who persevered always in doing what he thought was right. He was fighting for civil rights as far back as the mid-1940s and for the preservation of our environment as far back as the 1950s; advocating a nation of cultural diversity and arguing the importance of the preservation of Native American, African-American, and Latino heritages decades before the phrase "culture diversity" was coined. From the beginning of his career, he insisted on the rights of women, recognized their individuality, their abilities, and lauded their accomplishments; he encouraged their work and decried their subjugation or abuse.

He was a man who cultivated the qualities of kindness, consideration, and generosity. So many of our writers and poets of this century have, directly or indirectly (by showing their absence), written about the critical need for love, empathy, and kindness in our society, but it is truly remarkable to find a writer whose life and work were so closely joined in their expression. Perhaps Wallace Stegner's greatest creation was himself—a good man who always did the best he could. It isn't just his breadth of character and the diversity of his work that astonishes, it is also the quality of it all.

These final years were years of closure and review. As well as looking back over a nearly lifelong friendship in *Crossing to Safety,* Stegner was reviewing fifty years or so of his own life, and once again in a novel he was bringing together the past with the present. About this aspect of *Crossing to Safety* he said that

> the older you get, the more the relation of past and present grows on you, because you have more history to look at.... No matter how old you get, you don't feel old. You're still the same guy inside, and so there is a continuity there, within yourself. You can't ignore it.

The novel is a summing up, a review of past decades in terms of the values he felt were most important to live by. In the novel, looking back on his life and the lives of his wife and his friends, Larry says:

Lamely as I have limped the last miles of this marathon, I can't charge myself with real ill will. Nor Sally, nor Sid, nor Charity—any of the foursome. We made plenty of mistakes, but we never tripped anybody to gain an advantage, or took illegal shortcuts when no judge was around. We have all jogged and panted it out the whole way.

This is not something Stegner would have said of himself—he would have thought it untoward to boast of his own rectitude and was never self-righteous—but it is a bottom line that as observers we may be justified in attaching to his life—he jogged and panted the whole way.

Not the least wondrous in assessing Wallace Stegner's life and values was his marriage of nearly sixty years to Mary, a loving marriage that takes on added glow if one sees it as reflected in the relations of Larry and Sally in *Crossing to Safety*. Larry is a sensitive, responsive helpmate to a wife who has been crippled by polio, and she, although in braces much of their life together, has been of constant and spirited help to him. In every gesture and word, we can feel a mutual concern and respect. Many who have admired this aspect of the novel in particular have also wondered if the fictional marriage might not be too good to be true. But in life, Wallace's consideration was unwavering. Mary did not have polio, but she suffered through one illness after another during their marriage, with eight major operations. Wallace was untiring in his compassionate concern. In the care of his dying mother, a painful and demanding custody, he had his apprenticeship, his determined constancy a reaction to the inconstancy of his father, and he made caretaking a lifelong response to the woman in his life who often needed that care.

Despite health problems, Mary was a strong and determined woman with talent and intelligence. Although she made a life of her own in music, and had a circle of her own friends, much of Mary's life revolved around her husband and his work. When he gave his acceptance speech in 1990 for a lifetime achievement award from the California Arts Council, he thanked those during his life who had "out of love or friendship or plain goodwill given me a hand," and then added:

Most of all, I thank my wife, Mary, who for reasons known only to herself has put up with me for nearly sixty years, has planted and tended ideas in my head, has guarded my health and my working hours, has made me go back and improve the manuscripts I brought her looking for praise, and who remains the principal reason why I go on putting words on paper and taking an interest in a world that I am often inclined to disavow in disgust.

If *Crossing to Safety* was one closure, there were also many others. During the years of the final writing of the novel and its publication, Stegner was helping a bibliographer, Nancy Colberg, compile a book-length listing of his writings. He agreed to allow a Berkeley filmmaker, Steve Fisher, to do a documentary on his life with an emphasis on his environmental work, and in February 1989 he began the process of being interviewed in front of the camera and going to locations to be filmed. All of these activities took more of his time than he had antici-pated, but he dealt with them patiently and with good spirits. The year after his novel came out, a little book (which came out of his residence as a Montgomery Fellow at Dartmouth), *On Teaching of Creative Writing* (1988), was published that summarized his philosophy as a teacher of writing.

That March, in a nostalgic moment, Red Cowan, his high school and college buddy, wrote to Stegner about one of his earliest publications:

What it all doesn't give! Last week in our nation's capital I read a short story. "Blood-Stain." It had several typos and was obviously not done with a word-processor. Remember? *Hermitage 1930?* There was a modest introductory note. "We are under no illusions as to the contribution we are making to current literature: none of us expect to break into print in any other place." (3/15/88)

But although he was tying things up, Wally was far from resting on his laurels and spending all his time in wistful recollection of a time more innocent. He couldn't have been busier during these years, even though, as he told Page, he was hanging up his spikes as a novelist. From Ver-mont in the early fall of 1988, he reflected:

The days draw in, the color begins (not very good this year), the nights get down close to or below freezing. When I have fears that

I may cease to be before my pen can glean my teeming brain I wonder how I ever got into this ratrace. If I had lived a good normal respectable life I would have been loafing for the last fifteen years, with no more concern than the adequacy of my woodpile. But here I am writing lectures and preparing seminars for the University of Colorado, and writing a lit'ry speech for the New York Public Library, and writing another talk for the Dartmouth Bookstore and some Berkeley bookstore and the Stanford Bookstore, and the morning is gorgeous and my good wife would like to drive up to Lake Willoughby. Compromise: I will take her at eleven A.M. (9/9/88)

The last three years were devoted to travel, giving speeches, and accepting awards. At the same time, making all this activity difficult, he began an era of declining health, which he found irritating and inhibiting. His usual tack was to ignore illness as much as possible, and even when he did not feel well, to go ahead with his schedule.

Many of the speeches and readings came in connection with his final book publications, publications that in themselves signified closure: after *Crossing to Safety* (1987), he published his *Collected Stories* (1990) and *Where the Bluebird Sings to the Lemonade Springs: Living and Writing in the West* (1992), his last collection of essays. In the aftermath of the novel, he was invited to give a reading at Politics and Prose bookstore in Washington, D.C., where the crowd was so large they had to put out loudspeakers so that the overflow could hear him. But he had just come back from two weeks in Morocco and was not feeling at all well. The book signing that followed his reading turned out to be an ordeal.

During the fall and winter of 1989, his hip, which was disintegrating, became painful and he had to limp to walk. When it got so bad he couldn't stand it anymore, he was given anti-inflammatory drugs to ease the pain and reduce the swelling. The following spring he was to give a speech at an environmental conference at Park City, Utah, introduced by Robert Redford. Before leaving, he felt weak and vaguely ill, and Mary thought he should stay home. When he arrived, instead of resting, he found that he had to oblige Steve Fisher, who was working on the documentary and wanted photographs of Wallace in the western scenery.

Then the sponsors of the conference had stacks of the *Collected Stories* for Stegner to sign as part of a money-raising dinner, and they sat him down at a table. He signed a hundred, but instead of giving them out to the patrons as they told him they would do, the sponsors had the patrons come up before the dinner and bring additional copies up to be signed. Stegner had had no rest and almost nothing to eat since he arrived, but instead of giving him food while he was signing, they kept giving him glasses of wine. Mary recalled:

> So he drank the wine and signed [another] hundred and had to talk to the people, too. They were all Utah people, saying, "I remember you here . . . or, I remember you there." Then we had the dinner. . . . Finally, at the airport, I got a wheelchair to ride him to the car.

Then at home, as Wallace remembered it:

> I found myself one morning on the kitchen floor with my pajamas full of black blood. Mary called the doctor, the doctor called 911, the yard filled up with fire engines and ambulances, and I rode in state from here to Emergency, and in a gurney, after awhile, from emergency to Intensive Care. Very dramatic, considering I didn't even know I was sick. (10/17/90)

It had only been two days since he had returned, exhausted, from Utah. With very little food for many hours on the trip, the anti-inflammatory drugs he had been taking just ate his stomach out.

During these years he continued to grow quieter and more contemplative, and part of it was no doubt his need to suppress his reactions to pain. He was no longer the life of the party—indeed, he no longer went to parties. Except for receptions and public dinners where he would have a glass of wine, he had given up drinking as a before-dinner ritual. When his grandson, Page, asked him why, he told him that it had gotten to the point where he was looking forward to 5 o'clock too much.

Despite his experience of having to go into intensive care, he followed up the publication of his collected stories in 1990 with readings at the

National Gallery, the Library of Congress, and Trinity Church on Wall Street, where he read his story "The Traveler." Unfortunately, while getting settled on the airplane to fly to Washington, D.C., Stegner, compensating for his bad hip, sprained his back putting his luggage into an overhead compartment. The following year he had his hip replaced. He refused to use a cane during his recovery; instead, he worked hard to learn how to walk without a limp.

In 1992 he signed a deal with American Airlines that would give him free travel to wherever he and Mary wanted to go and then a fee for whatever article for their magazine that he might want to write as a result of his experiences. In June he and Mary took a trip on the superdeluxe (up to a thousand dollars a day, as Mary recalled) train through Scotland, which resulted in "Sailing the Royal Scotsman." That summer he suffered so much from back pain while he and Mary were in Vermont, he was unable to do any work at all. Toward the end of the summer his hands began to hurt as well. The doctors thought at first it might be carpal tunnel syndrome, then they suspected gout. But it turned out to be a blood disease, very painful, called polynalgia, and he had to take cortisone for it for the rest of his life. Unfortunely, that changed his appearance, and during the last years a very handsome man would look bloated and puffy.

There were many honors during this time, including an honorary doctorate from the University of Montana in 1987, the PEN USA West lifetime achievement award in 1990, the Governor's Award for lifetime achievement from the California Arts Council in 1991, and then in 1992 he went to Bozeman to help inaugurate a chair in history named after him at Montana State University. Fifteen minutes after he had begun his speech, he collapsed onstage. He had been hit with a virulent intestinal flu and, as usual, had neglected the warning signs in order to fulfill his commitment. While he was in Bozeman, he was given the Freedom to Write Award by PEN USA West for his turning down of the National Medal for the Arts that was to be presented to him by President Bush. He had refused the medal on the grounds that the National Endowment for the Arts had had its freedom to support the arts restricted by political pressure. The award was accepted by a proxy, who read his short speech to the gathering in Los Angeles. It said, in part:

I believe that government should support the arts. I also believe that its function stops with support—it has no business trying to direct or censor them. Art must be left to the artists. If they sometimes make mistakes, or press too hard, or test too strenuously the boundaries of the accepted, that is part of the commitment and the excitement: creation by definition deals with what has not yet been made.

Then, in March 1993, the Stegners were in Santa Fe, New Mexico, to accept an award from the Montana & Plains Booksellers Association. On the evening of the twenty-eighth, they had just taken some friends home and were on their way back to where they were staying, when they had the automobile accident that would prove fatal to Wallace. They were in a rental car in an unfamiliar city, and their route took them on a street that crossed the main highway at the top of a hill. A car was coming from the left very fast, and it was almost impossible to see until it was nearly on top of them as Wallace pulled out from the stop sign. The car hit them broadside, breaking the corner post and smashing in the driver's-door panel. Cars stopped, and a woman who identified herself as a nurse had Mary, who was unhurt, put her cape over Wallace, who was bleeding profusely and in shock. Sadly, it was some time before word could be relayed to the authorities and an ambulance finally came to the scene. Mary rode in the ambulance and watched while the orderlies cut off her husband's clothes and sought to stem the flow of blood.

At Emergency it was discovered that Wallace had suffered a broken collarbone, all the ribs on his left side had been broken, and his lung had collapsed. Even though Wallace was in the Intensive Care Unit, the doctor was cautiously optimistic, and after the first day transferred him to a regular ward and a day later had him walking around. On the third day he had a relapse: he had contracted pneumonia and was back in Intensive Care. Mary thought that it had all been too fast and that he should not have been moved out of there in the first place. At that point the situation became critical when Wallace suffered a heart attack and a possible stroke.

The first time Mary saw him in the hospital the next morning after the accident, he said to her, "How could I have done this to you?" In the two days prior to the relapse, the family came and was allowed to see him. Then on April 12, he died from his injuries and resulting complications. When she got home, Mary saw this list, pinned on the wall above his desk:

TO DO

1. Introduction to Page's essays.
2. Remarks for Santa Fe.
3. Introduction for B.O.M. trilogy.
4. Remarks for Earth Day.
5. Remarks for Cyril Magnin luncheon.
6. Remarks for BABRA meeting.
7. Nature Conservancy foreword.
8. Bright Edge foreword.

Wallace Stegner's career as a novelist followed a pattern of lifelong growth, reaching its zenith near the end. Commenting on the possibility of such growth during a seminar at Dartmouth College, he said:

Largeness is a lifelong matter—sometimes a conscious goal, sometimes not. You enlarge yourself because that is the kind of individual you are. You grow because you are not content *not* to. You are like a beaver that chews constantly because if it doesn't, its teeth grow long and lock. . . . If you are a grower and a writer as well, your writing should get better and larger and wiser.

As he grew older, Stegner began to think he had grown wiser, but during the last decade of his life, he tended to discard that notion. He told Terry Gross during an interview on National Public Radio:

There was a time when I thought I was wise, and I don't think so any more. I think we're all more confident of ourselves in our youth, because confidence goes with physical competence and energy and the rest of it. I'm not that confident anymore, and I'm not so sure that I was ever wise.

His later storytellers seem to reflect this growing doubt. But one of the things that draws us most to them—Joe Allston, Lyman Ward, and Larry Morgan—is that their wisdom is certified by their fallibility, their uncertainty. All of them, even at a late stage of life, are learning and growing: while they have strong values and carefully nurtured, strong personalities, they nevertheless remain open to experience. In this they reflect their creator, who, until the day of the auto accident, was active and curious, reading, writing, traveling, and giving speeches. Throughout his last years, Stegner gave himself almost entirely to his art and to his life as a writer, investing his knowledge and experience, as well as his doubts, in those "ventriloquist dummies," as he called them, who spoke for him.

One of his strengths as a writer of fiction was the relationship he formed with his readers, a relationship that evolved gradually and became stronger as his career progressed and he found the narrative voice that allowed him a deeper participation in his work. By giving so much of himself, risking so much of himself, he bound his readers to him, and it is this quality, above all, that will lead to a wider recognition of his greatness of spirit and the rich vibrancy and continuing relevance of his fictional creations. As an essayist, historian, biographer, and short story writer he was among the very best of our time. As environmentalist his works persist and his words continue to inspire. But it is as novelist that he would want to be remembered—that was his aim, his delight, his real life's work.

In *All the Little Live Things*, no doubt speaking for the author, Marian tells an anguished Joe Allston:

> Don't feel bad. I'm glad you love me, but I hope you and Ruth won't grieve. It's right there should be death in the world, it's as natural as being born. We're all part of a big life pool, and we owe the world the space we fill and the chemicals we're made of. Once we admit it's not an abstraction, but something we do personally owe, it shouldn't be hard.

If we were to hike up to the picnic site at the top of Barr Hill used in *Crossing to Safety*, on property deeded by the Grays to the community as a park, we would be high enough so that "those who lifted eyes could count / Five mountain ranges one behind the other / Under the sunset far into Vermont." Just below, on Baker Hill, Wallace Stegner's ashes have been spread among the ferns near his summer cottage. There, on a westward-facing slope, he could be seen to stand guard, not just on the West but on a whole continent. He became more joined to the land as he grew older: now he will become that land. Look for him under the soles of your boots.

NOTES AND DOCUMENTATION

On the following pages, sources and notes for each chapter are listed under the following categories (when applicable): (1) Interviews, (2) Published Material by Wallace Stegner, (3) Unpublished Material by Wallace Stegner, (4) Published Material About Wallace Stegner or Related Topics, and (5) Notes and Sources for Quotations and Topics (listed by page number and introductory phrase). Items in sections (2), (3), and (4) are listed in order of their initial appearance in the text of the chapter. No notes are provided for the quoted letters; instead, the source for letters (almost all of them are by Stegner himself) and the recipient are indicated in the text and the date of the letter given in parentheses at the end of the quotation. The dates for the letters are given to provide a further guide to the chronology of the life.

Wallace Stegner's books (the specific editions) referred to in the various sections in the following chapter listings are abbreviated as follows:

NOVELS

Remembering Laughter. Boston: Little, Brown, 1937 = *RL.*

On a Darkling Plain. New York: Harcourt, Brace, 1939 = *DP.*

Fire and Ice. New York: Duell, Sloan and Pearce, 1941 = *FI.*

The Big Rock Candy Mountain. Lincoln: University of Nebraska Press, 1983 [first Published in New York: Duell, Sloan and Pearce, 1943] = *Rock.*

Second Growth. Lincoln: University of Nebraska Press, 1985 [first published in Boston: Houghton Mifflin, 1947] = *Growth.*

Joe Hill: A Biographical Novel. Lincoln: University of Nebraska Press, 1980 [first published as *The Preacher and the Slave* in Boston: Houghton Mifflin, 1950] = *Hill.*

A Shooting Star. New York: Viking Press, 1961 = *Star.*

All the Little Live Things. Lincoln: University of Nebraska Press, 1979 [first published in New York: The Viking Press, 1967] = *Live.*

Angle of Repose. Garden City, New York: Doubleday, 1971 = *Angle.*

The Spectator Bird. Garden City, New York: Doubleday, 1976 = *Bird.*

Recapitulation. Garden City, New York: Doubleday, 1979 = *Recap.*

Crossing to Safety. New York: Random House, 1987 = *Safety.*

SHORT STORY COLLECTIONS

The Women on the Wall. Boston: Houghton Mifflin, 1950 = *Women.*

The City of the Living and Other Stories. Boston: Houghton Mifflin, 1956 = *City.*

The Collected Stories of Wallace Stegner. New York: Penguin Books, 1991 [first published in New York: Random House, 1990] = *CS.*

HISTORIES

Mormon Country. Lincoln: University of Nebraska Press, 1981 [first published in New York: Duell, Sloan & Pearce, 1942] = *Mormon.*

DISCOVERY!: The Search for Arabian Oil. Beirut, Lebanon: An Export Book, 1971 = *Disc.*

The Gathering of Zion: The Story of the Mormon Trail. Salt Lake City: Westwater Press, 1981 [first published in New York: McGraw-Hill, 1964] = *Zion.*

Wolf Willow: A History, a Story, and a Memoir of the Last Plains Frontier. Lincoln: University of Nebraska Press, 1980 [first published in New York: The Viking Press, 1962] = *WW.*

BIOGRAPHIES, AUTOBIOGRAPHY, LETTERS, AND INTERVIEWS

Beyond the Hundredth Meridian: John Wesley Powell and the Second Opening of the West. Lincoln: University of Nebraska Press, 1982 [first published in Boston: Houghton Mifflin Company, 1954] = *Powell.*

The Uneasy Chair: A Biography of Bernard DeVoto. Garden City, New York: Doubleday, 1974 = *DeVoto.*

The Letters of Bernard DeVoto [edited]. Garden City, New York: Doubleday, 1975 = *Letters.*

Conversations with Wallace Stegner about Western Literature and History (with Richard Etulain). Salt Lake City: University of Utah Press, 1983 = *Convers.*

On the Teaching of Creative Writing, ed. Edward Connery Lathem. Hanover, New Hampshire: Dartmouth College, 1988 = *Creative.*

ESSAY COLLECTIONS

One Nation (with the editors of *Look*). Boston: Houghton Mifflin, 1945 = *Nation.*

The Sound of Mountain Water. Lincoln: University of Nebraska Press, 1985 [first published in Garden City, New York: Doubleday, 1969] = *Water.*

This Is Dinosaur: Echo Park Country and Its Magic Rivers [edited]. Boulder, Colorado: Roberts Rinehard, 1985 [first published in New York: Alfred Knopf, 1955] = *Dino.*

One Way to Spell Man. Garden City, New York: Doubleday, 1982 = *One Way.*

American Places (with Page Stegner). Moscow: University of Idaho Press, 1983 [first published in New York: E. P. Dutton, 1981] = *Places.*

The American West as Living Space. Ann Arbor: University of Michigan Press, 1987 = *Living.*

Where the Bluebird Sings to the Lemonade Springs. New York: Penguin Books, 1992 [first published in New York: Random House, 1992] = *Bluebird*

References to Wallace Stegner's agents, Brandt and Brandt, have been abbreviated throughout the notes as "B & B." In the following listings the volume number for periodicals will be given only for scholarly journals, and items have been put into footnote form, rather than in bibliography form. Complete publication information for Wallace Stegner's books is given in the preceding list—subsequent reference is only to the titles.

INTRODUCTION: AGAINST THE GRAIN–
A Heritage of Integrity

2. *Published Material by Wallace Stegner:*

One Nation

"Pop Goes the Alley Cat," *CS,* 247–265.

"Born a Square," *Water,* 170–185.

Conversations with Wallace Stegner

"Autobiography: Wallace Stegner," *Contemporary Authors: Autobiography Series,* 9 (Detroit: Gale Research Company, 1989), 257–271.

All the Little Live Things

Crossing to Safety

The Big Rock Candy Mountain

Recapitulation

Angle of Repose

Fire and Ice

A Shooting Star

"That New Man, the American," *One Way,* 75–83.

4. *Published Material About Wallace Stegner:*

Doris Grumbach, "The Grace of Old Lovers," review of *Crossing to Safety, New York Times Book Review,* 9/20/87, 14.

5. *Notes and Sources for Quotations:*

5 Endowment for the Arts, *Los Angeles Times,* 5/25/92, F-14.

6 "in a box," "Born a Square," *Water,* 170, 175–176.

7 "I knew nothing," *Convers,* 13.

8 "doesn't love," "Mending Wall," *Complete Poems of Robert Frost* (New York: Henry Holt, 1949), 47.

13 "I'll tell you," *Star,* 365.

13 "We are all likely," "That New Man," *One Way,* 82.

14 "Little as I want," *WW,* 132–33.

15 "I was trying to," Ernest Hemingway, *Death in the Afternoon* (New York: Charles Scribner's Sons, 1932), 2.

1: THE LAST HOMESTEAD FRONTIER:
A Prairie Childhood

1. Interviews. My thanks to:
Wallace Stegner, David L. Freed

2. Published Material by Wallace Stegner:
"Bugle Song," *CS,* 13–20.
Wolf Willow
"Finding the Place: A Migrant Childhood," *Bluebird,* 3–21.
All the Little Live Things
"Autobiography: Wallace Stegner," *Contemporary Authors: Autobiography Series,* 9 (Detroit: Gale Research Company, 1989), 257–271.
"The Colt," *CS,* 179–190.
"The Chink," *CS,* 191–203.
"That Great Falls Year," *Montana Spaces,* ed. William Kittredge (New York: Nick Lyon Books, 1988), 121–134.
The Sound of Mountain Water
The Big Rock Candy Mountain
Conversations with Wallace Stegner

3. Unpublished Material by Wallace Stegner:
"Growing Up Western," 18-page manuscript.

4. Published Material About Wallace Stegner and Related Topics:
Paula Simons, "Reclaiming Wallace Stegner," *Alberta Report,* 3/6/89, 42.

5. Notes and Sources for Quotations:
18 "a tough old Lutheran," WS, 5/7/87.
18 "Saskatchewan is," *Bluebird,* 30.
19 "What we did," *WW,* 268.
20 "had a seven-foot," WS, 5/7/87.
20 "had read," *WW,* 274.
21 "You don't get," *WW,* 8.
22 NOTE: The term "rugged individualism" was coined by Herbert Hoover in *American Individualism* (1922) and entered into the common vocabulary during the presidential election campaign of 1928 according to *The Oxford Dictionary of Modern Quotations,* ed. Tony Augard (New York: Oxford University Press, 1991), 105.
23 Eastend, *WW,* 11, *Bluebird,* 7.

23 "I caught lice," *Bluebird*, 6.

24 "sponsored," *WW*, 129.

24 "would have been," *WW*, 129.

24 "After almost," *CS*, 191.

25 "I remember," *CS*, 193.

25 "It was . . . the cowboy," *WW*, 134.

25 "Nothing . . . could have," *WW*, 259.

26 "I should think," *Live*, 59.

26 "My adult," "Autobiography," 260.

26 "A man named," WS, 6/2/87.

26 "I can remember," WS, 6/2/87.

27 "School," *WW*, 132.

27 Eastend school, WS, 6/2/87.

27 "made up," *WW*, 290.

28 chores, WS, 6/2/87.

28 "I can remember," Convers., 21.

28 "some novels," *WW*, 27.

29 "It seems to me," *WW*, 112.

29 "they lived," WS, 6/2/87.

30 "Everyone in town," *WW*, 262.

30 "forty bushels," *Bluebird*, 11.

30 "the fields were," *Bluebird*, 11.

31 "this dung-heeled," *WW*, 24.

31 "I wouldn't," "Reclaiming," 42.

31 "I was desolate," "Autobiography," 261.

31 "bloated," *CS*, 190.

31 "I think I might," *WW*, 35.

32 "In my first days," *Bluebird*, 12.

32 "it had a little," "Great Falls," 124.

33 "But I never forgave," "Great Falls," 132.

33 "I thought . . . he," WS, 6/2/87.

34 "summer 1921" NOTE: 1921 would seem to better fit the chronology, although WS and Robinson both list this date as 1920.

34 "our camp beds," *Bluebird*, 15.

34 "How it lies," *Water*, 159.

NOTE: Of course this has all changed. In a trip back to the city in 1979, WS found the changes "profound and disheartening" (*Water*, 160).

35 "The Mormons," *Bluebird*, 15.

35 reading, *Bluebird*, 10.

35 "always volunteering," WS, 7/20/87.

35 "What I most wanted," *Bluebird*, 16.

35 "made to order," "Growing Up," 14.

35 "I suppose," "Growing Up," 14.

36 "went up," "Growing Up," 14.

36 "across lots," *Water*, 162.

36 a good school, "Rocky Mountain Country," 75.
37 "I had my moment," "Growing Up," 14.
37 tennis, Freed, 5/25/89.
38 "I was always," WS, 6/2/87.

2: FROM PRIMITIVE TO INTELLECTUAL:
The Education of Wallace Stegner

1. *Interviews.* My thanks to:
Wallace Stegner, Robert Irvine, Milton Cowan, David L. Freed, Harold Hoyle Smith.

2. *Published Material by Wallace Stegner:*
"The Iowa Years," *Communications Research—A Half Century Appraisal,* eds. Daniel Lerner and Lyle M. Nelson (Honolulu: University Press of Hawaii, 1977), 305–310.
The Big Rock Candy Mountain
Recapitulation
"Literary by Accident," *Utah Libraries,* Fall 1975, 7–21.

3. *Unpublished Material by Wallace Stegner:*
"Autobiography," essay ms.
"Growing Up Western," 18-page manuscript.

4. *Published Material About Wallace Stegner:*
Forrest G. and Margaret G. Robinson, *Wallace Stegner* (Boston: Twayne, 1977).

5. *Notes and Sources for Quotations and Topics:*
40 "Perhaps that was," *Rock,* 563.
40 "It was," "Growing Up," 14.
41 "Simultaneously," *Recap,* 114.
42 "What he liked," *Recap,* 265.
42 "spell to banish," Malcolm Cowley, "Nightmare and Ritual in Hemingway," the introduction to *The Portable Hemingway,* ed. Malcolm Cowley (New York: Viking, 1945) as reprinted in *Hemingway: A Collection of Critical Essays,* ed. Robert P. Weeks (Englewood Cliffs, New Jersey: Prentice-Hall, 1962), 48.
42 "walked double," *Recap,* 19.
43 "Yes, absolutely," WS, 7/20/87.
44 "The humiliation," Cowan, 8/4/86.
44 "good . . . because," WS, 7/20/87.
45 "He [Bruce] would," *Recap,* 103.
45 "Sunday was," WS, 7/20/87.
45 "was very competitive," Freed, 5/25/89.
45 Ellsworth Vines, WS, 3/22/90.
46 "one of those teachers," *Convers,* 25.
46 "Tillicums," Cowan, 8/4/86.
46 "the common people," *Webster's Third New International Dictionary* (Springfield, Massachusetts: G. & C. Merriam, 1968).

47 "three sunburned," *Recap*, 22.

47 "pretty abstract," WS, 7/20/87.

47 "a good bone," WS, 7/20/87.

48 "I don't think," WS, 7/20/87.

48 "rather exotic," Cowan, 8/4/86.

48 "He was making," *Recap*, 124.

48 "I didn't know," *Convers*, 24.

48 "who was sort of," *Convers*, 25.

49 senior year, WS, 3/22/90.

49 "Why don't you go," "Literary by Accident," 10.

50 "Two roads," "Autobiography," ms., 13.

50 NOTE: paraphrase of "The Road Not Taken," *Complete Poems of Robert Frost* (New York: Henry Holt, 1949), 131.

50 "just like poor," Robinson/Bib., 12.

50 "which I then thought," "Literary by Accident," 10.

50 "I [was an] . . . incomparably," "Iowa Years," 305.

50 "Homesickness is," "Growing Up," ms., 15.

51 learned more in Iowa City, "Growing Up," ms., 15.

52 "That made me mad," "Literary by Accident," 11.

52 "hopelessly chasing," "Autobiography," ms., 14.

52 "he wanted to know," Schramm, 3/4/87.

3: FROM STUDENT TO PROFESSOR:
The Further Education of Wallace Stegner

1. *Interviews.* My thanks to:
   Wallace Stegner, Mary Stegner, Wilbur Schramm, Milton Cowan.

2. *Published Material by Wallace Stegner:*
   "The Iowa Years," *Communications Research—A Half Century Appraisal*, eds. Daniel Lerner and Lyle M. Nelson (Honolulu: University Press of Hawaii, 1977), 305–310.

   "Literary by Accident," *Utah Libraries*, Fall 1975, 7–21.

   "Letter, Much Too Late," *Bluebird*, 22–33.

   "The Blue-Winged Teal," *CS*, 231–246.

   Clarence Edward Dutton: An Appraisal, Salt Lake City: University of Utah Press, 1936.

   "C. E. Dutton, Explorer, Geologist, Nature Writer," *Scientific Monthly*, July 1937, 83–85.

3. *Unpublished Material by Wallace Stegner:*
   "Growing Up Western," ms.

   "Autobiography," ms.

   Letter from WS to MS, n.d.

4. *Published Material About Wallace Stegner and Related Topics:*
   Ben Merchant Vorpahl, "Roosevelt, Wister, Turner, and Remington," *A Lit-*

erary History of the American West, eds. J. Golden Taylor, et. al. (Fort Worth: Texas Christian University Press, 1987), 273–302.

5. *Notes and Sources for Quotations and Topics:*

54 "That first reduction," "Autobiography," ms., 14.

55 "at least it was," "Autobiography," ms., 14.

55 "in certain curious," WS, 1/28/88.

55 "I looked outside," "Autobiography," ms., 13–14.

56 "a strange interlude," "Autobiography," ms., 16.

56 Cowan remembered, Cowan, 8/4/86.

57 the pain, WS, 3/22/90.

57 "Somehow I," "Letter," *Bluebird*, 21, 20.

58 "I was," "Autobiography," ms., 16.

58 "At Augustana," $900 a year, WS, 1/16/88.

58 hitchhiked, WS, 3/22/90.

59 "a great place," Cowan, 8/4/86.

59 "Fisher immediately," Cowan.

59 "I had gone," MS, 11/18/88.

60 "Having japed," letter from WS to MS, n.d.

61 "My wife," "Autobiography," ms., 17.

62 "I was back," *Convers*, 26.

63 "Then I sat down," "Autobiography," ms., 18.

63 "a connected," *Literary History*, 284.

64 NOTE: Turner—Frederick Jackson Turner, "The Significance of the Frontier in American History," *The Early Writings of Frederick Jackson Turner*, compiled Everett E. Edwards (Freeport, New York: Books for Libraries Press, 1938).

64 "Turner ... had," Rideout, et al., interview with WS, at the University of Wisconsin, 5/86.

64 "It turned out," Rideout, 5/86.

65 "By pure accident," "Literary by Accident," 12.

66 "Six ... parks," *Scientific*, 84.

66 "People recognize," *Scientific*, 85.

67 salesman, WS, 3/22/90.

4. BECOMING A NOVELIST:
Write a Novel and Win a Prize

1. *Interviews.* My thanks to:

Wallace Stegner, Mary Stegner, Stuart Brown, Mark Eccles, Theodore Morrison.

2. *Published Material by Wallace Stegner:*

Remembering Laughter

Conversations with Wallace Stegner

"Literary by Accident," *Utah Libraries*, Fall 1975, 7–21.

Crossing to Safety

"Can Teachers Be Writers?," *Intermountain Review of English and Speech* 1, 1/1/37, 1, 3.

The Letters of Bernard DeVoto

The Uneasy Chair: A Biography of Bernard DeVoto

3. Unpublished Material by Wallace Stegner:

"Autobiography," ms.

4. Published Material About Wallace Stegner:

Forrest and Margaret Robinson, *Wallace Stegner* (Boston: Twayne, 1977).

Theodore Morrison, *Bread Loaf Writers' Conference: The First Thirty Years (1926–1955)* (Middlebury, Vermont: Middlebury College Press, 1976).

5. Notes and Sources for Quotations and Topics:

68 Wallace didn't have any classes, *Convers*, 27.

69 "in hands," Robinson, 99.

69 "I just sort of," WS, 1/26/88.

69 "Their eyes," *RL*, 7.

70 "There is something," *RL*, 23.

71 "we're dealing," *Convers*, 37.

72 telegram, WS, 3/22/90.

72 "We had a party," "Autobiography," ms., 18.

72 Virgin Islands, "Literary by Accident," 14.

72 "that butcher," Page Stegner, 11/17/88.

73 "Take that little," "Autobiography," ms., 18.

73 Europe, bicycle, WS, 6/2/87; 7/20/87.

74 "We were all interested," WS, 6/2/87.

75 "very kind," WS, 5/7/87.

75 "Benny was," WS, 5/7/87.

76 "actually help"; 77 "And if, in the first," "Can Teachers Be Writers?," 23.

77 "In two years," "Autobiography," ms., 19.

78 WS's teaching, Eccles, 4/9/87, Brown, 3/4/87.

80 professionalism at Bread Loaf, Morrison, 8/3/86.

80 "I have been talking," WS, 3/22/90.

81 "emphasized work," Morrison, *Bread Loaf*, 45.

81 Bread Loaf routine, Morrison; *DeVoto*, 124.

81 "Evenings," *DeVoto*, 124.

82 tennis, Morrison, 8/3/86.

5: ACCOMPLISHED WRITER, HARVARD TEACHER, AND FRIEND TO THE FAMOUS:
What More Do You Need?

1. Interviews. My thanks to:

Wallace Stegner, Mary Stegner, Theodore Morrison, Mark Eccles.

2. Published Material by Wallace Stegner:

The Sound of Mountain Water

The Uneasy Chair

The Letters of Bernard DeVoto (edited)

The Potter's House

"The People Against the American Continent," *Vermont History* 35, Autumn 1967, 177–185.

"The Sweetness of Twisted Apples," *CS*, 221–229.

On a Darkling Plain

A Shooting Star

Angle of Repose

Crossing to Safety

3. *Unpublished Material by Wallace Stegner:*

"Growing Up Western," ms.

5. *Notes and Sources for Quotations and Topics:*

84 "the image," *Convers*, 31.

85 "He sort of," WS, 11/4/87.

85 DeVoto description, *DeVoto*, 47.

86 "incomparable," *Water*, 252.

87 "Brilliance," *Water*, 258.

87 "It is entirely," *Water*, 259.

87 "before girls," *Water*, 259.

87 "western history," *Water*, 261.

88 "demonstrates," *DeVoto*, 204.

88 Frost . . . liking, Morrison, 8/3/86.

89 "to walk and talk," *DeVoto*, 205.

89 "He was a friend," *DeVoto*, 206.

90 "What began," *DeVoto*, 207.

90 "For God's sake," *DeVoto*, 207.

90 "he was too magnanimous," *DeVoto*, 209.

90 "You're a good poet," (WS quoting Lawrence Thompson), *DeVoto*, 209.

91 "Everybody who grows," *Vermont History*, 59–60.

91 population pressures, *Vermont*, 60.

91 "within a few feet," *CS*, 222.

92 "The Last Mowing," *The Complete Poems of Robert Frost*, 338; "The Wood-Pile," 126; "The Witch of Coos," 247.

92 "there would be a day"; "She stood up," *CS*, 226.

93 "After Apple-Picking," *Complete Poems*, 88.

95 "brute luck," WS, 1/26/88.

95 had the highest," WS, 1/27/87.

96 "a little jejune," "Growing Up," ms., 18.

97 "standing" guard, MS, 9/24/94.

98 "Cambridge was," WS, 3/22/90.

6: HARD WORK AT HARVARD:
Climbing the Big Rock Candy Mountain

1. *Interviews.* My thanks to:

Wallace Stegner, Mary Stegner, Walter Rideout, Theodore Morrison.

2. *Published Material by Wallace Stegner:*

Fire and Ice

The Big Rock Candy Mountain

"A Field Guide to Western Birds," *CS*, 311–359.

Angle of Repose

A Shooting Star

The Preacher and the Slave

"Goin' to Town," *CS*, 75–84.

"Two Rivers," *CS*, 115–127.

"Chip Off the Old Block," *CS*, 205–219.

"The Iowa Years," *Communications Research—A Half Century Appraisal*, eds. Daniel Lerner and Lyle M. Nelson (Honolulu: University Press of Hawaii, 1977), 305–310.

Mormon Country

Recapitulation

" 'Truth' and 'Faking' in Fiction," *Writer* 53, February 1940, 40–43.

"The Shaping of Experience," *Writer* 55, April 1942, 99–102.

5. *Notes and Sources for Quotations and Topics:*

99 "If you are," WS, 11/4/87.

100 "Nobody . . . got to know," WS, 11/4/87.

101 "When he [Wally]," Rideout, 4/10/87.

101 "Tell other people's," WS, 1/26/88.

102 "Just an enjoyment," Morrison, 8/3/86.

102 "very lively character," WS, 1/20/89.

102 "I had a sense," WS, 1/27/89.

102 "DeVoto, Frost," WS, 1/27/87.

107 "After the night's," *CS*, 75.

108 "Standing in the yard," *CS*, 75.

109 "All his sullenness," *CS*, 117.

109 "there wasn't," "It's funny," *CS*, 125.

110 "things that made," *CS*, 125.

110 "something bothersome," *CS*, 120.

110 "over the whole canyon," *CS*, 123–24.

110 " 'Okay,' he said," *CS*, 219.

111 "Mining men," *Mormon*, 200.

111 "As if wheels," "Iowa Years," 309.

113 "Willard's wife," WS, 1/28/88.

113 "kind of a literary," WS, 1/28/88.

114 "the story gets lost," " 'Truth' and 'Faking,' " 42.

114 "the safe system," " 'Truth' and 'Faking,' " 43.

114 "The technical problems," "The Shaping of Experience," 100.

115 "changes dictated," "Nothing in nature," "The Shaping of Experience," 102.

7: LOOKING BACK AT THE WEST FROM CAMBRIDGE

1. Interviews. My thanks to:

Wallace Stegner, Mary Stegner, Leonard Doran, Walter Rideout.

2. Published Material by Wallace Stegner:

Mormon Country

"The Saw Gang," *CS*, 69–74.

The Uneasy Chair

The Big Rock Candy Mountain

4. Published Material About Wallace Stegner:

Forrest and Margaret Robinson, *Wallace Stegner* (Boston: Twayne, 1977).

Nancy Colberg, *Wallace Stegner: A Descriptive Bibliography* (Lewiston, Idaho: Confluence Press, 1990).

George R. Stewart, "Land of the Mormons," *New York Times Book Review*, 10/25/42, n.p.

Marjorie Leet Ford, "Remembering Wallace Stegner," *San Francisco Examiner: Image*, 5/30/93, 21.

William C. Baurecht, "Within a Continuous Frame: Stegner's Family Album in *The Big Rock Candy Mountain*," *Critical Essays on Wallace Stegner*, ed. Anthony Arthur (Boston: G. K. Hall, 1982), 98–108.

Howard Mumford Jones, "World Out of Nowhere," review of *The Big Rock Candy Mountain*, *Saturday Review*, 10/2/43, 11.

5. Notes and Sources for Quotations and Topics:

116 "Well, I suggest"; "You need to," Doran, 8/5/86.

117 "I took," Frost as quoted by William H. Pritchard in *Frost: A Literary Life Reconsidered* (New York: Oxford University Press, 1984), 222.

120 "who dealt," *DeVoto*, 239.

120 "I admired," Rideout et al., 12.

121 "What is admissible," Robinsons, 57.

121 "His kind of history," *DeVoto*, 240.

123 "In general," "There is some," Robinsons, 56.

124 "Within the United States," *Mormon*, 187.

124 "It would be fatal," *Mormon*, 187–8.

124 "seems to loom," "Land of the Mormons," n.p.

125 "he expands," Robinsons, 56.

125 "could endure," *Mormon*, 242.

125 "He was one," *Mormon*, 294.

126 "he had been betrayed," *Mormon*, 317.

127 Short story prizes, Colberg, 235–39, *passim.*

128 Frost, "Drumlin Woodchuck," *Complete Poems*, 365.

129 "Contemplating," Baurecht, "Within a Continuous Frame," 101.

129 "vast, living," Jones, "World Out of Nowhere," 17.

131 "I could give all," Frost, *Complete Poems*, 447.

8: FROM THE FIGHT AGAINST
RUGGED INDIVIDUALISM TO THE FIGHT
AGAINST PREJUDICE AND RACISM

1. Interviews. My thanks to:
Wallace Stegner, Mary Stegner.

2. Published Material by Wallace Stegner:
Where the Bluebird Sings to the Lemonade Springs
The Big Rock Candy Mountain
"Get Out of That Story!" *Writer*, December 1942, 360–362.
"The Naturalization of an Idea," *Delphian Quarterly*, October 1942, 31–36, 43.
"The Cooperatives and the Peace," *Delphian Quarterly*, April 1943, 15–18.
"Colleges in War Time," *Delphian Quarterly*, April 1942, 2–7.
"Who Persecutes Boston?" *Atlantic*, July 1944, 45–52.
One Nation
"One Man's Rediscovery of America," *Saturday Review*, 8/17/46, 5–6, 26–27; "Rediscovering America: Part II," *Saturday Review*, 8/24/46, 12–13; "Rediscovering America: Part III," *Saturday Review*, 10/19/46, 21–23; "Rediscovering America: Part Four [*sic*]," *Saturday Review*, 11/23/46, 200–221, 47.

3. Unpublished Material by Wallace Stegner:
"Autobiography," ms.

4. Published Material About Stegner:
Nancy Colberg, *Wallace Stegner: A Descriptive Bibliography* (Lewiston, Idaho: Confluence Press, 1990).
Orville Prescott, "Books of the Times," review of *The Big Rock Candy Mountain*, *New York Times*, n.d., n.p.
Joseph Warren Beach, "Life-Size Stegner," review of *The Big Rock Candy Mountain*, *New York Times Book Review*, 9/20/43, 4.

5. Notes and Sources for Quotations and Topics:
134 "In the more," *Bluebird*, 21.
134 "He was not," *Rock*, 30.
135 "he was born," *Rock*, 83.
136 "There were things," *Rock*, 563.
137 "It was all familiar," *Rock*, 552.
137 "love and know," *Rock*, 519.
138 "Long afterward," *Rock*, 374.
138 "it was not permanence," *Rock*, 374.
138 "a childhood hunter," *Rock*, 511.
138 "It was good," *Rock*, 563.
139 *Big Rock* publication, Colberg, 26–33.
140 "a novel that commands," Orville Prescott, "Books of the Times," n.d., n.p.
140 "the patient, realistic," Joseph Warren Beach, "Life-Size Stegner," 4.
140 "There had been," *Rock*, 185.
141 "he approaches," "Get Out of That Story," 262.
142 "growing increasingly," "Naturalization," 31.
142 "this is a nation," "one half," "Naturalization," 31.

142 "the *consumer* is," "Naturalization," 31.

142 "If we don't produce," "Cooperatives and the Peace," 15.

143 "approach world problems," "Cooperatives and the Peace," 15.

144 "It was a melancholy," WS, 1/27/87.

144 "most likely," "The Colleges in War Time," 3–4.

144 duties teaching, letter, WS, 10/15/43.

145 "one of the gravest," "Foreword," *Nation*, v.

145 "all the sociology," WS, 3/22/90.

146 "messing around," WS, 3/22/90.

146 "snubbed, bought and sold," "Who Persecutes Boston?," 47.

146 "it could do," "Who Persecutes," 52.

148 "I cannot say," "Autobiography," ms., 22.

149 "The schools not only," *Nation*, 10.

150 "the Indian's right," "We already," *Nation*, 142–3.

150 "None of us," *Nation*, 5.

9: BACK TO FICTION, ON TO STANFORD

1. Interviews. My thanks to:

Wallace Stegner, Mary Stegner, Page Stegner, Richard Scowcroft.

2. Published Material by Wallace Stegner:

"Four Hundred Families Plan a House," *'47 Magazine*, April 1947, 63–67.

"Wallace Stegner on the Stanford Writing Program," *American Literary Almanac*, ed. Karen L. Rood (New York: A Bruccoli Clark Layman Book, 1988), 98–99.

"Volcano," *CS*, 107–113.

"The House on Cherry Creek," *Collier's*, 8/11/45, 16–17.

"Balance His, Swing Yours," *CS*, 61–68.

"The Women on the Wall," *Harper's*, April 1946, 366–376; *CS*, 41–59.

The Preacher and the Slave

A Shooting Star

"One Man's Rediscovery of America," *Saturday Review*, 8/17/46, 5–6, 26–27; "Rediscovering America: Part II," *Saturday Review*, 8/24/46, 12–13; "Rediscovering America: Part III," *Saturday Review*, 10/19/46, 21–23; "Rediscovering America: Part Four [*sic*]" *Saturday Review*, 11/23/46, 200–221, 47.

"Packhorse Paradise," *Atlantic*, September 1947, 21–26.

"Backroads River," *Atlantic*, January 1948, 56–64.

"Navajo Rodeo," *Woman's Day*, November 1949, 48–49, 106–108.

"Why I Like the West," *Tomorrow*, July 1950, 5–9.

"Backroads of the American West," *Tomorrow*, October 1950, 9–14.

"One-Fourth of a Nation: Public Lands and Itching Fingers," *Reporter*, 5/12/53, 25–29.

Angle of Repose

Second Growth

"Hostage," *Virginia Quarterly Review* 19, July 1943, 403–411.

"Jews Are the Most Misunderstood Minority," *Glamour*, July 1946, 75–78.

3. Unpublished Material by Wallace Stegner:

"Autobiography," ms.

4. Published Material About Wallace Stegner:

Page Stegner, "A Brief Reminiscence: Father, Teacher, Collaborator," *Montana*, Autumn 1993, 54–56.

Pamela Feinselber, "Giants," *Peninsula*, March 1987, 52–55, 84–93.

5. Notes and Sources for Quotations and Topics:

151 "the business," WS, 1/26/88.

152 "beyond my depth," WS, 1/26/88.

152 "I came out," WS, 1/26/88.

153 "as things went," Scowcroft, 11/5/87.

155 "on the rocky isle," *CS*, 42.

156 "but that trip," *Water*, 45.

156 "where Powell," *Water*, 58–59.

156 "My father," Page Stegner, "A Brief Reminiscence," 55.

158 "There is something," *Water*, 92.

159 "a bad life," *Water*, 101.

159 "there is no," "for upon the lack," "Why I Like," 6, 7.

159 "All around us," "Backroads," 11.

159 "reflect almost," "Backroads," 13.

160 "Benny was," WS, 5/7/87.

160 "There is," "One Fourth," 25.

160 "who for years," "One Fourth," 26.

161 "it may be taken," One Fourth," 28.

162 Stanford, WS, 1/26/88.

163 "He would shower," MS, 1/19/88.

163 Burdick and O. Henry Memorial Awards, *American Literary Almanac*, 98.

163 "it was impossible," "Autobiography," ms., 22.

164 "Instead of green," "Autobiography," ms., 22.

164 "We have to do something," "Giants," 54.

164 "fellowships," "Autobiography," ms., 23.

164 "when we moved," "Autobiography," ms., 24.

165 "wished he'd," "Giants," 54.

165 "For years," "Giants," 54–5.

166 "the stage apparatus," *American Literary Almanac*, 99.

168 "live down," *Growth*, 115.

10: ABANDONING THE NOVEL AND EMBRACING THE SHORT STORY

1. Interviews. My thanks to:

Wallace Stegner, James Houston, Boris and Edda Ilyn, Mrs. R. E. Cameron.

2. Published Material by Wallace Stegner:

Second Growth

The Preacher and the Slave

"On the Writing of History," *American West* 2, Fall 1965, 6–13.

"I Dreamed I Saw Joe Hill Last Night," *Pacific Spectator* 1, Spring 1947, 184–187.

"Joe Hill: The Wobblies' Troubadour," *New Republic*, 1/5/48, 20–24, 38.

"A Problem in Fiction," *Pacific Spectator*, Autumn 1949, 368–375.

"The City of the Living," *CS*, 513–525.

Conversations

3. **Unpublished Material by Wallace Stegner:**

"Autobiography," ms.

4. **Published Material About Wallace Stegner:**

Nancy Colberg, *Wallace Stegner: A Descriptive Bibliography* (Lewiston, Idaho: Confluence Press, 1990).

Israel Shenker, "Whither the Short Story?," *New York Times*, 11/20/70, n.p.

5. **Notes and Sources for Quotations and Topics:**

172 "The making of fiction," *Growth*, copyright page.

173 "glittered," Edwin Arlington Robinson, "Richard Cory," in *Twentieth Century American Writing*, ed. William T. Stafford (New York: The Odyssey Press), 1965, 21.

174 "Despite his reserved," Houston, 1/10/90.

174 "I think I got," WS, 11/5/87.

175 could not teach them to write, Mrs. R. E. Cameron, 6/8/88.

175 "But it was simply," Boris Ilyn, 12/28/86.

176 "in his comments," Houston, 1/10/90.

177 "Boris came out," Edda Ilyn, 12/28/86.

178 "About two or three," Etulain, speech at University of Montana, 9/17/93; *Convers*, 194.

178 "so that I would," "On the Writing of History," 28.

178 "was kind of hair raising," WS, 1/26/88.

179 "the less I thought," WS, 1/26/88.

179 "soft-spoken," "resembling a certain," "I Dreamed," 186.

180 "Sir: I wish," *New Republic*, 2/9/48, 38.

180 "proletarian novel," WS, 1/26/88.

181 short stories, Colberg, *Bibliography*, 235–239.

182 "before two mornings," "A Problem," 370.

182 "The problem," "A Problem," 370.

183 "the way everybody," "A Problem," 374.

183 "idyllic and wistful," "A Problem," 374.

184 "so much," "A Problem," 373.

184 "I thought that," "A Problem," 372.

185 "six weeks in England," "Autobiography," ms., 25.

186 Kawabata, MS, 9/24/94.

187 "the first trip," MS, 1/20/89.

187 "from the age," Page, 11/17/88.

189 "When the gimlet," *CS*, 376.

190 "he drew into his lungs," *CS*, 515.

190 "I am just beginning," *CS*, 515.

190 "the chlorine bite," *CS*, 521.

190 "was innocent," *CS*, 523.

190 "all the Nile's," *CS*, 523.

191 "Yet the praying," 524–25.

191 "Chekhov," Israel Shenker, "Whither the Short Story?," n.p.

11: FROM SHORT STORY WRITER TO ENVIRONMENTALIST

1. Interviews. My thanks to:

Wallace Stegner, Mary Stegner, Stuart Brown, Marvin and Leah Chodorow, Kenneth Arrow, Virginia Page, Stuart Udall, Froehlich Rainey.

2. Published Material by Wallace Stegner:

"The Traveler," *CS*, 3–11.

"The City of the Living," *CS*, 513–525.

All the Little Live Things

"The Book and the Great Community," *Library Journal* 93, 1 October 1968, 3513–3516; reprinted in *Water*, 276–286.

Beyond the Hundredth Meridian

"Powell and the Names on the Plateau," *Western Humanities Review* 7, Spring 1953, 105–110.

"One-Fourth of a Nation: Public Land and Itching Fingers," *Reporter*, 5/12/53, 25–29.

"Battle for the Wilderness," *New Republic*, 2/15/54, 13–15.

"We Are Destroying Our National Parks," *Sports Illustrated*, 6/13/55, 28–29, 44–46.

This Is Dinosaur (edited)

"Quiet Earth, Big Sky," *American Heritage*, October 1955, 22–27.

"A Field Guide to Western Birds," *CS*, 311–359.

4. Published Material About Wallace Stegner:

Don Kazak, "What Wallace Writes," *Palo Alto Weekly*, 5/2/90, 29–30.

T. H. Watkins, "Typewritten on Both Sides: The Conservation Career of Wallace Stegner," *Audubon*, September 1987, 88, 90, 92, 94–97, 99–101, 103.

Tracy Minkin, "Where Will the Animals Run at Night?," *American Way*, 6/1/89, 91–96, 130–131.

"Western Heroes," *New Yorker*, 5/10/93, 41.

"A Very Special Event," *Green Footnotes*, Summer 1987, 1.

5. Notes and Sources for Quotations and Topics:

192 "overcome by a feeling," *CS*, 513.

193 "For all of this," *CS*, 6.

193 "The ways a man," *CS*, 10.

193 "looked back once," *CS*, 11.

194 "No risk," *Water*, 282–3.

194 "It was . . . about 20 below," Don Kazak, "What Wallace Writes," 29.

194 "Something long buried," *CS*, 5.

194 "are places," Don Kazak, "What Wallace Writes," 30.

194 "loved books," Brown, 3/4/87.

195 "We were trying," Watkins, "Typewritten," 99.

195 "your enemies," "A Very Special Event," 1.

195 told him off, Chodorow, 7/23/87.

196 NOTE: "The Cremation of Sam McGee," *The Complete Poems of Robert Service* (New York: Dodd, Mead, 1940), 33–36.

197 concerts in San Francisco, MS, 11/16/93.

197 "the house," Minkin, "Where Will the Animals," 92.

199 "All these hills," MS, 1/20/89.

199 Walking, Virginia Page, 6/9/88.

199 "listening attentively," Watkins, 95–96.

203 "Thomas Moran," WS to agents, 9/9/54.

204 "the fact the Reclamation," "Battle," 15.

204 "an effective," *Dino*, Foreword, vi.

207 "When I was rebuilding," Rainey, 11/7/90.

207 "Across its empty," "Quiet Earth," 24.

208 "I was sufficiently aware," Watkins, 99.

208 But Udall had already read, Udall, 5/22/89.

208 "when I first read," "Western Heroes," 41.

209 "the reason," DeVoto, "Introduction," *Powell*, xvi.

12: TO THE BARRICADES FOR THE ENVIRONMENT

1. Interviews. My thanks to:

Wallace Stegner, David Brower, Stuart Udall, Harold Gilliam.

2. Published Material by Wallace Stegner:

Beyond the Hundredth Meridian

This Is Dinosaur (edited)

Conversations

Where the Bluebird Sings to the Lemonade Springs

"The War Between the Rough Riders and the Bird Watchers," *Sierra Club Bulletin*, May 1959, 4–11.

4. Published Material About Wallace Stegner:

Michael P. Cohen, *The History of the Sierra Club: 1892–1970* (San Francisco: Sierra Club Books), 1988.

T. H. Watkins, "Typewritten on Both Sides," *Audubon*, September 1987, 88–101, 103.

Tracy Minkin, "Where Will the Animals Run at Night?," *American Way*, 91–96, 130–131.

5. Notes and Sources for Quotations and Topics:

211 "Losing one's right," *Powell*, 17.

212 "He was made," *Powell*, 3.

212 "What distinguishes," *Powell*, 16.

212 "driving will," *Powell*, 16.

212 "went clear under," *Powell*, 109.

212 "As a last," *Powell*, 72.

213 "There are characteristic," *Powell*, 66.

213 "He had nerve," *Powell*, 6.

215 "Nine men," *Powell*, 111.

215 "in finding," *Powell*, 3.

215 "who before," *Powell*, 6.

216 "Both Powell and Twain," *Powell*, 152.

216 "almost alone," *Powell*, 224.

216 "acute political," *Powell*, 176.

217 "lunatic counterpoint," *Powell*, 50.

217 "and from there," *Powell*, 70.

217 "His career," *Powell*, 50.

217 "whatever his education," *Powell*, 9.

218 "in most things," *Powell*, 249.

218 "his friends," *Powell*, 249.

218 "If he had," *Powell*, 249.

219 "Powell respected," *Powell*, 131.

219 "substituting," *Powell*, 258.

219 "a complete revolution," *Powell*, 212.

219 "as rooted," *Powell*, 212.

220 "it might," *Powell*, 229.

220 "Every generation," *Powell*, 255.

221 "the learning," *Powell*, 292.

221 "a character out of fiction," *Powell*, 284.

222 "He had one central," *Powell*, 292.

222 "in his way," *Powell*, 304.

223 "did not want," *Powell*, 336.

223 "with it much," *Powell*, 342.

225 "We only wanted," *Dino* (new edition), vi.

225 "words are," Brower, 6/19/89.

226 a pamphlet, *Dino* correspondence.

226 "it . . . constituted," Cohen, 193.

226 "to conserve," *Dino*, vii.

227 "It is legitimate," *Dino*, 17.

227 "We really whipped," *Convers*, 169.

228 "We did have," Brower, 6/19/89.

228 "If the national," *Bluebird*, 128.

229 "In wilderness," *Bluebird*, 121.

229 " 'Man . . . is everywhere,' " *Bluebird*, 123.

229 "the philosophical," *Bluebird*, 130.

229 "He wanted," *Bluebird*, 130–31.

229 "Like Leopold," "Autobiography," ms., 26.

230 "When, after innumerable," *Bluebird*, 131.

230 "In the decades to come," *Dino*, 17.

230 "this bill," "Bird Watchers," 7.

231 "In spite of," "Bird Watchers," 11.

231 "had plenty of supporters," Watkins, 97.

231 "elicited the wonder," Minkin, 95.

231 "It is a lovely," *Water*, 153.

232 "These are some," *Water*, 153.

232 wilderness letter, Udall, 5/22/89.

232 "it's been made," Minkin, 96.

13: TRAVEL, TRAVEL LITERATURE, AND THE SEARCH FOR NARRATIVE VOICE

1. Interviews. My thanks to:

Wallace Stegner, Mary Stegner, Kenneth Arrow.

2. Published Material by Wallace Stegner:

"Cairo, 1950," *Pacific Spectator* 5, 1951, 42–47.

"Asian Literary Articles," *The Indian P.E.N.* 17, 1/1/51, 2–4.

"Literary Lessons Out of Asia," *Pacific Spectator* 5, 1951, 413–419.

"Queen of the Salmon Rivers," *Sports Illustrated* 3, 8/8/55, 38–41.

"America's Mightiest Playground," *Holiday* 20, July 1956, 34–43, 122–125.

"Ordeal by Handcart: The Mormon Trek," *Colliers* 138, 7/6/56, 78–85.

DISCOVERY!: The Search for Arabian Oil (Beirut, Lebanon: An Export Book, 1971).

"The World's Strangest Sea," *Holiday* 21, May 1957, 76–77, 176–185.

"California's Gold Rush Country," *Holiday* 24, August 1958, 64–69, 127.

"A Love Affair with the Heber Valley, U.S.A.," *Vogue* 131, 2/1/58, 132–133, 192–193.

"The Rocky Mountain West," *The Romance of North America*, ed. Hardwick Mosley (Boston: Houghton Mifflin, 1958), 363–392.

"Field Guide to Western Birds," *The City of the Living and Other Stories* (Boston: Houghton Mifflin, 1956). [Also published in *New Short Novels 2* (New York: Ballantine Books, 1956).]

On the Teaching of Creative Writing.

4. Unpublished Material by Wallace Stegner:

"Garden Made for Snow" (short story)

5. Notes and Sources for Quotations:

235 beginnings and endings, WS, speech for Author's Coffee: Stanford University Women's Club, ca. 1990.

238 "In some ways," "America's Mightiest," 122.

239 "When we arrived," MS, 5/7/87.

239 "I got to go out," WS, 5/7/87.

240 "It was kind of nice," WS, 5/7/87.

240 "Even in a region," *Disc*, 43.

242 "Those who live," "Rocky Mountain," 380.

243 "I am beginning," "Field Guide," *CS*, 313.

243 "It is all out of," "Field Guide," *CS*, 332.

244 "If she weren't," "Field Guide," *CS*, 329–330.

245 "this movie set," "Field Guide," *CS*, 334.

246 "Why would he?" "Field Guide," *CS*, 358.

246 "for the forty years," "Field Guide," *CS*, 359.

246 "I don't know," "Field Guide," *CS*, 359.

247 "any work of art," *Creative*, 22.

14: AN ALL-STAR CAST

1. Interviews. My thanks to:

Wallace Stegner, Page Stegner, Nancy Packer, Steven Tanner, Al Young, Ed McClanahan, Ernest Gaines, Ian Watt, Richard Scowcroft, James Houston, Wendell Berry, Kay House.

2. Published Material by Wallace Stegner:

"The Book and the Great Community," *Water*, 276–286.

"A Letter to Wendell Berry," *Bluebird*, 207–213.

"The Sense of Place," *Bluebird*, 199–206.

4. Published Material About Wallace Stegner and Related Topics:

Martin Lasden, "Wallace Stegner on His Own Terms," *Stanford* (Spring 1989), 24–31.

Bruce Carnes, *Ken Kesey* (Boise, Idaho: Western Writers Series, 1974).

Stephen L. Tanner, *Ken Kesey* (Boston: Twayne Publishers, 1983).

Stephen L. Tanner, "The Western American Context of *One Flew Over the Cuckoo's Nest*," manuscript to be published in *Writing the American Classics*, *II*, ed. Tom Quirk and James Barbour.

Gordon Lish, "What the Hell You Looking in Here for, Daisy Mae?—An Interview with Ken Kesey," *Genesis West* 2, 1963, 17–29.

John C. Pratt, ed., *One Flew Over the Cuckoo's Nest: Text and Criticism* (New York: Viking Press, 1973).

Malcolm Cowley, "Kesey at Stanford," in *Kesey*, ed. Michael Strelow and staff (Eugene, Oregon: Northwest Review Books, 1975), 2 (single-page photocopy).

5. Notes and Sources for Quotations and Topics:

249 "I think they," WS, 6/12/89.

250 "the build of," Cowley, "Kesey at Stanford," 2.

250 "hoping to sign," Tanner, "The Western American," ms., 15.

250 "that the best reason," Lish, 25.

251 "A man becomes," Lish, 25.

251 "Stegner would have," Tanner, "The Western American," ms., 16.

251 "he said," Packer, 6/3/87.

252 "You go back," Lish, 24–25.

252 Malcolm Cowley, Tanner, "Western American," ms., 16–17.

253 "youth-cult," Tanner, 15.

253 "As soon as," Kesey, speech at Claremont-McKenna College, 9/17/93.

253 "Stegner saw Kesey," Lasden, 28.

254 "he [Wally]," Kesey, speech, 9/17/93.

254 "McMurphy's the name," Ken Kesey, *One Flew Over the Cuckoo's Nest* (New York: Viking Press, 1962), 11.

254 "the intellectuals," Packer, 6/3/87.

255 other writers and history, Carnes, 12, 13, 16, 17.

255 "Thought is," *Water*, 284.

255 "No young person," *Water*, 281.

256 "I am beginning," Pratt, 338–339.

257 NOTE: Cowley on Faulkner, "Introduction," *The Portable Faulkner* (New York: Viking Press, 1951); Cowley on Hemingway, "Introduction," *The Portable Hemingway* (New York: Viking Press, 1945).

258 "Robert Mitchum," Lasden, 24.

258 "the kind of guy," Page Stegner, 11/17/88.

258 "about the most," Packer, 6/3/87.

258 "Who's your favorite," Packer, 6/3/87.

258 "A representative," House, interview by tape and letter, 12/5/90.

259 "All sins," House, 12/5/90.

259 "Wally was very businesslike," Young, 6/12/90.

259 "Wally wrote," Young, 6/12/90.

260 "We're not going," Gaines, 6/15/90.

260 "full of gung-ho," Houston, 1/10/90.

261 "He just called," Gaines, 6/15/90.

262 "As the would-be," Berry, 4/12/87.

262 "seeing how," Berry, 4/12/87.

262 "By bestowing," Berry, 4/12/87.

262 "I'd describe," Berry, 4/12/87.

263 "I don't think," Berry, 4/12/87.

263 "If you don't," *Bluebird*, 199.

264 "the expression," *Bluebird*, 208.

264 "the value," *Bluebird*, 212.

264 "far beyond," Berry, 4/12/87.

264 " 'Just take care,' " Young, 6/12/90.

265 "Mr. Stegner," McClanahan, 4/12/87.

265 "everybody was," McClanahan, 4/12/87.

1 5: THE STRUGGLE TO LOCATE ONESELF

1. Interviews. My thanks to:

Wallace Stegner, Mary Stegner, Nancy Packer, Virginia Page, Stewart Udall, Harold Gilliam, Emilie Perry.

2. Published Material by Wallace Stegner:

A Shooting Star

Wolf Willow

Conversations
The Gathering of Zion
3. **Unpublished Material by Wallace Stegner:**
   "All About a *Shooting Star*," ms., n.d.
   "Autobiography," ms., n.d
   Notes from *The Eastend Enterprise*, n.d.
4. **Published Material About Wallace Stegner and Related Topics:**
   Albert J. Guerard, *The Triumph of the Novel: Dickens, Dostoevsky, Faulkner* (New York: Oxford University Press, 1976).
   Larry McMurtry, "Power of a Place," [clipping], n.d., n.p.
   Claude Simpson, "Stegner Explores Past in Blend of Fact, Fiction," [clipping], n.d., n.p.
5. **Notes and Sources for Quotations and Topics:**
   267 told Packer, Packer, 6/4/87.
   270 "as we were driving," *Convers*, 73.
   271 "without any preliminary," WS, "All About," ms., 1.
   272 "Give me," *Star*, 100.
   273 " 'I'll tell you,' " *Star*, 465.
   273 "I guess," *Star*, 397.
   274 "His kind," *Star*, 321.
   274 "walking a tightwire," *Convers*, 76.
   275 "The concept," Guerard, 136.
   276 "He seemed to me," "Autobiography," ms., 27.
   276 Stewart Udall, Udall, 5/24/89.
   276 "I didn't just," Udall, 5/24/89.
   277 "I knew that," Udall, 5/24/89.
   277 "another learning," "Autobiography," ms., 27.
   277 "a quick, deep look," "Autobiography," ms., 27.
   277 Mary in Washington, MS, 1/20/89.
   278 "was to send," WS, 11/4/87.
   278 "Well, I'm not," WS, 5/24/89.
   279 "It was the best," Udall, 5/24/89.
   279"This is fiction," *Convers*, 19.
   279 "It is with me," *WW*, 18.
   280 "My wife and I," *Convers*, 162.
   281 "the reason," WS, 3/22/90.
   281 "Jan. 10, 1917," Notes from the *Eastend Enterprise*, n.d.
   283 "I found," "Autobiography," ms., 28.
   283 "is as good," McMurtry, n.p.
   283 "keenly observant," Simpson, n.p.
   284 "On that monotonous," *WW*, 7–8.
   285 "were the most," *Zion*, 6.
   285 "If I have a home," *Zion*, 314.
   287 "the Mormons get," *Convers*, 111.
   288 "growing up without," "Autobiography," ms., 25.

288 "a revelation," "Autobiography," ms., 25.

288 "A message," Perry, 7/4/90.

289 sick at heart, WS to B & B, 11/26/63.

16: HISTORIAN AND "CONTEMPORARY"

1. Interviews. My thanks to:

Wallace Stegner, Mary Stegner, Page Stegner, Harold Gilliam, Mrs. R. E. Cameron, Richard Scowcroft, Joseph Houghteling, Tom Moser.

2. Published Material by Wallace Stegner:

The Gathering of Zion

"Fiction: A Lens on Life," published as a pamphlet by The Viking Press, 1960.

"Foreword," to Don Moser, *The Peninsula: A Story of the Olympic Country in Words and Photographs* (San Francisco: Sierra Club, 1962), 9–11.

"Quiet Crisis or Lost Cause," *Saturday Review*, 9/19/64, 28, 50.

"Whatever Happened to the Great Outdoors," *Saturday Review*, 5/22/65, 37–38, 97–98.

"Lake Powell," *Holiday*, May 1966, 64–68, 148–151.

All the Little Live Things

"Field Guide to Western Birds," *The City of the Living and Other Stories* (Boston: Houghton Mifflin, 1956); reprinted in *CS*, 311–359.

"Willa Cather: *My Antonia*," *The American Novel from James Fenimore Cooper to William Faulkner*, ed. Wallace Stegner (New York: Basic Books, 1965), 144–153.

"The Clouded Skies of Lotus Land," *St. Louis Post-Dispatch*, 9/26/65, n.p.

4. Published Material About Wallace Stegner and Related Topics:

Forrest and Margaret Robinson, *Wallace Stegner* (Boston: Twayne, 1977).

Philip C. Sturges, "History Over the Back Fence," review of *The Gathering of Zion*, [clipping], n.p., n.d., 18.

David Levin, *Exemplary Elders* (Athens, Georgia: University of Georgia Press, 1990).

5. Notes and Sources for Quotations and Topics:

290 "I write," *Zion*, 314.

291 "They traveled," *Zion*, 102.

291 "What I was trying," *Convers*, 117.

291 "the novelist," Sturges, "History Over," 18.

292 "Suffering, endurance," *Zion*, 12–13.

293 "in the rude shelter," *Zion*, 59.

293 "one feels," *Zion*, 71.

293 "Working like," *Zion*, 177.

294 "The fiction writer," "A Lens," 5.

294 "The ideas, the generalizations," "A Lens," 5.

295 "Until morning," *Zion*, 248.

295 "the harshest testing," "The story," *Zion*, 222.

295 Frozen heads, *Zion*, 194.

297 "fatigue," *Zion*, 245.

297 "It is hard," *Zion*, 255.

298 "a gaunt image," *Zion*, 255–56.

300 "It just mattered," Gilliam, 11/20/88.

300 "O.K., these areas," WS, 11/20/88.

301 "gave a very eloquent," Gilliam, 11/20/88.

301 "Fort Walsh," Gilliam, 11/20/88.

302 "he was very eloquent," Gilliam, 11/20/88.

302 "Everyone spoke," Levin, 118.

303 "This book is like," Moser, i.

303 "In no sense," "Quiet Crisis," 50.

303 "It will no longer," "Great Outdoors," 38.

303 "You cannot," "Great Outdoors," 38.

304 "they are the indispensable," "Great Outdoors," 38.

305 Don Gold, WS to B & B, 5/4/65.

305 "that does not challenge," "Powell," 151.

305 "From every evening," "Powell," 151.

306 "Save this tributary," "Powell," 151.

306 "was interested," *Convers*, 75.

306 NOTE: "I bequethe myself," from Walt Whitman, "Song of Myself," 52, *Leaves of Grass* (New York: The Modern Library, 1921), 103.

307 ostensibly a student, MS, 9/24/94

307 marijuana, Page, 11/17/88.

308 "got onto the Joe Allston," *Convers*, 76.

309 "Oh, yes, but," *Convers*, 77.

309 "knowing him," Scowcroft, 11/5/87.

310 "In essence," Houghteling, 8/13/88.

1 7: TROUBLE IN THE SIXTIES

1. *Interviews.* My thanks to:

Wallace Stegner, Mrs. R. E. Cameron, Harold Gilliam, David Brower.

2. *Published Material by Wallace Stegner:*

All the Little Live Things

"The Class of '67: The Gentle Desperadoes," [WS's essay is one of an anthology of essays in one article], *Nation*, 6/19/67, 780–781.

"California: The Experimental Society," *Saturday Review*, 9/23/67, 28.

"The Law of Nature and the Dream of Man: Ruminations on the Art of Fiction," *Bluebird*, 214–227.

"We have met the enemy and he is us," [*sic*] *Life*, 8/3/70, 2 pp. between pp. 32 and 33.

"The People Against the American Continent," *Vermont History* 35, Autumn 1967, 177–185.

"Sensibility and Intelligence," *Saturday Review*, 9/13/58, 24.

"Ansel Adams and the Search for Perfection," *One Way to Spell Man*, 144–160.

3. *Unpublished Material by Wallace Stegner:*

Manuscript of speech given at dedication of Mt. Ansel Adams.

Transcription of an interview conducted in 1982 by Ann Lage entitled "The Artist as Environmental Advocate," for the Sierra Club History Series and housed at the Bancroft Library, University of California, Berkeley.

4. *Published Material About Wallace Stegner:*

John Daniel, "Wallace Stegner: A Remembrance," *The Bloomsbury Review*, July/August 1993, 9.

Michael P. Cohen, *The History of the Sierra Club, 1892–1970* (San Francisco: Sierra Club Books, 1988).

5. *Notes and Sources for Quotations and Topics:*

311 "I was pondering," *Live*, 7.

311 "I am a tea bag," *Live*, 4.

312 "as a group," "Desperadoes," 781.

312 "the hippie poet," "Desperadoes," 780.

315 "I had no," *Bluebird*, 223.

315 "He was grumpy," Snyder to author, postcard, 4/1/94.

316 "Like the rest," "Experimental," 28.

317 "is in the midst," "The People," 180.

317 "this green sanctuary," "The People," 181.

318 "The hill that once," *Live*, 15.

319 "Oh, he was alert," *Live*, 23.

319 "It's his *temperament*," *Live*, 164–165.

320 "The hippie just wandered," *Convers*, 75.

321 "I don't mind," Cameron, 6/8/88.

321 "was taken completely," Cameron, 6/8/88.

321 "Never have," Cameron, 6/8/88.

321 "it's self-indulgent," WS, 1/28/88.

321 "which he composes," *Live*, 13.

322 "He understands," *Live*, 14.

322 "It used to comfort me," *Live*, 19.

322 "mother and daughter," *Live*, 101.

322 "Ruth was staring," *Live*, 206.

322 "a tiny procession," *Live*, 217.

322 "as volubly unintelligible," *Live*, 218.

322 "There ought to be," "Sensibility," 24.

323 " 'I should think,' " *Live*, 59.

323 "The suit was," *Live*, 21.

324 "Each new storm," *Live*, 124.

324 "Where you find," *Live*, 54.

325 "In nearly fifty," Daniel, 9.

325 "Once I found him," Daniel, 9.

326 "the most interesting," MS, 11/19/93.

326 "whose inaugural," *One Way*, 146.

326 "unfailingly open," "feels deeply," *One Way*, 152.

327 "it was the sound," dedication speech, ms., 1.

327 "It was a mistake," Lage, 24.

327 Mineral King, Cohen, 343.

328 "unswerving partisan," Lage, 28.

328 "wallow down," WS, 7/3/88.

328 Colorado River, Gilliam, 11/20/88.

328 Mineral King vote, Cohen, 342–44.

329 Litton, Adams, WS-Adams correspondence.

329 "up the coast," Cohen, 366.

329 "either false," "And whether," Cohen, 370.

330 Ansel Adams thought, Cohen, 373.

330 Litton felt, Cohen, 369.

330 "I wasn't very pleased," Lage, 26.

330 "open warfare," Cohen, 374.

330 "Some members," Lage, 27.

331 "that didn't scare," Lage, 25.

331 "Question Authority," Cohen, 413.

331 "he was taking the club," Lage, 26.

332 cocktail party, Gilliam, 11/20/88.

332 board election, Cohen, 423.

18: A NEW LIFE

1. Interviews. My thanks to:

Wallace Stegner, David Brower, Harold Gilliam, Janet Lewis, Richard Scowcroft, Ian Watt, Tom Moser, Nancy Packer, Wilfred Stone, Albert Guerard, George Sensabaugh, John Loftis.

2. Published Material by Wallace Stegner:

Angle of Repose

Conversations

"Some Worm of Power," letter to *Palo Alto Times*, 2/11/69, 27.

3. Unpublished Material by Wallace Stegner:

Transcription of an interview conducted in 1982 by Ann Lage entitled "The Artist as Environmental Advocate," for the Sierra Club History Series and housed at the Bancroft Library, University of California, Berkeley.

4. Published Material About Wallace Stegner and Related Topics:

David Levin, *Exemplary Elders* (Athens, Georgia: University of Georgia Press, 1990).

Irving Howe, *A Margin of Hope: An Intellectual Autobiography* (New York: Harcourt Brace Jovanovich, 1982).

H. Bruce Franklin, *Back Where You Came From: A Life in the Death of the Empire* (New York: Harper's Magazine Press, 1975).

5. Notes and Sources for Quotations and Topics:

333 Earth International Park, Cohen, 424.

333 announcements, WS, "Worm," 27.

334 "as Brower," "Worm," 27.

334 "a new breed," "Worm," 27.

335 "I notice," Brower, 6/19/89.

335 "pretty upset," Lage, 27.

335 "Later . . . I regretted," Lage, 27.

335 "It does seem to me," Lage, 30.

336 Relations got so bad, Packer, 6/3/87.

337 "Kittredge," Levin, 134.

337 "a poet of the minor theme," *Yvor Winters on Modern Poets* (New York: Meridian Books, 1959), 192.

337 volunteered, Guerard, 11/17/93.

338 Stegner . . . disliked, Watt, 6/2/87.

338 detested the label, Watt, 6/12/87.

338 Voice Project, Scowcroft, 11/5/87; Packer, 6/4/87; Guerard, 11/17/93.

338 "Wally did not," Guerard, 11/17/93.

339 Stegner felt threatened, Moser, 5/26/94.

339 "would not teach," Levin, 124.

340 NOTE: Irving Howe identified himself as part of a group, "New York Jewish intellectuals," which throughout his autobiography (*A Margin of Hope*) he declares to be superior to other Americans in intellect and taste.

340 "Where is Palo Alto," Stone, 6/3/87.

340 "was the rudest," Stone, 6/3/87.

340 "Something about California," Howe, 288.

340 "been protesting," Stone, 6/3/87.

341 teaching . . . impossible, Sensabaugh, 6/15/87.

341 "I told him," Scowcroft, 11/5/87.

341 arrogant, know-it-all, Packer, 6/3/87.

341 "a whole sense," Page, 11/17/88.

342 Bruce Franklin, Moser, 5/26/94.

342 Now a Maoist, Moser, 5/26/94.

342 "My purpose," WS, 1/27/88.

342 "He said, 'That ends it,' " Stone, 6/3/87.

343 "There was a real," WS, 1/27/88.

19: THE PULITZER AND BEYOND

1. Interviews. My thanks to:

Wallace Stegner, Evelyn Foote Gardiner, Froehlich Rainey, Wallace Page Stegner.

2. Published Material by Wallace Stegner:

The Sound of Mountain Water

Angle of Repose

"Western Record and Romance," *Literary History of the United States*, ed. Robert Spiller, Willard Thorp, Thomas H. Johnson, Henry Seidel Canby, Volume II (New York: Macmillan, 1948), 862–877.

Selected American Prose: The Realistic Movement, 1841–1900 [edited, with an introduction by Wallace Stegner] (New York: Rinehart, 1958).

"The Great Amazonian Plain," *Travel and Leisure*, February 1974, 31, 47–49.

Conversations

3. Unpublished Material by Wallace Stegner:

"The West: A Culture?," ms., n.d.

4. Published Material About Wallace Stegner and Related Topics:

T. H. Watkins, "Typewritten on Both Sides: The Conservation Career of Wallace Stegner," *Audubon*, September 1987, 88–90, 92, 94–97, 99–101, 103.

Mary Ellen Williams Walsh, "*Angle of Repose* and the Writings of Mary Hallock Foote: A Source Study," *Critical Essays on Wallace Stegner*, ed. Anthony Arthur (Boston: G. K. Hall, 1982), 184–209.

William Abrahams, "The Real Thing," review of *Angle of Repose*, *Atlantic Monthly*, April 1971, 96–97.

William Dubois, "The Last Word: The Well-Made Novel," *New York Times Book Review*, 8/29/71, 31.

Page Stegner, "A Brief Reminiscence: Father, Teacher, Collaborator," *Montana: The Magazine of Western History* 43, Autumn 1993, 54–56.

5. Notes and Sources for Quotations and Topics:

345 "I was creating," WS, 1/28/88.

346 "What really interests," *Angle*, 211.

346 "progressive decline," *Convers*, 94.

347 "In my mind," *Angle*, 17.

347 "the first-person," WS, 1/26/88.

347 "you're making half," *Angle*, 266.

348 "They didn't give a damn," *Convers*, 88.

348 "It was . . . like," *Convers*, 83.

349 "It's perfectly clear," *Convers*, 48.

352 "one of the best," *Convers*, 85.

352 "Reading her quaintly," "The West," n.p.

353 "I thought he would," Gardiner, 8/3/93.

356 "For years I have," "The West," n.p.

356 "continuities, contacts," *Angle*, 41.

356 "intractable self-reliance," *Angle*, 134.

357 "written a superb," Abrahams, 96–97.

357 "Had one of Mr. Stegner's," DuBois, 31.

358 Leonard blasted, *Convers*, 96.

358 "having left Harvard," *Convers*, 98.

359 "Through his efforts," Rainey, 11/7/90.

359 "My father," Page, 54.

360 Page decked him, Page, 54.

360 young Page, Wallace Page, 8/14/93.

360 "the magazine article," Wallace Page, 8/14/93.

361 "Always messing," Wallace Page, 8/14/93.

361 "He hated those thistles," Wallace Page, 8/14/93.

361 "spitting out," Wallace Page, 8/14/93.

362 "The entire history," *Water*, 19–20.

362 "to a noble," *Water*, 38.

363 "The number," Watkins, 103.

363 "I'm going to sound," Watkins, 103.

363 "By such a river," *Water*, 41.

20: BACK TO BIOGRAPHY AND ANOTHER PRIZEWINNING NOVEL

1. Interviews. My thanks to:

Wallace Stegner, Page Stegner, Mary Stegner, Nancy Packer, Wallace Page Stegner.

2. Published Material by Wallace Stegner:

"Bernard DeVoto," *A Literary History of American West*, ed. J. Golden Taylor, et al. (Fort Worth: Texas Christian University Press, 1987), 899–911.

The Uneasy Chair

"The Coast of Oregon," *Travel and Leisure*, Autumn 1971, 41–43.

"DeVoto's Western Adventures," *American West*, November 1973, 20–27.

"The Law of Nature and the Dream of Man: Ruminations on the Art of Fiction," *Bluebird*, 214–227.

"The Book and the Great Community," *Library Journal* 93, 10/1/68, 3513–3516; *Water*, 276–286.

4. Published Material About Wallace Stegner and Related Topics:

James R. Hepworth, "The Art of Writing: An Interview with Wallace Stegner," *The Bloomsbury Review*, March/April 1990, 6–7, 9–10.

"Angle of Repose," *San Francisco Opera Magazine 1976* (San Francisco: A Performing Arts Publication, 1976).

Critical Essays on Wallace Stegner, ed. Anthony Arthur (Boston: G. K. Hall, 1982).

5. Notes and Sources for Quotations and Topics:

364 "When Bernard DeVoto," *Literary History*, 899.

367 "*The Uneasy Chair* was," Hepworth, 10.

367 "biographies of *careers*" WS to author, 8/24/87.

368 "when he created," Page, 11/17/88.

370 "I'll type," WS, 11/5/87.

371 Blixen had been digging, transcript of an interview by Walter Rideout, et al., at the University of Wisconsin 8/86.

372 "Getting old," *Bird*, 171.

373 "I can read," *Bird*, 11.

373 "It is not arthritis," *Bird*, 89.

373 "They are not hostile," *Bird*, 117.

374 "If you were black," *Bird*, 120.

374 "old people," *Bird*, 10–11.

374 "These days," *Bird*, 195.

375 "It has seemed to me," *Bird*, 209.

375 "I've always thought," Packer, 6/4/87.

375 "terminate my," Page, letter to author, 10/6/94.

376 "Writers are far," *Bluebird*, 217.

377 "vigorously inventive," Thomas N. Walters, review of *The Spectator Bird*, in *Magill's Literary Annual 1977*, ed. Frank Magill (Englewood Cliffs, New Jersey: Salem Press, 1978), II, 769–775, as reprinted in *Critical Essays on Wallace Stegner*, ed. Anthony Arthur (Boston: G. K. Hall, 1982), 37–43.

378 "No society," *Water*, 285.

379 "with an American," *Opera*, 63.

379 "couldn't wade," *Opera*, 76.

379 "To cut yourself off," *Opera*, 26.

2 1: THE PAST THAT COMES BACK TO HAUNT US

1. *Interviews*. My thanks to:
Wallace Stegner, Page Stegner, Nancy Packer, Tom Moser, Robert Irvine, Milton Cowan.

2. *Published Material by Wallace Stegner*:
Recapitulation
American Places [with Page Stegner]
"Will Reagan Ride with the Raiders?," *Washington Post*, 1/20/81, 25, 33, 35, 37.
"If the Sagebrush Rebels Win, Everybody Loses," *Living Wilderness*, Summer 1981, 30–35.
"Land: America's History Teacher," *Living Wilderness*, Summer 1981, 4–13.
"Water Warnings, Water Futures," *Plateau*, Fall 1981, 2–3.
"Ask the Dust," *California*, December 1981, 188–189.
"The Twilight of Self-Reliance: Frontier Values and Contemporary America," *The Tanner Lectures on Human Values*, ed. Sterling M. McMurrin (Salt Lake City: University of Utah Press, 1981), 193–222.
"Tribute to Ansel Adams," *Update*, Winter 1986, 4–5.
"The Best Idea We Ever Had," *Wilderness*, Spring 1983, 4–13.
"Living on Our Principal," *Wilderness*, Spring 1985, 15–21.
"The Sense of Place," *Bluebird*, 199–206.
"Water in the West: Growing Beyond Nature's Limits," *Los Angeles Times*, 12/29/85, V, 3.
"The Spoiling of the American West," *Michigan Quarterly Review* 26, Spring 1987, 293–310.
"The Function of Aridity," *Wilderness*, Fall 1987, 4–18.

3. *Unpublished Material by Wallace Stegner*:
Notes for "A Conversation Between Ansel Adams and Wallace Stegner," presented at Stanford University, 10/15/82.
Video for "A Conversation Between Ansel Adams and Wallace Stegner," courtesy of the Stanford University Libraries, Special Collections.

4. *Published Material About Wallace Stegner and Related Topics*:

Joseph Hooper, "Gilbert Sorrentino: Writer Spurns Fame for Personal Vision," *Palo Alto Weekly*, 10/20/82, 29.

T. H. Watkins, "Typewritten on Both Sides: The Conservation Career of Wallace Stegner," *Audubon* (September 1987), 88–90+.

"Dick Scowcroft: Professor Emeritus," *Newsletter*, Department of English, Stanford University, 1 (Autumn 1979), n.p.

5. *Notes and Sources for Quotations and Topics*:

382 His son's advice, Page, 11/17/88.

382 "The girl from Utah," Crawford to author, 1/4/94.

383 "When Red Cowan," WS to author, 8/24/87.

384 "You take something," *Bluebird*, 227.

385 "could also be an art form," *Recap*, 265.

385 "He felt like," *Recap*, 274.

386 "When Mason is having," "I certainly do," *Convers*, 78.

386 "I think that's what," *Convers*, 78.

387 "Utah boys," *Newsletter*, n.p.

387 Gilbert Sorrentino, "Gilbert Sorrentino," 29.

387 "a direct, virile sort," "Gilbert Sorrentino," 29.

388 "Over my dead body," "I said, 'I'm sorry,' " Packer, 6/4/87.

388 "You just can't," Packer, 6/4/87.

389 "an attempt," *Places*, vii.

390 "We are the unfinished," *Places*, vii–viii.

390 "have not been inviting," *Places*, 105.

391 "Great Salt Lake," *Places*, 102.

391 "Like Aldo Leopold," *Places*, 106.

392 "He does not feel the need," Notes, 3.

392 "while standing," Notes, 3.

392 "We work in different," Notes, 5.

392 NOTE: Frost quotation from "Birches," *Complete Poems of Robert Frost* (New York: Henry Holt, 1949), 153.

392 "the fast approaching," video.

393 "Many of us agree," Notes, 3.

393 "The ranchers," "Sagebrush," 35.

394 "Let us not forget," "Frontier," 221–222.

394 NOTE: Frost quotation from "The Gift Outright," *Complete Poems of Robert Frost* (New York: Henry Holt, 1949), 467.

394 "The only real success," "Principal," 21.

395 "I have not been," Watkins, 100.

22: CROSSING TO SAFETY

1. *Interviews*. My thanks to:

Wallace Stegner, Mary Stegner, Page Stegner, Phil Gray (Jr.), Sherry Gray, Lewis and Nancy Hill, Langley and Nancy Keyes, Mrs. Penelope Lewis, Mrs.

Emilie Perry, Mrs. Marion Stegner, Froehlich Rainey, Mary Stone, Gwen Mann.

2. Published Material by Wallace Stegner:

On the Teaching of Creative Writing: Responses to a Series of Questions, ed. Edward Connery Lathem (Hanover, New Hampshire: University Press of New England, 1988).

The American West as Living Space

"Introduction," *Selected American Prose*, ed. Wallace Stegner (New York: Rinehart, 1958), v–xxvi.

Conversations, Second Edition, 1990.

Crossing to Safety

5. Notes and Sources for Quotations and Topics:

397 "risk superficiality," *Living*, v.

397 "the West is," *Living*, 3.

398 "If there is such," *Living*, 4.

398 "the West is defined," "Aridity," *Living*, 6, 8.

398 "Two lessons," *Living*, 19.

398 "no more fixed"; "has hindered," *Living*, 19–20, 22.

398 "the principal," *Living*, 23.

398 "bacterial cultures," *Living*, 24.

399 "original sin,"; "land monopoly," *Living*, 36, 56.

399 "the West in a relatively," *Living*, 38, 40.

399 "a higher duty," *Living*, 43.

399 dominate nature, *Living*, 45.

399 "lived alone," *Living*, 72.

399 "who really fired," *Living*, 73.

400 "The Western culture," *Living*, 65, 68, 69–70.

400 "her mining camps," *Selected*, xi.

400 "external, objective," *Selected*, v.

400 "not of cleverness," *Selected*, v.

401 "Actually, I didn't," *Convers*, Second Edition, xi.

401 *Crossing to Safety* started, letter to author, 6/26/89.

401 "there was no 'shape,' " letter to author, 6/26/89.

402 long lawns of lakefront, from a letter to WS from Sam Vaughan, 10/2/86.

402 "If there are such," *Convers*, Second Edition, xiv.

403 "There was nothing very dramatic," *Convers*, Second Edition, xii.

404 "It is a road," *Safety*, 5.

404 "wonders if," "There it was," *Safety*, 6.

405 "It was not a big serpent," *Safety*, 139.

406 "I could give all," *Complete Poems of Robert Frost*, 447.

407 "From the high porch," *Safety*, 10.

407 "Though I have been busy," *Safety*, 10.

407 best conversationalist, Phil Gray, 7/2/90.

407 writer's need for self-discipline, Sherry Gray, 7/1/90.

408 "always took seriously," Nancy Keyes, 7/3/90.

408 get out his hoe, Sherry Gray, 7/1/90.

408 "Two Tramps in Mud Time," *Complete Poems of Robert Frost*, 357–359.

409 "Perfect Picnic," Phil Gray, 7/2/90.

409 meat well-done, Nancy Keyes, 7/3/90.

409 "*Molly!* Don't," Nancy Keyes, 7/3/90.

410 "just sort of," Nancy Keyes, 7/3/90.

410 "I rose at six," *Safety*, 124.

410 "hired baby-sitters," Nancy Keyes, 7/3/90.

411 Phil Gray (Sr.), Nancy Keyes, 7/3/90; Sherry Gray, 7/1/90; Phil Gray (Jr.), 7/2/90.

411 "Life here," letter to author, 8/24/87.

2 3: GIVING ALL TO TIME

1. Interviews. My thanks to:

Wallace Stegner, Mary Stegner, Wallace Page Stegner.

2. Published Material by Wallace Stegner:

Conversations

All the Little Live Things

Crossing to Safety

On Teaching of Creative Writing (Hanover, New Hampshire: University Press of New England, 1988).

3. Unpublished Material by Wallace Stegner:

Acceptance Speech for Lifetime Achievement Award from California Arts Council (1990).

Acceptance Speech for PEN-West Freedom to Write Award.

"To Do" list left at WS's death.

Transcript of interview of WS by Terry Gross, *Fresh Air*, National Public Radio, n.d.

5. Notes and Sources for Quotations and Related Topics:

413 "the older you get," *Convers*, Second Edition, xiii.

414 "Lamely as I have limped," *Safety*, 11.

414 "Most of all," California Arts Council speech, 1–2.

415 "The days draw in," letter to author, 9/9/88.

416 speeches and readings, MS, 9/24/94.

416 environmental conference, 417 "So he drank," MS, 9/24/94.

417 "I found myself," letter to author, 10/17/90.

417 readings, MS, 9/24/94.

418 Royal Scotsman, blood disease, Bozeman, MS, 9/24/94.

419 "I believe that government," PEN-West speech, n.d.

419 the accident, the hospital, MS, 9/24/94.

420 "To Do," list provided by MS.

420 "Largeness," *Writing*, 38.

420 "There was a time," interview by Terry Gross, National Public Radio, n.d.

421 "Don't feel bad," *Live*, 287.

422 "those who lifted," from " 'Out, Out—,' " *Complete Poems of Robert Frost* (New York: Henry Holt, 1949), 171.

INDEX

☐ RECAPITULATION
Essays, memoirs, letters, and speeches, written over a period of twenty-five years, which expound upon the rapid changes in the West's cultural and natural heritage.

ISBN 0-14-026673-9

☐ REMEMBERING LAUGHTER
In the novel that marked his literary debut, Stegner depicts the dramatic, moving story of an Iowa farm wife whose spirit is tested by a series of events as cruel and inevitable as the endless prairie winters.

ISBN 0-14-025240-1

☐ A SHOOTING STAR
Sabrina Castro follows a downward spiral of moral disintegration as she wallows in regret over her dissatisfaction with her older and successful husband.

ISBN 0-14-025241-X

☐ THE SOUND OF MOUNTAIN WATER
Bruce Mason returns to Salt Lake City not to perform the perfunctory arrangements for his aunt's funeral but to exorcise the ghosts of his past.

ISBN 0-14-026673-9

☐ THE SPECTATOR BIRD
Stegner's National Book Award–winning novel portrays retired literary agent Joe Allston, who passes through life as a spectator—until he rediscovers the journals of a trip he took to his mother's birthplace years before.

ISBN 0-14-013940-0

☐ WHERE THE BLUEBIRD SINGS TO THE LEMONADE SPRINGS
Sixteen brilliant essays about the people, the land, and the art of the American West.

ISBN 0-14-017402-8

☐ WOLF WILLOW
In a recollection of his boyhood in southern Saskatchewan, Stegner creates a wise and enduring portrait of a pioneer community existing on the verge of the modern world.

ISBN 0-14-013439-5

FOR THE BEST IN PAPERBACKS, LOOK FOR THE

In every corner of the world, on every subject under the sun, Penguin represents quality and variety—the very best in publishing today.

For complete information about books available from Penguin—including Puffins, Penguin Classics, and Arkana—and how to order them, write to us at the appropriate address below. Please note that for copyright reasons the selection of books varies from country to country.

In the United Kingdom: Please write to *Dept. JC, Penguin Books Ltd, FREEPOST, West Drayton, Middlesex UB7 0BR.*

If you have any difficulty in obtaining a title, please send your order with the correct money, plus ten percent for postage and packaging, to *P.O. Box No. 11, West Drayton, Middlesex UB7 0BR*

In the United States: Please write to *Consumer Sales, Penguin USA, P.O. Box 999, Dept. 17109, Bergenfield, New Jersey 07621-0120.* VISA and MasterCard holders call 1-800-253-6476 to order all Penguin titles

In Canada: Please write to *Penguin Books Canada Ltd, 10 Alcorn Avenue, Suite 300, Toronto, Ontario M4V 3B2*

In Australia: Please write to *Penguin Books Australia Ltd, P.O. Box 257, Ringwood, Victoria 3134*

In New Zealand: Please write to *Penguin Books (NZ) Ltd, Private Bag 102902, North Shore Mail Centre, Auckland 10*

In India: Please write to *Penguin Books India Pvt Ltd, 706 Eros Apartments, 56 Nehru Place, New Delhi 110 019*

In the Netherlands: Please write to *Penguin Books Netherlands bv, Postbus 3507, NL-1001 AH Amsterdam*

In Germany: Please write to *Penguin Books Deutschland GmbH, Metzlerstrasse 26, 60594 Frankfurt am Main*

In Spain: Please write to *Penguin Books S. A., Bravo Murillo 19, 1° B, 28015 Madrid*

In Italy: Please write to *Penguin Italia s.r.l., Via Felice Casati 20, I-20124 Milano*

In France: Please write to *Penguin France S. A., 17 rue Lejeune, F–31000 Toulouse*

In Japan: Please write to *Penguin Books Japan, Ishikiribashi Building, 2–5–4, Suido, Bunkyo-ku, Tokyo 112*

In Greece: Please write to *Penguin Hellas Ltd, Dimocritou 3, GR–106 71 Athens*

In South Africa: Please write to *Longman Penguin Southern Africa (Pty) Ltd, Private Bag X08, Bertsham 2013*

Be a Good Friend

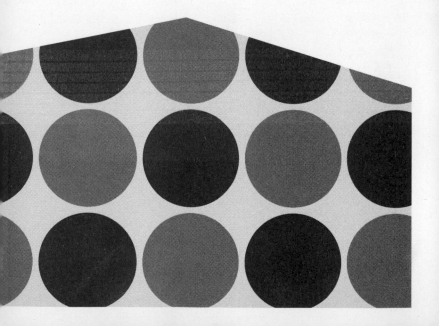

Forgiving others when they have done something mean isn't easy.

Sometimes I get so mad that I just want to scream. Maybe a friend calls me a mean name behind my back. Or worse, maybe she makes up a story about me that isn't true, but everyone believes it. So I promise I will stay mad at her forever. The problem with being mad forever is that forever never ends. And even though she was wrong in what she did, I miss hanging out with her. This is a real dilemma.

What can I do when something like this happens? I can talk my feelings over with my mom or my grandmother. Grandma always has a good suggestion for me. She believes that staying mad causes me more harm than my friend did. She suggests I try to see the situation differently. That isn't easy, but it's better than staying mad forever.

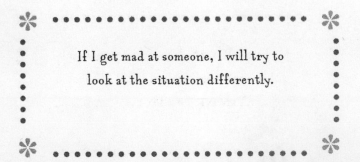

If I get mad at someone, I will try to
look at the situation differently.

Feeling left out is no fun.

When my friends get together to do something, I hate getting left out. Don't you? Once in a while all the kids on my block go down to the park and nobody remembers to ask me. I always wonder if they just forgot or if they didn't ask me on purpose. David, my stepdad, says kids sometimes don't notice when somebody's missing from the group. It hurts anyway. It's no fun being left out.

I know sometimes I forget to include someone when I invite kids to come over to my house, but I don't do it on purpose. Mom says we don't have room around the table for everyone. But they probably feel hurt anyway, just like I do.

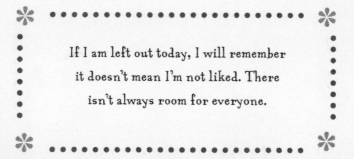

If I am left out today, I will remember it doesn't mean I'm not liked. There isn't always room for everyone.

How we treat others is like a boomerang.

My cousin Justin says that how we treat other people comes back to us like a boomerang. For example, if I am really kind to him, he will be really kind back. If I am polite to my teacher, she treats me politely, too. If I am nasty to my older brother, he usually gets mad and chases me. Remembering the boomerang idea saves me a lot of trouble.

The good part about the boomerang idea is that I know what I'll get back from people by how I treat them first. If I'm nice to other people in my life, pretty, happy experiences can happen. I'm going to practice first on my older sister by French-braiding her hair.

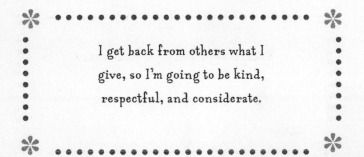

I get back from others what I give, so I'm going to be kind, respectful, and considerate.

Sharing with others is a good
way to honor them.

There are so many ways to share with other people. Can you think of some? How about giving half of your candy bar to a friend? Or maybe helping Reshma study her social studies? Aren't those good ways to share your friendship? Maybe inviting the new girl from down the street over to play computer games is the best way to share today.

Sharing whatever I have with another person makes me feel really good. You probably know someone at school who is really selfish and doesn't like to share. Does she seem very happy? Sharing changes people. Maybe you can share something with a selfish person today. It may make her want to try sharing, too.

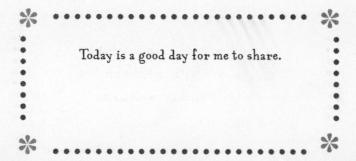

Today is a good day for me to share.

> I will be there as your sounding
> board whenever you need me.
>
> —Sandra Lamberson

If you fall down and scrape your knee, making it bleed, you want someone to take a look at it, don't you? If you get an F on a project you did for science class, you want someone to console you and help you understand that you can get better than an F next time. If you're nervous about a party you've been invited to, you want someone to talk to you about being brave. Everybody feels better when others show they're concerned. It means they care about us.

It's just as important to show others I care about them too. If one of my friends falls off her bike or gets the flu and has to miss school, I know it's nice to stop by her house to see how she is. Making an effort to be really kind and considerate to others is always good.

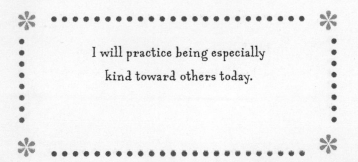

I will practice being especially
kind toward others today.

Do you express your appreciation to others?

It makes me really happy when my mom says she loves me. It assures me that everything is okay. But I forget to do the same for her. I get in such a hurry that I can't remember she likes hearing she is loved as much as I do.

I know I don't always show my friends how much I care about them, either. For instance, yesterday Beth brought an extra dessert for me in her lunch, but it had raisins in it, so I didn't eat it. Before I even thought about what I was saying or doing, I spit it out. I didn't even say thanks for thinking about me. I apologized later, which felt good, and she promised that she wasn't mad. The most important thing is that I really love having her for a friend, and I didn't show that. I don't think I will make that kind of mistake again.

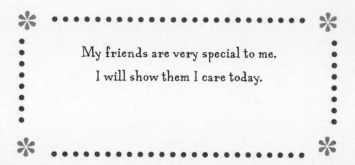

My friends are very special to me.
I will show them I care today.

New friends can make our
lives more interesting.

Have you ever been the new girl at school? Maybe you haven't ever moved into a new neighborhood, but lots of kids move around a lot. Sometimes it's because their mom and dad quit living together, and the mom moves to a different house. Or sometimes the dad gets a new job in another town, so the whole family has to move. It isn't easy being the new girl at school or in the neighborhood.

If there's a new girl in the classroom today, why not go up to her and say hi? Tell her your name and ask her to sit next to you at lunch. She'll feel a lot better if she's not alone. And you'll feel good about this too. Every time we make a connection like this with someone else, it gives us a warm, fuzzy feeling inside.

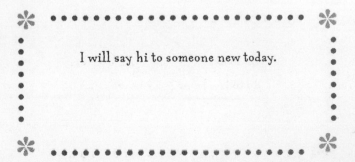

I will say hi to someone new today.

> What's important in life is
> how we treat each other.
>
> —Hana Ivanhoe

When you tell a friend you will take good care of her bike, are you really careful, or do you drop it when you get off instead of using the kickstand? How about when you borrow Sophie's Gameboy? Do you remember to turn it off as soon as the game is over, like you said you would?

How do you feel when a friend says she will keep a secret you told her, and then you find out she told everyone at the lunch table, and now they're all looking at you? Being able to trust another person is important. Making certain that someone else can trust you is important too.

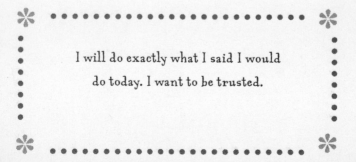

I will do exactly what I said I would
do today. I want to be trusted.

Making a new friend can be hard.

Do you ever wish a certain girl would be your friend, but you don't know how to ask her? Did anybody ever ask you to be her friend? Sometimes kids don't really ask, they just start talking to each other. When Jamie and I became friends, she just walked up to me and asked if I wanted to play jacks. I said yes, and we've been friends ever since.

My teacher says it's good to make friends with someone new in our class. It would be pretty lonely to move to a new school where you didn't know anyone. I'm so glad I have a lot of friends.

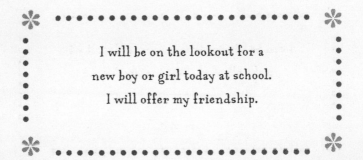

I will be on the lookout for a
new boy or girl today at school.
I will offer my friendship.

Best friends can make the day more fun.

Did somebody choose you as a best friend? Sometimes when I look at my classmates, they all seem to be paired up with a best friend already. That's probably just my imagination, though. Plenty of girls ask me to come over for parties and stuff.

Being a best friend doesn't just happen. It takes work. If I want a best friend, I have to be kind. I have to be willing to share my favorite things. I have to be willing to take turns. If I'm not anybody's best friend right now, maybe I should just enjoy all the good friendships I already have.

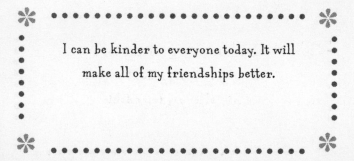

I can be kinder to everyone today. It will make all of my friendships better.

You don't have to like everybody,
but you can still be considerate.

There's a big difference between not liking someone and being mean to them. Just because I don't like the boy who sits behind me at school, or the girl who lives across the street, I don't have to call them names or play mean tricks on them.

What I do when I don't like someone is pay extra attention to the kids I like a lot instead. Sometimes I watch my friends who like the kids I don't like. Mom says I can learn something I need to know that way. My best friend at school actually likes the boy who sits behind me. Maybe I can learn why.

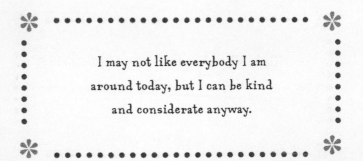

I may not like everybody I am
around today, but I can be kind
and considerate anyway.

Show others that they matter to you.

Sharing a treat that Mom sent in my lunch shows Maia that she's my friend. Asking Jackie to sleep over this weekend is a nice way of telling her she's important to me. Helping Mom clean up the family room and bringing in all the toys from outside shows her I love her.

My teacher says we all need to know that we matter. If we aren't noticed on the playground or chosen to join a dodgeball team, we can forget that we matter. But we do, she says.

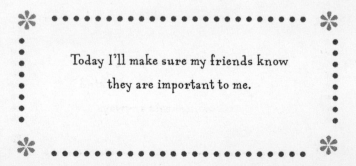

Today I'll make sure my friends know they are important to me.

All that is necessary to make this world
a better place to live is to love.

—Isadora Duncan

Molly didn't get to come to our school Halloween party because she was sick, so Mrs. Smith sent some pumpkin sugar cookies home with Molly's brother. I wonder if she was too sick to eat them. Mother said that even if she couldn't eat them, they might have made her feel better. She said that when somebody does something really nice for us when we are sick, it helps us feel better. Knowing we're really missed and loved helps us heal.

I guess this means I can help someone who's sick by being thoughtful toward them.

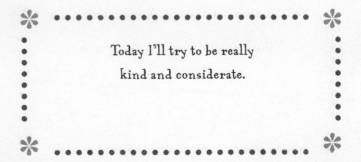

Today I'll try to be really
kind and considerate.

Compromise is part of getting along with others.

My dad always says, "It's the human condition to want everything your own way." But getting your own way all the time isn't even a possibility in most families. For instance, do you get mad when your mom says you and your brother have to take turns riding in the backseat of her van? Deciding who gets to go first when the class is playing T-ball can cause an argument too. Taking turns is the only fair way, isn't it? Not always having to be first in line means you're growing up. It means you're learning to compromise. Mom says grownups compromise all the time, especially when they're solving problems at work.

You will have a chance to compromise with a friend today, probably while playing a game. Try it and see how grown-up it makes you feel.

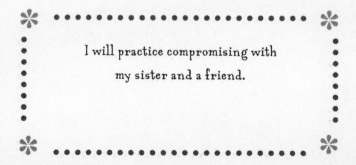

I will practice compromising with my sister and a friend.

Love one another!

Do you love everyone you know? I don't. Dad says I should try to love everyone. But when Theresa chases me for no reason or when Sandy laughs at me for getting a bad grade in math, I really don't feel like loving them. I don't want to love anybody who isn't really nice to me.

I don't even understand how you can love someone who is mean. Mom says people are only mean when they are afraid. She says mean people even need extra love. That's not easy to do! Mom says if I can't be loving, the next best thing to do is to not hurt them back at least. Maybe I can do that part.

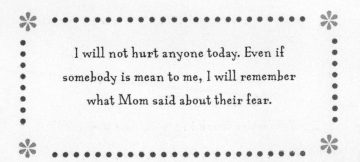

I will not hurt anyone today. Even if somebody is mean to me, I will remember what Mom said about their fear.

Friends notice each other's strengths.

I can do certain things better than Rusty, the girl who lives across the street. I can climb the apple tree much higher than she can. She's a lot better at jumping rope than me, though. I stumble too often. Rusty's mom says each one of us has special abilities, so we can do at least one thing better than anyone else. Reading and playing Scrabble are also things I am really good at.

If my friend Sara needs help in something I'm good at, it's fun for me to help her. Then I can ask her for help with math in return. She nearly always gets a perfect score when we have a math quiz. Helping one another makes all of us a little bit better at everything. That's what friends are for.

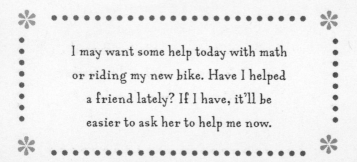

I may want some help today with math
or riding my new bike. Have I helped
a friend lately? If I have, it'll be
easier to ask her to help me now.

Staying mad at a friend hurts both of you.

One time I stayed mad at my friend Torry for two years! She had made fun of me at her birthday party in front of all the kids. She told everybody that Ben was my boyfriend, and he was at the party too. I never spoke to her at school or on the playground, and I didn't even go to her eighth birthday party the next year. She asked me to come too.

Staying mad isn't any fun. Even when it seems like we have a good reason for it, it makes life harder. I never knew what to do when a friend I wanted to play with was playing with Torry. I just had to walk away. I'm glad I finally got over being mad. One day I just stopped feeling mad. I don't even know why. Torry seemed glad too.

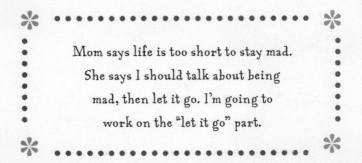

Mom says life is too short to stay mad.
She says I should talk about being
mad, then let it go. I'm going to
work on the "let it go" part.

I can change only myself, but
sometimes that is enough.

–Ruth Humlecker

Don't you wish you could make every one of your friends
do exactly what you want them to do? Everybody wishes
that, my stepmother says. She wishes we all would come
to the dinner table on time, just once! Dad wishes we
would get our bikes out of the driveway before he comes
home from work. My brother wishes I'd let him play with
my friends and me more often.

Changing someone else is hard work. Actually, it can't
be done. Sometimes a friend will do what you want her to
do, but that doesn't mean you changed her. All it means is
that she changed her mind about what she was going to
do. Trying to get someone else to change wastes a lot of
time. It's a lot easier just to change yourself.

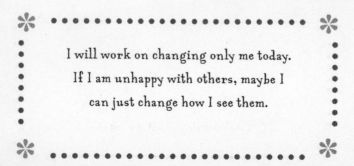

I will work on changing only me today.
If I am unhappy with others, maybe I
can just change how I see them.

Love your friends—they are very special.

How hard is it to think before doing something? Once in a while, it seems there just isn't time to think first. For instance, when Melissa suggested that we ignore Kira at recess because she hadn't shared her cookies with us, I did it before I even thought about it and then felt sorry later. After all, Kira has always been a good friend, and what I did was not loving at all. My mother explained to me that love is about giving to others first, not just getting something from them, and I forgot this. It's difficult to remember this, but it's not impossible.

Each day it's a good idea to think about a way to express love to a friend. Maybe I can help someone in my reading group who is having trouble with phonics. For sure, I can avoid doing something mean. That's another way of being loving.

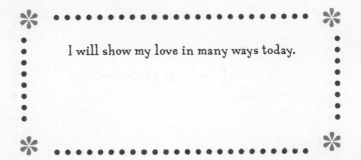

I will show my love in many ways today.

Open hearts can get hurt. Asking
for help is not always easy.

Sometimes the box of toys is too big to move by myself.
Maybe the bed is too wide to reach across to pull the sheets
straight. Maybe I keep forgetting how to spell certain
words for my spelling test. Every single day, there are
things I have to do that are too hard for me to do alone.
I'm lucky that I have friends and family and teachers who
can help.

Asking someone for help is a really good idea for another reason too: everyone likes to feel important. When I
get asked for help, I know I'm needed. And when someone
helps me out, I feel cared for. It's a great two-way deal.

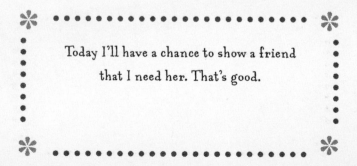

Today I'll have a chance to show a friend
that I need her. That's good.

21

Being angry with friends is not easy.

When I have a fight at school or with one of my friends who lives close by, it makes it hard to even see them. That's how I felt after Molly and I fought over who had the most jewelry. It's okay to feel like this for a while. Even adults sometimes feel this way. But I can't stay mad forever. What's the solution?

Deciding to say I'm sorry is not easy, but it's one solution. Asking Mom or Dad for help with working out a solution is another good idea. After talking it over with my dad, I realized I was angry at Molly because she had become so mean in the argument we had. And I realized I had been mean also. My dad promised that if I apologized for my mean words, I would feel better. I practiced saying I'm sorry to one of my stuffed animals. Then, when I saw Molly, I pretended I was still saying it to the stuffed animal, and I got the words out just fine. In no time at all, we were playing again and laughing. The jewelry argument was forgotten.

Everybody gets angry sometime.
It's important to find healthy,
respectful ways to talk about
anger and then to move on.

Fighting with a friend
always makes me sad.

When you can't get your best friend to play the board
game you have been asking her to play every day for a
week, do you get mad? Maybe she has a good reason for
wanting to play something else. Maybe she doesn't know
how to play the game you prefer, or has forgotten how to
play it. Did you ask her? If you want to spend time with
her, why not go ahead and play what she wants instead of
fighting over it, or make a deal to take turns getting your
way? Fighting is never any fun. At least I don't think so.
In fact, fighting makes my stomach upset.

When I'm about to fight over a difference of opinion,
sometimes I decide instead to let the other person have
her way. It really isn't so bad to give in once in a while. It's
better than having an upset stomach!

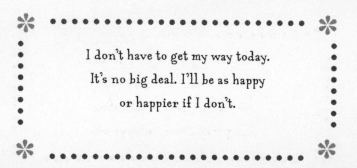

I don't have to get my way today.
It's no big deal. I'll be as happy
or happier if I don't.

I feel we have picked each other from
the crowd as fellow-travelers.

—Joanna Field

Mother says every friend I have is very important. She even says the reason for my many different friends is because of all the things I need to learn. For instance, Hannah is very pushy and always wants me to do things her way. She gets me to do things I might not do on my own, like the day we rollerbladed to the store. We laughed so much! I'm also learning how to say no to Hannah when it's something I really don't want to do.

From Joyce I am learning that it's better to share than to be stingy. She never wants to share anything with the rest of us. My big sister teaches me many things too. The first one that comes to mind is how important practice is for learning things. She practices her piano every day, and she is getting so good!

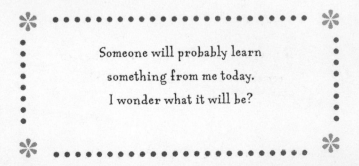

Someone will probably learn
something from me today.
I wonder what it will be?

Harmony exists in difference
no less than in likeness.

—Margaret Fuller

Sometimes Hayley makes me so mad! She always has to play at her house. She never wants to come to my house. She says she has more computer games than I have. I think she does, but it still isn't fair. Maybe I just have to make another best friend. When I asked Mom about this, she said I could decide it's okay to play at Hayley's house all the time.

Disagreements aren't any fun, but sometimes it seems like we can't avoid them. Maybe I can learn that disagreements aren't so important and that they are a part of friendships. My mom and dad have disagreements, but they're still married and laugh a lot. I'm not sure I understand how this works. But it helps me to think of my disagreements as a small part of a big picture. The bigger picture includes laughter, fun, good talks, and great company.

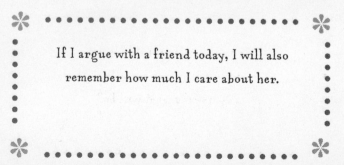

If I argue with a friend today, I will also
remember how much I care about her.

Sharing secrets requires trust.
–Kathy Andrus

Don't you love it when a friend shares a secret with you?
It makes me feel special when I have been chosen to hear
a secret. Knowing something that my friend has told no
one else usually means we're special friends.

Secrets can be about many things. A common secret is
sharing who we like among the boys. Maybe we share that
we miss our dad and wish he would move back home. Pretty
often the clothes I wear to school came from a garage sale,
but I am afraid to tell that secret to anyone. Mom says it is
good to tell at least one other person the secret things that
make me uncomfortable. She says my grandmother would
keep any secret I needed to tell someone.

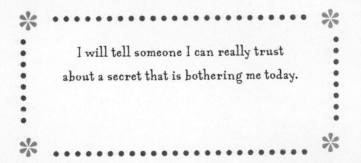

I will tell someone I can really trust
about a secret that is bothering me today.

Practice random acts of kindness.

There are so many ways to help. Most of them don't even take very long. For starters, I can help my mother or dad by picking out my own clothes for school. I can gather up all the things I need to put in my backpack. One of the easiest ways to help is by putting my dishes in the sink after I have eaten.

There are lots of ways to help at school too. How about when somebody spills milk at lunch? I can run and get a towel. I can lend Katey a pencil if she has forgotten hers. Last week I saw Zak go up to the new boy in our class and offer to show him where the bathroom was. The more often I do helpful things, the more I am a part of making the world a kind and gentle place.

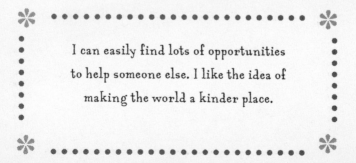

I can easily find lots of opportunities
to help someone else. I like the idea of
making the world a kinder place.

The most exhausting thing
in life is being insincere.
—Anne Morrow Lindbergh

Being sincere isn't all that easy sometimes. What do you do, for instance, when a friend asks you if you like her new winter jacket, and you actually don't like the color or the style very much? Gushing over it, saying you love it, isn't being sincere. Can you say something else instead? For instance, that you think the color looks good on her (if it does) or that it looks like it will keep her really warm? Feelings won't get hurt this way, and you won't feel like you have been dishonest.

Responding to friends insincerely makes me feel tired. Mother suggested my conscience gets worn out from insincerity. It's much easier on our minds and on our hearts, she says, if we give honest and loving answers to our friends and siblings.

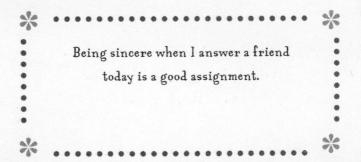

Being sincere when I answer a friend
today is a good assignment.

There are lots of ways to show respect.

Showing respect for others can be done in thousands of ways. Listening and paying attention to my teachers is one example. Picking up the umbrella Mrs. Brown dropped by my fence and taking it to her is another. Asking for seconds on the mashed potatoes at dinner is better than just reaching across the table for them. Holding the door open for an elderly man or woman shows respect too.

One of the easiest ways to show respect is to not interrupt while someone else is talking. I interrupt a lot! I often have to remind myself to wait for my turn to speak. It's not really very difficult to learn to be respectful. It just takes practice.

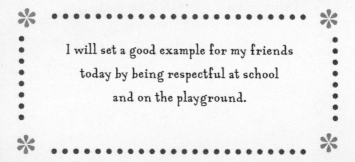

I will set a good example for my friends today by being respectful at school and on the playground.

How I see my world is different from how you see yours.

Have you ever noticed how many times a day you and a friend feel differently about something? For instance, I really love to play Scrabble. Finding words to make from the letters I have chosen is like doing a puzzle. My friend Robyn doesn't like Scrabble as much as Pictionary. Mother says our differences are because I like to read more than Robyn does and she likes art better than I do. That makes sense.

Most of us don't feel exactly the same way about anything. Miss Lubovitch says that's what makes this such a fun world. We are like colors in a rainbow, all different. Our differences make us special.

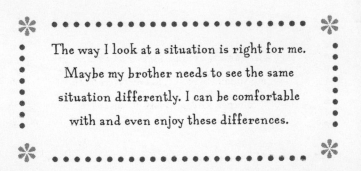

The way I look at a situation is right for me. Maybe my brother needs to see the same situation differently. I can be comfortable with and even enjoy these differences.

Being in charge is seldom fun for long.

Bossing my friends around hasn't made me very popular. They probably didn't like it when I insisted they play a game by my rules when they'd rather be doing something else. When a friend starts bossing me around, I don't like it either. Nobody is very happy when someone else tries to take charge. Why do people always want to take charge of others?

My stepmother says that's how people are. Everybody wants to be in control. It just doesn't work though. Everybody can't be in control. Some of us have to just follow along, or learn to take turns.

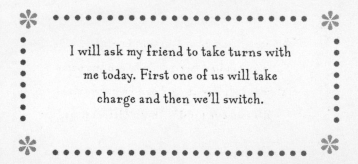

I will ask my friend to take turns with me today. First one of us will take charge and then we'll switch.

Be a Part of
Your Family

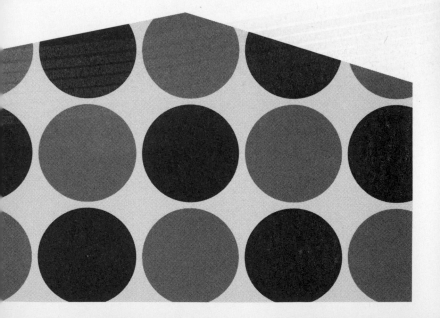

Love is all around, if only you look for it.

Sometimes I think receiving gifts for my birthday and other holidays is the most important sign of love from my family. Everybody likes gifts, but there are lots of other signs of love surrounding us throughout the day. And sometimes absolute signs of love don't actually look that way.

For instance, when Mom told me I couldn't go to Rachael's house after school, that sure didn't seem like love, but there was a reason she said no. Rachael's older sister has been in a lot of trouble with the police because of shoplifting, so Mom doesn't want me around her. Mom is protecting me, and that's certainly love. Having to go to bed by a certain time and eating breakfast before leaving for school are also signs of love. Moms and dads want us to be healthy, and that's a kind of love. Love is often more than a gift in a box.

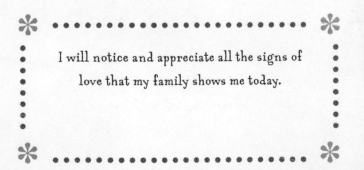

I will notice and appreciate all the signs of love that my family shows me today.

Let's notice the loving acts of others.

My mother told me that love can be expressed in many ways. She said there are as many small ways we can show others we love them as there are colors of crayons to choose from. So I thought about this, and here's what I figured out:

When I pull a clean blouse out of the closet today, it's because somebody lovingly washed it for me. They may have ironed it, too. When I was thirsty, there was milk or juice in the refrigerator because someone loved me enough to go shopping. Mom comes to get me when a friend calls on the phone, and even something that small is a very loving act.

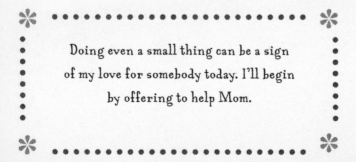

Doing even a small thing can be a sign
of my love for somebody today. I'll begin
by offering to help Mom.

> People rarely feel good about themselves
> for being unkind to others.
>
> —Mildred Newman

I just don't stop to think before I act sometimes. Yesterday my little brother used my bike without asking me, and I really yelled at him and made him cry. I was sorry afterward because he's so young. I wish I had thought first before getting mad.

When Mother told me I couldn't go to the park with Emily, I was really awful. I threw my jacket and stomped out of the kitchen. She never even yelled at me, but I felt bad anyway. I knew I was wrong. I wouldn't have done it if I had thought about it first. I get myself in trouble way too often just because I don't take time to think through my actions. Will I ever learn?

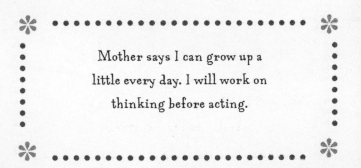

Mother says I can grow up a
little every day. I will work on
thinking before acting.

When it comes down to it,
we all just want to be loved.

—Jamie Yellin

How many ways do you know to show your dad you love him? Is responding immediately when he calls one way? How about pulling weeds around the flowers? Setting the dinner table without being asked, or playing with your little sister or brother so they don't bug him when he is on the phone or fixing dinner? One of the best ways, and it's pretty easy to do, is to listen very carefully every time he talks to you. Giving Dad your full attention is giving him a gift. He's probably saying something you need to know.

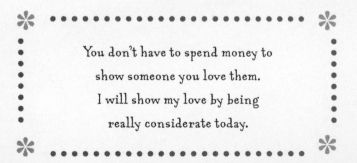

You don't have to spend money to
show someone you love them.
I will show my love by being
really considerate today.

> We can build upon foundations anywhere
> if they are well and firmly laid.
>
> —Ivy Compton-Burnett

Everybody has a family. The family acts as our foundation, Ms. Glasser says. It provides our security. Some families are much larger than others. My friend Sara has three brothers and two sisters. She has a big foundation! My foundation is small. There is just my dad, my brother, my grandmother, and me. My mother doesn't live with us anymore, but she is still part of my family.

My grandmother says it doesn't really matter how large or small a family is if its members are willing to help one another feel brave during the scary times and secure about being loved. In my family, we are really good at both of these things. Dad tells us he loves us every night when we go to bed.

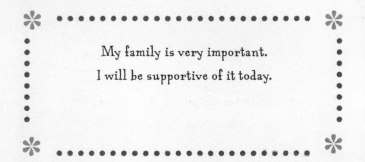

My family is very important.
I will be supportive of it today.

Showing others we love them is like giving them a gift.

Even in very small ways I can show my stepmom Stella that I really love her. I can help her by clearing the kitchen table after breakfast. I can pull the covers up on my bed. I can hang up my towel in the bathroom. I can pick up all my games, my books, and all my shoes from the middle of the living room.

When I pick up after myself, I save my parents from having to do extra work. That's a good way to show them I love them.

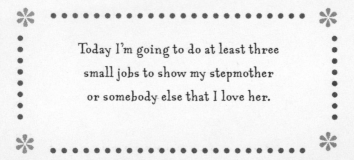

Today I'm going to do at least three
small jobs to show my stepmother
or somebody else that I love her.

Every person is your teacher.

—Florence Scovel Shinn

Does your mother ever have to remind you that everyone in your life is very special? Once in a while, I just don't like my sister. I have even wished she had never been born. And then I felt really scared for wishing it. Has that ever happened to you? It's hard to remember she is special when she breaks my hairbrush just before I need to use it, or when she gets into my favorite markers.

Mom says every single one of us is special to God and that means we are special to each other too. My sister made a beautiful drawing for me, and sometimes on hard days she can make me laugh in a way that no one else can. It's harder to understand what's so special about people I don't like. But Dad says I can learn kindness from the mean-spirited and generosity from those who are selfish.

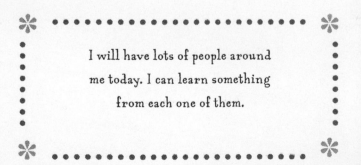

I will have lots of people around me today. I can learn something from each one of them.

To get help you usually must ask for it.

Do you ask for help when you need it, or do you think you should be able to do everything all by yourself? My little sister refuses to let me help her put her shoes on. Dad says that's because of her age.

Some things are really hard for me to do alone, like getting my new jeans buttoned. Putting my bike in the garage when Mom's new car is there can be hard too. She warned me not to scratch it! Even getting all my homework done is hard some days.

It's fine to ask for help. I can ask for help with anything, in fact. If my teacher or my mom thinks I should do it alone, they say so.

There are lots of people around
who can help me.
All I have to do is ask!

Being part of a family is like playing on a team.

I get an allowance, but I have to do certain jobs, and I have to do them really well if I want to get paid. Last year, all I had to do was put my toys away before I went to bed. This year, I have to clear the dinner table and sweep the kitchen floor every night. And I have to put my toys away too! Mom says the additional responsibilities are building my character as well as adding to my piggy bank.

My older sister even helps cook. I guess I will, too, when I get older. Mom says everybody has to help out because she doesn't have time to do everything and be a doctor too. She says it's part of being a family, like being on a team together.

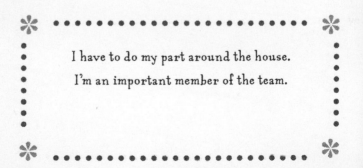

I have to do my part around the house.
I'm an important member of the team.

Love is all around us.

—Marianne Williamson

Do you know what it means to love somebody? Love is a pretty hard word to explain, isn't it? Even moms and dads and other adults can't always explain it. But most of us know love when we feel it. When your dad surprises the family with a pie from the bakery, isn't that showing love? Another time we can feel love is when a parent or maybe a grandparent tucks us into bed at night, especially if they sit there a while and chat with us.

Love makes me feel cozy and safe inside. Love helps me know that other people want to be close to me. Love is being treated in kind ways. Sometimes love is being held close when I'm scared.

Do you show others that you love them? Do you notice the love coming to you?

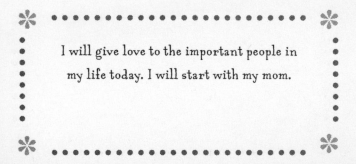

I will give love to the important people in my life today. I will start with my mom.

> The greatest gift we can give one
> another is rapt attention.
>
> —Sue Atchley Ebaugh

Have you noticed there are times when you can't get anyone to pay attention to you? Maybe you're having a problem with your homework, or you've had a fight with a friend, and you want to talk it over with your mom or dad. Some days they are just too busy with their jobs and all the work around the house to listen. You could ask your teacher, but she gets very busy too.

What do you do when you're bursting inside with the need for someone to talk to? Sometimes I have to say it's really important that you listen, right now. And when she says I need to listen to her, whether it's about the next day's schedule or about my aunt who's very sick, I should give her my full attention too.

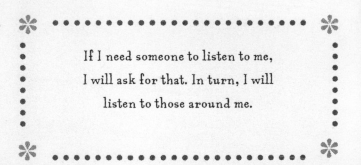

If I need someone to listen to me,
I will ask for that. In turn, I will
listen to those around me.

I am learning how to help others.

Does your mother have a job away from your house? Mine does. Most moms have to work at jobs because food and clothes cost so much. Moms generally want us to have all the things we need and, unless they work, we can't have those things. Does your mom ever ask you for help since she is so busy? Are you willing and eager to help her?

Some kids whine when their mom asks for help. Maybe you have whined a lot in the past, but you don't have to whine anymore. Part of growing up is being willing to help when there is work to be done. Being asked to help is a sign your mom thinks you are growing up. That's a compliment! You can even offer to help before being asked.

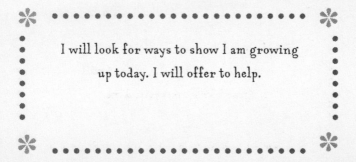

I will look for ways to show I am growing up today. I will offer to help.

There is no healing without forgiveness.
—Helen Casey

Forgiveness is a difficult idea for many kids my age. When somebody lets me down, it can take me a while before I'm ready to forgive.

Last week my dad forgot to come to my school program. He had promised he would be there, and I kept watching for him. When he got home that night, he said he was sorry. It made me feel better, but I was still sad he missed hearing me sing "Amazing Grace." He asked me to sing it just for him, but I was too upset and mad at him. The next night, he asked again and when I sang it, he had tears in his eyes. I could see how much he loved me, and my heart opened and I felt ready to forgive him.

My Aunt Karen says that asking for forgiveness can heal broken relationships. Do you understand what she means?

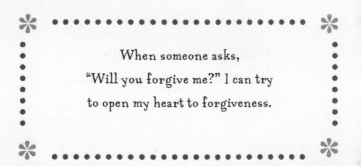

When someone asks,
"Will you forgive me?" I can try
to open my heart to forgiveness.

> It is healthier to see the
> good points of others.
>
> —Françoise Sagan

My younger brother often makes lots of noisy engine sounds when he's playing with his trucks. This can really get to me. He also sometimes tries to start fights with me by making faces, grabbing at my arm, or taunting me.

Often all I can see is that my little brother is trouble with a capital T. It's harder to also notice how much he wants to hug me and tell me a story when I've been gone overnight. On the night I burst into tears because I lost my student council election, he hugged me and offered to give me his soccer trophy.

It's really easy to notice the faults of people in our family. But it's important to pay attention to the loving gestures that are meant just for us. That's the way to open up our hearts to give and receive more love.

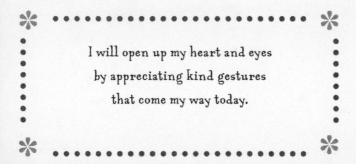

I will open up my heart and eyes
by appreciating kind gestures
that come my way today.

Be Your Best Self

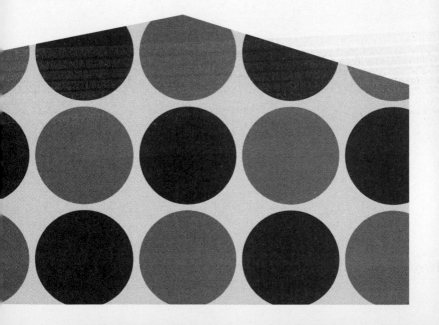

Encouragement helps me move ahead.

The first time I tried to ride my bike, I was sure I couldn't do it right. I was lucky that someone could help me. My mom was at work, so my friend Susie hung onto the seat while I tried to ride down the sidewalk. It worked! One of the main reasons was that she told me, over and over, that I could do it. She was right. After that, all I needed was lots of practice.

I can encourage my friends, just like I've been encouraged, when they're trying something for the first time. I don't have to be a grownup to encourage others. All I need to do is tell them again and again that I know they can do it. Pretty soon they'll believe it too!

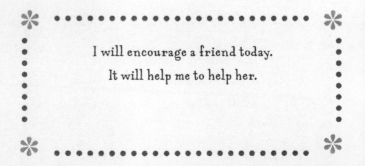

I will encourage a friend today.
It will help me to help her.

Needing help is okay.

Most of us need help with stuff every day. It can start with getting dressed in the morning. Maybe the zipper on my jeans is broken. Maybe I need help pouring milk for my cereal.

Mrs. Carl says asking for help with math is better than trying to copy off somebody else's paper. I know that's right. When I looked on Sheila's paper last week, I got the answer wrong, Sheila did too, and we both got in trouble. Next time, I'll ask for help instead.

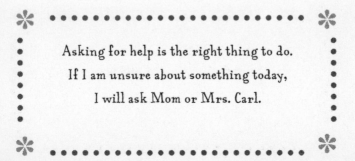

Asking for help is the right thing to do.
If I am unsure about something today,
I will ask Mom or Mrs. Carl.

Be willing to give in.

Trying to make my twin brother Jake or my friend Samantha play cards my way isn't easy. Everyone has their own rules, and they don't agree with mine. No matter how hard I try to convince Jake or Samantha, they won't give in. That means we're stuck unless I give in. Does that seem fair to you?

It's hard to give in when I think I'm right about something. But I guess I can do it. My foster mother says it's good practice to give in, at least once in a while. She says I'll understand this when I get older. She says if we try it a few times, we'll see it's not such a big thing after all. I'm not so sure. But it's worth a try.

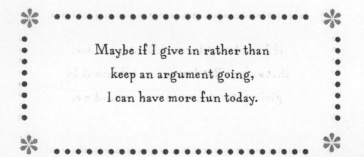

Maybe if I give in rather than
keep an argument going,
I can have more fun today.

There are good and bad ways
to seek attention.

Do you ever show off to get attention? Just last week, I rode my bike really fast down the street without touching the handlebars to show off in front of the new girl who moved in across the street. I know she was watching. Once in a while I wear my very best clothes to school because I want Mrs. Hadley to give me a compliment.

It's okay to want attention. Everyone likes it when people notice them. But there are good ways and bad ways to get attention. Bad ways get people's attention at other people's expense, like by interrupting them or making jokes about them or teasing them.

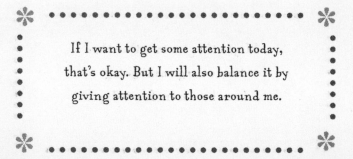

If I want to get some attention today, that's okay. But I will also balance it by giving attention to those around me.

I am learning to accept responsibility for my behavior.

Every day I'll probably have to say I'm sorry to someone. If I'm grouchy when I wake up, I may say something mean to a member of my family. They aren't the reason I'm grouchy, so I should say, "I'm sorry." Maybe in my rush to get ready for school, I spill my milk. If so, I should help to clean it up and say, "I'm sorry.

Running into a classmate because I'm not watching where I'm going is another reason for being sorry. Being mean to the person behind me in line in the lunchroom or laughing when someone misses a question the teacher asks are also very good reasons for saying I'm sorry. Whenever I do something I wouldn't want someone else to do to me, it's time to say, "I'm sorry."

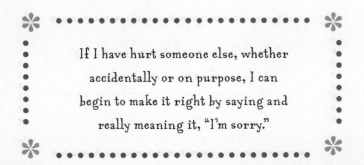

If I have hurt someone else, whether accidentally or on purpose, I can begin to make it right by saying and really meaning it, "I'm sorry."

Growing up happens in many ways.

Brittany is the tallest girl in my class at school. She almost comes up to the teacher's shoulder. I'm still the shortest one in my whole row. Will I ever grow up? I heard my mom tell my brother to grow up, and he's a lot bigger than me. Maybe "growing up" is not just about being bigger. What else does it mean?

When I asked Dad, he said growing up sometimes means thinking like an older person. For instance, stopping to consider what might go wrong before trying an activity that I've never tried before. He says it can mean not being selfish too, and saying "Please" and "Thank you" every time I get the chance.

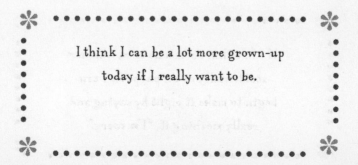

I think I can be a lot more grown-up
today if I really want to be.

Do you know what it means to have a healthy lifestyle?

Nobody can always prevent sickness. But everyone can learn how to take better care of herself, according to my Aunt Sandra. She is overweight, and she wishes she had been more careful with what she ate when she was younger. She frequently makes suggestions to my mother about what she should be feeding my sister and me so we don't gain too much weight.

I am not very fond of carrots and broccoli, but I love the dip my aunt makes for them. It's a good way of getting used to them, Mom says. Abbey and I recently enrolled in gymnastics too. I didn't want to go at first, but now I like it. Mom says it's important to be strong and gets even more important as women get older. She goes to a gym every day for a workout. I think I may want to do that when I get older too. She has a lot of energy, which she says comes from exercise.

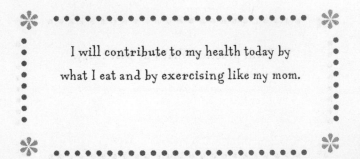

I will contribute to my health today by what I eat and by exercising like my mom.

Comparing yourself with a friend can make you feel insecure.

Everyone's good at something. Laurie jumps rope really well. She can even jump a double rope. Bryan can outrun most of the kids on the block. Caitlin can paint really beautiful birds and flowers.

We're all good at some things. When I remember this, I don't feel as bad when I see I can't paint as well as Caitlin or run as fast as Bryan. Bryan probably wishes he could read as well as I do. None of us does the same at everything. That's what makes this an interesting world, my dad says.

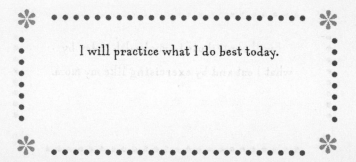

I will practice what I do best today.

It's a simple formula: Do your best
and somebody might like it.

—Dorothy Baker

Are you as well behaved as your mother wants you to be?
For instance, would you feel okay having your mother
watch you during the day? I know that sometimes I do
mean things that I wouldn't want my mother to see.

Kyle, one of the boys in my room at school, is pretty
mean all the time. I wonder what his mother taught him.
I'll bet she doesn't know how he acts. I wonder if he ever
feels afraid she'll find out.

Worrying about whether my mom will find out
taught me to think twice before doing many of the things
that pop into my head. I guess that's good.

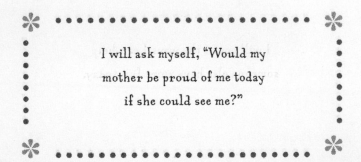

I will ask myself, "Would my
mother be proud of me today
if she could see me?"

Spreading joy around is good work.

You know what's really fun to do? Helping other people have more fun. Sometimes Mom is pretty tired in the morning if my baby sister cried all night. Teasing her a little about something gets her to smile. Maybe I'll give some attention to the dog, or better yet, my little brother or sister. Helping someone else have fun is really important.

There are places I go every day where I can help others have fun. Maybe at recess, or maybe I can crack some jokes at lunchtime. Playing tag after getting home from school or surprising Mom with a big hug when she didn't expect it can be fun too.

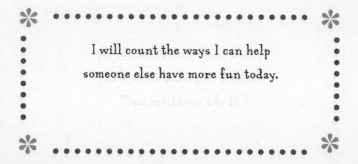

I will count the ways I can help
someone else have more fun today.

Let's make life less difficult for each other.

—George Eliot (Marian Evans Cross)

"What have you recently done to help out one of your parents?" This is a question we had to write an answer to in school last week. My mom and dad both have jobs, so my brothers and I have lots of chores at home. I wrote a pretty long list of ways I had helped. The next question asked how we had helped a friend. Just the day before, I had helped Samantha draw a map of the United States. It wasn't really that hard because we could copy it from a book, but I am better at drawing than she is. She shared her dessert with me at lunch that day.

My mom says that anytime we help someone else, we are helping ourselves at the same time. This is how it works: Helping others makes you feel good about who you are. And feeling good about yourself makes it easier for you to be successful when you try a whole new activity. Our confidence grows when we help others.

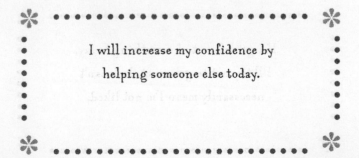

I will increase my confidence by
helping someone else today.

Everybody gets left out sometime.

Last week Whitney asked everybody in our swimming class except me to come to her pizza party. I felt really sad when she left me out. Mom said maybe she just forgot. I could have asked her if she forgot, but I was scared to. What if she said she just didn't want me to come?

Everybody gets left out once in a while. Mom said the other day her two best friends didn't ask her to go for a walk with them. She felt bad too. Why do we feel such pain if we are left out? Probably we think it means we aren't liked. But then I've never asked Samantha to sleep over. And I like her. So maybe not getting invited to do something isn't really such a big deal.

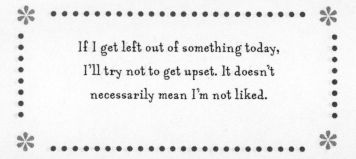

If I get left out of something today,
I'll try not to get upset. It doesn't
necessarily mean I'm not liked.

Criticism is hard to listen to.

When Dad says I haven't cleaned my room very well or my teacher calls me to her desk to talk over mistakes on my math test, I feel pretty uncomfortable. I want praise for everything I do, even though Dad says this isn't realistic. When I'm not praised, my feelings get hurt.

Part of growing up is being able to listen to criticism without getting angry or hurt. I need to remember that part of learning to do something better is first seeing what I've done wrong.

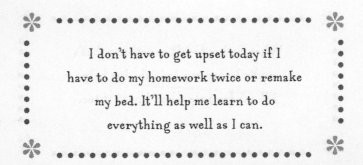

I don't have to get upset today if I have to do my homework twice or remake my bed. It'll help me learn to do everything as well as I can.

Needing help is human.

I need help a lot. Often I can't read all of the words in the book I get at the library. Sometimes I need help buttoning my shirt because the buttons are so tiny they're hard to hold onto. If it's completely full, the gallon milk container is too hard to lift by myself.

Knowing when to ask for help is part of growing up. I can do lots of things alone, but it's smart to ask for help when I really need it. And for sure I'll ask for it in an emergency.

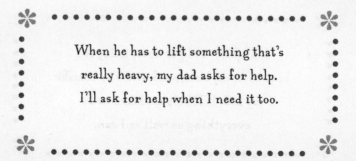

When he has to lift something that's really heavy, my dad asks for help. I'll ask for help when I need it too.

Sometimes I think I am the
luckiest person in the world.

—Jane Fonda

Last week I really wanted to be Molly because she got a new bike. This morning I want to be my baby sister because she gets to stay home. I have to go out in the cold, rainy weather to school. Wanting to be someone is natural. Not many girls think they are lucky to be who they are.

But it is really important to realize I'm exactly who I need to be already. God only made one of each of us, so we're all unique and important. My aunt often says, "Turn your eyes toward all that you have, rather than toward what you don't have." When I do this, I can see many ways in which I am lucky.

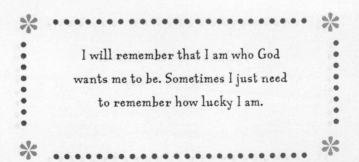

I will remember that I am who God
wants me to be. Sometimes I just need
to remember how lucky I am.

Life is about avoiding jealousy,
overcoming ignorance, and
building confidence.

—Katie Leicht

I had dinner with my dad last night. He noticed I was often quick to say I couldn't do something that my friends were all good at. He asked me how I felt about my abilities. I told him I was scared a lot of the time and embarrassed when I couldn't keep up.

I'm not as embarrassed about feeling uncomfortable now that I know he felt the same way when he was younger. The first thing we are going to do is work together on rollerblading. He said he puts little messages on his mirror when he is trying to change how he is feeling about something.

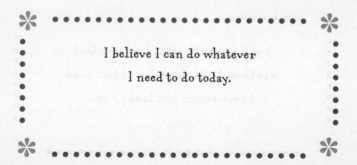

I believe I can do whatever
I need to do today.

Wanting to be noticed is okay.

When I wear a new dress to school or put on my patent leather shoes to go to the movie with Jennifer and Emily, I hope someone notices and tells me they like what I am wearing. My grandfather says it's normal to want others to notice us. He also says it's normal to not always notice what others are wearing or doing, so I shouldn't expect my friends to always notice me. I'm glad he lives with us because he explains many things to me.

Sometimes I get loud when I want others' attention. Dad pointed out to me that I seem to get bossy and loud when my brother or a friend hasn't asked me to play. When I want others to notice me, for whatever reason, and they are too busy with someone else, I feel left out. I even wonder if they can't see me! Isn't that silly? I am sure I haven't really disappeared.

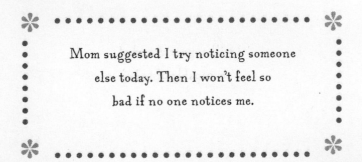

Mom suggested I try noticing someone
else today. Then I won't feel so
bad if no one notices me.

Do not compare yourself with others.
Make your own beautiful
footprints in the snow.

—Barbara Kimball

My grandmother says that God needs every one of us to be a little bit different because there are so many jobs to be done on this Earth. I need to remember this, I think, because I often wish I were more like someone else.

Dad says we all make different footprints in the sand and the snow. I am not sure I understand what he means, but he says I will when I grow up. For now, I am trying to be glad I am who I am. One of the things about me that is different from all of my friends is my ability to play the piano. I can actually play a song after hearing it only a couple of times. Leah and Holly both wish they could do this.

I will appreciate what
I am capable of today.

Feeling shy is common.

Starting at a new school is not the easiest thing to do. I had to do it twice last year! Going by myself to the YWCA for swimming lessons takes courage too. Even going to my cousin's tenth birthday party, where I won't know any of the kids but her, scares me a little. Why do I have all of these feelings?

Dad says it's because I am shy. He says nearly everybody feels shy when they go someplace for the first time. Even he felt shy when he started his new job at the phone company. I'm just like everyone else, I guess. That makes me feel a little bit better.

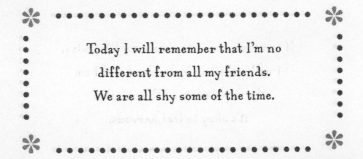

Today I will remember that I'm no different from all my friends. We are all shy some of the time.

Being the new girl in class can be hard.

It's pretty hard for me to go up to a bunch of kids when I don't know any of them. I'm afraid they won't talk to me or worse, they may chase me away. I can remember when my mother started her new job. She had "butterflies" in her stomach, she said. Having butterflies means you are feeling scared on the inside about doing something new.

It's nice to know that everyone has a hard time being the newest person in a group. Do you know what would be a nice thing to do? The next time a new girl shows up in your class, go up to her right away and say "Hi." She will feel so much braver then.

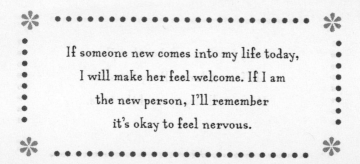

If someone new comes into my life today,
I will make her feel welcome. If I am
the new person, I'll remember
it's okay to feel nervous.

If you have made mistakes, even serious ones, there is always another chance for you.

—Mary Pickford

Making mistakes is part of living, according to my teacher Ms. Banks. She says that no one can expect to be perfect in everything all of the time. Even though she knows all of the words in our books, she even mispronounces one sometimes because she's thinking about something else. Doing our best is what really matters, she says.

I don't always do my best. Sometimes I watch television instead of studying for a test in math. When I miss some problems in class the next day, I know why. This morning I didn't make my bed very well, either. I just threw the covers over my pillow and left all of my stuffed animals on the floor, and I didn't really like coming home later to that mess. I always tell my mother I will try harder from now on.

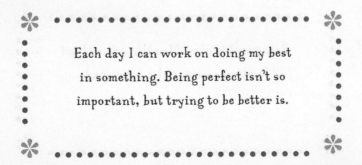

Each day I can work on doing my best in something. Being perfect isn't so important, but trying to be better is.

Anger is natural. Try to handle it constructively.

Is there one thing that makes you really angry? When my brother turns off the light while I'm in the basement, I get really angry. I'm afraid of the dark. My imagination gets the best of me, according to Mom. After he did this for the tenth time last week, I went wild in his bedroom and threw his favorite toys against the wall. He got the idea. Mom set us both down for a family meeting. She said anger was a natural feeling and she feels it too sometimes, but handling it in more constructive ways was a sign of growing up. She asked us to think of some.

I remembered a book Grandmother once read to us. It told about a girl who planted a flower in her backyard every time she got really mad at someone. By the end of the book, she had a beautiful garden.

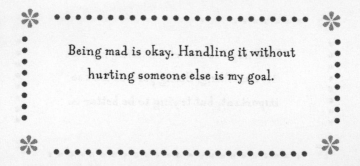

Being mad is okay. Handling it without hurting someone else is my goal.

Praising others can bring
praise back to us.

Having the teacher notice how carefully I wrote my spelling lesson made me feel really good. Doing a really careful job of making my bed, pulling the sheets extra tight, will get noticed by Mom, I hope. Whenever I do a job around the house really well, she usually tells me how glad she is. I love having people notice my good work. Am I different from my friends?

Mom says not. She says everyone likes to be praised. I am sure I'll see a friend do something today that I can praise her for. Sherry is usually the neatest printer in the whole room. Maggie makes us all laugh. Sue can talk to everyone in our class, even the shy and quiet ones.

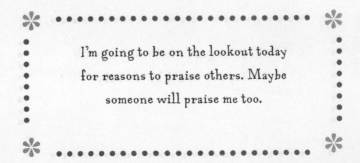

I'm going to be on the lookout today
for reasons to praise others. Maybe
someone will praise me too.

Be gentle, like a mother cat
with her kittens.

It's easy to be gentle when I touch a baby kitten or the little yellow chick I got at Easter time one year. When I get to hold a newborn baby, it's easy to be gentle too. Mom says I can learn to be gentle in other ways as well. I can answer people's questions with a gentle voice. I can speak to my friends and family in a gentle way. I can help set the table for dinner gently too.

Being gentle is more than just a way of touching something. It's a way of thinking and speaking and even listening. It means I'm trying to be soft and full of love. When my mom is soft and loving toward me, I feel special. I can show that kind of softness to others too.

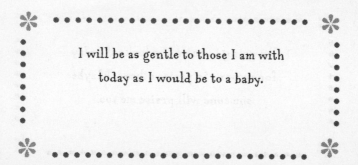

I will be as gentle to those I am with
today as I would be to a baby.

Everyone is shy sometimes.

If you've never played with a certain girl before, are you shy about asking her to jump rope with you? Maybe that hasn't happened to you, but maybe you've tried to find a place to sit in the lunchroom when your friends have filled up their table already. Are you nervous about sitting with a group of kids you don't know very well?

Feeling a little bit scared is what shyness is. But there really isn't anything to be scared of. I've been told that we always have a guardian angel who will never leave our side. So even when I end up having to sit by a stranger at lunch or on the bus, I'm not sitting there alone. My "best friend" is right next to me. That's really nice to know.

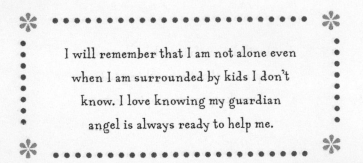

I will remember that I am not alone even when I am surrounded by kids I don't know. I love knowing my guardian angel is always ready to help me.

People see things very individually.

If you've ever watched a car accident or a friend falling off a bike, you probably thought you saw exactly what happened. But if someone standing right next to you was watching the same thing, you may have argued over what really happened. That is because we all see things differently.

Each of us sees through our own eyes. Miranda and I are always together, so we see the same things all of the time. And we often see things just a little bit differently. Sometimes this drives me crazy, but mostly, I feel like we learn a lot from each other. She always surprises me!

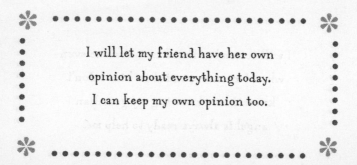

I will let my friend have her own
opinion about everything today.
I can keep my own opinion too.

Worrying solves nothing.

I am really a worrywart sometimes. A worrywart is someone who worries all the time over really silly things. They worry about the dog getting loose even though they know he is safe in the yard. Or they worry about whether it will rain two weeks from now, when the school picnic is planned.

Do you ever worry about whether a particular friend will stay your best friend forever? Some kids worry that their clothes are not as nice as everyone else's. There are so many things to worry about. But worrying never helps, according to my stepmother Laura. She says it drains our energy!

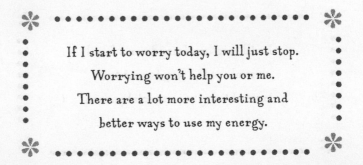

If I start to worry today, I will just stop.
Worrying won't help you or me.
There are a lot more interesting and
better ways to use my energy.

I want to feel myself part of things.

—Joanna Field

I'll bet you hope the teacher likes you the best of all the girls in your room! That's the way most of us feel. Adults like to be considered special too. Everybody wants to be an important part of the action. And do you know what? You are important. You are special!

Every one of us is special. Do you know why? Because there is no one exactly like you. There are no two people exactly alike in all the world. Every one of us is needed to make the rest of the world complete.

If you are special, that means your friend Emily is special too. Do you always treat her like you think she is special? Maybe this would be a good thing to do: show the people you care about that you know they are special.

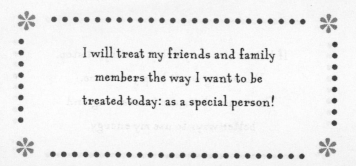

I will treat my friends and family members the way I want to be treated today: as a special person!

Meeting new people comfortably
is a sign of maturity.

Have you ever been invited to a birthday party where you didn't know many of the girls and boys and you felt scared to go? It's scary sometimes to meet new people. But if we can remember that these kids are just as scared as we are, we will feel better. When we say hello and they answer back, we begin to feel better. It's kind of magical. And before you know it, you are having fun.

It is good if we can learn how to meet new people because they will always be coming into our lives. A new family may move in next door. New kids will come into our classroom at school. That happens every year a few times. The after school program will mix us up with a lot of kids we don't know from all over town. If we decide to look forward to meeting them, our lives will be more fun. We can do it!

If a new girl comes into my room today,
I will try to be the first one to say
hello at recess. I will remember
that she might be scared.

Crying is okay.

Do you ever start to cry even when you can't think of a single reason for it? That happens to me sometimes. Mom says maybe I had a bad dream even though I can't remember it. I always feel sad when my dad has to cancel our plan to go out for supper. I only see him two times a week. Things can happen in a day that make me feel bad, and crying is a natural reaction. It can make me feel better. Some people even think it washes away the sadness.

My older sister cries at sad movies. Moms cry when their children have been gone a long time and they don't know where. My dad sometimes cries when he hears a beautiful piece of music in church or at a concert. My brother cried when he got dropped from the A-team in basketball. Tears are good for all of us. They help move the sadness out of our bodies.

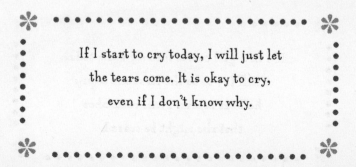

If I start to cry today, I will just let
the tears come. It is okay to cry,
even if I don't know why.

Be yourself!

Melissa is an excellent reader. She sounds out all the new words without help. Kerry is really good in spelling. She says she doesn't even have to study. My teacher says I will find something I am really good at too. But for now, it doesn't seem I am very good at anything. I sure can't run as fast as Mark. I can't paint as well as Susan. Seth subtracts faster than anyone in our class. I wonder if I will ever really be the best at anything?

Do you ever feel like this? If so, here's what you can do. You can talk over your feelings with one of your parents. I talk to my grandmother when my mom is too busy to listen. She helps me see how really good I am at being me! She says that's all I have to be good at right now, and nobody can do that as well as me. I know your parents would tell you the same thing.

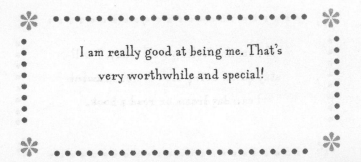

I am really good at being me. That's
very worthwhile and special!

Feeling sick can ruin
what you have planned.

It's not unusual to have an occasional day when you don't feel so good. Maybe you wake up with a headache or a toothache. Or worse, maybe you have the flu and feel like throwing up. That happened to me last week. Yuck!

If you have planned a special activity, it's really a bummer to be sick. The school picnic is something I hate to miss, and so is a field trip. Being sick may mean I need to get more rest. While I'm in the middle of it, the sick feeling seems like it will last forever, but it never does.

Taking time out for my body to get well is good for everyone. I don't want to spread my germs to others. And I need to remember that the more rest I get, the quicker I'll get well.

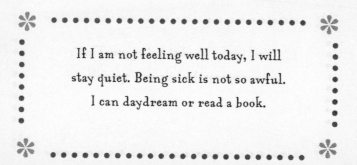

If I am not feeling well today, I will
stay quiet. Being sick is not so awful.
I can daydream or read a book.

Hope can change how a situation looks.

Do you worry over big and little things? I do. Mom says I worry way too much. Yesterday I worried about the science lesson. There were lots of different words in it. I worried about my fish too. I was afraid he would die while I was at school. Some days I worry about my mom at her job. Last week she was upset because her boss corrected her in front of her friends. I know how she felt. My teacher corrects me lots too.

If I feel some worry starting to come into my mind, I can think of an angel. That's what my Aunt Sarah does. Then I give the angel some of my worries. I ask the angel to watch over my fish while I'm at school, which helps me feel calmer. Having a picture of an angel in my mind doesn't leave so much room for worry pictures.

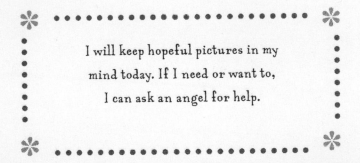

I will keep hopeful pictures in my
mind today. If I need or want to,
I can ask an angel for help.

Privileges come with responsibility.

It is not unusual to want to be liked by the teacher. I think I know who she likes a lot by who she calls on. Emma always gets called on to clean the boards. Does that mean she is the "teacher's pet"? Maybe it just means she does the best job. After all, the teacher wants to make sure the boards are really clean before she goes home every day.

If you want to be noticed by the teacher and called on to do special things, like taking a message down to the principal, you need to show her you can be counted on to do them carefully. It is always up to each of us if we want to have special privileges. We have to earn them.

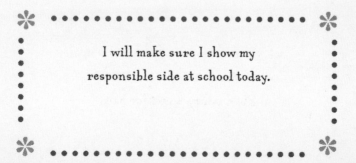

I will make sure I show my
responsible side at school today.

I always feel sorry for people who
think more about a rainy day
ahead than sunshine today.

—Rae Foley

My dad calls my mom a worrywart because she worries about everything. She even worries about my spelling tests! I know she worries a lot about my brother and me when we are at the park. Worrying keeps her from having fun with my dad and her friends.

I don't like to worry. It ruins whatever I'm doing. Mr. Sylvester, my third grade teacher, said worry means we aren't trusting that everything will work out okay. Some people walk out into nature and notice a beautiful sunset, and that helps them trust that all is okay. Some people pray. Sometimes a hug from my mom helps me to trust that everything is going to be okay.

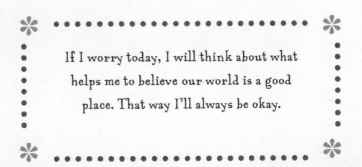

If I worry today, I will think about what
helps me to believe our world is a good
place. That way I'll always be okay.

Telling the truth is harder than it sounds.

Sometimes I pretend I'm telling the truth when I'm really not. For instance, If I break a brand-new toy, one that cost a lot of money, I've sometimes said I didn't know how it got broken. Or if I came home late from school, I've pretended that I lost a book or a jacket and had to go find it.

Probably everybody tells a lie once in a while. But it isn't good to do it. Why? Because afterward I feel guilty and worry about the truth coming out. Telling the truth, even when I've made a big mistake, doesn't hurt as bad as telling a lie. I learned this the hard way!

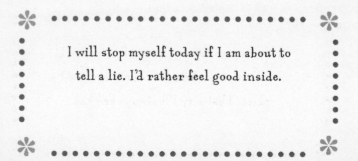

I will stop myself today if I am about to tell a lie. I'd rather feel good inside.

It's always best to think
before taking action.

It's not so easy to remember to think a minute before yelling at someone who makes me mad. Sometimes I've even hit a friend and then I've felt really sorry or even scared that I've done it. I always end up remembering Mom or Dad or my teacher saying, "Don't speak or act before thinking over what you are about to do." Why is it so hard for me to slow down?

Mrs. Powers, the principal at my school, says she sometimes counts to ten before she answers a person who has made her mad. Counting to ten isn't too hard for anyone who knows how to count—we do it all the time during math period and when we are playing hide-and-go-seek. Now we can practice it in a new way, and this way will help us calm down and do the right thing.

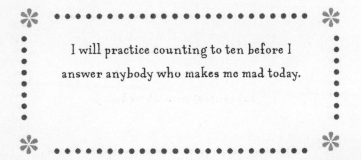

I will practice counting to ten before I
answer anybody who makes me mad today.

Laughter changes our whole perspective.

—Jan Pishok

Laughing over a good joke makes my body feel good all over. Does it have that effect on you? Occasionally, I wake up a little sad, or like one day last week, a little scared because I had not finished my science project for school and it was due that day. When I went into the kitchen for breakfast, the first thing I noticed was my cat all tangled up in some yarn. She looked so cute and funny that I laughed really hard. Instantly, my fear left me and I felt really good about everything. My project was still unfinished, but I felt calmer about being able to explain that to Mr. Jerome, my teacher.

My grandmother has always said that more laughter could change the direction of the world. I never really understood what she meant. I think I have a better sense of her meaning now.

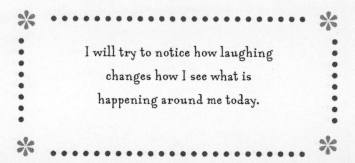

I will try to notice how laughing changes how I see what is happening around me today.

Jealousy is a very uncomfortable feeling.

What if your best friend gets a beautiful new bike, and it isn't even her birthday? How does her good fortune make you feel? Are you happy for her or are you jealous because your old, beat-up bike is the one your brother used to ride? It's pretty normal to be jealous, to envy what other kids have. My older sister is jealous because her best friend has a really cute boyfriend, and she doesn't have a boyfriend. You may even have heard your mom or dad say they were jealous because the neighbors got a new car. I guess jealousy is everywhere.

If we are jealous, it doesn't mean we are bad, according to my dad, but it's so much better if we can learn to be glad for other people. To do that, it helps to notice what we ourselves have. For instance, I may ride a beater bike, but my rollerblades are the best on the block. My sister made the cheerleading team, and her best friend didn't. When we appreciate what we do have, it's easier to be happy for what others have or get.

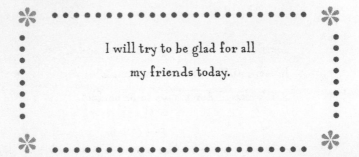

I will try to be glad for all
my friends today.

Making mistakes is common.

It's a good thing that making mistakes is something everybody does. Otherwise, whenever I made one I would be really embarrassed. Yesterday even my teacher made a mistake: she added up a list of numbers and got the wrong answer. We all had a good laugh over that. Brad told her she better take some homework home. That made her laugh really hard.

Usually I make mistakes when I am doing one thing but thinking about something else. Ms. Carl was probably thinking about going to lunch because the bell had just rung for us to go to the cafeteria. We loved her mistake because it reminded us that nobody is perfect.

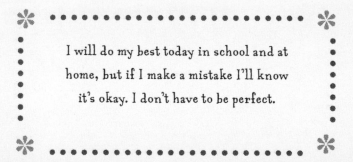

I will do my best today in school and at home, but if I make a mistake I'll know it's okay. I don't have to be perfect.

Life isn't always fair.

My best friend Annie gets invited to every party held by our classmates. I get invited to a few of the parties, but not all of them. Just last week I found out she was going to Leah's party. Leah is the newest girl in our fourth grade class. She moved here from New Jersey. I really don't understand why I was left out, and I wish Annie wouldn't go either. I sometimes feel afraid Annie will end up choosing to be someone else's best friend. Do you understand how I feel?

My dad is famous for saying, "Life isn't always fair." Every time I whine or complain about how a situation has upset me, he says it. I get so tired of his saying this. Mom says he is right though. She told me how she felt about being left out when she was young too. I realized her feelings were just like mine. That made me feel better. I guess Dad is right: things happen just because they happen. Usually no one intends to hurt your feelings. That's just how life goes, he says.

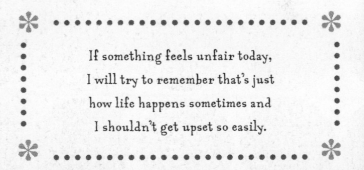

If something feels unfair today,
I will try to remember that's just
how life happens sometimes and
I shouldn't get upset so easily.

Be Kind

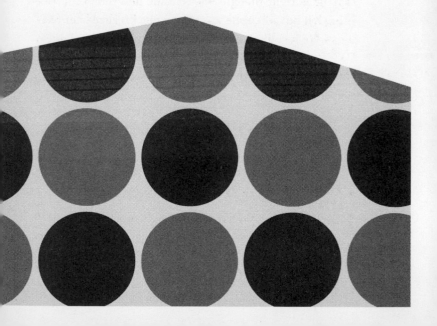

Even on a rainy day,
I can feel the sunshine.

–Jill Clark

Attitude is a pretty important word. I can remember hearing my mom say, "Watch your attitude if you want to go to the movie." Maybe we can't always remember what attitude means, but we probably do remember having our mom change her mind about letting us go to the park or over to a best friend's house because she didn't like how we were acting. Attitude, when it isn't good, can cause trouble.

Having a good attitude means we are pleasant toward all the kids in the neighborhood. It means we are respectful of everybody who crosses our path. A good attitude keeps us out of trouble. We can have so much more fun playing with our friends when we have a good attitude.

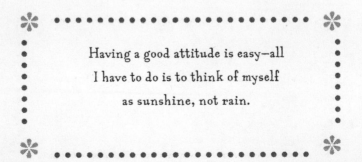

Having a good attitude is easy—all
I have to do is to think of myself
as sunshine, not rain.

Happiness comes from
having a positive attitude.

Making the decision to be happy when something crummy happens is pretty hard. I had an opportunity to try this last week, but I didn't do so well. First, my dog Gorky disappeared. I was sure he had been stolen because he is so cute. I frantically looked for him all over the neighborhood. My grandmother came for a visit, but I couldn't stop worrying. She left before I had a chance to talk to her. I didn't even thank her for the birthday present she brought because my mind was filled up with fear that Gorky would be forever gone. That night after supper a man came to the door with Gorky. So all my worries had been for nothing.

I have learned, though, that some situations can't keep me from feeling happy. When Mom forgot to buy my favorite dessert, it didn't keep me from laughing over the silly stuff my baby sister did when we were having dinner. Last night, she poured her peas all over her head.

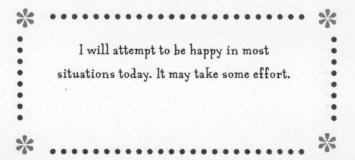

I will attempt to be happy in most
situations today. It may take some effort.

You can't get your way all the time.

Mom says I get into too many fights with my sister. Does your mom ever say that to you? I wonder why I fight so much. Mom says it's because I want my way too often. I haven't learned how to take turns. But I don't always get my way at school, and I don't fight there. Maybe because I know my teacher is watching me.

Learning to take turns isn't all that easy. Most people, even moms and dads, want everybody to follow their rules. I don't like it when Jody wants to make all the rules. I guess that's why I can't make them all either. Taking turns isn't a rule just for kids!

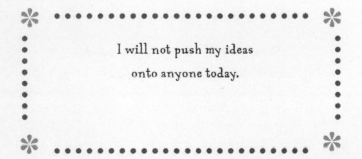

I will not push my ideas
onto anyone today.

Be generous.

I used to be afraid that sharing a favorite possession meant losing it. One time, I let my friend Jessica borrow my favorite CD to play for her sister, and her sister lost it and refused to replace it. My best friend and I just started sharing part of our lunch every day. It has almost become a game to guess which part she may want. My mom recently suggested that everyone in our family choose three things from our closet to share with another family. Then we took them to the homeless shelter. I chose my favorite sweater to give away. At first I hesitated, then it felt right. Every time I think about it now, I imagine another girl loving it as much as I do, and the thought makes me happy.

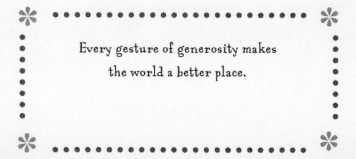

Every gesture of generosity makes
the world a better place.

Being quiet can help us
hear important messages.

Sometimes I get really frustrated because I can't stay in the lines perfectly when I'm coloring a special picture in art class. If I fall off of my bike while Brian is watching, I get upset too. When I am really embarrassed or frustrated, my mind seems like it's going to burst because of all the things I am thinking to myself.

Mom says getting really quiet inside, letting my thoughts just float away, helps. If I get upset with a friend or with Mom because she won't let me go to the park with Amanda, I'll go to my room and get quiet for a while. When I feel calm inside, my peaceful feelings grow stronger than my upset feelings.

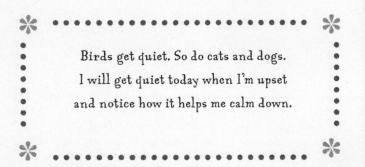

Birds get quiet. So do cats and dogs.
I will get quiet today when I'm upset
and notice how it helps me calm down.

Nobody can keep you mad but yourself!

Sometimes I get mad at my little brother for messing up my bed right after I have made it. Telling Mom doesn't really help. She thinks I get upset with Sammy too easily. After all, he is only two years old. I have many other reasons for getting mad too. I get mad when my dad forgets to show up for our special night out. That happened twice last month. And I get mad when my friends laugh at me for missing the bus. It happened three times last week.

When I am mad, I can't seem to think of anything else. Being mad just takes over my thoughts. We had a party at school last week, and I was still so mad at my friends that I refused to join in when they were all laughing and popping balloons. When I complained to Mom, she reminded me that nobody can keep me mad. I made that decision all by myself. She said the sooner I learned this piece of wisdom, the better. She is still trying to remember it, she said, and she is forty years old!

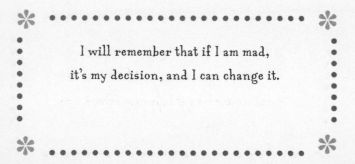

I will remember that if I am mad,
it's my decision, and I can change it.

Expressing gratitude
improves one's outlook.

—Susan Atchley Ebaugh

Walking down the street gives me a lot of things to be grateful for. I'm glad to have a safe, uncluttered street to walk on and that I'm not living in a violent city. I'm glad I can walk, that my legs hold me up and move me forward and backward. I know someone in a wheelchair, and she's glad she can go out for a walk in her chair. I've learned there's more than one way to walk since Jenna and I became friends. I feel good about being able to see, and that I have a few good friends. And that I have clothes to wear. And that every single night I sit down to a good dinner. Not every kid does.

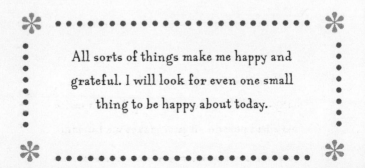

All sorts of things make me happy and grateful. I will look for even one small thing to be happy about today.

Admitting you're wrong can develop your character.

Nobody likes to admit being wrong. Mom and Dad don't like to be wrong. My teacher doesn't, either. But all of us are wrong part of the time. Maybe I miss a word on the spelling test or forget to make my bed after promising to. It's good to learn that being wrong isn't such a big deal. But it is a big deal to be able to admit when you're wrong.

It's better not to wait too long after realizing you've made a mistake. Admitting you're wrong right away is much easier than waiting a day or two.

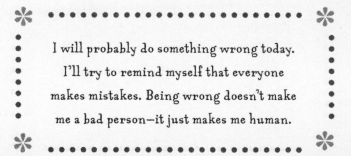

I will probably do something wrong today. I'll try to remind myself that everyone makes mistakes. Being wrong doesn't make me a bad person—it just makes me human.

Blaming someone else for a situation you don't like is too easy.

I am too quick to blame others, according to my stepfather. One night, I left my bike outside and a neighbor kid borrowed it without asking. I couldn't find it in time for school the next day and had to walk, which made me late, which meant I had to stay after school for being late, which meant I had some explaining to do at dinnertime. I kept insisting that it was actually Timothy's fault because he had moved my bike. My stepdad said, "No way!" If the bike had been in the garage where it belonged, this wouldn't have happened.

Blaming others becomes a habit, I think. My stepfather says it's not easy, but it's so much more peaceful to simply take responsibility for our mistakes. He says when we quit blaming others we're mature. I do want to show him I'm maturing. I never hear him blame anyone.

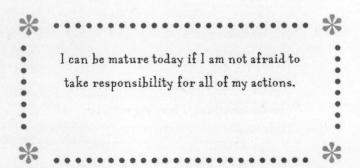

I can be mature today if I am not afraid to take responsibility for all of my actions.

It's good to talk about sad and mad feelings.

Do you ever wish you had kept quiet instead of yelling at your friend? Like when Molly chose someone else to sleep over, did it help me to yell at her? I usually yell or get mad when I am feeling hurt about something. The problem is that my reaction doesn't make me feel any better. Often I feel even worse.

Actually, I can always go to my mom or some other grown-up and tell them how I feel. That way I won't need to yell at someone else. It helps to share with someone I can trust when my feelings are hurt. It's a safe way to get rid of them so I can feel happy again.

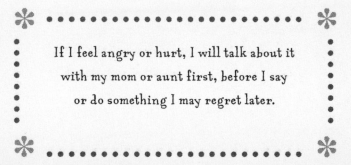

If I feel angry or hurt, I will talk about it
with my mom or aunt first, before I say
or do something I may regret later.

We do not always like what is good
for us in this world.

—Eleanor Roosevelt

One day last year, Mother wore her bedroom slippers to her new job. She forgot she had them on! The people in her office laughed and laughed. She said the experience was good for her because it helped her make friends with some of the other women in the office.

A number of things can happen to me that I don't like at the time, but they may be good for me in the long run. For instance, I forgot my homework one day last week. So I had to do it over. This turned out to be good because I had misunderstood the directions. What I had done at home was wrong.

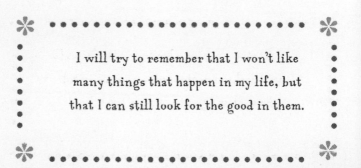

I will try to remember that I won't like
many things that happen in my life, but
that I can still look for the good in them.

Changing your mind is okay, but it's important to do it carefully.

When my friend Holly decided to go home instead of coming home with me after school, I got mad. My feelings were hurt. When people change their minds it affects us, doesn't it? When I'm about to change my mind, it's good to remember that someone else may be hurt by the change too.

It isn't wrong to change my mind. It wasn't wrong when my friend changed her mind and decided to hang out with someone else. But everyone should think about how others will feel before changing things.

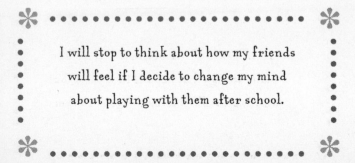

I will stop to think about how my friends will feel if I decide to change my mind about playing with them after school.

Fighting is never the best solution.

I don't like to fight. I get slightly afraid when the older kids fight on the playground at school. Mom says it's good that I don't want to fight, but what if some mean girl or boy starts to chase me? What should I do then? The first thing to do is run, I guess.

I don't like to be chased unless I'm playing a game. If someone starts to chase me and won't stop even after I ask them to, I guess the thing to do is go talk to the teacher or some other grown-up. Some kids like to fight. Maybe it's because they aren't very happy. I've noticed that the kids who like to fight don't have many friends.

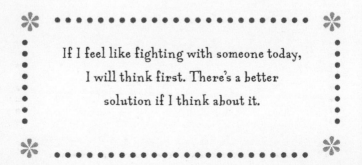

If I feel like fighting with someone today,
I will think first. There's a better
solution if I think about it.

You don't have to be bored.

Do you ever feel like there's nothing you really want to do? You've finished reading *Harry Potter* and you can't get another book until you go to school Monday. Your best friend is at her grandmother's, so she can't come over. It's too cold to go bike riding and besides, it's starting to rain. What a bummer! That's how boredom is.

My teacher said I never had to be bored unless I wanted to be. She said I could study for the science test or work on memorizing the multiplication tables. Mom says I can always straighten up my room if there's nothing else to do. She said that she wrote make-believe stories when she was young. She never, ever got bored then.

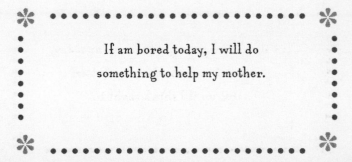

If am bored today, I will do
something to help my mother.

It's good to be thankful for all that we have.

Did you have enough to eat yesterday? Some girls didn't. Do you have shoes and socks to put on today? Some girls don't. If you look around yourself right this minute, you'll see many, many reasons for being thankful. Being able to read these words is one reason. Having fingers and arms that can move is another.

You have big and tiny reasons for being thankful. You have people who love you—that's big. You have your very own toothbrush—that's tiny. You have a sweater you can wear if it is cold—that's kind of big. You have some toys that belong just to you—that's pretty big too.

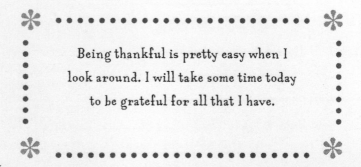

Being thankful is pretty easy when I look around. I will take some time today to be grateful for all that I have.

Growing up means finding
better solutions to problems.

I sure feel sorry for myself when things don't go my way. Yesterday I was supposed to be the monitor and hand out the papers at school, and my teacher forgot. She asked Kelley instead. I felt sorry for myself for a while, then I talked to my teacher. She let me feed the hamster instead. I was glad I just asked instead of keeping to myself and pouting.

Mom says I need to handle difficult things more gracefully. When I feel sorry for myself, I need to look for a graceful way to take care of my feelings. That may be by talking to my teacher, my mom, or my best friend.

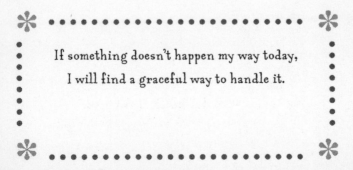

If something doesn't happen my way today,
I will find a graceful way to handle it.

Laughter helps me feel better inside.

My brother makes me laugh a zillion times a day. Sometimes he makes me laugh when I really shouldn't, like when he makes a face behind the babysitter's back after she has scolded him. Mostly he does really funny things that make my mom and dad laugh too. Last night he put all of his clothes on backward before coming to the dinner table. He even wore a pair of my dad's shoes, since he couldn't get his own on backward. Mom took his picture when we couldn't stop laughing.

Laughing can make us feel good all over. Don't you wish you could laugh more of the time? Hey, maybe you can. Maybe we all can! There aren't any laws against it! Mainly we have to be willing to laugh.

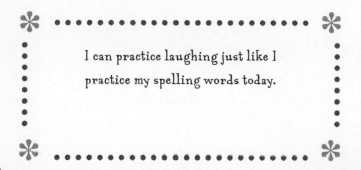

I can practice laughing just like I practice my spelling words today.

Do you feel lucky?

I do. I have a school to go to. I have clothes to wear, warm ones when it's chilly, and shorts for the hot days. I have cereal for breakfast and hot lunches at school every day. Some days my mom leaves a treat for me after school too. I have lots of reasons to feel lucky.

Not all kids are as lucky as me. Kirsten comes immediately to mind. Her mother was killed in an accident last year. Some days Kirsten doesn't have on really clean clothes. Probably her dad doesn't have time to get all of the work done. I can't imagine how much I would miss my mom if anything happened to her.

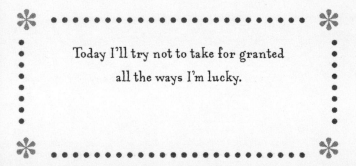

Today I'll try not to take for granted
all the ways I'm lucky.

You can *choose* to be happy!

Sometimes I wake up excited because something really special has been planned for the day. Maybe my class is going on a field trip or my dad is taking me out for dinner all by myself, just the two of us. Or maybe my mom promised that I could wear my new shoes to school. Lots of things make me excited and full of joy.

I can decide to be excited even if nothing really special has been planned. Getting excited is something I can do for no reason at all, perhaps just by looking forward to all the good things that can happen. Each day is lots more fun if I decide to look forward to it.

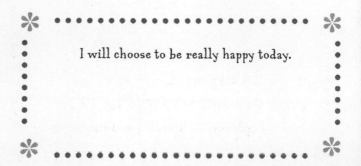

I will choose to be really happy today.

Opinions are individual ideas.

Do you know what opinions are? They're what you believe about certain things. Like my mom's opinion that video games are too violent. She doesn't want me playing them at Cassie's house. My dad has an opinion about camping. He thinks it's the best activity families can do together.

My teacher's opinion is that all children should be quiet unless called on to answer questions. That's a hard one for most of us to go along with, especially Brittany. She talks out of turn all of the time. My opinion is that school is pretty fun. I love to learn new words.

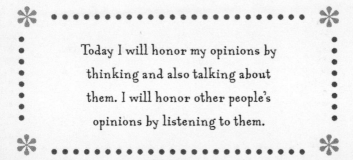

Today I will honor my opinions by
thinking and also talking about
them. I will honor other people's
opinions by listening to them.

I'm wrong almost as often as I'm right.

Nobody's right all the time. The principal at my school may be right more often than us kids, but even she makes mistakes. Sometimes the clerk at the grocery rings up the wrong price, and Mom has to point it out to get the correct change. When Dad ran the stop sign, he was wrong. It's a good thing there were no cars there, or he might have hit somebody. That would have been a very sad wrong.

Being wrong isn't the end of the world. It helps to remember that mistakes don't need to be hidden—they're okay.

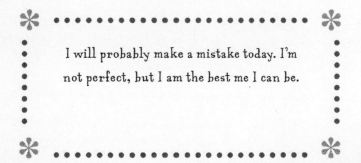

I will probably make a mistake today. I'm not perfect, but I am the best me I can be.

Time will bring the good to us as
well as take away the bad.

—Amy E. Dean

When I'm doing homework or sweeping the kitchen floor
or putting the supper dishes in the dishwasher, time seems
to drag. All I think about is getting done, and the more I
think about that, the longer it seems to take to finish whatever I have to do.

But time goes by quickly when I'm at a movie, at the
park, or over at a friend's house playing with her toys. Playing a game on the computer makes time whiz by too. Isn't
it weird that time goes by slowly sometimes and quickly
at other times?

Mr. Hazzard, my teacher, says that time doesn't change.
It's how I think about what I'm doing that changes.

Slow time, speedy time . . .
I will try to enjoy it all.

> It is wonderful how quickly you get used
> to things, even the most astonishing.
> —Edith Nesbitt

Have you recently looked at any pictures of yourself when you were a little girl? It is fun to see how you've changed. When I was a baby, I was totally bald. Now I have lots of hair. It's so long I can wear it in braids, a ponytail, curled, or straight with barrettes. Mom said she thought I would be bald forever because I didn't have any hair by my first birthday!

We change in many ways, not just in how we look. I used to get really scared when Mom turned out my bedroom light. I like the dark now. I can make better pictures in my mind in the dark. My sister used to hate reading because she wasn't very good at it. My aunt took her to a special class where she learned how to sound out words. Now she loves to read. She reads even when it's time to help make our beds.

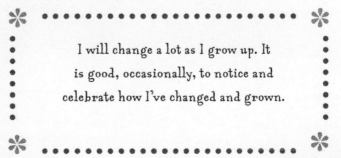

I will change a lot as I grow up. It
is good, occasionally, to notice and
celebrate how I've changed and grown.

Laughing feels good.

Having a great big laugh feels really good. It tickles my insides. Does it do that to you? Funny jokes make me laugh. So does watching my dad play a trick on my mom. Last week, just for fun, he hid all the dinner plates and left a note in the cabinet saying the plates and the family were at her favorite restaurant, waiting for her. Sometimes my little brother puts his shoes on the wrong feet. That makes all of us laugh.

When I forget to comb my hair sometimes, I laugh when I look in the mirror. One time I wore one brown shoe and one black shoe to school. That really made me laugh! It's good to be able to laugh at ourselves. Mother says that can be the best time of all to laugh.

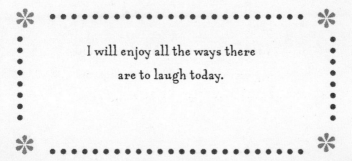

I will enjoy all the ways there
are to laugh today.

You can have fun alone.

When I was little, I thought for me to have fun somebody had to play with me or maybe read to me. Now that I'm older, I realize I can have fun all by myself. This is good because there isn't always somebody around to entertain me.

One of the things I like to do when I'm alone is pretend I'm grown up. Some days I put on my mother's lipstick, fingernail polish, and perfume. When I was younger, I even dressed up in her old clothes. I like to write stories too. Now that I've learned to use the dictionary, I don't have to make pictures for the words I can't spell. Sometimes I have more fun all by myself than with other kids.

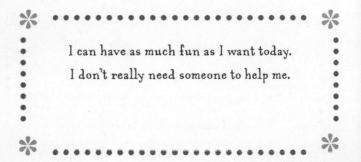

I can have as much fun as I want today.
I don't really need someone to help me.

How you see a situation is up to you.

Have you ever been sure you saw a grey car that your mom said she thought was green? You wonder if your eyes were playing tricks on you. Eyes don't always see the same things. If my mind was on something really important to me when a car went by, I might not have seen its real color at all.

Sometimes I think someone is making a face at me when she really wasn't. I think sometimes this happens because I was expecting her to act that way. Like one day I was sure that an older kid at my bus stop was making fun of me, but my mother said he was laughing at something down the street behind me. My eyes and mind can play tricks on me.

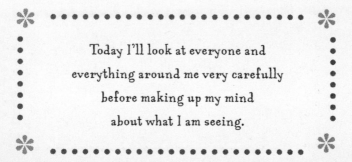

Today I'll look at everyone and
everything around me very carefully
before making up my mind
about what I am seeing.

Being lonely can push us
toward new friends.

Some days it just seems all my friends are gone. Last week, Suzanne was at her grandmother's house all week long. And Jackie was at the dentist. And Roberta was sick with the flu for three days. I was lonely and bored. Having someone to play with is really important.

I am not the only one who gets lonely. My stepdad says feeling lonely is pretty common. When I was at the park last week, I noticed a girl who was by herself all afternoon. I wonder now if she was lonely. If I see her the next time I go, maybe I'll ask her to play on the slide. That way maybe I'll have another friend to play with when Suzanne and Jackie and Roberta aren't around.

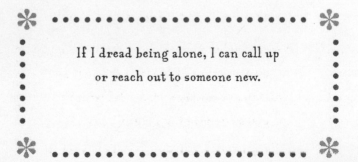

If I dread being alone, I can call up
or reach out to someone new.

Blaming others doesn't
allow me to grow up.

I couldn't find my pencil box at school yesterday, and I was really sure that Sophie had taken it. After telling my teacher what I thought Sophie had done, I found my box under the red table. Too often, I blame someone else when I can't find something. Mom gets upset when I do this. My teacher was kind of disappointed too. I wonder why I did that?

I get blamed for things too. When Joey lost his hat, he accused me of putting it somewhere. Then he found it under his bed! Mom even thought I had hidden her purse for a joke, but then she remembered leaving it in the car.

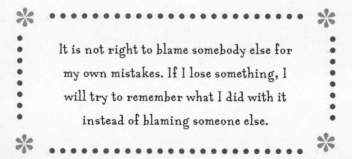

It is not right to blame somebody else for
my own mistakes. If I lose something, I
will try to remember what I did with it
instead of blaming someone else.

Thanksgiving can happen
a little bit every day.

There are hundreds of ways to say thanks. I can simply say thank-you to everyone who does something kind for me. For instance, when my babysitter offers to check my homework, I can say thanks. Maybe she'll help me get an **A** on the assignment! I can offer to help my little sister braid her hair, just like my stepdad used to help me. There are lots of opportunities. I can even take a little gift to the neighbor who has been kind enough to return my soccer ball that I kicked into her yard.

One of the ways my mom taught me to say thanks is through prayers. She says thanking God for helping me out every day is a wonderful way to show my thanks. I think I will tell her how thankful I am that she's my mother.

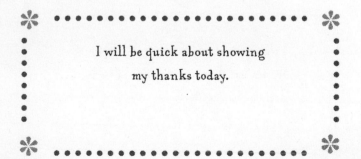

I will be quick about showing
my thanks today.

Are you a good sport when situations don't turn out as you had hoped?

Life seldom happens in exactly the way we envisioned it. In fact, my mom has a great saying. She says, "Life is what happens while you are making other plans." This is certainly what happened to me last week. First of all, I had asked Grace to come for an overnight. At the last minute, she cancelled because her grandmother unexpectedly came for a visit. The next day, I had planned to bicycle to the park for the harvest festival. It rained. But that's not all. On Sunday, my dad had promised he would come over and take my little brother and me to dinner. He didn't. Mom felt sad for us, so she took us to Friday's, which was fun, but I was disappointed.

Accepting whatever happens as okay takes effort. Mom says she struggles with this too. But she says the better we get at it when we are young, the easier our lives will be when we grow up.

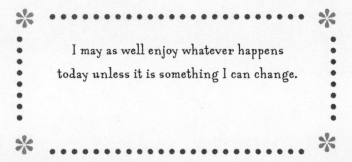

I may as well enjoy whatever happens today unless it is something I can change.

Respect yourself . . . and others.

I hate it when someone calls me a "wuss." Don't you? Mother says it bothers me because it's embarrassing to be made fun of. She also says that the person who is making fun of me is no doubt scared of many things. They feel better when others are afraid too, she says. Even adults do this, I've noticed.

I never see my parents do this to each other or anyone else, either. So it's possible to be a person who doesn't make fun of others and who is always respectful. That's the kind of person I would rather be. Some things may still make me afraid, but I don't have to make others feel afraid too. Using my mom as a model can help me be more respectful of others.

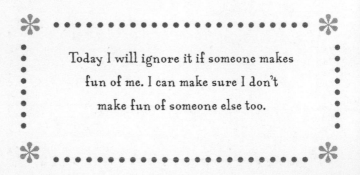

Today I will ignore it if someone makes
fun of me. I can make sure I don't
make fun of someone else too.

The change of one simple behavior
can affect other behaviors and
thus change many things.

—Jean Baer

Ms. Henry read a story to our class last week. In it, there was a really mean girl named Shelly who chased all the first graders out of the school yard. One of them almost got hit by a car. Shelly got sent home from school. But the next day, she came back and announced over the loud-speaker to the whole school how sorry she was. The principal asked everyone to forgive her.

At first I didn't want them to, but the story showed how she was just very lonely and didn't know how to make friends. After she apologized, one of the other girls in her class asked her to play at recess. The story ended with everyone being happier. The teacher said that was a good lesson for all of us.

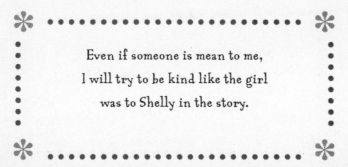

Even if someone is mean to me,
I will try to be kind like the girl
was to Shelly in the story.

Accepting whatever happens as okay is a sign of maturity.

Every day something happens that I don't expect. Maybe it rains, and I was going to ride my new bike to school. Or a button comes off a favorite blouse, and I have to wear something else. Maybe I'm really counting on having pancakes for breakfast, but Mom is running late for work and doesn't have time to make them. Things just happen. I can get really upset and pout or even cry, but that won't make the rain stop or put the button back on my blouse.

Being able to accept whatever is happening will probably make me feel better about the rest of the day. Getting no pancakes is not the end of the world! My aunt, who is a dancer, says it's about meeting life's surprises gracefully. When her ballet teacher changes the beat unexpectedly, it is her job as a dancer to keep her balance and gracefulness.

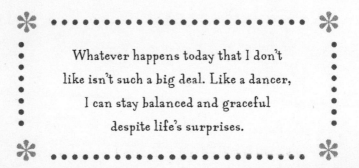

Whatever happens today that I don't
like isn't such a big deal. Like a dancer,
I can stay balanced and graceful
despite life's surprises.

Choose to be kind.

Are you always kind to your friends? Probably not. Some days my mother says I act like I woke up on the wrong side of the bed. Those days I'm a grouch toward everyone. Even when my brother or sister or a friend is really nice to me, sometimes I just seem to say mean things or ignore them completely. I don't feel happy when I act this way.

Some of my friends are kind most of the time, especially Shawn. I've never seen her be snotty to anyone. When I'm feeling kind, I don't say mean things to others. Maybe I can pretend to feel kinder, even when I want to be a grouch. When a friend treats me in a kind way, I feel really good. When I decide to treat someone else with kindness, I'll help that person feel good too.

I will spread good feelings
by being kind today.

> It is of immense importance to
> learn to laugh at ourselves.
> —Katherine Mansfield

My mom says there are times when laughing isn't using good sense, like when my friend Timmy made a face at our teacher. Sometimes I laugh before I really think about what I am doing. As long as it's done at the right time, laughing is good for us. My grandmother says laughter is particularly good when we've made silly mistakes. She made one last week that we all laughed at. She tried to throw a cup of water out of her car window. Guess what? The window was closed!

Laughing makes me feel bubbly all over. When I laugh at a funny movie or a joke in a book I'm reading, I feel like being nice to everyone I meet. My mother says laughing can even help us get well when we're sick.

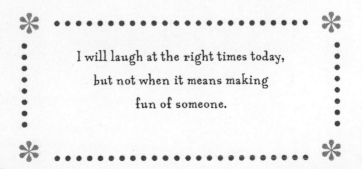

I will laugh at the right times today,
but not when it means making
fun of someone.

What most of us want is to be heard.

—Dory Previn

Does it seem that the teacher doesn't notice you very often? Maybe she's always helping Wendy or Kyle or somebody else when you have your hand up. When you can't get her attention, what do you do? Maybe you feel like crying, or you slam your book closed. It's hard not getting attention when you really need it.

What can you do when you need some attention? In school, maybe you can talk to the teacher during recess and tell her how you feel. Or talk it over with your mom. Maybe she can help you. There's something you can do. Sometimes it just takes some thinking or talking to figure it out.

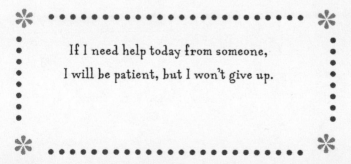

If I need help today from someone,
I will be patient, but I won't give up.

Nobody likes a grouch.

Are you frequently a grouch? How do you know? Maybe someone's called you one. My mom is grouchy once in a while, particularly when nobody comes to the breakfast table on time and she's late for work. When kids at school act up, even the teacher gets pretty grouchy. I think being a teacher must be pretty hard. Kids in my class act up all of the time. My dad is a grouch when I leave my bike out all night!

How does it feel to be grouchy? Some people are grouchy so often that I think they must like the feeling. But I don't like how it feels. I would rather smile and laugh than be grouchy. Sometimes I think of Oscar the Grouch and he helps me laugh at myself. This is a good thing to remember.

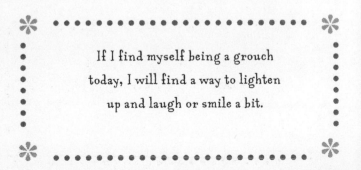

If I find myself being a grouch
today, I will find a way to lighten
up and laugh or smile a bit.

"If onlys" are lonely.

–Morgan Jennings

Lots of things happen in a normal day that can upset me. For instance, yesterday I couldn't find my favorite pair of shoes, and it was almost time for the bus. All I could think of was "If only I could find my shoes!" Mom said, "That's life." She meant that we can't always have things the way we want them. Growing up means learning to accept things we can't change.

We get lots of opportunities to accept how things happen every day. I am not so bothered by some things that happen. For instance, last week I had counted on going to a movie with Kimberly, but she changed her mind. I was in the middle of a really good book, so I didn't even care. I don't always act this grown-up, though. Sometimes when things turn out differently than I had planned, I have a tantrum! At least that's what Mom calls it.

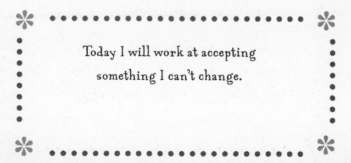

Today I will work at accepting something I can't change.

Attitude and perspective are everything.
—Kathy Kendall

Some people whine and complain all the time. You probably know somebody who does that. My friend Jasmine complains a lot. I don't really like to spend much time with her or with other people who always complain. Their poor attitude ruins my fun. Kids who laugh a lot or maybe play a lot of jokes on others are much more fun to be with. My older sister says kids like that have a better perspective on life. That's a big idea, but it means they see life more positively.

I wonder why some people complain so much. My sister Rebecca says that complainers are just afraid. Maybe they're afraid other kids don't like them, or maybe they're afraid they can't learn what everyone else already knows. I know that when I'm afraid or tired, I whine a little bit too.

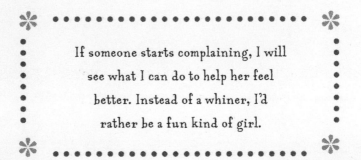

If someone starts complaining, I will
see what I can do to help her feel
better. Instead of a whiner, I'd
rather be a fun kind of girl.

When you notice what you don't have, pay attention to all that you do.

Do you know what it means to compare yourself to others? It means matching what you have with what they have and deciding who has more. For instance, Judy got a new bike for her birthday. Brad got one for being such a big help while his mom was in the hospital having his baby sister. And I've never had a brand new bike. I got caught up in the unfairness of it without stopping to think that I have a dog and a cat and my friends have neither.

Not everyone has the same number or kinds of things. I guess as long as I have certain things, like a bed to sleep in and plates to put food on and shoes to wear when I go out to play, I'm pretty lucky. You know, some kids don't have nearly as much as I have. Just look around and see what all is in your house and in your bedroom. Lots of stuff. You actually have enough, don't you?

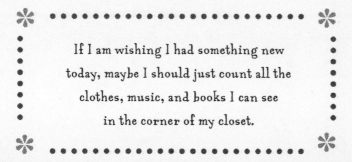

If I am wishing I had something new today, maybe I should just count all the clothes, music, and books I can see in the corner of my closet.

I truly want to be part of the solution.

–Kathy Kendall

Have you ever heard an adult describe a friend as always seeing the glass as half-empty? That sounds weird, but its meaning is simple. It means the friend always sees the negative side of a situation, not the positive side. That person sees only problems, not solutions.

I have three best friends. My problem is that two of my friends don't like each other very much. When I want to have a sleepover, I have to choose Susan or Kelley but never both. I talked this problem over with Dad, and he suggested that I talk to each girl privately about my feelings and ask them for a solution. I was nervous about doing this at first, but I did it. Guess what? They agreed to try to be better friends to each other. Last week was the first sleepover with all of us, and we had fun! I can hardly believe it. My dad is pretty smart.

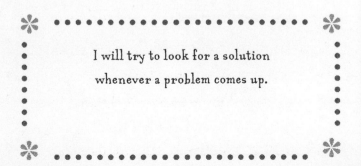

I will try to look for a solution
whenever a problem comes up.

Never lose hope.

"Never lose hope." That's written in big letters on our refrigerator. I'm not sure I understand what it means. I do hope for a lot of things. Like I hope I pass to the next grade in June. I hope I get all **A**'s on my report card. I hope my baby sister learns to leave my CDs alone. I hope my older sister comes back home. She ran away last year to my aunt's house. Mom says that is one hope that might not get answered until my sister gets out of high school.

Having hope means you don't give up. But lots of things I hope for are going to take effort, or they won't really happen. I can't just hope to pass my spelling test. I have to study. I can't even just hope that Stacy will leave my CDs alone. I have to tell her what I expect her to do. Hope doesn't take care of everything without some work from me. But hope makes me feel like all good things are possible.

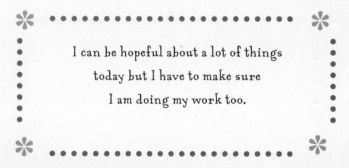

I can be hopeful about a lot of things
today but I have to make sure
I am doing my work too.

> The future is made of the same
> stuff as the present.
>
> —Simone Weil

Do you spend a lot of time thinking about tomorrow or maybe next week? Sometimes I even think about when I'm going to be old enough to get married. My mother says I am missing out on today because I spend so much time thinking about the future. But when my birthday is coming up or maybe Christmas, it's hard not to dream about it. For me, at least.

I guess she is right, though. When my mind is on the future, I am not able to really think about what is happening around me. Just yesterday, I was thinking about planning a sleepover with Anna while Erin was playing here. It took me a while to realize I was wasting my playtime with Erin by thinking too far ahead.

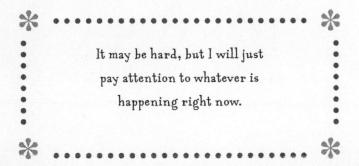

It may be hard, but I will just
pay attention to whatever is
happening right now.

A good attitude usually makes a good day.

Do you believe you can be happy no matter what's going on? I didn't until my older sister taught me how. When I was in second grade, Miss Temper was my teacher, and she really lived up to her name! No matter what I did, she always seemed to be yelling at me. I started hating school. Then I started getting sick to my stomach Sunday night, just thinking about being in her classroom on Monday.

My sister Janna told me that maybe I was setting myself up to feel bad. Because I was so tense, Miss Temper probably watched me extra closely, so she saw even my smallest mistakes. Janna wrote out a list of things for me to read every morning before school to make me happy and relaxed. She told me to read that list whenever I felt scared or worried. And you know what? It worked. I still do this but now I call it my gratitude list.

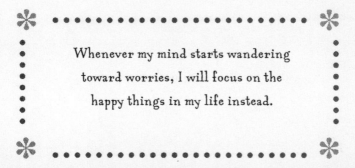

Whenever my mind starts wandering
toward worries, I will focus on the
happy things in my life instead.

Taking a time-out can help when I've gotten emotional about something.

My mother, dad, and teacher often make me take a time-out when I've misbehaved. I have had zillions of time-outs. Getting quiet when I have behaved inappropriately actually helps me. Most recently I was really upset because my brother got into my colored chalks and broke most of them. I needed them for a special picture I was making for science class. I screamed and threw the remaining chalk at him, and I got a time-out. It didn't seem fair, but it did help me to feel calm.

Taking a time-out gives me a chance to think about what I was doing. Almost every day I do something that isn't very nice. I don't always get a time-out for it, but I always know when I deserved one. Stopping to think before I do anything can help me avoid time-outs. This is good advice to follow, don't you think?

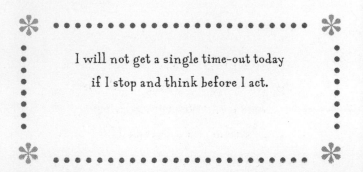

I will not get a single time-out today
if I stop and think before I act.

Feeling sorry for myself is okay once in a while.

Sometimes it feels good to feel sorry for yourself. Like the day it was raining and I couldn't go to the playground. Or when my little sister was sick and my dad decided it was better if Betsy didn't come for a sleepover. When something doesn't go as I thought it would, feeling sorry for myself almost makes it easier to accept. Isn't that weird?

Mom says feeling sorry for myself is normal when disappointing things happen. She also says, "Don't make a career out of it." Sometimes, I shift my focus just a little bit, so I can see that things aren't bad. For instance, that rainy day, we ended up having an Outburst tournament—it was a blast. And the night my sister was sick, I got to watch a movie, and the next week I had Betsy over. Feeling sorry for myself keeps me from seeing that the best thing generally happens, even though I may not understand it at the time.

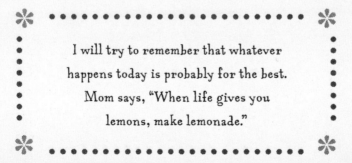

I will try to remember that whatever
happens today is probably for the best.
Mom says, "When life gives you
lemons, make lemonade."

Being rude is never a good choice.

Do you know what it means to be rude? It means not answering someone very nicely. Or it may mean not answering the person at all. Like when your mom calls you to dinner and you are busy at your computer and don't answer her—that is being rude.

Adults are sometimes rude to kids perhaps because they are feeling crabby or tired. It never feels very good to be at the receiving end of rude behavior. The opposite of being rude is being considerate of others. All of us can learn from one another. You are never too young to be a good example.

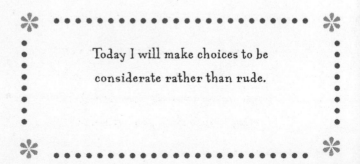

Today I will make choices to be
considerate rather than rude.

A good attitude has to be cultivated just like a garden.

Attitude is important. You may have heard your mom or dad say, "You have a bad attitude, young lady!" Maybe you didn't know exactly what that meant, especially when you were young, but you could tell by the tone of their voices that it wasn't good. Being pleasant to all the members of your family is one way of showing a good attitude. This can be done in simple ways, like saying " Good morning" or "How was your day?"

A good attitude means being friendly and warm. It also means expecting good things to happen, not bad things. Families are a great place to practice having a good attitude.

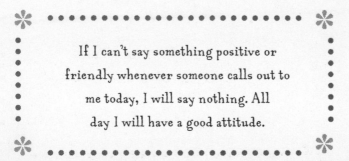

If I can't say something positive or friendly whenever someone calls out to me today, I will say nothing. All day I will have a good attitude.

Look for happiness: it's often nearby.

What makes you happy? Does having your favorite dessert make you happy? How about getting to go to a movie when you thought it was too late? My dad is happy when my sister and I get good report cards. Mom is happy when Dad surprises her with a bouquet of flowers. My teacher seems really happy when our class is very quiet, especially when the principal comes to our room. My friend Melissa is the happiest when her dad comes over for dinner.

All of us feel happy for different reasons. My grandmother says it is often the simple things in life that bring us the most happiness. The simple happy things I noticed after she said this were a hug from my mom, the taste of a crunchy apple, sun sparkling across the water near where I live. I would like to be the kind of person who easily finds happiness all around me.

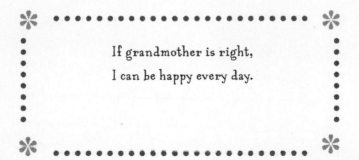

If grandmother is right,
I can be happy every day.

The thoughts we carry around in our minds influence our behavior.

When I am feeling happy about my experiences, like when Betsy and I have had a great time over at her house, I am willing to be more helpful to my little sister and brother. My happiness makes it easier for me to be nice to them. I'm not sure how the two things are related, but Mom said that what's in our mind more or less takes charge of our behavior. Here is how she explained it to me:

When I play with Matt, I often come home angry and take it out on whoever is close by. Yesterday it was my mom. Matt had called me mean names because I wouldn't play a game by his silly rules, which were wrong, by the way. I left his house really mad, just as his mother was bringing in some cookies for a treat. When Mom asked what was wrong, I stomped up to my room and slammed my door. When we talked about it later, she suggested I spend more time with friends like Betsy.

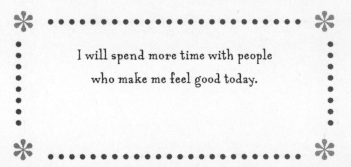

I will spend more time with people
who make me feel good today.

Small disappointments don't mean you have to feel sorry for yourself.

Maybe the birthday present I expected to get didn't come. Or the special bike I asked Santa for wasn't under the tree last year. The babysitter was supposed to rent a movie, but she forgot again. So many things can happen that I don't like. But does feeling sorry for myself make it any better?

At first I thought feeling sorry made me feel better. It doesn't change anything, though. When the babysitter forgot the movie, I was really disappointed until we got out the Monopoly game and played a huge tournament. Maybe not getting what I want is not as big a deal as I make it.

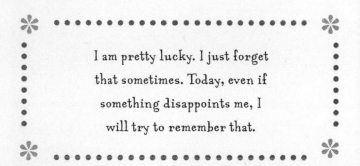

I am pretty lucky. I just forget
that sometimes. Today, even if
something disappoints me, I
will try to remember that.

Laughter changes everything.

I love to laugh. Whenever my brother tells a joke, we all laugh, partly because he usually gets the joke all mixed up. I love it when my dad teases me and sings me silly songs. That always makes me laugh and feel loved.

Our teacher makes me laugh sometimes when she gets the twins mixed up. They play a joke on her once in a while by sitting in each other's seat. The whole class laughs then. Laughing makes me feel good all over. Robyn's dad is a doctor, and he says it is really good for us to laugh. Laughing makes our bodies healthier, he says.

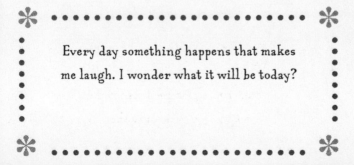

Every day something happens that makes me laugh. I wonder what it will be today?

We are all different, yet equal.

Did you ever look carefully at everyone in your room at school? No two people look much alike, except for the twins Sam and Max. Many aren't even the same color. Antonio has darker skin than me. Lauren is even darker than Antonio. Emma has the curliest hair. Three kids wear glasses. We really are all different.

Mother says it's good there are so many differences. She says we need to understand that looking one way or another isn't a very big deal. Our differences are important, but they don't make any one of us better or worse than anyone else. We are equal, no matter what our differences are.

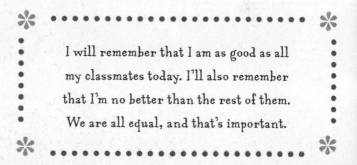

I will remember that I am as good as all my classmates today. I'll also remember that I'm no better than the rest of them. We are all equal, and that's important.

Be Brave

Sometimes life seems unfair.

Are you ever ignored by your friends? It doesn't seem fair, does it? Maybe they all went on a bike ride and didn't ask you, but probably each one thought someone else was going to invite you. They probably didn't realize that no one had until they were on their way home.

A lot of things can happen in a day that seem unfair. Recently my aunt got sick and had to cancel our big shopping trip. She couldn't help it. I had done extra chores to earn money to spend, and was bummed out. Even worse things happen sometimes. Dad can't always make it to my ball game because his boss needs him to work late occasionally. That doesn't seem fair, but it can't be helped.

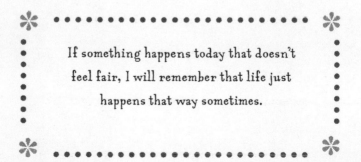

If something happens today that doesn't feel fair, I will remember that life just happens that way sometimes.

Bravery can be a decision.

What does it mean to be brave? It might mean we aren't afraid to sleep in the dark. Or it could mean we have studied all the spelling words and are ready for the test on Friday. Being brave can mean we are ready to admit a mistake we made to whoever is around. Being brave means we can face whatever is about to happen. We know we will be okay and that being a little scared is no big deal.

How do you get braver? That's the big question. My stepdad says bravery happens more or less by itself as we get older. Mr. Simpson says praying helps him feel braver. My grandmother says the more we practice being brave, the braver we become. My older sister, Hannah, says she decided to be brave one day, and she has felt braver ever since.

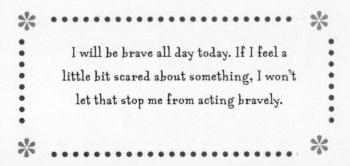

I will be brave all day today. If I feel a little bit scared about something, I won't let that stop me from acting bravely.

Let your tears come.

Do you ever cry when you don't understand something that's happening? I do. And I cry when I get punished for hitting my sister. Getting punished hurts my feelings. Mother cries when my stepsister doesn't come home at night. Last night, she and my stepdad were both up all night worrying. My little brother cries a lot, but that's what babies do.

My grandmother says tears can wash away sad memories sometimes. Maybe that's a good reason to cry. Grandma cries when she remembers my grandfather. He died last year. I miss him too.

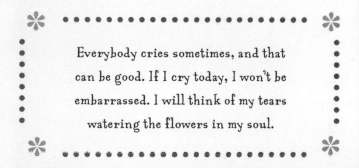

Everybody cries sometimes, and that can be good. If I cry today, I won't be embarrassed. I will think of my tears watering the flowers in my soul.

Mistakes happen.

Nobody is perfect! Even Katy, my best friend and the smartest girl in my class at school, isn't perfect. She left her permission slip for going on the field trip at home and had to stay at school. She missed an exciting trip to the history museum.

Making mistakes is normal. Adults make them all the time too. Just ask my dad. Mistakes can be big or little. Forgetting to turn the stove off when a pan is on it can be a big mistake. That's one my dad can tell you about. Knocking over a vase can be a big or little mistake, depending on what spills. My little sister knows about that one. Forgetting to bring homework to school can be a big mistake, especially if a project is due.

Mistakes can be forgiven and forgotten if I'm willing to accept responsibility for them and try harder the next time.

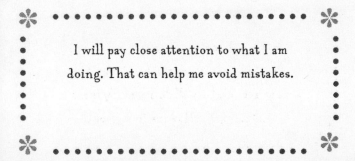

I will pay close attention to what I am doing. That can help me avoid mistakes.

Fear is a common feeling.

What are you most afraid of? Ruby is really afraid of spiders. They don't scare me, though. My mother is afraid of snakes. They kind of scare me, but my dad says most snakes are harmless. My grandmother says she gets a little bit afraid when strangers come to her door. I am afraid when I hear my parents fight, because I wonder if they'll get divorced like Jenny's parents.

Feeling afraid is normal, but I don't have to stay that way. We can learn to watch where we walk and avoid snakes and spiders. We can refuse to let strangers into our houses. We can tell Mom and Dad how we feel about their fights. I guess there are lots of things we can do to stop being afraid.

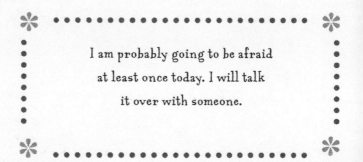

I am probably going to be afraid
at least once today. I will talk
it over with someone.

Blaming someone else doesn't make us feel better.

When I fell down next to my friend Akeesha, I wanted to blame her for tripping me even though I knew it wasn't her fault. When I can't find my coat or hat and it's time to catch the bus, I really want to yell, "Who hid my coat?" My mother says becoming responsible for my own accidents, lost toys, books, and misplaced clothes is part of growing up.

Not blaming someone else is really hard, but it helps me feel like I'm more grown-up. I want my parents and the other people in my life to notice that I'm growing up. It's okay for little kids to blame others. But I'm not really a little girl anymore.

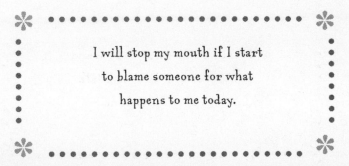

I will stop my mouth if I start
to blame someone for what
happens to me today.

I get anxious when I forget that God is in charge.

I can get nervous so easily, and so many things trigger my nervousness. I worry that I will miss my ride to school. I get nervous that the girls in my class will leave me out when they play at recess. I often get nervous while trying to fall asleep at night.

Being nervous occasionally is normal. Staying nervous all of the time isn't healthy, according to my mother. I think I will try what she suggested. If I feel even a little bit nervous about anything, I will think about something comforting. That's what she does. She says it helps. I wonder if other people do this too.

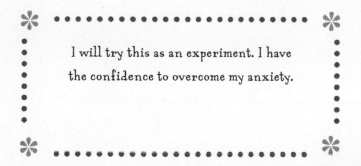

I will try this as an experiment. I have the confidence to overcome my anxiety.

Sadness is natural.

Being sad is a natural thing. Lots of things make me sad. If I don't get invited to Katy's after school I am sad, particularly if I know that my other friends were invited. Did I do something to make Katy mad? If Mom cancels her plan to take me shopping, I feel sad. I've saved up from my allowance, and I really want a new book. I've read all the books under my bed already.

When our parakeet flew away, I was sad. I wondered if it would know how to survive outdoors. We had always fed it and given it water. I definitely learned how important it is to keep the front door closed. Mom said maybe it would join another group of birds, and that made me feel a little bit better.

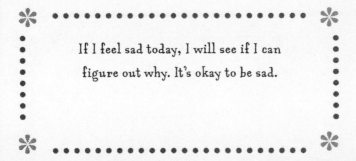

If I feel sad today, I will see if I can figure out why. It's okay to be sad.

The world is a wheel always turning.

—Anzia Yezierska

It seems like every year one of my best friends moves away. Last year, three friends moved. That was the worst year so far. I wish nothing had to change, but my step-mom says if nothing changed, I would never grow older, my braces would never come off, and my little sister Hannah would never outgrow getting into my favorite things. Some changes are good, I guess.

My teacher says that without change, flowers would never bloom, trees would never grow new leaves, chickens would never lay fresh eggs, we wouldn't have summer vacation, and I'd have to reread the same books over and over again. I guess change is good, even though I don't always like it.

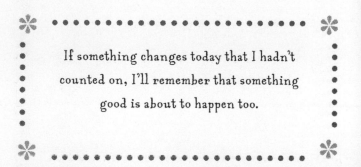

If something changes today that I hadn't counted on, I'll remember that something good is about to happen too.

We can learn what to do with our fears.

Thunder made me really scared when I was little. I always wanted to crawl into bed with my parents. Maybe it affected you too. If it's really loud, with lots of lightening, even now I sometimes get a little bit afraid, but I don't like to admit it to anyone. I usually snuggle up with one of my teddy bears and try to keep my eyes closed. Sometimes I turn on the bedroom light.

When I first started crossing the busy street by my house or went to the store all by myself, I often felt a tiny bit afraid too. But after doing it a few times, I really felt brave. I learned how to handle many things.

Even adults are afraid once in a while. I've heard my mom talk about her fears to her best friend. Maybe I should talk about my fears with Mom or my friend Caitlin.

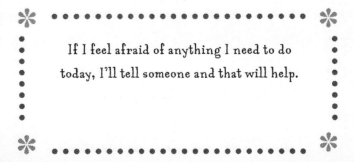

If I feel afraid of anything I need to do today, I'll tell someone and that will help.

Problems teach us things.

There are many kinds of problems. There are math problems every day. There are science problems on Friday. There is the problem of who to play with when both Margo and Jamie ask me to come over after school. Even what to eat for lunch can be a problem because some days I like everything the cafeteria has. Sometimes deciding whether to spend the weekend with my dad or my mom is a big problem.

Mom says solving problems of any kind is good practice. She says problems are one thing you can count on having for the rest of your life. When I'm older, I wonder if my problems will get any harder than knowing who to spend the weekend with.

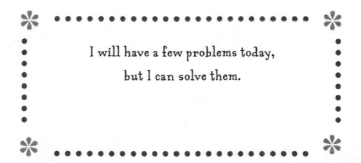

I will have a few problems today,
but I can solve them.

Being scared is normal.

Everybody is scared part of the time. Even my parents get scared by some things. Maybe riding a roller coaster is too scary for them. A loud thunderstorm may scare me, but not them. It's a good thing everybody isn't scared by the same things because we can help each other feel brave.

Teachers and parents often tell kids to stay away from strangers. They don't mean to scare us, but they want us to be careful. Going to a new classroom or playing with some new kids in the neighborhood may make me feel shy or even a little scared. That's okay. Lots of people, kids and adults, are a little shy when meeting people for the first time. I just have to remember this is how it is, even for Mom and Dad, to feel a little braver.

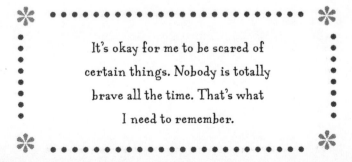

It's okay for me to be scared of certain things. Nobody is totally brave all the time. That's what I need to remember.

Some days we feel happier than other days.

Some people believe you are as happy as you make up your mind to be. My grandmother has this idea. She said she adopted this idea from Abraham Lincoln, a former president from more than a hundred years ago! I am not so sure I agree with my grandmother. Yesterday I was not one bit happy. My dad cancelled our dinner plans at the last minute. How could I be happy about that! When I mentioned this to my grandmother, she said maybe I could find another reason to be happy. For instance, she was willing to play Monopoly with me after we had dinner at home.

My grandmother said sadness was perfectly normal. But she said we could always look for something to feel good about even when a bad situation has occurred. The good thing was that my friend didn't run after her dog when it chased the squirrel. If she had, she might have gotten hit by the car too.

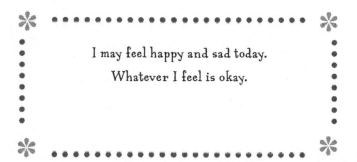

I may feel happy and sad today.
Whatever I feel is okay.

Often when we're being tough
and strong, we're scared.

—Dudley Martineau

Sisters and brothers fight. Moms and dads fight too. Neighbors sometimes fight. Fighting upsets me. When I fight, I end up with a stomachache. I guess fighting is bad for my health! There are many reasons why people fight. My stepdad thinks people fight because they're scared. I know when I fought with Hannah yesterday, it was because I was angry that she was taking all the cookies.

Fighting sometimes happens because one person wants to be in charge. When Mom and I fight, it's because she wants me to do something I don't want to do. When the neighbors fight, Mom says it's because Mr. Gray stays out too late at night.

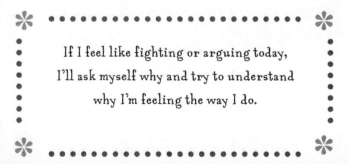

If I feel like fighting or arguing today,
I'll ask myself why and try to understand
why I'm feeling the way I do.

Having problems is a sign of being alive.

Nobody's free of problems. At least that's what Tiffany's grandmother says. Part of everybody's job is to learn how to solve problems. The problems you have at school are easy compared to the problems adults have to solve. For instance, my dad got fired from his job. Now he has to find a new one—really quickly, Mom says. Lots of people got fired where he works, so they'll all be looking for new jobs.

The only problem I had yesterday was how to sound out some new words in reading. They were hard words, but I managed to figure them out. Making my mind get really quiet is the first thing to do when solving any kind of problem, whether it's a small problem or a big one.

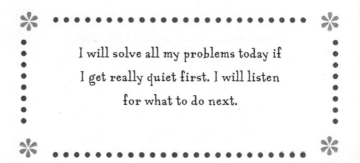

I will solve all my problems today if
I get really quiet first. I will listen
for what to do next.

Change is an everyday experience.

Have you ever had to change schools in the middle of the year? I haven't, but my friend Lisa has already changed twice since December. She says it isn't hard, but I think I'd be scared. What if nobody liked me?

My teacher says we make changes all of the time, but mostly we don't notice them. For instance, she changed our reading group from the morning to the afternoon and I never realized it until it was time to go home. She changed the bulletin board too before we came to school this week and only Stephanie noticed. It's good to remember that everything changes.

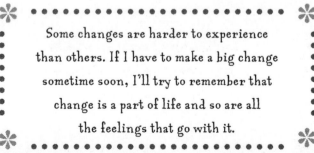

Some changes are harder to experience than others. If I have to make a big change sometime soon, I'll try to remember that change is a part of life and so are all the feelings that go with it.

There is body pain and
heart pain—they both hurt.

There are many kinds of pain. Last week, my mother stubbed her toe on the stove, and did she yell! I went to the dentist to get a cavity filled and after the numbness went away, my jaw hurt. My dad got rear-ended in his car almost six months ago. He's had pain in his neck ever since.

The minister at church says that some pain can't even be seen. That kind can be the worst of all. My grandmother has been in pain ever since my grandfather died. But I can't see what hurts. My mother says it's her heart. She's lonely. I think I'll bring her a flower today.

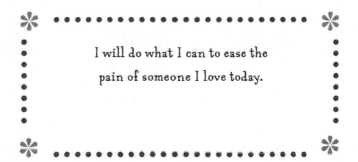

I will do what I can to ease the
pain of someone I love today.

When you are lonely, you will feel better if you do something nice for someone else.

Do you ever feel lonely? Most people do. I can tell my mother is lonely ever since her boyfriend got transferred to another city. I've heard my grandmother talk many times about being lonely since her neighbor died. It's nice to have companions and friends, isn't it?

I know some things I can do if I'm feeling lonely. I can call the new girl in my class and ask her to come over and hang out. I can go visit the neighbor who always seems to be in her yard all alone. Sometimes reading a good book helps—it's like the characters are keeping me company. I can ask my mom if I can help her do something around the house. Just being busy with something makes my loneliness disappear.

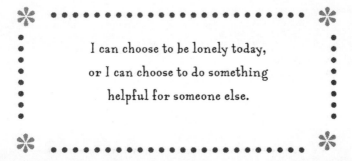

I can choose to be lonely today,
or I can choose to do something
helpful for someone else.

> All my trouble with living
> has come from fear.
>
> —Angela L. Wozniak

Nobody is brave all the time, even Dad. I know my mother doesn't like it when it storms really hard after dark. Sometimes she makes us go to the basement in case a tornado is close by. Sometimes I think there's something creeping around my bedroom after Mom has turned out the light. Then I have to get up and check to make sure nothing is there.

Dad says people generally get braver as they get older. He also says it's okay to be scared part of the time, no matter how old you are. Talking to God helps him when he feels afraid, and sometimes that helps me too. Fear is normal.

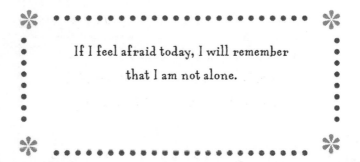

If I feel afraid today, I will remember
that I am not alone.

Blaming others is how
we avoid responsibility.

I always want to blame someone else for my mistakes. Last week, I forgot to turn the water off in the bathroom sink, and water ran into the living room. At first, I said I didn't do it, that my little sister must have, but Dad knew better. None of us wants to admit when we are wrong. Mom says that it is "human nature" to blame others, but that doesn't mean it's the right thing to do. I must be afraid I'll get yelled at for mistakes because I always think first about blaming someone else.

It isn't honest to blame someone else for what I did, or to claim I knew nothing about it. It isn't fair to the person I blamed. They know I'm lying, and I know it too. We both know I'm pretending I had nothing to do with something I did.

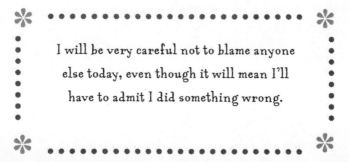

I will be very careful not to blame anyone else today, even though it will mean I'll have to admit I did something wrong.

Compromise is a grown-up way to handle differences.

Taking turns is important. I'm glad my grandmother lives with us because she told me how important this was before I started school. I won't mention names, but one of the girls in my class never wants to take turns, and no one wants to play with her. I'm glad nobody feels that way about me.

Of course, I don't always like to take turns either. For instance, when I trip during jump rope, I want another turn right away. The teacher says, "No dice." What a weird saying that is. But rules are rules! I have to go to the end of the line. Taking turns is right for all of us, I guess.

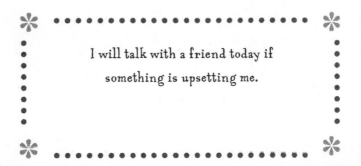

I will talk with a friend today if
something is upsetting me.

Sometimes there is no clear answer to the question "Why?"

I can't understand why bad things happen to people. Why did Rachel's baby brother die? Megan says God punishes people, so maybe the baby did something bad? My grandfather says this isn't true. He says God never punishes us, that no matter what we do, God never stops loving us. But then why do bad things happen? It isn't easy to understand.

Some things just happen, my dad says. It just isn't possible to understand why bad things happen.

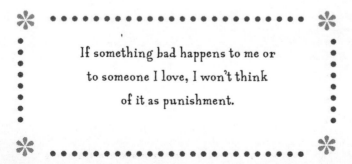

If something bad happens to me or to someone I love, I won't think of it as punishment.

Talking about what bothers me
usually makes it shrink.

Almost every day something happens that bothers me a little. For instance, yesterday my dad seemed mad at me for no reason at all. He didn't smile once while we were eating dinner. He didn't really talk to any of us. After we finished eating, I asked my mother if Dad was mad at me. She said he was just upset about something that happened at work.

It is really important to talk my feelings over with Mom or another grownup or a friend. Just talking to somebody about how I feel helps me feel a little better. I'm glad Dad wasn't mad at me, though. I gave him a big hug right after the talk I had with Mom. He kind of smiled then.

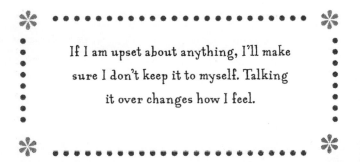

If I am upset about anything, I'll make
sure I don't keep it to myself. Talking
it over changes how I feel.

Illness can happen to anyone, anytime.

Most people feel sick occasionally. My mother stays home from work once in a while when she gets a bad headache. Sometimes she has to miss work because my baby brother is really sick with a temperature. I get a stomachache when I get too hot. Some kids can't drink milk because it upsets their stomachs. Since ice cream is made from milk, I wonder, does that mean they can't ever eat ice cream? What bad luck!

Feeling sick once in a while can happen because we need to rest more. Sometimes I play too hard and then stay up really late at night. Sometimes I catch colds this way. Sickness can be caused by many things, but usually resting and eating healthy foods make me get well.

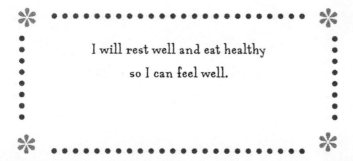

I will rest well and eat healthy
so I can feel well.

> I have accepted fear as a part of life.
>
> —Erica Jong

What are you most afraid of? Have you ever thought about this? Tommy, my baby brother, is afraid of shadows. My dad says he's afraid he will get sick and have to quit working like Grandpa did. My grandmother says she was afraid of people, getting a job, and dating boys when she was younger, but now she lets God have her fears, and they seem to disappear.

At school last week we talked about fear. I enjoyed the discussion. Mr. Penny said people sometimes get afraid because they forget to tell others what is bothering them. He says if we tell someone what fear is in our minds, it will help it to disintegrate. I've thought about telling God my fears, like Grandma does. I notice when I talk to Mom or Dad about my fears, I feel less afraid.

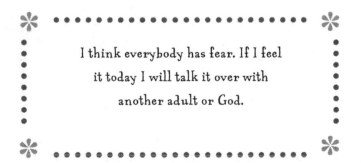

I think everybody has fear. If I feel it today I will talk it over with another adult or God.

We all have dark days of fear and doubt.

—Jo Ann Reed

My dreams wake me up some nights. They seem so real. Once I dreamed we had moved away to a new house in a new town. I didn't know anybody in my class at school, and whenever I walked into a room, it went dead silent and everybody turned away from me. Was I ever glad when I woke up and went to the bathroom! I could see it was the same old house, which meant my dream was not true and I didn't need to be afraid.

My dreams can help me sometimes, Mother says. They can show me what was on my mind before I went to sleep. Maybe I was feeling afraid about something when I went to bed that night. My dream was about fear, but when I woke up, everything was okay. Knowing that things are okay is a good feeling.

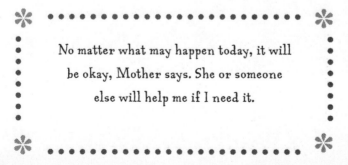

No matter what may happen today, it will be okay, Mother says. She or someone else will help me if I need it.

Shy feelings are common.

Walking onto the school yard where a bunch of kids are already gathered can be hard to do sometimes, especially if there's someone I don't know in the group. I feel a little shy some days. Is there anything wrong with that? I don't like to feel shy.

What is it that makes me feel shy? Maybe I had a bad dream during the night and it made me a little upset. Or I had a fight with Mom about what I was going to wear to school. Really small things that aren't even important can make me a bit upset, and these can then cause me to feel shy. Feeling shy is very normal. Everybody feels it part of the time, even the most popular girl in the class.

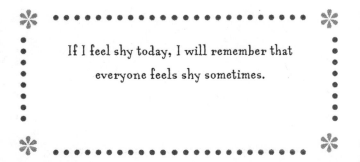

If I feel shy today, I will remember that
everyone feels shy sometimes.

Happiness is often close at hand.

What makes you happy? Does having your mother wake you up for school make you happy? Does having your favorite warm cookies waiting for you when you get home from school make you happy? I feel happy when I have done something nice for Grandma and she gives me a big hug.

My mother says I have a tendency to notice what I don't have rather than all that I do have. I am working on this, and when I look at my world this way, I do see many reasons to be happy. Last night I drifted off to dreamland listening to music and curling up with my favorite stuffed animal. Today my mom is picking me up at school. All those things make my heart happy.

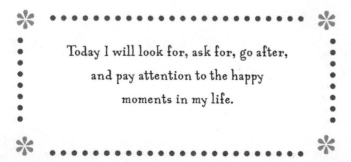

Today I will look for, ask for, go after, and pay attention to the happy moments in my life.

Worrying never helps.

Moms worry that kids may get hurt on the playground. And sometimes we do. Both dads and moms worry when we're on our bikes after dark. And that can be dangerous, especially if we aren't wearing reflective clothes and don't have lights.

Do you worry much? Sometimes I worry if a certain friend really likes me or if I will remember all the multiplication tables for the big test. Even teachers worry. Ms. Hanson said she worried Monday morning that she would be late for school because her car wouldn't start. She called her brother for help, she said.

Even though most people worry about something, it never helps. In fact, it can make things worse. One time I worried so much about a spelling test that I couldn't remember a bunch of words.

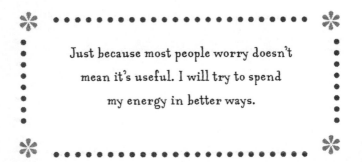

Just because most people worry doesn't mean it's useful. I will try to spend my energy in better ways.

Have the courage to act instead of react.
—Darlene Larson Jenks

When a friend makes fun of you, how do you feel? Do you get mad, or pout, or hit her, or maybe refuse to play with her ever again? It isn't very easy to just walk away, is it? My older sister says that only sissies walk away. But really smart grown-ups say it's better to walk away from a fight than risk getting hurt or hurting someone else. It isn't easy to walk away, maybe, but I can learn to do it.

Fighting with a friend or a brother or a kid at the park I hardly know always upsets me. It's good to know I don't ever have to fight. It's okay to walk away. In fact, sometimes the best thing to do is to walk away. That way nobody gets hurt.

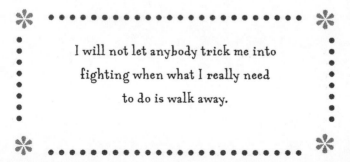

I will not let anybody trick me into fighting when what I really need to do is walk away.

Death is natural.

It isn't very pleasant to think about dying. My foster mom says that's probably because we don't know how it will feel, and we're afraid. Some of my friends have been to funerals, but not me. Have you been to a funeral? Looking at a dead body would be sort of weird, I think. But when I remember that birds and leaves and flowers die, it's easier to understand why people die too.

Some adults believe a part of us never dies. The body dies, but not the part that talks to God. If that is true, then all the dead people are still alive, in a way. I guess my foster parents and I will stay alive too. I like this idea.

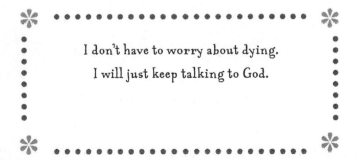

I don't have to worry about dying.
I will just keep talking to God.

Confusion is a normal human feeling.

I get confused sometimes. Last week in school my teacher asked us to hand in our math assignments. I couldn't find mine, and I knew I had finished it the night before. I looked everywhere. I even looked in my lunch box. I was confused. Later in the morning, we had science. Guess what? In the middle of my science book I found my math assignment. I am still confused about this. I hadn't even taken my science book home. How did it get there?

The best thing about confusion, according to my stepdad, is that it reminds me to pay closer attention to what I'm doing each minute. He thinks most confusion comes from not watching very closely. He suggested that the mysterious reappearance of the math paper was probably due to my sticking it in the science book and then thinking it was my math book when I got to school. He could be right. I was really excited to talk to my friend Hannah when I got to school that day. Maybe I wasn't watching very closely.

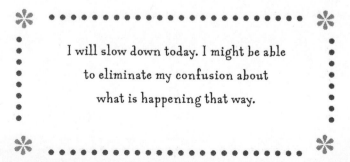

I will slow down today. I might be able
to eliminate my confusion about
what is happening that way.

Each day provides its own gifts.

—Ruth P. Freedman

Some days I seem to wake up feeling a little bit troubled. I wonder if my unhappiness is because I had a bad dream I can't remember. Or maybe I know my dad will be upset because I don't want to go to his house this weekend. The more I think about my feelings, the deeper my unhappiness goes. I learned a trick from Grandma, though, that I can always use when I feel unhappy.

First, I get a pencil. Next, I make a list of all the good things that happened yesterday. I could put down the **A** I got in spelling on my list. I could also mention the good cookies Mom made for dessert. Grandma says when I begin to count up all of the good things that happen, the few things that made me unhappy won't seem so big.

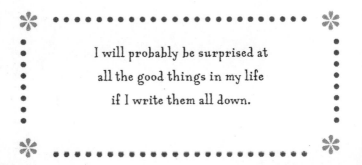

I will probably be surprised at
all the good things in my life
if I write them all down.

Sickness happens to everyone.

Is someone you know sick? Maybe it is just a case of the flu or a bad cold, and we all know that flu and colds go away in time. Emma's mother has something more serious, though. She was in the hospital for many weeks and is in a nursing home now. Emma says she may not be able to come home for a few months.

It's scary when someone I know is sick. Often there isn't very much I can do. My grandmother believes prayer is important. My dad says spending some extra time with Emma right now would be helpful too. Making a special get-well card for Emma's mother, maybe baking some cookies for Emma's family are a couple of things that would help too. According to my mother, the important thing is to extend myself in some way. I should think of something that would make me feel better in this situation, and then do it for my friend.

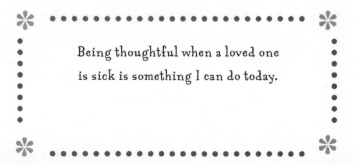

Being thoughtful when a loved one
is sick is something I can do today.

Fear affects every person in some way.

Everybody is afraid some of the time. When Mom had to give a speech in front of her club, didn't she say she was scared? And when Jason's dad got arrested for speeding, I bet Jason was afraid his dad might go to jail. Being afraid right before a math test or when the principal comes into the room just as the teacher calls on you to read happens to all of us.

What does being afraid feel like? I get the feeling of butterflies in my stomach. I feel all jumpy inside. Usually I can't eat when I am afraid, either. Stacy says she gets a headache when she's scared. My mom says her hands shake. It seems like something happens to everyone who is scared.

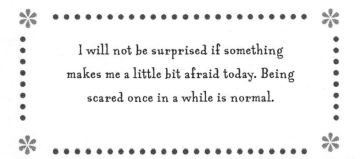

I will not be surprised if something makes me a little bit afraid today. Being scared once in a while is normal.

Our fears change as we grow.

Is there something in particular that you are afraid of? My aunt is afraid of big dogs. When she was a young girl, a German shepherd chased and bit her. He drew blood. Big dogs have been a problem for her ever since. Little kids are sometimes afraid of big kids. Most of the time they don't need to be, but I remember when I was little and a big kid named John beat me up for no reason. I was afraid of big kids for the rest of that year.

Sometimes I'm afraid of the dark, but not every night. Were you afraid the first time you went to the dentist? I was. I was afraid the first day of school too. I cried for about a week before the first day. It seems silly now to think of all the times I used to be afraid. It's nice to grow out of some fears.

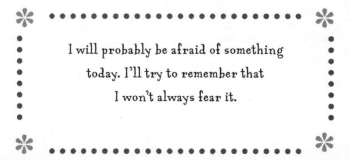

I will probably be afraid of something today. I'll try to remember that I won't always fear it.

Everyone experiences sadness.

Last week, I was really sad because I lost my favorite pair of mittens, and my grandmother gave them to me. Probably somebody picked them up and is now using them.

I was even sadder when my hamster died. Her name was Hilda. We called her Henry at first, until she had babies! What a joke on us. At least we still have two of her babies. Feeling sad makes me want to just sit by myself in my room or crawl into my mother's lap.

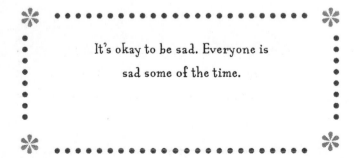

It's okay to be sad. Everyone is
sad some of the time.

Sharing something personal
can be a good idea.

Yesterday my friend Amanda was feeling hurt because she hardly ever gets chosen to play on either team at recess. I felt sad for her and told her about the time the same thing happened to me. It seemed to make her feel better. Sometimes just sharing a little story about ourselves can help someone else feel better.

My big sister says one of the reasons we all have hard experiences is so we can help other people when they have the same kind of experience. She calls sharing something that makes another person feel better getting a turn at being God's special angel. Sad feelings are a part of having a warm and open heart. Sharing these feelings is how people connect with each other: human to human, heart-to-heart. It's an important part of friendship.

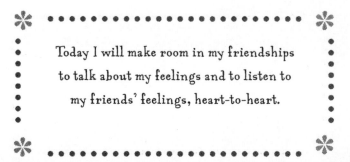

Today I will make room in my friendships to talk about my feelings and to listen to my friends' feelings, heart-to-heart.

> Life is perfect just the way it is
> and just the way it is not.
>
> —Peggy Bassett

Mom and my stepdad Ted are often telling me "Don't worry." But I still do. I wake up worrying. I worry about getting the states in order on Friday's geography test. I worry about all the multiplication tables. Every Wednesday we have a surprise test that includes some of them. I worry about whether or not Tammy will invite me for another overnight. The last time I went, I had a nightmare and woke up her whole family. Right now I worry about whether or not I'll get invited to Alexandra and Anne's eighth birthday party.

My mind seems to worry about things like this all the time. It is always wondering if I will be included or left out of special activities. I wish I could quit worrying so much.

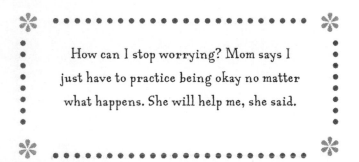

How can I stop worrying? Mom says I
just have to practice being okay no matter
what happens. She will help me, she said.

Life is sometimes painful.

–Thelma Elliott

What makes you sad? How about when your mom makes you go to bed even though your favorite television show isn't over yet? If I can't find my favorite DVD, I am pretty sad. I sometimes suspect my little brother hid it. One of the times I feel saddest is when Dad says he is going to come over after school and take me to dinner, and then he doesn't show up. This has happened two weeks in a row. Why doesn't he even call?

Mom feels sad when her boss isn't very nice to her at work. That would make me sad too, if I were a grown-up. When my teacher scolds me, I get sad. I think she's like my boss. Being sad happens to all of us, I guess. If I talk to a friend about it, I usually begin to feel better.

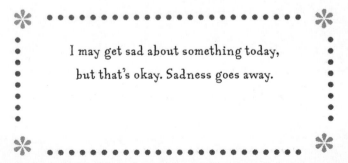

I may get sad about something today,
but that's okay. Sadness goes away.

I can stand what I know. It's what I don't
know that frightens me.

—Frances Newton

Everybody is frightened sometimes. Loud thunder and a
bright flash of lightning scare my little sister Hannah. My
mom says she is a little bit afraid when she has to drive
our brand-new van. Do you ever get afraid when you are
trying to cross a busy street on your bike? Maybe that's
because you can't see very well around the big tree on the
corner. Maybe a car is coming from the other direction.
That is probably a good time to be afraid. It can help you
be more cautious.

I don't want being scared to keep me from doing
something I really want or need to do. I'll just go slow, be
brave, and do it anyway. When being scared means I need
to be careful, I will pay attention and be careful.

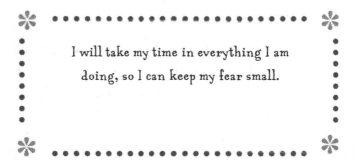

I will take my time in everything I am
doing, so I can keep my fear small.

Birds sing after a storm.

—Rose Fitzgerald Kennedy

Something may happen today that will make you sad. Maybe your favorite angel fish will die. Or perhaps Samantha will be absent from school today, which means she can't return your comic book. Losing my neck scarf while walking home from school made me sad last week because my aunt had just sent it to me from California.

Things happen that make everyone feel sad. If you never felt sad, though, you wouldn't appreciate nearly as much the times you feel like singing. For instance, when my cat died, we had a burial service in the backyard. My friends and I threw glitter and flower petals where we buried her, and I talked of all my fondest memories of our cat. Pretty soon we were all laughing because she had been a pretty funny cat. In the middle of the laughing and my friends' understanding and the beautiful sparkly glitter, I felt happy again.

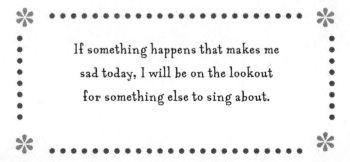

If something happens that makes me sad today, I will be on the lookout for something else to sing about.

> It's astonishing in this world how
> things don't turn out at all the
> way you expect them to.
>
> –Agatha Christie

Yesterday I planned on going to my friend's house after school to play with her new computer, but she got sick, so I had to come home. What a bummer! Mom said I needed to look for the "silver lining" in my disappointment. I couldn't see it.

But then, an hour later, my big sister came home early from school and asked me to go to a movie. If I had been at my friend's house, I would have missed seeing the new Godzilla movie. I think that was the silver lining!

Adults say there is always something good that can come out of every disappointment. Sometimes it takes a while to see it.

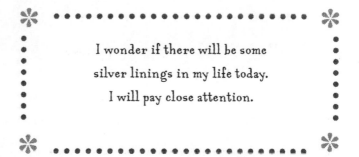

I wonder if there will be some
silver linings in my life today.
I will pay close attention.

We all have bad hair days.

Does it seem like nothing goes the way you want some days? Maybe it starts out with your hair sticking out really funny because you slept on it crooked. Or you counted on wearing a favorite skirt, and the zipper broke when you were getting dressed. But worst of all, you get all the way to school and remember that you left your homework on the kitchen counter.

Mom says I have to learn to "roll with the punches." What a funny picture that makes in my mind! Probably at least one thing will happen every day of my life that I don't like, she says. She also says, "Don't make a mountain out of a mole hill."

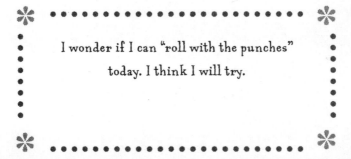

I wonder if I can "roll with the punches"
today. I think I will try.

Be Willing to Learn

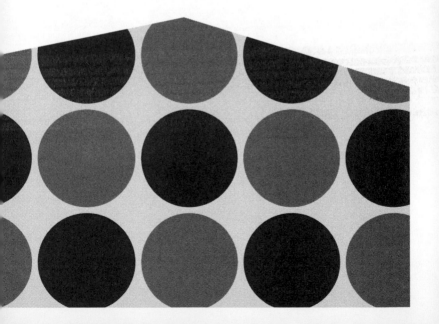

Developing good habits
can be a full-time job.

I have some very good habits. My grandmother Sara recently helped me see what many of them are. While I recalled them, she wrote them on a fancy piece of paper and taped them on her refrigerator. She said that seeing them often keeps them fresh in our minds too. Because I open her refrigerator door dozens of times a day when I stay at her house, I get lots of reminders!

At the top of my list is remembering to say thank you. She said not everyone does this as well as I do. I was surprised to hear that. I also am a very good listener. I think I learned this from my dad. He never interrupts me, even when I am telling a long story. I also make my bed nearly every day without a reminder, and I am very careful with my mother's nice dishes. I am not sure how I learned that habit. Not from my older sister, that's for sure!

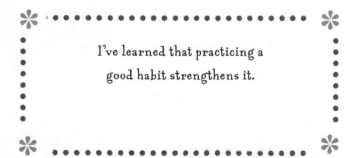

I've learned that practicing a
good habit strengthens it.

Every skill takes practice.

—Susan Atchley Ebaugh

Every teacher I've ever had said we have to practice skills we want to be good at. That's what my parents say too. Mom is always asking me to practice my spelling words. Sometimes I even ask her to help me practice my subtraction tables. Since I started to take piano lessons, I have to practice piano thirty minutes every night. I don't have very much time to watch TV anymore. That doesn't seem to bother my mom at all.

I really want to read at a higher grade level, so I make sure I read at least a half-hour every day. My brother likes hockey—he goes to practice a lot, and I can see what a good skater he's becoming.

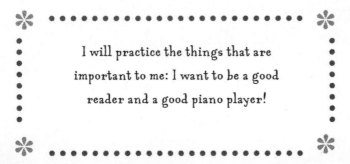

I will practice the things that are important to me: I want to be a good reader and a good piano player!

Making a mistake can teach me something.

I make many mistakes every day, like everyone else. Some are little ones. Maybe I forgot to brush my teeth before leaving the house, or I put on my old sneakers instead of my new ones when I was getting ready for school because I forgot it was Friday and not Saturday.

Do you ever make mistakes when you're doing addition? That's a bigger mistake, I think. When I know the right answer, it really makes me mad when I miss. I guess I hurry too much sometimes. Lots of mistakes happen when I hurry. Adults even make mistakes when they hurry. Last week my mom went off to work so fast that she forgot her purse. She had to borrow money when she got there for parking.

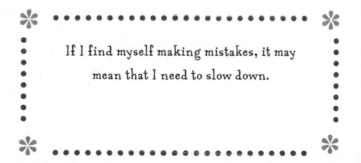

If I find myself making mistakes, it may mean that I need to slow down.

Imagination is mind power.

Pretending I am Spiderman or Catwoman or even a big sister or the teacher is one of my favorite games to play. My dad says when he was little he often pretended he was a gardener like his neighbor. Imagination can help a person quite a bit. It can change whatever is in my mind. I can become brave when I actually feel scared. I can act strong when I feel weak. And best of all, I can act confident when I feel nervous. This is one of the ways I use my imagination regularly.

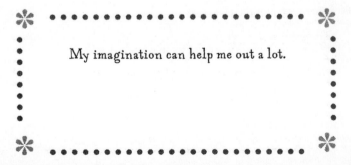

My imagination can help me out a lot.

How we see ourselves
isn't always accurate.

–Marge Reed

Do you like how you look when you stand in front of the mirror? Lots of kids—even lots of adults—are very picky about how they look. My brother Jason thinks he's too short. I know this because I heard him complain to Dad. My sister thinks her hair is ugly. It's pretty curly, but I like it. Being overweight or having too many freckles bothers some kids. None of us is perfect, I guess.

My parents say that being short or pudgy or having lots of pimples doesn't affect what we're like on the inside. And that the inside is what's most important.

How we act and think shows our insides. On the inside, are we kind? Patient? Generous? Expressing important inside qualities is what counts, not our freckles.

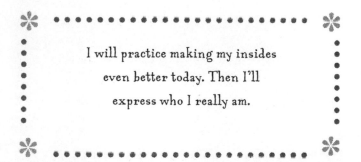

I will practice making my insides
even better today. Then I'll
express who I really am.

Know when and how to help others.

What do you do when a friend wants to copy your answers on a math test? I don't want my friend to be mad, but I don't want to cheat, either. I've thought about why my teacher tells me to cover my answers. It's because whenever I do someone else's work for them, they aren't learning what they need to know. They'll suffer in the next grade if I help them too much now.

Wanting to help others is a good quality. I just have to be choosy about who and when to help. I could help my friend with her math after school instead of giving her the answers. That's the best way I can help.

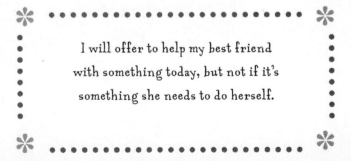

I will offer to help my best friend
with something today, but not if it's
something she needs to do herself.

We will never hear anyone else's thoughts
if we are only listening to our own.

—Cathy Stone

My teacher sometimes accuses me of daydreaming. What does she mean? Probably she means she can tell I'm not really listening to her because I'm staring out the window at a dump truck going by while she is explaining how to do a new kind of math problem. Having my mind someplace other than on what someone is saying to me means that I miss the thought the other person is sharing with me.

Every day each of us has specific jobs to do. Maybe it's pouring the juice for breakfast or bringing in the newspaper. One job each of us can do really well every day is to listen to what others are saying. That may be the most important job we have all day.

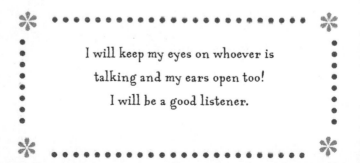

I will keep my eyes on whoever is
talking and my ears open too!
I will be a good listener.

Our own gentleness is a
powerful force in our lives.

—Patricia Hoolihan

I can easily recognize gentleness in others. For instance, when my grandfather offers to take a walk with me, I know he's wanting to share a gentle story. He has lots of them from when he was a boy growing up on a farm. The easiest way for me to express gentleness is toward my cat Sophia. She is very soft and extremely quiet. She is also pretty old. I have had her since I was a tiny girl and she was a tiny kitten. When I am gentle toward Sophia or my mom or even my brother, who is always getting into my stuff, I feel good inside. Grandmother says practicing gentleness makes each person a better person.

Being gentle can help me
in many ways today.

I do not have to always be right!
–Mary Zink

Why do some people think they have to be right all of the time? I hate hearing my parents argue. They do it a lot too. I don't like to hear Joannie and Rachael argue, either. They are both my best friends, but they don't seem to like each other very much. Arguing makes me a little nervous. Sometimes I want to tell my dad to be quiet, and once I took Joannie's side because Rachael can be really bossy. That didn't make me feel any better, though. Actually, they got mad at me when I took sides. Boy, was I surprised! I wasn't even in the argument.

This is what I notice when I watch an argument: nobody is listening! If each side really listened to the other side, that would help a lot. Sometimes, both sides are a little bit right.

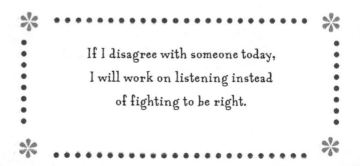

If I disagree with someone today,
I will work on listening instead
of fighting to be right.

Do you ask for help when you need it?

It's okay to ask someone to braid your hair or help you make the bed. When you want your bedroom or your hair to look extra neat, getting help is good. I ask my teacher to help me understand science experiments all the time. The more I learn at school, the better my life will be. Nobody knows everything, and everybody needs help with some things.

When your mom comes home from work, she may ask you to help her by setting the table for dinner. Maybe the neighbor needs help raking his leaves, now that he uses a walker. Someone learning to ride a bike may need help to balance while pedaling. People are all the same— we all need help with something. So we can all feel good by helping someone else too.

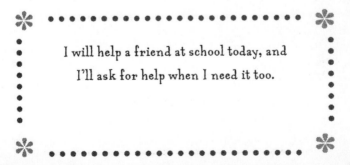

I will help a friend at school today, and
I'll ask for help when I need it too.

Can you be trusted?

If I tell a secret about my family to Kaitlin and ask her not to tell anyone, and then I learn she has told the secret to Megan, the biggest gossip in our school, I have learned the hard way that I can't trust Kaitlin. Being able to trust my friends is very important. Having them know they can trust me too is just as important.

I have been untrustworthy a few times, and I don't feel very good about it. For example, just last week Mother sent me to the corner store for milk she forgot on her way home from work. I bought a candy bar too, and ate it before I got home. She asked me where the rest of the change was, and I said I must have dropped it on the walk home. She gave me a funny look, and I felt pretty uncomfortable. Even a little lie interferes with how I feel about myself.

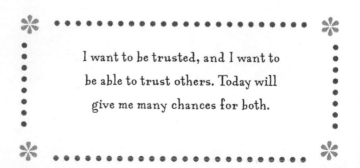

I want to be trusted, and I want to be able to trust others. Today will give me many chances for both.

Thinking before acting
saves trouble and time.

Does your mother ever say, "Don't be so impulsive"? Do you know what she means by impulsive? She means reacting to a situation before thinking about what to do. If you act in a hurried way before thinking it through, you may make a big mistake. For example, after my dog got loose and ran through the mud, it wasn't a good idea for me to call him inside. He tracked mud all over the carpet. It's a good thing I grabbed him before he jumped up on the couch, but Mom got mad anyway. Lots of times I end up wishing I hadn't done something after it's too late.

Thinking first is something I can learn to do. For instance, if the new girl at school asks me to play a trick on my friend, I can take the time to think first about how it will make my friend feel. If I'm impulsive instead, I'm going to hurt my friend's feelings.

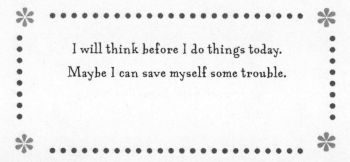

I will think before I do things today.
Maybe I can save myself some trouble.

Taking responsibility for behavior is a sure sign of growing up.

Admitting when I've done something wrong, no matter how slight, is a good habit to develop. For example, I spilled orange juice all over the kitchen floor while pouring from a really full carton. I cleaned it up a little bit, but I knew it would be sticky to bare feet. When Mom asked what had happened, I was very, very slow to admit my carelessness. It wasn't a big deal, but I didn't feel very good about holding back the truth for a time.

Another time I was hesitant to admit I intentionally left the newspaper under the bushes during a rainstorm. I had time to get it before the rain started, but I was mad at Mom for not letting me go to Emma's house, so I "paid her back." When the rain stopped and Mom got the paper, she could tell by how I acted what I had done. She didn't say anything, but she didn't need to. I still have some growing up to do, I think.

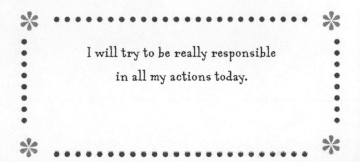

I will try to be really responsible
in all my actions today.

Showing respect and love for others exercises my heart.

It is really easy to love an innocent kitten. Kittens are so soft and willing to cuddle! It is pretty easy to love a newborn baby too, because it's innocent and not really able to hurt you. Not all individuals in our lives are easily loved, however. And that's okay. Sometimes we have to steer clear of people who have hurt us. I stay as far away from Bobby, the new kid on our block, as I can. He has a temper!

Mom says learning to show respect and love for people who treat me kindly are good habits to develop. She says the more I practice this, the easier it becomes. Practice makes everything better, she says. She reminds me that my soccer playing got lots better when I practiced. My expressions of love and respect will flow more easily from me with practice too, she says. She calls it exercising the heart. I like that idea.

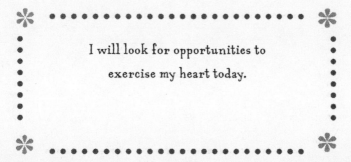

I will look for opportunities to exercise my heart today.

You can learn to be a good sport.

Are you good at sports? I'm a pretty fast runner. Even though boys can usually run faster than girls, the twin sisters who moved into our school district last year can outrun every boy in our whole school! My mom said their parents are good athletes too.

I'm not good at everything I try. Nobody is. I have worked really hard at shooting baskets, but I still don't get very close to the rim most of the time. Sara has the magic touch: she's always making baskets. The other day I told her she was really good, and her whole face lit up. That made me happy too. It's actually nice when our friends are better at some things than we are. That way we can trade praises for the things each of us is good at.

Being glad for how good others are is good sportsmanship. Are you a good sport around your friends?

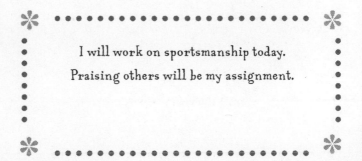

I will work on sportsmanship today.
Praising others will be my assignment.

Learning to be understanding can be developed like a habit.

I counted on my brother Tim to help me with my multiplication tables, but he couldn't because he got sick. Now I probably won't get an **A** on the test. Mom says I have to be understanding. She says being understanding means that I should show concern for his sickness rather than think only about myself.

I want others to be understanding of me too. For instance, after I told my friend Heather that I could work on the play we are writing for our after school program, I had to go someplace with my aunt instead. Heather didn't get angry. She was very understanding, and I appreciated that. I really want others to show me understanding, so I'll work on showing it too.

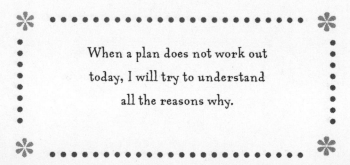

When a plan does not work out
today, I will try to understand
all the reasons why.

Teaching is the royal road to learning.

—Jessamyn West

Did you know that our teachers aren't just the ones we have at school? Jacob's mom said that everyone who speaks to us every single day is actually one of our teachers. What a funny idea this is. How can my friend Samantha be a teacher? She's younger than me. But Hank's mom says we learn from one another all the time. For instance, we learn what not to do sometimes. I sure don't want to sass the neighbor like Leah did. She got into lots of trouble. That taught me a lesson.

I wonder if this means I'm my sister Julia's teacher. She always wants to do what I'm doing. I better think about what I'm teaching her.

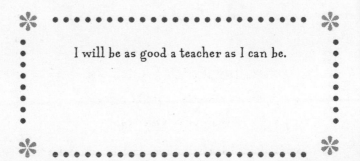

I will be as good a teacher as I can be.

Learning is fun and necessary.

Everything that happens today can teach me something. When I get washed up for school, I can watch how the soap bubbles up on my arms and takes the dirt away. I can listen for the birds chirping and notice if they are calling to warn their friends that I am walking under their tree. We are studying the sky at school, and I am noticing all the different stages of the moon and how the sun is setting later and later. I'm actually beginning to understand how this world works!

Learning to do arithmetic is hard sometimes, but it helps me when I want to buy candy. Since I have learned to be a good reader, it really is fun to travel by car or bus. It gives me a chance to read all the signs we pass. My mom was really impressed yesterday because I knew the word *authority*. Just to prove I understood its meaning, I used it in a sentence for her. Maybe today would be a good day to write a letter to Grandma. I can expand my vocabulary by doing that too.

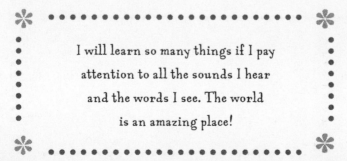

I will learn so many things if I pay
attention to all the sounds I hear
and the words I see. The world
is an amazing place!

You don't have to be perfect, but you can always be getting better.

Nobody is perfect all of the time, even Jenny, who never gets into trouble at school. I get jealous of her sometimes. Do you ever feel jealous because a classmate is really good at something?

Mom says we all make mistakes and they are not such big deals, as long as we are willing to admit them. Pretending we didn't make a mistake, especially one that affects others, is a big deal, like forgetting to close the freezer door so the ice cream melts. Instead of feeling bad for my mistake, I apologized and told myself I'd remember to close it next time.

Making an apology is part of growing up. Making mistakes must be part of growing up too. They go together, according to my mom.

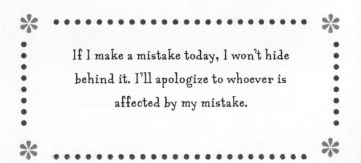

If I make a mistake today, I won't hide behind it. I'll apologize to whoever is affected by my mistake.

Growing up goes hand in hand with becoming more responsible.

As you get older, you are given more responsibility. What does that actually mean? If you ask a teacher, she will probably say it means she can depend on you to erase the boards very carefully if that's your assigned job. Or maybe it means she can trust you to go down to the principal's office to get something without supervision.

Mom says being more responsible means that as I get older, she can count on me watching the baby. She can trust me to make my bed without her having to come in and check my room. Learning to be more responsible is one of the things that's expected of me when I grow up.

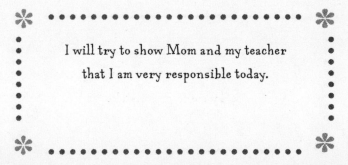

I will try to show Mom and my teacher
that I am very responsible today.

"You are what you eat!"

My mom has this saying in big, bold, red letters across our refrigerator. She has been dieting for a few months, and she says she doesn't want to forget and absentmindedly start to eat something that isn't on her diet. But Dad says he thinks she has it up there as a message to all of us. He has a sweet tooth, which means he really loves sweets. I have a sweet tooth too. And so did my mom before she started dieting. She claims her sweet tooth is what got her into so much trouble.

Now she works out four times a week and eats carrots every time she wants a snack. She looks a lot different than she did last year. She keeps a picture of herself before she started dieting on the refrigerator right along with the saying. It's a good reminder, she says. She has suggested that I go with her to work out so I can develop good exercise habits while I am young. It would be fun to spend the time with her, I think I will. Do you exercise and eat healthy foods?

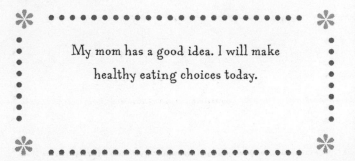

My mom has a good idea. I will make
healthy eating choices today.

Not everything that goes across my brain needs to come out of my mouth.

I get myself into trouble pretty often because I don't stay quiet when I should. My thoughts sometimes tell me to criticize or make fun of someone. Do your thoughts push you to make a mean comment to a friend when she doesn't do something the way you like to do it? What happens next? If your experience is like mine, you end up without your friend to play with because she went home hurt or angry.

Probably your mom and your dad told you to try being quiet rather than doing what your thoughts tell you to do. Everybody says things they wish they hadn't. When my dad yelled about the yard not being raked, he was sorry and apologized. I bet he wished he'd kept his mouth shut then.

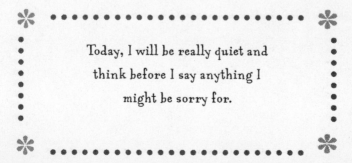

Today, I will be really quiet and
think before I say anything I
might be sorry for.

> The fragrance always remains in the
> hand that gives the rose.
>
> —Heda Bejar

Some people believe giving something away that you really love is one of the kindest things you can do. One of my grandmother's best friends when she was young was a Native American girl, and her tribe believed this. They called it a giveaway. On the occasion of a wedding, gifts were given to every person who came to celebrate the marriage. And on the anniversary of someone's death, that person's family gathers all of the tribe together and gives them gifts to honor the dead person, even though he lives in the Spirit world now.

At my church, they say that whenever we give something away, we get back something even better, maybe not immediately, but soon. Maybe you can discuss this idea over dinner at your house tonight.

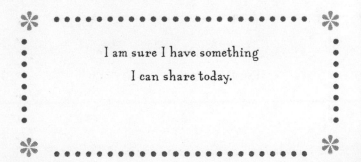

I am sure I have something
I can share today.

Cooperating with others is a sign
we are growing up.

My mother says cooperation is necessary in our family because she has a very hard job at the newspaper, and she works overtime two or three times a week. She needs my sister and me to help get dinner, set the table, do dishes, and do the laundry too. Some days I hate to help. I just want to curl up on my bed and read.

In school last week, Mr. Andrus asked our class to make a list of the ways we had cooperated in the last week. I ended up with more examples than anyone! It made me glad that Mom expects me to help out at home. Mr. Andrus said that learning to cooperate now will help us when we grow up. I think I would like to be a dentist like my Uncle Hank. I wonder if he cooperates with others at his clinic?

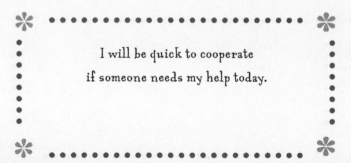

I will be quick to cooperate
if someone needs my help today.

Handling your temper takes a lot of effort.

Occasionally I feel like yelling and throwing my books across the room, particularly when I am doing homework and can't remember how to do the assignment. When I get mad at my brother, it seems to make me feel better to yell. Mom says it would be productive if I learned other ways to handle my temper besides throwing things and yelling. One of the easiest ways is by talking about my anger to her or my grandmother, who lives with us. Another is by talking to one of my Barbies. I can even yell at the doll if it helps. When Mom was young, she loved to go outside and run as fast as she could up and down the street when she was really mad. Eventually this made her the fastest girl on her track team!

Letting my temper push me to be better at some activity is a good way to handle anger, I think. I like the story Mom told me about running track. Maybe I should try the same thing.

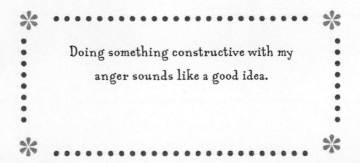

Doing something constructive with my anger sounds like a good idea.

> Every person is responsible for all the
> good within the scope of her abilities.
> —Gail Hamilton

Mother says that every single person I come into contact with has a lesson to teach me. I'm not sure I know what she means. I can understand that my teacher has lessons for me. But she says that even Cory, the boy next door who is often mean to me, can teach me some lessons too. I guess he shows me how not to treat other people. That may seem like a funny way to teach and learn a lesson, but Mother says we learn in many ways.

It can be fun to see if I can figure out what lesson each person is trying to teach me today. One lesson I can teach everybody else is that I'll look for the good in them and praise it.

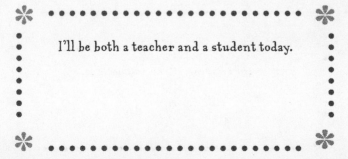

I'll be both a teacher and a student today.

The ordinary human being thinks about twelve thousand thoughts a day.

—Susan Smith Jones

Mom has to remind me to slow down and think first before I do stuff. For instance, when I finish breakfast and jump up from the table, accidentally knocking her cup of coffee over, usually I can't even remember what was in my mind at the time. Whatever thought it was, it didn't help me avoid an accident!

My teacher reminds us to think before writing down answers on the science test. Why? If I don't think about the answer first, I might write down the wrong thing. I always have some thought in my mind. During science, my thoughts should be on the question my teacher asked.

Almost everything I do would be done better if I stopped and thought about it first. Even making my bed or getting dressed in the morning could be done better.

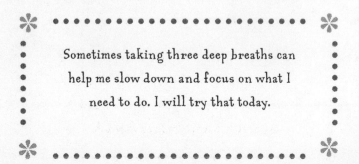

Sometimes taking three deep breaths can help me slow down and focus on what I need to do. I will try that today.

Deciding on the right thing to do isn't always easy.

There's always a right thing to do. Like if a friend is mean, should you be mean back? My foster mother says the right thing is to just walk away and find someone else to play with. If a friend wants to copy from your math paper, what's the right thing to do? The teacher says everybody needs to learn how to do the work alone. Maybe you can help your friend later. Letting her copy isn't the right thing because she won't learn anything that way.

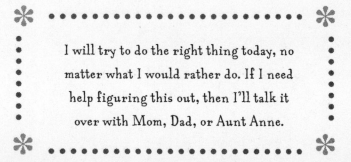

I will try to do the right thing today, no matter what I would rather do. If I need help figuring this out, then I'll talk it over with Mom, Dad, or Aunt Anne.

We all have unique strengths and talents.

I want to be really good at everything I try. I remember when I first tried ice skating. I kept falling down, and it made me so mad. My best friend Amy never fell. It didn't seem fair. She didn't practice any more than me, but she still never fell, at least while I was watching.

Being good at dodgeball or basketball takes practice too, even though I think I should be able to play as well as the best kid in my class. I'm never going to be an expert at some stuff, though. Even though I study hard, I may never be an expert in math. My dad said math was always his hardest subject too.

Not everyone can play the piano very well, even with lessons. I heard Mom say her aunt wasn't a very good cook. You don't have to be good at everything, I guess. That's a relief!

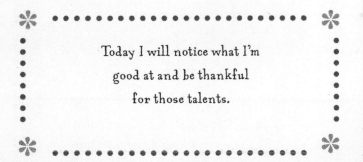

Today I will notice what I'm
good at and be thankful
for those talents.

Good deeds help make the world a better, kinder place.

Doing a favor for someone who has not even asked for one is a good deed. Maybe I can do a good deed for a neighbor and make her very happy. I can sweep her walks. I can carry the fallen tree limbs from her yard out to the street. If her newspaper goes into the bushes instead of onto her porch, I can get it for her.

Mom and Dad are easy to do good deeds for. Picking up the baby's toys and cleaning up the food the dog spilled around his dish are good deeds. So is making sure I clean up all the messes in my bedroom, the kitchen, and the backyard. Anything I do that Mom or Dad would have to do if I wasn't around counts as a good deed.

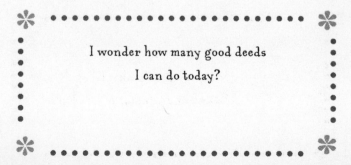

I wonder how many good deeds
I can do today?

Kindness is a state of mind.

—Thelma Ebaugh

My grandfather says people can never be too kind. He says the nicest thing I can do for anybody is to treat them as if they're very special to me. Last week, I told Olivia how much I liked her, and she seemed so happy to hear it. I think it stayed in her mind all day because she was smiling every time I looked at her.

It isn't very hard to be kind. Just saying "Please" or "Thank you" whenever I can is one way of being kind. So is not gossiping about a friend, even when I'm angry at her. There are many small ways to show kindness. I will practice this by being very kind to my mom, my dad, my sister, and the new bus driver.

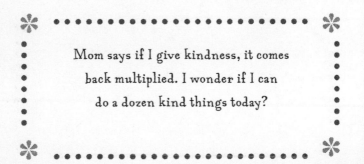

Mom says if I give kindness, it comes back multiplied. I wonder if I can do a dozen kind things today?

Helping someone else makes the world a kinder place.

No matter where I go today, I'll see someone who needs some kind of help. Maybe the neighbor can't bend over very well to reach her newspaper in the bushes. Maybe the little girl next door is learning to ride her bike or trying to catch a beach ball, and I can help by showing her how I do it. Lots of mornings Mom is in a hurry to get my breakfast so she can get to work on time. I can help by putting the milk away, the dishes in the sink, and by wiping off the table.

Helping others doesn't take a lot of time. I can help in lots of ways if I really want to. Maybe I can start by asking Mom what I can do for her right after she has helped me zip up my dress.

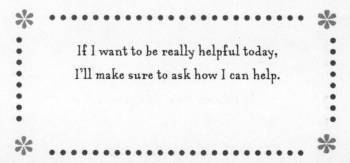

If I want to be really helpful today,
I'll make sure to ask how I can help.

Slowing down can actually
save a lot of time.

—Robyn Halsema

Do you know what it means to be impulsive? You may not hear that word very often, but it means doing something too quickly, before thinking it through. I can remember my dad yelling at my brother last week, saying, "Why didn't you think first before slamming the car door?" He was upset because my brother locked his keys in it, and Mom was gone with the spare set.

I showed up at my swim meet last week without my suit because I was in such a hurry to get there. It was a scramble to find a suit in time, and that made me more nervous than usual. Mom says the trick is to slow down. Count to ten or even five before doing things, and your mind will slow down enough to remember what you need to remember. You'll save yourself a lot of trouble.

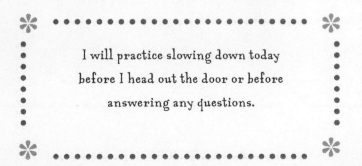

I will practice slowing down today
before I head out the door or before
answering any questions.

Listening to a friend is like
giving her a gift.
—Hayley Halsema

What are you thinking about right this very minute? Are you thinking about what you're reading? Are you thinking about school or what your teacher said yesterday about being quiet during class? Maybe you are thinking about your birthday and what you hope grandmother will buy you. Our minds seem to fill up with thoughts, don't they?

There is a time for thinking, and a time for listening. Mom says sometimes we just have to let the thoughts in our mind float away so we can hear what someone is saying. Listening requires being truly interested in what another person thinks and feels. Listening is a very important part of friendship and family life.

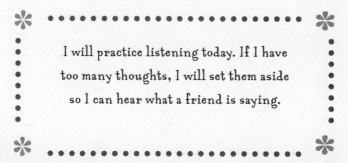

I will practice listening today. If I have
too many thoughts, I will set them aside
so I can hear what a friend is saying.

Needing help is one way of honoring other people's skills.

Do you enjoy helping out a friend? My best friend Sara may not get promoted into seventh grade if she doesn't get better grades in math and science. I overheard Mr. Smith speak to her about it last week. That would be really sad because next year we go to a new school, and she wouldn't be going with our class. I am sure this would affect our friendship.

I am very good in both science and math. In fact, they are probably my best subjects. Maybe I could offer to help her after school. Mom says trading our skills with others is good practice for adulthood. When she bakes, she always makes an extra batch of cookies for Jenny's mom, and Mrs. Spencer does errands for Mom on Tuesdays. They both get some help this way. Mom says I should try to think of what Sara might be able to help me with. I have noticed that she can braid hair really well, and my hair is finally long enough for a braid.

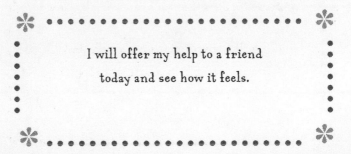

I will offer my help to a friend
today and see how it feels.

Patience is a virtue.

Tolerance is a new word for me. It means patiently accepting situations and people as they are. My mom has asked me to "just be patient!" for a few minutes pretty often. Most people struggle when we don't get what we want right away. Being impatient doesn't make me a bad person, but it can make it hard for others to be around me. When my baby sister is hungry, she cries. Mom says she doesn't know how to tolerate the time it takes to get ready to feed her. Even my dad gets impatient if the newspaper carrier is late getting to our house in the mornings.

Learning to be patient and tolerant is something everybody has to learn. Some of us learn it faster and better than others. Some grown-ups haven't ever learned it. Maybe I can be a good example to one of them.

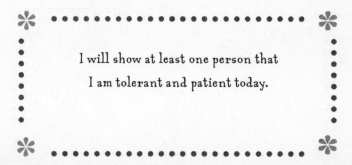

I will show at least one person that
I am tolerant and patient today.

Be able to apologize.

Every single day, I say or do something for which I feel sorry or guilty. Sometimes it's a little thing, like making a face behind someone's back. Or I take something that doesn't belong to me. Maybe I yell at Mom or my best friend for no reason at all, except that I'm in a bad mood. I always know when I need to make an apology; I can feel it inside.

If an apology is necessary today, I won't avoid it. The quicker I take care of it, the better I'll feel. The better all of the other people around me will feel too.

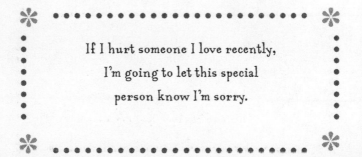

If I hurt someone I love recently,
I'm going to let this special
person know I'm sorry.

> We can't take any credit for our talents.
> It's how we use them that counts.
>
> —Madeleine L'Engle

My brother can hit a softball really hard and far. He is probably the best player on our school softball team. My dad plays the harmonica. He isn't as good as he wants to be, but he practices a lot. He plays when he's stuck in traffic. Mom thinks he's getting better, but I'm not so sure. I'm not as good at Spanish as the other kids in my group, but the teacher says I'm getting better. I think doing more homework helps.

We're all good at different things. I am best at drawing pictures. In fact, I think I'm the best painter in my art class this year. For the last three weeks, one of my pictures has been up on the main hall bulletin board next to the cafeteria. I feel proud and happy every time I walk by it.

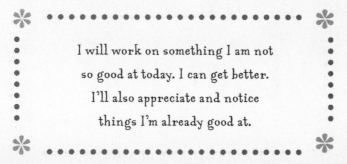

I will work on something I am not so good at today. I can get better. I'll also appreciate and notice things I'm already good at.

Generosity is a very good habit to develop.

Sharing my toys with my little sister or brother is a nice thing to do. I may not want to share them because I may be afraid a special toy will get broken. But when I remember how good it feels when a friend lets me ride her bike or read her favorite book, I know why it's good for me to share too.

Sharing gets easier the more I do it. I begin to enjoy making other people happy. It begins to make me really happy too. After all, it's more fun to have friends than untouched belongings.

Today I will let a friend play with
one of my favorite things.
Sharing will feel good.

To be trusted by those who love us,
we need to tell the truth.

Sometimes, almost before I realize it, I find I haven't told my mother the truth about why I'm late coming home from school. Once I remember saying that Melinda lost her sweater and I had stayed to help her find it. Was I ever scared when we ran into Melinda's mother at the store and my mother mentioned the lost sweater!

The reason people lie is because they're afraid that telling the truth will get them into trouble. My dad says it works just the opposite of that. If I tell him a lie and he catches me at it, then I'm in trouble for sure. But he promised not to get mad if I always tell the truth, even if what I did was not so good.

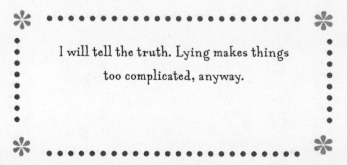

I will tell the truth. Lying makes things
too complicated, anyway.

I like to feel good about my own behavior.

I'm not always proud of how I act. When I threw my tennis ball really hard at the bedroom wall because my dad said I couldn't go over to Lauren's house, I knew my behavior was crummy. I'm certain my dad heard the thud. He didn't say a thing, but he didn't need to. I felt bad about it anyway.

I don't like feeling bad about my behavior. It affects everything else I try to do the rest of the day. But with the help of my grandmother, I have learned that when I apologize for bad behavior, I feel much better almost right away! She says there is always a resolution to the bad feelings we get from our behavior. Owning them and then making amends for them changes the rest of the day. I am so glad she taught me this.

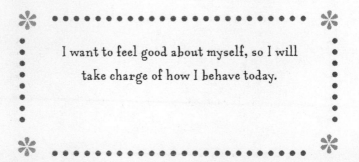

I want to feel good about myself, so I will
take charge of how I behave today.

Generosity makes at least
two people feel good.

Sharing my favorite doll with Chelsea is a nice idea. She has lots of sisters and brothers, so she doesn't get as many gifts for her birthday and at holidays as I usually do. Sharing with her shows that I really like having her as a friend. It also shows that I trust her to take good care of my favorite things.

Generosity can be shown in other ways too. I can show a generous spirit with my words, for example. Why not tell Jerrilyn that I really like her? I can be generous in my prayers also. I do this by praying for all the members of my family, all of my friends, my neighbors, even those kids I don't like so very much. Mom says it's the most generous thing I can ever do!

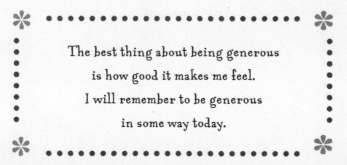

The best thing about being generous
is how good it makes me feel.
I will remember to be generous
in some way today.

Making an apology where it's needed is a good habit to develop.

Are you quick to say you are sorry when you've been bossy toward your brother? What about when you push ahead in line at school? Do you apologize then? Lots of girls need to make apologies for talking behind a friend's back. Is this something you've ever done? Did you apologize for it? There are possibly many times every day that you act before thinking, and sometimes that creates a need for an apology.

Learning when to apologize and being willing to do it without being reminded by your teacher or your mom is a sure sign that you're growing up. In time, it will seem natural to say "I'm sorry" and really mean it. And when you are older, you will even be able to stop yourself from doing the very thing you're apologizing for today.

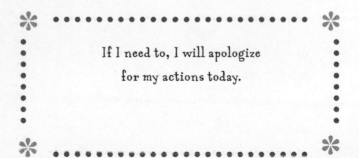

If I need to, I will apologize
for my actions today.

Being patient is a sign of growing up.

Waiting for dinner makes me antsy. So does waiting in line at the movies for popcorn, especially when the show has already started. Sometimes Mom gets home late from work, and the rule is that I can't go to a friend's house until she says I can. Waiting then is really hard too.

"Be patient!" That's what I often hear from adults. Maybe it will be easier to be patient when I get older. Right now it seems hard, but I can't make anything happen faster by being antsy. Sometimes it helps to do something to fill the waiting time: play the piano or read a comic book or imagine my next birthday party.

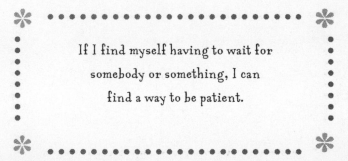

If I find myself having to wait for somebody or something, I can find a way to be patient.

Being able to think is one
of your special gifts.

There is so much to think about! For instance, I have to think about what to wear to school. I have to think of the right answers to all of the questions the teacher asks. I have to think about who to invite to sleep over. Mom said I could ask two friends. I have to think about which book to write my book report on. I have to think about not saying the mean things I said yesterday to my brother anymore. Life feels complicated sometimes with all of this thinking.

There are lots of other things to think about too. Sometimes I think about the other planets. Do you suppose people live there also? In small ways and big ways, my mind is always at work. There is so much to wonder about and figure out in this world—I'm glad to have a mind that works.

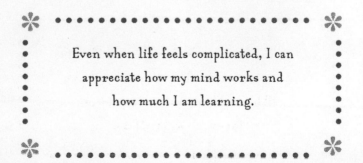

Even when life feels complicated, I can
appreciate how my mind works and
how much I am learning.

How do you get and give attention?

Wanting my parents to notice my room after I clean it or wishing I would be the first person chosen for a softball team is normal, my teacher says. We all want to be special, and getting attention makes us feel special. But we can't get all the attention we want all of the time. Attention has to be shared, just like so many other things.

Even adults want lots of attention. We're no different from them. So I guess we all need to feel special. Maybe if I make someone else feel special, she will take a turn at making me feel special too. What can I do? Maybe just listen closely or compliment Mary Beth; that will show her I think she's special.

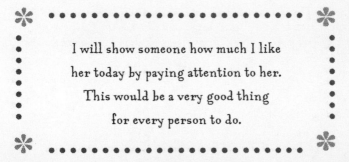

I will show someone how much I like
her today by paying attention to her.
This would be a very good thing
for every person to do.

Experience is a good teacher.

—Minna Antrim

I wasn't sure if I'd like swimming or not. So I joined the swim team but ended up in tears at the end of my first swim meet. After talking it over with my mom, I decided to keep going to swim practice because I really like swimming with my friends. I decided not to go to the meets— I simply didn't enjoy that kind of competition, although I do love skating competitions. My mom reminded me that in the future, if I changed my mind, I could always try a meet again.

I'm learning what I love through experiences. It's important to try activities and see which ones fit me and which ones don't. It usually helps to talk this over with my mom, dad, or another grown-up.

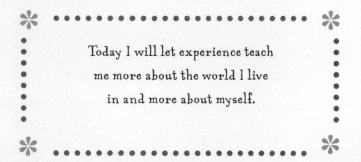

Today I will let experience teach
me more about the world I live
in and more about myself.

More work means I'm growing up.

As I get older, parents and other adults are starting to ask me to do more chores and take on more responsibility. I don't know if I'm glad or if I dread doing grown-up work. Some kids are both glad and mad at the same time. My friend Hayley has to sweep the kitchen floor after dinner every night. She complains that it's too hard, but I can see she kind of likes having a big job. Her brother's job is a lot smaller—all he does is carry the dishes to the sink. I think Hayley's job makes her feel important even though she likes to complain about it.

Carrying out the trash, watching the chicken fry so it doesn't burn, and putting the clothes in the dryer are all jobs I've done this week for Heather, my stepmom. My jobs are changing just like I'm changing. By the time I go away to college, I will know how to take care of myself.

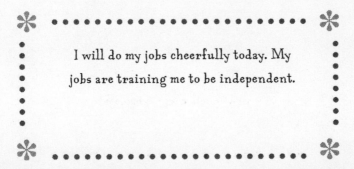

I will do my jobs cheerfully today. My jobs are training me to be independent.

Be a Dreamer

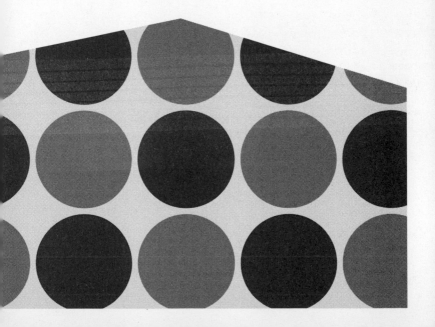

Dreams can be meaningful for our future.

Dreams can be significant. My mom has read many books about dreams. She is most interested in nighttime dreams, but she said I need to dream about my goals for life too, during the daylight hours. She explained that when she was a girl, she wanted to be a good athlete, so she practiced running, playing tennis, and joined the basketball team. She said her hard work coupled with the dream gave her the opportunity for a scholarship to college.

I read the biography of Amelia Earhart, and she dreamed of flying a plane around the world. She didn't make that dream, but she was the first female pilot to fly across the Atlantic Ocean. Think how much dreaming it took to make that happen! Trying to make our dreams come true gives us direction, energy, and hope. I bet Amelia Earhart had a lot of fun flying!

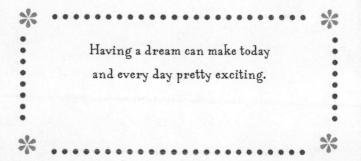

Having a dream can make today
and every day pretty exciting.

> No one can become a winner without
> losing many, many times.
> —Marie Lindquist

Do you hate to make mistakes? I guess most people do. But I heard in school last week that Thomas Edison, the man who invented the lightbulb, failed more than 100 times while he was trying to make the first lightbulb. I guess he mustn't have hated failure too much.

Failing at something just means I need to try again. It's no big deal. Even my teacher has to do lots of things a second time, like when she tried to draw a picture the class needed to copy for the front of our reading folders. She had to erase it and start over three times yesterday. We all laughed. She did too.

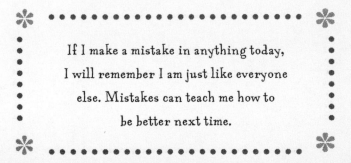

If I make a mistake in anything today,
I will remember I am just like everyone
else. Mistakes can teach me how to
be better next time.

> You must do the thing you
> think you cannot do.
>
> —Eleanor Roosevelt

The swimming coach at the YWCA recently asked our team to swim from one end of the pool to the other, underwater. I knew I could go from one side to the other with no trouble, but from one end to the other seemed impossible. We all groaned, me the loudest. The coach said we had to be able to do it by the end of the class, so we had better start practicing. At first, Sandra and I both refused. And then Sandra gave in. I was the only one sitting on the sidelines. It was embarrassing.

Finally I jumped in and dove underwater, thinking all the while that I'd make it only halfway to the other end before my lungs gave out. Before I knew it, though, my fingers touched the end of the pool. I had made it! Ms. Henry, the coach, said she wished she had a camera to catch the surprised look on my face.

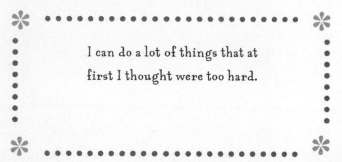

I can do a lot of things that at
first I thought were too hard.

Choices are not irrevocable.
They can be remade.

—Julie Riebe

What are you going to do today? If it's a weekday, I'll bet you're going to be in school. But you still get to make lots of choices. For instance, who are you going to sit with at lunch? Are you going to ask the new girl to join you? Which book are you going to read during free time?

I never used to think about how many choices I had to make in a day. My dad says that's something that never changes. Choices keep coming at us. Some are hard to make too. For instance, how should I act when someone treats me poorly, and what should I do when two friends move away in the same week? It's a good thing I can talk over my choices with Dad or my best friend.

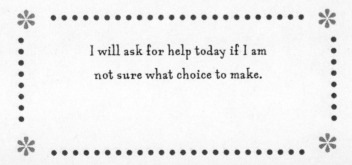

I will ask for help today if I am
not sure what choice to make.

My imagination is my friend.

Do you ever pretend you're older than you are? I do. Sometimes I pretend I am a teacher, and I line my stuffed animals up in the bedroom and pretend we are having a math lesson. Last week I pretended I was a doctor and that my favorite doll was a very sick little girl, and then I made her well.

My teacher says it's good to make up dreams. She says it can help in lots of ways. For instance, if I'm afraid of reading out loud, I can practice at home, pretending I am sitting in the circle at school. She says that when we see ourselves doing something, even just in our minds, it helps us when the real experience comes along.

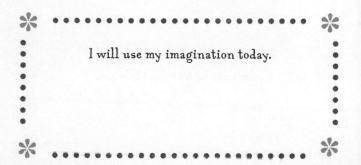

I will use my imagination today.

What does being successful mean?
Does it mean being rich?

I heard Alex say the new family next door to him is really rich. They have a boat and a giant television. My Aunt Carolyn said her new friend must be rich and successful because she has a very fancy house and a new Corvette. My teacher says you can be successful in lots of different ways and it doesn't necessarily mean having money at all. Mom agrees with her.

Mom says having really good friends is one kind of being rich. She says using and developing our talents is a way to share a rich mind. It's nice to know there are lots of ways to be successful besides money. Maybe I won't ever have extra money, but that doesn't mean I won't be rich and successful in other ways.

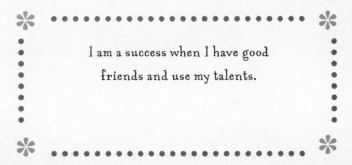

I am a success when I have good
friends and use my talents.

Believing in ourselves means
we have confidence.

How many times a day do you start to say, "I can't do this"? Most kids and even many adults don't believe they can do what is expected of them. I remember when Mr. Gerard, my second grade teacher, put a new kind of math problem on the chalkboard. My first thought was, "Oh, no, I can't do that." But he helped me. And I did learn it.

Putting fear out of mind helps me try new things. I can change my thoughts, and pretty soon, I discover that nothing is too hard for me if I go slow and ask for a little help.

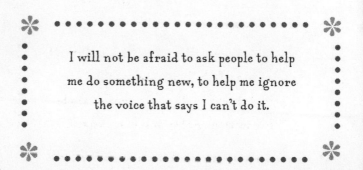

I will not be afraid to ask people to help
me do something new, to help me ignore
the voice that says I can't do it.

Jealousy is usually a dissatisfaction with yourself.

It seems that no matter how good I am at math or how many library books I've read or how quickly I get picked for a side at recess, I always wish I was the very best. Usually, some other boy or girl seems to be better than me at everything! Adults say that's just how it is. They also say I need to learn I'm good enough just as I am.

Wanting to be as good as Abbey in my reading class or as fast as Tom when we're running a race isn't wrong, but maybe I can learn to be glad for them instead of sorry for me. They must have practiced a lot to be so good. Maybe my feelings are telling me what's important to me, and I can set a goal for myself about practicing.

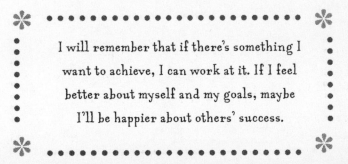

I will remember that if there's something I want to achieve, I can work at it. If I feel better about myself and my goals, maybe I'll be happier about others' success.

I don't always know what I want,
but I do know what I don't want.

—Helen Neujahr

Do you ever dream about who you may want to be when you grow up? Most kids do. My friend Holly wants to be a doctor like our neighbor Dr. Russell. Her brother says he wants to draw plans for houses and other buildings. That's what his dad does. There are so many people and jobs to choose from! You can work outdoors or indoors. You can have the kind of job where you wear a uniform, like a bus driver or pilot. My cousin Alison is a pilot. She flies planes all over the world. Being a teacher like Melissa's mom looks like fun too. I would really like the summer vacations.

Thinking about what you like to do best will help you know what to do when you grow up. The happiest people are the ones who enjoy what they do.

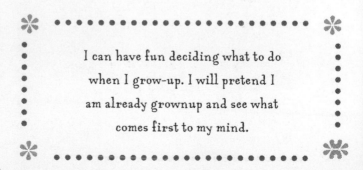

I can have fun deciding what to do
when I grow-up. I will pretend I
am already grownup and see what
comes first to my mind.

All acts performed in the world
begin in the imagination.

—Barbara Grizzuti Harrison

Dreaming isn't just for sleeping. Our imagination, which is where dreams live, can give us the ideas that will point us in certain directions. Samantha's Aunt Karen says we need to have dreams about what we can be when we grow up. She dreamed of being a pediatrician. And she is! My mom dreamed of being a doctor, too. She didn't have enough money to go to school that long, so she became a nurse instead and is a good one.

Last week I imagined I was a robot. What a funny daydream that was! I don't think that's what I will actually be, but maybe I will be a scientist who develops a special kind of robot. Hank, my stepdad, says that dreams indicate where our talents lie. He is exceptionally good at drawing and has been good at that since he was my age. Today he is an architect. I love to draw too. Maybe that job is in my future.

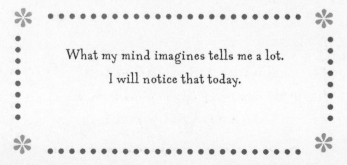

What my mind imagines tells me a lot.
I will notice that today.

Creativity is part of being alive.

There are lots of ways to be creative: drawing a picture of an elephant and picking up pretty leaves on the way home so that I can make a design on paper. My teacher says it's good to be creative. She says everybody is creative in some way. She can play the piano. My brother is learning to tap dance. My mother writes poetry, and my dad tries to put music to her poems with his guitar. He hits a lot of sour notes, though, and that makes us laugh. Mom says creativity is what makes us most alive. And it's fun!

I'll watch how other people are being creative today. Maybe I can even try some new ways to be creative myself.

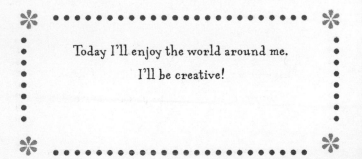

Today I'll enjoy the world around me.
I'll be creative!

Your mind can help your body do lots of things: Think positive!

Did you know that you can do almost anything you think you can do? It works like this. Let's say you really want to be able to ride a two-wheeled bike. First, imagine yourself riding by imagining just how you get on it. Now imagine yourself pedaling slowly, moving down the street. Don't go too fast. Now put the brakes on and put one foot down on the ground. See, you can do it in your mind. Now it's time to try the real thing!

This is how you can learn to do anything new. Imagine how it will go first. What a neat trick! Look at all the new things you can learn this way.

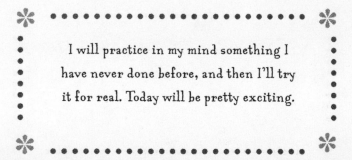

I will practice in my mind something I have never done before, and then I'll try it for real. Today will be pretty exciting.

Hope helps me keep going.

Do you know what it means to have hope? Last year my teacher said we should never give up hope. She said if we had hope, it helped every part of our lives. She told us to sit quietly and make pictures in our minds of what we hoped for. Every day I hope I don't miss any words when my teacher calls on me to read. My mother hopes she gets a new job soon. She isn't very happy at her office. My big sister hopes her boyfriend takes her to the movies.

I wonder what hope does? It seems like it mainly gives me something to put in my mind in place of fear. Hope makes everything seem a little easier. Being quiet and letting my mind and heart fill up with hope makes my world brighter.

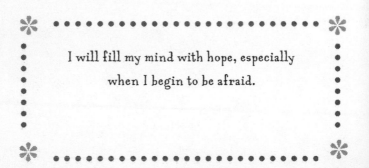

I will fill my mind with hope, especially when I begin to be afraid.

> If I work hard for what I want,
> if I keep trying after I've been turned
> away, my dreams can come true.
>
> —Lisa Gumenick

Most of the things we want in life require our effort. For instance, if I want to get good grades in school, and I do, I have to study really hard. Actually I have to study harder than my sister, Abby. She is in the advanced class in almost every subject. My grandmother says Abby is gifted academically. But she is quick to tell me that I am gifted in other ways. For instance, I am a natural at the piano. I hardly even have to practice a song to master it.

Neither Abby nor I are very good at sports. We tried out for the softball team but didn't make it. Abby didn't really care, but I did. Mom has promised to play catch with me every night for a week so I can try out again. I know I can make the team if I really work hard.

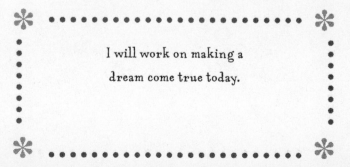

I will work on making a
dream come true today.

Our hearts speak to us every minute.

My mom says she can tell what the right thing to do is by listening to her heart. That seems like a strange idea to me. I am not aware of my heart talking. Are you? But she explained it this way: She says her heart speaks by making her feel a certain way. For instance, if she is snotty to a friend, her heart feels some pain. When she goes out of her way to be helpful, her heart feels like it is smiling.

She also says her heart seems to nudge her toward doing the right thing. Very quietly, it urges her to go forward with a good idea. One example she gave me was when she decided to marry my stepfather. He had been really nice to her and my sister and me. He helped paint our house. He often brought groceries over and even fixed dinner as a surprise once in a while. And he made all of us laugh a lot. That was the best. Ever since my dad died, we hadn't laughed very much. She said her heart helped her to know that Jack would make a good husband for her and a good dad for us.

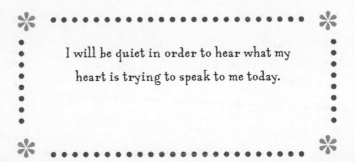

I will be quiet in order to hear what my heart is trying to speak to me today.

Find something of your own to do.

—Sheila Thomsen

Some days I am bored. I have read all my books, most of them two or three times. My markers are mostly dried up so it's no fun to use them. My best friend Sandra is at her grandmother's for the weekend, so we can't play with her Playstation. Dad is cleaning the garage, and my mom isn't here. I don't know where she is. I really hate to be bored!

My teacher says if we are bored it's because we are not using our imagination. Dad says if I am bored I should offer to help him in the garage. Maybe I could make some cookies for our dessert. Maybe I could even fry the potatoes for dinner. Once, after being bored all morning, I wrote a play and acted it out all by myself. It was so fun. Being bored is a decision, according to Dad. There is always something to do, and if I think hard enough, I can come up with something really productive.

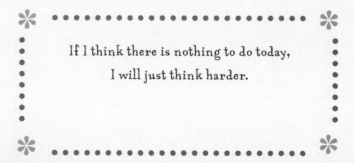

If I think there is nothing to do today,
I will just think harder.

Heroes set examples for all of us to follow.

During second grade, Mr. Schmidt talked to our class about the importance of heroes. I wasn't even sure I knew what a hero really was. I had been taught that Abraham Lincoln was a hero for his role in freeing the slaves during the Civil War. And Amelia Earhart was a hero too. She was the first woman to attempt to fly around the world. She never made it but is considered a hero anyway. Heroes are people who do extraordinary things. But Mr. Schmidt said common, ordinary people can be heroes too.

He suggested that we notice the people in our lives who are always available to help others. From his perspective, they are the real heroes. That made me think of Mrs. Simons next door. Whenever my mom is sick, which is often, Mrs. Simons brings over some meal she has cooked. I also thought of my grandfather. He never fails to show up when our family needs help with something. Last week we needed help getting Tabby out of the tree. Guess who climbed the ladder?

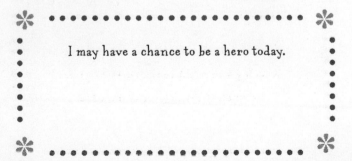

I may have a chance to be a hero today.

> No trumpets sound when the important
> decisions of our life are made.
>
> —Agnes De Mille

Making up my mind about who to play with today is only one of many choices I will make. Beth's birthday is Saturday and I am invited to her party, which means I need to choose a gift for her. If her best friend Bryce is there, I will have to decide if I will talk to her. She and I had a big fight last week.

My parents and I have to decide which camp I will go to next summer. Mom says we will visit three possibilities and ask lots of questions. Getting a feel for each place and knowing as much as I can will help me decide. Making any kind of choice is a big responsibility. I'll make the best decisions if I am thoughtful about them first.

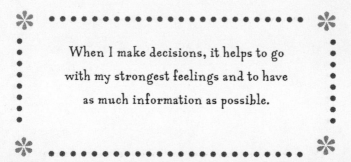

When I make decisions, it helps to go
with my strongest feelings and to have
as much information as possible.

It is often the small, simple things
we do in life that really matter.

Everyone has a lot to be proud of. For instance, did you help your parents a little bit this morning before you went to school? Maybe last night you did the dishes. Did you give a friend some help in reading a word that was too difficult for her? Maybe there are other things you can think of that you feel proud of. Why not write down two or three?

Mom feels proud when she gets a raise at work. It means she has worked really hard. Do you get an allowance for doing chores? Some kids do, and when they start doing more work at home, maybe they get a raise too. You can feel proud just because you're able to read this message. It means you care about making your life better.

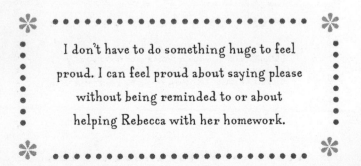

I don't have to do something huge to feel proud. I can feel proud about saying please without being reminded to or about helping Rebecca with her homework.

Choices give us a chance to practice growing up.

When both Heidi and Sandy ask me to come for sleep-overs on Saturday night, it's hard to make the choice between them. Heidi has more video games than Sandy, which makes her house really fun, but Sandy's mom is so funny, and she always makes fudge or brownies or some other dessert for us, and I love that. I don't want to hurt either girl's feelings. It's probably best to go where I was invited first. That would make it fair for everyone.

Not all choices are so easy. One choice I had to make last year was whether to go to my dad's for Christmas or stay home with my mom. He lives in Florida now, and the weather would have been warm. However, my grand-mother was going to be at our house, and she really makes me feel good when she is around. Mom said the decision was up to me. This was a very hard choice. What would you have done?

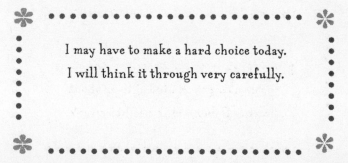

I may have to make a hard choice today.
I will think it through very carefully.

Admitting mistakes is a sign of maturity.

Mistakes, even big ones like forgetting to ride your bike home from the park, may not be too serious if you admit them before your bike gets stolen. Most mistakes can be corrected if we don't ignore them. What is much worse is to lie about them. I wanted to lie about losing the twenty-dollar bill Mom gave me last week to pay for groceries.

I feel bad when I make a mistake, which is why lying seems like a good solution. I don't want anyone else to know about my mistakes. Sometimes I try so hard to be perfect that I forget nobody is perfect.

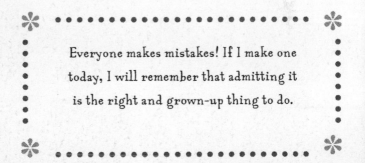

Everyone makes mistakes! If I make one today, I will remember that admitting it is the right and grown-up thing to do.

Be Inspired

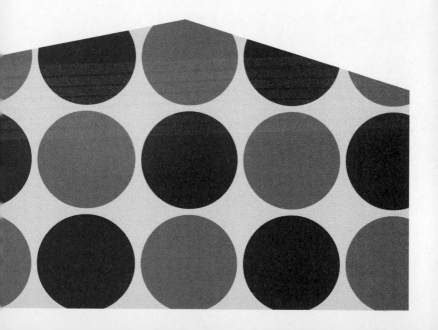

Do you wake up filled with wonder?

I love to look up at the stars at night and wonder how many there are. When we're at Grandma's house, we see even more stars. Dad says it's because there are no city lights to outshine the stars out where she lives. I saw a scientist on television who said there are more stars in our universe than grains of sand on all the beaches in the world. That's a lot of stars!

I love lying on the ground and looking at all the blades of grass in one tiny space and then watching ants crawl through those blades too. Don't you wonder if ants think about what they're doing? There's so much to think about. We're so lucky to be able to think. It means there's always something to do. Even when all of my friends are somewhere else, I can still be busy with my thoughts.

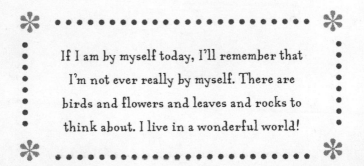

If I am by myself today, I'll remember that I'm not ever really by myself. There are birds and flowers and leaves and rocks to think about. I live in a wonderful world!

What is Spirit?

Spirit is the part of me that feels safe and joyful. It's the part of me that wants to be kind to others. Spirit helps me listen when my teacher or some other grown-up is talking. It helps me be polite to a neighbor who hasn't always been so pleasant.

Someone, I think it may have been my grandfather, told me that my guardian angel and my Spirit are the same thing. But even if they aren't, I know they are both with me every minute of the day. I don't have to worry about school, or if my best friend Jamie still likes me, or if my mother is mad at me. My Spirit will protect me and comfort me all day today.

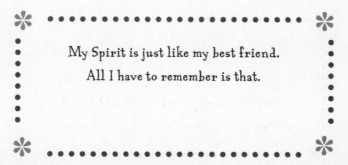

My Spirit is just like my best friend.
All I have to remember is that.

Often God shuts a door in our face,
and then subsequently opens the
door through which we need to go.

−Catherine Marshall

Sometimes I ask God for help with a certain problem, but the problem still doesn't go away. I wonder why grownups tell me to ask God for help? When I asked Mom, she told me that God does answer our prayers every time. They just aren't answered until the time is right. She says there's always a right time for every problem to be solved.

Last week I really needed help from God because I was afraid to go to my first gymnastics class. I wanted to stay home, but Mom said I had to go because she had already paid the money. That time I was lucky, and God helped me right away. I walked in the gym and saw Bridget, a friend from second grade. I wasn't afraid anymore.

God will always help me.
It just may not be right away.

> What a strange pattern the
> shuttle of life can weave.
>
> —Frances Marion

My dad jokes that bad luck is better than no luck at all. What is bad luck, anyway? Mom says it might be when it rains during a picnic. When Robyn won the best prize, the ticket to the circus, at my birthday party, we all yelled, "Lucky!" But it was bad luck for the rest of us.

Is it bad luck to miss the school bus? Maybe not if the bus slid in the rain. When things happen that we don't want to have happen, we generally say, "Bad luck." But maybe it's good luck instead. Mother says that whatever happens is really what is supposed to happen. If that's right, can there be such a thing as bad luck?

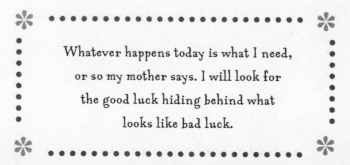

Whatever happens today is what I need,
or so my mother says. I will look for
the good luck hiding behind what
looks like bad luck.

There is a divine plan of good
at work in my life.

—Ruth P. Freedman

Lots of things confuse me. For instance, I'm confused by the new math we're learning in school. I'm confused by why girls in my circle can read better than boys. Grown-ups are confused by lots of things too. I heard my dad say only yesterday he didn't understand why Mr. Brown got another new car when their house needs new windows and a paint job.

Maybe it's not so important to understand everything. Mom says I can always ask her when I'm confused and she'll try to make sense of things for me.

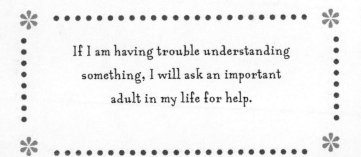

If I am having trouble understanding
something, I will ask an important
adult in my life for help.

Praying is as important
as eating breakfast.

When I am scared about the test we are having at school or about going on a field trip, I say a prayer. Mother says that God always hears our prayers. I sometimes wonder how God has time to hear the prayers of so many people. Maybe not everybody prays, but in my family, everybody does. That means God has to listen to at least nine people every day!

When I talk to God, no matter what about, it makes me feel better. I don't feel so alone, and I feel like I can handle what I need to do. Isn't it wonderful having a friend like God, who never gets tired of listening, who is always there to help or comfort me?

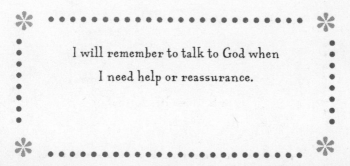

I will remember to talk to God when
I need help or reassurance.

Hope makes us believe in possibilities.

I hope for lots of things. Sometimes I get lost in my thoughts because I'm hoping for so many things. How about you? Do you ever hope your best friend asks you to sleep over? Do you hope you get a new computer for your birthday? Do you hope you will grow up to be as smart as your older sister? I do.

Sometimes even small hopes count. Maybe you hope for chocolate milk with dinner, or that you can stay up an hour past your bedtime. Hoping is something we all do. Our grandparents hope for our safety. Our parents hope they have enough money to buy the clothes we need for school. Our brothers and sisters hope we will leave their things alone. Hope gives us something to do when we are afraid of what might happen.

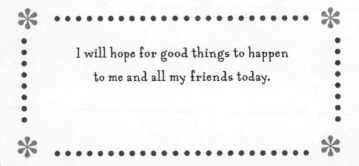

I will hope for good things to happen
to me and all my friends today.

Everyone in this universe is important.

—Josie Bryant

God needs every one of us! Just because you don't like Boyd, the older boy who lives across the alley, or the crabby woman who clerks at the drugstore on the corner, doesn't mean God doesn't love both of them as much as God loves you and me. According to my grandfather, God loves each of us the same amount. God needs every one of us too, because we all have specific information we need to teach and learn from each other. This doesn't mean that every single person alive has something to teach you, but people who cross your path each day do.

Maybe you can learn that it's better not to be crabby from the lady who is crabby a lot of the time. You know how others feel when you're crabby by how you feel when she talks to you.

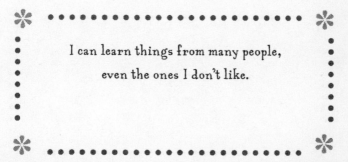

I can learn things from many people,
even the ones I don't like.

Be still and listen to the stillness within.

—Darlene Larson Jenks

Sometimes there's too much noise in my head. I can't listen when my teacher is saying what to do with our math paper because of all the things I am thinking about. Even worse, I don't hear what my best friend is saying about the party she's planning. Mother says this kind of noise happens to her too. She says it comes from not knowing how to be really still inside. She says if she closes her eyes for a minute, it helps. Noticing her breathing helps too.

I wonder why I have so many thoughts running around in my head? I suppose it's because I am curious. It's good to be curious, my teacher says, but maybe it isn't so good when she wants me to just think about math. Many of my thoughts are silly ones too, not ones that are making me one bit smarter.

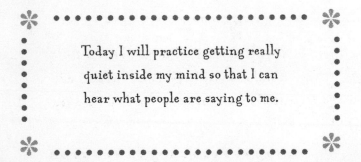

Today I will practice getting really quiet inside my mind so that I can hear what people are saying to me.

Spirit is part of what we are made of.

My friend Elliot says that the Spirit that lives inside of us makes our skin soft to touch. He figured this out after his grandfather died. He noticed when he touched his grandfather's body at the funeral that his grandfather didn't feel soft anymore.

It's comforting to know that our Spirit is as close as our skin all the time we're alive. I believe that our Spirit never dies—it just floats away from our body when the body dies. Our minister says that each Spirit goes to be with God after the body dies, which means we will all be together again someday. I don't miss my grandmother as much when I remember this.

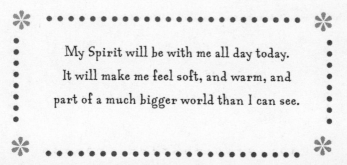

My Spirit will be with me all day today.
It will make me feel soft, and warm, and
part of a much bigger world than I can see.

Seek only peace.

Almost every day most moms say at least once, "Give me some peace and quiet, will you?" What does that mean? Usually it means she wants you to let her alone so she can think. Do you ever want to be left alone the same way?

Sometimes my mind is just too busy. I'm thinking about what someone said to me yesterday or where I want to go tomorrow. Maybe I'm worrying about whether Rachael is going to invite me to her birthday party. I get tired when my mind is so busy. Maybe I need to ask for some peace and quiet too.

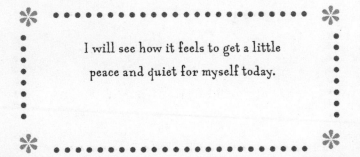

I will see how it feels to get a little peace and quiet for myself today.

Praying for others helps
us as well as them.

Have you ever heard someone say it's good to pray for whoever you're angry at? That seems kind of silly. When I'm mad at someone, I either want to ignore her or maybe yell at her. Why should I pray for her?

Adults have funny ideas about things but maybe they are smarter because they are older. My dad says praying for someone we're mad at takes away our anger, and then we feel better. I don't always want to feel better when I'm mad.

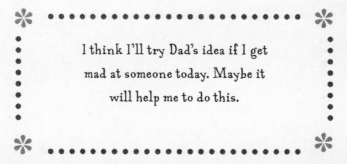

I think I'll try Dad's idea if I get
mad at someone today. Maybe it
will help me to do this.

To show great love for God and our
neighbor, we need not do great things.

—Mother Teresa

Does it make you feel good when your mother reminds you that she loves you? If you have just done something pretty obnoxious, like stomping out of the kitchen because you didn't like what she made for breakfast, it may surprise you that she loves you. Maybe she even says that she loves you but doesn't love how you are behaving.

Mom is like God in that way. God loves us no matter what we do, according to my Sunday school teacher. God notices all of our efforts toward goodness and accepts our imperfections. If we make a mistake and do something that is not very nice, God won't decide to quit loving us.

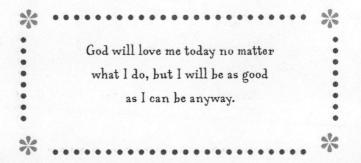

God will love me today no matter
what I do, but I will be as good
as I can be anyway.

What is a miracle?

When someone wins the lottery, everybody says, "It's a miracle!" Or when my friend Sara got her new bicycle, she thought it was a miracle, especially because her mom and dad had gotten divorced. What about waking up from a bad dream? That seems like a miracle too because the dream seems so real. Are all these things really miracles?

How do I decide what's really a miracle? I can ask my teacher or my mom, but they won't necessarily know. Maybe all that counts is if I'm happy about what's happening in my life. If I think about a miracle as my ability to be happy, then I can have miracles every day.

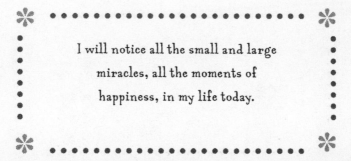

I will notice all the small and large
miracles, all the moments of
happiness, in my life today.

Dying is part of living.

Dying is really hard to understand. I wonder what actually happens? Does your heart just suddenly stop beating? Sometimes I watch people die in the movies or on television. One of my grandparents got really sick and died many years ago, but I still see her in my dreams some nights. Dead birds in the street or even dead cats sometimes make me think of my grandmother who died. I wonder if their Spirits are all together in one place?

I like to think people go to heaven when they die. I imagine they're all there, having a lot of fun, laughing together, and just waiting for the rest of us. That's a good picture to have in my mind.

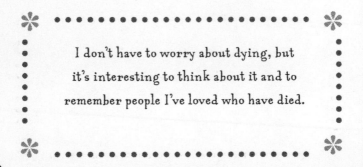

I don't have to worry about dying, but it's interesting to think about it and to remember people I've loved who have died.

To be courageous is to be filled
with the strength of Godpower.

–Mary Helen Smith

Courage is a pretty important word. My teacher asked us to draw pictures of courage, and I drew one showing a girl climbing a tree to rescue her cat, who was afraid of the dog chasing it. My friend Joannie drew a picture of a big girl yelling at a group of mean-looking kids who were chasing a little girl.

My Sunday school teacher said courage is when you put your own fear aside for a time. She says it helps to ask God to feel brave in those scary situations. I think everyone is afraid some of the time. My dad says he is even afraid occasionally. He also said that praying helps him.

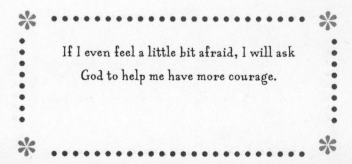

If I even feel a little bit afraid, I will ask
God to help me have more courage.

Prayer is not a science.
—Mary McDermott Shideler

Praying is something you can do a hundred times a day if you want to. Some people pray as soon as they wake up. Some families pray before they eat every meal. Lots of kids pray before going to sleep. I know a girl who prays before she takes the reading test every Friday. Are there times you would like to pray? You can, you know. Just close your eyes and talk softly to God. No one needs to hear you. You can tell God anything.

Praying makes lots of people feel better. Particularly when you're feeling scared or alone, you'll feel better if you pray. You don't have to tell anyone you are doing it either. You can just quietly, privately, do it.

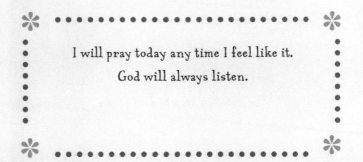

I will pray today any time I feel like it.
God will always listen.

> Everything has its wonders,
> even darkness and silence.
>
> —Helen Keller

Do you ever look up at the Big Dipper at night? Isn't it beautiful? When I was younger, I wondered how all the stars got up there and why they didn't fall down. Now I know they stay in place just like the Earth does. One day I watched a mother bird feed worms to her babies in a nest, and I wondered how she knew she was supposed to do that. There are so many things to wonder about.

Cats seem to understand they are supposed to chase mice. Dogs know they are supposed to bark if people come into the yard. Birds chirp loudly when you climb the tree they're in. How does everything know what its job is?

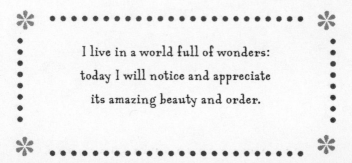

I live in a world full of wonders:
today I will notice and appreciate
its amazing beauty and order.

Praying can help us when we
are scared or confused.

We don't have to know a certain prayer by heart. We can say something really simple like, "Dear God, please help me not be so afraid right now." And everybody says a prayer sometimes. Praying before eating a meal is called "saying grace." Some families always say grace. Saying a prayer when we go to bed at night makes us just like millions of other kids. Everybody has their own way of praying.

There is no law that says we have to pray. It's nice that we don't have to do it. It's better if we pray because we want to. Praying is something my father does every morning.

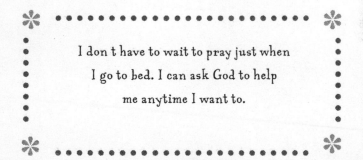

I don't have to wait to pray just when
I go to bed. I can ask God to help
me anytime I want to.

A miracle can be almost anything.

When we have planned a picnic and it doesn't rain, my grandmother Rinny says, "This is a miracle!" Last week, when I got an **A** in math even though I'm not very good at multiplying big numbers, I thought, "Wow, a miracle!" Mom says it was a miracle she remembered everything she went to the store to buy because she forgot her list.

I wonder if all these things are really miracles. Does a miracle have to be some big deal? When I fell down the stairs at school and didn't even tear my skirt, I called it a miracle. Mr. Temple, my old art teacher at Sunnyside, said miracles live in our minds. How we see an experience is the miracle, he says.

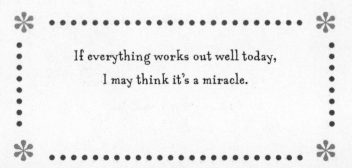

If everything works out well today,
I may think it's a miracle.

Where is God?

Some people say that God is everywhere. I wonder if that means God is in the pretty leaf I picked up on the way home from school. Is God also in my angel fish? If God is in everything, why is Shawn so mean? Wouldn't God keep Shawn from chasing the little kids?

Sometimes it is hard to understand how all this works, but some grown-ups say that God can always help you do the right thing if you ask for help and you really want the help. It seems like a good idea to ask for help. I wonder if all the fish and rabbits and trees ask for help.

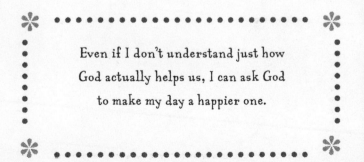

Even if I don't understand just how
God actually helps us, I can ask God
to make my day a happier one.

The more I force things,
the tougher my life.

—Helen Neujahr

What makes you mad? Think about this for a minute. Do you get mad when you can't force a friend to play your way? Or when your mom says no to something you want to do? I recently got mad when Tricia didn't ask me to come over after school, especially after I found out she had asked Blythe, the new girl in our class.

Getting mad at others is something everybody does, adults too. I get maddest when others don't do what I want them to. It's like I want to force everybody to let me be their boss. My aunt has a favorite prayer that begins with "God grant me the serenity to accept the things I cannot change." When I bump into something I don't like and can't change, thinking about my aunt's prayer helps me.

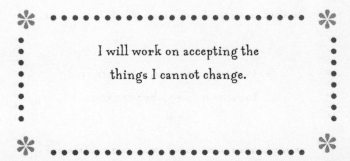

I will work on accepting the
things I cannot change.

I am in God's care and if I trust,
all of my fears will subside.

—Michele Fedderly

Everybody feels a little afraid part of the time. A bad
storm may make even your older sister a little bit afraid,
especially if all the lights go out. Even my dad doesn't like
storms. And he says I don't have to be ashamed of being
afraid. It will make me feel better if I tell someone how I
am feeling. Maybe that person will admit to being afraid,
too, and then we'll both feel better.

Being afraid of some things is good. For instance, running across very busy streets should feel scary and make
you extremely cautious. If you weren't a little bit afraid,
you might run right out in front of a car. That's what my
dog did. Being afraid to pet a dog that growls every time
you walk by its house is good too. He could bite you. But
there is no need to be afraid of everything. Most things
really won't hurt us.

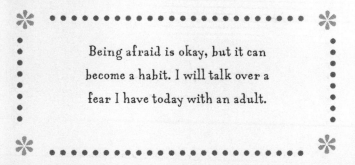

Being afraid is okay, but it can
become a habit. I will talk over a
fear I have today with an adult.

Feeling peaceful comes and goes.

Being peaceful means that I feel quiet and not afraid. Lots of times I am not very peaceful. For instance, last week I wondered for three days if Dad would be mad at me for breaking his hammer. I was trying to hang up a picture in my bedroom when I dropped the hammer, and the handle broke off. Every time I thought about what had happened, my stomach tightened up.

When I'm scared that my teacher will think I cheated on the spelling test because I got all the words right, I certainly don't feel peaceful. Sometimes I feel like thoughts are racing through my mind at a hundred miles an hour, and most of them keep me from being quiet.

Mom says I should remember that God will help me handle any problem that comes up. Even the big ones, like when she or Dad is mad at me. When I think about God, I feel more peaceful instantly. Other things that help me feel peaceful are painting, playing the piano, and going for a bike ride.

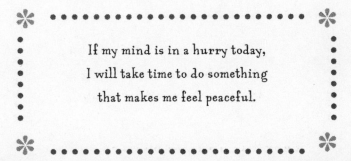

If my mind is in a hurry today,
I will take time to do something
that makes me feel peaceful.

It's good to take our questions to God.

Every time I wonder what I should do or say when a friend does something that upsets me, like when Stephanie hid my coat under hers so I couldn't find it, I can close my eyes and speak softly to God. God can help me respond to a mean act in a way that isn't hurtful. Hurting someone back is usually not the best thing to do.

There are many times I don't know what to do. That is true for everybody. Even my parents get confused. Some dads wonder if they should quit a job. Maybe my mother wants to go to college, but she isn't sure she has time. I heard the teacher say he would like a new car but was afraid it cost too much. Some questions are bigger than others.

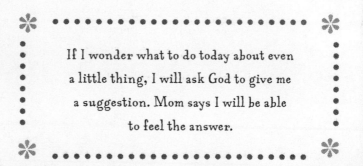

If I wonder what to do today about even
a little thing, I will ask God to give me
a suggestion. Mom says I will be able
to feel the answer.

> "May the Force be with you."
> —*Star Wars*

Did you ever see the first *Star Wars* movie? My mom rented it recently. My parents had seen it when they were much younger, and they said it had a good message. Mom popped popcorn and my stepdad made fudge, and then we all sat down together to watch it. The part about "the Force" was really neat. Mom said she always thought of the Force as God. My stepdad said he thought of the Force as a guardian angel smoothing the way for him. I'm not sure what it means to me, but in the movie it made me feel safe. It made the characters seem stronger too.

After the movie, my stepdad wondered what I thought about it. I really haven't decided yet, but I do like the idea that there is a power around me all of the time that can help me. Mom believes we can call the power anything we want. The important thing is to remember that it's there waiting for us to express our need for it.

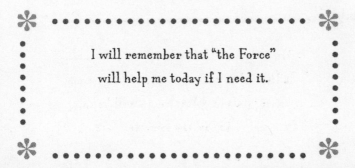

I will remember that "the Force"
will help me today if I need it.

God insists that we ask.

—Catherine Marshall

What are you most uncomfortable about? Do you know what makes me most uncomfortable? It's being afraid. I hate feeling afraid, and there are lots of times when I am afraid. Mother says it would help if I kept the thought of God in my mind more often. She says I can't think of two things at once. There isn't room for fear and God too. If I ask God to stay in my mind, then fear has to leave.

Sometimes fear just seems to come, even when nothing seems to be causing it. And sometimes I forget to ask for help with my fear. But when I do ask my mom or God for help, my fear melts away.

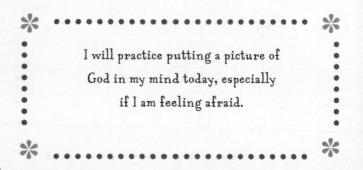

I will practice putting a picture of God in my mind today, especially if I am feeling afraid.

The idea of God is different
for every person.

–Angela L. Wozniak

Did you know that you can talk to God as often as you want? And even more important, you can picture God any way you want. I have decided that God looks like my grandmother. I can't hear her voice, but I can get a feeling about what she is thinking. I talk to my God when I wake up in the morning before getting out of bed. I ask her to help me be really kind to all my friends and my family too. My grandfather says that people talk to God in their own way. He gets down on his knees beside his bed at night and in the morning. God makes him feel hopeful that he will have a good day.

It is good to ask God for help if you are feeling unsure about something. God can make you courageous right away. Everybody needs to get God's help once in a while.

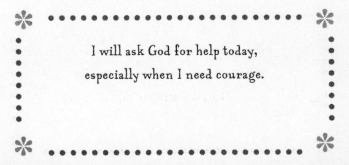

I will ask God for help today,
especially when I need courage.

One needs something to believe in.

—Hannah Senesh

Do you ever wonder what God looks like? Mom says he looks different to each of us, but that doesn't mean there is more than one God. I think he looks kind of like Santa Claus, except he doesn't wear a red suit. He looks that way to my friend Janet too. Mom says God looks like a whirling cloud to her. My friend Alicia said she thinks of sunrises, sunsets, and trees as God. I have an African friend who says the tribe her grandmother grew up in worshiped the sun. My Sunday school teacher said God isn't necessarily a man. God could be a woman.

One thing I do know, and that's because my grandmother told me, is this: God loves me regardless of what I do. This love shows itself in beautiful trees, breathtaking sunsets, the warmth of the sun on a sunny day, and a hundred people joined in song. God's love is all around me.

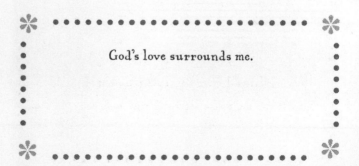

God's love surrounds me.

We were not born accidentally.

Everybody has a purpose, or she would not have been born. Everything that happens has a purpose too. Do you know what that means? It is a pretty difficult idea, but here is what it means. Nobody is in this world by accident. Nobody crosses your path today by accident. Everything that happens around us can teach us something. For instance, when Erin's cat got run over it was sad that Snuggles died. His death made all us kids realize how busy our street was. Now we are all more careful when we cross the street.

I like thinking this way. It makes me feel like my life is important and that everyone around me is special. It also helps me look for lessons in what happens at home, at school, and in my neighborhood.

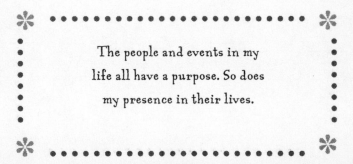

The people and events in my
life all have a purpose. So does
my presence in their lives.

God is everywhere every minute of the day.

Wouldn't it be nice to be able to see God? Maybe you think about God a lot. I do. Maybe even your parents think about God. My best friend's name for God is the Great Spirit. My friend is Indian and has told me a lot about her beliefs. She says when the wind blows into her from the south, north, east, or west, each direction brings special strengths. She and I agree we're lucky that God wants to help us in everything we do.

The Great Spirit never goes away. Sometimes friends move away. A parent sometimes has to leave too. Maybe your dad has to move to another city for a while, like Melanie's dad did. Many things can change even when we don't want them to. But we are really lucky that God never changes and never goes away. Ever. If we want to talk to God or the Great Spirit, all we have to do is close our eyes. We will always be listened to.

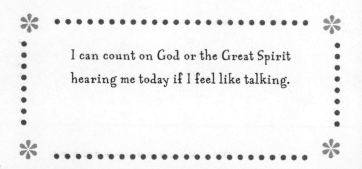

I can count on God or the Great Spirit
hearing me today if I feel like talking.

Knowing God isn't as hard as it sounds.

I bet you don't think you know God. I didn't think I knew God either. But my Auntie Maria said all I needed to do was look around me to know God. She said God was every-where, every minute of the day. Just because we can't see a godly person doesn't mean that God isn't present. She says she sees God in every tree she looks at and in every flower, every bird, every sunset, every child, even in grouchy old men.

We took a walk right after she told me this, and she pointed out all the places she knows God lives. She point-ed out hundreds of places in just a three-block walk. Wow! When I told Mom what Auntie Maria said, she said she found God most easily in friendly people. She also said that she learned as a child that we could all help God a great deal by our kindnesses to each other. Her church taught that God loves us all, and by being kind to each other, we are helping God do his work. That's a good way of knowing God better because it shows us how God feels all of the time.

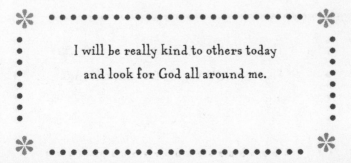

I will be really kind to others today
and look for God all around me.

Quiet moments replenish our souls.

—Sue Atchley Ebaugh

Some days it seems like my mind just won't shut up. Does your mind ever feel like that? It just seems to be talking to me all the time. It tells me I am scared when it is thundering really loud outside the bedroom window. It tells me I am not very smart when I miss a bunch of words on the spelling test. Yesterday it told me I was nobody's friend.

Mother says it is good to tell my mind to just be quiet! She says when my mind seems to be saying things that make me sad or afraid, I should imagine a peaceful picture instead. Sometimes I picture our favorite beach, and I can actually feel the sun and hear the waves. Sometimes I picture Grandmother Sylvia because she is so kind to me. If I picture quiet and peaceful places or people, my mind calms down.

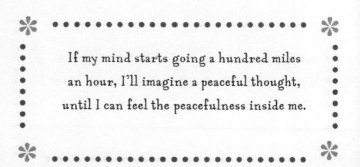

If my mind starts going a hundred miles
an hour, I'll imagine a peaceful thought,
until I can feel the peacefulness inside me.

> You don't have to seek God in church.
> I find God within my heart.
>
> —Sandra Lamberson

Do you sometimes wonder what God looks like and where God is? No one I know has actually seen God, but everyone has an idea of what God looks like. I used to think God looked a little like Santa. My friend Molly is sure God looks like an angel. She even says she saw God. Mom thinks God is a really bright light that shines everywhere. Her sister says she sees God all over in Mother Nature.

What counts is asking God for help when I am scared or lonely. Talking to someone who I can't really see may sound silly, but I don't have to talk out loud. I can talk just in my mind. God will hear me and I will feel so much better.

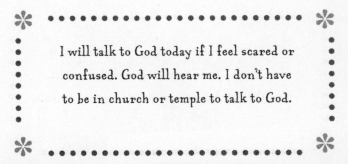

I will talk to God today if I feel scared or confused. God will hear me. I don't have to be in church or temple to talk to God.

Remember the Spirit inside you.

There is something very special inside all of us. Maybe you already know what it is. Have you ever heard of Spirit? That is what is inside every person. Even grouchy old Mr. Lynch next door has Spirit. Heidi, my aunt's newborn baby girl, and Dustin, the mean kid across the street, have Spirit too. Every one of us has it.

Do you wonder what Spirit does? I've heard that it helps us be kind to others. It helps us remember that everyone is special. It helps me remember that I am special. I sometimes think of God as the Great Spirit. The Spirit inside of me can talk and listen to the Great Spirit whenever the world around me feels confusing or too hard. This almost always makes me feel better and like I'm not alone.

I will let my Spirit help me
today by connecting me to the
Great Spirit in this world.

3 1901 04830 1677

who you feel comfortable talking to, there is always someone available to listen. Close your eyes and imagine your
guardian angel. Picture what she looks like. Give her a name,
if you like. She is always there, whenever you need her.
She will never leave your side, no matter where you are
or what's going on. I promise you this. But you'll have to
find her by yourself. Perhaps you can find her today.

Your friend forever,
Karen Casey

P.S. If you want to write to me, I would love to hear
from you. You can contact me through my Web site,
www.womens-spirituality.com, or in care of my publisher,
Conari Press, 500 Third Street, Suite 230, San Francisco,
CA 94107.

Dear Reader

I've always wanted to write a book to help young girls handle the kinds of feelings that troubled me when I was young. When I was your age, I often felt afraid and confused. I didn't feel comfortable asking questions, and sometimes everyone else seemed to understand things that baffled me. Sometimes I dreaded going to school and sometimes I felt confused or hurt because my friends didn't include me in their plans and activities. My parents argued a lot and I really hated that. I had stomachaches all the time because of these worries.

If you sometimes find yourself getting confused or angry, try reading one of the pages of this book each day before you go to school. I can almost guarantee it will help you feel better. If you want to, you can share the book with your mom or dad, or a teacher or other adult you trust. It almost always feels better to talk over your thoughts with another person. And it's good for them to hear what's going on with you.

Remember: You don't have to handle your problems all by yourself. Even if you don't have an adult close by

Contents

First published in 2007 by Conari Press,
an imprint of Red Wheel/Weiser, LLC
With offices at:
500 Third Street, Suite 230
San Francisco, CA 94107
www.redwheelweiser.com

ISBN: 978-1-57324-308-7

Library of Congress Cataloging-in-Publication Data available
upon request

Cover and interior design by Maija Tollefson.
Cover photograph © Comstock/Corbis.

Printed in Canada
TCP
10 9 8 7 6 5 4 3 2

Be Who You Want to Be

Dealing with Life's Ups & Downs

Karen Casey

Conari Press